women's lives ▪ men's laws

CATHARINE A. MacKINNON

women's lives ▪ men's laws

THE BELKNAP PRESS OF HARVARD UNIVERSITY PRESS

Cambridge, Massachusetts, and London, England ▪▪▪ 2005

Printed in the United States of America

Library of Congress Cataloging-in-Publication Data

MacKinnon, Catharine A.
Women's lives, men's laws / Catharine A. MacKinnon.
p. cm.
Includes index.
ISBN 0-674-01540-1 (alk. paper)
1. Women—Legal status, laws, etc.—United States 2. Women—United States—Social conditions. 3. Sex role—United States. I. Title.

KF478.M26 2004
342.7308'78—dc22 2004052086

Preface

The cases of my women clients form the spine of this collection. Their lives, what I learned from them, grounded the theory and practice of these past three decades. From statutory law in the 1970s, to constitutional law in the 1980s, to international law in the 1990s and beyond, they were the close context of this work.

Starting in the mid-1970s, many women who had been sexually harassed at work and in school, including Ronni Alexander, Pamela Price, and Mechelle Vinson, worked with me. Sexual harassment law took root because of them.

Beginning in 1980, in collaboration with the writer Andrea Dworkin, survivors of sexual abuse through pornography became the work's center of gravity. Linda Borman (previously Linda Marchiano), coerced as "Linda Lovelace" into the pornography film *Deep Throat*, was my colleague until she died in 2002. The estate of Dorothy Stratten, who was murdered by her pimp-husband after she was used in *Playboy*, and the surviving families of Kristin French and Leslie Mahaffey, who were murdered in Ontario, Canada, by Paul Bernardo after he made pornography violating them, fought for women's lives beyond the grave. Representing dead women taught me how much live ones give to my capacity to go on.

Starting early in the 1990s, as lessons from the struggles against sexual harassment and pornography were applied to the Violence Against Women Act, new ones were learned representing Bosnian Muslim and Croatian women seeking justice for Serbian genocidal sexual atrocities committed against them, and my focus shifted to the international arena. The concerns of that period mark the pieces in this book indelibly, as does extended involvement in constitutional equality litigation in Canada. The resulting essays on comparative and international law and politics will be published in a companion collection to follow, *Women's World, Men's States.*

Urgency to respond to the injuries in specific women's lives, no preconceived theories, propelled the arc traced here. Their needs and requests, over entrenched, well-funded, at times violent opposition, summoned the combative and contemplative, analytical and argumentative, embattled and elegiac voice you hear in these writings, most of which were spoken first. Looking back, it was the critical location of these women's experiences in fundamental divisions of social power that positioned them, hence our legal initiatives framed in those terms, on a leading edge of change in this period.

In addition to the debts acknowledged in each piece, Martha Nussbaum's early reading of the manuscript was extremely helpful. Joan Davis contributed an accessible index. The technical work of John Stoltenberg and Charlotte Croson, aided by Lori Watson and Amna Akbar, was invaluable. Pat and Twiss Butler, Kent Harvey, Nancy Ruth, Lindsay Waters, and the University of Michigan Law School, especially its phenomenal law librarians, backed me up in ways that counted over the long haul. For your generous help and belief in this work, I cannot thank you enough. To the survivors, I thank you for your trust in me.

This volume is in honor of my father, who wrote men's laws, and in memory of my mother, who lived a woman's life.

Catharine A. MacKinnon
June 25, 2004

Contents

women's lives ▪ men's laws

Introduction: Realizing Law

I think [judges] have failed adequately to recognize their duty of weighing considerations of social advantage. The duty is inevitable, and the result of the often proclaimed judicial aversion to deal with such considerations is simply to leave the very ground and foundation of judgments inarticulate, and often unconscious. . . . [They need to] see that really they [are] taking sides upon debatable and often burning questions. So much for the fallacy of logical form.

—Oliver Wendell Holmes[1]

Over the last thirty years, the lives of women, newly visible as such, cast a bright critical light on laws constructed by men. Women's insistence that law respond to them, too, has exposed the sex of those the law empowers as male, in the main, and the gender of laws, even the law itself, as masculine. Sex inequality was found built into mainstream sex equality law's oscillation between denying that the sexes are human equals and pretending that they are social equals.[2] Sexual abuse, found commonplace and effectively widely condoned by laws against it, began to be understood as a systemic form of sex discrimination.[3] Pornography was unmasked as a practice of misogyny masquerading as a constitutional entitlement to freedom of expression.[4] Prostitution was exposed as a violation of the human rights of the prostituted misconceived as a crime they committed.[5] The racism and sexism of law and society emerged as often mutually constituting.[6] The essays in this volume, impelled by public moments[7] and collective movements, reflect and refract that blaze of light.

During the same period, the women's movement in the United States—without which nothing in this book would exist—went at once mainstream and underground. In the process, injuries to one-half the human race,

From a talk at Harvard Law School, November 20, 2000, delivering "Disputing Male Sovereignty," infra at 206.

formerly submerged from public view and excluded from legal systems, began to surface and be recognized as political issues and legal claims. Sexual harassment was established as sex discrimination,[8] framing public conflagrations[9] as well as private disputes.[10] Attempts to make mainstream sex equality law into a useful tool against the subordination of women persisted.[11] The harms of pornography were spoken in public, recasting what to do about them in less moral and more real terms.[12] As proposed civil rights remedies for injuries inflicted in and through pornography were debated, the pornography issue redefined women's politics.[13] The expendability of those used by the pornography industry was the new bottom line, dividing the politics of abolishing male dominance from doing better under it. Congress, in passing the Violence Against Women Act (VAWA), recognized rape and battering as gender-motivated violence.[14] The crime of rape, with international law in the lead, began to be defined in terms more commensurate with women's experience of sexual violation.[15] The outlines of the practical possibilities for changing the forms as well as the content of law's tenacious gender bias began to be seen.[16]

The essays in this volume, with the public engagement that produced them, took part in these changes. As this work progressed, revealing time and again men's power over women as fundamental, a substantive theory of sex equality, grounded on particular women's experiences, contextualized by data showing that they were far from alone, was taking shape in the world and in my mind. That theory is: sex inequality is a hierarchy that is substantively sexual at base and merges especially crucially with inequalities of race and class.[17] A theory of sex equality must thus encompass sexual violation, although no equality theory had before.[18] By contrast with existing theories, and through the heavy weather encountered, it became clear that not only was this theory new in its focus on substance and in content; its method of constitutional interpretation, and its jurisprudential notion of the relation between life and law, even its vision of law itself, were departures as well. This collection, arranged chronologically within large themes, shows that theory being born.[19]

"Formalism" in legal interpretation is frequently berated and repudiated, but substance in the sense of the substantive division, organization, and distribution of social power is not commonly the focus of legal theorizing, whether by legal academics or judicial actors. This book takes up that challenge on the subject of law affecting women and men as such. The resulting substantive theory is not textualist but is text-based. It is not doctrinal but analyzes doctrine and has doctrinal implications. It is not structural in the technical sense, legally or philosophically, but is attentive to both. It is not historicist in the sense of arguing something should be as it is because it has long been that way, but it is deeply aware of history. It is neither abstract in the sense of being disconnected from reality nor originalist. It is principled in its own way and critically respectful of constitutional values.

Substance, on this theory, centers on society's divisions of power. If it is perhaps evident that power divisions drive cases where inequality is involved, where is inequality not involved? This general theory of inequality is that inequalities are particular. To have a substantive theory of an inequality requires having an explanatory analysis of its particular content, function, and driving dynamics: what makes it go and why it exists. If society systematically divides women from men, poor from rich, people of color from white, gay from straight, young and old from adult, human from nonhuman animals (among others, not necessarily in that order), to pursue equality on these grounds, one needs to know, in fact, what racism is really about, where homophobia comes from, why humans treat nonhuman animals as lesser beings,[20] why children are kept so socially powerless and elder adults have less power than middle-aged adults, why the rich get richer and want to, and all the interconnections between the forces so set in motion. Substance, in other words, is not an abstraction.

From the crossroads of the substance of women's lives with men's laws, with sexually abused women in its crosshairs, a general theory of law, including of constitutional interpretation, formed in turn. Law is substantive first, everything else it is and claims to be second. Surely this is true in equality cases, arguably so in other cases that affect the distribution of power in society as well. Most do. One of law's main functions is to organize social power among groups. Most legal conflicts, whatever else is at stake, involve social ranking and distribute social resources and treasure for the living of life; most have dimensions of, or effects on, "who gets what, when, and how."[21]

In this view, the consequences of each legal provision or interpretation for organized divisions of social power, for stratifications of advantage and disadvantage, animate, and may be seen ultimately to define and determine, legal struggles. In strongest form, what a case *does* in the world of these social systemic realities is what it is, in reality, about, both for those who decide it and for those who decide what was decided. This substance can take the form of political party, as where the power of the presidency was at stake,[22] or of gendered sexual power, where sexual power[23] or sexual freedom[24] is at issue. When cases raising such issues are litigated as abstract legal questions of election law, federalism, or due process privacy, their substance is obscured and evaded, not controlled or eliminated.

To illustrate, *United States v. Morrison*'s adjudication of the constitutionality of the Violence Against Women Act (VAWA), substantively interpreted, is about male dominance in physical relations between the sexes, specifically about the state's position on and in the exercise of physical force by men over and against women. Interpreting the doctrine of federalism to hold that intimate violence was necessarily under state not federal jurisdiction provided abstract cover for finding the VAWA unconstitutional.[25] In a subsequent case concerning federal legislative power raising almost identical formal issues, but substantively giving men more resources in the family, another traditional preserve of states under U.S. doctrine of federalism, a statute was found constitutional.[26] Being for or against white supremacy, and how strongly, can similarly be seen to underlie positions for or against affirmative action[27] and the regulation of cross-burning.[28]

Norms of judicial self-restraint prescribe that substantive views are not supposed to dictate or even be involved in juridical outcomes. So the relation between reality's substance and legal abstraction's air provides the torque, undertow, tension, interest in deciding cases and commenting on them. *Women's Lives, Men's Laws* gives those underlying realities first-order analytic place. It at once argues for a substantive theory of equality in equality cases and takes a substantive equality-sensitive approach to reading other cases and law in these terms, whether those questions are presented on the surface or not. If what is learned about men's laws from their confrontation with women's lives is not confined to a ghetto of legal scholarship on women, far more than sex equality cases are illuminated.[29]

It is an illusion, I think, that law is not on some level substantive first—from the social epistemology of the reality conceptions that power permits, to the structures of logic considered to define the reasonable, to the doctrinal dictates that frame the questions asked, to the results of cases and their extended consequences. Facts, relief, and context are substantive. On this reading, doctrines like abstract equality or speech absolutism are epiphenomenal smokescreens for outcomes that are in fact, consciously or not, predicated on the substance of historical experience or group identification or power interest. The fact that little scholarly commentary is devoted to analyzing opinions in such substantive terms (with exceptions) only demonstrates the extent to which the illusion is successful and shared.

Such an analysis is often thought to be nonlegal (not to mention inferior). On the contrary, it goes to the essence of the law. This does not make it simple. Sometimes, a case is decided the way it is because a judge is substantively worried about another case or group or sphere of life that, because precedent and doctrine interact, will be affected down the line. The U.S. Supreme Court's obsession with hypotheticals at oral argument can be understood in this light. The underlying dynamic remains substantive; it is just some other substance. Imagine how this makes the litigants feel.

Formalism can be undeniably powerful for those who make effectively final decisions at lower levels of a legal system constrained from the top. It does sometimes matter very much into what bottle the wine is poured. But form remains, as Holmes observed, a much-overused excuse, even a mask, for substance, even as it is a guise substance takes. Where there is latitude for interpretation, and usually there is, most purported commitment to form is a commitment on some level to substance in disguise or one step removed.

The theory built and exemplified here is its own species of legal realism—one not previously been applied to women and men as such. Built through systematic attention to *cui bono*, it stands opposed to the "neutral principles of constitutional law"[30] that have been so influential in defining principle and method in that field. The basic idea of neutral principalism is that who one substantively is or what is substantively at stake in constitutional interpretation should not matter to who wins. Substantively, "neutral principles" began in a rejection of the Supreme Court decision in *Brown v. Board of Education* that invalidated official segregation of schools on the basis of race.[31] By submerging substance—the people and facts and outcome in *Brown*—in abstractions, where none of those can matter, neutrality, far from being neutral in the simple sense of favoring neither side, has made outcomes more manipulable by powerful substantive interests that can not be exposed or countered by the less powerful, except by indirect means that have no legitimated role in the process.[32]

Critique of the approach taken here is usually reduced to a charge of bias or naked pursuit of interest or allegation of bad faith or attribution of conspiracy. It is not a theory of motive in the individual psychological sense but of social system and consequence. It certainly is what lawyers talk when they talk strategy, the disreputable underside of legal interpretation. Anyone who has ever practiced law knows that the real issues of a case—its gut, how it plays on the street—are one thing; the legal issues, into which these real issues must somehow be shoehorned, are commonly another. Rarely do the two coincide; often they do not even overlap. Legal theory, in my opinion, should analyze the legal issues in terms of the real issues, and strive to move law so that the real issues *are* the legal issues. Legal scholarship should accordingly analyze the real life behind the legal curtains and how the back story and the window dressing interact. Apart from being more democratic and honest, this could help women a lot, and other members of socially disadvantaged groups as well.

Because confronting reality directly is not abstract, this approach has not qualified as a legal theory worthy of the name. In received Theories of constitutional interpretation, to theorize *is* to abstract. Reality gets one dirty and involved, and talking about it requires knowing something about the world, which is harder than knowing something about the law of that aspect of the world. Theory is formal; substance is finger-pointing, politics. However, to return the favor, substantively speaking, not only are "neutral principles" substantive in actuality, they are also oxymoronic, even self-canceling. Some judges and legal commentators seem genuinely to believe they are called upon to apply their minds neutrally to abstract legal questions. While the attempt may rein in their biases to some extent, it more surely conceals them, even from themselves, and permits unconscious commitments on substance, which tend to favor the status quo and established interests, to control. No wonder legal change is so intractable. Besides, what is principled about not permitting real effects on real people in real life to matter to law? By these lights, principle is ultimately substantive, the more so if its substance is express, its group grounds showing and democratically contestable.[33] Substantive principles of constitutional law, embraced as norms as well as inevitabilities, would enhance judicial transparency as well as realism.

Consider free speech doctrine, addressed in part two of this book. Although the substance of "speech" was once the class politics of communism and leftist dissent, in recent times it has become largely code for sexuality and money, often standing in for gender and class. On my observation, positions on issues of free speech today are largely predictable based on the life experiences and identifications that result in the fears, hopes, loyalties, and sensitivities that determine one's sex and class and sometimes other group politics, such as religion. Those views, not positions on overbreadth or artistic versus commercial speech, determine predispositions on First Amendment questions, shaping the heuristic and casting the template in terms of which the facts of cases are made meaningful and determining outcomes. Thus, the First Amendment is usually interpreted so men can have their pornography—sometimes due to their attachment to it; sometimes due to their view of its abstract connection to other things to which they are substantively attached; sometimes because, given pornography's pervasiveness, its unavailability is unthinkable; and so on.[34] Pornography in the concrete controls law's "speech" in the abstract, not the other way around. Yet discourse on the subject, from scholarship to litigation, remains overwhelmingly couched in free speech's abstractions, often elaborated through unreal hypotheticals, as welcomed as pornography's realities are shunned.

Privacy, another abstract doctrine, is regularly code for sexuality, which mobilizes sex and gender as a power division between women and men, including lesbian women and gay men.[35] Views on the realities of homosexuality and abortion determine views on privacy, not the other way around. On a substantive reading, judicial opinions in abortion cases turn on (surprise) views of abortion, which on a sex equality reading derive in turn from views on the substantive realities of the relative status and treatment of women and men with a stop en route at "the fetus,"[36] producing what is talked about as "privacy." Views on sodomy laws similarly reflect experiences and emotions and conclusions predicated on who people know and love and identify with. "Privacy" becomes the second-order derivative abstract vehicle for that substance. The point of this discussion is simply to identify which is the tail and which is the dog, and to observe that legal analysis often has them reversed or feels constrained to pretend that it does.[37]

One source of resistance to openly facing this way law is made sub rosa, hence to this way of reading and writing legal opinions, stems from the experience of the *Lochner*[38] era. In the early part of the twentieth century, the U.S. Supreme Court struck down as unconstitutional provision after legislative provision passed to protect working people from excesses of capitalism. Common wisdom holds that, if substance is allowed to drive outcomes, as occurred in that line of cases, the wrong substance may win; so the lesson learned was to preclude substantive decisionmaking and avoid substance at all costs. Missed is that the legislation was not invalidated in the name of its substance, unbridled capitalism, but in the name of a legal abstraction, freedom of contract. Abstract doctrines embody substantive assumptions and tilt outcomes, but form in itself did not then, and does not now, ultimately dictate those outcomes. It does and did put their real determinants, which were and remain substantive, off the table, out of view, and sometimes out of reach. In substance, *Lochner* and its progeny advanced the class interests of upper economic classes at the expense of lower ones. What was wrong with these cases, in the view advanced here, was not their substantivity but their substance. What was problematic was not that substantive decisions were made. Ineluctably, they are. What was wrong was that abstractions obscured both the substance of the decisions and the fact that the decisions were substantive.

That substance drives outcomes and moves people is inevitable. There really is no way around it. This is why it is so essential that it be accessible to law and legitimate in legal discussion, available to be grappled with by theorists as well as practitioners on all sides: on the table. The only question is whether it will be engaged out front or behind the scenes, in court and in the press or at lunch and in chambers and corridors where only those with legal power can get at it and no one else can engage with it. It has to be conceded that the abstraction dodge has not restrained judicial power. The pretense of formal constraints *has* triangulated dialogue and made the exercise of legal power less transparent and accountable.

Much the same can be said of activist versus passivist institutional notions of judicial role and of related norms of positive and negative constitutional rights. The real issue is what substantive ends the action or inaction will produce, and who is accordingly afraid of whom and why. Passivists become notoriously activist when something that greatly matters to them in substance can be achieved, even as discussion of that substance by litigants—those directly effected—is prohibited in the course of the legal confrontations in which it will be decided.

The related concern that substantive disputes are ipso facto unresolvable has a similar answer. They *are being* resolved. Why formal abstract disputes are considered resolvable—or, more to the substantive point, *what* is resolved when they are addressed—is the better question, seldom asked. If one is attentive to the consequences, it is no easier to decide whether the fetus is a form of human life than whether abortion is a privacy right. In reality, to decide the latter is to decide the former, under systemic norms that effectively let the judge make up his own mind without briefs or argument. The essays in this book proceed on the notion that real conflicts can only be resolved, and are only resolved, on real ground. The rest is sleepwalking and gaslighting, smoke and mirrors.

At this point, the substance that determines legal judgments is buried beneath such a deep layer of the institutional ideology of its impermissibility that it is not just unarticulated and inaccessible, it is largely beyond the consciousness of most legal actors and interpreters, even the most candid and self-reflective. It is seen as insulting and reductive, hitting below the belt, to point out. But substantive commitments and priorities, which come from walking through life, with the resulting intuitions and sensitivities and reflexes, can no more be controlled or eliminated from legal thinking than objectivity in the sense of point-of-viewlessness can be achieved.[39] They can either be denied or they can be made conscious, visible, transparent, informed, and accessible, hence open to evidence and argument and accountable to the public. If it was openly conceded that law qua law is on some level necessarily a substantive pursuit, as women's engagement with it shows, not mechanistic or scientific or abstract or finally formal, its functionaries and decision makers could less easily hide and legitimate what they do and its levers of power could be more widely shared. The point is not to trade covert for overt licencing of personal bias and hidden for blatant evisceration of precedent as part of the rule of law. The point is to permit opinions and precedents to be confronted accountably on the level on which they are actually determined.[40]

Unlike many interpretive theories, the one that runs through this volume truly is a theory of interpretation. It does not dictate outcomes, although facing disagreements on their substance rather than by posturing for abstract authority or dealing from a formally stacked deck may help reverse existing patterns of privilege. But the normative and interpretive dimensions are kept separate. That an argument is substantive does not necessarily mean that it will or should win, only that this is what will, openly, be decided. The purpose is not to end discussion but to begin the real one in public.

For example, interpretively, the VAWA civil remedy, by permitting women to sue men civilly for assaulting them, substantively intervened in the distribution of social power between women and men as institutionalized under law. The VAWA was thus found unconstitutional not because, as the Supreme Court contended, the ties of gender-based violence to commerce were insufficient, or because, as some have thought, the Court did not see the clear analogies to race that the case posed.[41] It was invalidated because federalism institutionalizes male dominance and the VAWA provision deinstitutionalized it. This is to criticize the *Morrison* opinion for deploying male dominance in substance in the form of the structural doctrine of federalism. Substantively, the decision could be defended, for example, by defending male dominance's place in structuring state power. If avoiding such substance for talk of federalism made it easier to invalidate the provision, and confronting its substance would make invalidating it harder by making taking the VAWA civil remedy away from women look like what it was, surely this is not the theory's fault.

In other words, legal interpretation, for technical equality cases as well as for cases that affect equality in the world, really *is* about "whose ox is gored."[42] Under law, reality is on the side of the unequal in an unequal world with equality rules. This presents a problem only for those who wish to maintain inequality in reality while purporting to embrace it on principle. The only question is whether that reality will be excluded and denied, so fought over at a remove, or will be admitted, theorized, evidenced, and argued over, so the same oxen may not be gored forever. At least, this is a conviction that has grown in the period encompassed by this collection, as the burning questions of women's lives brought whose laws these really are ever further into the open.

part one

equality re-envisioned

SECTION A. ■ WOMEN'S LIVES UNDER MEN'S LAWS

1

Unthinking ERA Thinking

As June 30, 1982, drew to a close and the Equal Rights Amendment expired unratified, American women did not riot in the streets. They did wipe the asses of children and put them to bed, lurk on street corners warily until a car circled and slowed and they got in, finish typing the last page of transcription for the following day, begin the night shift sewing plastic handbags or cleaning downtown offices, fight for their lives as fist met face and lay their lives down as penis sliced in and out and in and out, scurry across the street with their eyes down to avoid the man coming the other way, and give up on covering June's bills. Not noticing as the shadows disappeared over TVs in mental hospitals and IVs in nursing homes, they removed their mascara, locked their doors if they had them, set their alarm clocks, and let the day go, largely unmarked. A few went to well-behaved demonstrations, largely unreported. In the noise and in the silence, some picked up pens and wrote.

Why an explicit guarantee of women's equality was rejected as part of the constituting document of the United States is a good question, one it takes some courage to ask. The answers are bound to be as unnerving, challenging, even anguishing as they are crucial and urgent for law and politics. The ERA came to mean the equality of the sexes to those who sought it, to those who abhorred it, and to those who found saying it in law somewhat obvious if not yet redundant. It is hard for women to face the fact that we live in a country that rejects our equality. In Canada, when women's demands for good sex equality guarantees in the proposed *Charter of Rights and Freedoms* were not met, and a national convocation of women to discuss women's rights under the proposed Charter was threatened with cancellation, Canadian women spontaneously rebelled nationwide. Not only was the meeting held; not only were the sex provisions left meaningful; but an additional provision guaranteeing the Charter's rights "equally to male and female persons" was added.[1] Granted, culture

Book Review, Jane Mansbridge, *Why We Lost the ERA* (1986). First published, 54 *University of Chicago Law Review* 759 (1987).

and process differ. Still, one wonders why American women, a majority of whom were said to have wanted it,[2] let ERA go so quietly.

Jane Mansbridge's *Why We Lost the ERA* is less an analysis of this loss than an example of the kind of thinking that produced it. This book is not a searching criticism of the approach to law, gender, and politics that failed to mobilize the masses of women in favor of a legal guarantee of their own equality; it assumes it. It is not an indictment of a legal regime that is stacked to require that the sexes already be equal before sex equality can be guaranteed to women by law. It is not an inquiry into the way those disempowered by the structure and content of a system designed to exclude them have difficulty making it work for them. Nor is the book an autopsy of crushed hopes or a rallying call against a despair that grows at once more rational and more luxurious daily. It is not even a case study of how a system that seldom recognizes women's existence, denigrates women's needs as women,[3] and is hostile to women's perspectives[4] goes about rejecting a law to guarantee women's rights. Rather, it is a wake, an almost relieved if mordant celebration of an inert fact: after a long and tormented life, old ERA is dead. "It is beyond harm now." Now, we can think about it. Academics seem to prefer their subjects as dead as possible.[5]

According to Mansbridge, the ERA lost because its proponents did not play the conventional political game conventionally enough. Feminists did not undermine or abandon our position consistently or loudly enough to assuage the fears of the opposition, did not cave in on sex equality enough, but instead kept giving the impression that guaranteeing sex equality would encourage or even mandate real social change: "[l]egislators in wavering states became convinced that the ERA might, in fact, produce important substantive changes—and the necessary votes were lost." The leadership of the ratification movement is accordingly faulted for lacking that all-American virtue, unprincipled pragmatism. As Mansbridge puts it, "they preferred being right to winning." The volunteer activists, the lifeblood of the effort, are faulted, by contrast, for wanting to win at all costs, for having such an emotional stake in recognition of women's full citizenship by their government that it was "worth almost any sacrifice." Mansbridge, who was one of them, portrays the volunteers as pathetic and childish for being wounded by expressions of misogyny; their commitment is presented as fanatical, their solidarity likened to that of a religious cult. Their problem was that they "care[d] even more about winning than about being right." It is my experience that when women fail to sell women out—when the opposition fails to get you to commit suicide before they murder you, so to speak—it is said that your failure to submit is a reason you deserve to be destroyed. Too, when you are committed enough to women to be willing to do what it takes to win—a posture once given some dignity by men under the phrase "by any means necessary"—people say that you care about winning too much. It seems that women who want to win something that is right should care very passionately neither about winning nor about being right. What in politics is there to care about more? It is worth noting that Mansbridge's book does sincerely intend to be a sympathetic insider's account of the ratification movement.[6]

In many ways, *Why We Lost the ERA* is to the ERA effort what the ERA effort was to sex equality. Both are conventional about law and politics. Both assume that politics as usual sets the real ground rules for politics for women. At the core of both is the same strange resignation garbed as realism: both wear like a tight undergarment the assumption that most Americans do not really want sex equality and that this view cannot be changed,[7] so that to get an equal rights law, something sort of has to be put over on them. Instead of facing the status quo in all its misogyny, and accepting that part of the process of winning involves changing it, both pretend that it doesn't exist while assuming that they can do nothing about it. Apparently both books and laws must get over in the system as it is, although one gets the persistent impression that both Mansbridge's book and the ERA aspire to something better.

Of course realism is desirable. But accepting the status quo as the only reality that can be, and the other side's myths as characterizing it, is not realism for a political movement for equality; it is closer to suicide. Neither Mansbridge's book nor the ERA effort systematically comprehends that sex inequality is a problem of male dominance,[8] a distinctive political system that—for feminists both to be right and win—calls as much for a new political science as a new politics. Mansbridge seems to imagine neither. For one example, in all her assessments of what influenced (male) legislators to oppose the ERA, she never considers that they might have had a real stake in sex discrimination—an economic, social, psychological, institutional, and sexual stake, the more determinative to the degree that it may be nonconscious. ERA's failure is consequently presented not as yet another male victory but as a female defeat. Indeed, both Mansbridge's book and the ERA effort—because they do not face up to male dominance and therefore cannot face it down—condescend to and blame the victim while purporting only concern for her welfare. Mansbridge blames the ERA effort for failing to win more than she blames what it was up against for defeating it, much as ERA activists blamed conservative women for failing to support their version of sex equality more than they blamed what such women were up against for undermining the ERA's appeal to them.[9] Neither analyzes how the dispossessed can be maneuvered into doing themselves in, a feature proponents and opponents of ERA share.

Because neither Mansbridge's book nor the ERA effort seriously confronts male supremacy as the problem with which ERA had to contend, but accept it implicitly as fish accept water, the book is no clearer in evaluating ERA strategy than the ERA effort was in pursuing it. Was the aim of ERA more to move the powerless or to placate the powerful? On what analysis of sex inequality are these emphases in tension? Is sex equality a real change or isn't it? Is it about altering power and powerlessness on the basis of sex or isn't it? If women are no longer to make 59 cents to men's dollar, will men make 20 cents less so the sexes can meet around 80 cents or what?

The sense the ERA effort too often communicated of trying to slide one by, its frequent aura of contempt for audiences, the feeling it was hiding its real agenda—none of this was lost on the opposition. But the continual revisions of the public image of what the ERA "would do," equivocations designed to win over the opposition by reassurance, *did* effectively vitiate the potentially explosive organizing effect the ERA might have had on those who had the world to gain from actual sex equality. The longer the campaign went on, the more this happened, and the more this happened, the less ERA meant. No amount of PR could keep ERA from communicating to those with power that under ERA, yes, women would matter. Now, that *would* be a change. Opponents knew this no matter how much proponents denied it, but the denying only confirmed what most powerless potential supporters already most deeply felt: nothing can make a difference, surely not a law. Essentially, then, Mansbridge criticizes the ERA effort for failing to follow the very strategy her book documents it pursued: the one that defeated it. The misunderstanding that sex equality can be made nonthreatening and still be real, the misidentification of what women are up against and the resulting waffling, the incredible spectacle of feminists denying that sex equality would make much difference while urgently demanding to be given it, all this made ERA's latest demise a major tragedy of lost political possibilities—unmourned in these terms by Mansbridge, however.

Mansbridge recounts the campaign's search for a sex equality issue that would present the ERA as an appealing solution to some aspect of women's inequality. She does not ask what made this search so hard and largely futile in a society in which women's subordination is so pervasive. The reason for the ERA effort's failure of analysis, and the reason for Mansbridge's failure to analyze that failure, is that both the ERA—at least in its leading interpretation[10]—and Mansbridge—at least here—implicitly apply liberalism to women and call that feminism. In both the ERA campaign and Mansbridge's analysis, the liberal agenda sets the direction and limits of ERA's agenda. In a central instance, Mansbridge traces the way the perceived need for a new constitutional provision was undermined as the ERA campaign progressed and more and more sex equality rights were won under the Equal Protection Clause—rights mostly for male plaintiffs,[11] neither notes. Why did the country need a new constitutional amendment to solve a problem that the existing Constitution was already solving? This only posed a problem for a provision that had no legal or political agenda of its own, beyond carrying the conventional liberal interpretation of the Equal Protection Clause to its extreme. That ERA had none—a fact neither the ERA forces nor Mansbridge's book faces—has not yet been solved.

Although not all ERA's supporters took so limited a view of what they were fighting for, the mainline liberal interpretation of the ERA, one that reduced the problem of the subordination of women to men to a problem of gender classification by law, was never seriously questioned by the pro-ERA movement.[12] Mansbridge never questions it either. This is an approach to sex equality that leaves out the social institutionalization of practices through which women are violated, abused, exploited, and patronized by men *socially*—in collaboration with the state, but not only or even primarily by the state as such. This approach leaves out practices that have never needed to be enacted into sex classifications in law because they are plenty powerful in civil life, practices that the state is often kept *out* of *by law* in the name of individual rights. It is one thing for lawyers to urge this approach as an interpretation; it is another for a movement to embrace its results and limits as unquestionable; it is still another for a postmortem of the political failure of the measure based on such a theory to accept it so implicitly as not even to consider that its legal theory, and the political strategy based on it, might have contributed to its loss.

Mansbridge acknowledges that the existence of the ERA would have had a political impact that might have changed the way existing laws are interpreted.[13] She does not see that ERA's legal impact need not have been confined to being the women's auxiliary of the Equal Protection Clause. As a result, she fails to analyze the specifics of ERA's potential impact so as to take into account what a constitutional amendment could do to the entire balance of forces on the political landscape and hence to specific cases. As ERA doctrine did, Mansbridge assumes that legal doctrine immaculately produces its own progeny without messy political intercourse. As ERA doctrine did, she assumes a definition of equality doctrine based on comparisons with men. As ERA doctrine did, she assumes an essentially male definition of what issues are sex equality issues. In other words, both not only assume that sex equality issues come down to women's sameness or difference from men rather than to men's dominance over women;[14] both tacitly accept a model of sex equality that is limited to those issues men recognize as equality issues because they arise in contexts in which men now know they sometimes treat *other men* arbitrarily and irrationally. This approach, while some improvement, nevertheless precludes the distinctive abuses of women as a sex—for example, rape, denial of reproductive control, and prostitution—from being considered sex equality issues *at all.*

It seems to me that a new constitutional amendment both signals and calls for a new departure. Probably as many people were for ERA as against it because they had a breathtaking vision of all the legal possibilities Mansbridge keeps finding "difficult to imagine." I see no reason to accept her legalistically conventional prognostications about what ERA "would do" over these people's hopes and fears. Perhaps one sees this differently from Mansbridge if one thinks the ERA is not "politically dead"[15] but only comatose.

All these analytical difficulties converge tellingly in her treatment of the issue of abortion rights. Dominant abortion rights and ERA strategies on reproductive control have been based on treating forced sterilization, maternity leave and related benefits for women, pregnancy surcharges in health insurance, and abortion rights as anything but issues of sex discrimination (except when women are advantaged by them). Mansbridge describes the decision not to litigate the abortion funding case of *Harris v. McRae*[16] on a sex discrimination theory as a political choice to avoid associating sex equality with abortion rights in order to help ERA's chances of ratification.[17] Unmentioned is that the choice was also the result of a Supreme Court equal protection decision that discrimination on the basis of pregnancy was not discrimination on the basis of sex, but rather a gender-neutral choice not to ensure against all the risks that members of that third sex—"pregnant persons"[18]—might face.[19] By the time *McRae* arrived at the Supreme Court, Congress had repudiated this result under Title VII in the case of pregnancy, but had explicitly excluded abortion[20] and considered that it could not change the constitutional result. An Equal Rights Amendment could have.

Instead of acknowledging that no man under existing technology will personally be deprived of needed abortion funding, reuniting abortion with pregnancy and pregnancy with sex—which is how its benefits and deprivations are largely experienced by women—both Mansbridge and the ERA effort move heaven and earth to keep them apart in the name of strategy. But once abortion was decriminalized, this is exactly the approach that has legalized denial of support for women's reproductive needs.[21] An analysis of reproductive issues that placed them in the context of sex inequality would locate the debate in the context in which the problem is lived: a context of lack of choice by women of the terms of sexual access to our bodies, a context of forced sex. If something were done about male sexual aggression and intrusion on women as the paradigm of sex, there would be no abortion problem as we know it, if only because dramatically fewer abortions would likely be needed. Real sex equality would mean real sexual freedom, including the power to have no mean no, hence the freedom to have yes mean yes. Until then, women need abortions and are denied access to them as women in a context of sex inequality, as an act of sex inequality. An ERA could have given women crucial support in such a resituated argument.

Abortion *is* a sex equality issue. Everyone knows it.[22] Denial of access to abortion denies women, and only women, a final act of control over the reproductive consequences of male sexuality as it largely seals women's lack of control over their time, which is what a life is made of. Mansbridge bemoans only the extent to which such realities were not able to be fully manipulated out of the ERA debate.[23] But the current lack of success in securing access to federal abortion funding, in making the abortion right real for those who otherwise have least access to it, suggests that denying women's experience and ignoring gender divisions in legal doctrine may make not only bad law and lousy politics but also ineffective strategy.[24] It is even worth considering that here, as elsewhere, Mansbridge may attribute ERA's death to failing to go far enough in the direction that killed it.

Neither the ERA effort nor Mansbridge's book inquires into whether an ERA that addressed the deep realities of women's condition might have mobilized the kind of uprising of women that only a new vision of society can do. In a teleological approach to political explanation, when Mansbridge asks why ERA failed, she does not look at what did not happen but only at what did. What if sex equality were not limited, as the ERA effort and her book assume, to the way the white male liberal cabal of lawyers, publishers, professors, the media, and their "domesticated" feminists have defined it? What if, instead, issues of sexual abuse of children, denial of the abortion choice, rape, battery, prostitution, pornography, and sex-based de facto job segregation were core examples around which a critique of the denial of civil rights to women were forged? What if, when we talked ERA, we talked about state complicity in male violence against women through writing and administering rape laws from the viewpoint of the reasonable rapist; misogynist police practices in domestic violence calls that relegate assault on women to the lowest category of concern; collaboration of law enforcement and law itself in the terrorization and stigmatization of child victims of sexual abuse, many of them girls; biased enforcement of biased laws against prostitution so that prostitutes (most of them women) are harassed and violated while pimps and johns (men) are allowed to ensure that prostitution, something men made a crime, will continue to exist for their pleasure; useless and dangerous obscenity laws that cover for the pornography industry, provide its design format, and allow public officials to decry pornography in public while nonenforcement and built-in unenforceability guarantee its availability in private, ignoring documented harms to women from its production and consumption?[25] What if we called all this "state action" in the sex equality area?

What if, when we talked ERA, we criticized the legal standards under Title VII that essentially assume that the status quo is nondiscriminatory, stacking the burden of proof so that the tools we are given embody the problem they are supposed to solve?[26] What if, when we talked ERA, the equal protection requirement that discrimination be proved intentional were criticized as a protection for bigots, a good many of whom so sincerely believe that women are a lower form of life that hurting us never crosses their minds as they hurt us, who do not even take account of our existence as human enough to form an intention to discriminate against us?[27] What if, when we talked ERA, we talked about how it might support laws that recognize abuses of women that have never been recognized, abuses just now coming out of our silence, abuses that have previously been guaranteed as *rights* to men under existing law, abuses like pornography? Just as slaves once had nothing to weigh against the laws that made them property, women abused through pornography now have nothing—certainly nothing of comparable constitutional magnitude—to weigh against the laws that make them "speech."[28]

Strikingly consonant with the general direction of this critique is the active, positive, embodied rights language of Alice Paul's original Equal Rights Amendment as submitted in 1923: "Men and women shall have equal rights throughout the United States and every place subject to its jurisdiction."[29] The, by comparison, passive- and negative-voiced, disembodied 1943 revision—"Equality of rights under the law shall not be denied or abridged by the United States or any State on account of sex"[30]—arguably introduced surely strengthened, the structural liberalism that undermined ERA legally and politically. In 1923, equal rights were to be affirmatively granted to men and women by name. Wherever they did not then exist, which in its purview, was certainly somewhere they were to be given. In 1943, equality of rights in a category called sex were to be precluded from denial by government. Seemingly, no one was given rights where government was not involved. Women and men became "sex," a move toward relative abstraction, equality of which already seemingly existed somewhere where government was not.

What if the original language and the stance it suggested had been pursued? Might we have been able to mobilize women's physical and economic insecurity and vulnerability and desperation? Women's personal indignity, boredom, and despair? Women's fear and invisibility and hopelessness and exhaustion and silence and self-hate? If all that were loosed, what could stand against it? If the question is more why we did not win than why we lost, could not the failure to mobilize women's pain and suppressed discontent due to sex inequality be at least part of the answer? At a minimum, I believe that this real damage of sexism is what women were dealing with the night ERA went down, too submerged in the problem probably even to notice the passing of what might have been part of its solution—especially since almost no one who took up pens and wrote, that night or since, has imagined how it might have helped.

2

From Practice to Theory, Or What Is a White Woman Anyway?

And ain't I a woman?

—Sojourner Truth, *Black Women In Nineteenth-Century American Life: Their Words, Their Thoughts, Their Feelings* 235 (Bert Loewenberg and Ruth Bogin eds. 1976)

Black feminists speak as women because we are women. . . .

—Audre Lorde, *Sister Outsider*, 60 (1984)[1]

It is common to say that something is good in theory but not in practice. I always want to say, then it is not such a good theory, is it? To be good in theory but not in practice posits a relation between theory and practice that places theory prior to practice, both methodologically and normatively, as if theory is a terrain unto itself. The conventional image of the relation between the two is first theory, then practice. You have an idea, then act on it. In legal academia you theorize, then try to get some practitioner to put it into practice. (More accurately, you read law review articles, then write more law review articles.) The closest most legal academics come to practice is teaching—their students, most of whom will practice, many regard as an occupational hazard to their theorizing.

The postmodern version of the relation between theory and practice is discourse unto death. Theory begets no practice, only more text. It proceeds as if you can deconstruct power relations by shifting their markers around in your head. Like all formal idealism, this approach to theory tends unselfconsciously to reproduce existing relations of dominance, in part because it is an utterly removed elite activity. On this level, all theory is a form of practice, because it either subverts or shores up existing deployments of power, in their martial metaphor. As an approach to change, it is the same as the conventional approach to the theory/practice relation: head-driven, not world-driven. Social change is first thought about, then

Talk to Women of Color and the Law, 9 February 1991, Yale Law School, New Haven, CT. First published, 4 *Yale Journal of Law and Feminism* 13 (1991).

acted out. Books relate to books, heads talk to heads. Bodies do not crunch bodies or people move people. As theory, it is the de-realization of the world.

The movement for the liberation of women, including in law, moves the other way around. It is first practice, then theory. Actually, it moves this way in practice, not just in theory. Feminism was a practice long before it was a theory. On its real level, the women's movement—where women move against their determinants as women—remains more practice than theory. This distinguishes it from academic feminism. For women in the world, the gap between theory and practice is the gap between practice and theory. We know things with our lives, and live that knowledge, beyond what any theory has yet theorized. Women's practice of confrontation with the realities of male dominance outruns any existing theory of the possibility of consciousness or resistance. To write the theory of this practice is not to work through logical puzzles or entertaining conundrums, not to fantasize utopias, not to moralize or tell people what to do. It is not to exercise authority; it does not lead practice. Its task is to engage life through developing mechanisms that identify and criticize rather than reproduce social practices of subordination and to make tools of women's consciousness and resistance that further a practical struggle to end inequality. This kind of theory requires humility and it requires participation.

We who work with law need to be about the business of articulating the theory of women's practice—women's resistance, visions, consciousness, injuries, notions of community, experience of inequality. By practice, I mean socially lived. As our theoretical question becomes, What is the theory of women's practice? our theory becomes a way of moving against and through the world, and methodology becomes technology.

Specifically—and such theory inhabits particularity—I want to take up the notion of experience "as a woman" and argue that it is the practice of which the concept of discrimination "based on sex" is the legal theory. That is, I want to investigate how the realities of women's experience of sex inequality in the world have shaped some contours of sex discrimination in the law.

Sex equality as a legal concept has not traditionally been theorized to encompass issues of sexual assault or reproduction because equality theory has been written from men's practice, not women's. Men's experiences of group-based subordination have not centered on sexual and reproductive abuse, although they include instances of it. Some men have been hurt in these ways, but they are few and are not usually regarded as hurt because they are men, rather in spite of it or in derogation of it. Few men are, sexually and reproductively speaking, "similarly situated" to women but treated better. So sexuality and reproduction are not regarded as equality issues in the traditional approach.[2] Two intrepid, indomitable women, determined to write the practice of their lives onto the law, moved the theory of sex equality to include these issues.

In her case, *Meritor Savings Bank v. Vinson*,[3] Mechelle Vinson established that sexual harassment as a working environment is sex discrimination under civil rights law. Her resistance to her supervisor Sidney Taylor—specifically, her identification that his repeated rape, his standing over her in the bank vault waving his penis and laughing, were done to her because she was a woman—changed the theory of sex discrimination for all women. In her case, *California Federal Savings and Loan Association v. Guerra*,[4] Lillian Garland established that guaranteeing unpaid leaves for pregnant women by law is not discrimination on the basis of sex, but is a step in ending discrimination on the basis of sex. Her resistance to her employer, the California Federal Savings and Loan Association, in its refusal to reinstate her in her job after a pregnancy leave—her identification of that practice as illegal treatment of her because she was a woman—gave sex equality law a decisive spin in the direction of promoting equality, away from its prior status quo—mirroring regressive neutrality. The arguments that won these cases were based on the plaintiffs' lives as women, on insisting that actual social practices that subordinated them as women be theoretically recognized as impermissible sex-based discrimination under law. In the process, sexual assault and reproduction became sex equality issues, with implications for the laws of rape and abortion, among others.

So what is meant by treatment "as women" here? To speak of being treated "as a woman" is to make an empirical statement about reality, to describe the realities of women's situation. In the United States, with parallels in other cultures, women's situation is made up of unequal pay combined with allocation to disrespected work, sexual targeting for rape, domestic battering, sexual abuse as children, and systematic sexual harassment together with depersonalization, demeaned physical characteristics, use in denigrating entertainment, deprivation of reproductive control, and forced prostitution. To notice that these practices are done by men to women is to see these abuses as forming a system, a hierarchy of inequality. This situation has occurred in many places, in one form or another, for a very long time, often in a context characterized by disenfranchisement, preclusion from property ownership (women are more likely to be property than to own any), ownership and use as object, exclusion from public life, sex-based poverty, degraded sexuality, and a devaluation of women's human worth and contributions throughout society. This subordination of women to men is socially institutionalized, cumulatively and systematically shaping access to human dignity, respect, resources, physical security, credibility, membership in community, speech, and power. Comprised of all its variations, the group "women" can be seen to have a collective social history of disempowerment, exploitation, and subordination extending to the present. To be treated "as a woman" in this sense is to be disadvantaged in these ways incident to being socially assigned to the female sex. To speak of social treatment "as a woman" is thus not to invoke any abstract essence or homogeneous generic or ideal type, not to posit anything, far less anything universal, but to refer to this diverse and pervasive concrete material reality of social meanings and practices such that, in the words of Richard Rorty, "a woman is not yet the name of a way of being human."[5]

Thus cohering the theory of "women" out of the practice of women produces the opposite of what Elizabeth Spelman has criticized as a reductive assumption of essential sameness of all women that she identifies in some feminist theory.[6] The task of theorizing women's practice produces a new kind of theory, one that is different from prior modes of theorizing in form, not just content. As Andrea Dworkin said quite a long time ago, women's situation requires new ways of thinking, not just thinking new things.[7] "Woman" as abstraction, distillation, common denominator, or idea is the old way of thinking, or at most a new thing to think, but it is not a new way of thinking. Nor is thinking "like" a woman, largely a misogynist slur for reproducing one's determinants when thinking like a victim, all there is to thinking "as" a woman, as one embodiment of a collective experience.

Some recent work, especially Elizabeth Spelman's, could be read to argue that there is no such thing as experience "as a woman" and that women of color prove it.[8] This theory converges with the elevation of "differences" as a flag under which to develop diverse "feminisms."[9] To do theory in its conventional abstract way, as many do, is to import the assumption that all women are the same or they are not women. What makes them women is their fit within the abstraction "woman" or their conformity to a fixed, posited female essence. The consequence of such theorizing is to reproduce dominance on the level of theory. While much work subjected to this criticism does not do this,[10] one can trace it, surprisingly, in the works of Simone de Beauvoir and Susan Brownmiller.

De Beauvoir, explaining why women are second-class citizens, says:

> Here we have the key to the whole mystery. On the biological level a species is maintained only by creating itself anew; but this creation results only in repeating the same Life in more individuals. . . . Her [woman's] misfortune is to have been biologically destined for the repetition of Life, when even in her own view Life does not carry within itself its reasons for being, reasons that are more important than Life itself.[11]

Here women are defined in terms of biological reproductive capacity. It is unclear exactly how any social organization of equality could change such an existential fact, far less how to argue that a social policy that institutionalized it could be sex discriminatory.

Susan Brownmiller argues the centrality of rape in women's condition in the following terms:

> Man's structural capacity to rape and woman's corresponding structural vulnerability are as basic to the physiology of both our sexes as the primal act of sex itself. Had it not been for this accident of biology, an accommodation requiring the locking together of two separate parts, penis and vagina, there would be neither copulation nor rape as we know it. . . . By anatomical fiat—the inescapable construction of their genital organs—the human male was a natural predator and the human female served as his natural prey.[12]

Exactly how to oppose sexual assault from this vantage point is similarly unclear. Do we make a law against intercourse? Although both theorists have considerably more to offer on the question of what defines women's condition, what we have in these passages is simple biological determinism presented as a critical theory of social change.

The problem here, it seems to me, does not begin with a failure to take account of race or class, but with the failure to take account of gender. It is not only or most fundamentally an account of race or class dominance that is missing here, but an account of male dominance. There is nothing biologically necessary about rape, as Mechelle Vinson made abundantly clear when she sued for rape as unequal treatment on the basis of sex. And, as Lillian Garland saw, and made everyone else see, it is the way society punishes women for reproduction that creates women's problems with reproduction, not reproduction itself. Both women are Black. This only supports my suspicion that if a theory is not true of, and does not work for, women of color, it is not really true of, and will not work for, any women, and that it is not really about gender at all. The theory of the practice of Mechelle Vinson and Lillian Garland, because it is about the experience of Black women, *is* what gender is about.

In recent critiques of feminist work for failing to take account of race or class,[13] it is assumed that there is such a thing as race and class, although race and class are generally treated as abstractions to attack gender rather than as concrete realities, if indeed they are treated at all. Spelman, for example, discusses race but does virtually nothing about class.[14] In any event, race and class are regarded as unproblematically real and not in need of justification or theoretical construction. Only gender is not real and needs to be justified. Although many women have demanded that discussions of race or class take gender into account, typically these demands do not take the form that, outside explicit recognition of gender, race or class do not exist. That there is a diversity to the experience of men and women of color, and of working-class women and men regardless of race, is not said to mean that race or class is not a meaningful concept. I have heard no one say that, without sex or gender specificity, there can be no meaningful discussion of "people of color." Thus the phrase "people of color and white women" has come to replace the previous "women and minorities," which women of color rightly perceived as not including them twice, and as embodying a white standard for sex and a male standard for race. But I hear no talk of "all women and men of color," for instance. When women of color refer to "people who look like me," it is understood that they mean people of color, not women, in spite of the fact that both race and sex are visual assignments, both possess clarity as well as ambiguity, and both are marks of oppression, hence potentially of community.

In this connection, it has recently come to my attention that the white woman is the issue here, so I decided I better find out what one is. This creature is not poor, not battered, not raped (not really), not molested as a child, not pregnant as a teenager, not prostituted, not coerced into pornography, not a welfare mother, and not economically exploited. She doesn't work. She is either the white man's image of her—effete, pampered, privileged, protected, flighty, and self-indulgent—or the Black man's image of her—all that, plus the "pretty white girl" (meaning ugly as sin but regarded as the ultimate in beauty because she is white). She is Miss Anne of the kitchen, she puts Frederick Douglass to the lash, she cries rape when Emmett Till looks at her sideways, she manipulates white men's very real power with the lifting of her very well-manicured little finger. She makes an appearance in Baraka's "rape the white girl,"[15] as Cleaver's real thing after target practice on Black women,[16] as Helmut Newton's glossy upscale hard-edged, distanced vamp,[17] and as the Central Park Jogger, the classy white madonna who got herself raped and beaten nearly to death. She flings her hair, feels beautiful all the time, complains about the colored help, tips badly, can't do anything, doesn't do anything, doesn't know anything, and alternates fantasizing about fucking Black men with accusing them of raping her. As Ntozake Shange points out, all Western civilization depends on her.[18] On top of all of this, out of impudence, imitativeness, pique, and a simple lack of anything meaningful to do, she thinks she needs to be liberated. Her feminist incarnation is all of the above, and guilty about every single bit of it, having by dint of repetition refined saying "I'm sorry" to a high form of art. She can't even make up her own songs.

There is, of course, much too much of this, this "woman, modified," this woman discounted by white, meaning she would be oppressed but for her privilege. But this image seldom comes face to face with the rest of her reality: the fact that the majority of the poor are white women and their children (at least half of whom are female); that white women are systematically battered in their homes, murdered by intimates and serial killers alike, molested as children, actually raped (mostly by white men); and that even Black men, on average, make more than they do.[19] If one did not know this, one could be taken in by white men's image of white women: that the pedestal is real, rather than a cage in which to confine and trivialize them and segregate them from the rest of life, a vehicle for sexualized infantilization, a virginal setup for rape by men who enjoy violating the pure, and a myth with which to try to control Black women. (See, if you would lie down and be quiet and not move, we would revere you, too.) One would think that the white men's myth that they protect white women was real, rather than a racist cover to guarantee their exclusive and unimpeded sexual access—meaning they can rape her at will, and do, a posture made good in the marital-rape exclusion and the largely useless rape law generally. One would think that the only white women in brothels in the South during the Civil War were in *Gone with the Wind*.[20] This is not to say there is no such thing as skin privilege, but rather that it has never insulated white women from the brutality and misogyny of men, mostly but not exclusively white men, or from its effective legalization. In other words, the "white girls" of this theory miss quite a lot of the reality of white women in the practice of male supremacy.

Beneath the trivialization of the white woman's subordination implicit in the dismissive sneer "straight white economically-privileged women" (a phrase that has become one word, the accuracy of some of its terms being rarely documented even in law journals) lies the notion that there is no such thing as the oppression of women as such. If white women's oppression is but an illusion of privilege and a rip-off and reduction of the civil rights movement, there is no such thing as a woman, our practice produces no theory, and discrimination on the basis of sex does not exist. To argue that oppression "as a woman" negates rather than encompasses recognition of the oppression of women on bases such as race and class is to say that there is no such thing as the practice of sex inequality.

Let's take this the other way around. As I mentioned, both Mechelle Vinson and Lillian Garland are African American women. Wasn't Mechelle Vinson sexually harassed as a woman? Wasn't Lillian Garland pregnant as a woman? They thought so. The whole point of their cases was to get their injuries understood as "based on sex," that is, it happened because they are women. The perpetrators, and the policies under which they were disadvantaged, saw them as women. What is being a woman if it does not include being oppressed as one? When the Reconstruction Amendments "gave Blacks the vote," and Black women still could not vote, weren't they kept from voting "as women"? When African American women are raped two times as often as white women, aren't they raped as women? That does not mean their race is irrelevant and it does not mean that their injuries can be understood outside a racial context. Rather, it means that "sex" is *made up of* the reality of the experiences of all women, including theirs. It is a composite unit rather than a divided unitary whole, such that each woman, in her way, is all women. So, when white women are sexually harassed or lose their jobs because they are pregnant, aren't they women too?

The treatment of women in pornography shows how the category "women" is constructed in real life in graphic relief. One way or another, all women are in pornography. African American women are featured in bondage, struggling, in cages, as animals, insatiable. As Andrea Dworkin has shown, the sexualized hostility directed against them makes their skin into a sex organ, focusing the aggression and contempt directed principally at other women's genitals.[21] Asian women are passive, inert, as if dead, tortured unspeakably. Latinas are hot mommas. Fill in the rest from every demeaning and hostile racial stereotype you know; it is sex here. This is not done to men, not in heterosexual pornography. What is done to white women is a kind of floor; it is the best anyone is treated and it runs from *Playboy* through sadomasochism to snuff. What is done to white women can be done to any woman, and then some. This does not make white women the essence of womanhood. It is simply a reality that this is what can be done and *is* done to the most privileged of women. Privilege as a woman gets you most valued as dead meat.

Each woman is in pornography as the embodiment of her particularities. This is not in tension with being there "as a woman"; *it is part of what being there as a woman means.* Her specificity helps make up what gender *is.* White, for instance, is not a residual category. It is not a standard against which the rest are "different." There is no generic "woman" in pornography. White is not unmarked; it is a specific sexual taste. Being defined and used in this way defines what being a woman means in practice. As Sartre answered the question, What is a Jew? start with the anti-Semite.[22] Applied to the question of theory and practice, Robin Morgan once said, "[P]ornography is the theory, rape is the practice."[23] This is true, but Andrea Dworkin's revision is more true: "Pornography is the theory, pornography is the practice."[24]

In my view, the subtext to the critique of oppression "as a woman," the critique that holds that there is no such thing, is dis-identification with women. One of its consequences is the destruction of the basis for a jurisprudence of sex equality. An argument advanced in many critiques by women of color has been that theories of women must include all women, and when they do, theory will change. On one level, this is necessarily true. On another, it ignores the formative contributions of women of color to feminist theory since its inception. I also sense, though, that many women, not only women of color and not only academics, do not want to be "just women," not only because something important is left out, but also because that means being in a category with "her," the useless white woman whose first reaction when the going gets rough is to cry. I sense here that people feel more dignity in being part of any group that includes men than in being part of a group that includes that ultimate reduction of the notion of oppression, that instigator of lynch mobs, that ludicrous whiner, that equality coattails rider, the white woman. It seems that if the oppression that is done to you is also done to a man, you are more likely to be recognized as oppressed as opposed to inferior. Once a group is seen as putatively human, a process helped by including men in it, an oppressed man falls from a human standard.[25] A woman is just a woman—the ontological victim—so not victimized at all.

Unlike other women, the white woman who is not poor or working-class or lesbian or Jewish or disabled or old or young *does not share her oppression with any man.* That does not make her condition any more definitive of the meaning of "women" than the condition of any other woman is. But trivializing her oppression, because it is not even potentially racist or class-biased or heterosexist or anti-Semitic, does define the meaning of being "antiwoman" with a special clarity. How the white woman is imagined and constructed and treated becomes a particularly sensitive indicator of the degree to which women, as such, are despised.

If we build a theory out of women's practice, comprised of the diversity of all women's experiences, we do not have the problem that some feminist theory has been rightly criticized for. When we have it is when we make theory out of abstractions and accept the images forced on us by male dominance. The assumption that all women are the same is part of the bedrock of sexism that the women's movement is predicated on challenging. That some academics find it difficult to theorize without reproducing it simply means that they continue to do to women what theory, predicated on the practice of male dominance, has always done to women. It is their notion of what theory is, and its relation to its world, that needs to change.

If our theory of what is "based on sex" makes gender out of actual social practices distinctively directed against women as women identify them, the problem that the critique of so-called essentialism exists to rectify ceases to exist. And this bridge, the one from practice to theory, is not built on anyone's back.

3

Law in the Everyday Life of Women

For most women, life is little but everyday, a constant cycle of minutiae with few landmarks or dramatic demarcations of time, a litany of needs served but never satisfied, time spent but seldom occupied, lines drawn that, like the horizon, recede on approach. Across time and culture, and in individual biographies, the sameness in women's lives is as striking as the diversity of conditions under which it is lived. Men rise and fall. Their dynasties and revolutions and intellectual fashions come and go. Things happen. In the lives of women, men are served, children are cared for, home is made, work is done, the sun goes down.

Most women will tell you that law has little to do with their everyday lives. They seldom hit walls that look legal—they do not get that far. The lives of women in poverty are circumscribed by rules and regulations that they know are stacked and enforced against them and could be different, but nothing so majestic as "the law" is accessible to them. Many women encounter official obstacles, but few have the law in their hands. If a woman complains to the police of a crime against her, the law is in the hands of the prosecutor. On the civil side, it usually takes money to get the law to work for you. Even when a woman's injury is recognized by law, which is seldom, most women lack the resources to use it.

To most women, the law is a foreign country with an unintelligible tongue, alien mores, secret traps, uncontrollable and unresponsive dynamics, obscure but rigid dogmas, barbaric and draconian rituals, and consequences as scary as they are incomprehensible. Actually, this is true for most men as well.[1] The difference is that the people who can and do make law work for them, who designed it so it would work for them as if they were the whole world, are men—specifically, white upper-class men. Women reflect this reality in their view that if you try to use the law, it is as likely to blow up in your face as to help. Law is Kafka's trial, Dickens's *Bleak House*. Mostly women feel that the law is not about them, has no

First published, *Law in Everyday Life* 109 (Austin Sarat and Thomas R. Kearns, eds., 1993).

idea who they are or what they face or how they think or feel, has nothing to say to them, and can do nothing for them. When the law and their life collide, it is their life that gets the worst of it.

Women in conflict with the law show this relation in highest relief. Most become criminals for responding in kind to male violence against them, for crimes of poverty, for being involved with a man who committed a crime (what might be called first-degree bad choice of boyfriend), or for prostitution—being sold by men to men for what men value women for, and then being devalued and considered a criminal for it. On my observation, most imprisoned women who are not inside for crimes of self-defense *against* men who batter them are in for crimes committed *with* men who batter them.[2] The law does little to nothing about the crimes against women that position them to commit the crimes that do matter officially. For instance, women's imprisonment in their homes by violent men who batter them is not thought official, even though it is widely officially condoned.

The law operates most visibly in the lives of women in officially recognized captivity. They are surrounded, defined, debased, and confined by the law. Their everyday lives are taken over by it. It swallows them up: their liberties, their children, their bodies, their community ties, what initiative and self-respect they had managed to salvage, and sometimes their lives. To be in prison is what it is for women to live their everyday lives entirely inside the law. Even when women criminals do the same things and get the same sentences as men, which is not the norm,[3] their crimes are the crimes of women. They commit them as women, are punished as women, and, when the law is finished with them, are thrown back onto society's trash heap for women.

The law that is applied to them and to all women was not written by women, white or Black, rich or poor. It has not been based on women's experiences of life, everyday or otherwise. No one represented women's interests as women in creating it, and few have considered women's interests as women in applying it.[4] Unlike men, many of whom are also estranged from the law—especially unlike white upper-class men—no women had voice or representation in constituting this state or its laws, yet we are presumed to consent to its rule. It was not written for our benefit, and it shows.

The exclusion of women from a formative role in the law has meant that much legal intervention in women's lives is unconstructive, to say the least, while most of women's lives is carried out beneath explicit legal notice. Crimes and civil injuries do not imagine most harms distinctive to women, such as the stigma of female sexuality, which pervasively imposes inferiority on women in everyday life. Canons of legal interpretation in laws that might apply to real events in women's lives are shaped to assume the validity of the male point of view. An example in the law of sex discrimination is the "intent" requirement, which bases a finding of discrimination on the perspective of the alleged discriminator rather than on the consequences of his actions for the discriminated-against. Burdens of proof and evidentiary standards as well as substantive law tacitly presuppose the male experience as normative and credible and relevant. An example is the mens rea requirement in the law of rape, which bases its determination of rape on the perspective of the accused rapist as opposed to that of the victim. Proceeding by analogy, as the law does, means that new crimes and injuries committed against women must be like old ones (read: those committed against men) before they can be recognized as crimes and injuries at all. Crimes women distinctively commit, they seem to have figured out. When a woman tries to raise her voice, precedent often requires decisive deference to a law built on the silence of women, a law that originated when we were not even permitted to vote or to learn to read, in a society premised on women's subjection.

No law addresses the deepest, simplest, quietest, and most widespread atrocities of women's everyday lives. The law that purports to address them, like the law of sexual assault, does not reflect their realities or, like the law of domestic violence, is not enforced. It seems that either the law does not exist, does not apply, is applied to women's detriment, or is not applied at all. The deepest rules of women's lives are written beneath or between the lines, and on other pages.

Yet the actions and inactions of law construct and constrict women's lives, its consequences no less powerful for being offstage. Focusing on the areas the law abdicates, its gaps and silences and absences, one finds that women's everyday life has real rules, but they are not the formal ones. They have never been legislated or adjudicated. They have not had to be. They effectively prescribe what girls can be, what the community encourages and permits in a woman, what opportunities are available and hence what aspirations are developed, what shape of life is so expected that it is virtually never articulated. These rules go under the heading of socialization, pressure, religion, popular culture, masculinity and femininity, everyday life. The rules of everyday life, in this sense, are that law which is not one, the law for women where there is no law.

The content of the formal legal system, the output of legislatures and courts, has a real effect on these processes, but, from the vantage point of life being lived, it seems a distant one. Whether sex discrimination in athletics is illegal, whether women's supposed "interests" make occupational segregation nondiscriminatory,[5] whether pornography is protected by the state,[6] whether legal abortion is available[7]—all deeply shape women's realities, but from high up and a long way off. Women seldom have much say in these matters yet live their consequences every day in factories, behind counters, in beds, on streets, in their heads, and in the eyes and at the hands of men, where the everyday lives of most women are largely lived out. Women's exclusion from law and marginality within it does not make the law inactive in women's subordination day to day. The fact that women have nothing to say about a sphere of life does not mean that it does not affect us—to the contrary. Especially if one thinks of everyday life as not having to be the way it is, the role of law in keeping it the way it is becomes visible, compelling, imperative.

Of all of everyday life, sexual relations between women and men may seem the farthest from the reach of law. Sex occurs in private, in presumed consent, in everyday intimacy. Sex is thought of as a sphere to itself with its own rules, written by desire or individual taste or mutual negotiation or tolerance, not by law. Yet the law of sexual assault in the United States has a very real everyday impact on sexual life. Rape is supposedly illegal. Yet the rape that the law actually recognizes as illegal is a far cry from the sex forced on women in everyday life. The law's rape is by a stranger, in a strange location, with a weapon, which the woman resisted within an inch of her life. Preferably the woman is white, the rapist Black. Most rapes that actually happen are by someone the woman knows, of the same race, often to women of color. Rape happens at home or on a date, without weapons other than hands and a penis, and the woman is too surprised or too terrified or too learned in passivity or wants to get it over with too badly or has heard too much about men who kill women who resist to fight back. Or she does fight back and loses and is not believed, either by the rapist or in court, because sex is what a woman is for.

To the extent your reality does not fit the law's picture, your rape is not illegal. The implications of this for everyday sex life are that any man who knows a woman of the same race can probably get away with raping her. The better he knows her, the more likely he is to get away with it. Married women in states that do not have a law against marital rape are the ultimate example. Until the early 1970s, a woman was not considered a reliable witness about her own rape, but the defendant was.[8] Unless someone besides the woman saw it, it was not legally real. Many jurisdictions, like California and Canada and England, still require that the state prove that the accused rapist honestly believed that the woman did not consent, no matter how much force was used.[9]

What does all this mean for having no mean no? When no can legally mean yes, what does yes mean in everyday life? When rape passes legally as intercourse, what is sexual intimacy? The law of rape deeply affects sexual intimacy by making forced sex legally sex, not rape, every night. Every day, because women know this, they do not report rapes nine times out of ten.[10] When a woman does report, the media have the legal right to print her name and picture, making her into everyday pornography.[11] The racism of the criminal justice system is an everyday reality for women of color, who do not report their rapes by men of color because of it. In reality, there are no laws against what can be done to them. Many women, no matter how violated they were, do not call what happened to them rape if they do not think a court would agree with them. In this ultimate triumph of law over life, law tells women what happened to them and many of us believe it. When asked, "Have you ever been raped?" many women answer, "I don't know."[12]

A similar combination of utter neglect with malignant concern animates the law of reproduction. Women get pregnant every day without wanting to be and at the same time are prevented from having children they want to have. The question here is who controls the reproductive uses of women, a process to which controlling the fetus is instrumental. When a woman is sterilized against her will and even without her knowledge, as has most often been done to women of color and to "mentally disabled" women, no law prohibits it or even compensates it after the fact.[13] Does law then have no relation to each day of the rest of their lives, on which they now cannot have children? If a woman dies from a desperation-induced self-abortion because a funded, safe one is not available by law—and most such women have been Black or Hispanic[14]—did law not end her everyday life?

Pornography suffuses women's everyday life, crisp in cellophane at your child's eye level in the 7–11, dog-eared and hidden at the back of your boss's drawer at work, smack in your face on the wall of your car repair shop or your school's film society's trendy spring roster, soggy under your son's mattress. Under the law of obscenity, pornography is supposed to be against the law. In the real world of everyday life, it is effectively legal because it is pervasively there, available without sanction or fear of sanction. This is what a dead-letter law looks like: everyday life is lived as if it is not there. But the pretense of law being there also has a distinctive effect. The combination of pornography being putatively forbidden but totally available, decried in public but permitted and used in private, intrudes the law deeply into women's everyday lives. The allegedly forbidden quality of pornography sexualizes it by surrounding it with power and taboo and makes defending and using it appear to be an act of daring and danger, a blow for freedom against repression. Meantime, its actual availability belies the taboo and promotes the power, spreading it and supporting it as a model for women's everyday lives.

The everyday reality of pornography, particularly of adults, supersedes any formal law currently in force and becomes the real rules for women's lives, the sacred secret codebook with directions about what to do with a woman, what everything she says and does means, what a woman is. All the sexual abuses of women's everyday lives that are not recognized by the law are there in the pornography: the humiliation, the objectification, the forced access, the torture, the use of children, the sexualized racial hatred, the misogyny. As Andrea Dworkin has said, "Pornography is the law for women." Open your mouth this far. Spread your legs this wide. Put your arms like this. Talk dirty to me. Now smile.[15]

In this way, visual and physical intrusion on women—a normative experience of objectification and dehumanization made to seem deviant and marginal when medicalized as voyeurism and other exotic paraphilias—becomes the paradigm for sex. Sex in this sense is not just an activity at a time and place but a pervasive dimension of social life as lived every day. A woman's physical condition (*Knocked-Up Mamas*, *Milky Tits*), occupation (lady lawyer, hot housewife), racial or ethnic or religious heritage (*Geisha Gashes*, *Black Bondage*, *I Was a Gestapo Sex Slave*), age (*Cherry Tarts*, *Ten*), family status (*Daddy's Girl*), pets (*Doggie Girl*), facts of everyday life to her, become sex to the consumer in the world pornography creates, along with everyday objects like telephones, cucumbers, beer cans, ropes, paper clips, razors, candle wax, police uniforms, plumber's helpers, lollipops, and teddy bears. In this process, the law helps constitute what is called desire by defining what amounts to sexual use and abuse of women and children as illegal and out of bounds and then doing nothing about it. Women realize that reporting sexual assaults is futile because this is a society that considers them freedom. When the state goes a step further and declares that pornography is affirmatively protected after all, and its harm to women is real but does not matter as much as the pornography of us matters,[16] women's despairing relation to the state and its laws—our belief that they will never see us as real—becomes total.

Even in the world pornography has made, it never occurs to most women, living their lives day to day, that having sex with a man to whom one is married is part of being a good mother. The law of child custody in general, of lesbian child custody in particular, reveals that there are sexual requirements for the legal adequacy of women's parenting. If a woman has a sexual relationship with a woman, she can lose her children,[17] "lesbian" being pornography for men, to which they do not think children should be exposed. The everyday sexuality of many women is thus controlled every day through fear due to the recently strengthened possibility of men seeking custody of children.[18] This is not to say that the men actually want the children, although sometimes they do. More commonly, they want to use the threat of challenging custody as a financial lever to reduce support payments, and as control generally. The new norm of joint custody has a similar effect. Day to day, the mother has the major responsibility and does most of the work, but because of joint custody, the father can still control the big decisions. In other words, now not even divorce disturbs the power relation of marriage. And women who were raped in their marriages face sharing custody of their children with their rapist.

Family law keeps a lot of women in place and in line, fearful of altering their lives because of how it could be made to look in court. Some do not go public with past abuse through pornography for this reason. Many stay with men who abuse them because they fear the man would try to take their children away, and he would look better under existing legal standards—high income, intact new family, white picket fence—than they do. Most women feel they married an individual but find on considering divorce that he represents the law and the law represents him. He is the law of the state in the home.

The realm in which women's everyday life is lived, the setting for many of these daily atrocities, is termed "the private." Law defines the private as where law is not, that into which law does not intrude, where no harm is done other than by law's presence. In everyday life, the privacy is his. Obscenity is affirmatively protected in private. Wives are raped in private. Women's labor is exploited in private. Equality is not guaranteed in private. Prostitution, when acts of sex occur out of public view, is often termed private. In private, women who can afford abortions can get them, but those who cannot afford them get no public support, because private choices are not public responsibilities.[19]

Women in everyday life have no privacy in private. In private, women are objects of male subjectivity and male power. The private is that place where men can do whatever they want because women reside there. The consent that supposedly demarcates this private surrounds women and follows us wherever we go. Men seem to reside in public, where laws against harm exist—real harm, harm to men and whoever has the privilege to be hurt like men—and follow them wherever they go. Having arranged the law against rape and battering and sexual abuse of children so virtually nothing is done about them, and having supported male power in the home as a virtual absolute, the law then proclaims its profoundest self-restraint, its guarantee of liberty where it matters most, in "the right to be let alone."[20] This home is the place Andrea Dworkin has described from battered women's perspective as "that open grave where so many women lie waiting to die."[21] As a legal doctrine, privacy has become the affirmative triumph of the state's abdication of women.[22] Sanctified by the absolution of law, the private is the everyday domain of women in captivity, abandoned to their isolation and told it is what freedom really means.

This is to say that the law is complicit in the impoverishment of the average woman who makes nowhere near the income of the average man,[23] in the everyday aggression against the 44 percent of women who are victims of rape or attempted rape at least once in their lives,[24] in the assaults of the quarter to a third of women who are battered in their homes,[25] in the denial to women of the choice not to have children and the choice to have children and not to have them stolen, and in every act of violation or second-class citizenship that involves pornography. The law of rape collaborates with rapists to the extent it precludes recognition of the violations it purports to prohibit. The law of discrimination collaborates with perpetrators of discrimination to the extent its doctrines reproduce inequality rather than remedy it, requiring that equality already effectively exist before it can be guaranteed. The law of pornography collaborates with pornographers by protecting their right to abuse women behind the guarantee of freedom of speech, at the same time participating in their marketing strategy of sexualizing pornography by making it seem forbidden. The law of child custody collaborates with patriarchy in imposing male dominant values on women in the family, and the law of privacy collaborates with whoever has power by guaranteeing spheres of impunity in which the law leaves men to their own devices. Even when the law does nothing—and it does nothing in so many ways—it is responsible for not working for women, whether law permits nothing when it pretends to do something, is inadequate, is not enforced, or does not exist at all. If it does not work for women, it does not work.

The same people who have power in life have had power in law, and the reverse. This relation is a process, though, not an inert or static fact, as one counterexample serves to reveal. Women have made at least one law: the law against sexual harassment. Before sexual harassment became actionable as a form of sex discrimination, it was just everyday life. The sex role norm that empowers men to initiate sex to women under conditions of inequality is intensified in sexual harassment. Women are pressured and intimidated into sexual compliance and raped as the price for economic survival. This has been done for centuries with virtual impunity. When women's experience was made the basis for the law against sexual harassment, everyday life altered as well. Men kept doing it, but the experience had a name, an analysis that placed it within the collective reality of gender, a forum for confrontation with some dignity and the possibility of relief. Most important, women's own sense of violation changed because the harm had legal expression and legitimacy and public sanction. Law told women back what they knew was true. Sexual harassment was against the law against treating women as unequals, the law of sex discrimination. This law told the truth: sex inequality is the problem, this problem. In going from everyday life to law, sexual harassment went from a gripe to a grievance, from a shameful story about a woman to actionable testimony about a man. Changing what could be done by law changed the way it felt to live through it in life, and the status of women took a step from victim to citizen.

To wonder whether women will ever become full citizens is partly to ask whether law in women's hands can mean what law in men's everyday hands has meant. For better and worse, probably not. For worse, even when clothed in law, no woman escapes the female body when she is in court, not yet. This may be why sexual harassment complainants still do better on paper than they do on the witness stand. For better, the extent to which law in women's hands could improve upon law in men's is suggested by the pornography example. Obscenity law is the closest men have come to an attempt to address the problem of pornography. It is not very close and has been an abject and total failure. It is clear that men do not want to restrict pornography very much or they would treat it seriously, as they treat air traffic control, for instance. In ignoring abuse to women entirely, obscenity law invites pornographers to violate women and run, sheltered by the First Amendment. The obscenity definition, which requires the materials be "taken as a whole,"[26] invites surrounding abuse with literature, making the abuse look more legitimate. The "community standards" rule invites flooding communities with pornography, so that their standards will come to conform to it. The "prurient interest" requirement invites juries to deny the sexual appeal of the most violent materials, supporting their protection. Even given these built-in difficulties for applying obscenity law to anything, its vague definition invites prosecution of nearly anything with sexual content. Given its large potential sweep, from the fact that the pornography industry has nearly quadrupled in size since this definition was promulgated, it is reasonable to conclude that men do not want to do anything about pornography. If one assumes that the law can only work as it has worked in men's hands, the failure of obscenity law makes a good case for the limits of the law in this area. If one has an alternative, that failure shows that the law is impotent in men's hands when it helps men be potent in everyday life. In other words, men's law has been constructed and applied to conform to a deeper logic that supports male power.

By contrast, the civil rights law against pornography that Andrea Dworkin and I, working with others at their request, designed, puts the legal power to oppose the pornographers in the hands of women, and those men who are also hurt by it on the basis of their sex. Because it is based on the reality of women's everyday lives, this law gives women the power of law to act against pornography's real abuses. It names the harm: sexual subordination on the basis of gender. It permits women to act without prosecutors' permission or police discretion. It does not forbid pornography, which keeps it sexy; it makes it actionable as a sexualized practice of bigotry, which is detumescent. Its down side is neither as unlimited, nor its up side as limited, as obscenity law. This is because the civil rights law against pornography has a real relation to the lives women live. Once women are empowered to expose its harms in their everyday lives, there is no place left to hide its abuses.

The only question is: will the law permit this everyday abuse to be stopped? The fact that this law directly confronts male power where it lives means it will be slated for extinction. This does not mean it should not exist; it merely means its existence will be opposed. Making it possible for women to stand against the pornographers in court would be a change in itself. Maybe the lesson here is that law is not monolithic, that what it is depends on *how* it is used, on its social substance and interface. Perhaps antidiscrimination initiatives are unlike other laws in that they confront the real issue—social inequality—more directly and potentially more constructively than other laws do.

Among left-leaning academic lawyers in particular, there is a big controversy over whether law matters to life and whether those who care about everyday life should care about law at all. Does life make law or does law make life? they wonder. When men make both, and you are a woman, the distinction may not count for much, except that law purports to have rules other than force and pretends to be accountable, whereas life does not. At this point, the case for giving up on law is even stronger than the case for giving up on life. Women giving up does seem to be the point.

There is a legitimate question, though, about the relation between law and the power that produces it, and the degree to which change in one produces change in the other. Whatever we know about how change is made, we do know that *no* change in one produces no change in the other. Women's experience makes us suspicious of making women's legal exclusion and marginalization and invisibility into a radical virtue, even as the antistate position usually stops short of opposing pornography, which the state is clearly for. Women's everyday lives make us suspicious of the view that rights, especially equality rights, do not matter, even as many who take this position have rights while women in general do not.[27] Our lives make us suspicious of abdicating the state—in favor of what? those bastions of sensitivity and receptivity to women, the media and organized labor? Besides, what does it mean to abdicate a society you are excluded from, besides further exclusion? It does not stop affecting you when you stop trying to affect it.

Surely one of the most effective strategies for maintaining a system of dominance is to convince those who seek to end it that the tools of dominance must be left in the hands of the dominant. Women need institutional support for equality, both because of and in spite of the fact that power in women's hands is different from power in men's hands. Getting power is not the same as transforming it, but how are we supposed to transform it if we cannot get it? How can it be changed if it is authoritatively defined in male terms and retained in male hands? I am tired of people who have power—whether they identify with it or not—telling women that we can only have power if we transform it. They might begin by insisting it be transformed in the hands of those who already have it. They might also explain how they plan to produce equality without institutional support, indeed while leaving in place present legal structures that enforce women's inequality. It's like telling women we should transform the state in the face of a law that deprives us of the right to vote. What are we supposed to do? Picket and hope they listen? Start a new state? Get the bomb? Why aren't any of these critics doing any of these things or their equivalent? I would also really like to hear their argument against the franchise. Not why it is limited; why its limits mean we should not fight for it and be able to vote at all. Maybe they think it is only symbolic.

Whoever says law cannot make change so we should not try might explain why the law should be exempt in the struggle for social transformation. Some of us suspect that women, in particular, are being told that not much can be done with law because a lot can be. If law were to be made to work for women, the relation of law to life, as well as its content, might have to change in the process. As more women become lawyers and maybe the law starts to listen to women, perhaps the legal profession will decline in prestige and power. Maybe women using law will delegitimize law, and male supremacy—in its endless adaptability and ingenuity—will have to find other guises for the dominance it currently exercises through law.

This is not to urge a top-down model of change or to advocate merely inverting or reshuffling the demographics of existing structures of power, or to say that law alone solves anything. It is to say that putting power in the hands of the powerless can change power as well as the situation of the powerless. It is also to urge a confrontational engagement with existing institutions: one that refuses to let power off the hook. Integral to a larger political movement on all levels, this is a demand that law recognize that women live here, too. Every day of our lives.

4

Toward a New Theory of Equality

Equality is valued nearly everywhere but practiced almost nowhere. As an idea, it can be fiercely loved, passionately sought, widely vaunted, legally guaranteed, sentimentally assumed, or complacently taken for granted. As a reality, in lives lived or institutions run, it hardly exists anywhere.

This is true among men but it is nowhere more true than between women and men. Sex equality is fairly common as a legal guarantee, its application varying widely in meaning and meaningfulness, as a principle ranging in acceptance from obvious to anathema, with the inequality of the sexes thriving alongside it. Sex inequality is diverse empirically, ideologically, and legally, varying in extent, form, and degree,[1] with some places far worse for women than others, but nowhere is sex equality achieved. Equality between women and men, in realms from the institutional to the intimate, remains more dream than fact.

The goal of legal equality is to end discrimination and produce social equality. After about thirty years of trying, very hard in some places, it has yet to succeed. There is no equality between women and men, and there is little among men either, certainly not on an ethnic or racial basis. Economic measures document this failure particularly clearly; discrimination on combined grounds illustrate it especially vividly. Of the many possible explanations, legal equality theory itself needs to be considered. On the view that the existing approach is consistent with the outcomes it has produced—that it is determinately connected with its results or lack of them—I will examine the dominant legal equality theory, its assumptions and consequences, and offer and explore a responsive alternative.

I

Equality animates law both implicitly and explicitly. Implicitly, the whole idea of "the rule of law" embodies one idea of equality. Law as law means

Unpublished talk, Institute for Advanced Study, Berlin, Germany, July 12, 1994.

the kind of equalization that comes from elevating rules over force and status, a leveling principle that treats everyone the same, no favorites and no exceptions, except when distinctions can be justified. Legal method involves reasoning through analogy and distinction,[2] that is, treating things alike based on their similarities and unalike based on their differences. Most elaborately in common law systems that proceed through cases, but also in systems that reason from authoritative principles, law itself works through treating the same that which is the same and treating differently that which is different.

On the more explicit level, equality is often guaranteed positively as a right. International treaties and conventions, constitutions, and statutes provide for it in governments' relations with each other, in government's relation to the governed, and in citizens' relations among themselves. Constitutional and treaty-based equality favors prohibiting inequalities imposed by official action and centers on unequal laws, although there are exceptions and many attempts to expand it beyond that. Statutory equality treats selected spheres of civil society, typically employment and education.

In an unbroken line, mainstream equality thinking, systemic and doctrinal, flows from Aristotle's analysis in the *Ethica Nichomachea* that equality means treating likes alike and unlikes unalike.[3] To be the same is to be entitled to the same; to be different is to be treated differently. At any rate, this concept is the meaning universally attributed to his sometimes obscure discussion. Aristotle's distributive justice, from which legal mainstream equality primarily flows, is "a species of the proportionate."[4]

Less important for present purposes than what Aristotle actually thought is what has been made of the equality concept drawn from him, as applied in law over time. In the United States, bedrock to Fourteenth Amendment equality is that one must be the same as a relevant comparator to be entitled to equality of treatment. Equality was not part of the original Constitution; it was added after the Civil War to help eliminate official racism and was not applied to sex until 1971.[5] Its threshold requirement is that equality claimants must be "similarly situated" to those not treated unequally before an equality claim can be made. This language was used under the Fourteenth Amendment for the first time in 1884: "Class legislation, discriminating against some and favoring others, is prohibited, but legislation which . . . within the sphere of its operation . . . affects alike all persons similarly situated, is not within the amendment."[6] Another case soon after formulated the concept concisely in the form in which it has been used since. In its terms, under the Fourteenth Amendment, "the classification must be reasonable, not arbitrary, and must rest upon some ground of difference having a fair and substantial relation to the object of the legislation, so that all persons similarly circumstanced shall be treated alike."[7] The reasonable relation came from earlier due process cases; treating likes alike derived from Aristotle, his translators and transliterators. One hundred years later, when civil equality for African Americans still had not even remotely been achieved, Congress passed the Civil Rights Act of 1964, prohibiting discrimination based on race, color, national origin, religion, and sex in accommodation and employment.[8] That act has been interpreted through an analytically parallel requirement of comparability.

Termed "formal equality," this principle has become the familiar equality calculus of sameness and difference, of identity and distinction, requiring same treatment if one is the same, different treatment if one is different. Inequality means different treatment for likes, same treatment for unlikes. This approach, which tracks Aristotle's concept but is not usually cited to him, has been embraced as obvious by legal institutions worldwide, defining the core and ambit of legal equality in constitutions, statutes, and international law. It is the ruling approach to equality in the United States and, if anything, tends to be adhered to more strictly in Europe. An exception is Canada's interpretation of its new Charter of Rights and Freedoms since 1989.

While some progress has been made using this sameness/difference equality concept—most of it for small elites of men and a few privileged women, which is more than nothing—some of the historical uses of this approach—applications, not misapplications—give one pause. Aristotle, his concept of equality apparently undisturbed, defended slavery and lived in a society in which prostitution (sexual slavery) thrived and no women were citizens.[9] This approach readily supported official racial segregation by law in the United States, African Americans being construed as different from whites; equality under the Fourteenth Amendment meant legally imposed segregation of Black from white in the schools, courthouses, parks, pools, prisons, hospitals, restaurants, trains, and cemeteries of civil society.[10]

The same equality reasoning and language was used under the Third Reich to justify hierarchy of so-called Aryans over Jews.[11] In a discussion that explicitly embraces this same equality model, respected German constitutional scholar Ulrich Scheuner said, "From the racial foundation of today's German laws follows inevitably the cutting off of foreign elements, especially the Jews, from the German body politic, and their differential treatment."[12] One sign over a Nazi extermination camp—these signs specialized in vicious twists on homely phrases—stated "*Jedem Das Seine*," an eerie echo of Aristotle's formulation that equality means "each has one's own."[13]

This is not to hold Aristotle responsible for the Nazi atrocities, nor to say that a proper concept of equality in law alone could necessarily have stopped them. However, the ease with which this equality logic, which by then had taken on a life of its own, rationalized these extremes of social inequality, at just the points at which law was most needed to stand against them, encourages deeper scrutiny. Combined with the fact that legal equality guarantees promise and aim for a social equality they have yet to produce, even under less cataclysmic circumstances, while at the same time producing perverse outcomes with perfect logical consistency—the invalidation of affirmative action programs designed to reverse decades of racial exclusion are another example[14]—it is as ominous as it is curious that the same equality logic that was used to legalize apartheid and genocide remains legally fundamental in an American law that has repudiated segregation and a European law that has rejected fascism. Germany rejected all Nazi law by applying its current constitutional equality approach,[15] while continuing to use the same approach to equality itself that the Nazis used. At least as remarkable is the fact that the identical sameness/difference approach remains the equality concept in use in international human rights law, which arose largely to make sure that nothing like the Holocaust ever happened again.

Equality law and its results have not gone entirely unquestioned. Some of its conceptual absurdities and human costs have been sharply contested, largely in the racial context.[16] But the critique has stopped well short of questioning this standard approach to equality itself. No political theorist has argued that Aristotle was wrong: that treating likes alike and unlikes unalike is not what equality is all about, nor is treating likes unalike or unalikes alike what the problem of inequality really looks like. In over thirty years of progressive litigation on race and sex in the United States, no court of law has squarely been asked to assess whether requiring the parties to be alike—in doctrinal language "similarly situated," the threshold for equal protection scrutiny—perpetuates social inequality, as was argued in Canada in 1989. Unchallenged, the approach's underlying assumptions have been submerged from view.

These assumptions include the reference points for sameness (the same as whom?), the social creation and definition of differences (how is difference created and perceived?), and the comparative empirical approach itself (why not measure treatment and status against a principle or a standard or an outcome rather than measuring people's attributes against each other?). Aristotle says that "if they are not equal, they will not have what is equal."[17] But how do we know or measure who "are" equal? What defines who is equal, so we know inequality when we see it? Moreover, why can differences justify inequalities? Because some people cannot walk up stairs, thus are "different" from those who can, are buildings constructed so they cannot enter them not unequal? What is "one's own" anyway? What if the goods of societies are systematically maldistributed as far back as the eye can see, or merely today from cradle to grave? Relative to what is maintaining a certain distribution "equality"?

Further, why should unequal groups have to be "like" groups who have not had this problem before their inequality can be complained of? Socially dominant groups never have to meet any comparative test to acquire or retain the privileges and advantages they have. How can a subordinate group be seen as, or be, "like" dominant groups if society has organized inequalities along the lines of the group's socially perceived "unalikeness"? The worse conditions of inequality are, the more disparate are the circumstances in which people are placed—circumstances that at once reflect inequality and create and define difference. In any case, what does sameness have to do with entitlement to equal treatment? And who is the relevant comparator? Should the best athletic facilities go to the most athletically talented, those who need the most help, those who have had the worst facilities to date, those who can improve the most from using them, or should everyone have the same facilities, despite their differences? Why shouldn't people be treated alike, say admitted to schools, on the basis of their unalikeness from each other? On all these questions, the Aristotelian theory offers no guidance.

The result has been that so long as Blacks are socially constructed as different from whites, or Jews from "Aryans," or women from men, they can be treated differently, even if that "difference" has meant systematic disadvantage from indignity to apartheid to liquidation—and this equality principle has been satisfied. Treating members of disadvantaged groups as well or better based on their unalikeness, the value of diversity, is contrary to the theory, making affirmative action squarely contrary to it, even as treating disadvantaged groups less well never seems to be seen as treating advantaged groups better based on their unalikeness. These are outcomes to which this reasoning has demonstrably led and to which it is conceptually open. In this light, the historical examples of the applications of this principle are not isolated excesses. The principle is consistent with its practice. Nothing in it defines all human beings as being equal. Nothing in it requires that the definition of human be equally comprised of the defining qualities of all groups of people. Judgments like this—what does merit look like? who is deemed human?—Aristotle left to individual character. Political systems since have left these same kinds of judgments to the political realm—to power and force. At the same time, this equality principle has been presented as equality-producing, a counterbalance to, rather than a vehicle for, the power politics that forcefully shape the unequal status quo.

If socially unequal groups, in order to demand equal treatment, must first be situated the same as groups not afflicted by inequality, many of the worst injuries of inequality will be obscured and few will be corrected. It seems you have to first have equality before you can get it, expanding the implications of Anatole France's trenchant irony that "law, in its majestic equality, forbids the rich as well as the poor to sleep under bridges, to beg in the streets, and to steal bread."[18] Only the already disadvantaged will be made worse off by laws that are equal in this sense, because the advantaged ipso facto will never be in a position to run afoul of them. By the same token, the disadvantaged will never be made better off by this equality because they will never be in a position to take advantage of it. Who that needs this equality can get it? Under it, just as those who can least afford it can continue to be treated worse, those who most need it can continue not to receive its help. If situated differences must be elided to gain access to equal benefits, how will the consequences of inequality be exposed in order to rectify them? If equal treatment requires the same treatment for those who have and those who have not, for those who need and those who are not in need, how will their status relative to one another ever change?

Whatever Aristotle intended, those who see the way out of these traps as different treatment for differences should first notice that same treatment for sameness has been the fundamental equality rule in every legal equality regime. Equality in this approach has meant, first, same treatment based on relevant empirical sameness, equivalence, symmetry with a relevant comparator. To get what we have, be like us. Different treatment for differences, treating unalikes unalike, in Aristotle's formulation on a par with the main rule, as applied in legal systems, has been in some tension with the main rule, indeed is widely regarded as second-class equality. In reality, experience with it has not, in the main, been good. Different treatment, from the Nazi's "special treatment,"[19] a euphemism for extermination, to arguments that women's weakness and incapacity require "special protection,"[20] have mostly operated as the opposite of equality, to put it mildly. U.S. sex discrimination law's "special benefits" rule has often been seen to be in tension with, not complementary to, the fundamental rule of equal treatment, called "gender neutrality." Affirmative action, cast as "different treatment" for differences, is seen by its critics to be in tension with the fundamental equality principle of same treatment (whether in fact it is or not). Different treatment is thought to be where the double standard lives. Affirming differences sometimes has, in any case, not overcome the imposed homogeneity and affirmation of privilege of the sameness model. If "same treatment" for sameness has offered an illusory equality, "different treatment" for differences has been demeaning and dangerous, at times catastrophically so.

II

So far, the analysis here has considered social inequality in general, including among men, focusing on the way this mainstream equality approach has limited the pursuit of equality through law. As to issues of sex in particular, Aristotle thought of the sexes as different. Perhaps his abstract equality formulation took sex as an underlying concrete template for an unlikeness that could, consistent with equality, be treated unalike. He believed that "the excellence of character . . . the temperance of a man and of a woman, or the courage and justice of a man and a woman, are not, as Socrates maintained, the same: the courage of a man is shown in commanding, of a woman in obeying. And this holds of all other excellences. . . ."[21] The sexes are different: men tell women what to do, women do it, and so on. Gender is defined as a difference, the sex difference. This has been as much social construct, imposed social fact, as philosophical argument. Human societies have tended to define women as such in terms of just such differences from men, whether real or imagined, generally enforced to women's detriment in resources, roles, respect, and rights.

If equality is a sameness and gender a difference; if first-order equality is defined in terms of sameness, and women as such are "not the same" as men, women cannot be equal to men until they are no longer women. This is neither to affirm women's sameness to men, the usual approach, nor to affirm women as "different," a currently fashionable strategy in some circles (although conservatives beat the fashion by a couple of centuries). This is to point out the collision between the existing equality paradigm and the social definition of women and men as such. How sex equality can be produced if sex is a difference and first-class equality is predicated on sameness is problematic. Sex equality becomes something of an oxymoron, a contradiction in terms.

In practice, legal systems attempting to be progressive try to get around the drawbacks of this equality approach by carving out what are seen as exceptions to it. Predominantly allowed is different treatment where differences are seen to be real but valuable—such as pregnancy and maternity leaves even though no man needs one, or affirmative action although members of dominant groups do not qualify for it. The problem with this kind of exceptionalism, however practically helpful in cushioning the impact of the standard equality approach, is that the same principle—different treatment for real differences—has not only squarely rationalized the worst human rights abuses in history; it continues to be used to justify systematic forms of disadvantage like paying women in the most sex-segregated jobs less money. Women do different jobs, so they can be paid differently, meaning less. Nothing in Aristotle's approach prevents treating someone less well who is "differently situated" or "different" by virtue of being already less well off. That tautology is precisely equality under this approach, and precisely inequality, worse and more of it, in the real world.

A system-level consequence of this mainstream approach, rectified nowhere, is the failure to see as inequality issues many that are, especially those that are sexual or reproductive. Sexual violence, because of the overwhelming predominance of male perpetrators and female victims, and its rootedness in normative images of sexuality seen as naturally gendered, has tacitly been construed as an expression of the sex difference, therefore not an issue of sex inequality at all. Because overwhelmingly one sex is the perpetrators and the other is the victims, sexual violence is not sex discrimination, it is sex, that is, a "difference." The law of sexual harassment, which recognizes one form of sexual aggression as sex discrimination, is a bit of a miracle in this light, and in some tension with the mainstream structure, which hives off sexual abuse into the criminal law, ignoring its inequality dimensions. Similarly, because women and men contribute differently to reproduction, women's needs for reproductive rights have been brought under equality law only partially, as exceptions, with severe doctrinal strain, or, in the case of the right to abortion, not at all.

Women had no voice in contesting Aristotle's formulation in his day and have had little institutional power in shaping its legal applications since. Despite this lack of representation, including in democracies, women have in the last twenty years begun to articulate their condition in public. The facts that have emerged in this way, taken together, have revealed a grim system of unequal pay, allocation to disrespected work, sexual stigmatization, sexual violation as children and adults, and domestic battering. Women are attributed demeaned physical characteristics, used in denigrating entertainment, depersonalized as objects, deprived of reproductive control, and forced into prostitution[22]—all this in the civilized West. Elsewhere, if women are permitted gainful employment at all, it can be all that and chattel status, early and forced marriage, inability to divorce, compulsory veiling, genital mutilation, honor killings, ritual murder as in suttee, and more.

These abuses have occurred, in varying forms, for a very long time in a context characterized by disenfranchisement, preclusion from property ownership, possession and use as object, exclusion from public life, sex-based poverty, degraded sexuality, and devaluation of worth and contributions throughout society. Like other inequalities, but in its own way, the subjection of women is institutionalized, including in law, cumulatively and systematically shaping access to human dignity, respect, resources, physical security, credibility, membership in community, speech, and power. Composed of all its variations, the group women has a collective social history of disempowerment, exploitation, and subordination extending to the present, such that, in the words of the philosopher Richard Rorty, to be a woman "is not yet the name of a way of being human."[23]

This is not all there is to every woman's life, any more than racism is all there is to every Black American's life or class oppression is all there is to every working person's life under capitalism. Too, oppressive social systems legitimate themselves by individual exceptions. Many people enjoy the illusion that they, and most everyone they know, live their lives in freedom, in their minds anyway, or in exceptionality, in circumscribed areas at least. Thus can women have a feeling of freedom and dignity, and men a sense of nonparticipation in sex inequality, even as women's unequal status relative to men goes largely unchallenged.

We can choose to call this reality "the sex difference"—as, in their way, many sociobiologists, conservatives, postmodernists, and members of the religious right, consistent with the deep structure of conventional equality theory, do. It can be represented as Aristotle's level line disproportionately divided, which so long as each has their own, is equality. In this equality tradition, to describe something as a difference means it does not need to be changed, cannot be changed, is not produced by inequality, and is not unequal. So, although few openly defend mass rape in war or husbands slaughtering their wives in so-called peacetime as "just the sex difference," this is the reigning default conceptualization of such occurrences, insofar as they are not conceived as violations of sex equality rights. If the reality of women's status and treatment described merely refers to sex differences, equality already exists and the existing legal approach is in no need of change. Alternatively, these facts can be represented as a hierarchy, a top-down arrangement of imposed superiority and inferiority, of better off and worse off, advantaged and disadvantaged. To this, difference is relatively indifferent. For instance, the sexes could be "different" to the degree they are hierarchically (i.e., differently), situated and treated, without making that hierarchy equal in any sense except as so deemed under the mainstream model. To describe the facts as representing a hierarchy also means to see them as changeable, as overwhelmingly produced by inequality, as unequal, and as in need of change.

Once women are seen as men's human equals—an assumption presumably made when a legal sex equality standard is adopted, at the same time making it more possible to notice that the sexes are social unequals—systematically fewer material resources and life chances and more sex-specific victimization for one sex become difficult to justify. In addition, although equality is not only a second-order right to other rights, entitlements to life, liberty, property, security, dignity, and self-determination are thereby violated, to mention a few. And if the sexes are different, they are equally different. Once the hierarchy of social outcomes is noticed, it becomes difficult to explain why men are not paid less and assaulted by women more for *their* "differences." Measuring the equality approach created in women's silence and exclusion against the realities of women's lives, as women have begun to articulate them, the analytical and practical shortcomings of the existing approach thus emerge, revealing the need for a reconstructed equality theory to remedy them. The new paradigm moves behind and beyond sameness and difference to the subordination and dominance that has been the real problem of inequality all along.

Take Aristotle's "difference" between commanding and obeying, tracking sex. Giving and taking orders is one of the most universally recognized hierarchies known, including among men. In other words, his "difference" is a hierarchy. The embedding of hierarchy in relations that do not attract equality scrutiny makes predictable what has happened when this approach is applied in legal systems. Sex equality for the "similarly situated" best provides equality for whoever is "the same as men." Actually, these people have *been* men: white men have brought most of the leading Supreme Court sex discrimination cases.[24] Next in line are women whose biographies most closely approximate those men, elite women with privileges (white skin, money, education, and so on). Unrecognized here is that it is hierarchy, not difference as such, that is the opposite of equality. The inequality that is hierarchy, existing theory builds in as difference, meaning something that can be treated differently—that is, less well, hierarchically as lower—thus making the theory systematically unable to identify the one thing it needs to be able to identify and eliminate, in order to do what it has to do.

III

The implications of this critique are far-reaching and transformative. In politics and law, they range from state theory to doctrine, from jurisprudential theory to positive law, from epistemology to constitutional interpretation. Once the reality of gender is faced, it becomes clear the extent to which the laws, the legal system, the state as such, and relations between states have built in the experiences of the dominant and have been built from the perspective of those who created them. In the sociology of knowledge, this is a common kind of observation. Those who have created these systems have been the dominant gender group, the naming of which—men—becomes what is considered an extreme position, particularly when it is noted that the result has been their systematic hegemony over half the human race. To be clear: this equality theory is not a conspiracy theory; it relies on no conscious invidious motivation. It assumes, as other political theories do, only that people act in their own interest, as they see it, when they can. Why they see their interest as they do, and why they are permitted to act on it unchecked, is a separate question. The present analysis merely observes a political system of institutionalized interest supported by social facts of patterned behaviors and its embodiment in legal doctrine and philosophy. Nor is it a moral theory of who should do what. It is a political analysis of who gets what, how, and why, when that is dramatically differentially distributed, it is also a critique of terming "equality" the maintenance of that system and embodying it in legal equality doctrine. It should be noted that the conflict between ranks in a hierarchy need not be intractable. The sex hierarchy is merely big, old, pervasive, tenacious, denied, and a good many people are in love with it. Once it is faced as posing a certain division of interest enforced by force, like other serious inequalities such as race and class (and inextricably interconnected with them), it can be faced as in need of change through its own solutions.

The Supreme Court of Canada expressly adopted this alternate theory of equality in its first equality decision under the new Charter of Rights and Freedoms in 1985, in *Law Society v. Andrews*, a case adjudicating whether noncitizens could be made to wait longer than citizens before becoming lawyers.[25] Interpreting the Charter to effectuate its purposes, the Court determined that the purpose of an equality provision is to "promote equality." This does not sound like much, but it is everything: given social inequality, it requires that law has to move the world to be legal. It no longer leaves equality law standing neutrally in the face of an unequal world, sorting sameness from difference, reinforcing social inequalities by law. It requires courts to interpret laws so as *actually to produce* social equality. One might have thought this was obvious. The point of equality law is to produce equality. What else is it for—to produce inequality? That this stance is regarded as a major departure supports the indictment of the prior theory as status quo—reinforcing.

The *Andrews* Court explicitly repudiated the "similarly situated" test for equality, noting that this approach had justified racial segregation in the United States and could have supported the Nuremberg laws.[26] Aristotle and 2,000 years of equality abstractions based on him, including the Enlightenment's elevation of universality over particularity, came tumbling down, at least in Canada. That Court rejected the logic of the mainstream approach for having treated pregnancy less well than other nonwork reasons for not working because pregnancy is a difference, for treating First Nations women worse than men because Canadian Indians were a special class, and for treating all Native Peoples worse than non–Native Peoples because all Indians were treated alike. In its place was put a concrete, substantive, openly social-context–sensitive test of "historical disadvantage." The sky did not fall. At last report, women and men continued to go on dates, babies continued to be born, and so forth.

This decision is a tectonic shift, a fundamental movement in the ground. One effect is to expose hierarchy where it has not been seen before, as in the areas of sexual assault and reproductive rights. Canada's new equality principle has been used to extend statutes of limitations in incest cases,[27] to sue a city for failing to warn women of a known serial rapist,[28] and to give credibility to battered women.[29] Less explicitly, but no less potently, it has influenced outcomes that include preventing men from vetoing abortions,[30] keeping a midwife who delivered a baby that died from being convicted of negligent murder,[31] and keeping raped women's names and identities out of the media.[32] It may also provide real rights for gay men and lesbian women.

If equality theory had been written to end women's inequality to men, it would certainly have included employment and education, but it would not have left out the street and the family, as the existing equality approach has. Sexual coercion (including sexual abuse of children, sexual harassment, rape, prostitution, and pornography) and deprivation of reproductive control (including forced sterilization, lack of sex education and contraception, misogynist gynecology, female infanticide, forced sex, and criminalization of abortion) are arguably central to the ways in which women, as a group, have been historically disadvantaged. In this light, the laws of rape and abortion are equality laws in disguise—deep disguise. More precisely, they are unequal laws that have never been held to an equality standard on social problems where group-based inequality is enacted. If rape is really a practice of sex discrimination, existing positive law and patterns of nonprosecution for sexual assault must meet constitutional sex equality standards. If reproductive control is a sex equality issue, deprivation of reproductive control is a sex equality violation, and prohibitions on abortion must sustain sex equality scrutiny or be found illegal under existing constitutions and international conventions.

This same new equality theory can be discerned beneath the U.S. Congress's law against gender-motivated violence, which makes rape and battering federal sex discrimination claims,[33] as well as in proposals to make pornography civilly actionable as sex discrimination.[34] The jurisprudence of the approach observes that sex inequality occurs in civil society, between women and men, and is then backed up and enforced through law. In many areas of its application, it names equality as the issue there for the first time. This is changing not only the content of law but potentially law's relation to unequal social life. Given that the state form has traditionally embodied male authority, a jurisprudence of equality cannot simply rely upon further empowering the state. It cannot rest with rules with different content, as big an improvement as that could be. It must also work structurally to redistribute the state power, by enabling women, with institutional support, to confront and remedy inequalities they encounter, including in intimate settings. Recognizing women's human rights on this level has major implications for the law of family, contract, and crime, as well as for constitutional and international law. As to equality as legal method, this substantive approach to equality reveals that the "rule of law" has not meant the same equalization for women that it has meant among men, at least for some of them. Assessment of the logic and outcomes of formal equality suggests that its "rule of law" form will never produce real positive equality either.

Effectively addressing the realities of social inequality between women and men requires addressing all inequalities. Indeed, much gender inequality is inextricable from inequalities women share with some men. On this point, consider two Canadian milestones: cases holding that hate propaganda and pornography threaten equality rights. One case involves a man who taught Holocaust denial to high school students;[35] the other involves a pornographer.[36] The Supreme Court of Canada found that the equality of Jews and women, recognized as historically disadvantaged groups, was more important than the speech interests restricted by criminalizing expression that promoted their inequality. It found that racist and anti-Semitic hate propaganda produces and reinforces social subordination from segregation to genocide. Parliament, it held, may justifiably conclude that pornography, in its making and through its use, contributes to violation of and discrimination against women individually and as a group, harming the community's interest in equality. Thus both can be restricted. The United States, firmly in the grip of the traditional equality approach and blind to the hierarchy of systematic group-based disadvantage, remains unable to see that inequality is involved in issues of hate speech and pornography at all.[37]

The point of the new equality jurisprudence is to institutionalize social equality, rather than inequality, through legal equality initiatives. It begins by articulating the systematic, pervasive, and cumulative absence of equality throughout society, including in democracies, and by moving to put legal power to redress it into the hands of affected groups through law. In this vision, law can be something people do, not just something states do to people. This democratic shift in legal form as well as content—called civil rights as pioneered by the Black movement in the United States, with echoes in the human rights of transnational law—is appropriate to an aspiration to transform social hierarchy from the bottom up. Beyond clarifying unnoticed dynamics in law and history, and stimulating needed scholarship and analysis, the goal of this theory is to close the gap between legal promise and social reality in the equality area. This approach could be adopted anywhere. A legal regime capable of producing equality of women to men—half the human race to the other—made up as they are of all existing inequalities, might learn what it needs to know to produce equality among men as well.

5

Law's Stories as Reality and Politics

Law's way of appropriating reality—that vexed, even beleaguered notion—grounds it as a distinctively potent form of text. Case law starts with stories called "facts." The sense that its facts have not felt real enough, that something has gone missing in them or was struggling to break through them, has called law's embrace of reality into question and has largely impelled the specific movement back toward the world that has taken the form of narrative.

The lack of felt verisimilitude in the law has arisen not only in going from thick to thin—in other vocabularies, from specific to general, from particular to universal, from concrete to abstract, from case to rule. Nor has the urgency behind the shift toward narrative as a form arisen only to avoid abstracting trauma or, to extrapolate Elaine Scarry's phrase, to reverse a movement from the one to the many.[1] Storytelling entered legal discussion at a prior moment: upon realizing that the analytic-argumentative engine has been running on particulars that have not been particular enough, and on submerged or entirely absent specifics. Legislation has been predicated on too many elided voices as the common law has marched majestically past unbringable cases. In the relative absence of women, children, people of color, and working people, the legal mill has been grinding a grist that is too thin to begin with. To adapt Lévi-Strauss's terms, the raw of the law, not only its cooking, has been a problem.

As a practitioner of narrative, the first thing I do when I take a case is do, or redo, the account of the facts. As it comes to me, the story is never right: never based on what happened deeply or directly enough, never showing the blood of the injury vividly enough, never embodying the theory of the case sharply enough. Often the way the facts are framed, and framing intensifies what it focuses, tacitly concedes much of what matters most to the result. The facts as told, which represent and stand in for the client's story, also seldom resonate with the client.[2] This sense of imposed

Response, conference on Narrative and Rhetoric in the Law, February 11, 1995, Yale Law School, New Haven, CT. First published, *Law's Stories: Narrative and Rhetoric in the Law* 232 (Peter Brooks and Paul Gewirtz, eds., 1996).

unreality to be broken through, of gloss of form burying urgency of substance, of prefabricated concepts begging to be remade from the ground up through the more real account emerging, has given birth to legal storytelling.

Stories start over to put back in what has been left out. But there is more to their politics than that. As Paul Gewirtz delicately put it, there has been a relation between storytelling as method and a particular point of view.[3] The systematically excluded accounts, the pervasively silenced voices, have a particular point of view because they are the voices of certain people: the unequal. Movements for equality have noticed the elision in law's stories, and it is the legal claim for equality that has given the world as reconstituted by stories some standing in the yet-to-be reconstructed legal system. Thus Robert Ferguson's oral Gabriel, movingly resurrected and speaking for himself and his community,[4] embodies the politics of subordinated communities denied literacy.

Social inequality, Alan Dershowitz's protestations to the contrary notwithstanding, is not random;[5] it is determinate as well as cumulative and systematic. Stories that are persuasive rely on its teleology. For example, as he said, most men who batter women do not kill them—if they all did, a third to a half of American women would be murdered by male intimates.[6] But few battered women who are murdered are likely to be killed by anyone other than their batterers.[7] (Fewer still are the innocent battering husbands of murdered wives who drive around, as O.J. Simpson did, with her DNA all over the inside of their cars.) Granting the credibility of individual stories that fit group regularities, Jean-François Lyotard, considering the controversy over whether that extreme in inequality, the Holocaust, occurred, rightly observed that reality is the plaintiff's problem.[8] No matter now emblematic an individual story of inequality is of the larger unequal story, the burden is on those who are hurt and seek accountability to establish their account as having happened. Crucially, if you are the one whose story's ending needs to be changed, you need to show that what got you there is both determinate enough to fit the larger pattern and contingent enough to have been, and to deserve to be, different.

It is thus no coincidence that storytelling—bearing witness, giving account as we know and practice it—took shape within civil rights movements. Since 1968, the women's liberation movement contributed distinctively to this tradition through its speak-outs and consciousness-raising. Women analyzed women's condition in this form because there was no other way. Women's reality is what was missing, all the way down to the ground. Women's experience, not exclusively but crucially experiences of sexual abuse, had simply been left out of account. Existing concepts denied it—they still largely do—so it came out as story, howling and broken. These original victim-impact statements had the narrative structure of machine language: and then he, and then he, and then he.

This process and its products—nerves exposed, inelegant by comparison with glossy abstractions—was, and continues to be, stigmatized and denigrated in the hierarchy of public discourse. It is actually a bit startling to find what women have been doing all this time called narrative and given some dignity, even literary cachet. Women's accounts have been more commonly called anecdotes, impressions, although they are at the very least testimony and, as such, evidence. Regarding a paper I wrote on sexual harassment—a legal concept that did not exist in the early 1970s—an editor of the *Yale Law Journal* told me at the time that the legal argument was terrific, but all those personal accounts at the beginning "just did not add all that much." Take them out, you have a law review article. Never mind that without them, so far as anyone knows, you made the whole thing up.

Related to filling the gaps, much of the contemporary storytelling impulse has sprung from resistance to the claim of exclusivity of the single dominant version of social reality.[9] Enlightenment "truth" has accordingly taken considerable heat for flattening reality's many dimensions. It is an old point. By capturing multiplicity, nuance, situatedness, perspectivity, storytelling teaches a new version of the old rule that at least two realities must inhabit any account. Reality lies in interpretation; in postmodernity, where no one actually lives, interpretations become infinite.

It is time to ask whether this is all there is to the storytelling movement in reality appropriation. Are all stories equal so long as they are stories, *Rashomon* lurking in the underbrush as nineteenth-century objective/subjective epistemic regresses inhabit our method forever? Is the most pointed contribution of narrative to law its challenge to the singleness of the dominant version—or is it to the domination in the substance of that single version, hence its likely falsity, or at least its interestedness? Has the shift in form masked an abdication of content, showing up in just another guise as storytelling? Maybe only one thing *did* happen, just not the one thing we were told.[10] Moreover, if the whole story has not been told before, the principles that have been predicated on the assumption that the story *was* whole cannot be unbiased principles. Which makes them, to some degree, wrong. In telling stories and stopping there, have we abandoned principle for counterpoint, our claim of right for the jester's place at court?

The contribution of narrative to law so far centers on defiance of canon.[11] Storytelling has opened up legal discussion, giving it sweep of gesture, depth, ambiguity, connection, vaulting it toward literature. The breath of human life animates stories as it never did "the facts"; a human face is envisaged in them. Empathy is encouraged, which victims of inequality could use. But there is no reality magic to the story form as such. Perpetrators of inequality—often at just the point of being held accountable for what they have done to their victims—claim that they, too, have stories. And they do. Stories can support accountability by telling a reality that dominant concepts have not accommodated. They have been a vehicle for the down and out. But the form itself is no guarantee of a view from the outside or the bottom. Stories break stereotypes, but stereotypes are also stories, and stories can be full of them. Do not mistake form for content, as abstracting narrative as method away from its origins in the critique of inequality that substantively impelled it does. Disembodied and decontextualized stories are also stories.

Even when accounts remain rooted in a critique of hierarchy, storytelling has real dangers, one of which is accepting a place at the margin. Storytelling as method originated in powerlessness and can bring a fear of power with it. Instead of telling power it is wrong, tell it a story. Avoid finger pointing. No offense; everyone can be right. Storytelling can be ingratiating in ceding reality to power this way, presenting itself as just another version, becoming a grace note to the main account. When one dare not argue, storytelling can be a strategy for survival. But it can ask too little. Dominant narratives are not called stories. They are called reality.

To push this point a step further, storytelling hazards becoming entertainment. The point of telling stories is to make law more real, but because a story is a story, it can also be less real. It cannot only be taken as fiction, it can be fiction. When story becomes fantasy, the account passes into a different order of experience in which reality can be hidden, distanced, occluded, or denied.[12] A related risk is excess credibility, resulting from the suspension of critical faculties.[13] Sometimes the audience is having too good a time, particularly when the story tells power what it wants to hear. Freud was all story—many mythological, many, it turns out, false.[14] Stories can be powerful, evocative, resonant, death-defyingly influential, yet cover up the most relevant of possible facts—such as, in Freud's case, the realities of child sexual abuse. How do you counter the appeal of a story that power wants to believe? A story on the other side, of which there has been no lack, has not been enough. This brings us full circle to the point where there is much to be said for data. As to child abuse, we have it.[15] Freud did not. Of course, the basis for the data is accounts of being sexually abused as children, stories which remain largely unbelieved and overwhelmingly not acted upon, while the baseless stories of Freud continue to ground much psychology and policy. Similarly on the literary side, accounts of why real prostituted women went into prostitution have never been given the credibility and gravity of Rousseau's fantasies of why Marion did.[16] The issue remains not form but content, specifically the politics of the content.

Lies are the ultimate risk of storytelling as method. This may be embarrassingly nonpostmodern, but reality exists. Of this the law, at least, has no doubt. Something happened or will be found to have happened. You can still be tried for perjury even though there supposedly is no truth. You can still be sued for libel, so somewhere reality exists to be falsified.[17] Therefore, each side's story cannot simply be assumed equally spoiled by the law's masks or equally dependent on an excluded reality for its power. There is still such a thing as a lie. The contrary position offers the joy of the half-imagined fact, the justice of the good read.[18] Fiction can be closer to reality than nonfiction, or it can be lying as art.

Storytelling in law is regressive when it promotes the notion that there is no such thing as "what happened" in a society that is still determinately unequal and a legal universe that will either find that inequality or cover it up. No one who seeks change can afford to pretend that they live in Gertrude Stein's Oakland, where there is no there there.

It is my view that the major conflicts of our time are over the real and only secondarily over versions of it and methods for apprehending it. The struggle over reality is conducted through contending versions and debates over verification but it is reality, not versions or verification, that is in contention. For instance, the discussion of pornography and prostitution can be seen as a debate in two stories. In story 1, a woman wakes up in the morning and decides, Today is my lucky day. I can choose whether to become a brain surgeon or whether to go find a pimp and spread my legs for a camera. In story 2, a girl is sexually abused at home, runs to the street thinking nothing can be worse, is picked up by a pimp, is molested, raped, beaten, starved, drugged, threatened, and sold for sex. Story 1 is a story of choice, equality, liberation; story 2 is a story of force, inequality, slavery. As story, there is no way to distinguish between the two. The fact that most women in the industry were sexually abused as children, entered it as children, are desperately poor, report massive violence against them, and say they want to leave but cannot[19] supports story 2, but all this is extrinsic to the narrative form as such. Story 1 is fantasy, entertainment, lie—it is propaganda—but its support for power widely makes the real story of story 2 into just another story. Storytelling as method requires only the story form for validation. Pimps and tricks have stories, too, and they own the means of production. Story as method is thus located at a critical expansion joint in legal and political discourse as well as in a position to ensure that it gets nowhere.

Narrative's future in legal scholarship is an open one. Comparing first-person narrative with that of other personas, including the off-stage omnipotent deus ex machina, would further its growth. Lawyers usually work through stories that are not their own. Sometimes this is representation in the legal sense; sometimes it is representation in the aesthetic sense; sometimes it is plain using other people's lives in the everyday sense. The location of the author in relation to the story emerges in varied voices in judicial opinions as well as in naked advocacy. In Canada, even judges writing for the majority will use "I"; in the power-obsessed, objectivity-sensitive United States, the first-person singular virtually never appears in majority opinions. Probably in democracies in particular, the illusion that no one is present in a narrative gives it more rather than less credibility. Some stories have more clout when their authors leave invisible tracks.

Further analysis of the role of first-person accounts could give us a tighter grip on the crucial issue of credibility. What is it about some such stories that makes them so believable? The observation that narrative has more persuasive force than statistics could productively be furthered in this context. As someone who bursts into tears at columns of figures, the realities that produced them parading before my eyes, I have no idea why it can be known for a decade that 85 percent of federal workers are sexually harassed,[20] but not until one of them embodies the experience on national television (as Anita Hill did) does sexual harassment in the federal work force become real in some sense. I want to know. Why is it not real that 38 percent of girls are sexually abused before they reach the age of majority?[21] Why the stories behind facts like these are not taken as real when presented as data is the other side of why narrative has a peculiar capacity to make them real. This may be especially true in individualistic cultures, where biography is imagined to be singular. But with no lack of first-person narratives of child sexual abuse, no narrative has yet made it as publicly real as it is privately pervasive.

In this connection, one form narrative can take, the example, needs to be theorized within and beyond the common law. What does "case by case" really mean? What is the point and function and consequence of moving onto that level and back? What *is* an example? When does an example produce a paradigm and when does it limit a case to its facts? In connecting one particular with another, what is the relation between metaphor and knowledge:[22] what is it that allows us to see some things as similar to other things, and to know one through knowing another? Crucial growth in human rights has occurred through this process; through seeing racism as a metaphor for inequality, as well as a prime instance of it, inequalities on other grounds have been exposed and understood. Pursuit of law's poetics could deepen understanding of this feature and its function in the legal process.

Finally, close analysis of specific rhetorics that work as legal fictions may serve to unmask law's devices for legitimacy. My favorite candidate for this role is the "I so regret to do this" of the judicial opinion.[23] This ubiquitous trope of bench in extremis serves up the source of authority as "not me," such that the more you hate to do what you are doing, the more authoritative and principled you become in doing it. Operating by compulsion behind a fig leaf of moral regret apparently transforms atrocity into principle. The more egregious cases, like *Collin v. Smith*, in which the Nazis were permitted to march in Skokie because the First Amendment was said to require it, lean heavily on this, as in, "[W]e feel compelled once again to express our repugnance. . . . Indeed, it is a source of extreme regret. . . ."[24] Why legitimacy is enhanced by revulsion is the question here. Why does the posture of caving in to power validate? Perhaps it hides the power that law does have—to intervene or not, to equalize or not, not to slide down any slope it does not want to (or that may not exist), to be restrained or to abandon restraint—behind the resigned passive pose of *Ich kann nicht anders*. In these specific rhetorics inhere much of law's story per se, of how law makes our lives into cases. Analysis of them[25] could help expose how law imposes itself on a world whose stories are never the same again.

6

"Freedom from Unreal Loyalties"

On Fidelity in Constitutional Interpretation

Does the Constitution deserve our fidelity? To briefly consider that normative question, I will ask of the Constitution the question Rousseau asked of the inequality he observed around him: "What can make it legitimate?"[1] In so doing, I decline to theorize morally, meaning to pontificate on what I feel, and therefore "we" should think, is good and bad. This is not my project, nor is my project a disguised version of that project. In the process, I sketch an alternative approach to Ronald Dworkin's "moral reading" of the Constitution, like his one centered on the equality question, but more descriptively accurate of constitutional process and less elitist and exclusionary in method and content. I also hope to show that the fidelity I practice is not what Jack Balkin has warned us against, yet is a reading of the Constitution—an aggressive reading, but a reading nonetheless.

The reading I propose stands against moralism, constitutional or otherwise. The moralism criticized[2] is evident in Balkin's discussion of "constitutional evil,"[3] his "really bad stuff."[4] I am not saying those things are good. Rather, the main problem Balkin seeks to solve is not a problem I have. He is conflicted over faith to a document that originally considered the ancestors of my colleagues and friends to be three-fifths of a person, to be bought and sold as "property."[5] Then, after keeping people like me from practicing law because we were not fully "persons,"[6] and, after strictly scrutinizing for racism, locking up the families of my colleagues and friends in concentration camps,[7] this same document arrives today at a point where my colleagues and friends can still be bought and sold, this time as "speech."[8] I am not torn over fidelity to that document. Behind the angst over infidelity in Jack Balkin's engaging paper lurks an identification with the Constitution that masks a deeper identification with those who have authoritatively interpreted it. This identification, I do not share; I do not recognize myself, or feel my power implicated in, the "we" of his discussion.

Conference on Fidelity in Constitutional Interpretation, September 20–21, 1996, Fordham Law School, New York, New York. First published, LXV *Fordham Law Review* 1773 (1997).

To state this directly, no one asked women about the Constitution. We never consented to it. This, I take it, is, or should be, a big legitimacy problem. The so-called majoritarian premise of the Constitution so widely invoked, including by Ronald Dworkin,[9] began by assuming about 53 percent of the population out. Add to this the excluded male slaves then, men of color largely now; non–property owners then, poor people almost entirely now; and what is left of the majority in the premise? It refers to the holders of the majority of power, an elite, who are a tiny minority. Why should I be torn between loyalty to them and other loyalties?[10]

At risk of oversimplification, contrast two dramatically divergent accounts of constitutional interpretation to explain why the location I am claiming produces constitutional fidelity. In one account, Ronald Dworkin floats above social life, transcending it, accompanied by Herbert Wechsler.[11] He sees words in the Constitution. He reads Supreme Court opinions. He thinks. He theorizes. He decides what is good and bad. He distills principles by sanitizing value judgments to the point where no one's name is discernible on them. He says: This is good. He sees how particular facts—a gritty, low-level notion not much in use—fit under what he calls principles. Through this top down approach to constitutional interpretation, he pronounces what is faithful to the Constitution and what violates it.

An alternative: You walk through life, this life. You notice some people—sometimes you, your colleagues, your friends—systematically treated worse than others. It is actually rather hard to miss. People tell you what happens to them, themselves. You remember what they tell you and who they are. You try to make sense of what has been done to them. Nobody needs to be told that there is a problem here, because you deny neither the equality of these people nor the inequality imposed on them. You and they want to end it. You remember that there is, supposedly, "no caste here,"[12] no second-class citizenship under the Constitution.

So a conflict is posed: Does the Constitution permit the practices you have encountered? It does in reality: here is the Constitution, and here are these practices being done. Do you give up on the Constitution, in a crisis of faith, ceasing to believe in God because there is evil in the world? Or do you decide to hold the Constitution to its promise, for the first time if necessary? If you take this bottom up approach, it is not because you believe in the Constitution, although you might, but because you believe in the equality of your people, and you are not going to let the Constitution make them less.

Gradually you articulate the equality principle in terms of ending the inequality you see. You know that those who interpreted the Constitution before you did not see it the way you do, but you never allow them to think that they cannot understand what you are saying—no fancy epistemological dodges. They may not have come to see what you see on their own, unaided, but they can sure get their minds around it now.

Gradually you learn that inequality, as lived, keeps people down because of who they are. You decide that if constitutional equality does not mean ending this, it does not mean anything at all. Nobody says you are wrong about that, that the equality principle really permits denigrating subordinated groups, supports trafficking human flesh, imposes inferior status. Then one day you run into Ronald Dworkin trying to get in your way. And calling that "fidelity."

Using the bottom up approach to illuminate the "top down" one clarifies some otherwise murky issues in the fidelity discussion. Consider first the confusion between what would be good to encompass in constitutional equality and what equality means. Arguing that a practice is unconstitutionally unequal is not the same as arguing that it is a bad thing in the moral sense. Many things are no doubt bad, but only being part of systematic subordination on a group basis makes something unequal. Bad things may or may not be unconstitutional, but unequal things are.[13] Expanding the standards for cognizable inequality by getting new groups and practices recognized under the Constitution is interpretation. If expanding the meaning of a constitutional term like "equal protection of the laws" to prohibit the reality of second-class citizenship of formerly excluded peoples is regarded as a rather large interpretive step by some, it may be because those doing the interpretation want to keep their practices and privileges, or have limited imaginations or narrow lives. But we are still talking interpretation: what is and is not inequality. We are not talking what it would be good to be against: the task of moral theory and legislation.

Take, as an example, the question whether sexual harassment violates the equality principle. Before, it did not. Now it does, by interpretation.[14] That was not done by arguing that sexual harassment is a bad thing. It was done by arguing that sexual harassment is unequal treatment, sex discrimination. Consider how to argue that acts that are already supposedly considered bad and criminal, like rape, are also inequalities constitutionally. Not by arguing that being raped by state actors is a bad thing; by arguing that being raped by state actors is a distinctively female form of second-class citizenship, gendered injustice. That rape is bad does not make it unequal or gendered. That rape is sex-based violation that, when officially allowed, deprives citizens of their rights to equal protection of the laws does.[15] That rape is bad is not an argument of constitutional interpretation; that rape is a practice of gender inequality is.

My point here is: as a matter of method, moralism is not interpretive. Its referent is not a constitution or a law, it is the person taking the moral position, the "I" of the moralist. Moralism asks, Is rape bad? Is sexual harassment wrong? This is not a question of constitutional interpretation. The Constitution does not prohibit the bad and the wrong. It does prohibit the unequal. Even being *really* bad does not make rape and sexual harassment unequal; being unequal based on sex does. Certainly, whether rape or sexual harassment is wrong is an important question, and denial that sexual harassment or rape is wrong or harmful is often involved in adjudications of it. From my own point of view, what is wrong with rape is that it is unequal. If men were raped equally with women (which I am not recommending), I might even get interested in what is wrong with rape apart from its inequality. But so long as sexual assault violates women as women and keeps them inferior, and violates men on the woman model when men are raped, it is an act of sex inequality. And this analysis is an interpretation of a text to which it is being faithful.

Another confusion in Ronald Dworkin's work, as well as in Jack Balkin's, concerns the matter of internal and external standards for validation of an interpretation. It seems, in their view, that having external standards for interpretational validity is a form of infidelity to the text. They tend to assume that you are faithful to the Constitution only if you can validate your interpretation of it by standards that are wholly internal to the document itself. Gödel showed that internal standards for validation do not work in mathematics,[16] and we are unlikely, in a social discipline like law, to do better on this score. Besides, law is *supposed* to have its feet in the world. It is not supposed to be a closed system, a set of abstract postulates and empty axioms from which determinate conclusions are deduced. The best thing about the legal process, particularly the common law, is that, within principled limits, it is open to reality. Certainly it is muscle-bound with power, resistant to change, status quo and status driven, but it is still also fact based. And facts are where people live. To require that only internal standards validate interpretation methodologically excludes from the system its most democratic, least solipsistic, and most creative feature. Legal change comes from life, not from the brow of moral readers.

In the "moral reading," interpretation is also, in a sense, literary.[17] I used to think that it was my *criticism* of law professors that they acted as if law were a novel. The fact is, law isn't fiction, folks. With all respect to the real-world clout of literature, heads roll in legal cases, and I don't think it's a virtue, called "principle," to position yourself to transcend that. There is no virtue in adjudicating child custody cases to better develop character and plot—it makes a better story about "the best interests of the child" to give the little girl to Daddy even though he is sexually abusing her. Deciding that law is something this "we" makes up, some collective story by its high theorists, takes authorship from people's lives. Law does not need more of this.

So how is my view of interpretation principled? Because equality is not, pace "the moral reader," an abstraction, my equality principle is thick with reality. This *is* its principle.[18] As it happens, the actual constitutional process of equality adjudication has been more open to reality than the "moral reading" appears to be. Courts are a great deal less afraid of substantivity than are some who theorize equality out of court—and courts hold themselves faithful to a text. Some courts, who practice interpretation while preaching it, understand that legal principles animated by life can still be principled—indeed, in their closeness to reality, precisely their thickness, may inhere much of their principle.

My view also faces the fact that social location and accountability—who you are and who you answer to—are central to interpretation. A legal interpreter has to be all people at all times in all places and social positions before his reading qualifies as "the moral reading." With all respect to Ronald Dworkin's stature, this is impossible. Not only *is* no one this person, no one *can* do this, and trying denies reality and validates power.[19] Would our floating everyone, the no one in particular who is capable of the "moral reading," have known in 1857 what was wrong with *Dred Scott*? This same reader knows that sexual harassment is a practice of inequality today,[20] but would he have known it before the courts did? Forgive me if I doubt it, given that "the moral reader" today, along with law today, tells us that women can be bought and sold as sex called speech and constitutional equality is troubled not at all.[21] The "moral reading" of equality knows only what power has already been brought to concede. If this is constitutional fidelity, count me an adulterer.

Observe that, in the discussion of whether the Constitution deserves fidelity, equality is not just an artifact or a convenient example. Equality keeps coming up not only because it is a dynamic doctrine with big interpretive shifts, or because the mainstream equality idea about sameness and difference also animates legal method's reasoning by analogy and distinction, making equality law a fair stand-in for law itself. The reason is that equality makes the Constitution legitimate, so its treatment is central to answering the question of why we should be loyal to the Constitution.

Equality comes up in the fidelity discussion precisely because, to the degree the Constitution is not equal, it is not legitimate, hence not deserving of adherence, so it becomes unacceptable merely to interpret it. If there were no equality guarantee in the Constitution, or in the fundamental understandings with which it is interpreted, I would be trying to get one in. Would that make me faithless? I do know I could not work in the position of interpretation I do now, a luxury I owe to those who got equality in there in the first place, because there would be no equality to interpret. And I would have less faith in a Constitution that would deserve less.

The Constitution became more legitimate the day it guaranteed equal protection of the laws. It will become more legitimate, and deserve greater fealty, the day it delivers on this promise. It became more legitimate the day it prohibited facial sex discrimination by interpretation. It will become more legitimate, and more worthy of faith, the day it recognizes that discrimination against gays and lesbians in all its forms is unequal. It will be more legitimate still the day it interprets all its other amendments in light of a serious equality guarantee, so that just as no one's slavery can any longer be someone else's property, no one's slavery can ever again be someone else's speech.

Lawyers think we have to legitimate our legal arguments by asserting that all we ask of law is interpretation. My point is that, in a democracy, a constitution also has to legitimate itself with people, and as to women it has quite a lot to answer for. In this sense, fidelity, in law as in life, is a relationship, a two-way street: our fidelity to the Constitution is bound up with its fidelity to us.

The last big concrete discussion that I was around for of what is interpretation and therefore a reading, thus faithful, versus what is imported or made up or brought in or effectively legislated, therefore lacking faith—in Jack Balkin's terms, what is "on the table" or "off-the-wall"[22]—was whether the Fourteenth Amendment could or would expand to provide sex equality, or whether we needed an Equal Rights Amendment saying in so many words that women are constitutionally equal. The question remains whether a Constitution that does not facially guarantee women's equality deserves women's fidelity. The Constitution is less legitimate today than on the day ERA becomes part of it. Women cannot get full equal rights, nor does the Constitution deserve their faith, to the degree it would if ERA were there. Until that day, women's equality is less legitimate in constitutional interpretation, but the Constitution is also less legitimate from women's point of view. So it is a repository of less of our faith. Where is democratic legitimacy grounded, in people or in texts?

I think that an equality mandate requires refusing to reflect back to the law the limits its powerful interpreters have set on the lives of the unequal, and seeing instead your own face in terms that reflect you whole—terms like citizen, like person. To interpret an equality guarantee faithfully is to embody this aspiration in law and society. If it is instrumentalism or consequentialism, as opposed to principled, to care about the outcome of this process, then call what I do something other than principled. Alternatively, show me someone who is indifferent to the human consequences of their principles and I will show you someone who is in great need of what the word integrity implies.[23]

Fidelity, in moralism, is about the constitutional equivalent of, Do you believe in God? The alternative view begins with asking, Who are your people? It requires finding those to whom you are accountable. You can listen to everyone, be in dialogue with everyone, be fair-minded to everyone, but you cannot be equally accountable to everyone at once in an unequal world. This perspective reframes the fidelity question as a lawyer's question I have long wanted to ask "the moral reader": Who *do* you represent?

7

What *Brown v. Board of Education* Should Have Said

MacKinnon, J. (concurring in the judgment).

Beneath and beyond the victory for Black schoolchildren in these five cases[1]—and a step for all toward what Mr. Silas Hardrick Fleming, a plaintiff testifying in *Brown*, called "the light"[2]—lie hazards for the principle of equality under law and for the social equality it aims ultimately to promote.

The risk we run today is not of going too far too fast, as defendants fear, but of going too slowly and not far enough. Ensuring a future consistent with the Fourteenth Amendment's purpose and promise, as my colleagues document and interpret it, calls not only for dismantling racially segregated public schools but for squarely facing why official separation on the basis of race ever was seen as consistent with a constitutional equality rule in the first place. This deeper history has roots and remains in legal concepts, as well as in the social dynamics and political events my colleagues report. Because this case requires us to define no less than what equality, as guaranteed in the Constitution, means, I write separately to draw out and repudiate this theoretical legacy, which began long before slavery on this continent.

Plaintiffs in these five cases argue that public school segregation on the basis of race, officially permitted or required, relegates Negro children to inferior status, denying them equal protection of the laws within the meaning of the Fourteenth Amendment by depriving them of equal educational opportunities. On reargument before this Court, plaintiffs[3] squarely challenge the rule of "separate but equal," as formulated in *Plessy v. Ferguson*, 163 U.S. 537 (1896), a transportation case under the aegis of which racially segregated public schools were permitted so long as they were substantially equal in facilities. Plaintiffs argue, in this and in *Bolling v. Sharpe*, post, challenging racial segregation in schools in the nation's capital, that "separate but equal" is intrinsically inconsistent with the Fourteenth Amendment's guarantees of equality and due process of law.

Delivered to American Association of Law Schools panel, January 9, 2000, in mock Supreme Court argument. First published in *What Brown v. Board of Education Should Have Said* 143 (Jack Balkin, ed., 2001)

Specifically, they contend that our rulings in *Sweatt v. Painter*, 339 U.S. 629 (1950), and *McLaurin v. Oklahoma State Regents*, 339 U.S. 637 (1950), effectively vitiate racial segregation in higher education even with equal facilities. Our principled opposition to drawing official race-based lines in *Shelley v. Kraemer*, 334 U.S. 1 (1948), and *Buchanan v. Warley*, 245 U.S. 60 (1917), a due process case; our repudiation in doctrine, if not result, of racial distinctions except in extremity of *Hirabayashi v. United States*, 320 U.S. 81 (1943), and *Korematsu v. United States*, 323 U.S. 214 (1944); and against the larger backdrop of the emancipatory purpose of the Fourteenth Amendment as articulated in the *Slaughterhouse Cases*, 16 Wall. 36 (1872), properly understood, and *Strauder v. West Virginia*, 100 U.S. 303 (1879)—this context, they argue, compels a ruling in their favor. Given these precedents, they say the "separate but equal" rule of *Plessy* is incorrect on principle, out of step and out of line with our Fourteenth Amendment jurisprudence, and, at the very least, distinguishable from the cases before us. They also argue that its standards were unmet in the South Carolina and Virginia cases, in which educational facilities were concededly (one could add grotesquely) unequal.

The plaintiffs' principal argument is that *Plessy* was wrong the day it was decided: that to separate on the basis of race in the circumstances of these cases is intrinsically to treat equals unequally. Secondarily, even assuming the Fourteenth Amendment does not invalidate racial distinctions per se, they argue that the racial segregation of schools bears no reasonable relation to any valid legislative purpose or educational goal, given the predicate of the equality clause of the Fourteenth Amendment that intellectual capacity is equal by racial group.

The official defendants for their part do not explicitly argue that racial segregation in education is reasonable. Rather, they seek shelter under *Plessy*'s rule that racial segregation is permissible state behavior under the federal Constitution, supported by this Court's decisions in *Berea*, *Cumming*, and *Giles*. *Berea College v. Kentucky*, 211 U.S. 45 (1908) (finding school segregation statute does not violate due process when applied to a state-chartered corporation); *Giles v. Harris*, 189 U.S. 475 (1903) (refusing to remedy violation of Fifteenth Amendment right to vote by ordering Blacks put on voter registration lists); *Cumming v. Board of Education of Richmond County*, 175 U.S. 528 (1899) (holding denial of injunction against funding school for whites, where no equivalent school for Blacks existed, did not violate Equal Protection Clause). They claim, with emphasis varying among the cases at bar, that the Fourteenth Amendment was never meant by its drafters or ratifiers to integrate public schools racially; that school segregation by race does not arise from or promote racial prejudice but was benevolently meant and "presented a way of life," Transcript of Oral Argument of Justin Moore, Dec. 10, 1952, at 25; that said segregation does no harm when educational facilities are materially equal; that there is no showing of individual harm to students in any of the cases; that state policy is powerless to affect whether individuals feel inferior; and that ending segregation would produce dislocation and chaos, interracial violence and social unrest. Finally, they assert that federalism mandates leaving to states and localities the policy choice of how to administer schools. In short, they do not defend segregated education as a reasonable classification, but rather contend that it is harmless and even constitutionally privileged.

We find for the plaintiffs in law and in fact in the state cases. No one on this Court supports the view that our doctrines of federalism permit states to do what the equality clause of the federal Constitution forbids them from doing.[4] In the District of Columbia case, we find no valid reason that federal authorities should be permitted to violate the constitutional equality principles to which states are held. In the process, my colleagues implicitly adopt a variety of positions on the legal meaning of equality. Convinced that emphasis is all, see *Bethlehem Co. v. State Board*, 330 U.S. 767, 780 (1947) ("In law also the emphasis makes the song") (Frankfurter, J.), I attempt to clarify my colleagues' common implicit substantive ground. I have also come to believe that it is difficult to err in speaking too plainly of who has done what to whom on this question.

I

The question of the harm of school segregation by race where physical facilities are comparable (as in fact they seldom are) is the central question of this litigation. The Kansas court, where substantial equality of facilities was conceded, found as fact in *Brown* (Finding no. 8):

> Segregation of white and colored children in public schools has a detrimental effect upon the colored children. The impact is greater when it has the sanction of the law; for the policy of separating the races is usually interpreted as denoting the inferiority of the negro group. A sense of inferiority affects the motivation of a child to learn. Segregation with the sanction of law, therefore, has a tendency to [retard] the educational and mental development of negro children and to deprive them of some of the benefits they would receive in a racial[ly] integrated school.

Brown v. Board of Education of Topeka, 98 F. Supp. 797 (D. Kan. 1951) (No. T-316).

In a similar finding left undisturbed by the Supreme Court of Delaware, the chancellor in the Delaware case found as fact that "in our Delaware society," state segregation in education "itself results in the negro children, as a class, receiving educational opportunities which are substantially inferior to those available to white children otherwise similarly situated," *Belton v. Gebhart*, 87 A.2d 862, 865 (1952)—in essence finding that racially separate schools, ipso facto, provide inferior educational opportunities for Black children.

Expert witnesses also testified without contradiction in the South Carolina case, *Briggs v. Elliott*, that compulsory racial segregation injured Negro students by impairing their ability to learn, deterring their personality development, depriving them of equal status in the school community, destroying their self-respect, denying their full opportunity for democratic social development, subjecting them to the prejudices of others, and stamping them with a badge of inferiority. Brief for Appellants in nos. 1, 2, and 4 and for Respondents in no. 10 on Reargument at 29. The same view of racial segregation in higher education was reflected in the opinions of this Court in the *Sweatt* and *McLaurin* cases. Certainly, it is difficult to see how the educational deprivation done by separate education with equal facilities that intrinsically harms graduate and professional students does no injury to younger children. The reverse is more likely to be true.

This record documents injuries to public education by official action done through injury to the children's status as human beings in society. In my view, it is a misnomer to label these injuries "psychological," if by that is meant that the harm to equality is to be found in the children's inner response to the conditions imposed upon them, rather than in the imposition of the conditions themselves. The damage to which the experts testified in these cases[5] is one measure of the consequences of authoritative relegation of equals to a social status of inferiority. Being categorically ranked low among humanity on a hierarchical scale on a group basis by operation of law is a harm in itself: the quintessential harm of official inequality. It is always harmful, although some individuals deal with it better than others. We dare not fall into the trap of *Plessy*, in which whether or not "the colored race chooses to put that construction upon it," 163 U.S. at 551, is seen to constitute the harm or not. It is the construction put upon the colored children by the imposed arrangements that constitutes the harm of the segregation that forms the core of the injury to equality rights in these cases. Nothing the children thought or felt—their construction of it, as it were—created or could have changed that.

Indeed, what the children were found to have thought and felt was simply what that practice, in social reality, meant: they were assumed inferior, their presence contaminating, to white children. The children's response is also one measure of what that practice, in reality, did to them: it imposed inferior status and often inferior education on them in life. The tracks left on their hearts and minds are real damage; it is useful to have it documented. But the injury itself is done *to* them in the outward social world they inhabit, not in any sense *by* them or solely inside their heads.

The equality injury, hence the violation of law in these cases, thus lies not in the children's response to the state practice but in the practice itself. When a man is cut, he bleeds. Here, it is as if experts had to be called in to study the blood before the cut that produced it would be seen to be an injury. Simply put, the injury is one thing, the damages are another. Although injuries to equality typically do inflict, inter alia, psychic harm, inequality injuries are not subjective ones. Even if Black children do not think they are inferior, and many do not think so, they are still injured by the school segregation that makes that official assumption about them on a racial basis. That injury happens in the real world. The inequality takes place not when the children feel hurt by the unequal arrangements. That they often do is one real and intolerable measure of its damage. But they feel hurt because they are *being* hurt. The inequality takes place in material, not merely psychic, space. In these cases, the inequality inheres in the official imposition of unequal status on equal persons—that is, in the arrangement of racial segregation itself.

II

Mr. Justice Harlan, early in his dissent in *Plessy* vindicated today, observed: "Every one knows that the statute in question had its origin in the purpose, not so much to exclude white persons from railroad cars occupied by blacks, as to exclude colored people from coaches occupied by or assigned to white persons. . . . The thing to accomplish was, under the guise of giving equal accommodations for whites and blacks, to compel the latter to keep to themselves while traveling in railroad passenger coaches. No one would be so wanting in candor as to assert the contrary." 163 U.S. at 557. The candor to which he referred could not be taken for granted, beginning with the *Plessy* majority. So, too, here. The statutes in question in these cases originated in, and accomplish, not a symmetrical exclusion of all children from all but their own racial group, but an exclusion of

Black children from schools for whites. The thing for white people to accomplish, under the guise of equal educational facilities for all, was to keep white children, in particular white girls—in large part for reasons that implicate that distinguishability that makes the color line, hence white privilege, visually possible—from being educated with Black children, in particular young Black men.[6]

The segregation in the cases before us is no more equal a separation than the one in *Plessy*. The reason it is unequal is not that Black children felt bad about themselves as a result of it. One reason is, as plaintiffs put the point on reargument, "that the plain purpose and effect of segregated education is to perpetuate an inferior status for Negroes which is America's sorry heritage from slavery." Brief for Appellants in nos. 1, 2, and 4 and for Respondents in no. 10 on Reargument at 17. The point and premise of segregation laws, as they argue, was "to organize the community upon the basis of a superior white and an inferior Negro caste." Id. at 50. Segregation excludes Negro children from state public schools created for the children of dominant white groups. "Such a practice can only be continued on a theory that Negroes, *qua* Negroes, are inferior to all other Americans." Id. at 198. The United States recognized the same reality when it observed in these cases that the school systems litigated presented an instance of "[t]he subordinate position occupied by Negroes in this country as a result of governmental discriminations ('second-class citizenship,' as it is sometimes called)." Brief for the United States as Amicus Curiae at 31. The American Jewish Congress, in unvarnished terms, called the racial segregation of schools in these cases what it plainly is: "white supremacy."[7]

The point is that the evil of segregation we confront here is not one of mere differentiation but of hierarchy; not a categorization as such but an imposed inferiority; not an isolated event but an integral feature of a cumulative historical interlocking social and legal system; not a separation chosen by a subordinated group to seek their equality, but a segregation forced on them by a dominant group; not an abstract distinction made on the basis of race, but an officially imposed ordering of one race, white, over another, people of African descent. And note that "white," as pointed out by Thurgood Marshall in oral argument, is undefined by these school systems except by default; in South Carolina, he observed, the term in practice means everyone but Blacks. Transcript of Oral Argument of Thurgood Marshall, Dec. 9, 1952, at 12–13.[8] In these cases, Black students are treated one way, worse, and everyone else is treated another, better. The sting of the state-imposed segregation we invalidate in these cases is that it is imposed by white people on Black people and imposes and validates daily the discredited theory of superiority of the so-called white race over people of African descent—the same theory that long served to justify the institution of ownership of Black people by white people as their chattel property.

The cautionary note being sounded is that we avoid taking the ringing indictment of the Brief of the United States as Amicus Curiae at 13 of "separate and hence unequal" schools, or their equally correct observation that, "'separate but equal' is a contradiction in terms," id. at 17, as stand-ins for the concrete conditions and groups and history and context and substantive social status—the reality of experience—that gives these phrases their meaning. Those conditions, to repeat, have been the institutionalization by white Americans of inferior status for persons of African heritage, a rule of white supremacy. The policies invalidated today institutionalize white supremacy as public policy in education. Because supremacy of one race over another is inimical to an equality rule, we invalidate these policies. A premise of human equality and a premise of natural group-based hierarchy or valid racial social ranking cannot occupy the same space.

This is not to limit the Fourteenth Amendment's reach to these facts alone, but to establish that it is group dominance in historical space that is the enemy of equality. Our observation in *United States v. Carolene Products*, 304 U.S. 144, 153 n.4 (1938), that, for purposes of equal protection solicitude, the treatment of "discrete and insular minorities" deserves heightened scrutiny compared with other types of official distinctions, is animated by this same awareness. Group-based disadvantages other than to Negroes have been, see, e.g., *Yick Wo v. Hopkins*, 118 U.S. 356 (1886), and, when appropriate, will be prohibited. Expectably, which groups are "discrete and insular minorities," even whether it is only minorities who are unequally treated, has changed over time, see, e.g., *Leser v. Garnett*, 258 U.S. 130 (1921) (holding the Nineteenth Amendment, granting suffrage to women, validly part of the federal Constitution), and will properly continue to evolve.[9]

Conversely, however, not every official notice of the situation of Black people will be prohibited as discriminatory, although all, because of a history that is far from over, must be treated with "immediate suspicion," *Korematsu*, 323 U.S. at 216, and grave concern. But an embargo on official notice of race could, given widespread racial inequality, preclude official attention to the very substantive realities of racism that have made us rightly suspicious of race as a designation. In sum, our ruling today should be read to hold not that separate is inherently unequal in the abstract but that, as these facts substantiate, forced segregation of Black from white in a racially hierarchical society of white supremacy is a practice of inequality and cannot stand.

Fortunately, the Fourteenth Amendment was passed to dismantle precisely the substantive reality of imposed systematic inferiority of Black to white. More words on the history of the Thirteenth, Fourteenth, and Fifteenth Amendments can scarcely make this clearer. As we noted in *Strauder*: "The very fact that colored people are singled out . . . is practically a brand upon them, affixed by the law, an assertion of their inferiority, and a stimulant to race prejudice," 100 U.S. at 308. *Strauder* speaks further of the Fourteenth Amendment's granting "the right to exemption from unfriendly legislation against them distinctively as colored, exemption from legal discriminations, implying inferiority in civil society," 100 U.S. at 307–308. In *Ex Parte Virginia*, 100 U.S. 339, 344–345 (1879), we stated that "[o]ne great purpose of these amendments was to raise the colored race from that condition of inferiority and servitude in which most of them had previously stood, into perfect equality of civil rights with all other persons within the jurisdiction of the States." And in *Virginia v. Rives*, speaking of the Reconstruction statutes, we noted that "[t]he plain object of these statutes, as of the Constitution which authorized them, was to place the colored race, in respect of civil rights, upon a level with whites." 100 U.S. 313, 318 (1879).

Many of our precedents in this area can be read as rejecting abstraction severed from substance and as insisting on the relevance of the substantive content of concrete inferiority as socially imposed. In a salient recent example given surprisingly little attention in my colleagues' opinions today, this Court in *Shelley v. Kraemer* firmly grasped substance and repelled the argument from abstraction in rejecting the potential equality of application of restrictive covenants against any race. We said: "It is . . . no answer [to plaintiff's claim] . . . to say that the courts may also be induced to deny white persons rights of ownership and occupancy on grounds of race or color. Equal protection of the laws is not achieved through indiscriminate imposition of inequalities." 334 U.S. 1, 21–22 (1948). Put affirmatively, we have long rejected a presumption of hierarchy among humans on particular group grounds as the gravamen of the Fourteenth Amendment's equality clause. Put another way, we must not take the road of building a better Fourteenth Amendment law of "rational" discrimination on the ashes of *Plessy*, vitiating segregation today but leaving standing *Plessy*'s rule of "reasonable" differentiation—a rule of categorization by correspondence that makes equality law tautologous with social inequality rather than resistant to it.

III

It is time to admit that the notion of equality that found race-based segregation by law congenial has ancient roots and a beachhead in our jurisprudence in the "similarly situated" requirement. Well before *Plessy*, this Court in *Barbier v. Connolly* stated that while "class legislation, discriminating against some and favoring others, is prohibited . . . legislation which, in carrying out a public purpose, is limited in its application, if within the sphere of its operation it affects alike all persons similarly situated, is not within the amendment." 113 U.S. 27, 32 (1885). In 1920, we similarly distinguished the wide legislative discretion to classify from that which the Fourteenth Amendment prohibits in these terms: "[T]he classification must be reasonable, not arbitrary, and must rest upon some ground of difference having fair and substantial relation to the object of the legislation, so that all persons similarly circumstanced shall be treated alike." *F. S. Royster Guano Co. v. Virginia*, 253 U.S. 412, 415 (1920). See also *Hayes v. Missouri*, 120 U.S. 68, 71 (1887).

This "similarly situated" test will be recognized as a restatement of Aristotle's principle of formal equality, long thought axiomatic, even obvious, that "things that are alike should be treated alike, while things that are unalike should be treated unalike in proportion to their unalikeness," Aristotle, *The Nicomachean Ethics* V.3, 1113a–13b (W. Ross trans., 1925), a notion recently embraced and formulated by Joseph T. Tussman and Jacobus tenBroek, "The Equal Protection of the Laws," 37 *California Law Review* 341 (1949), written while *Plessy* was still good law.

The logic of Aristotle, who supported slavery, was followed precisely in *Plessy*: segregating those seen as likes from unlikes constitutes equality. In the racist mind, race is always a relevant unalikeness, and nothing in the notion of treating "likes alike, unlikes unalike" requires the assumption of equal humanity across racial or any other lines, or clarifies when (if ever) race is relevant to policy and when it is not. This inherited approach to equality from the Greeks through the Enlightenment, one that has been treated as common sense in our law until today, ratifies legal categories that are hand in glove with social inequalities. In the present cases, a rule of "likes alike" would support segregated schools, overlaying "unalikeness" of race from nineteenth-century theories of "scientific racism" drawing on Darwin and Spencer that purported to prove race-based intellectual inferiority and superiority with schools legally divided on the same lines. Just as consistently, Aristotle's equality reasoning justified the Nuremberg laws of the Third Reich. See Ulrich Scheuner, "Der Bleichheitsgedanke in der völkischen Verfassungsordnung," 99 *Zeitschrift für die gesamte Staatswissenschaft* 245, 260–267 (1939). Similar treatment—ultimately, extermination—was contemplated for all Jews, seen as "alike" by virtue of being Jewish and "unlike" so-called Aryans. The American Veterans Committee aptly observes that the segregation at bar is cut of the same cloth as the racism over which we just prevailed in World War II. Brief of American Veterans Committee Inc., Amicus Curiae, at 2. See also *The Yellow Spot* (1936) (documenting official segregation and other inequalities imposed on Jews in Germany).

Nothing in *Plessy*'s equality rule requires an assumption that all racial groups possess equal humanity or equal capacities. Nothing precludes imposing by law a condition of inferiority upon a group that is deemed inferior in society—in fact the opposite is true. Nothing in its notion of "rationality" stops giving a group less on the grounds that, having been given less in the past, it might appear less deserving today. Nothing, in other words, precludes law from simply replicating the consequences of social inequality and calling that "equal protection of the laws." Rather, the *Plessy* rule encourages, and *Plessy* achieved, precisely that.

Examples of the circular relation between this equality rule and unequal social reality are numerous. The thin guise of equal facilities that has been formally necessary for confronting the "separate but equal" rule as such is one. The "separate but equal" doctrine placed litigants challenging segregation as such in the perverse position of having to show that segregated facilities were equal when, because of the racism that produced the segregation that they wished to confront, facilities virtually never were equal. To have to deny an inevitable component of the harm of segregation in order to be able to challenge its legality is a litigation posture engendered by the approach to equality that produced the legal fiction that, under existing conditions of inequality, imposed separation along the same unequal lines can be equal in the first instance. It plays out the "similarly situated" approach in requiring that litigants must first present themselves as being in an equal situation before they are heard to complain of unequal treatment—when, in fact, due to the very inequality they challenged, they could not be "similarly situated." To be required first to have material equality before one can complain of unequal treatment, and then be told that due to material equality there is no harm, is a classic vicious circle.[10]

Plessy's "reasonableness" test provides another example. In *Plessy*, separation with equal facilities was justified as having a reasonable basis in the "established usages, customs and traditions," 163 U.S. at 550, of the surrounding society. On the sad record before us, experts were thus constrained to document, see Transcript of Oral Argument of Louis L. Redding, Dec. 11, 1952, at 25, what should go without saying: there are no racial differences in inborn intellectual capacity. There is, thus, no rational basis for educational differentiation on a racial basis. However, an ominous indication that the reasonableness approach of *Plessy* is not interred can be found in the amicus brief for the United States on reargument here. The government speculates that had the issue of rationality of separate schools been raised shortly after the Civil War, "constitutional justification for such action might conceivably have been found in the illiteracy and retarded social and economic status of a race so recently liberated from the bonds of slavery" Supplemental Brief for the United States on Reargument at 142. In other words, social inequality could rationalize legal inequality.

Applying *Plessy*, the doll studies in this record, Testimony of Dr. Kenneth Clark, Record of Trial at 2:87096, *Briggs v. Elliot*, 103 F. Supp. 920 (E.D.S.C. Mar. 13, 1952) (No. Civ. T-316); Appendix to Appellants' Briefs, The Effects of Segregation and the Consequences of Desegregation: A Social Science Statement at 3–7; Transcript of Oral Argument of John W. Davis, Dec. 10, 1952, at 6–7 could be read not as we do, to show the damage of segregation, but as finding a race-based inferiority or difference, to justify segregation. Permitting what might be called rational discrimination was what *Plessy* was all about. By implication, under *Plessy*, when enough social equality had been achieved over imposed inequality, official segregation would be rendered "unreasonable." Equality, on this approach to reasonableness, could be achieved by law only when it was no longer socially necessary to seek it.

We are not constrained to reproduce the inequality the Fourteenth Amendment aimed to end. To escape the hall of mirrors—the endless regress in which inequality in society makes "rational" inequality by law, which imposes inequality on society, which makes "rational" further inequality by law—we must take a substantive, principled, contextual approach. Guided by a record of harm, we need not pretend not to know as judges what we know as members of our society. Treating equals equally does not reduce to treating likes alike. The value of groups may lie in their variety, just as the value of individuals may lie in their singularity. But it is not for us to judge their value. An equality rule presumes it to be equal. Our equality question is not whether groups are alike or unalike in the abstract, but whether, assuming human equality on a group basis, a practice or statute promotes the social disadvantage of a historically disadvantaged or subordinated group. This contextualized determination mobilizes the clear purpose of the framers of the Fourteenth Amendment to *promote* equality, not merely to preside passively over a Constitution that reflects social inequality by sorting people by law in the same order into which an unequal society has ranked them. That *Plessy* would see that process as making a regulation reasonable, hence equal, is what we overrule when we overrule *Plessy* today.

On the view that "[t]hat which is unequal in fact cannot be equal in law," Brief on Behalf of ACLU et al., as Amicus Curiae at 5 emphasizing one part of our tradition and rejecting another, in an attempt to ensure that the reality of social inequality never again becomes a constitutional reason that equality rights can be denied, this analysis of basic principles is offered so that, fifty years from now, we have no cause to wonder why nothing has changed.

IV

Change is not slow; it is resistance to change that makes it take a long time. At oral argument, Kansas laudably conceded that eliminating segregation would not have serious administrative or other consequences for them. The Supreme Court of Delaware in *Gebhart v. Belton*, 91 A.2d 137, 149 (1952), having already ordered admission of Black children into formerly white schools, observed that "[t]o require the plaintiffs to wait another year under present conditions would be in effect partially to deny them that to which we have held they are entitled." In Delaware, they have been attending those schools without incident. For these same reasons, I would give the schools a maximum of one year from the date of this decree to eliminate race-based segregation from their school systems. On account of segregated schools, let there be not one more "dream deferred." See Langston Hughes, "Harlem [2]," *Montage of a Dream Deferred* (1951).[11]

8

Keeping It Real

On Anti-"Essentialism"

Theorizing the juncture of critical race theory with feminism could begin by tracing the contributions of critical race feminism to feminism historically. Considering African American women alone would have to begin at least with their resistance to slavery and segregation, proceed through their formative participation in and critique of the Black civil rights movement, encompass groundbreaking initiatives such as the National Black Feminist Organization and Combahee River Collective, and observe their backbone role in the contemporary women's movement today. In these and in many other ways, women of color—African American, Latina, Asian American, and Native American women predominantly—have created feminism in their own image, a feminism of the real world that is largely obscured in academic feminism. The theoretical contributions of critical race legal feminists—their foundational concepts, such as multiple consciousness, outsider jurisprudence, and intersectionality—are also contributions to feminism. To the work of scholars like Kimberlé Crenshaw and Mari Matsuda, no secondary treatment can add or do justice. They make legal and social theory look and sound like women, and you can't get more feminist than that.[1]

The travels of central ideas of critical race theory and their effects on women could also be traced. Critical race theory's critique of racism has had a major impact on equality and liberation thinking and practice around the world and, unlike some versions of feminism, has yet to be twisted into a defense of dominance. Critical race theory's rights theory has moved toward reconstructing the shape of the container, toward making rights nonindividualistic, nonatomistic, contextual, substantive entitlements, challenging and changing the abstract, status quo—preserving, state-power-based concept of rights that we inherited. As it is articulated by Patricia Williams in her *Alchemy of Race and Rights*, for example, this concept of rights remains unrebutted by the right and uncorroded by the left (for no

Talk at Critical Race Theory Conference, Yale Law School, New Haven, CT, November 14, 1997. First published, *Critical Race Theory: Histories, Crossroads, Directions* 71 (Francisco Valdes, Jerome Culp, Angela Harris, eds., 2002).

lack of trying).[2] As critical race theory, with the feminism that has been part of it from inception, becomes part of transforming human rights, human rights begin to be claimed as women's rights everywhere.

Storytelling, a key contribution of critical race theory to method, could also be retold. Widely appropriated, it may have lost some edge. But in the hands of its authentic practitioners, flowing together with feminism's consciousness-raising, storytelling remains a powerful direct means of grasping and exposing dominant realities and sharing subordinated ones. Critical race theory also could be located in the larger world of theory by exploring propositions like "critical race theory without race plus feminism without sex with a dash of Marxism without class gives you (presto) post-modernism!" Under current historical conditions, appropriating the approach while abstracting away the content is one of power's adaptations to challenge by transformative theory.

Asked to explore the interface between feminism and critical race theory, I will instead consider the origins and consequences of one criticism of feminism by some critical race theorists during critical race theory's first decade: the notion that feminism is "essentialist." In my view, this notion is often wrong and, when wrong, has created a false antagonism with regressive consequences, one of which has been to surround analysis of gender with an aura of suspicion and stigma. "Women," I will argue, is not a racist term. Most critical race thinkers see straight through the charge that feminism is essentialist to feminism's analysis of the reality of male dominance as a social system. But, having become something of a reflex and fixture in postmodernist litanies,[3] the misrepresentation of feminism as intrinsically "essentialist" has been going on for a decade now, is often repeated, and has at times been leveled regardless of its accuracy.

In philosophy, essentialism refers to a core essence inherent in something—a word, a person, a group—defining what that thing is.[4] Historically, being essentialist on sex or race has meant being biologically determinist: as if people are the way they are, act and think and feel the way they do, have the abilities and resources and occupy the social status they have because of their sex- or race-specific physiology. What is deemed the essence of race or sex—hence, the people who are raced or sexed—are biological facts like hormones, body type, and skin color. These so-called natural traits, in the essentialist view, determine social outcomes and individual qualities. Essentialism in this sense has long been central to the ideology of racism and sexism in its most vicious forms.

Contemporary thinkers have used the term in a variety of ways, its pliability and chameleon properties proving adaptive. I will focus on its use by some to claim that feminism is racist. "Essentialism" in this sense means taking white women as the model of "woman," taking white women's status and treatment as paradigmatic of women as such. In this criticism, white solipsism produces a category, "sex," in which white women are mistaken for all women, in which women who are white define what gender means for all women. As to particular work, this characterization either is or is not accurate; it has been both. What it has become is something more: the claim that it is racist to speak of "women" at all.

Elizabeth Spelman criticizes the white template for women she finds in feminism by criticizing its "essentialism" as finding that "some 'woman' substance . . . is the same in each of us and interchangeable between us."[5] In her view, feminism assumes and imposes a unit of analysis called "women" that is presupposed, internally uniform, fixed in nature, and rigid, by distinction with the diverse, heterogeneous, and fluid reality women are said to inhabit. Here, feminism is implicitly biologist and racist. While treating women as if they are a biological group is not necessarily easy to avoid,[6] to say that a biologically determinist theory of gender is not very feminist is not very controversial. Contemporary feminism began by resisting biology as destiny. If women's bodies determine women's inferior social status, the possibilities for sex equality are pretty limited. On this simplest level, one cannot be essentialist and feminist at the same time.

Angela Harris's widely cited critique of feminism in the *Stanford Law Review* defines "essentialism" as "the notion that a unitary 'essential' woman's experience can be isolated and described independently of race, class, sexual orientation, and other realities of experience."[7] Professor Harris's use of this term is predicated on Elizabeth Spelman's enumerated "assumptions of feminism."[8] These assumptions include "that women can be talked about 'as women,' . . . are oppressed 'as women,' . . . that women's situation can be contrasted to men's" and so on.[9] Professor Spelman is wrong to call these assumptions. They have been hard-won discoveries. Calling feminism "essentialist" in this sense thus misses the point. Analyzing women "as women" says nothing about whether an analysis is essentialist. It all depends on *how* you analyze them "as women": on whether what makes a woman be a woman, analytically, is deemed inherent in their bodies or is produced through their socially lived conditions.

An analysis of women that is predicated on women's experience is based on observed social conditions, hence can assume no uniformity of gender, biological or otherwise, because women's concrete social experience is not uniform. Any regularities the analysis finds, it finds, its findings are then subject to examination by others. Discerning commonalities in experience is not the same as searching for an "essence." The socially constructed "woman" has no "essence." If women "as women" are social and concrete, they must encompass all of women's experiences of social hierarchy, because race, class, and sexual orientation (for instance) contribute to making women's concrete situation and status as women be what it is. A genuinely feminist method is thus open to real women in the social world and builds its category, "women," from them.

If, by contrast, an analysis of women proceeds from an abstract idea—a category that is not predicated on and built of women's social reality but is a priori or biological or otherwise pre-fixed in asocial space (here Woman makes her appearance)—it is likely to be factually inaccurate as well as to impose a false sameness on women and to obscure power divisions within the group. Elizabeth Spelman asks, "Is it really possible for us to think of a woman's 'womanness' in abstraction from the fact that she is a particular woman?"[10] I don't know who her "us" is, but she writes as if to analyze women "as women" requires abstracting from women's particularities. But analyzing women "as women" can also require encompassing women's particularities. Professor Spelman assumes that feminist method is abstract in the sense of beginning with an idea of women rather than with women's material realities. Philosophers often do. But "sex" can be an abstract category or it can be a concrete reality. It is concrete in feminist work. "Essentialism," by contrast, has become an abstraction.

Further, feminism does not take the view that gender is all there is. It takes the view that gender is almost never not there. Feminism claims not that all women are affected the same by male power or are similarly situated under it. It claims that no woman is unaffected by it. Feminism does not see all women as the same; it criticizes this view. It claims that all women are seen and treated as women in some way under male supremacy. This is not to say that feminism is always practiced, even by feminists. It certainly is not to say that feminism does not need to be more race-conscious; it does. Nor is it to say that some work, claiming to be feminist, has not been racist; it has. It is to say that some of the feminist analysis that has been dismissively tagged with what has become the academic epithet of "essentialism," as exemplary of the "straight, white, and economically privileged,"[11] is not.

My work, for example,[12] is socially based to the ground and built on women's realities, including those of women of color, from the ground up. It pioneered the theory that sexuality is socially constructed, for example.[13] Its theory of gender is explicitly nonunitary and nonhomogenous. While facing the fact that gender affects all women, this work is clear that not all women are affected by male dominance in the same way or to the same degree. For example, it argues that "feminism seeks the truth of women's commonality out of the lie that all women are the same."[14] It systematically addresses racism and makes point after point that it is said to miss.[15] The least privileged women, not the most, are its center and foundation.[16] It is not, as Professor Harris claims, a "color-blind"[17] theory. It does not employ or embody a "nuance" theory of women of color.[18] The fact that women of color in the United States are the worst-off women, due to racism, and are in fact hit harder by virtually every social problem that also afflicts white women, problems like poverty and sexual assault, is hardly an invidious white observation, although its reality reflects plenty of invidious white practices.[19] I do not relegate women of color to footnotes and brackets.[20] I do not assume that all women are white. I do not require women to choose between their ethnic identification and their gender, and then to choose gender.[21] I do not say or think that sex is more fundamental than race, more important than race, worse than race; that gender is primary and race is not; or any of a host of related assertions about my work that shouldn't have survived a cite check.[22] The misrepresentations in Professor Harris's Stanford article[23] are particularly hard to explain in light of her nearly contemporaneous draft of a review of my *Toward a Feminist Theory of the State*, in which she observes that the book "tellingly points to the contradictions, paradoxes, and multiplicities hidden in every seeming unity."[24]

The "essentialism" charge has become a sneer, a tool of woman-bashing, with consequences that far outrun its merits. The widespread acceptance of the claim seems due more to its choice of target than its accuracy in hitting it. Male power is ecstatic; its defenders love the accusation that feminism is "essentialist," even though they don't really know what it means. They do know that it has divided women, which sure takes a lot of heat off.[25] The charge brings the moral authority of opposition to racism to the support of male dominance. "Essentialist" name-calling has become a weapon of choice against those who oppose pornography, prostitution, clitoridectomy, dowry burning, and other misogynist cultural practices, practices that target and harm women as women across cultures, although often in culturally specific forms. Avoiding "essentialism" has become a politically and intellectually respectable pretext for dismissing and ignoring gender and the realities of sexual politics.

One deep project of anti-"essentialism" appears to be to undercut resistance to sexual oppression. First, it is implied that the feminist protest against women's sexual definition and mistreatment is a protest against nature. In fact, it is the avatars of anti-"essentialism" who, when they read "sexuality," so deeply think biology that no amount of social, relational, and political analysis and observation deters them from the view that the biological is what is being analyzed and observed.[26] Then, it is more than suggested that political resistance to sexual abuse is a white thing. The idea here is that only white women (having no more significant problems to worry about) have the luxury of minding sexual objectification and sexual atrocities enough to make a big deal of them, so a feminism of resistance to sexual use and abuse is a white women's feminism.

What I want to say here is this: Sexual abuse is a real problem in the real world, not a move in an ideological or academic parlor game. Women of color are severely, pervasively sexually abused, including in racist ways worldwide. They are violated by it, resent it, resist it, want justice for it, and they want it to stop. Sexually abused women tend to know with real clarity that sexual abuse has everything to do with being women. It is mainly academics and perpetrators who, along with the law, deny it.

Fear of being labeled "essentialist" for identifying the role of gender in sexual abuse has far-reaching consequences. Those within and outside the academy who know that male power in all its forms remains entrenched also know they face defamatory attacks and potential threats to their economic survival if they say so. As "essentialism" has become a brand, a stigma, a contagious disease that you have to avoid feminism to avoid catching, it has become one more way that the connections and coherence of the ways women are oppressed as members of the group "women" can be covered up. It is silencing when women cannot tell the truth of what they know and survive; Professor christi cunningham is among the few who explore the dilemmas of discussing these subjects in public.

The defenders of dominance know, even if its postmodernist pretenders don't, that you can't change a reality you can't name. There is an ever growing, almost entirely unpublished body of writing on the sexual subordination of women of color. Some women send it to me. When it takes a lot of courage to look at crucial intersectional issues—for example, the racist treatment of women of color in pornography, including its place in hate crimes, ground prepared by Richard Delgado and others[27]—when one risks being shunned in one's own critical community for raising issues of the sexual subordination of women of color, it becomes necessary to ask who is doing this and why.

The "essentialism" charge, which has become a vehicle for misogyny, has also undermined the contributions that dominance theory, as developed in feminism, could make to antiracist work. Feminist dominance theory is a theory of social and political inequality as such. It builds on antiracism and builds it in. It is time for it to come home. Instead, in strenuous attempt to avoid the hated label of "essentialism," the revulsion at the "sameness" of all women falsely said to be inherent in gender analysis has produced a reflexive affirmation of "difference" in much critical race theorizing during the past decade or so. During this time, there seems to have been little or no awareness that sameness and difference are the two roads to nowhere that mainstream equality theory confines the unequal to walking.[28] In my opinion, failure to see this has crippled much antiracist legal work, including the fight for affirmative action, miring it in the sameness/difference equality trap that can only maintain white male power as is and fail to confront white male supremacy as such.[29]

Anti-"essentialism," as practiced, thus corrodes group identification and solidarity and leaves us with one-at-a-time personhood: liberal individualism. What a coincidence. With the inability to assert a group reality—an ability that only the subordinated need—comes the shift away from realities of power in the world and toward the search for "identity," excuse me, "identities."[30] It changes the subject, as it were, or tries to. But who wins? Can a postmodern humanism be far behind? "Identity" in its currently psychologically shrunk sense is not women's problem. Reality is: a reality of group oppression that exists whether we identify with our group or not.

It is not really necessary to say most of this to most of the critical race community. I therefore hope, and dare to believe, that critical race theory will avoid being diverted—as so much of academic feminism has been—into careerism, posturing, and seductive elite agendas. We need to theorize the place of the academy in the movement, to resist the forces that have created an elite that is accountable to power and principally responsive to its demands to de-realize reality. It would sound a lot less academic to call racism "racism" than to obscure that diagnosis under "essentialism." It wouldn't be as high-sounding. But a lot more people would be involved in much larger discussion, the focus would be kept on dominance of some people over others where it belongs, and none of the regressive consequences of the "essentialism" slur would result. This seems a good moment to reaffirm the injunction to keep it real.

9

Of Mice and Men

A Fragment on Animal Rights

Nonhuman animals in man's society are more than things, less than people. If the father of all social hierarchies, or the mother of all social distinctions, is the animate/inanimate division, it is closely followed by the human/animal[1] dichotomy, and then (for present purposes) the male/female line. When the three hierarchies are analyzed together—even, as here, tentatively and incompletely—the ordering of humans over animals appears largely retraced within the human group at the male/female line, which in turn retraces the person/thing dichotomy, to the detriment of animals and women. To unpack and pursue this analysis in the context of theorizing animal rights in law, the ways nonhuman animals are seen and treated by human animals need to be considered in gendered terms. Comparing humans' treatment of animals with men's treatment of women illuminates the way the legal system's response to animals is gendered, highlighting its response to women's inequality to men as well. Interrogating how animals are treated like women, and women like animals, and both like things, can shed reciprocal light.

Beneath the inquiry lurk large issues. Is the fact that, from the human side, the animal/human relation is necessarily (epistemically and ontologically) a relation *within* human society more problematic than it has been seen to be? Is the inquiry into what can be done for animals in human society and law limited when women's social and legal subordination to men is overlooked—specifically, is missing the misogyny in animal use and abuse detrimental to gaining rights for animals? Under existing law, are animals in any respects treated better than women are? On these questions, my operative suspicion is yes. The resulting further suspicion is that the primary model of animal rights to date—one that makes animals objects of rights in standard liberal moral terms—misses animals on their own terms, just as the same tradition has missed women on theirs. If this is right, seeking animal rights on the "like us" model of sameness may be misconceived, unpersuasive, and counterproductive.

Talk delivered at Conference on Animal Rights, University of Chicago Law School, April 13, 2001. First published in *Animal Rights: Current Debates and New Directions* 263 (Cass Sunstein and Martha Nussbaum, eds., 2004).

I

People dominate animals, men dominate women.[2] Each is a relation of hierarchy, an inequality, with particularities and variations within and between them. Every inequality is grounded and played out and resisted in unique ways, but parallels and overlaps can be instructive. One prominent similarity between these two hierarchies is ideological: in spite of the evidence that men socially dominate women and people dominate other animals, the fact that relations of domination and subordination exist between the two is widely denied. More precisely, it is widely thought and practiced and said that people are "above" animals, whereas it is commonly thought and practiced but denied that it is thought and practiced that men are "above" women. And while a hierarchy of people over animals is conceded, and a social hierarchy of men over women is often denied, the fact that the inequality is imposed by the dominant group tends to be denied in both cases. The hierarchy of people over animals is not seen as imposed by humans, because it is seen as due to animals' innate inferiority by nature. In the case of men over women, either it is said that there is no inequality there, because the sexes are different, or the inequality is conceded but is said to be justified by the sex difference, that is, women's innate inferiority by nature. Religion often rationalizes both.

In place of recognizing the realities of dominance of humans over animals and men over women is a sentimentalization of that dominance, combined with endless loops of analysis of sameness and difference. We see denial that each hierarchy involves socially organized power, combined with justifications of why one group, because of its natural superiority, should have what is, in substance, power and dominion and sovereignty over the other. The denial often takes the form of the assumption that the groups are equal just different, so their different treatment, rather than being a top-down ranking, is not unequal treatment but merely an appropriate reflection of their respective differences. It is as if we are confronting Aristotle's level line unequally divided, treating unlikes unalike—that is, equality.[3]

The denial of social hierarchy in both relations is further supported by verbiage about love and protection, including in what have been termed "the humane movements." The idea is, love of men for women or people for animals, motivating their supposed protection, mitigates the domination. Or, by benign motivation, eliminates the dominance altogether. One recalls Justice Bradley's concurring language denying Myra Bradwell's petition to be admitted to the bar that permitted persons: "The humane movements of modern society, which have for their object the multiplication of avenues for women's advancement, and of occupations adapted to her condition and sex, have my heartiest concurrence."[4] Difference rationalized dominance despite support for movements for advancement. Organized attempts to prevent cruelty to animals or to treat them "humanely" echo a similar underlying top-down paternalism, one most vivid in some social movements of the past to uplift prostituted women.[5] Neither with women nor animals has redress of abuses of power changed power's underlying distribution. Loving women is an improvement over hating them, kindness to animals is an improvement over cruelty, but neither has freed them nor recognizes their existence on their own terms.

Women are the animals of the human kingdom, the mice of men's world. Both women and animals are identified with nature rather than culture by virtue of biology. Both are imagined in male ideology to be thereby fundamentally inferior to men and humans. Women in male dominant society are identified as nature, animalistic, and thereby denigrated,[6] a maneuver that also defines animals' relatively lower rank in human society. Both are seen to lack properties that elevate men, those qualities by which men value themselves and define their status as human by distinction. In one vivid illustration that condescends to women and animals at once, James Boswell recounts Samuel Johnson saying, "Sir, a woman's preaching is like a dog's walking on his hind legs. It is not done well but you are surprised to find it done at all."[7] Using dogs imitating people as a simile for women speaking in public, a woman engaging in democratic discourse becomes as inept, laughable, unnatural, and imitative as a dog trying to walk upright. Qualities considered human and higher are denied to animals at the same time as qualities considered masculine and higher are denied to women.

In a related parallel, both animals and women have been socially configured as property (as has been widely observed), specifically for possession and use. Less widely observed, both women and animals have been status objects to be acquired and paraded by men to raise men's status among men, as well as used for labor and breeding and pleasure and ease. Compare beauty pageants with dog and cat shows. Men have also appointed themselves women's and animals' representatives without asking and have often defined both as to be protected by them. In law, this has often meant that injuries to animals and women—if seen as injuries at all as opposed to breaches of moral rules—are seen as injuries to their owners, just as seduction of a young woman (which was often rape) was legally considered an injury to her father.[8] In neither case has protection worked.

In a point of overlap and convergence between the two hierarchies, women have been dominated by men in part through the identification of their sexuality with their bodies, and their bodies with nature, meaning with animals. Women are attributed "naturalness," hence proximity to supposedly lower life forms. When your name is used to degrade others by attribution, it locates your relative standing as well, such as when "girl" is used as an insult among boys. Animality is attached to women's sexuality; the most common animal insults for women are sexual insults. Women are called animal names—bunny, beaver, bitch, chick, and cow—usually to mark their categorically lesser humanity, always drawing on the assumption that animals are lower than humans.[9] In pornography, women are often presented as animals and copulating with animals. The more denigrated the woman among women, prominently on racial grounds, the more and lower animal names she is called. This dynamic insults women, reinforces the notion that being like animals is a denigration, and denigrates animals.

Both women and animals are seen as needing to be subdued and controlled. Both are imagined as dangerously powerful, so must be kept powerless; if not locked up and kept down and in place, and killed when they step out, they will take over, overrun civilization, make chaos, end the known world. Both can be subjected to similar treatment, often by the same people in the same course of conduct, including torture, battering, terrorizing, taunting, humiliation, and killing.[10] Nowhere are the powerless as powerful as in the imaginations of those with real, not imaginary, power.

A related ideological parallel is the endless moralism of people with power in contending how good "we" are to be good to "them," surrounded by the resounding silence of the powerless. Consider the repeated retracing of the "As we treat them, so go we" trope.[11] We can tell how civilized we are by how well we treat our—fill in the blank with the unfortunates, the lessers. Take Senator Jennings Randolph in congressional debate in 1963 over the Equal Pay Act: "Emerson wrote that one of the measures of a civilization is the status which it accords women."[12] Or Mahatma Gandhi: "The greatness of a nation and its moral progress can be judged by the way its animals are treated."[13] Treating the low well, raising up women and animals within their limits, shows how civilized and great humans and men are. The ranking of noblesse oblige, who and what matters, in whose eyes, who is great, civilized, and progressing could not be clearer or more self-referential.

Men's debates among themselves over what makes them distinctively human have long revolved around distinctions from women and animals. Can they think? Are they individuals? Are they capable of autonomous action? Are they inviolable? Do they have dignity? Are they made in the image of God? Men know they are men, meaning human, it would seem, to the degree their answer to these questions is yes for them and no for animals and women. In response to this definition-by-distinction, many who seek rights for women and for animals have insisted that they do, too, have these qualities men value in themselves. If men have dignity, women and animals have dignity. If men can think, women and animals can think. If men are individuals, so are women and animals. That women are like men and animals are like people is thought to establish their existential equality, hence their right to rights.

So the question becomes, are they like us? Animal experimentation, using mice *as* men (so men don't have to be) is based on degrees of an affirmative answer.[14] The issue is not the answer;[15] the issue is, is this the right question? If it is the wrong question for women—if equality means that women define the human as much as men do—it is at least as wrong for nonhuman animals.[16] It is not that women and animals do not have these qualities. It is why animals should have to be like people to be let alone by them, to be free of the predations and exploitations and atrocities people inflict on them, or to be protected from them. Animals don't exist for humans any more than women exist for men.[17] Why should animals have to measure up to humans' standards for humanity before their existence counts?

II

Bearing in mind the limitations of dominant standards, following Mari Matsuda's injunction to "ask the other question,"[18] the woman question can be asked of animals in the animal law area. Relatively little attention has been paid by animal law scholars to the sexual use and abuse of animals.[19] Most states have provisions against bestiality, which in substance are laws against doing sexually to animals what is done to women by men on a daily basis. These laws define it as immoral for men to treat animals as they treat women free of legal restraints.[20] To the degree an injured party is envisioned in bestiality laws, though, it is structurally imagined to be the human or the community. Only Utah categorizes the laws against sexual contact by humans with animals under cruelty to animals.[21]

Why do laws against sex with animals exist? Their colonial roots indicate a preoccupation with debasement of the self, a lowering of the human to the animal realm.[22] In contemporary times, these laws are barely enforced, if they ever were. Commercial pornography alone shows far more sex with animals than is ever prosecuted for the acts required to make it. Much as with laws on sodomy (not a random parallel; in some sodomy laws, gay men are sub silentio lumped in with beasts). So little is done with it, one wonders what the law is doing there. Moralism aside, maybe the answer is that people cannot be sure if animals want to have sex with us. Put another way, we cannot know if their consent is meaningful.[23] Other than in some feminist work, the question whether the conditions of meaningful consent to sex exist for women has not been seriously asked. Whether it is possible, under conditions of sex inequality, to know whether women fully and freely consent to sex or comply with much sex without wanting to, (not to mention whether they consent to other things, like the form of government they live under) is a neglected question of inequality among people. So, too, it is neglected between people and animals, although the substance of the inequalities is not identical. Surely animals could be, and are, trained to make it appear that they enjoy doing what people want them to do, including having sex with people. Pornographers train dogs to sexually penetrate women on signal; other pimps train donkeys to have sex with women in stage shows. Pornographers joke that women would have more sex with animals in their films but that would be cruelty to animals; putting a mouse in a woman's vagina would be cruel to the mouse, ha ha. Now whose status is higher?[24]

Laws against "crush videos" illustrate the comparative public ethos on this point. In this genre of pornography, mice or other (often small furry) animals are "taunted, maimed, tortured and ultimately crushed to death under the heel of a shoe or bare feet of a provocatively dressed woman"[25] to make a fetish film. The sex in the movie centers on the slow killing of the animals, called "pinkies" when they are baby rodents. Congress made crush videos a federal crime recently in a bill providing "punishment for depiction of animal cruelty."[26] It covers any visual or auditory depiction in which a living animal is "intentionally maimed, mutilated, tortured, wounded, or killed" if the conduct is illegal under federal law or the law of the state in which the "creation, sale, or possession" of such materials occurred.[27] There is no such law against depicting cruelty to women—a multibillion-dollar industry with considerable constitutional protection. In movie-making, someone must be on the set to monitor the safety of the treatment of nonhuman animals. No such requirements practically exist for women (or men) in, for example, the making of pornography.

There was some dissent to the federal bill, largely by the American Civil Liberties Union (ACLU), on First Amendment speech grounds, and some opposition to it in committee. The essence of the objection: "films of animals being crushed are communications about the act depicted, not doing the acts."[28] That it often takes the doing of the act to create the communication about the acts depicted is as obvious as the fact that the film itself is not the killing of the animal, although it would not usually exist without it. To the question "whether protecting animal rights counterbalances citizens' fundamental constitutional rights" to speech, the dissenters concluded that they did not.[29] But the bill passed. No prosecutions under it have yet been reported, so no occasion has arisen to consider any issues of freedom of expression further. There still is no equivalent statute prohibiting *a depiction in which* a living human is intentionally maimed, mutilated, tortured, wounded, or killed in order to make the film. The First Amendment protected status of such films, including snuff films, in which a human being is murdered to make a sex film, remains contested even in theory, making it unclear whether such a statute would be found constitutional.

In California, a bill was introduced in February 2000 that would have prohibited both crush videos of animals and torture and snuff films of human beings. For animals, it sought to prohibit an "image that depicts . . . the intentional and malicious maiming, mutilating, torturing, or wounding of a live animal" or the similar "killing of an animal" when the "killing of an animal actually occurred during the course of producing the depiction and for the purpose of producing that depiction."[30] For humans, the bill defined as a felony "the intentional or malicious killing of, or intentional maiming, torturing, or wounding of a human being, and intentional killing or cruelty to a human being actually occurring in the course of producing the depiction and for the purpose of producing the depiction."[31] A massive public First Amendment hue and cry, principally by the ACLU, was raised about the human part of the bill only.[32] No part of the bill passed. However, the makers of a crush video were successfully prosecuted for the underlying acts under the California law this measure had sought to amend, a provision that prohibits malicious mutilation, torture, or killing of a living animal.[33] In the prosecution, the videotape—for which rats, mice, and baby mice were slowly killed "for sexual gratification of others and for commercial gain"[34]—was evidence.

Instructively, the joint crush/snuff bill had a consent provision only for people.[35] Welcome to humanity: while animals presumably either cannot or are presumed not to consent to their videotaped murder, human beings could have consented to their own intentional and malicious killing if done to make a movie, and the movie would be legal. Even that was not enough to satisfy the avatars of freedom of speech. One wonders anew if human rights are always better than animal rights. Many laws prohibit cruelty to animals, but no laws prohibit cruelty to women as such. There are prohibitions on behavior that might be said to be cruel that at times are applied to women, such as laws against battering and torture. And laws against cruelty to animals are not well enforced. But then the laws against battering and torture of people are not well enforced either, especially where women are the victims. Consider the outcry if California's criminal law against negligent and intentional "torture" of animals—defined as any act or omission "whereby unnecessary or unjustified physical pain or suffering is caused or permitted"—was sought to be extended to women.[36] One has to go to Canada's criminal law on pornography[37] to find a law against "cruelty" to women, sexual or otherwise.

Having asked a woman question—sexuality—about animals, it is time to ask the animal question of animals. What is the bottom line for the animal/human hierarchy? I think it is at the animate/inanimate line, and Carol Adams and others are close to it: we eat them.[38] This is what humans want from animals and largely why and how they are most harmed. We make them dead so we can live. We make our bodies out of their bodies. Their inanimate becomes our animate. We justify it as necessary, but it is not. We do it because we want to, we enjoy it, and we can. We say they eat each other, too, which they do. But this does not exonerate us; it only makes us animal rather than human, the distinguishing methodology abandoned when its conclusions are inconvenient or unpleasant. The place to look for this bottom line is the farm, the stockyard, the slaughterhouse. I have yet to see one run by a nonhuman animal.

The overarching lesson I draw for theorizing animal rights from work on women's issues is that just as it has not done women many favors to have those who benefit from the inequality defining approaches to its solution, the same might be said of animals. Not that women's solution is animals' solution. Just as our solution is ours, their solution has to be theirs. This recognition places at the core of the problem of animal rights a specific "speaking for the other" problem. What is called animal law has been human law: the laws of humans on or for or about animals. These are laws about humans' relations to animals. Who asked the animals? References to what animals might have to say are few and far between. Do animals dissent from human hegemony? I think they often do. They vote with their feet by running away. They bite back, scream in alarm, withhold affection, approach warily, fly and swim off. But this is interpretation. How to avoid reducing animal rights to the rights of some people to speak for animals against the rights of other people to speak for the same animals needs further thought.[39]

A related absence is the lack of serious inquiry into animal government, including political organization in the sense of patterns of deference and command, and who gets what, when, how, and why. Ethologists and animal behaviorists have provided observations that might be put into that category,[40] but lawyers have devoted little attention to the emerging rules and forms of governance in animal societies that might illuminate entitlement, remedy, ethics, justice, community. The point of this inquiry would not be to see how "they" are like "us" or different. One point is to see whether, not having made such a great job of it, people might have something to learn. Maybe hierarchy and aggression and survival of the fittest are systematically focused upon by people in animal studies because those dynamics are so central to the organization of human affairs by male humans. How animals cooperate and resolve conflicts within and across species might be at least as instructive. How do they define and distribute what we call rights, or is there some other concept? Do they recognize and redress injuries? While animals aggress, so far as I know there has yet to be an animal genocide. This inquiry would be into animals' laws, not just what the two-leggeds say about the four-leggeds. Inventing what is not known across power lines has not worked well between men and women. I do not know why it would work any better between people and animals.

The question is (with apologies for echoing Freud's infamous question of women), what do they want from us, if anything other than to be let alone, and what it will take to learn the answer. Instead of asking this question, people tend to remain fixated on what we want from them, to project human agendas onto animals, to look for and find or not find ourselves in them. Some see economics. Some see Kant-in-the-making. Some see women. People who study animals often say more about themselves than about animals, leaving one wondering when the road kill will rise up off the page and say: stop making me an object of your analysis. What it would do to the discussion if they spoke for themselves is the question. The animal communicators are working on it.[41] People joke about dolphins' having discursive democracy but miss whether people will ever be able to communicate collectively as well as whales and blackbirds—who seem not to have our collective action problems—do.

Women are doubtless better off with rights than without them. But having rights in their present form has so far done precious little to change the abuse that is inflicted on women daily, and less to change the inferior status that makes that abuse possible. Like women's rights, animal rights are poised to develop first for a tiny elite, the direction in which the "like us" analysis tends. Recognizing rights for chimpanzees and bonobos,[42] for instance, would be like recognizing them for the elite of women who can preach in public—perhaps at the expense of, and surely in derogation of, the rights of that rest of women who are most women. Establishing animal individuality, agency, and rationality as a basis for their rights goes down that road.

Predicating animal rights on the ability to suffer is less likely to fall into this trap, as it leads more directly to a strategy for all.[43] Indeed, capacity to suffer may be closer to women's bottom line than liberal legal approaches to women's rights have yet reached. But women's suffering, particularly in sexual forms, has not delivered us full human status by law—far from it. It has gotten us more suffering. Women's suffering has also been sexualized. That women feel, including pain, has been part of stigmatizing them, emotions in particular traditionally having been relegated to the lower, animal, bodily side of the mind/body split. What will it do for animals to show that they feel?[44] Calculations of comparative suffering weighted by status rankings, combined with the inability to register suffering on the sufferer's terms, have so far vitiated the contribution Bentham's recognition might make. The ways women suffer as women have been denigrated and denied and, when recognized, more often used to make us seen as damaged goods than humans harmed. But fundamentally: Why is just existing alive not enough? Why do you have to hurt? Men as such never had to hurt or to suffer to have their existence validated and harms to them be seen as real. It is because they are seen as valid and real to begin with that their suffering registers and they have rights against its harm.

Women have been animalized, animals feminized, often at the same time. If qualified entrance into the human race on male terms has done little for women—granted we are not eaten, but then that is not our inequality problem—how much will being seen as humanlike, but not fully so, do for other animals? What law resists doing is taking anything they want away from those at the top of hierarchies. It resists effectively addressing the inequality's material bottom line.

III

Rereading Steinbeck's play *Of Mice and Men*[45] in this context—seeing mice as animals in the animal rights and crush video sense, and men as men in the sense of exercising gender dominance—offers insights in hierarchy, power, and love among people and between people and animals. Three interlocking hierarchies structure the play. Lenny, the slow, caring guy who doesn't know his own strength, is above animals. Curly, the boss's son who only wants to have a level conversation with the boys in the bunkhouse, is above his recently wed young wife, initially presented as a sexualized tart. George, Lenny's buddy, the guy's guy, is the smart one: shutting Lenny up, he will speak for him, he will make everything come out right. You know Lenny cares about animals. You question whether Curly cares about his wife. You never doubt that George, with condescension and comprehension, loves Lenny, who returns that love with unquestioning trust, adulation, and adoration.

With his love, Lenny kills the mice he dotes on, then the puppy his heart and hands adore; eventually, by accident and in panic, he kills Curly's wife. Curly's masculinity is desperate; he has to make himself a place among men. He is ultimately responsible for his wife's death, because he set her up for it: he stifled her, made her have to leave, run away, by depriving her of the ability to have her own life. He made Lenny rightly fearful of her making noise, of exposing her plans to flee, of them being together. Curly put her in the position where Lenny, always stronger than he knows, stifles her life out of her because he so loves her silky hair and to keep her leaving from being found out once she starts screaming. She is an animal to him. Once George realizes what Lenny has done, knowing Lenny will be hunted down like an animal and will not survive men's legal system, because he loves him, George kills Lenny himself. As we say of animals, including those who attack humans, he put him down.

On this reading, the play is about men's love: unknowing, gentle, soft, sensual love; sexual and explosive and possessive love; protectionist and "humane" love. Every relationship here is unequal: between humans and animals, between women and men, between some men and other men. It is about unequal love. In Steinbeck's context, one I am calling socially male, loving means death. Specifically, it kills.

Read this way, *Of Mice and Men* is a morality play about loving to death: the relation between affection and aggression. It shows the stifling lethality of protective love in society ordered hierarchically, where no one but George gets to be who he is without dying for it. In the interlocking connections among hierarchies among men, women and men, and people and animals, between love in its male dominant form and death-dealing, each man with the best of intentions kills what he most loves. Men's love did not save Curly's wife, the mice, or Lenny—quite the contrary. The good intentions of the powerful, far from saving the powerless, doom them. Unless you change the structure of the power you exercise, that you mean well may not save those you love. Animal rights advocates take note.

Central dilemmas in the use of law by humans to free women—men's pets, their beasts of burden, their living acquisitions—from male dominance have included analyzing structural power in intimate settings, meeting and changing standards simultaneously, redefining power while getting some, gaining protection without strengthening its arbitrary exercise,[46] and supporting caring and empathy while enforcing accountability. And we supposedly speak the same language. In the effort to use law to free animals from the species domination of human beings, the most socially empowered of whom are men, these and other challenges remain unmet.

10

The Power to Change

As women have moved to end women's inequality to men, we have found law to be a wall as well as a tool for taking down walls. Sometimes we have made law a door.

Variously potent in all cultures, law is particularly used in the United States to distribute and negotiate resources, rules, and power itself, making it at once a powerful medium and a medium for power. A form of force, law is also an avenue for demand, a vector of access, an arena for contention other than the physical, a forum for voice, a mechanism for accountability, a vehicle of authority, and an expression of norms. Although law has operated in ways socially male, women seeking change for women have found that its consequences and possibilities cannot be left to those elite men who have traditionally dominated in and through law, shaping its structures and animating attitudes to guarantee the supremacy of men as a group over women in social life. Women who work with law have learned that while legal change may not always make social change, sometimes it helps, and law *un*changed can make social change impossible.

Historically, women in the United States have not been permitted the tool of law in our own hands. We had no voice in writing the U.S. Constitution. When, one hundred years and a civil war later, an equality provision was added in 1868, it was without any expectation that the legal status of the sexes would be affected. Equality for women under the Constitution has been late, slow, and slight. Severely undertexted—all that is there are the five words "equal protection of the laws,"—it applied to women as such only by interpretation. In 1920, the women's movement gained passage of the Nineteenth Amendment, formally institutionalizing women's equal citizenship: the right to vote, to decide who governs; the right to serve on juries, to decide what happened when people do not agree; and the right to practice law, to use this lever of power directly. Even with that, it took until 1971 for the U.S. Supreme Court to decide

First published, *Sisterhood is Forever: The Women's Anthology for a New Millennium* 447 (Robin Morgan, ed., 2003).

for the first time that explicitly different rights for women than for men could violate the constitutional equality principle.

The 1970s saw women moving into the legal profession in ever greater numbers, determined to end law's sexism, root and branch. The women's movement of the 1980s and 1990s applied equal protection doctrine to women where it fit and exposed its male bias where it did not. It became clear that its main interpretive doctrine—while a big improvement on no constitutional sex-equality guarantee at all—works best for women's problems that arise least: where sex discrimination is explicit on its face, or where an elite individual woman meets male standards but is not treated as men are. But most laws that promote sex inequality do not discriminate on their face and most women in unequal societies do not have the advantages of being similarly situated to men. Existing equality rule thus works best for problems, however important, that fewest women have.

Despite the shortfall in the Equal Protection Clause, a federal Equal Rights Amendment (ERA), originally proposed in 1923, narrowly failed of ratification in 1982 after several attempts at passage.[1] The international Convention on the Elimination of All Forms of Discrimination Against Women (CEDAW), which could help compensate for the lack of an explicit sex-equality guarantee in the U.S. Constitution, has yet to be ratified by the U.S. Senate. After 1973, most U.S. women who needed abortions were no longer criminals, but those who could not pay for an abortion were still effectively deprived of access to them by lack of federal funding for this medical procedure. At the beginning of the twenty-first century, no explicit words yet granted overarching legal equality to U.S. women.

Statutory law, passed by elected representatives of the people in a political system far from flawless at conveying the will of the governed, attempts to address some of the problems unremedied because of the absence of constitutional and international rights. In the late nineteenth century, married women secured the right to own property in their own name, so their material existence no longer had to be dependent on husbands by law. But a sex-unequal marketplace still did not necessarily provide them economic independence—and does not today. In 1963, the Equal Pay Act guaranteed equal pay on the basis of sex for work that requires equal skill, effort, and responsibility. But most women have been and remain segregated into occupations that mostly women do—jobs that either are different or are seen as different from those men do and that pay less. Title VII of the Civil Rights Act of 1964, propelled by the civil rights movement, prohibited discrimination on the basis of sex in employment, although it had been introduced in Congress for partly racist reasons. Later Congresses did take sex discrimination seriously—for example, by prohibiting discrimination on the basis of pregnancy in employment in 1978 and extending Title VII to the federal labor force. Under the aegis of Title VII, sexual harassment and sex stereotyping as an employment standard were made actionable as violations of sex-equality rights, and intersections of race and sex discrimination were increasingly recognized as a joint or combined basis for legal action. But despite more than 30 years of legal guarantees of workplace sex equality—and some progress, mainly for elites—the workplace remains overwhelmingly gender-unequal, to women's disadvantage.

Law functions also as a form of politics. On this level, law has required that women use its rules to be effective, even as part of women's political agenda has been to challenge and change those rules—rules women had no voice in making. In its analysis of politics *as* sexual, the women's movement in our time has illuminated law's dynamics from beneath, casting new light on law as such. Before this movement, women, defined as the denizens of the private, were not thought of as a political group at all. So law, embodying the rules by which public power is distributed, was thought inappropriate for addressing women's situation as members of a sex—certainly a convenience for male supremacy. Once women exposed the line between public and private as gendered—revealing that masculine is to public as feminine is to private—the male bias built into the definition of the public by law was also exposed. The public/private line that distinguished the properly legal from the legally exempt stood revealed as a barrier that excluded and marginalized women from law, and under and within it as well. Women thus began to claim a place in the public world of law, to redefine the legal as already involved in the private and as a determinant of women's status and treatment, top to bottom and society-wide. As women thus became subjects of law, the hidden and denied ways women had been subordinated to men prior to law and under law became revealed to public view, requiring accountability for the first time.

One example of this theory in action is the way Title VII's prohibition on sex discrimination in employment was used by women in the 1970s to forge the first civil right created by women: the prohibition on sexual harassment, a formerly subterranean practice considered a private privilege of powerful men. By 1980, Title IX of the Education Amendments of 1972, which guaranteed women equal access to the benefits of an education, was authoritatively interpreted to prohibit sexual harassment in education, giving young women some legal rights against sexually exploitive teachers and coaches. Under Title IX, young women also routinely came to take part in organized athletics on a mass scale for the first time in U.S. history. Whether in so doing they reclaimed their bodies (becoming strong, self-possessed, and physically self-respecting) or whether their bodies were further claimed on male terms (competing to dominate rather than excel, striving to meet new sex-object standards, and having their victories co-opted as trophies for male triumphs), or whether some of both, remains debatable and to be seen.

Also during the latter quarter of the twentieth century, some aspects of rape law were reformed in an attempt to make them more effective. The numbers of rapes reported soared for a time, but conviction rates rose barely, if at all. Initiatives were taken to shelter women from battering in their homes, and to contain and educate the men who attacked them, but the rate of physical assault of women by men in intimate relationships did not significantly drop. Pornography's harms were legally confronted as a form of sex discrimination,[2] but the pornographers retained their First Amendment right to violate women's civil rights through pornography—at least for now. The Violence Against Women Act—a legal tool to empower survivors by holding batterers and rapists directly accountable to them for sex-based violence—was passed by Congress in 1994, but was invalidated (as a violation of states' rights) in 2000 by the U.S. Supreme Court. And while some statutes and international protocols have begun to address international sex trafficking, little to nothing has been done by law for women in prostitution.

Until effectively addressed, all these issues will remain new questions for law, even as further issues loom. Will international law, uniting women globally in rights as they are currently united in inequality, prove capable of supporting changes in women's human rights that domestic laws have not? Will ever-new technological forms and social configurations be used to traffic women and children, or will the predators be stopped? Will family be created and defined in new ways? Whose genetic material can be used how? As women participate in the armed forces, will aggression at home and abroad decrease or increase, and will the laws and customs of war change in response? Will national and religious strictures allow women to define our cultures equally with men? What new definitions and markers of gender will emerge in society and law? Will any existing ones truly fade? Will anything shift the unequal division of power between women and men?

In working with law, women have learned that the system of male supremacy is like a vampire: it thrives on women's blood but shrivels in the light of day. Male dominance is exposed in public when made subject to law. The private is a place, but it is also a mode, a dimension of being as well as a location. A formally lawless site to which women are relegated, the private is both where and how women are defined as women, what and where we have been tossed instead of having access to a whole life and a wider world. Law is the private's antithesis, the quintessential public place and mode.

When women claim and use law *as* women, women go public. This in itself challenges the hierarchy of men over women that has been built into law. For women to speak in a legal voice—including to represent people effectively—requires something beyond the ways in which women, socialized as private beings (as women, as feminine), are trained and allowed to speak: apologetic, soothing, imitative, pandering, approval-seeking, risk-averse, ineffectual, deprived of consequence. Law requires skills of contention—including standing one's ground—and persuasion—including touching and moving others onto one's ground—abilities that are still widely stigmatized, even demonized, in women. But law is not only combat; it is also cooperation, and here women's training under inequality becomes skill.

As more and more women graduate from law schools,[3] legal culture will adjust to accommodate them. Perhaps it will respect them and women's status will rise. Perhaps the status of the legal profession will sink as more women move into it, or women's legal ghettos will form within it. Possibly women in law—who will remain a small minority of all women—will become lawyers as men have, using its advantages as an elite profession over other women and men. In any case, these women, once lawyers, will likely never have to beg for an abortion from a back-alley butcher or sell themselves for sex on street corners to men numbering in the thousands. They will either forget or remember the fact of their privilege, however earned, among women. But they will neither be insulated nor exempted from the rest of women's status, a fact they will either deny or will use their power to work to change. Whether their practice of law reflects a consciousness of these facts of sisterhood under male dominance until it is ended is up to them.

Most women think of law as alien, subject to influence they do not have, ignorant of the realities they live. Many conclude that law can do nothing for them, so they should stay as far away from it as possible. One result of this turning away, however realistic its reasons, is that male power continues to own law unopposed. When law is abandoned to the powerful, corruption and physical force remain the real law, a fact ignored by those who, having a choice, urge abdicating this ground. It is hard to avoid the feeling that women are urged to think law can do nothing for them precisely because it can do so much.

The movement for women through law is not a movement content to rest with dissent on the margins. It intends to change the mainstream, to make ordinary everyday rules work for ordinary everyday people—women included—and to give them tomorrow what they do not have today. In whose interest is it for women to leave a power like this to men? Law can mean community: your people stand behind you, hear you, support you. It can mean reality: what you say happened is found to have happened; your knowledge is validated. It can mean vindication: it is wrong that you were wronged; someone took something that belongs to you; you count. It means hope: what happened to you might not happen again.

Women who use law for women in our time have tried to ensure accountability for the unspeakable and the unnamed. Law names authoritatively. Survivors of sexual abuse, torture, genocide, trafficking in human beings, have taken tremendous risks to say what happened to them to ensure that law calls their abuse by its real name in public. Often they get little else. Consider the almost-unbelieving ecstasy on the faces of the tortured when former Chilean dictator Augusto Pinochet was extradited in 1999. Recall the stoicism replaced by bitter uplift on the faces of surviving families when racist murderers in the U.S. South were brought to justice even decades later. Remember the crumpled blankness on the faces of raped women when their violators are exonerated, the look of hope vanquishing disbelief when they are convicted. This—not closure, not incarceration, not money—is what law can mean. It can give people back the humanity that the violation took away. This is what gives law the power to change.

SECTION B. ■ SEXUAL ABUSE AS SEX INEQUALITY

11

Sexual Harassment

The First Five Years

[A] new voice is beginning to be heard on behalf of the gaps in the socio-symbolic order, on behalf of the unsaid, the unmeaningful, the repressed holes in masculine discourse.

—Xaviére Gauthier, "Pourquoi sourciéres?" in *New French Feminisms*, 200 (Elaine Marks and Isabelle De Courtivron eds. 1980)

As the first legal wrong to be defined by women,[1] sexual harassment has been called a feminist invention. Women were subjected to sexual attention they were not in a position to refuse long before the state recognized it as an injury under some circumstances. Sex discrimination law now prohibits requiring sexual compliance in exchange for material survival or educational benefits[2] and tolerance of sexual propositions or byplay as a condition of work,[3] as well as compulsory provocative uniforms that make women appear to "ask for it" on the job.[4] Sexual objectification, the unifying dimension of these prohibitions and a central dynamic of gender inequality, is to this extent illegal, women's resistance to it to this degree legitimized. But it took a women's movement to expose these experiences as systematic and harmful in the first place, a movement that took women's point of view on our own situation as significantly definitive of that situation, as the basis for beginning to embody it in the law of sex equality.

Sexual harassment, now a legal term of art, permits the claim that sexual initiatives that men may perceive as "normal and expectable"[5] sex role behavior—just as men may see as "sex" the same encounters women experience as rape, or as erotic the same graphic materials women find violating—can be damaging to women. Legal doctrine has tended to identify with socially male perspectives on these injuries. From the standpoint of a male harasser, and that taken in some cases, there is no harm if none is meant.[6] In the same view, damages would implicitly be assessed by what a male victim of heterosexual harassment might suffer and imagine being

First published as "Introduction," *Sexual Harassment: A Symposium Issue*, 10 *Capitol University Law Review* 1 (1981).

made whole by: pay, promotion, grades, and other such measures of concrete loss.[7] Burdens of proof would effectively presume a non–sex-discriminatory social universe (the one men largely occupy) and would require a plaintiff to prove herself exceptional.[8] Women who meet the "good girl" standard of asexual respectability would merit protection; "bad girls" would not be believed. These questions of the nature of sexual injury,[9] adequacy of remedy,[10] attachment and scope of liability,[11] and implicit standards for credibility at trial[12] are beginning to be adjudicated in the sexual harassment context. Advances reflect some acceptance of women's standpoint. Failures at the dismissal stage often reveal corresponding noncomprehension. Losses at trial expose a lack of fit between the court's image of a proper victim and a real one.[13] These doctrinal questions presuppose a substantive view of the relations between the sexes, the role of sexuality in work and education, and a theory of the state, as well as the existence or not of a neutral ground between women's and men's perspectives on sexual issues and the proper posture of the law as a result.

This volume provides an opportunity for progressed reflection upon the effect of the injection of the issue of sexual harassment into sex discrimination doctrine and equal protection theory. Whatever merit might exist in the Supreme Court's distinction between "differential treatment" and "disparate impact" as types of discrimination cases,[14] the division is inapt in instances of sexual harassment. The disparate treatment of an individual woman based upon a prohibited criterion (female sexuality as a badge or incident of gender) converges with the disparate impact of an arguably sex-neutral criterion upon one gender group (the requirement of sexual delivery sanctioned by material or other deprivations or threats, often supported by lack of an effective institutional remedy). This conceptual convergence occurs because of the social convergence of male sexual initiation toward women with the hierarchy between employers and teachers, who tend to be heterosexual men, and women workers and students, who tend to be considered desirable and available sex objects on the basis of their femaleness and position of hierarchical vulnerability.[15] Further, the distinction between treatment and impact relies upon an underlying sense that individual and group claims are somehow different. This difference can be attenuated under a legal theory of group-based injury in a legal system that requires representatively injured individual plaintiffs. Although sometimes injured one at a time, women are not discriminated against *as* individuals. Indeed, the absence of treatment based upon personal differential qualities is part of the harm of discrimination. At the same time, sexuality is no less individual to a particular woman for being an attribute of women as a gender. In short, there is no individual/group distinction here.[16]

Although sexual harassment claims are implicitly brought under a "disparate treatment" theory, in which one must prove discriminatory motivation,[17] no court has required or inferred it in order to find the behavior sex-based. This doctrinal omission is appropriate and progressive from women's standpoint, since so much sex inequality is enforced by unconscious, heedless, patronizing, well-intentioned, or profit-motivated acts—acts that are no less denigrating, damaging, or sex specific for their lack of conscious specific sex-based motivation or intent. To hold that a woman target of unwanted heterosexual advances would not be in that position if she were not a woman is both the point and very different from requiring a plaintiff to prove that she was victimized as a woman because a man made sexual advances to her meaning to discriminate against women. Hopefully, courts will learn that an intent requirement is equally inappropriate in analogous contexts, rather than reimpose it here, or confine the impact of sexual harassment doctrine on this point to their facts.

Sexual harassment cases have also avoided making the largely conclusory determination of whether sex distinctions, to be permissible, may be only "rationally related" to purposes of varying validity or whether they must sustain "strict scrutiny" or something in between the two.[18] This may be because few would argue that the practice of sexual harassment is validly related to any degree to any acceptable governmental (or, for statutory purposes, business) purpose. But such determinations often presume, or devolve back onto, the validity of the relation between the differential practice and *gender*.[19] Short of a substantive prohibition on sex subordination, any rationality test, however stringent, turns on whether a distinction is validly applied, while tending to collapse, in the process of necessarily adjudicating, the prior issue of whether the differential is validly sex-based (meaning, whether it consistently tracks the gender line). Unconfronted in any doctrinal guise is the validity of requiring that the sexes be "similarly situated" before an equality rule applies, when different situations may be the precipitate of, as well as an excuse for, social inequality. The issue is whether the analytical starting point for antidiscrimination law is gender *differences*, which may or may not validly create unequal outcomes, or gender *inequality*, which may or may not validly create sex differences.[20]

Do male and female sexuality more express sex differences or sex inequality? If coercive sexual advances are seen as expressions of male love, attraction, or sex drive—differences—the fact they are unwanted or intolerable becomes their recipient's problem. They are not arbitrarily sex-based and would not constitute harassment if the woman did not resist or resent them. Sexual harassment law, while altering the iconography of doctrine significantly, has been inexplicit on this underlying tension between the equality principle as law and the unequal social reality to which it refers: When the two conflict, should law rationally reflect society or change it? From whose point of view? Sexual harassment law has avoided the doctrinal morass that failure to resolve this issue has produced. It may at the same time have avoided establishing clear policy connecting sexuality with gender that will survive continued attack and affect equally crucial areas for women, such as rape, abortion, gay and lesbian rights,[21] and, potentially, pornography.

Equally significant issues include political concerns of trial strategy, racist abuse of the cause of action, and organizing in connection with legal initiatives. Should plaintiffs be presented to fact finders as exceptionally and uniquely abused by a deviant male, or as examples of abuses common to women, the more outrageous for being pervasive, with which a properly selected jury is encouraged to identify? This is a question both of a plaintiff's facts and preferences and of political principle. The history of the racist use against Black men of vague sexual misdeeds, particularly with white women, raises problems of similar magnitude. This heritage haunts *any* attempt to use this state to support women's control over access to our sexuality. Even when white women are believed, should antiracist feminists support them? Is the question, Did he do it? decisive, irrelevant, or somewhere in between? What if Black women are sexually harassed by the same man but refuse to come forward—perhaps because of well-grounded apprehension of being disbelieved or insensitivity by institutions with a reputation for racism, or to protest the selective pursuit of a Black man for actions that white men get away with regularly? Institutions have been known to take the opportunity of a white woman's accusation against a Black man suddenly to support women's rights, however tepidly. What is it to win under such conditions—a victory against sexism or a victory for racism? Or, what is worse, both?

The question whether this state can make change in women's interest arises in some form for all feminist goals. The law against sexual harassment often seems to turn women's demand to control our own sexuality into a request for paternal protection, leaving the impression that it is more traditional morality and less women's power that is vindicated.[22] Can organizing prevent what has happened with rape, in which legal proof requirements reflect a vision of the injury that is far from the actuality of rape, yet women tend to feel they have not been raped if they could not prove it to the law's satisfaction? The law against sexual harassment has helped many women name their oppression and has reduced the stigma of victimization. Restrictions on the cause of action and losses at trial could take back this sense of legitimate outrage.

Creating and pursuing a legal cause of action for the injury of sexual harassment has revealed that different social circumstances, of which gender is one, tend to produce different stakes, interests, perceptions, and cultural definitions of rationality itself. This awareness neither reduces legal rules to pure relative subjectivity nor principle to whose ox is gored.[23] It does challenge the conception that neutrality,[24] including sex neutrality, with its correlate, objectivity, is adequate to the nonneutral, sexually objectified, social reality women experience. It urges the priority of defining women's injuries as women perceive them. Andrea Dworkin has written: "One can be excited *about* ideas without changing at all. One can think *about* ideas, talk about ideas, without changing at all, people are willing to think about many things. What people refuse to do, or are not permitted to do, or resist doing, is to change the way they think."[25] Whether traditional legal approaches to discrimination are a way of thinking or something thought about, the law may need to confront not only what, but also the way, it thinks about women to achieve its commitment to sex equality.

12

Reflections on Sex Equality Under Law

I

There is a wrong way of thinking that one has rights, and a wrong way of thinking that one has not any.

—Simone Weil, 1 *The Notebooks Of Simone Weil* 152 (Arthur Wills trans. 1956)

No woman had a voice in the design of the legal institutions that rule the social order under which women, as well as men, live.[1] Nor was the condition of women taken into account or the interest of women as a sex represented. To Abigail Adams's plea to John Adams to "remember the ladies" in founding the United States, he replied, "We know better than to repeal our Masculine systems."[2] Mostly, one senses, women as such were beneath notice at the time.[3] The political theory that formed the principled backdrop for the new American republic certainly did not encourage their visibility. Hobbes grounded natural equality in the ability to kill.[4] Locke argued that whoever did not leave a regime consented to it.[5] Rousseau once posited the primitive passions as "food, a female, and sleep."[6] It seems unlikely that the female role then, any more than now, socially empowered women to defend themselves effectively, far less to aggress, or that they had any place to go to escape male supremacy, even if they had the means of exit. And whatever need they conceived for "a female" probably went largely unfulfilled. Yet the applicability of these reigning conceptions of equality, consent, and human need to at least half the population went unquestioned as women—including those owned neither in marriage nor in slavery—were deemed in theory to be participants in the social compact, while most women in life were not allowed to sign a contract.[7]

Equality was not mentioned in the Constitution or the Bill of Rights. The constitutive mind felt no need to guarantee it explicitly. It was ap-

First published, 100 *Yale Law Journal* 1281 (1991).

parently neither structurally essential to government nor in danger of loss to the federal power being created. Women who were not slaves were counted as persons, without being mentioned, for purposes of apportionment; slaves of both sexes were explicitly counted as three-fifths of a person.[8] The only purpose of counting either of them was to divide power among white men, who kept the vote, that primitive exercise of citizenship, to themselves. The exclusion of all women as such from the polity was so far a given that the absence of half the population from the founding process was not seen as compromising its legitimacy—a legitimacy claimed on behalf of "we, the people"[9] no less.

One hundred years and a war among men over equality among men later,[10] the Fourteenth Amendment guaranteed "equal protection of the laws." Racial inequality was its crucible, its paradigm, its target, and its subtext. Sex-based denials of equal rights were not covered.[11] It is thus a misnomer to say that the Reconstruction Amendments gave Black people even formal constitutional equality. To the extent gender inequality limited it—no woman could vote—that ostensible equality was reserved for Black men.[12] One hundred years later, women in the meantime having extracted the franchise,[13] sex discrimination in private employment was forbidden under federal law as a result of a last-minute "us boys" amendment proposed by a senator hostile to Title VII's prohibition on racial discrimination.[14] Maybe the commitment to ending racial inequality was strong enough to survive the insult of adulteration; maybe the fear of what Black men would do if the law did not pass was stronger than the fear of what women would do if it did; maybe Congress was equally against both bases for discrimination on principle or in recognition of reality; maybe some members glimpsed that race and sex inequality were inextricably interconnected, fundamentally and in the lives of many people; maybe some members even found women's humanity not laughable.[15] Maybe a bit of each. There is evidence that protecting white women from discrimination based on sex appealed to some, if Black women were to be protected from discrimination based on race.[16] There is also evidence that some members who did not favor the prohibition on race felt that, if it were to pass, they preferred it with a prohibition on sex discrimination as well. All this missed that sex discrimination affected Black as well as white women and that white women were already largely protected from racial discrimination by being white.

Whatever Congress saw in 1964, it was not until 1971 that the United States Supreme Court deigned to conclude that unequal treatment of women on the face of the law could violate the constitutional guarantee of equal protection of the laws.[17] With the subsequent failure of ratification of the proposed federal Equal Rights Amendment, which would have prohibited states or the federal government from denying or abridging equality of rights "on account of sex,"[18] this recognition has remained a matter of interpretation rather than a mandate of express constitutional dimension. Thus has the legal entitlement to sex equality, tenuous and limited when there at all, ranged from anathema to afterthought.

An account of sex inequality under law in the United States must begin with what white men have done and not done, because they have created the problem and benefited from it, controlled access to addressing it, and stacked the deck against its solution.[19] Women, for their part, have registered dissent to second-class citizenship to a surprising degree, given that they have been precluded from most means of effective resistance and excluded from many of its arenas.[20] Women have often refused to accept the premises, limits, and rules of the law written by male dominance while having little choice but to live under it. Given that the majority of women were and are poor and working-class and many were slaves and are members of racially subordinated groups, this is even more impressive.

That women have voluntarily engaged law at all is a triumph of determination over experience. It has not been an act of faith. Determined to leave a trace, to make sex equality ordinary, to live under social conditions that reflect and reinforce their aspirations rather than suppress or extinguish them, to live in respect and safety rather than indignity and terror, to redefine social standards in the image of their values, to participate fully in their own times, to save their own lives and those of generations to come, women have long demanded legal change as one vehicle for social change.[21] Treacherous and uncertain and alien and slow, law has not been women's instrument of choice. Their view seems to be that law should not be let off the hook, is too powerful to be ignored, and is better than violence—if not by much.

In recent years, the contemporary movement among women for civil equality has created a new political practice and form of theory with major implications for law.[22] The distinctive theory forged by this collective movement is a form of action carried out through words. It is deeply of the world: raw with women's blood, ragged with women's pain, shrill with women's screams. It does not elaborate yet more arcane abstractions of ideas building on ideas. It participates in reality: the reality of a fist in the face, not the concept of a fist in the face. It does not exist to mediate women's reality for male consumption. It exists to bear witness, to create consciousness, to make change. It is not, in a word, academic.[23]

Legal practice and legal scholarship have not, on the whole, led this movement but have attempted to respond to it. The initial transmutation of the feminist impulse into law lost a lot in translation, creating an approach that has not changed much to the present. Remaining largely within traditional legalism, early practice and scholarship tended to accept reigning legal assumptions and method: laws developed when women were not allowed to learn to read and write, far less vote, enunciated by a state built on the silence of women, predicated on a society in which women were chattel, literally or virtually. In these early legal forays, existing doctrine was largely accepted as given—with the not minor exception that it be applied to women. Creativity meant shoehorning reality into doctrine.

The first step in these legal attempts to advance women was to demand women's inclusion on the same terms as men. Laws that had provided "special protections" for women were to be avoided.[24] The point was to apply existing law to women as if women were citizens—as if the doctrine was not gendered to women's disadvantage, as if the legal system had no sex, as if women were gender-neutral persons mistakenly trapped in bodies that happened to be female. The women's movement claimed women's control over their procreative lives from intercourse to child care. In legal translation, this became state nonintervention in reproductive decisions under the law of privacy. The women's movement demanded an end to the sexual plunder that is rape, meaning to include an end to sex acts forced by conditions of unequal power on the basis of sex. In legal translation, this became the argument that rape had nothing to do with sexuality or with women and must be considered a gender-neutral crime of violence like any other.[25] The women's movement exposed and documented the exploitation and subordination of women by men economically, socially, culturally, sexually, and spiritually. Legal initiatives in the name of this movement called for an end to legal classifications on the basis of sex.[26]

Equality, as translated here, merely had to be applied to women to be attained. Inequality consisted in not applying it. In legal settings, *the content of the concept of equality itself was never questioned.* As if there could be no other way of thinking about it, the courts adopted that content from Aristotle's axiom that equality meant treating likes alike and unlikes unalike,[27] an approach embodied in the Constitution's "similarly situated" requirement,[28] which under Title VII became the more tacit requirement of comparability.[29] Inequality is treating someone differently if one is the same, the same if one is different. Unquestioned is how difference is socially created or defined, who sets the point of reference for sameness, or the comparative empirical approach itself. Why should anyone have to be like white men to get what they have, given that white men do not have to be like anyone except each other to have it? Since men have defined women as different to the extent they are female, can women be entitled to equal treatment only to the extent they are not women? Why is equality as consistent with systematic advantage as with systematic disadvantage, so long as both correlate with differences? Wouldn't this reasoning support Hitler's Nuremberg laws?[30] Why doesn't it matter if the differences are created by social inequality? Never mind that Aristotle defended slavery and lived in a society in which prostitution—the buying and selling of women for sex—thrived, and in which no women were citizens.[31]

Rather than designing a solution indigenous to the problem of sex inequality, the early feminist legal view was, implicitly, that if equality meant being the same as men—and being different from men meant either no rights at all or sex-based deprivation circumscribed and rigidified by inadequate and patronizing compensation—women would be the same as men. Embarrassments to this analysis such as pregnancy, insurance, women's schools,[32] and women-only prisons were minimized as unimportant or lone exceptions or problems to be treated under some other rubric. Sexual assault and reproductive control were not considered legal issues of sex inequality at all, not in the doctrinal sense.[33]

The essentially assimilationist approach fundamental to this legal equality doctrine—be like us and we will treat you the same as we treat each other—was adopted wholesale into sex cases from the cases on racial discrimination. The judicial interpretation of sex equality, like its predicates the Fourteenth Amendment and Title VII, has been built on the racial analogy. So not only must women be like men, but sexism must be like racism, or nothing can be done.[34] Where the analogy seems to work, that is, where the sexes are reasonably fungible and the inequalities can be seen to function similarly—as in some elite employment situations, for example—this equality law can work for sex. Where the sexes are different and sexism does not readily appear to work like racism—as with sexual abuse and reproductive control, for example—discrimination as a legal theory does not even come up. Along with these issues, the reality of inequality for those women for whom racism and sexism are too inseparable to be subject to a relation of analogy—those who are apparently too both to be regarded as fully either—has also been obscured.

The African American struggle for social equality has been the crucible for equality law in America. "That race and that emergency"[35] has provided the deep structure, social resonance, and primary referent for legal equality, however abstractly phrased. Although racial equality has not been achieved, to say the least, law has periodically been induced to recognize some of the realities of white supremacy and has, at times, sustained these recognitions with results.[36] The political analysis developed by the civil rights movement was substantive not abstract, self-respecting not comparative, and opposed hierarchical disadvantage rather than differentiation as such, yet in racial equality cases courts have largely confined themselves to the Aristotelian framework: qualification for admission into liberal humanity implicitly meant being like the white man. In *Plessy v. Ferguson*, for example, where segregation with equal facilities was held to be equality, the reason given was that Blacks were different from whites, so could be treated differently.[37] When *Brown v. Board of Education* repudiated *Plessy* and held that educational segregation with equal facilities was inherently unequal,[38] what changed was that *Brown* implicitly considered Blacks to be the same as whites. At least, Black schoolchildren were viewed as potentially so. This was a substantive shift in the political and ideological ground beneath the case law, not a pure doctrinal development. What was different was now the same. Difference could still justify differentiation, presumably including exclusion and subordination as well as segregation (maybe even affirmative action). Being the same as the dominant group remained the equality test.

The insult to Black culture inherent in the assumption, being made that to be different is to be inferior, meaning properly outside the reach of guarantees of equal treatment, lies coiled like a snake in *Brown*'s ringing axiom that separate but equal is inherently unequal. The invidiousness of the assumption has been overlooked for the most part in the name of the practical benefits of integration, combined with the pragmatic consideration that separate Black schools were less likely to be equal to schools also attended by whites in a white supremacist society.[39] That the failure to end discrimination by whites against Blacks may signal a defect in the whole approach, rather than merely its inadequate delivery, is suggested by the Court's march to deinstitutionalize racial equality, flawlessly predicated as it is on earlier progressive precedents.[40] What did it also undoes it; differences, including products of social inequality, make unequal treatment not unequal at all.[41]

As a further illustration, legal initiatives for sovereignty by indigenous peoples presumably do not complain of inequality because no attempt is made to meet the white man's standard or to be compensated for not meeting it. Yet in seeking an end to nonrecognition as nations, indigenous peoples may be seen to claim another kind of equality: that of meeting their own standards, as other cultures recognized as nations meet theirs.

Nationhood is a concept defined, ostensively at least, by those included in it, not in any state of nature. Seeking recognition through inclusion within that concept affirms a particularity that being the same as any other nation would efface, yet also asserts a right of place within the concept that is no different from any other nation. Legal recognition as sovereign is thus based neither on correspondence nor distinction, but on an equal entitlement of self-determination. Yet such an argument is not regarded as an equality argument because it is predicated upon neither sameness nor difference.

Whatever the defects of the Aristotelian model when applied to race and nation—and they are substantial—it is stunningly inappropriate to sex. Society defines women as such according to differences from men: hence the sex difference, as gender is customarily termed. Then equality law tells women that they are entitled to equal treatment mainly to the degree they are the same as men.[42] The inadequacy of the sameness/difference model, and its consequences for equality under law, are strikingly revealed by the law's treatment of women of color. Discriminated against on the basis of race and sex, interactively and synergistically,[43] women of color should have seen their situation improved the most under laws addressing both. Instead, the law seems to have them least in mind. First the doctrine had apoplexy trying to decide if their inequality was sex or race. When it faced the fact that it is both at once, women of color were sometimes regarded as different twice over: from the male standard of race and the white standard of sex.[44] This reveals a racism in the law of sex and a sexism in the law of race. White women meet the white male standard as white, if not male, and men of color meet the white male standard as male, if not white. Although a good many women of color can meet any substantive standard around, women of color as such meet neither. This treatment of women of color serves to support the view that the implicit standard for equality is what white men value about themselves and each other—an irreducible minimum of which is often that you be one.[45]

Attempts to redress women's inequality through law have almost exclusively continued to adhere to the Aristotelian model rather than challenge it.[46] In the older cases on sex, women as a group were legally seen as different from men to the point of lacking legal personhood; thus, for example, in *Bradwell v. Illinois*, qualified women were not permitted to practice law under a rule that admitted qualified "persons" to the bar.[47] The Court in the meantime having recognized that facial sex classifications may violate the Equal Protection Clause, women were given the chance to meet the male standard in some cases. In *Reed v. Reed*,[48] for example, the

Court invalidated facial statutory preferences for men, requiring that women be equally considered to administer estates. On this level, *Reed* is to *Bradwell* as *Brown* is to *Plessy*: women went from being categorically different to being putatively the same. Such a recognition looks like progress when it enables one to enter liberal humanity. But having to be the same as men to be treated equally remains the standard.[49]

So stress on sameness has shaped litigation strategies—which not surprisingly have often found male plaintiffs their ideal vehicle[50]—and provided the dominant interpretation and political strategy of the ERA.[51] The operative view has been that if classifications that distinguish by sex were eliminated from law, sex equality would be achieved. Some progress, largely but not totally[52] limited to elites, has been made in this way. Some compensation for sex differences, often termed "special protections," have also been won, but most of them arguably have been more ideologically denigrating than materially helpful.[53] While some situations have been improved, the conditions of inequality that made compensation seem necessary have been altered virtually not at all.

The harm of sex discrimination distinctively focused by this approach—the harm of facial classifications—has been largely the harm of stereotyping: assuming all women are the same and/or like some mythic feminine standard, and inherently and irredeemably different from men. To stereotype is to impose a trait or characterization that may be true of some members of a group upon all in the group. As an account of the injury of discrimination, this notion of misrepresentation by generalization is certainly partial and limited and can be trivializing and even perverse. What if the stereotype—such as women enjoy rape—is not really true of anyone? What if, to the extent a stereotype is accurate, it is a product of abuse, like passivity, or a survival strategy, like manipulativeness? What if, to the degree it is real, it signals an imposed reality, like a woman's place is in the home? What if the stereotype is ideologically injurious but materially helpful, like maternal preference in child custody cases? What if a stereotype is injurious as a basis for policy whether or not accurate, such as the view that women are not interested in jobs with higher salaries? Further, why is it an injury to be considered a member of a group of which one is, in fact, a member? Is the injury perhaps more how that group, hence its members, is actually treated? If sex-based generalizations are the problem of sex inequality under law, what can be done by law about those problems women generally *do* share? Will a law shaped to correct illusions rather than to confront the problems women have as women be able to face realities to the extent women have women's problems? If facial classifications are eliminated in the name of their exceptions, what becomes of those women the exceptions leave behind? This analysis suggests that the law of discrimination, to the extent it centers on empirical accuracy of classification and categorization, has primarily targeted inequality's inaccuracies of perception, such that full human value and variety is not recognized, above inequality's imposition of commonalities, such that full human value cannot grow and full human variety cannot exist.

As this doctrine developed, a grassroots practice of women's resistance to male dominance developed along side it, and with it a deeper confrontation with sex inequality. In rape crisis centers, battered women's shelters, incest support groups, and organizations of former prostitutes against prostitution, for example, nobody experiences anything so taxonomic and generic and neutral and analytic and abstract and empty as sameness and difference. The experiences that brought women there are not encounters with blank "different treatment," equally dangerous whether protective or invidious. They meet few illusions except their hopes for a better life. Stereotypes that see them as victims are overtaken by the reality in which they are victimized. Women face violent husbands, abusive fathers, violated children with venereal diseases, little food and no money, no jobs, a home on a shoestring if that, rats, cold, pushers, pimps, and cops. They are battered and raped indistinguishably, prostituted by force of violence and economics inseparably, already mothers and pregnant again without once having wanted to be. They live every day with fear, boredom, humiliation, deprivation, desperation, and dependency with no one to depend upon. Whatever sameness they share with men is not working very well, nor are their differences the precious kind. Their screams of pain and terror are not generally valorized as a "different voice."[54] Their difference lies in being on the bottom. It is this hierarchy that defines whatever difference matters, not the other way around, and defeats even most dreams of common humanity. As to the dimension of femaleness along which this is lived, what happens seems less exactly "based on sex" than because they are women. Tolerance of their differences or abolishing sex as a legal category or getting law more accurately to reflect their individuality is not even a watered-down approximation of what they need. What they need is change: for men to stop hurting them and using them because they are women, and for everyone to stop letting them do it because they are men.

Grounded in this world, law for women moved from seeking access to an unchanged legal regime to developing a substantively critical grasp of its tools, toward reshaping the law so that women can use it. Through such efforts, battered women's normal survival response to years of assault has begun to be reflected in the law of self-defense, so that those situations in which women are most likely to need to kill to save themselves are beginning to shape doctrine.[55] State by state, the law of rape is being expanded to include rape in marriage, so that some of the most common rapes in life become rapes in law.[56] Some protection has been extended to women testifying as rape victims, shielding their sexual history so they do not become cast as live pornography in court.[57] Abortion has been largely, if precariously, decriminalized.[58] Statutes of limitations in cases of incestuous sexual abuse of children have begun to be extended.[59] The law of the family has been confronted by practitioners and theorists alike as an enforcement of patriarchy, in an attempt to empower women in marital dissolutions and child custody disputes.[60] Tort concepts of harm and measures of damages have been scrutinized from the standpoint of women's situation, in an attempt to encompass women's injuries.[61] The law of contract has been criticized for abstracting from gender by assuming an at arm's length one-at-a-time atomism in transactions, and for presupposing behaviors and forms of power that imagine and favor men over women.[62] In these instances, women's legal initiatives have transformed inclusion into change. They have moved from a request to be permitted to play by the rules to an understanding that having no say in the rules means not being permitted to play the game. They have moved from the use of existing doctrine to a critical practice of reconstruction. They have begun to move from advancing within the gender hierarchy to subverting it.

Remarkably, sex equality doctrine has largely escaped this kind of critical scrutiny and pressure to reconsider its fundamental precepts.[63] Some changes have been made. In some tension with the doctrinal substructure, for example, the law of sex discrimination has been interpreted to cover sexual harassment and amended to cover pregnancy.[64] But the potentially larger implications for basic sex equality law of such initiatives—one involving sexual assault, the other involving reproduction—have been underestimated. If discrimination based on pregnancy is discrimination based on sex, one can be different in a way that perfectly tracks the gender line[65] and still be entitled to equal treatment. And if female sexuality is regarded as discriminated against rather than different when women are sexually harassed, given that the line of distinction tracks both biology and sex roles, the law of equality has taken a long step beyond the "similarly situated" requirement. Although implicitly undermined in these ways,[66] neither the "similarly situated" test, nor its statutory version, the comparability requirement, has been exposed as the doctrinal guise of dominance. I do not know of a single American case that has directly challenged them.[67]

As a consequence, legal sex equality theory has not been designed to address the substance of most lived sex inequality. At work, for example, most women do jobs that mostly women do.[68] So long as the extremity of this segregation can implicitly be considered a sex difference—whether caused by God,[69] the nature of things,[70] history,[71] the market,[72] Congress,[73] or what women are "interested in"[74]—sex equality law will be stymied in ending it. The worse the inequality is, the more like a difference it looks. Yet the connection is not often made that the same notion of difference underlies protectionism, rejection of the claim of comparable worth, refusal to address pregnancy as a discrimination issue, and the difficulty of proof in garden-variety sex discrimination cases, even ones in which huge hiring and promotional disparities exist.[75] The more perfect the disparity, the more difficult the showing of discrimination, so long as the basis for disparity is not mythic but real. Until this model based on sameness and difference is rejected or cabined, sex equality law may find itself increasingly unable even to advance women into male preserves—defined as they are in terms of socially male values and biographies[76]—for the same reason it cannot get courts to value women's work in spheres to which women remain confined. Such a law can prohibit holding women to feminine standards in the workplace but not holding them to masculine ones.[77] Designed for the exceptional individual whose biography approximates the male one, this approach cannot touch the situation of most women, where the force of social inequality effectively precludes sex comparisons.

Because the "similarly situated" requirement continues to control access to equality claims, the laws of sexual assault and reproductive control—areas as crucial in the social construction of women's inferior status as they are laden with misogyny—have not been seen as amenable to constitutional sex equality attack. Comparatively few men are raped and no men are denied abortions; gender comparisons are therefore unavailable or can be strained. So sexuality and procreation become happy differences or unhappy differences but never imposed inequalities. The legal system's treatment of rape, which is putatively illegal while overwhelmingly permitted,[78] is not regarded as state action that discriminates on the basis of sex, nor is criminalizing or refusing to fund a medical procedure that only women need. First there must be similarly situated men with whom to compare. Men's comparative lack of sexual and reproductive violation is not visible as a lack because it is relatively unthinkable that men would be hurt in these ways, although some men certainly are.[79] As a result, when sex inequality is most extreme—the vast majority of victims of sexual assault with impunity and all those denied legal or funded abortions are women—

it drops off the sex inequality map. These are the social practices of dominance that become, create, the gender difference as we know it. Once the "similarly situated" assumption is revealed as the white male standard in neutral disguise, the fist of dominance in the glove of equality, the continuity with *Plessy* and *Bradwell* beneath the victories of *Brown* and *Reed*, dominance essentialized as difference becomes first on the equality agenda rather than last, or not there at all.

II

it's not so good to be born a girl/sometimes.

—Ntozake Shange, *Three Pieces* 135 (1981)

Women don't get half as much rights as they ought to; we want more, and we will have it.

—Sojourner Truth, as quoted in Elizabeth Cady Stanton, Susan B. Anthony, Matilda Gage, *History Of Woman Suffrage* 568 (1882)

The inequality of women to men deserves a theory of its own. The status of women resembles other bases for inequality, but, like every inequality, is also particular and unique. Women's situation combines unequal pay with allocation to disrespected work; sexual targeting for rape, domestic battering, sexual abuse as children, and systematic sexual harassment; depersonalization, demeaned physical characteristics, and use in denigrating entertainment; deprivation of reproductive control; and prostitution.[80] These abuses have occurred, in one form or another, for a very long time in a context characterized by disenfranchisement, preclusion from property ownership, possession and use as object, exclusion from public life, sex-based poverty, degraded sexuality, and a devaluation of women's human worth and contributions throughout society. Like other inequalities, but in its own way, the subordination of women is socially institutionalized, cumulatively and systematically shaping access to human dignity, respect, resources, physical security, credibility, membership in community, speech, and power. Composed of all its variations, the group "women" has a collective social history of disempowerment, exploitation, and subordination extending to the present.[81] To be treated like a woman is to be disadvantaged in these ways as an incident of being assigned to the female sex. To speak of social treatment "as a woman" is thus not to invoke any universal essence or homogeneous generic or ideal type, but to refer to this diverse material reality of social meanings and practices such that to be a woman "is not yet the name of a way of being human."[82]

In this context, the failure of the law of sex equality to address sexual abuse and reproductive exploitation stands out. The law typically considers these abuses, cardinal experiences of sex inequality,[83] to be crimes or privacy violations, not acts of sex discrimination. Equality doctrine does not seem to fit them. Equality law privileges recognition of facial classifications, in which the group descriptor is the legal inequality, largely because such devices have enforced much racial inequality and race is the paradigmatic inequality in U.S. law. For the most part, the laws of sexual assault and reproductive control do not mention women or men, not anymore. Yet these laws are not exactly neutral with an adverse impact either, at least not in the usual sense. They are too gendered to be neutral, and any law on rape or pregnancy will affect the sexes differentially, without necessarily being discriminatory.

Existing legal equality templates utterly fail to capture the particular way in which the legal system organizes its participation in the subordination of women.[84] Consider whether the law of sex classifications has the same relation to the realities of women's subordination that the law of racial classifications has to the realities of racial subordination. Does a law preferring men as administrators of estates[85] have the same relation to women's subjection that a law prescribing "white only" railway cars has to racial subordination? Does a law prohibiting eighteen- to twenty-year-old boys in Oklahoma from drinking 3.2 percent beer while permitting it to girls[86] have the same relation to sex inequality that a law requiring Black children in Kansas to attend racially segregated schools has to racial inequality? I mention two seminal sex discrimination cases to suggest that facial sex classifications may be relatively peripheral to women's inequality, including by law. For claims based on sex, what the constitutional inequality net is made to catch has always been relatively rare and is now virtually extinct, while sex inequality, including through law, remains predatory and flourishing.

Much sex inequality is successfully accomplished in society without express legal enforcement and legitimation. Yet the law is deeply implicated in it. Law actively engages in sex inequality by apparently prohibiting abuses it largely permits, like rape, and by hiding the deprivations it imposes beneath ostensibly gender-neutral terms, like abortion. In the areas of sexual assault and reproductive control specifically, these legal concepts have been designed and applied from the point of view of the accused rapist and the outsider/impregnator respectively, and in the absence of the point of view of the sexually assaulted or pregnant woman. Most of the sexual assaults women experience do not fit the legal model of the ideal violation. Most rapes are by familiars not strangers, by members of one's own ethnic group not others, at home not on the street.[87] The notion of consent here, the law's line between intercourse and rape, is so passive that a dead body could satisfy it.[88] The law of rape is designed so that rape is what somebody else does and what almost never happens: so that what is done all the time, presumably including by those who design and interpret and enforce the laws, can be done.[89]

Similarly, when convenient to do away with the consequences of sexual intercourse (meaning children), women get abortion rights. Women can have abortions so men can have sex.[90] When not convenient—and for those men who seek to control women through controlling their childbearing and for those women (historically, women of color and mentally disabled women) for whom more drastic means are deemed somehow permissible—women are deprived of procreative choice through sterilization abuse the law either actively promotes or fails to recognize or redress,[91] forced obstetrical interventions the law permits,[92] fetal rights the law defines against women's rights,[93] and criminalized and unfunded and bureaucratically burdened abortions the law deems adequate.[94] In this light, the theme of the laws of sexual assault and reproduction is male control of, access to, and use of women.

Women are sexually assaulted because they are women: not individually or at random, but on the basis of sex, because of their membership in a group defined by gender.[95] Forty-four percent of women in the United States have been or will be victims of rape or attempted rape at least once in their lives.[96] Women of color experience disproportionately high incidence rates.[97] In one random sample study, only 7.5 percent of American women reported encountering no sexual assault or harassment at any time in their lives.[98] Females—adults and children—are most of the victims of sexual assault. The perpetrators are, overwhelmingly, men. Men do this to women and to girls, boys, and other men, in that order. Women hardly ever do this to men.

Sexual violation symbolizes and actualizes women's subordinate social status to men. It is both an indication and a practice of inequality between the sexes, specifically of the low status of women relative to men. Availability for aggressive intimate intrusion and use at will for pleasure by another defines who one is socially taken to be and constitutes an index of social worth. To be a means to the end of the sexual pleasure of one more powerful is, empirically, a degraded status and the female position.

In social reality, rape and the fear of rape operate cross-culturally as a mechanism of terror to control women. To attempt to avoid it, women are constrained in moving about in the world and walk down the street with their eyes averted.[99] Rape is an act of dominance over women that works systematically to maintain a gender-stratified society in which women occupy a disadvantaged status as the appropriate victims and targets of sexual aggression.[100]

Sexual aggression by men against women is normalized. In traditional gender roles, male sexuality embodies the role of aggressor, female sexuality the role of victim, and some degree of force is romanticized as acceptable.[101] Sexual assaults frequently occur in the context of family life or everyday social events, often perpetrated by an assailant who is known to the victim.[102] In one study, one-third of American men in the sample say they would rape a woman if assured they would not get caught. The figure climbs following exposure to commonly available aggressive pornography.[103] Pornography, which sexualizes gender inequality, is a major institution of socialization into these roles. The evidence suggests that women are targeted for intimate assault because the degradation and violation and domination of women is eroticized, indeed defines the social meaning of female sexuality in societies of sex inequality. Sexual assault thus becomes a definitive act of sexualized power and masculinity under male supremacy.

Only a fraction of rapes is reported, the most frequently mentioned reason for nonreporting being fear of the criminal justice system. Women of color fear its racism particularly. Only a fraction of reported rapes is prosecuted. Many rapes are "unfounded," to unfound being an active verb in police lexicon for a decision not to believe that a rape happened as reported.[104] Only a fraction of prosecuted rapes results in convictions. Rape sentences are often short. Most rapists therefore continue to live in society either undetected or unpunished and unrehabilitated. In many instances, one must suppose that they remain unaware that they did anything even potentially culpable.[105] Perhaps these data are viewed with complacency on the unconscious belief that sexual assault is inevitable or a constant that cannot be taken seriously because it is so common. Perhaps sexual assault would not be so common if it were taken seriously.

Seen in this way, sexual assault in the United States today resembles lynching prior to its recognition as a civil rights violation. It is a violent humiliation ritual with sexual elements in which the victims are often murdered. It could be done to members of powerful groups but hardly ever is. When it is done, it is as if it is what the victim is for; the whole target population cringes, withdraws, at once identifies and disidentifies in terror.

The exemplary horror keeps the group smaller, quieter, more ingratiating. The legal system is dominated by members of the same group engaged in the aggression. The practice is formally illegal but seldom found to be against the law. The atrocity is de jure illegal but de facto permitted.

Unlike the law of murder, however, before the rape law is administered, it is biased on its face.[106] Rape is typically defined as intercourse with force against one's will. Apparently this is not considered redundant, implying that women consent to sex with force all the time. Given this sadomasochistic definition of sex at the line between intercourse and rape, it is no wonder that the legal concept of consent can coexist with a lot of force. Crystallizing in doctrine a norm that animates the rape law more generally, the defense of "mistaken belief in consent" defines whether a rape occurred from the perspective of the accused rapist, not from the perspective of the victim or even based on a social standard of unacceptable force or of mutuality.[107] To a degree unlike any other crime to the person, the credibility of the victim is the issue on which turns whether any harm was done. Only in sexual assault cases is it believed, against the victim's statement to the contrary, that she may have consented to forced acts against her. The view that women seek out and enjoy forced sex is pure special pleading for the accused. Yet it is a perspective the law has often taken.

A major exception in application has been accusations by white women of sexual assault by African American men—a relatively rare event.[108] Here the usual presumption that the woman consented turns to the opposite on racist grounds: because the man is Black, she could not have wanted it. The possibility exists that prosecutions under such conditions can be successful independent of whether a rape occurred or of whether the particular defendant was the perpetrator. At the same time, women of color, overwhelmingly the victims of the sexual assaults men of color do perpetrate, are often faced with the necessity of siding with men of color on grounds of community self-preservation. Statistically, such a legal posture makes it more possible to convict when a sexual assault is less likely to have occurred, and next to impossible to convict when one is more likely to have occurred. It is not in women's interest to have men convicted of rape who did not do it, any more than it is in women's interest not to have men convicted of rape who did. Lives are destroyed both by wrongful convictions and the lack of rightful ones, as the law and the credibility of women—that rare commodity—are also undermined.

Women and men are not similarly situated with regard to sexual assault in the sense that the sexes are not equally subject to or subjected to it. But this is the inequality that indicts it, not the difference that exonerates it or exempts it from equality scrutiny. The one case in which the Supreme Court adjudicates the constitutionality of a sexual-assault statute in the sex equality context misses this point entirely. *Michael M.*[109] challenges the California statutory rape law as sex-discriminatory because it makes only males criminals for having sex with underage girls. The plurality upheld the statute on grounds that underage females could validly be protected from sex because they were likely to become pregnant. The dissent would have invalidated the statute, among other reasons, because it did not equally criminalize the two participants in the crime and because it embodied the invidious stereotype that men usually aggress in sex. The plurality opinion grasped the sex-differential reality at the cost of attributing it to biology. The dissent understood the reality of sexual assault of girls to be socially created rather than biological, at the cost of failing to understand it as nonetheless gender-based. The plurality saw a hierarchy but thought it was biologically fixed. The dissent saw the possibilities for change, but missed the hierarchy. The plurality allowed a sex difference—potential pregnancy—to render girls "not similarly situated" and to support a sex-differential statute that divides women by age. Never mind that many of those protected cannot become pregnant and more of those not protected can, that young boys are sexually assaulted too (usually but not always by older males), and that girls do not lose their vulnerability to sexual coercion upon turning eighteen. The dissent revealed more concern with avoiding the stereotyping attendant to the ideological message the law communicated than with changing the facts that make the stereotype largely true. In the interest of opposing facial distinctions and debunking the supposed myth of male sexual aggression, the fact that it is overwhelmingly girls who are sexually victimized by older males for reasons wholly unrelated to their capacity to become pregnant was completely obscured. The facts of social inequality, of sex aggravated by age, that could have supported particular legislative attention to the sexual assault of girls were not even considered. Underage girls form a credible disadvantaged group for equal protection purposes when the social facts of sexual assault are faced, facts that prominently feature one-sided sexual aggression by older males.[110] It seems that in order to imagine equality, one must first be blind to inequality, and to see inequality blinds one to seeing that equality is possible.

Perhaps this case reveals the reason that the law of sexual assault has never been held to sex equality standards, at the same time providing clues to the reason equality is defined in terms of sameness and difference in the first place. Sexuality, hence sexual assault, is believed by many to be biological, a natural part of the so-called sex difference. We are dealing here with the assumption that rape is inevitable in gendered biology. If explicitly embodied in law, such an assumption ought to violate equal protection of the laws. In fact, in *Dothard v. Rawlinson*, it has been found to be a nondiscriminatory reason for excluding women from some employment, equating capacity to be raped with membership in the female gender.[111] What it comes down to is that the most extreme instances of sex inequality in society are considered sex differences, hence reasons equality law does not apply, as in *Michael M.*, or reasons discrimination can be openly justified, as in *Dothard*. Men can be raped, and sometimes are. That alone should suggest that the overwhelming numbers of women in the rape-victim population expresses inequality, not biology. Will rape have to be comparably common in and definitive of men's status before women can be found deprived of equal protection of the laws when they are raped with legal impunity? How much legal impunity will it take before the law of sexual assault—its terms, enforcement, nonenforcement, and interpretation—is recognized as sex discrimination?

Sexual assault, in this argument, has a special place in women's social status, and the law of sexual assault has a distinctive place in the history of women's oppression by government. There is no lack of atrocities disclosing judicial bias by courts in sexual-assault adjudications.[112] Condescending, demeaning, hostile, humiliating, and indifferent judicial treatment of female victims of sexual assault is not uncommon.[113] Government commits this inequality and should rectify it. Law has a choice. It can inscribe this misogyny on society yet more authoritatively, promoting sex inequality, or it can move against it by promoting sex equality. Sexual assault cannot be treated as gender-neutral because sexual assault is not gender-neutral. The law of sexual assault cannot be treated as private action because it is government action.[114] Women are not receiving equal protection of the laws. The Equal Protection Clause is inconsistent with state law that promotes sex inequality. The law of sexual assault commands Fourteenth Amendment scrutiny.[115]

Sexual assault is already seen as gendered in the Supreme Court's treatment of the statute in *Michael M.* as facial sex discrimination against men, apparently as a result of its use of the term "sexual intercourse."[116] Sexual assault is squarely understood as a form of sex discrimination in the recognition that sexual harassment, which can include sexual assault, is actionable sex-based discrimination.[117] Just as women are sexually harassed based on their sex, women are subjected to sexual aggression in other ways based on their sex. Both forms of treatment (which overlap) are categorical and group-based. Men, usually heterosexual, harass and rape women.[118] Any woman within the ambit of such a man is his potential victim and, when she is harassed, is disadvantaged because of her sex. But for her sex, she would not be so treated.[119] Similar to the way Title VII governs the workplace, the criminal law of sexual assault, if governed by the Fourteenth Amendment, would set sex equality standards for state law, hence for society at large.

Deprivation of equal access to justice because one is a woman is deprivation of equal protection of the laws on the basis of sex. This analysis offers a constitutional basis for defending sexual-history exclusions from fair-trial attacks[120] and for upholding publication bans on names and identifying information of sexual-assault victims against First Amendment challenges.[121] It supports a constitutional appeal whenever a court engages in judicial sexism in a sexual-assault trial, a basis for massive civil litigation under federal civil rights statutes for nonenforcement and misenforcement of sexual-assault laws on the basis of sex, and a foundation for challenging the facial unconstitutionality of biased state criminal laws that adopt a male perpetrator's point of view to the systematic disadvantage of female victims. It squarely supports legislation making sexual assault actionable as a form of sex discrimination.[122]

Usually, sex precedes reproduction. In part through its connections with forced sex, procreation has also provided a crucial occasion, pretext, and focus for the subordination of women to men in society. Many of the social disadvantages to which women have been subjected have been predicated upon their capacity for and role in childbearing. Although reproduction has a major impact on both sexes, men are not generally fired from their jobs, excluded from public life, beaten, patronized, confined, or made into pornography for making babies. This point is not the biological one that only women experience pregnancy and childbirth in their bodies, but the social one: women, because of their sex, are subjected to social inequality at each step in the process of procreation. Encompassed are women's experiences of "fertility and infertility, conception and contraception, pregnancy and the end of pregnancy, whether through miscarriage, abortion, or birth and child-rearing."[123] As with most sex inequality, it is unclear whether an attribute distinctive to women is targeted for abuse and hatred because it is women's, or women are targeted for abuse and hatred because of a distinctive attribute. I suspect the former is closer to the truth. Either way, under male dominance, pregnancy—analyzed by Andrea Dworkin as "the primary physical emblem of female negativity"[124]—and the potential to become pregnant are socially fundamental in women's inequality to men.

Grounding a sex equality approach to reproductive control requires situating pregnancy in the legal and social context of sex inequality and capturing the unique relationship between the pregnant woman and her fetus. The legal system has not adequately conceptualized pregnancy, hence it has not adequately conceptualized the relationship between the fetus and the pregnant woman. This may be because the interests, perceptions, and experiences that have shaped the law have mainly not included those of women. The social conception of pregnancy that has formed the basis for its legal treatment has not been from the point of view of the pregnant woman, but rather from the point of view of the observing outsider, gendered male. Traditionally, fetuses have not fared much better under this vantage point than have women.[125] This may be changing at women's expense as increasingly, despite the explicit Supreme Court ruling to the contrary,[126] the fetus becomes endowed with attributes of personhood.[127] Men may identify more readily with the fetus than with the pregnant woman if only because all have been fetuses and none will ever be a pregnant woman.[128]

Accordingly, the law of reproductive issues has implicitly centered on observing and controlling the pregnant woman and the fetus using evidence that is available from the outside. The point of these interventions is to control the woman through controlling the fetus.[129] Technology, also largely controlled by men, has made it possible to view the fetus through ultrasound, fueling much of the present crisis in the legal status of the fetus by framing it as a free-floating independent entity rather than as connected with the pregnant woman.[130] Much of the authority and persuasiveness of the ultrasound image derives from its presentation of the fetus from the standpoint of the outside observer, the so-called objective standpoint,[131] so that it becomes socially experienced in these terms rather than in terms of its direct connection to the woman.[132] Presenting the fetus from this point of view, rather than from that which is uniquely accessible to the pregnant woman, stigmatizes her viewpoint as subjective and internal. This has the epistemic effect of making the fetus more real than the woman, who becomes reduced to the "grainy blur" at the edge of the image.[133]

The law of reproductive control has developed largely as a branch of the law of privacy, the law that keeps out observing outsiders. Sometimes it does.[134] The problem is that while the private has been a refuge for some, it has been a hellhole for others, often at the same time. In gendered light, the law's privacy is a sphere of sanctified isolation, impunity, and unaccountability. It surrounds the individual in his habitat. It belongs to the individual with power. Women have been accorded neither individuality nor power (nor a habitat truly their own). Privacy follows those with power wherever they go, just as consent follows women. When the person with privacy is having his privacy, the person without power is tacitly imagined to be consenting. At whatever time and place man has privacy, woman wants to have happen, or lets happen, whatever he does to her. Everyone is implicitly equal in there. If the woman needs something—say, equality—to make these assumptions real, privacy law does nothing for her, and even ideologically undermines the state intervention that might provide the preconditions for its meaningful exercise.[135] The private is a distinctive sphere of women's inequality to men. Because this has not been recognized, the doctrine of privacy has become the triumph of the state's abdication of women in the name of freedom and self-determination.[136]

Theorized instead as a problem of sex inequality, the law of reproductive control would begin with the place of reproduction in the status of the sexes. A narrow view of women's "biological destiny" has confined many women to childbearing and childrearing and defined all women in terms of it, limiting their participation in other pursuits, especially remunerative positions with social stature. Women who bear children are constrained by a society that does not allocate resources to assist combining family needs with work outside the home. In the case of men, the two are traditionally tailored to a complementary fit, provided that a woman is available to perform the traditional role that makes that fit possible. Law has permitted women to be punished at work for their reproductive role. The option of pregnancy leave mandated by law was not even regarded as legal until recently;[137] in the United States, it still is not legally required in most places. When women begin to "show," they are often treated as walking obscenities unfit for public presentation. Inside the home, battering of women may increase during pregnancy.[138] Pornography of pregnancy sexualizes it as a fetish, conditioning male sexual arousal to it.[139] Whether or not women have children, they are disadvantaged by social norms that limit their options because of women's enforced role in childbearing and childrearing. For a woman who does become pregnant, these consequences occur even when a pregnancy is wanted.

Women often do not control the sexual conditions under which they become pregnant, hence are deprived of meaningful control over the reproductive capacities of their bodies. Women are socially disadvantaged in controlling sexual access to their bodies through socialization to customs that define a woman's body as for sexual use by men. Sexual access is regularly forced or pressured or routinized beyond denial. Laws against sexual assault provide little to no real protection. Contraception is inadequate or unsafe or inaccessible or sadistic or stigmatized. Sex education is often misleading or unavailable or pushes heterosexual motherhood as an exclusive life possibility and as the point of sex. Poverty and enforced economic dependence undermine women's physical integrity and sexual self-determination. Social supports or blandishments for women's self-respect are simply not enough to withstand all of this.

After childbirth, women tend to be the ones who are primarily responsible for the intimate care of offspring—their own and those of others. Social custom, pressure, exclusion from well-paying jobs, the structure of the marketplace, and lack of adequate daycare have exploited women's commitment to and caring for children and relegated women to this pursuit, which is not even considered an occupation but an expression of the X chromosome. Women do not control the circumstances under which they rear children, hence the impact of those conditions on their own life chances.[140] Men, as a group, are not comparably disempowered by their reproductive capacities. Nobody forces them to impregnate women. They are not generally required by society to spend their lives caring for children to the comparative preclusion of other life pursuits.

It is women who are caught, to varying degrees, between the reproductive consequences of sexual use and aggression on the one side and the economic and other consequences of the sex role allocations of labor in the market and family on the other. As a result of these conditions, women are prevented from having children they do want and forced to have children they do not want and cannot want because they are not in a position responsibly to care for them because they are women. This is what a social inequality looks like.

Reproduction is socially gendered. Women are raped and coerced into sex. When conception results from rape or incest, it is a girl or a woman who was violated, shamed, and defiled in a way distinctively regarded as female. When a teenager gets pregnant because of ignorance or the negative social connotations of contraception, it is a young woman whose life is on the line. When miscarriage results from physical assault, it is a woman who was beaten. When there is not enough money for another child or for an abortion, it is a woman who is forced to have a child she cannot responsibly care for. When a single parent is impoverished as a result of childbearing, usually that parent is female.[141] When someone must care for the children, it is almost always a woman who does it, without her work being valued in terms of money or social status. Men, regardless of race, have not generally been sterilized without their knowledge and against their will, as have women of color. It has been held illegal to sterilize a male prisoner but legal to sterilize a mentally disabled woman.[142] Those who have been defined and valued and devalued as breeders and body servants of the next generation are not usually men, except under circumstances recognized as slavery. The essential social function of nurturing new life has been degraded by being filled by women, as the women who fill it have been degraded by filling it. And it is women who, for reasons not always purely biological, may pay for giving birth with their lives.

In this context, the relationship between the woman, gendered female, and her fetus needs to be reconsidered. Although it hardly presents new facts, this relation has never been accorded a legal concept of its own. Because legal method traditionally proceeds by analogy and distinction, attempts at analogy between the relationship between the fetus and the pregnant woman and relations already mapped by law are ubiquitous. Had women participated equally in designing laws, we might now be trying to compare other relationships—employer and employee, partners in a business, oil in the ground, termites in a building, tumors in a body, ailing famous violinists and abducted hostages forced to sustain them—to the maternal/fetal relationship rather than the reverse. The fetus has no concept of its own, but must be like something men have or are: a body part to the left, a person to the right. Nowhere in law is the fetus a fetus. Sometimes there are no adequate analogies.

Considering the fetus a body part has been the closest the law has come to recognizing fetal reality and protecting women at the same time. Since men have body parts over which they have sovereignty, deeming the fetus to be "like that" has seemed the way to give women sovereignty over what is done to their bodies, in which the fetus inevitably resides. Because persons are sovereign, deeming the fetus to be a person, "like me," has seemed the way to take away women's control over it, hence over themselves. The body-part analogy derives its credibility from the intricate and intimate connection between the woman and the fetus, which derives nourishment from her and is accessible only through her. From before viability until fully completed live birth, the fetus is within the person of the woman and at one with her bodily systems. What happens to it happens to her and what happens to her happens to it—if not always in the same way. By telescoping the fetus into the woman, the body-part analogy at once recognizes the unity of interest between fetus and pregnant woman that the personhood model is predicated on severing, and consolidates the woman as the decision-maker for the unit.

Yet the fetus is not a body part. The fetus is ordinarily created through intercourse, a social relation through which impregnation occurs. Although some body parts are donated (as are some fertilized ova), no body part is created from a social relation—one between the sexes at that. Physically, no body part takes as much and contributes as little. The fetus does not exist to serve the woman as her body parts do. The relation is more the other way around; on the biological level, the fetus is more like a parasite than a part. The woman's physical relation to her fetus is expected to end and does; when it does, her body still has all of its parts. She is whole with it or without it; a miscarriage leaves her body as such intact, although the loss may diminish her. On the level of feeling, she has lost a part of her, but this is also (sometimes even more) true of loss of children who are fully born alive. Fetal dependence upon the pregnant woman does not make the fetus a part of her any more than dependent adults are parts of those on whom they depend. The fetus is a unique kind of whole that, after a certain point, can live or die without the mother. Whatever credibility the body-part analogy has evaporates at the moment of viability, placing tremendous pressure on the viability line and its determination as a consequence.[143] No other body part gets up and walks away on its own eventually.

The fetus is not even like gendered body parts. Its cultural meaning, lived through by the pregnant woman through her pregnancy, is distinct. Pregnancy can be an emblem of female inferiority or adulation, of denigration or elevation; it can bring closeness or estrangement, can give hope and meaning to life and community, and depth or desperation to family. It attracts violence against women, sentimentality, attempts at control, gives rise to financial costs, and the need for difficult decisions.[144] Women have lost jobs and been stigmatized and excluded from public life because they are pregnant—jobs and access they had in spite of having breasts and uteruses. It seems that it is one thing to have them, another to use them.[145] No body part, including a uterus, has the specific consequences that pregnancy—as a rule a sign that a woman has had sex with a man—has on women's social destiny.

Now place the legal status of the fetus against the backdrop of women's tenuous to nonexistent equality. Women have not been considered "persons" by law very long; the law of personhood arguably falls short of recognizing the requisites of female personhood so far. Separate fetal status in a male-dominated legal system in which women have been controlled (inter alia) through the control of their procreative capacity, risks further entrenchment of women's inequality. If the fetus were deemed a person, it may well have more rights than women do, especially since fetal rights would be asserted most often by men—progenitors, husbands, doctors, legislators, judges—in traditionally male institutions of authority, prominently legislatures, hospitals, agencies, and courts. Fetal rights as such are thus in direct tension with women's sex equality rights.

Indeed, the only point of recognizing fetal personhood, or a separate fetal entity, is to assert the interests of the fetus *against* the pregnant woman.[146] There would be two persons in one skin—hers—the rationale being that its life depends upon her, but the reverse is not usually true. The fetus could be given the right to the use of the pregnant woman's body from conception to birth.[147] In arguments for fetal personhood, the fetus is "born in the imagination."[148] But it is not born in the world. Gestation and birth involve the mother and often entail considerable medical uncertainty.[149] Even well toward the end of pregnancy, the view that the fetus is a person vaults over this process in a way that is unrealistic and dangerous for the birthing woman, who can be made invisible and chattel in a situation in which she is deeply implicated.

Personhood is a legal and social status, not a biological fact. As gestation progresses, the fetus grows from something that is more like a lump of cells to something that is more like a baby. As the body-part analogy draws on the earlier reality to define the later one, the personhood analogy draws on the later reality to define the earlier one. In my opinion and in the experience of many pregnant women, the fetus is a human form of life. It is alive. But the existence of sex inequality in society requires that completed live birth mark the personhood line. If sex equality existed socially—if women were recognized as persons, sexual aggression were truly deviant, and childrearing were shared and consistent with a full life rather than at odds with it—the fetus still might not be considered a person but the question of its political status would be a very different one.[150]

So long as it gestates in utero, the fetus is defined by its relation to the pregnant woman. More than a body part but less than a person, where it is, is largely what it is. From the standpoint of the pregnant woman, it is both me and not me.[151] It "is" the pregnant woman in the sense that it is in her and of her and is hers more than anyone's. It "is not" her in the sense that she is not all that is there. In a legal system that views the individual as a unitary self, and that self as a bundle of rights, it is no wonder that the pregnant woman has eluded legal grasp, and her fetus with her.

The legal status of the fetus cannot be considered separately from the legal and social status of the woman in whose body it is. The pregnant woman is more than a location for gestation. She is a woman, in the socially gendered and unequal sense of the word. In an analysis of women's status as socially disadvantaged, the woman is not a mere vehicle for an event that happens to occur within her physical boundaries for biological reasons.[152] Women's relation to the fetus is not that of a powerful, fully capacitated being in relation to a powerless, incapacitated, and incomplete one. Indeed, it shows how powerless women are that it takes a fetus to make a woman look powerful by comparison. The relation of the woman to the fetus must be seen in the social context of sex inequality in which women have been kept relatively powerless compared with men. The fetus may have been conceived in powerlessness and, as a child, may be reared in powerlessness—the woman's.[153] The effects of women's inequality in procreation can range from situations in which the woman is prevented from conceiving, chooses to conceive and deeply desires to deliver but the baby dies, or does not choose to conceive but is forced to deliver.

The range of procreative events along which inequality is experienced contextualizes the fact that when women are forced into maternity, they are reproductively exploited. Short of achieving sexual and social equality—short of changing the context—abortion has offered the only way out. However difficult an abortion decision may be for an individual woman, it provides a moment of power in a life otherwise led under unequal conditions that preclude choice in ways she cannot control. In this context, abortion provides a window of relief in an unequal situation from which there is no exit. Until this context changes, only the pregnant woman can choose life for the unborn.[154]

Because the discussion of the political status of the fetus has been framed by the abortion controversy, it has proceeded from the premise that there is a conflict between what is good for the woman and what is good for the fetus. Sometimes there is. Usually there is not, in large part because when there is, women tend to resolve it in favor of the fetus. Women may identify with the fetus because, like them, it is invisible, powerless, derivative, and silent.[155] Grasping this unity in oppression, it has most often been women who have put the welfare of the fetus first, before their own. While most women who abort did not choose to conceive, many women who keep their pregnancies did not choose to conceive either. The priority women make of their offspring may be more true in the abortion context than it seems. Many women have abortions as a desperate act of love for their unborn children. Many women conceive in battering relationships; subjecting a child to a violent father is more than they can bear.[156] When women in a quarter to a third of all American households face domestic violence,[157] this motivation cannot be dismissed as marginal. Some women conceive in part to cement a relationship that later dissolves or becomes violent when the man discovers the conception.[158] Even where direct abuse is not present, sex inequality is. Many abortions occur because the woman needs to try to give herself a life. But many also occur because the woman faces the fact that she cannot give this child a life. Women's impotence to make this not so may make the decision tragic, but it is nonetheless one of absolute realism and deep responsibility as a mother.

Reproduction in the lives of women is a far larger and more diverse experience than the focus on abortion has permitted. The right to reproductive control I have in mind would include the abortion right but would not center on it. Women would have more rights when they carry a fetus: sex equality rights. Women who are assaulted and miscarry, women who are forced to have abortions and women who are denied abortions, women who are sterilized, and women who are negligently attended at birth all suffer deprivation of reproductive control. Under such circumstances, existing laws that regulate these areas should be interpreted consistent with constitutional sex equality mandates. If affirmative legislative pursuit of this principle were desired, this concept of reproductive control would encourage programs to support the fetus through supporting the woman, including guaranteed prenatal care, pregnancy leaves, and nutritional, alcohol, and drug counseling. If pursued in a context in which sexual coercion was effectively addressed, such programs would promote women's equality, not constitute inducements and pressures to succumb to women's subordinate roles. In this light, purported concern for the well-being of pregnant women and subsequently born children expressed by policing women's activities during pregnancy and forcing women to carry pregnancies to term is not only vicious and counterproductive, but unconstitutional.[159]

Because the social organization of reproduction is a major institution of women's social inequality, any constitutional interpretation of a sex equality principle must prohibit laws, state policies, or official practices and acts that deprive women of reproductive control or punish women for their reproductive role or capacity. Existing examples include nonconsensual sterilization, forced obstetrical intervention, supervision of women's activities during pregnancy under the criminal law, and denials of abortion through criminalization or lack of public funding where needed. Women's right to reproductive control is a sex equality right because it is inconsistent with an equality mandate for the state, by law, to collaborate with or mandate social inequality on the basis of sex, as such legal incursions do. It is at least as sex-discriminatory to exacerbate a pre-existing sex inequality as it is to impose a sex inequality that does not already socially exist. This is to argue to extend the meaning of constitutional sex equality based on the recognition that if it does not mean this, it does not mean anything at all.

Under this sex equality analysis, criminal abortion statutes of the sort invalidated in *Roe v. Wade* violate equal protection of the laws.[160] They make women criminals for a medical procedure only women need, or make others criminals for performing a procedure on women that only women need, when much of the need for this procedure as well as barriers to access to it have been created by social conditions of sex inequality. Forced motherhood is sex inequality. Because pregnancy can be experienced only by women, and because of the unequal social predicates and consequences pregnancy has for women, any forced pregnancy will always deprive and hurt members of one sex only on the basis of gender. Just as no man will ever become pregnant,[161] no man will ever need an abortion, hence be in a position to be denied one by law. On this level, only women can be disadvantaged, for a reason specific to sex, through state-mandated restrictions on abortion. Denial of Medicaid funding for medically necessary abortions obviously violates this right.[162] The Medicaid issue connects the maternity historically forced on African American women integral to their exploitation under slavery with the motherhood effectively forced on poor women, many of whom are Black, when their medically needed abortions are not funded and everything else that is medically necessary, for both sexes, is, as happened in *Harris v. McRae* in 1980.[163] For those who missed it, the abortion right has already been lost: this was when.

Although the sex equality argument for equal funding for abortions is doctrinally simpler than that for the abortion right itself, statutes that recriminalize abortion[164] would be invalidated under this argument as well. To recast the preceding argument in a more doctrinal form, statutes that draw gender lines are unconstitutional under the Equal Protection Clause if they do not bear a valid or substantial relation to an important or legitimate and compelling state purpose.[165] Initially, a state's purposes in passing criminal abortion statutes could be challenged as invalid. If states wanted to protect the fetus, rather than discriminate against women, they would help the woman, not make her a criminal. The most effective route to protecting the fetus—perhaps the only effective route—is supporting the woman. Further, the seeming appropriateness of forcing women to bear children when no such bodily impositions are made upon men by any state law—even after fetuses that men have participated in creating become children (persons) and even when no alternatives are available—is transparently based on the view that the purpose of women is breeding. If using women as a sex as a means to an end is discriminatory, if naturalizing as destiny a role that is rooted in the history of sex inequality is discriminatory, the state purpose in restricting abortions is discriminatory and not valid.

But even assuming the state purpose were found valid—the purpose was not to harm women but to help fetuses, and this need not be pursued in the best way but only nonpretextually—the issue would remain whether a statute that recriminalizes abortion is based on sex. Criminal abortion laws hurt women through a biological correlate of femaleness and a socially defining characteristic of gender long used to disadvantage women and keep them in a subject status. For this reason, criminal abortion statutes should be treated as closer to facially discriminatory than to neutral distinctions disparate in effect. By analogy, sexual harassment is legally treated more like facial than disparate impact discrimination, even though it is not done by express law or policy. Certainly, more men are sexually harassed than are denied abortions.[166] Criminal abortion laws hurt no men the way they hurt only women. They single out women exclusively. Criminalizing providers, which does affect men, is merely a pretextually gender-neutral means of accomplishing the same goal: depriving women and only women, by law, of relief from a situation of sex inequality that begins in unequal sex and ends in unequal childrearing. If criminal abortion prohibitions are treated as facial, not neutral, it is unnecessary, as doctrinally redundant, to prove that they discriminate intentionally.

If intent had to be proven in order to invalidate criminal abortion statutes, states would doubtless argue that they aim to help fetuses, not hurt women. But intent can be inferred from impact.[167] No men are denied abortions, even if some doctors, regardless of sex, are made criminals for providing them. Such a statutory impact would be far more one-sided than, for example, the impact of veterans' preference statutes, which have been found to lack the requisite discriminatory intent because, although most of those benefited by them are men, many men—nonveterans—are also harmed.[168] No men are damaged in the way women are harmed by an abortion prohibition. Even those who can be prosecuted are harmed for a procedure only women need, with the clear aim of keeping women and only women from access to it. Male providers can avoid liability by refusing to perform the procedure and be, as men, no worse off, while pregnant women who seek to abide by the law must continue the pregnancy, damaging them in a way that only women are or could be damaged.

Remaining as a barrier to this argument is the view that pregnancy, hence abortion, is implicitly not sex-based because no men get pregnant and are treated better. That is, there are no "similarly situated" men differently treated, so depriving women in this way cannot be sex discrimination.[169] Considering reproductive control as a sex equality right directly challenges the "similarly situated" requirement. In the pregnancy area, the notion that one must first be the same as a comparator before being entitled to equal treatment has been deeply undermined, although it remains constitutional precedent. After the Supreme Court held under Title VII that discrimination based on pregnancy was not discrimination based on sex,[170] Congress reversed this result by amending Title VII, requiring that discrimination based on pregnancy be recognized as discrimination based on sex.[171] As of this amendment, a cardinal difference between the sexes became an invalid reason for disadvantaging women in employment.[172] The theoretical implications of this shift are considerable. Most disadvantages can be construed as, and therefore become, differences.[173] The question is whether social disadvantages—like jail and deprivation of government funding—will be treated under the old model for biological differences, as not subject to equality law, or whether the new model, under which not even biological differences justify unequal social outcomes, will be applied.

Moving away from its earlier formalism in the pregnancy area, the Court has begun to interpret statutory sex equality mandates in light of substantive equality goals. In an early ruling construing the pregnancy-discrimination amendment to Title VII, the Supreme Court reached out explicitly in dicta, to a degree that was legally unnecessary, to repudiate its former *constitutional* reasoning on pregnancy, seeming strongly to signal its readiness to abandon its view under the Fourteenth Amendment that pregnancy is not gendered.[174] In a further Title VII ruling on pregnancy, the Court gave sex equality reasoning a strong pro-equality spin, holding that a state-mandated pregnancy leave was not sex discriminatory because it promoted women's equal access to the workforce.[175] Here the Court chose not to enforce gender neutrality where that would have meant invalidating or extending to men (via parental leave) a sex-specific reproductive benefit for women at work, noting that the consequence was neutral in the sense that, under the statute, "women, as well as men, can have families without losing their jobs."[176] The Court has not since had occasion directly to consider the issue of whether pregnancy is gendered in the legal sense.[177] Specifically, it has not confronted this question in the constitutional context since these newer developments in statutory sex equality law came into sharp conflict with its approach on the constitutional side. Adjudication of recriminalized abortion by state law could present such an opportunity.

Doctrinally, it is possible for criminal abortion statutes to be found sex discriminatory but nonetheless justified, for example, by the goal of protecting fetal life. Putting aside the question of whether sex discrimination should ever be justified, this inquiry would be the right context in which to balance fetal death from legal abortions with maternal death from illegal ones.[178] We would learn a lot about how much a woman's life is worth, hence about the reality of equality for women, from the answer.

Because forced maternity is a sex equality deprivation, legal abortion is a sex equality right. "Women's access to legal abortion is an attempt to ensure that women and men have more equal control of their reproductive capacities, more equal opportunity to plan their lives and more equal ability to participate fully in society than if legal abortion did not exist."[179] Sex equality would be advanced if women were permitted to control sexual access to their bodies long before an unwanted pregnancy. Sex equality would be advanced if society were organized so that both sexes participated equally in daily child care. Sex equality would be advanced by economic parity between women and men. Equality for women would gain from racial equality. All these changes would overwhelmingly reduce the numbers of abortions sought. The abortion controversy would not be entirely eliminated, but its ground would shift dramatically.

Those who support the abortion right in the name of "a woman's right to control her own body" might start earlier, before women are pregnant, with the issue of sexual access. If women cannot, socially speaking, control sexual access to their bodies, they cannot control much else about them. Those who think that fetuses should not have to pay with their lives for their mothers' inequality might direct themselves to changing the conditions of sex inequality that make abortions necessary. They might find the problem largely withered away if they, too, opposed sex on demand.

III

> When a system of power is thoroughly in command, it has scarcely need to speak itself aloud; when its workings are exposed and questioned, it becomes not only subject to discussion, but even to change.
>
> —Kate Millett, *Sexual Politics* 87 (1971)

The first part of these reflections takes on the complacency of the view that women have rights when we do not; the second part stands against the luxurious cynicism that despairingly assumes women have no rights when we do, or could. Both expose some of the workings of a gendered system of power whose command is maintained in part through being unspoken. In the process of the analysis, some broader implications for change in equality law and theory are suggested.

Inequality, as analyzed here, is not a bad attitude that floats in the sky but an embodied particular that walks on the ground. It is first concrete, historical, present, and material, only derivatively generic, and never abstract. Social inequality does not first exist in the abstract, in search of a basis or polarization or natural joint to carve or asymmetry to which to attach. It exists in the social reality of its particulars, such as the social dominance of men through which women are subjected. Sex equality as a norm comes into being through the resistance of women as a people to their subjection. The equality principle, in this approach, is properly comprised of the practical necessities for ending inequality in each of its real forms.

Such an analysis does not generate abstractly fungible categories. Inequality is not conceptually reversible, only concretely changeable. To be "similarly situated," a test that relies on and produces abstract counter-hierarchical comparisons as the essence of equality reasoning, thus cannot remain the threshold for access to equality guarantees. If inequality is concrete, no man is ever in the same position a woman is, because he is not in it as a woman. That does not mean a man cannot be recognized as discriminated against on the basis of sex. It does mean that it is no measure of virtue for an equality theory to accord the same solicitude to dominant groups as to subordinate ones, all the while ignoring who is who.[180] If the point of equality law is to end group-based dominance and subordination, rather than to recognize sameness or accommodate difference, a greater priority is placed on rectifying the legal inequality of groups that are historically unequal in society, and less priority is accorded to pure legal artifacts or rare reversals of social fortune. Although such a substantive interpretation is technically possible, indeed compelled, under existing law, the passage of an Equal Rights Amendment could help provide a political and textual basis for this rectification of constitutional emphasis. Sometimes emphasis is all.

Law furthering this equality norm would develop a new relation to society. In societies governed by the rule of law, law is typically a status quo instrument; it does not usually guarantee rights that society is predicated on denying. In this context equality law is unusual: social equality does not exist, yet a legal guarantee of equality does. If law requires equality, in a society that is structurally and pervasively unequal, and the social status quo were no longer to be maintained through the abstract equality model, then equality law could not even be applied without producing social change. For example, it is generally thought that nondiscrimination and affirmative action are two different things. Under the equality approach argued here, there is no difference between them. Equality law becomes a distinct species of law, in need of its own norms for its distinct relation to an unequal society.

One part of developing the jurisprudence of such law is creating new doctrine. Here, the existing laws of sexual assault and abortion are argued variously to constitute sex discriminatory state action. While existing state action doctrine readily accommodates these obvious forms of it, and existing discrimination precedent provides a possible basis for their recognition as discriminatory, the larger implications of this exposed interface between the state and women's everyday lives suggests the need for more commodious notions of both discrimination and state action. On a continuum of examples, denial of access to abortion, the marital rape exclusion, failure to enforce laws against domestic violence, the mistaken belief in consent defense in rape, and state protection of pornography[181] are all gendered acts of government. To the extent they are not recognized as sex discrimination or state action, those concepts are gender biased.

Doctrinally, these forms of discrimination look like much of the reality of sex discrimination looks: perhaps less provably purposeful than the existing model for intentional, but far from facially neutral and massively disparate in impact, they show a supportive interaction between government permission or omission and male aggression. More explicitly invidious than the neutral, but less superficially intentional than existing requirements for motive, such discriminations have social markers of sex written all over them and would arguably happen very differently were the stance of the government different.[182] Such laws and practices are simply biased, their one-sidedness diagnosable from reinforced subordinate group disadvantage, provable from invidious social meaning and damaging material consequences. To fail to see the state's hand in these examples is to miss much of the way law insinuates itself into social life, intruding on and structuring relations between the sexes, institutionalizing male dominance.

Equality approaches are often faulted as less powerful than other possible legal approaches to the same problems because they are inherently relative, while other approaches like liberty or security or privacy are thought more powerful because they are absolute. Existing absolutes have not proven particularly reliable; one suspects they are usually defined sub rosa in relative terms anyway. While equality never entirely escapes the comparative, substantive comparisons that recognize hierarchy and history pose few of the dangers that abstract Aristotelian comparisons do. Nor must the standard for comparison be conceded. Subordinate groups may challenge the dominant standard as a form of bias in itself. Equality allows critique of the social partiality of standards as well as opportunity to live up to existing ones. The socially contextual nature of this equality concept, its groundedness, seems to me a strength: what it seeks is always real, because it is real for someone. In one's zeal to make deeper change, it should not be overlooked that actually having the best any group currently has—for example, not being about to be raped at any moment—would be a big improvement for most of us.

I am also told that sex equality is not a desirable approach to reproductive control because it has a sunset built into it. Even if we had equality, wouldn't women still need abortions? If sex equality existed, there would be no more forced sex; safe effective contraception would be available and the psychological pressures surrounding its use would be gone; whatever womanhood meant, women would need neither men nor intercourse nor babies to prove it; abortions for sex selection as now practiced would be unthinkable; the workplace would be organized with women as much in mind as men; the care of children would be a priority for adults without respect to gender; women would be able to support themselves and their families (in whatever form) in dignity through the work they do. Now imagine the woman who is pregnant without wanting to be. True contraceptive failures would probably remain, as would fetuses with life-threatening disabilities, selective abortions (where too many fetuses in one uterus threatens the existence of all, the modern lifeboat situation), good old-fashioned not paying attention (but without all its currently gendered determinants), and the like. Perhaps some people would not want another child, but not for most of today's reasons. The point is, the politics of abortion would be so dramatically reframed, and the numbers so drastically reduced, as to make the problem virtually unrecognizable. If authority were already just and body already one's own, having an abortion would lose any dimension of resistance to unjust authority or reclamation of self-possession and bodily autonomy. At the same time, under conditions of sex equality, taking the putative father's view into account in the abortion decision would make sense it does not make now.[183] The issue of the pregnant woman's nine-month bodily commitment and risks would remain, and might have to be dispositive. But the privacy approach to the abortion question might begin to make real sense.

Given the pervasiveness of social inequality, imagination is the faculty required to think in sex equality terms. What would it be like if women had power, knowing what women know? Even under present conditions for women, two women with power under existing law, Madam Justice Bertha Wilson of Canada and Justice Sandra Day O'Connor of the United States, have written highly evocative abortion opinions. They are marked, on my reading, by a distinctively nonabstract and nonappropriative empathy. Both woman and fetus are real in their minds at once. Madam Justice Wilson, joining an opinion that invalidated Canada's criminal abortion law, speaks eloquently of the woman facing the abortion decision, highlighting the need to take her point of view seriously: "It is probably impossible for a man to respond, even imaginatively, to [the woman's abortion] dilemma not just because it is outside the realm of his personal experience . . . but because he can relate to it only by objectifying it. . . ." In the history of human rights, she sees "the history of men struggling to assert their dignity and common humanity against an overbearing state apparatus." The history of women's rights, by contrast, has been "a struggle to eliminate discrimination, to achieve a place for women in a man's world, to develop a set of legislative reforms in order to place women in the same position as men . . . *not* to define the rights of women in relation to their special place in the societal structure and in relation to the biological distinction between the two sexes." Reproductive control is properly "an integral part of modern woman's struggle to assert *her* dignity and worth as a human being."[184] In other words, it is a sex equality issue. Justice Wilson's decision also retains some state interest in fetal life.

Justice O'Connor is similarly alive to the predicament of the pregnant woman who needs an abortion yet is also unwilling to disregard the fetus, especially the potentially viable one.[185] She has expressed serious doubts about *Roe*, but her vote alone has prevented its repudiation.[186] Taken together, and interpolating what is unspoken from what is spoken, the views of these Justices could be seen to request an approach to abortion that values women unequivocally but does not trivialize fetal life. Why, they seem to be asking, must this life-or-death decision be, by law, in *women's* hands? Sex inequality is the answer.

Anticipating the full reach of the difference sex equality would make is another matter. The challenge of grounded thinking and keeping faith with silenced women means facing that we cannot know what women not unequal as women would want, how sexuality would be constructed, how law would relate to society, what form the state would take, or even if there would be one.

13

Prostitution and Civil Rights

The gap between the promise of civil rights and the real lives of prostitutes is an abyss that swallows up prostituted people.[1] To speak of prostitution and civil rights in one breath moves the two into one world, at once exposing and narrowing the distance between them.

Women in prostitution are denied every imaginable civil right in every imaginable and unimaginable way,[2] such that it makes sense to understand prostitution as consisting in the denial of women's humanity, no matter how humanity is defined. It is denied both through the social definition and condition of the prostituted and through the meaning of some civil rights.

The legal right to be free from torture and cruel and inhuman or degrading treatment is recognized by most nations and is internationally guaranteed. In prostitution, women are tortured through repeated rape and in all the more conventionally recognized ways. Women are prostituted precisely in order to be degraded and subjected to cruel and brutal treatment without human limits; it is the opportunity to do this that is acquired when women are bought and sold for sex. The fact that most legal prohibitions on torture apply only to official torture, specifically torture by state actors, illustrates the degree to which the legal design of civil rights has excluded women's experience of being denied them.

Security of the person is fundamental to society. The point of prostitution is to transgress women's personal security. Every time the woman walks up to the man's car, every time the man walks into the brothel, the personhood of women—not that secure in a male-dominated society to begin with—is made more insecure. Women in prostitution attempt to set limits on what can be done to them. Nothing backs them up. Pimps supposedly do, but it shows how insecure prostitutes' lives are that pimps can look like security. Nothing realistically limits pimps, and, ultimately, anything can be done to their property for a price. As Andrea Dworkin has

Talk at Symposium, "Prostitution: From Academia to Activism," October 31, 1992, University of Michigan Law School, Ann Arbor, MI. First published, 1 *Michigan Journal of Gender and Law* 13 (1993).

said, "whatever can be stolen can be sold."[3] In rape, the security of women's person is stolen; in prostitution, it is stolen and sold.

Liberty is a primary civil right. Kathleen Barry has analyzed female sexual slavery as prostitution one cannot get out of.[4] A recent study of street prostitutes in Toronto found that about 90 percent wanted to leave but could not.[5] If they are there because they cannot leave, they are sexual slaves. Need it be said: to be a slave is to be deprived of liberty, not to exercise it. To lack the ability to set limits on one's condition or to leave it is to lack consent to it. At the same time, liberty for men is often construed in sexual terms and includes liberal access to women, including prostituted ones. So while, for men, liberty entails that women be prostituted, for women, prostitution entails loss of all that liberty means.

The right to privacy is often included among civil rights. In the United States, one meaning privacy has effectively come to have is the right to dominate free of public scrutiny. The private is then defined as a place of freedom by effectively rendering consensual what women and children are forced to do out of the public eye. Prostitution is thus often referred to as occurring in private between consenting adults, as are marriage and family.[6] The result is to extend the aura of privacy and protection from public intervention from sex to sexual abuse. In prostitution, women have no space they can call off-limits to prying eyes, prying hands, or prying other parts of the anatomy, not even inside their own skin.

Freedom from arbitrary arrest is also a civil right. Criminal prostitution laws make women into criminals for being victimized as women, so are arguably arbitrary in the first place.[7] Then these laws are often enforced for bureaucratic, turf-protective, funding, political, or advancement reasons[8]—that is, arbitrarily, against women.

Property ownership is recognized as a civil right in many countries. Women in prostitution not only begin poor; they are systematically kept poor by pimps who take the lion's share of what they earn. They are the property of the men who buy and sell and rent them—placing the civil right, once again, in the hands of their tormenters.

Particularly in the United States, the right to freedom of speech is cherished. Prostitution as an institution silences women by brutalizing and terrorizing them so horribly that no words can form, by punishing them for telling the truth about their condition, by degrading whatever they do manage to say about virtually anything because of who they are seen as being. The pornography that is made of their violation—pimps' speech—is protected expression.[9]

One civil right is so deep it is seldom mentioned: to be recognized as a person before the law. To be a prostitute is to be a legal nonperson in the ways that matter. What for Blackstone and others was the legal nonpersonhood of the wife relative to the husband[10] is extended for the prostitute to all men as a class. Anyone can do anything to her and nothing legal will be done about it. John Stoltenberg has shown how the social definition of personhood for men is importantly premised on the prostitution of women.[11] Prostitution as a social institution gives men personhood—in this case, manhood—through depriving women of theirs.

The civil right to life is basic. The Green River murders, suspected to be of prostituted women; the serial murders of women in Los Angeles; the eleven dead African American women who had been in prostitution who were recently found under piles of rags in Detroit—what killed them is "gender cleansing." Snuff films are part of it. When killing women becomes a sex act, women have no right to their lives, lives women in prostitution are most exposed to losing as sex.

Equality is also a civil right, both equal humanity in substance and formal equality before the law. In the United States, constitutional equality encompasses equal protection of the laws under the Fourteenth Amendment and freedom from slavery or involuntary servitude under the Thirteenth Amendment. Prostitution implicates both.

The Fourteenth Amendment provides for equal protection and benefit of the law without discrimination. What little equality litigation does exist in the prostitution context to date misses the point of prostituted women's unequal treatment in a number of illuminating ways. Some older prostitution statutes, challenged as sex discriminatory on their face, made prostitution illegal only when a woman engaged in it. For example, Louisiana provided that "[p]rostitution is the practice by a female of indiscriminate sexual intercourse with males for compensation."[12] Applying the sex discrimination test at the time, the court ruled that "differences between the sexes does bear a rational relationship to the prohibition of prostitution by females."[13] In other words, defining prostitution as something only women do was found to be simple realism, a reflection of social reality. Women really do this; mostly only women do this; it seems to have something to do with being a woman to do this; therefore, it is not sex discrimination to have a law that punishes only women for doing this.

Here, the fact that most prostitutes are women is not a sex inequality, nor does equating prostitution with being a woman tell us anything about what being a woman means. That most prostitutes are women is the reason that legally defining the problem of prostitution as a problem of women is *not* a sex inequality. Thus does the soft focus of gender neutrality blur sex distinctions by law and rigidly sex-divided social realities at the same time. By now, most legislatures have gender-neutralized their prostitution laws[14] even as prostitution has gone on as anything but gender-neutral.

The cases that adjudicate equal protection challenges to sex-discriminatory enforcement of prostitution laws extend this rationale. Police usually send men to impersonate tricks in order to arrest prostitutes. Not surprisingly, many more women than men are arrested in this way.[15] The cases hold that this is not intentional sex discrimination but a good faith effort by the state to get at "the sellers of sex,"[16] "the profiteer."[17] Sometimes the tricks are even described by police as the women's "victim."[18] Courts seem to think the women make the money when, in most instances, they are conduits from trick to pimp, and the money is never theirs.[19] Sometimes the male police decoys wait to arrest until the sex act is about to happen—or, prostitutes complain, until after it happens.[20]

Another all-too-common practice is arresting accused prostitutes, women, while letting arrested customers, men, go with a citation or a warning.[21] This, too, has been challenged as sex discrimination, and it sure sounds like it. Yet this, courts say, is not sex discrimination because male and female prostitutes are treated alike[22] or because customers violate a different, noncomparable, law from the one under which the women are charged.[23] There are some men in prostitution, some who are preoperative transsexuals, some who are prostituting as women, some as men for men. You can tell you have walked into the world of gender neutrality when the law treats men as badly as women when they do what mostly women do, and that makes treating women badly non-sex-based. Of course, compared with users, when they are arrested, prostitutes also more often fail to satisfy the gender-neutral conditions of release: good money, good name, good job, good family, good record, good lawyer, good three-piece suit. . . .

Some states quarantine arrested women prostitutes but not arrested male customers. This, too, is not sex discrimination, according to the courts, because the women are more likely to communicate venereal diseases than the men are.[24] Where the women got the venereal diseases is not discussed; women are seen as walking disease vectors from which men's health must be protected. This was before AIDS, but the reality remains the same: the recipient of the sperm in sex is the one more likely to become infected.[25]

These cases represent the extent to which equal protection of the laws has been litigated for prostitutes to date.[26] The disparity between the focus of this litigation and the civil rights violations inherent in prostitution is staggering. Behind the blatant sex discrimination these cases rationalize is the vision of equality they offer prostitutes: the right to be prostituted without being disproportionately punished for it. As unprincipled as the losses in these cases are, if they had been won, this is the equality they would have won.

Criminal laws against prostitution make women into criminals for being victimized as women, yet there are no cases challenging these laws as sex discrimination on this ground. Criminal prostitution laws collaborate elaborately in women's social inequality;[27] through them, the state enforces the exploitation of prostituted women directly. When legal victimization is piled on top of social victimization, women are dug deeper and deeper into civil inferiority, their subordination and isolation legally ratified and legitimated. Disparate enforcement combines with this discriminatory design to violate prostituted women's Fourteenth Amendment right to equal protection of the laws.

This is not to argue that prostitutes have a sex equality right to engage in prostitution. Rather, it is to argue that prostitution subordinates, exploits, and disadvantages women as women in social life, a social inequality that criminal prostitution laws then seal with a criminal sanction. Prostitution cannot be decriminalized wholesale on this argument, however. While laws against the prostitution of prostituted people could be invalidated on these grounds, the argument from disadvantage on the basis of sex supports upholding and strict enforcement of laws against pimps, who exploit women's inequality for gain,[28] and against tricks, who benefit from women's oppressed status and subordinate individual women skin on skin.

Beyond eliminating discriminatory criminal laws and enforcing appropriate ones, it is time the law did something *for* women in prostitution. Getting the criminal law off their backs may keep the state from reinforcing their subordinate status but it does nothing to change that status. The Thirteenth Amendment, which applies whether or not the state is involved, may help.

The Thirteenth Amendment prohibits slavery and involuntary servitude. With its implementing statutes, the Thirteenth Amendment was passed to invalidate the chattel slavery of African Americans and kindred social institutions;[29] its language that slavery "shall not exist" gives support to slavery's affirmative elimination. The Thirteenth Amendment has been applied to invalidate a range of arrangements of forced labor and exploitive servitude.[30] The slavery of African Americans is not the first or last example of enslavement, although it has rightly been among the most notorious. Applying the Thirteenth Amendment to prostitution claims enslavement as a term and reality of wider application, which historically it has had.

To apply the Thirteenth Amendment to prostitution is not to equate prostitution with the chattel slavery of African Americans but to draw on common and often overlapping features of the two institutions of forcible inequality in the context of the Thirteenth Amendment's implementation. Compared with slavery of African Americans, prostitution is older, more pervasive across cultures, usually does not include as much nonsexual exploitation, and is based on sex and sex and race combined. For Black women in the United States, the relation between prostitution and slavery is less one of analogy than of continuity with their sexual use under slavery.[31] To analyze the two together is thus to take the view that the Thirteenth Amendment was intended to prohibit the forms slavery took for Black women as well as those it took for Black men.

Thirteenth Amendment[32] standards require a showing of legal or physical force, used or threatened, to secure service, which must be "distinctly personal service . . . in which one person possesses virtually unlimited authority over another."[33] Some cases predicated servitude on psychological coercion,[34] but the Supreme Court recently held that a climate of fear alone is not enough.[35] The vulnerabilities of the victims are still relevant to determining whether physical or legal coercion or threats compel the service, rendering it "slavelike."[36] Recognized vulnerabilities have included mental retardation, being an illegal immigrant, not speaking the language, being a child, and being stranded in a foreign city without means of support.[37] Poverty has been pervasively understood as part of the setting of force.[38]

The Thirteenth Amendment has often been found violated when a person is tricked into peonage or service through fraud or deceit and is then kept unable to leave, including through contrived and manipulated indebtedness.[39] Debt is not a requirement of servitude, but it is a common incident of it. One recent case found that victims—they are called victims in these cases—were forced into domestic service by enticing them to travel to the United States, where they were paid little for exorbitant work hours and had their passports and return tickets withheld, while they were required to work off, as servants, the cost of their transportation.[40] Corroborating evidence has included extremely poor working conditions.[41]

Indentured servitude has long been legally prohibited in the United States, even prior to the passage of the Thirteenth Amendment.[42] In interpreting the Thirteenth Amendment in contemporary peonage contexts, courts have been far less concerned with whether the condition was voluntarily entered and far more with whether the subsequent service was involuntary.[43] That victims believe they have no viable alternative but to serve in the ways in which they are being forced has also supported a finding of coercion and, with it, the conclusion that the condition is one of enslavement.[44] Involuntary servitude has embraced situations in which a person has made a difficult but rational decision to remain in bondage.[45]

If the legal standards for involuntary servitude developed outside the sexual context are applied to the facts of prostitution, most women in it are slaves, of most of their situations clearly prohibited. In prostitution, human beings are bought and sold as chattel for use in "distinctly personal service."[46] Many women and girls are sold by one pimp to another as well as from pimp to trick and for pornography. Prostitution was not formerly called "white *slavery*" for nothing.[47]

Prostitution occurs within multiple power relations of domination, degradation, and subservience[48] by the pimp and trick over the prostitute: men over women, older over younger, citizen over alien, moneyed over impoverished, violent over victimized, connected over isolated, housed over homeless, regarded over despised. All of the forms of coercion and vulnerabilities recognized under the Thirteenth Amendment are common in prostitution, and then some. No social institution exceeds it in physical violence. It is common for prostitutes to be deprived of food and sleep and money, beaten, tortured, raped, and threatened with their lives, both as acts for which the pimp is paid by other men and to keep the women in line.[49] Women in prostitution are subject to near total domination. Much of this is physical, but pimps also develop to a high art, forms of non-physical force to subjugate the women's will. Their techniques of mind control often exploit skills women have developed to survive sexual abuse, including mental defenses such as denial, dissociation, and multiplicity. They also manipulate women's desire for respect and self-respect.

Criminal laws against prostitution provide legal force behind its social involuntariness. Women in prostitution have no police protection because they are criminals, making pimps' protection racket both possible and necessary. In addition to being able to inflict physical abuse with impunity, pimps confiscate the women's earnings and isolate them even beyond the stigma they carry. The women then have no one but pimps to turn to to bail them out after arrest, leaving them in debt for their fines, which must be worked out in trade. Thus the law collaborates in enforcing women's involuntary servitude by turning the victim of peonage into a criminal.[50] Such legal complicity is state action, raising a claim under the Fourteenth Amendment for sex discrimination by state law.[51]

Although it is dangerous to imply that some prostitution is forced, leaving the rest of it to seem free, as a matter of fact, most if not all prostitution is ringed with force in the most conventional sense, from incest to kidnapping to forced drugging to assault to criminal law. Sex-based poverty, both prior to and during prostitution, enforces it; while poverty alone has not been recognized as making out coercion in slavery cases, it has been recognized as making exit impossible in many cases in which coercion has been found. If all of the instances in which these factors interacted to keep a woman in prostitution were addressed, it would be dramatically reduced.

Beyond this, the Thirteenth Amendment may prohibit prostitution as an institution. In the words of The Three Prostitutes' Collectives from Nice, "*all* prostitution is forced prostitution . . . we would not lead the 'life' if we were in a position to leave it."[52] In this perspective, prostitution as such is coerced, hence could be prohibited as servitude. At the very least, there is authority for taking the victims' inequality into account when courts assess whether deprivation of freedom of choice is proven.[53]

On a few occasions in the past, the Thirteenth Amendment has been used to prosecute pimps for prostituting women.[54] In these federal criminal cases, the prostitution was forced in order to pay a debt the women supposedly owed the pimp. In one case, the defendant procured two women from a prison by paying their fines and then forced them to repay him by prostituting at his roadhouse.[55] In another, young Mexican women were induced to accept free transportation to jobs that did not exist and then were told they could not return home until they repaid the cost of the transportation through prostitution.[56] These women were financially trapped, sometimes physically assaulted, always threatened, and in fear. Some complied with the prostitution; some were able to resist. In these cases, the prostitution as such was not considered involuntary servitude—the coercion into doing it was. But it is implicit in these cases that prostitution is not something a woman, absent force, would choose to do.

It is worth asking whether coercion of women into sex in a Thirteenth Amendment context would be measured by the legal standards by which courts have measured the coerciveness of nonsexual exploitation of groups that include men. The coercion of women into and within prostitution has been invisible because prostitution is considered sex and sex is considered what women are for. The standards for the meaning of women's "yes" in the sexual context range from approximating a dead body's enthusiasm to fighting back and screaming "no" to pleading with an armed rapist to use a condom.[57] If this is free choice, what does coercion look like? Sex in general, particularly sex for survival, is so pervasively merged with the meaning of being a woman that whenever sex occurs, under whatever conditions, the woman tends to be defined as freely acting.

Suits for prostitution as involuntary servitude confront the notion that women—some women who are "just like that" or women in general—are in prostitution freely. No condition of freedom is prepared for by sexual abuse in childhood, permits and condones repeated rapes and beatings, and subjects its participants to a risk of premature death of forty times the national average.[58] The fact that most women in prostitution were sexually abused as children,[59] and most entered prostitution before they were adults,[60] undermines the patina of freedom and the glamour of liberation that is the marketing strategy apparently needed for the users to feel free to use them and enjoy doing it. Such suits would also challenge freedom of choice as a meaningful concept for women under conditions of sex inequality. Women's precluded options in societies that discriminate on the basis of sex, including in employment, are fundamental to the prostitution context. If prostitution is a free choice, why are the women with the fewest choices most often found doing it?[61]

When a battered woman sustains the abuse of one man for economic survival for twenty years, not even this legal system anymore believes she consents to the abuse. Asking why she did not leave has begun to be replaced by noticing what keeps her there.[62] Perhaps when women in prostitution sustain the abuse of thousands of men for economic survival for twenty years, this will, at some point, come to be understood as nonconsensual as well. And many do not survive. They are merely kept alive until they can no longer be used. Then they are sold one last time to someone who kills them for sex, or they are OD'd in an alley or end up under those trash heaps in Detroit.

The fact that the coercion in prostitution will be difficult to establish in law when it is so overwhelmingly obvious in life is both why it would be difficult to win these cases and why it is crucial to try. It is helpful to be trying in a legal context, such as the Thirteenth Amendment, that has traditionally emphasized less the original means of subjection and more the barriers to leaving the subjected state.

The best thing about criminal law is that the state does it, so women do not have to. The worst thing about criminal law is that the state does not do it, so women still have to. Fortunately for women, the Thirteenth Amendment has a civil route, meaning women can use it ourselves. Under section 1985(3), prostituted women could allege that they have been subjected to a conspiracy to deprive them of civil rights as women. The conspiracy is the easy part—pimps never do this alone. In a supply-side conspiracy, they prostitute women through organized crime, gangs, associations, cults, families, hotel owners, and police. There is also a demand-side conspiracy, more difficult to argue but certainly there, between pimps and tricks.

Long unresolved is whether section 1985(3) applies to conspiracies on the basis of sex. In a recent case, the Supreme Court held that the group "women who seek and receive abortions" was not an adequate class for purposes of section 1985(3) because it was not based on sex.[63] The court did not say that sex-based conspiracies are not actionable under section 1985(3); several members of the court said that they are. Prostituted women form an even more persuasive sex-based class. How hard can it be to prove that women are prostituted as women? Not only is prostitution overwhelmingly done to women by men, but every aspect of the condition has defined gender female as such and as inferior for centuries. Evelina Giobbe explains how the status and treatment of prostitutes defines all women as a sex: "The prostitute symbolizes the value of women in society. She is paradigmatic of women's social, sexual, and economic subordination in that her status is the basic unit by which all women's value is measured and to which all women can be reduced."[64] As Dorchen Leidholdt put it: "What other job is so deeply gendered that one's breasts, vagina and rectum constitute the working equipment? Is so deeply gendered that the workers are exclusively women and children and young men used like women?"[65] The fact that some men are also sold for sex helps make prostitution look less than biological, less like a sex difference. Treatment that is socially and legally damaging and stereotypical that overwhelmingly burdens one sex, but is not unique to one sex, is most readily seen as sex discrimination.

A civil action under section 1985(3) would allow prostituted women to sue pimps for sexual slavery, refuting the lie that prostitution is just a job. Picking cotton is not just picking cotton. That slavery is a lot of work does not make it just a job. It is the enforced inequality of relations between people, as socially organized, that is the issue.

In addition to these legal tools, the law against pornography that Andrea Dworkin and I wrote gives civil rights to women in prostitution in a way that could begin to end that institution.[66] Pornography is an arm of prostitution. As Annie McCombs once put it to me, when you make pornography of a woman, you make a prostitute out of her. The pornography law we wrote is concretely grounded in the experience of prostituted women; women coerced into pornography are coerced into prostitution. It is also based on the experience of women in prostitution who are assaulted because of pornography. Beyond this, under its trafficking provision, any woman, in or out of prostitution, who can prove women are harmed through the materials could sue the pornographers for this form of trafficking in women. This provision recognizes the unity of women as a class rather than dividing prostituted women from all women. The precluded options that get women into prostitution, hence pornography, affect all women, as does the fact that pornography harms all women, if not all in the same way.

Subordination on the basis of sex is key to our pornography law. Pornography is defined as graphic sexually explicit materials that subordinate women (or, analogously, anyone) on the basis of sex. Women in prostitution are the first women pornography subordinates. In its prohibition on coercion into pornography, in making their subordination actionable, this law sets the first floor beneath the condition of prostituted women, offers the first civil right that limits how much they can be violated. It does not do all that they need, but it is a lot more than the nothing that they have.

This ordinance uses the artifactual nature of pornography to hold the perpetrators accountable for what they do. Before this, the pictures have been used against women: to blackmail them into prostitution and keep them there, as a technologically sophisticated way of possessing and exchanging women as a class. Under this law, the pornography becomes proof of the woman's injury as well as an instance of it.

Because pornography affects all women and connects all forms of sexual subordination, so does this law. And this law reaches the pornography. The way subordination is done in pornography is the way it is done in prostitution is the way it is done in the rest of the world: rape, battering, sexual abuse of children, sexual harassment, and murder are sold in prostitution and are the acts out of which pornography is made. Addressing pornography in this way builds a base among women for going after prostitution as a violation of equality rights.

It is difficult to know what to do, legally, about prostitution. State constitutions and human rights remedies could be adapted to use the argument sketched here. The Florida statute permitting civil recovery is beginning to be used.[67] Recent international initiatives build on long-term work and support domestic efforts.[68] Putting the power to act directly in women's hands is the goal.[69]

These thoughts are offered toward an institutional policy response to the reality of prostitution in the name of the civil rights all women are entitled to.

14

The Logic of Experience

The Development of Sexual Harassment Law

Sexual harassment law has been judge-made law. Formally predicated on statutory and constitutional text, the concept in substance was first recognized by federal judges who shaped thin equality laws to thick facts of women's lives. "[T]hat it should fit the facts" is what Oliver Wendell Holmes, speaking of the common law, observed to be "[t]he first call of a theory of law."[1] In the early sexual harassment cases, women told of being hounded for sex and fired when they refused and of years of private hell of sexual assault and molestation by their workplace superiors. In classic common law mode, judges hearing their cases crafted law to fit these newly spoken facts—and the District of Columbia's federal judges were the first to do it.

Through the D.C. Circuit's trial and appellate decisions, sexual harassment was first established as a cause of action for sex-based discrimination for which employers could be held civilly responsible. Beginning with *Williams v. Saxbe*[2] and *Barnes v. Costle*,[3] extending through *Bundy v. Jackson*[4] and *Vinson v. Taylor*,[5] this line of cases first cognized the harm of sexual harassment, authoritatively considered the rules of accountability for it, and judicially explored the parameters of the wider legal and social ramifications that the recognition of this injury was to generate. As women's pain broke through public silence, their resistance to sexual abuse became articulated as a deprivation of their entitlement to equality, and social movement became institutional change generating further social movement. Significant in its own right, this history also raises questions for explanation and offers lessons in the theory and strategy of promoting equality through law for historically subordinated groups.

I

Sexual harassment doctrine was initially predicated on Title VII of the Civil Rights Act of 1964.[6] It was later recognized under Title IX of the Edu-

Address, Bicentennial Celebration for the Courts of the District of Columbia Circuit, 9 March 2001, Washington, D.C. First published, 90 *Georgetown Law Journal* 813 (2002).

cation Amendments of 1972[7] and the Equal Protection Clause of the Fourteenth Amendment.[8] When each of these provisions was promulgated, however, sexual harassment as such was not publicly acknowledged to exist, nor had it yet been conceived to violate any publicly recognized principle of equal treatment of the sexes, legal or social. The Title VII Congress famously provided little to interpret beyond the monumental words that made it "an unlawful employment practice for an employer . . . to discriminate against any individual with respect to his compensation, terms, conditions, or privileges of employment, because of such individual's . . . sex."[9] Judicial determination that facts of sexual harassment violated sex equality rights postdated this statute's passage by over a decade. Similarly, the legal claim for sexual harassment in education was recognized well after Title IX's passage,[10] although the process moved more swiftly by building on Title VII precedents. In its constitutional dimensions, the prohibition of official sex-based discrimination under the Equal Protection Clause is also the product of latter-day judicial interpretation; over a decade after sex discrimination was recognized to violate the Equal Protection Clause, further interpretation applied this principle to official sexual harassment.[11]

The common law process interpenetrates law with society in both directions, cohering changing social standards and shaping precedents into new law in response to new or newly perceived facts.[12] Statutory interpretation proceeds from code or legislated text, usually guided to some extent by legislative direction. But in reality, the two converge. No law is self-interpreting. Whatever it is called, a decision whether a law applies to a set of facts is a kind of common law process, and social norms affect all cases, whether the cases arise under codes or prior case law. Each set of lived facts is unique in ways that can shift emergent rules as applied, and precedents tend to coalesce into principles and statutes. As a result, for one example, the distinction between civil law code systems and common law case systems is more one of degree than kind, and often largely a matter of point in time, particularly given mutual systemic influences.[13] The sexual harassment claim fits sex equality logic; it took sex equality guarantees for it to come into being. But sexual harassment doctrine did not historically arise because or when legislatures passed sex discrimination laws. It was judicial engagement with the experiences of sexually harassed women presented to courts on an equality theory, in phenomenological depth and one case at a time,[14] that made it happen. In this real sense, sexual harassment law is a women's common law.

The development of sexual harassment law is an anomaly in that the common law can hardly be said to have been a historical force for women's equality. The common law has historically reflected social structure, custom, habit, and myth to give legal sanction and legitimacy to men's social power over women.[15] Common law made tradition into law, and tradition did not favor sex equality. The common-law doctrine of coverture, for example, built in and on women's near-chattel status in marriage to become a legal fountainhead of all women's legalized subordination. It generated among other doctrines the marital rape exclusion (rape isn't rape if she's your wife), chastisement (beating isn't battery if she's your wife), the preclusion on women's property ownership (you own her so you own what she owns), and likely contributed to rape law's corroboration requirement and the instruction that rape complainants are particularly not to be believed. While the life of this law (to adapt Holmes's well-known aphorism) has concededly not been logic[16]—for instance, women have generally known, as coverture's fiction of marital unity did not, that a married couple is two people, not one[17]—neither has the life of the common law been women's experience. To this latter generalization, the development of the law against sexual harassment stands out as a striking exception.

Trial and appellate judges in the District of Columbia Circuit crafted the sexual harassment prohibition out of the life experiences of the women whose lawyers brought their clients' experiences to those courts. Holding contrary to rulings by judges elsewhere at the time,[18] the D.C. Circuit thus became an impelling force and organic participant in a transformative social movement for women's equality. By hewing closely to the facts of victimization that the women presented, grounding the developing principles on the realities of those experiences, the D.C. courts employed the common-law process to build a sex equality doctrine that, instead of reflecting the interests of the dominant—as both the historical common law and sometimes equality law had done before—advanced the interests of the less powerful.

Sexual harassment law is also largely exceptional in the degree to which it led social movements. In the last half of the twentieth century, litigation on issues that involve unequal social groups has rarely preceded social movements and legislatures. More typically, issues surfaced first through outspoken individuals and activist grassroots groups; protest then reached the public agenda and achieved momentum and public awareness through organized mobilization and media initiatives; official and private studies and more visible pressure groups followed. Legislative proposals and mass consciousness then emerged, resulting in beachheads in legislation and still later victories in courts. The abortion rights movement is an example of this pattern. The extent to which some breakthrough legal victories over segregation preceded large-scale mobilization against it is perhaps the only parallel to sexual harassment law's development, if a qualified one. Both show legally led social change: To a significant extent, antisegregation law and anti–sexual harassment law impelled social awareness of those issues rather than the reverse. The qualification is that, from the 1930s forward, the Black civil rights movement developed an organized approach to the use of courts to promote social equality based on race.[19] There was no such organized litigation campaign against sexual harassment. The few lawyers who first brought what came to be called sexual harassment cases as sex discrimination actions pleaded them as Title VII violations, but the establishment of sexual harassment as a legal claim for sex discrimination did not follow from a concerted plan of self-conscious legal elites, as so many legal civil rights advances had.

Consistent with the more usual framework, the civil rights movements in general,[20] and the women's movement in particular,[21] laid a foundation for the recognition of sexual harassment as a practice of inequality. In the mid-1960s, women on a large scale openly resisted sexual subordination.[22] Without both movements, the early sexual harassment cases would not likely have been brought and would not likely have prevailed. Individual victims and perpetrators privately knew that sexual harassment was real. But public knowledge that sexual harassment exists as a harm, a harm of sex bigotry, did not proceed first from widely mobilized social consciousness, extensive documentation and analysis, or major social outcry. The judicial recognition of sexual harassment as a form of sex discrimination *preceded* all of this. Social movements did not first define the issue of sexual harassment in the public mind to the degree that the courts did.

Nor did law by itself give rise to the sexual harassment claim by ineluctable logic or even appear especially propitious for its emergence. Until the D.C. Circuit's breakthrough rulings, laws against sexual abuse were mainly criminal rather than civil; their prohibitions focused on the breaking of rules rather than people. Other than sexual harassment law, they still primarily do. Forms of powerlessness or inequality other than age, and forms of force other than physical, had never been seen as legally integral to the injury of sexual assault. In the criminal law and the law of tort, formally speaking, they still are not. Before the legal claim for sexual harassment was recognized under Title VII, a handful of tort cases had confronted facts amounting to sexual harassment, but most had rejected them.[23] Even discrimination law had previously shown no understanding that inequality could be *sexually* enacted, enforced, and imposed, despite the realities of rape and molestation during slavery[24] and the vividly sexual dimensions of the lynchings that exploded during and after Reconstruction.[25] The racial analogy, as a result, was less available to support sex discrimination prohibitions than it would have been if the concrete experiences of sexual abuse within American racism had, in common-law fashion, been more central in defining the legal injury of race-based discrimination. Legal precedent, in other words, was not specifically favorable. Yet, by the mid-1980s, in direct line from the D.C. Circuit's path-breaking sexual harassment decisions, an inequality claim for unwanted sex at work had been established in law.

One way to capture this process and measure the distance traveled is to recall that, when the first cases were decided, there were two small grassroots women's groups working against the problem in the workplace, one of which used words other than sexual harassment to name it, and a single article on the subject in *Redbook*, a women's magazine.[26] Consider this further benchmark: In the early 1970s, I telephoned the women workers' organization "9-to-5" to see if any of their members would be willing to talk with me about their experiences of unwanted sex at work for a project to design a legal claim making it possible to sue. After a long wait, I received an apologetic return phone call declining to take part, explaining that the members were "afraid of giving up their only source of power." The gentle suggestion that it was a source of their powerlessness that was under consideration got nowhere. Needless to say, the plaintiffs who brought early D.C. Circuit cases—Diane Williams, Paulette Barnes, Sandra Bundy, and Mechelle Vinson—did not see it the way the organization's women did at that time, and neither did the judges who ruled on their cases. Soon, the women of 9-to-5 did not either.

II

The first cases to decide that sexual harassment violated sex equality law did not use that term.[27] Yet they achieved the key recognition that facts of sexual harassment constitute a practice of discrimination "based on sex." In so doing, the cases pioneered a new legal model of "sex" as a legal term of art and of inequality as well, grounded for the first time in women's experience—a model that equality law is only beginning to catch up with.

Diane Williams, an employee of a project of the U.S. Department of Justice, claimed that her supervisor harassed, humiliated, and then terminated her, allegedly for poor work performance, after she refused his sexual advance.[28] In 1976, Judge Charles Richey held that this practice was based on the sex of its victim and the supervisor's actions fell within Title VII. The practice was, in Judge Richey's language, "an artificial barrier to employment . . . before one gender and not the other, despite the fact that both genders were similarly situated."[29] Both sexes had sexuality; both had jobs; only the sexuality of one sex, that of Ms. Williams and other women at her workplace,[30] was made into a disadvantage in employment. That they were women was not a coincidence, in his analysis, but the reason they were subjected to abuse. At the time, Judge Richey's insightful ruling stood alone in concluding that the facts of what later came to be termed sexual harassment stated a legal claim for sex discrimination as a matter of law.

As *Williams* was not appealed on this issue,[31] *Barnes v. Costle* became in 1977 the first case to reach the Court of Appeals for the District of Columbia Circuit on this foundational question. At the time, a line of district court rulings in other circuits had all held that sexual preconditions for, or conditions of, work were not "based on sex" within the meaning of Title VII. Sexuality was not "sex." It was, those courts variously held, personal, biological, inevitable, universal, or not employment-related.[32] The most creative rationale for these early results was a counterfactual hypothetical: the assertion that because either sex *could* sexually harass or be sexually harassed, sexual harassment could not be based on sex as a matter of law.[33] It was as if white people and men could not be discriminated against, and that was why it was against the law to discriminate against Black people or women, when closer to the opposite is the truth. It was as if social inequality really *is* because of biology but discrimination law opposes it anyway. This judicial approach also militated against a claim for sexual harassment in same-sex settings. At the same time, most courts agreed that employment standards that made it harder for one sex or race to get or perform jobs violated equality requirements. It was strange. Courts seemed unable to connect sexuality with "sex"—or, rather, to separate the two long enough to see that their convergence in workplace abuse and disadvantage was arbitrary and biased and social, not natural and biological and inevitable. Until they could see "sex" and sexuality apart, they could not see them together.

What courts had not seen, or had refused to see, was that sexuality is socially gendered, meaning that demands for unwanted sex are most typically predicated on the fact that an employee is a woman or a man as that status and identification are marked and shaped in social space. It was this that Judge Spottswood W. Robinson III grasped in his lucid opinion in *Barnes v. Costle* for a unanimous panel that ruled that when Paulette

Barnes's job was abolished because she refused to have an after-hours affair with her supervisor, "retention of her job was conditioned upon submission to sexual relations—an exaction which the supervisor would not have sought from any male."[34] This, Judge Robinson wrote, constituted "the exaction of a condition which, but for his or her sex, the employee would not have faced."[35] The concurring formulation by Justice Ruth Bader Ginsburg, formerly of the D.C. Circuit, in *Harris v. Forklift Systems, Inc.*,[36] indicating that the critical issue in sexual harassment cases is "whether members of one sex are exposed to disadvantageous terms or conditions of employment to which members of the other sex are not exposed"[37]—subsequently embraced by the Supreme Court majority in *Oncale v. Sundowner Offshore Services, Inc.*[38]—vindicated this original *Barnes* formulation.

Most significant in reaching this result was the *Barnes* court's shift from what had been an abstract question of law—whether abuse based on sexuality, which was not a term of art, was abuse based on sex, which was—to a concrete question of fact: whether this complainant's sex was the reason she or he was subjected to sexual abuse at work. Before *Barnes*'s move to factual ground, defendants had prevailed in precluding the legal claim by litigating "various hypotheticals"[39] mostly of abstract hopscotch. These included invented variants of sex, sexual attraction, and orientation, for instance: "[T]he [male] supervisor could 'just as easily' have sought to satisfy his sexual urges with a male, and thus his actions were not directed only toward the female sex."[40] This sliding between hypothetical and actual also produced the view that if a bisexual person of either sex or a woman had done to a woman what a heterosexual man was accused of doing to a woman, the abuse would not in theory be sex discrimination, so the harassment could not be sex-discriminatory when it was in fact directed to one sex only. In this vein, the *Tomkins* district court, declining to permit the plaintiff's claim of supervisory sexual harassment, opined in a stunning non sequitur, "In this instance, the supervisor was male and the employee was female. But no immutable principle of psychology compels this alignment of parties. The gender lines might as easily have been reversed, or even not crossed at all. While sexual desire animated the parties, or at least one of them, the gender of each is incidental to the claim of abuse."[41] Why a woman *is* not harassed as a woman because a man *might* have been harassed as a man was not elucidated; why sexual desire makes gender irrelevant was not either. Fantasies about bisexuals harassing as it were indiscriminately and other phantoms of the legal imagination were thus employed to keep the victims of sexual harassment of one sex by another—usually women by men—from reaching a trier of fact for their injuries.

The *Barnes* panel further offered in dictum that if a bisexual imposed sexual requirements on both sexes, no sex discrimination could occur.[42] Given the absence of facts on the question, that court was in no position to recognize that both women and men could be sexually harassed based on their sex or gender by the same perpetrator. Judge Richey, with unerring compass in *Williams*, a case involving an allegation of harassment of a woman by a man, rejected "any argument that this cannot be sex discrimination because the application of the rule would depend upon the sexual preference of the supervisor, as opposed to some other reason."[43] Both opinions were clear on what was litigated: the *possibility* of harassment of people of both sexes by people of the same or different sexes from that of their victims did not mean that when a member of one sex *actually* imposed unwanted sex on another, sex-based discrimination could not, in fact, have taken place. *Barnes* held that the issue of Title VII coverage vel non turned on whether individuals were solicited for sex in each instance, in fact, because they were women or men: "But for her womanhood, from aught that appears, her participation in sexual activity would never have been solicited."[44] While much ink has been spilled on the "but for" part of this analysis, the earthmoving part is "from aught that appears." It moved the issue from the air of conjecture to the ground of reality, where both common law and women live. Other circuits followed *Barnes* reversing prior district court decisions to the contrary on the same grounds.[45]

Civil law adherents take note: This development was accomplished without sacrificing an iota of principle. On the contrary, the sex equality principle was vindicated more fully than hypothetical machinations or legislated principles had done. What might be observed of the distinction between civil and common law can be seen retraced here in the distinction between law and fact; indeed, they are species of the same distinction. Once questions of fact are perceived to form a pattern, they create legal rules and become matters of law, just as cases congeal into precedents into principles into codes. In sexual harassment law, factual questions and common law processes brought dynamism to equality law because, while women had been largely excluded from equality law, they had hardly been excluded from inequality in life.

The core comprehension of *Barnes* was the gendered—that is, social group—basis of the sexual harassment claim.[46] The effective presumption concerning unwanted sexual attention at work went from being not an inequality violation to being one, absent indications to the contrary. The *Barnes* court's observation that just because employment conditions between employees and superiors are constituted by sexual relations does not, ipso facto, exempt them from coverage under Title VII[47] is unremarkable today, but it was real news to many people at the time. Because of *Barnes*, courts approach sexual harassment as gender-based as a matter of law unless proven not gender-based as a matter of fact. This went from being largely unthinkable to being largely unthinkable any other way almost overnight. The rule that has emerged from *Barnes* in almost three decades of litigation since has sustained that core insight: if harassment is sexual, it is sex-based unless proven not to be. Once properly alleged, the issue of whether harassment that is sexual is based on sex has simply fallen out of most cases. As a panel of the Ninth Circuit put the animating understanding, "sexual harassment is ordinarily based on sex. What else could it be based on?"[48] Most defendants have declined to try to make their purported sexual harassment of both sexes into the defense it may or may not prove to be.[49]

This analysis—if it is sexual, it is gender-based, hence sex-based, unless shown otherwise—has yet to be explicitly acknowledged by most courts that apply it, and most do. It can be seen animating the Supreme Court's decision in *Oncale*, in which same-sex harassment was found covered by Title VII's sex equality component as a matter of law, even as the opinion distanced itself from that rule.[50] It has turned out to be socially obvious (even tediously so) that sex in the dual sense of biological sex and social gender is central in sex in the third sense of sexuality. Sexual orientation itself is largely defined in sexed and gendered terms. How one knows or proves that something sexual is "but for sex" can be conceptually complicated and interesting, but in most real, lived cases of sexual harassment, it has proven so simple and routine as to be a virtual nonissue as a practical matter. The D.C. Circuit law of two decades before laid the foundation for this outcome, one from which the same-sex harassment claim also follows directly.

Both Ms. Barnes and Ms. Williams complained of what has come to be termed quid pro quo harassment, in which an exchange of sex for economic benefit is proposed and job retaliation for refusal of a sexual advance often results. The case of Sandra Bundy in 1981 first permitted the circuit to confront "the novel question" of whether unrelenting sexual demands and pressures in themselves amounted to sex discrimination with respect to "terms, conditions, or privileges of employment."[51] In hostile environment cases, in contrast with quid pro quo cases, the harm is done to the equality interest of the woman herself, pure and simple, not only to her in her capacity as a worker. The injury is inflicted in and at work, but its impact on her is not confined to its impact on her work, hence its damage is not measurable in terms of indices of work alone. This explains why it was hostile environment sexual harassment cases that later impelled the amendment of Title VII to provide for damages for discrimination for the first time.[52]

In *Bundy v. Jackson*, Chief Judge Skelly Wright, joined by Judge Robinson and District Judge Swygert, held that a hostile working environment centering on a long-term pattern of sexual solicitations—including a superior who proposed she begin a sexual relationship with him and stated "any man in his right mind would want to rape you" when she complained to him[53]—was in itself sufficient to trigger the antidiscrimination protections of Title VII. In ruling that "sexually stereotyped insults and demeaning propositions . . . illegally poisoned that environment,"[54] *Bundy* established that there can be harm in asking. It made the D.C. Circuit the first court of appeals to hold that being treated as a sex object at work could be harmful in itself, and that harm was the harm of sex discrimination. The status harm at the core of an equality rule—the injury of being made a hierarchical subordinate in a location or relation governed by an equality standard—was authoritatively recognized on sexual facts. Once the issue of whether sexual harassment was properly sex-based discrimination under Title VII reached the U.S. Supreme Court in *Meritor Savings Bank v. Vinson*[55]—also a D.C. Circuit hostile environment case—the correct approach to the issue seemed so obvious as to be disposable in a single virtually circular sentence: "Without question," then-Justice Rehnquist wrote for a unanimous Court, "when a supervisor sexually harasses a subordinate because of the subordinate's sex, that supervisor 'discriminate[s]' on the basis of sex."[56] The D.C. Circuit, and women, had won. A new common law rule was established.

Mechelle Vinson's case, lost at trial in front of Judge John Garrett Penn and reversed on appeal in another of Judge Robinson's visionary but solid opinions, established sexual harassment as a legal claim for sex discrimination when the U.S. Supreme Court affirmed the court of appeals and remanded. Unprecedented, *Vinson* was all the more remarkable for being a hostile environment case, and thus an instance of the equality injury of sexual harassment in its relatively pure sexual form. Only two features of Judge Robinson's reasoning for the D.C. Circuit panel were not affirmed by the Supreme Court: his ruling that evidence of a victim's speech and appearance were irrelevant to whether or not she welcomed the harassing conduct and his embrace of then-EEOC guidelines on employer liability. As to the first point, Judge Robinson contended that "since, under *Bundy*, a woman does not waive her Title VII rights by her sartorial or whimsical proclivities, that testimony has no place in this litigation."[57] His analysis of the second point was that a supervisor's apparent or actual influence in job decisions "gives any supervisor the opportunity to impose upon employees" and that the power of supervisors as such "carries attendant power to coerce, intimidate and harass"; therefore employers were answerable for sexual harassment of any subordinate by any supervisor.[58] The Supreme Court, by contrast, held that victim speech and dress is potentially relevant to unwelcomeness. While declining to set standards for employer liability at that point in the law's development, it sent later courts in the direction of agency standards, reinserting tort law into equality jurisprudence at the crucial accountability stage.[59] The Supreme Court's subsequent judgments on employer liability clarified the applicable standards in compromises that did not put equality for violated women first.[60] The "unwelcomeness" requirement, while a big improvement on rape law's consent standard, may present a barrier to relief for sexually harassed women in exposing them to intimidation and threats of disclosure pretrial, thus particularly impervious to reviewing courts.[61] On both issues, the D.C. Circuit's positions were more attentive both to women's experiences and to the requisites of promoting equality. In general, when later courts conformed to D.C. Circuit precedent, for the most part they promoted equality; when they diverged from it, they tended not to, or less so.

The D.C. Circuit's early sexual harassment rulings gave women sex equality rights they had lacked, and in so doing provided legally enforceable standards that promoted self-respect and entitlement to inviolability and dignity that women did not have before. Why the D.C. Circuit was capable of this motion when other courts were not is well framed as a question of D.C. Circuit history. It happened here, not in other circuits, for no lack of trying elsewhere at the same time.[62] The plaintiffs elsewhere had compelling cases; precedent and social conditions were comparable; lawyers presented the arguments elsewhere. Passing why this change happened in the D.C. Circuit, why did it happen at all? The holding that sexual harassment was based on sex as a matter of law did not reflect a preexisting social consensus: the dominant social consensus was that the practice was harmless or nearly nonexistent. Nor did it recast moral disapproval of sex in civil rights garb, morphing sexual tut-tutting into inequality guise. The D.C. Circuit understood the injury as one of abuse in spite of, not because of, the fact that it was a form of sex, noting that "[t]he vitiating sex factor . . . stemmed not from the fact that what appellant's superior demanded was sexual activity—which of itself is immaterial."[63] Whatever one thinks of this latter point, the D.C. Circuit realized that sexual abuse under these circumstances was what second-class citizenship looked like: a form of human degradation and a harm in itself on the basis of membership in a social group defined by birth. The particularities of the women's cases powerfully conveyed this experience as being real in a way that nothing else had or can.

What led the women who sued to think that their abuse violated their rights when they had no such rights and as yet no substantial movement behind them on the issue is also worth considering, as is the question of what led the lawyers they consulted to frame their claims as violations of the law of sex discrimination when it was not recognized as such. That all of the early women plaintiffs in the D.C. Circuit, and many elsewhere, were African American and most of the men judges who produced this change had confronted their own group-based inequalities, may have something to do with it. For whatever reason, which certainly must include the women's movement as a whole, the relevant actors possessed vision, insight, conceptual acuity, principle, a sense of history, and indomitability. It was also necessary that the lawyers who brought the cases listened to their clients and were willing to call their injury what it was, as were the judges who heard their cases, although the law never had before. Perhaps, as the legal realists would have it, the cases that made the law simply reached the right desks on a roll of the clerk's dice.

III

Once predicated on the reality of women's experience, sexual harassment law largely continued developing through this method. As a result, certain distinctive features of the law of sexual harassment that have been largely sui generis prefigure a new model of equality law that better fits the inequalities of women's experience than does existing equality law, created largely in the absence of recognition of that experience. One example is sexual harassment law's treatment of intent or motive and its consequent approach to burden of proof. A requirement of proof of intent or bad motive—rooted in ancient superstitions concerning the animism of inanimate objects that underlie tort law[64]—continues to plague constitutional and statutory equality law alike, despite its irrelevance to the injury inequality does and to the dynamics of its infliction by often incompletely self-conscious human actors. As developed case by case, sexual harassment law has been essentially indifferent to intent requirements as they are known elsewhere in equality law, possibly because asking whether a perpetrator meant to discriminate against a woman or only meant to impose sex on her at work looks as beside the point of her inequality injury as it is. Partly as a result of this practical vitiation of "motive," burden of proof in sexual harassment cases is less tortured and torturing to plaintiffs than rote application of disparate treatment standards would be.[65]

As sexual harassment law became part of the law of sex discrimination, equality jurisprudence absorbed an active process of the subordination of women to men that the law had not confronted before. Until then, sex equality law had principally turned on an inquiry into whether women met male standards but were not treated as well as men were treated. Of course, men are infrequently treated like sexually harassed women, but that indicates a potential sex inequality without fully exposing the harm of the practice. With sexual harassment law, the focus turns away from sex difference and sameness to the real inequality problem: social hierarchy of status on the basis of sex. Because sexual abuse is gendered unequal, hierarchically not simply differentially, it is based on sex; no initial sex-sameness is required and no sex difference justifies it. As realities of dominance and subordination supplanted sameness and difference, the biological nose-counting test[66]—Are only women affected? Are more women affected than men? What if some men are also affected? What if there are no members of another sex around to compare with?—a helpful initial index to discrimination in many instances, became no longer the sine qua non of sex-based practices. Subordination because one is a woman or a man, variously inflected masculine or feminine, can be demonstrated in a variety of ways, of which sexual abuse is one. Women's sexuality can differ from men's without making sexual abuse non-sex-discriminatory. And, given the imbrications of sexuality with sex and gender, and all with social hierarchy, truly sex-neutral and gender-neutral—hence sex-equal—sexual abuse is virtually nonexistent. Indeed, sexual abuse is one way sex is gendered.

Same-sex discrimination law—law against abuse of people by people of the same sex and subordination of people because of chosen same-sexuality—thus emerged as part of sex-based discrimination law. When the U.S. Supreme Court recognized the basis in sex of same-sex as well as non–same-sex harassment, a sexual harassment case produced the first Supreme Court recognition of sex equality rights in a same-sex setting—in an opinion by none other than Justice Scalia, a former member of the D.C. Circuit.[67] Opposition to sexual harassment thus converged, appropriately and inescapably, with the movement for lesbian and gay civil rights. Hostile environment sexual harassment law, initially drawing on a lone Fifth Circuit precedent that prohibited racially hostile environments,[68] also became precedent for equality claims against racist bigotry in the working environment;[69] the number of those claims brought under Title VII grew. The recognition that racism and sexism are interpenetrated and convergent in many respects also grew through the many cases of sexual harassment brought by women of color in the D.C. Circuit and beyond—women who increasingly insisted that the real race-based dimensions of their sexual experiences of denigration be doctrinally visible together with, and integral to, its basis in sex.[70] Sexual harassment law thus became a central vehicle in exposing the reality of, and cementing the legal claim for, race and sex discrimination combined.

Sexual harassment doctrine also quickly and axiomatically came to encompass gender-based harassment, whether or not the abuse was specifically sexual. Abusive sexist remarks have always been part of sex discrimination prohibitions; they have long been used as signal indicators of sex-based motive and are stock evidence of sex stereotyping.[71] Distinguishing between sexist abuse that is sexual and sexist abuse that is not sexual is a dubious and, in most if not all real situations, a largely impossible venture. Almost all sexual harassment cases contain both, litigated indistinguishably. Thankfully, separating them was rendered unnecessary by an early leading D.C. Circuit precedent holding that gender-based harassment is gender-based discrimination, whether or not anything explicitly sexual was involved.[72] The obviousness of this position animated the U.S. Supreme Court decision in *Harris v. Forklift Systems, Inc.*,[73] in which the Court found such comments as "You're a woman, what do you know," "We need a man as the rental manager," and references to the plaintiff as "a dumb ass woman"[74] to be actionable violations of sexual harassment law. The Court could not have been clearer that sexual desire, at least, is not requisite for a sexual harassment claim than it was in *Oncale*: "[H]arassing conduct need not be motivated by sexual desire to support an inference of discrimination on the basis of sex."[75] A Ninth Circuit holding on a sex-stereotyping theory that harassing a man for being effeminate constitutes sex discrimination further underlines this point.[76] But make no mistake: the injection of the reality of specifically *sexual* abuse at work into sex equality law produced the expansion of a legal claim for *nonsexual* gender-based harassment as well.

Arguably, the core equality paradigm has also been affected by sexual harassment law's development. While early sexual harassment cases focused on the standard discrimination model of sameness and difference based on a biological definition of sex, the D.C. Circuit cases on sexual harassment contended with, and started down the path to recognizing, that it is the *social* definition of sex—gender—enforcing status hierarchy that is at the root of sex discrimination. Once the sexual facts of sex-based subordination became undeniably recognized by courts as part of gender inequality, the way was opened for a new model of discrimination to enter equality law proper, internationally as well as domestically. More group-based than individual, more socially based than biological, sensitive to hierarchy of power and status, relatively indifferent to biological sameness and difference except as an index to disparities in social treatment, this new model can be glimpsed taking root in various Supreme Court decisions[77] and in a growing understanding under international instruments that sexually abusive practices violate sex equality guarantees.[78]

In response to the sexual harassment rulings in the D.C. Circuit,[79] law changed around the country and ultimately around the world. In schools as well as at work, under labor contracts and international instruments, in states in the United States and in other countries such as Japan[80] and India,[81] sexual harassment became part of sex equality rights as a matter of common law interpretation. After the D.C. Circuit's early decisions, wherever a prohibition on sex discrimination exists, and there are many, and sexuality is used in life as a weapon of sex inequality, as it often is, the possibility exists for the common law development of a sexual harassment claim. Once sexual harassment rubrics are established by interpretation, other dimensions of equality law can begin to change as well, in typical common law form, as this example of inequality in the flesh becomes assimilated into its all-too-abstraction-prone jurisprudence. Building on the insights of the common law, some civil law jurisdictions, such as France[82] and Israel,[83] passed code provisions against sexual harassment, although they were not always equality laws. Perhaps when law is built less immediately on women's realities, unaccountable directly to women survivors and their experiences, it becomes easier to ignore the sex inequality involved in their experiences and to bow to other interests and constituencies, as is typical in the legislative process.

With the recognition of sexual harassment as a legal claim, the stage was set for some of the more significant social and political upheavals of the last quarter of twentieth-century United States. Had it not been for the development of sexual harassment law, it seems fair to say that Professor Anita Hill's testimony, with its attendant explosion of national and global consciousness on the issue, would unlikely have occurred, although *Bundy*, the closest controlling case in the D.C. Circuit to hers, was too fragile, isolated, and recent to have reliably helped her when it was handed down around the time of the injuries to which she testified.[84] Bill Clinton may well not have been elected President; women enraged at Professor Hill's treatment by the Senate may have supplied his margin of victory. In a certain live-by-the-sword, die-by-the-sword logic, the impeachment of President Clinton, and surrounding events, would also have been impossible without sexual harassment law, inasmuch as it all began with Paula Jones's allegations of sexual harassment and proceeded fueled to some degree by a heightened sensitivity to the place of extreme social inequality in sex, even though most women continue to have sexual relations with men who have more power in society than they do.

What common law gives it can also take away. What Professor Hill's allegations contributed to national consciousness, the dismissal of Paula Jones's case for legal insufficiency[85] seriously undermined. It is an irony that the acts Professor Hill alleged may well not have been recognized as actionable sexual harassment in the D.C. Circuit at the time that they happened, although publicly they were treated as sexual harassment allegations, but the acts Paula Jones alleged, when they happened to her, almost certainly would have been, but were publicly largely reviled and ultimately legally rejected as unactionable by sexual harassment law's standards. Women who saw that their treatment was at least as egregious as Professor Hill's resisted, increasing by the thousands the number of complaints to the EEOC and cases filed.[86] It remains to be seen whether the women whose treatment is as egregious as Paula Jones reported will stop resisting, turn their back on the courts, and return to silent despair. Holmes cautions: "We do not realize how large a part of our law is open to reconsideration upon a slight change in the habit of the public mind."[87] Whether women perceive the fact that the court that dismissed Paula Jones's claim was saying that what she said happened to her was not bad enough to be actionable is an empirical question. That the habits of women's minds partly constitute the public mind is some measure of progress.

The development of law against sexual harassment, and its transformation from private joke to public weapon, is one of the more successful legal and political changes women have accomplished. To a considerable extent, the legal change preceded—indeed, was instrumental in producing—mass consciousness on the subject. Perhaps it is difficult to expose some mass inequalities until they can authoritatively be addressed. Examining the history of sexual harassment law's development can help answer one systemic and strategic question that applies comparatively as well as domestically: What legal process more effectively promotes sex equality, common law's litigation or civil law's legislation? Countries with a strong civil law tradition seem to feel the need to pass a specific sexual harassment law—perhaps because the configuration of facts has a name of its own—while the more common law countries see no problem recognizing the claim under existing sex equality laws or norms. While the answer will vary with the legal system, culture, and strategic moment—and both legislation and litigation have been important in sexual harassment law's development—it is worth asking what legislature would pass a civil code provision giving women the scope of coverage of sexual harassment in rule form that common law case developments have so far given them by interpretation. To date, only Israel has come even close,[88] and it built on the extensive common law development in the United States. Individual women certainly are more likely to have access to a lawyer who can sue on their behalf than to have the resources and influence necessary to pass legislation. Once legislation exists, in many situations norms no doubt change, but in many situations people have to bring cases anyway, although under stronger legal circumstances than if no legislation existed. Codes, by virtue of explicitness, can also help reduce excuses (such as purported lack of knowledge of the rules) and distortions (such as bringing frivolous cases).

But the common law case-by-case process offers an edge for women that has so far gone unobserved. Comparing equality as a social value with equality as embodied in law further suggests that the society's notion of equality is more robust and substantive than the legal one traditionally has been. In life, people apply equality norms to their sexuality to a degree that outstrips the law's recognition of the inequality there. In addition, women have greater access to changing some of the de facto rules of social reality than they have had to changing the rules of law. As Baldwin noted in 1906, "[T]he common law of and for a particular people is made by that people from day to day as a natural growth of social life."[89] In this respect, in everyday life, the natural home of the politics of women's status, the common law process is in a potential position to make legal change for women, if only they can get into court.

In the sexual harassment context, something about confronting the empirical realities of women's lives, one at a time but in the conceptual context of women as a group (that is, under a sex equality rubric), has made it possible to extend equality rights to women, bringing about a shift in "public custom."[90] Once the foundational principle of equality between the sexes in relation to each other was made available, direct access of violated women to court processes has accomplished more change than legislatures have, in general, mandated or produced. It is worth asking whether this is because courts (at least in some countries) are more democratic and less elite—that is, less controlled by power and politics in which women are less, and less well, represented—than legislatures are.

This much is clear. When social inequality between women and men in the United States was more total than it was in 1975, women were more entirely excluded from representation and access to law, and public criticism of sexual abuse was muted at best, the common law worked their subordination. Once sex equality became recognized as a legal principle, and women began to be permitted to demand full human and civil status and gained a foothold in the legal system, and sexual abuse was socially exposed as systemic and gendered by sex, and women's resistance to it began to be validated to some extent, the common law process (principally federal but also inseparably in the states in interaction), predicated on concrete material realities of women's experiences, became progressive in promoting women's equality. The fact is, much of women's reality, if measured against a sex equality standard, looks overwhelmingly unequal. If law has seldom seen women's reality as unequal, it has been in part because equality standards have so seldom been applied to women's realities. In the late 1970s, when the women's movement made sexual subordination visible, it looked as unequal as it is. D.C. Circuit judges, confronted with the facts that women brought to court, calling them what they are, adapted equality doctrine accordingly.

One feature Holmes valued in the common law, possibly the reason he valued it, may have been its non-common touch: its operation as a counterweight to principled forces for equality in the law. While Holmes might be said to have loved the common law in part because of its antiegalitarianism, in the development of sexual harassment law, that same common law process served opposite ends—ends more like the Kantian ones Holmes opposed than the Darwinian ones he favored. Holmes also observed, "Everywhere the basis of principle is tradition. . . ."[91] In the instance of sexual harassment, it was old tradition exposed for what it was—unequal—and new tradition in the process of being born that became the basis for new principle. As women have lived their way toward creating a new tradition, and sought and obtained state support for their equality, new wine began to create a new bottle. In sexual harassment law's development, the common law became not a tool of the stronger but a principled mechanism for equality—from women's mouths to the D.C. Circuit's ear.

15

On Accountability for Sexual Harassment

Unwanted sex pressured by power became actionable as the sexual harassment claim for sex discrimination in employment in 1977 under Title VII,[1] and in education in 1980 under Title IX.[2] Sexual access to subordinates by superiors was no longer guaranteed as a perk of some positions, destabilizing traditional power arrangements. The precise terms on which institutions were to be held legally responsible for sex between unequals under their aegis were left open until three landmark Supreme Court decisions, one in education, two in employment, set these terms in the 1998 term.

In *Faragher v. City of Boca Raton*[3] and *Burlington Industries, Inc. v. Ellerth*,[4] the Supreme Court held companies liable in claims of sexual harassment by supervisors when the job is materially affected and, in claims for hostile environment, when the acts are reported (if reporting them is reasonable) and the employer did not correct the situation. No other kind of discrimination has a complaint requirement. But *Faragher* and *Ellerth* located institutional responsibility proximate to institutional reality: institutional hierarchy facilitates sexual use of subordinates by superiors in violation of the employer's duty not to discriminate. Employment superiors are the employer. When it came to schools, though, *Gebser v. Lago Vista*[5] ruled that before a school district may be held liable in damages to a student whose teacher had sex with her or him—acts that are often also statutory rape and child abuse—the correct school authorities must be told about the teacher's specific actions and treat them with deliberate indifference.

Surely this is wrong. Adult women have more power at work than girls do in schools, but women have more ready access to a legal right to be free from sex under conditions of inequality in employment than girls do in education. How can the responsibility be less where the inequality is greater, the danger more obvious, the population at risk more vulnerable,

Originally published by the American Bar Association as "New Developments in Sexual Harassment Law," 7 *Perspectives* 8 (Fall 1998).

the act itself often criminal, the danger well-known, the barriers to and punishments for reporting even bigger, the environment at least as controlled from the top, and the human consequences at least as disastrous?

Schools place teachers in a position of power over students. A score of pre-*Gebser* Title IX cases tacitly recognize that institutional power is largely responsible for sex between teachers and students, including sex that students "consent" to, and surely for damage to the student's education.[6] The failure to confront that reality squarely, however, particularly in cases where adolescents (most often girls) went along with or actively concealed the sex with authoritative adults (usually men), has clouded subsequent thinking on the responsibility of educational institutions. The "sex is personal" ideology, a dodge rejected in employment law early in the mid-1970s,[7] registers a comeback here. Evading the fact that teachers' power *as teachers* potentiates sex with students, the Supreme Court can imagine teachers who have sex with their students as acting "independently" (*Gebser*)[8] of their role.

In the work setting, some Title VII courts and employers openly recognize that hierarchy can coerce compliance with sex regardless of desire.[9] They grasp that the person with less power in the situation can be injured in and at work even if she wanted the sex at one point—for instance, if she wants to end it and is penalized, or if she is later punished when it ends.[10] They even have a clue that power can be sexualized. Courts interpret employment law to give workers a right to work in an environment that is not discriminatorily oppressive, one in which they can be productive and survive materially free of sexual exactions.

Schools are surely no less responsible for their environments. Yet, as a result of *Gebser*, we now do more for workers in a factory than for children in school—children whose educational and life prospects can be permanently derailed and destroyed as much by hierarchical sex and sexualization as by rape in the adult sense of the word. School authorities, using public funds and enforcing mandatory attendance, structure the teacher-student relationship on hierarchical lines and couple it with what amounts to proximity and opportunity for sexual access. Teachers' position of trust and authority, even intimacy—also encouraged, facilitated, and relied upon by the institution for good teaching to take place—makes the potential for sexual abuse of students constant and structural in the teacher-student relationship. The school creates and institutionalizes that structure.

The Supreme Court's *Faragher* and *Ellerth* decisions are properly clear that employers cannot escape liability by briefing their employees on the importance of not discriminating, and then treat whatever happens as the employee's own "independent" act if the victim does not use the complaint procedure. The *Gebser* decision's "hear no evil, see no evil, incur no liability" standard for schools allows this and worse: it affirmatively discourages institutional behavior that is known to deter sexual harassment—having a complaint procedure and encouraging reporting—because the less the school knows, the less it is liable for. The point of institutional liability in discrimination law is to make sure that institutional power is not abused to discriminate on the basis of sex. While employers move voluntarily to comply with *Faragher* and *Ellerth* by preventing and remedying sexual harassment at work, school authorities can breathe a legal sigh of relief as children all around them are silently sexually accosted, molested, and assaulted by their teachers. Post-*Gebser*, Congress should get busy amending Title IX so that young people whose sexual exploitation in education remains hidden can have a chance to grow and learn on equal terms.

The 1998 term's liability cases mark a larger shift in the discussion of sexual harassment as well: from whether it is a harm to who, if anyone, will be held responsible for it. The same shift has been taking place for some time in the political arena. The debate escalates depending not upon how much the woman is hurt, but upon how prominent the man is among men. The stakes rise not according to what he took from her, but according to what might be taken from him if she wins. The law of institutional liability accordingly focuses less on promoting equality between the sexes and more on how far up the food chain of each institution accountability for abusive sex will reach. In employment, responsibility in life is now reflected in a fair amount of responsibility in law. In education, where if anything the responsibility should be greater, one wonders whether the current accountability vacuum would be tolerated if the injury was anything but sexual.

The legal actionability of unwanted sex across hierarchical lines in employment and education has also led to a deeper questioning of how sexual desire is engendered in unequal settings in the first place. If one person has power over another, how can we know that sex between them is free and mutual, whether "consensual" or not? Why, for instance, would a thirteen-year-old girl want to be sexual with a forty-five-year-old man, if not in part that his power over her is eroticized? Most unsettled by this kind of questioning are people who are, however unconsciously, accustomed to the sexual acquiescence of their subordinates, and least aware of the effect of their institutional power in potentiating such acquiescence.

In addition, although Titles VII and IX both permit damage claims against institutions for sexual harassment of subordinates by superiors, neither allows direct suit against individual perpetrators.[11] As a result, focusing on who is being sued, courts think of discrimination as what institutions—meaning everyone but the sexual harasser—knew and did. This approach misses the simple underlying reality that individuals empowered by and within institutions also are the institution. They get much of their power to discriminate, and to harm through discrimination, from the institution. When they discriminate, the institution discriminates.

16

Beyond Moralism

Directions in Sexual Harassment Law

In the quarter century since some sex forced by power became illegal in the United States, what has changed?

The experience has been named, its injuries afforded the dignity of a civil rights violation, raising the human status of its survivors. Resentment of unwanted sex under unequal conditions is expressed more openly and given more public respect. Women may feel more valid and powerful, less stigmatized and scared, more like freedom fighters and less like prudes, when they turn down sex they do not want in unequal settings. Many more people know that a sexual harasser is a sex bigot and see that the use of power to leverage sexual access is a tool of dominance, whether the perpetrator knows that or not. Where sex equality laws apply—most employment and education, some housing—there is someplace to go to complain. Law is considerably more responsive to survivors than it was before, whether they refuse sexual bargains, resist sexualized environments, or comply with sexual demands they cannot avoid.

But sexual harassment is still not actionable every place it occurs;[1] zero tolerance is the rule virtually nowhere; resistance is far from safe or costless; perpetrators often protect one another, and sometimes victims protect them too. Institutions are often recalcitrant in taking responsibility and are often absolved of liability when they are oblivious. Victims seldom receive the support they deserve. Complaining about sexual harassment can be more injurious, if also more self-respecting, than suffering in silence.[2] Forms of power used to force sex other than economic, educational, or governmental power of position—common sources outside the context of warfare include age, familial relation, immigration status, racism, custodial position, drug addiction, and medical or spiritual authority—remain exempt from the facial reach of most equality laws. So far as is known, men sexually harass women as often as they did before sexual harassment became illegal.[3]

Originally published as "Afterword," *Directions in Sexual Harassment Law* 672 (Catharine A. MacKinnon and Reva B. Siegel, eds., 2003).

What has changed is the stakes. Sexually diddling the staff or the students used to be an open secret or joke, regarded as a perhaps deplorable but trivial peccadillo of some men, a tic of the person or perk of the position or both. Whatever else the man did or was outweighed the importance of whatever she said he did to her sexually. In many circles, such dismissive norms continue to reign. But, in going from a gripe to a grievance, in moving from whispers in secret to pleadings in federal court, sexual harassment went from an unnamed low-risk undertaking backed by a tacit understanding of tolerance among men to a public claim women could bring themselves under open rules with serious potential consequences for perpetrators.

The old tacit deal men had among themselves—to mutually overlook what other men did to women sexually unless an important man's claim was infringed, a deal that often encompassed the criminal law and authorities and often still does—was suddenly off. The calculation had to change. Once women could invoke and pursue civil process and sanctions for their own violation, the legality of coerced sex, and the costs to perpetrators of exposing it, newly depended on women. In a system in which even being subject to such a claim can have social weight, the fact that sexually aggrieved women were decision-makers in their own sexual grievances enhanced the civil rights law's function as a system of representation.[4] Sexual harassment became no longer something that journalists just knew about the powerful but kept quiet, or an experience by definition personal hence irrelevant to fitness for public office. Whether cynically or respectfully, as a pawn or a person, *she* suddenly counted.

Visible and audible, as an injured party, someone with relevant information, a woman could, at the least, make a man look bad, perhaps cost him a great deal. If the allegations are true, he is now potentially subject to real financial, reputational, and political as well as personal costs. Sexual harassment is serious business—or at least its exposure is. Women are not just bearers or objects of rights but actors in a sphere in which they had previously been acted upon. In this respect, women went from sexual objects of use and exchange to citizens. With women no longer absorbing the entire cost of this conduct in private, sexual politics went public, shifting the ground of political convention and becoming a visible part of politics as usual. In many instances, both on the individual level and for the polity at large, this change has made all the difference in the world.

Fundamentally, sexual harassment law transformed what was a moral foible (if that) into a legal injury to equality rights. What had been, if anything, reprehensible and deplorable, one of life's little joys or a minor rock in the road depending on your moral code or whether you were on the giving or receiving end, had real possible comeback attached. Sexually harassing conduct had been socially encouraged as masculine for perpetrators and further eroticized by being putatively but not really off-limits, while being an experience of shame for victims that kept them disempowered in the name of protection without protecting them. Now, sexual abuse remains sexualized. But sexual harassment law has changed this tut-tut no-no, a behavior that was essentially allowed while being decried only if embarrassingly displaced into public view, into an equality claim with collective meaning and the dignity of human rights that handed victims legitimate power to protect themselves, with sanctions backed by the state. To the question what is wrong with sexual harassment, previously to be answered with reference to a moral code for so-called private life, the law provided a new answer: sexual harassment is sex discrimination. That is, it is a practice of inequality on the basis of gender, an integral act of subordinate civil status because of sex, a practice of treating a person as less than fully socially human because that person is a woman or a man, a status-based treatment of hierarchy, of dominance, that is illegal.

Once the question became whether particular acts are or are not sexual harassment by legal standards—the threshold question being whether the behavior happened "because of . . . sex,"[5] meaning that it happened because of the victim's sex or gender—the question whether the behavior is morally bad was superseded, rendered obsolete and properly irrelevant to law, except perhaps for assessing punitive damages.[6] Judgments of magnitude, such as whether specific acts are sufficiently "severe" to be actionable as a hostile environment, correctly became questions of how severely discriminatory, how severely unequal, the acts are on a gendered scale, not how severely bad they are by moral compass. Judges and juries are thus called upon to ask not, is this bad? They are called upon to ask, is this unequal? While morality seeks to conform conduct to standards of right and wrong, whatever they may be, equality addresses the relative status and power of groups in society and is animated by an imperative of nonhierarchical treatment. Questions such as whether the other sex was subjected to similar behavior, whether the abuse was marked by gendered norms, and whether the treatment subordinated women or men as such, are determinative. How wrong, evil, or reprehensible the behavior or the parties are felt to be, becomes, within the inequality framework, properly inoperative.

Of course judgments of value remain involved. But they are equality values—not manners, civility, religion, propriety, decency, custom, or other value systems or sources of rules or codes or norms for interpersonal behavior. Once the legislative or constitutional judgment has been made to guarantee equality, whether it is good or bad to do so in particular cases is no longer a judicial question: whether a particular case presents inequalities is. Most fundamentally, the moral imperative to treat other people in a good way, *as if* they are fully human, is replaced by the requisite legal perception that, within the scope of the legal coverage, they *are* equal human beings—say, workers or students—whatever their sex or gender. In the case of sexual harassment, to use them as if they are sexual things becomes a category mistake, an instance of treating a human being as if she is not one, not a moral infraction about which people can differ, depending on their values. The argument that something is *good* is different from the argument that something *is*. While morality dwells in the normative, equality in this sense and setting is an empirical recognition, requiring not a judgment of how people ought to be treated but a cognition of the fact of their equal humanity across a specified line of particularity.

One obvious benefit of this approach, as befits a diverse society, has been that no moral agreement, community of belief, moral like-mindedness, or cultural convergence has been needed to apply sex equality standards to inequality's social harms. No particular moral sensitivity has been required to identify their existence. In any case, people with radically divergent moral commitments have to be able to implement equality laws or they will fail. While moral disagreements may underlie and be displaced onto equality questions, equality questions are properly resolved on equality grounds.

The transformation from moralism to equality, from treating people poorly or well to treating them without group rank, must occur for equality law to promote sex equality in substance. Among other reasons, this is because traditional morality upholds dominance in sex, which it genders, by defining men dominating women as "good" sex—as institutionalized for instance in the patriarchal family. This morality, with exceptions for extreme cases, tends to refuse to recognize that events empirically exist that it normatively rejects. Child sexual abuse, for instance, is considered exceptional rather than common because conventional morality finds it "bad," with the result that the fact that it is done to more than a third of all girls under eighteen, and many boys, in the United States, mostly by heterosexually identified men, is regularly denied.[7] Just as traditional morality defines certain sexual behavior as right, such as male dominance in sex, even though members of powerless groups are systematically and disproportionally endangered or violated by it, sexual behavior that takes place outside favored institutional structures is defined as wrong, regardless of whether anyone is harmed. Same-sex sexuality and prostitution are both deemed "bad" by traditional morality, for instance, although the former can be for both partners not only unharmful but validating, loving, affirmatively desired, and a resistance to male dominance, while the latter, for the one prostituted, tends toward the opposite on every score. Conventional morality tends to value people unequally on the basis of sex, sexuality, race, age, class, and other unequal stations in life. Their sexual abuse thus is often attributed to the moral character of the actors rather than to their relative positions of inequality, making sexual injuries of inequality difficult or impossible to see.

Conservative moralism holds that any nonprocreative sex is bad, liberal moralism that all sex is good—although neither fully owns up in public. Most conservatives do not want to oppose the secular religion or appear uncool or passé; most liberals do not want to be identified with sexual abuse, at least not in all of its forms. Neither morality adequately addresses sexual abuse because neither faces it as a practice of inequality: a reality of social condition, situation, status, and treatment rather than bad acts by bad people. The conventional morality of sexual regulation, whether of the left or the right, may at times decry the abuse of power by the powerful, but it systematically resists criticizing or undermining the fact of that power and its unequal distribution. Commonly, unequal power in private is defended, including by opposing the entry of equality law into the so-called private realm, which tends to be anyplace sexuality happens.[8] Most conventional morality in practice permits women and men of all ages who are seen by power as less valuable, thereby designated for use, to be sexually violated and exploited with relative impunity by those, most of them adult straight men, seen as more valuable and positioned higher up on the social food chain. Sexual morality thus traditionally entrenches what it purports to regulate or prohibit while punishing sexuality that challenges its hegemony, which is the hegemony of power itself. The misogyny characteristic of traditional morality—ranking vanishingly small numbers of women whose abuse matters and will be believed above the multitudes whose does not; imposing heterosexuality so as to make invisible anyone whose abuse either fits traditional norms (is "just sex") or deviates from them (is "perverse" rather than injurious)—puts the role of morality compared with equality in this body of case law at the heart of the question of whether anything that matters has changed.

The inquiry is thus framed: Has the sexual harassment claim, as applied, shed moralism—the normative calculus of right and wrong, good and bad—to emerge fully as a legal injury of discrimination, an injury defined by social harm of unequal treatment? Does sexual harassment law prohibit harm to members of socially subordinated groups through sex, no more and no less? Specifically, is the inequality of power between women and men that the traditional moral approach to sex keeps in place—an approach that remains as socially dominant as sex inequality—being altered by the law of sexual harassment, or have sexual harassment law's doctrines, applications, and dynamics internalized, replicated, and extended sexual morality? If the latter, the question of whether sexual injury is a recognized wrong of discrimination is being effectively relitigated in case after case, courts finding discrimination when injuries meet the standard moral code's rules for the "bad" and not when they do not, even when the behavior is sex-discriminatory, while finding sexual behavior that they rate immoral to be sex-discriminatory even when it does not violate sex equality standards. The question is, is sexual harassment law transforming social inequality into equality of status, or merely mutating moral prohibitions into equality guise?

The concern is whether sexual harassment law updates, disguising in civil rights skin, the same underlying moral dynamics that continue to drive sexual morality in the interest of male dominance and against the interests of women and all subordinated peoples. If sexual harassment law has mapped itself onto these underlying moral dynamics, hijacking human rights rhetoric to further sexual repression and sexual stigma while permitting the sexual abuse of power with impunity, it is morality's wolf in the sheep's clothing of equality. The incomplete yet real changes sexual harassment law has brought about, read against twenty-five years of case law and political upheaval, suggest that this is not the case.

Sexual harassment law originated the recognition that sexual abuse is a practice of inequality of the sexes, a recognition increasingly embraced and expanded, even taken as given, in the laws of nations around the world and in international forums.[9] In changing the understanding of sexual harassment's facts from morality to equality—from religious to human rights referents, from internal psychological and ideal predicates to external material ones—the cornerstone has been the conceptualization of the injury as sex discrimination.

To qualify as a legal injury of sex discrimination, the challenged behavior must be "based on sex," meaning that it happened because of the victim's gender. Ever since the breakthrough cases of the mid-1970s, in which facts of sexual harassment were first found to state a claim for sex discrimination as a matter of law, the question whether a claim is "based on sex" has not usually been extensively litigated when the alleged perpetrator is a man, the victim is a woman, and the activity complained of is sexual. As a Ninth Circuit panel put the animating understanding, "sexual harassment is *ordinarily* based on sex. What else could it be based on?"[10] In practice, unless challenged, the individual parties are taken as exemplars of the sex groups of which they socially present as members, and the challenged behavior is understood as gendered on the usually inexplicit, perhaps not fully conscious, view that sexual aggression is socially gendered male and sexual victimization, female.

With the allegations thus made not by individuals as such (as they were in tort precursors)[11] but by individuals in their capacity as members of groups—and no longer of "bad" behavior but of practices integral to a social system of gendered group-based inequality that produce injuries of second-class citizenship—the typical parties become no longer bad men and virtuous women but dominating men and subordinated women. With the gravamen of the offense changed from sin to injury, its identification from moral judgment to reality perception, the questions raised change from whether anything is wrong to what has occurred, in a context that moves from private to public and from morality to politics: sexual politics.[12] Sexual harassment doctrine squarely entrenches in law the position that moral valuations of relative personal worth and sexual propriety are not the point in this legal claim. Harm because of one's membership in a gender group is.

In jurisdictions where the claim for sexual harassment is not clearly located in law as a form of sex discrimination, as in France,[13] the doctrine continues in society as well as law to be confused with traditional moral strictures, and to be socially delegitimated by that confusion. In this setting, laws against sexual harassment are likely to be misconstrued as repressive, as restrictions on what is reflexively considered the sexual freedom of perpetrators, rather than as liberating and enhancing to the sexual freedom of those who need no longer be their victims. Where the law construes sexual harassment as a tort, but one of sex discrimination, as in Japan, the understanding is accordingly mixed.[14] India regards sexual harassment as sex discrimination but in some respects continues to treat it as a moral issue,[15] to the detriment of effective change for women, although the judicial trend is in the equality and human rights direction. Much of the shape of the claim's development can be seen to reflect the strength and focus of the women's movement in each country, specifically whether that movement has addressed the realities of sexual abuse. Many have not. To the degree that voice is absent or muted, moralism fills the void to the detriment of victims and the legal claim's development as a force for equality.

If so-called antisex attitudes of traditional male dominant moralism were driving the law of sexual harassment—that is, if sexual harassment has been recognized as a civil right because male dominant moralists are sex-negative—stronger prohibitions might be expected to be applied against expressly sexual forms of harassment because they are sexual than to other forms of harassment that are not sexual.[16] This has not happened.[17] So long as they were not expressly sexual, many forms of seemingly nonsexual abuse that might be construed as gender-based harassment have been integral to sex discrimination law all along—whether as verbal abuse showing intent or motive, direct evidence shifting the burden of proof to defendants, sex stereotyping, or gender harassment itself.[18] In fact, it was the recognition that expressly sexual forms of harassment are sex-based discrimination that led to expanded judicial recognition of gender-based forms of harassment that are not expressly sexual.

Of course, the analytical relation between sexual and not-explicitly-sexual-but-gendered harassment is complicated by the reality of their near inextricability in the world. Given that sexuality is socially gendered and gender socially sexualized,[19] separating the two forms of harassment is problematic as well as difficult. Even conceptually separable facts almost always occur together and are thus adjudicated in the same cases. Determining whether acts of abuse that are gendered but not sexual are ignored where the comparably severe act, if sexual, would be recognized approaches the impossible. Comparing the severity of sexual with apparently-nonsexual-but-gendered abuse is an abstract and speculative venture. Distinguishing between sexist abuse that is sexual and sexist abuse that is not clearly sexual has thankfully been rendered legally unnecessary by express judicial recognition that gendered abuse need not be expressly sexual to be actionable as harassing, which has generally made gender harassment axiomatically (if not completely or always, anymore than sexual abuse is) covered under sex discrimination law as sexual harassment.[20]

If sexual harassment law were animated by an antisexual hostility, that law would be unlikely to extend, as it has, to gender-based abuse that, while demeaning or derogatory or belittling, is not expressly sexual.[21] The fact that it does so extend is more persuasively explained by equality law's being antiabuse. Surely it means something that conventional morality has been, if fairly superficially, antisex for easily a couple of hundred years, without being antiabuse (sexual or otherwise), and without seeing sexual harassment as wrong. While admitting to neither, conventional morality and its legal regime have been both pro-sex (in the hegemonic hierarchical heterosexual or at least procreative sense) and pro-abuse during this entire period, as the equally long absence of effective laws against sexual forms of intrusion testify. Only when the behavior became framed as a harm of unequal gender status on the basis of sex, that is, as a material injury of inequality, was its harm recognized as legally significant.

Certainly courts and agencies often fail to recognize simple sex discrimination in particular cases, such as when women are deprived of less favorable work assignments or training opportunities because they are women.[22] This observation hardly indicts sexual harassment law as such or suggests an overweening emphasis on specifically sexual forms of abuse at work. If courts and agencies are not as sensitive as they should be to simple sex discrimination, including to gendered harassment in particular cases, they also expressly tolerate much egregious *sexual* behavior in employment and education because it resembles customary sexual practices that conventional morality tolerates, or because they judge the victim as morally bad or worthless.[23] A law that was simply antisex would not do this. A law that was not yet sufficiently sensitive to abuse, tolerating it, including when sexual, so long as it conforms to traditional morality, would. Any emphasis on sexual abuse in sexual harassment case law over other forms of gender-based abuse, should it exist, may also be due to the particularly transparent misogyny of much harassment that is sexual, or to a choice of sexual forms of abuse by some especially misogynist perpetrators, rather than to a judicial slighting of nonsexual forms of inequality in harassment cases.

Analysis of sexual harassment law's treatment of racist sexual abuse supports the view that sexual harassment law is not moralism redux. Standing against the racist dimensions of sexual denigration that traditional sexual morality builds in are the early successful sexual harassment cases brought by women of color.[24] Far from supporting the enforced sexual availability of women of color on white men's terms, sexual harassment law in these cases opposed the stereotyping of women of color by traditional morality that stigmatizes their sexuality so as to make it insusceptible of being seen as violated. In so doing, sexual harassment law thus became a central vehicle in exposing the reality of, and cementing the legal claim for, race and sex discrimination combined. Although racist sexual abuse is not adequately recognized nearly as often as it occurs, traditional morality would not, and does not, support such a recognition at all. The reach of Title VII to racial and religious harassment was similarly predicated on sexual harassment precedents, opposing conventional morality's myriad racist and religious biases in both sexual and nonsexual forms.[25] The cases reveal that, while an undercurrent of traditional morality's tolerance of sexual abuse of women by men can be seen in some cases—and may even be an undertow that will have to be fought by plaintiffs in most cases on some level, so long as inequality exists—antisex moralism can hardly be said to be driving sexual harassment law. On the contrary, sexual harassment law stands against traditional morality's tolerance of the sexual abuse of women with less power by men with more.

Sexual harassment law also stands against the abuse of men with less power by men with more. In the area of sex equality law, where precedents have so often been set by men claiming equality with women, rather than the other way around, the fact that male victims of men would be seen to have the same legal rights as women victims of men would stand to reason. It was news in sexual harassment law, however. Traditional morality has largely suppressed the possibility of recognizing that men can be sexually violated or subordinated, at once making sexual violation of men inconceivable and naturalizing women's sexual vulnerability as biological, obscuring the social function of both forms of abuse in male supremacy. Sexual harassment law, in recognizing that men also dominate and harm men through sex, took a step traditional morality never has, indeed a step that adherence to traditional morality largely precludes. Most cases of sexual harassment are male-on-female on their facts, but given the fixation of sex discrimination law with sex differentials as the method for discerning sex-based treatment, it was by no means obvious that sexual harassment in a same-sex context of man-on-man, or men-on-man, would be found to be sex-discriminatory.

The *Oncale* case, which so found,[26] marks the first time the sex equality principle was held violated in a same-sex factual setting by the U.S. Supreme Court, and one of the precious few such findings ever. Although we do not yet know if the same rule will be applied when an out gay man is harassed, it should, at pain of violating the constitutional rule of equal protection of the laws as well as sexual harassment holdings.[27] And although we do not yet know if the prohibition on same-sex harassment will extend to protect mutually desired same-sex intimacy when that is the predicate for homophobic discrimination, it also should. Thus sex equality law, having protected people with less power from unwanted sex in a same-sex setting, may, by building on sexual harassment precedent, come to protect wanted sex by groups with less power in a same-sex setting as well.[28]

In paving the way for protection of gay men from specifically sexual gay-bashing as sex discrimination (as well as for putatively nonsexual gay-bashing, which predictably will be easier to address by law as well as hard to separate from the sexual forms), and ultimately in recognizing that sex discrimination prohibitions require nondiscrimination against gay men and lesbian women as such, sexual harassment law, far from internalizing traditional morality, will have helped produced outcomes that traditional morality squarely opposes. Sexual harassment law's counterhegemonic logic may conceivably be reversed or twisted backward by dominant moral forces,[29] although in general it has yet to be. But this particular concern may more exemplify a reassertion of dominant moral rules[30] insofar as sexual harassment's equality rule tolls the bell on the sexual pleasures of a sex-discriminatory gender-hierarchical social order, specifically on the eroticism of the top-down unequal definition of sexuality that traditional morality has long guarded.

Tensions between morality and equality can also be discerned beneath sexual harassment law's "unwelcomeness" doctrine. The consent rule of traditional morality builds inequality of power into the criminal law of sexual abuse by tending to authoritatively assume, under conditions of inequality, that whatever sex happens is mutually desired unless proven otherwise. Apart from statutory presumptions based on age differentials, usually only physical forms of force (and typically quite extreme force) are recognized by the rape law as making sex nonconsensual.[31] The *Vinson* case exposed how inequality between a male supervisor and a female subordinate could produce sex that was consensual under this criminal law but unwelcome to the woman—hence unequal under sex discrimination law. In Mechelle Vinson's case, sex forced by inequality was found illegal.[32] Morality's "consent" was thereby exposed as consistent with inequality, as a fictional synonym for desire or choice but consistent with forced sex all along. "Unwelcomeness" was correspondingly framed as consent's equality-based, non-double-talking, alternative. The doctrine of unwelcomeness *could* become what the doctrine of consent is now: a pretend stand-in for desire and choice that in application means its opposite, sex the woman does not desire and in which she has no choice. Whether legal unwelcomeness becomes what it was created to oppose—for example in findings that some women welcome abuse they could not refuse—thus becomes another face of the question of the continuing force of moralism in sexual harassment law.

Whether a woman wants sex is a question of fact, posing the question of who proves what in a case that raises it. Why the so-called hypersensitive woman, who may simply have high dignitary standards, becomes the reviled Puritan instead of a miners' canary or a thin-skulled plaintiff has never been explained. Yet few reported sexual harassment cases reveal unwelcomeness as problematic in practice.[33] After *Harris*, courts generally assess the substance of unwelcomeness as part of whether a hostile environment was "subjectively abusive,"[34] inviting inquiry into the woman's standards and potentially her moral status as defined under male supremacy, rather than remaining focused on the harasser's actions in social context. Courts quite often find abusive conduct unwelcome even when defendants try, in customary moralistic fashion, to smear the plaintiff as a bad woman, hence uninjurable.[35] It is surprising that this attempt to turn inequality into noninjury has not succeeded more often in reported cases. Of concern is moralism may be being smuggled into sexual harassment litigation beneath the surface pretrial,[36] clawing unwelcomeness back to consent, potentially devastating plaintiffs and disabling their resistance to sex forced on them by inequality and excluding them from access to justice in a way that is insulated from appellate review. One creative proposal would require an accused harasser to prove that the woman indicated that she wanted the sexual attention she is suing for, of which affirmative initiation and statements of desire would be good evidence.[37] Certainly, to the extent unwelcomeness is reinterpreted in traditional consent terms—violating *Vinson*, regressing to traditional moralism, and supporting dominant power—sexual harassment law becomes no longer a sex equality instrument.

Strong evidence that sexual harassment law to date is not merely replicating male dominant morality is provided by the virtual nonexistence of a defense of sexual harassing behavior as "speech." If the law of sexual harassment was to protect this form of abuse by protecting one form dominant power takes, sexual harassment would be protected speech, as pornography is under U.S. First Amendment law, and no harm done to women through it would be recognized as illegal.[38] In Canada, by contrast, pornography's harms to adult women and its destructive effects on equality of the sexes, as well as the illegality of hate speech as a form of inequality, are constitutionally recognized.[39] Given the absence of such recognitions in the United States, the fact that U.S. law has so far approached the experience of sexual harassment through pornography by way of its toll on the unequal, rather than through speech—a legally protected artifact for inflicting this abuse by the powerful—is nigh on miraculous. And given the extent to which existing law of freedom of speech in the United States tracks dominant morality by effectively guaranteeing that the powerful (whether based on race, wealth, sex, age, or a combination) get what they want, unlimited by legal equality guarantees, perhaps the strongest evidence available that sexual harassment law does *not* build in power's morality is the fact that calling sexual harassment "speech" has so little traction in sexual harassment law[40] as barely to have surfaced in case law to date. Calling sexual harassment protected speech does not pass the straight-face test. Not yet. Perhaps it only awaits the right facts to call it art.

The major clouds on the immediate horizon are the cases on liability. They, too, can be read as shaped by a moralistic undertow. Under traditional moral rules, sexual harassment qua sexual is deemed an individual and private act, presumptively exempt from public accountability, not an act that conventional morality is comfortable referring to public authorities or attributing to group membership or to institutional entities. Intimacy guarantees impunity, and the more power the perpetrator has, the more his so-called intimacy insulates him from account. By extension, forms of violation that happen to women as women, especially the intimate kind, are deemed personal and private and cultural; forms of violation that happen also to men are more likely to be called public and institutional and political, eventually. Once the group-membership hurdle was cleared in considering sexual harassment sex-based, the accountability question loomed. In the last quarter of the twentieth century, the center of gravity in U.S. sexual harassment litigation shifted from a dispute over whether sexual harassment, if it happened, is legally sex-based to a contest over whether, given that it happened, anyone will be held responsible for it.

For decades, it has been assumed in U.S. law that if an institutional actor discriminated, the institution discriminated; if the act was discriminatory, the employer was accountable for it. In one narrowing move, many courts have now held that individual perpetrators cannot be held responsible under Title VII if they are not the employer.[41] Since Title IX arises under the Spending Clause, monitoring a contractual relation between Congress and recipient entities, only institutional recipients can be defendants,[42] focusing explicitly the question of what actions put the school on the hook. It is no accident that the Title VII cases establishing that individuals were not liable for discrimination under it were brought for sexual harassment rather than for any other kind of discrimination: traditional morality deems sex quintessentially personal and as such exempt from public accountability. It is also no accident that the hurdles sexual harassment plaintiffs must clear for institutional liability in either work or school are now distinct in kind and higher in height from those any other kind of discrimination plaintiff must clear. Again, sex is morally regarded as quintessentially personal, making it uniquely difficult to attribute responsibility for it to entities. As neither Title VII nor Title IX yet runs to individual perpetrators, and institutional entities often do not meet the Court's stringent (and often unlikely) prerequisites for so-called vicarious liability,[43] current Supreme Court doctrine restricts employer or educational institution accountability so that sexual harassment by legal definition can happen and no one will be held liable for it. Under these conditions, sexual harassment can be a violation without a violator, a legal injury without a legal remedy.

The cases on liability thus track traditional morality in a number of ways. Institutions that are oblivious to what is taking place on their watch tend to be insulated from responsibility. The implicit assumption seems to be that if the institution does not know, it cannot be bad, so the victim is not injured, or at least no injury of inequality is attributable to the institution. See no evil, hear no evil, incur no liability. Apart from the disconnection between the morality-based intent requirement and the unequal consequences that flow regardless of intent, the rationale for why institutions are assumed not responsible for what goes on under their aegis remains murky and elusive—particularly in the workplace, where the existence of a liability rule for sexual harassment that is different from other forms of employment discrimination has never been explained. Giving more legal power to the more socially powerful, adult working women, and less legal power to the less socially powerful, schoolgirls, the liability cases also track conventional morality by making it more difficult for children in schools to hold school districts accountable for their sexual harassment than it is for working women to hold their employers accountable for theirs.[44] These rules, by operating in reality counter to traditional morality's protectionist protestations, but consistent with its predilections for power, go far to subvert the equality principles established in the substance of the claim, smuggling conventional morality's unequal power relations in through the back door of liability.

Under the guise of a liability ruling, the Supreme Court holding in the *Ellerth* case, for example, altered the substantive law of sexual harassment for the worse. There it held that a threat of a quid pro quo followed by a constructive discharge—a woman's having to leave her job because it was discriminatorily unbearable—was what the Court termed an "incomplete" quid pro quo.[45] Under the EEOC Guidelines from 1980 through 1998, proposing an exchange of sex for a job indulgence was actionable in itself. In the language of the guidelines: "Unwelcome sexual advances, requests for sexual favors, and other verbal or physical conduct of a sexual nature constitute sexual harassment *when* submission to such conduct is made either explicitly or implicitly a term or condition of an individual's employment."[46] Most courts held accordingly, whether or not employment consequences followed from having or not having sex.[47] Before *Ellerth*, a threat of a quid pro quo, meaning an offer or a demand to exchange sex for employment benefits, was a quid pro quo. *Ellerth* rendered sexual threats, unless sufficiently severe or pervasive to create a hostile environment, mere puffery.

Kim Ellerth's supervisor, in a sexualized context, told her that he could "make your life very hard or very easy" on the job, and followed up by making it very hard for the sexually recalcitrant Ms. Ellerth; later he said, as he rubbed her knees at her promotion interview, that he hesitated about promoting her because she was not "loose enough" for him.[48] Rather than recognizing such sexual conditions on work as actionable discrimination, hanging like Damocles' sword over only some employees because the supervisors' power was being heterosexually deployed, the Supreme Court took the view that until the quid completes the quo, or the environment is made severely or pervasively hostile, sexual threats do no harm of discrimination at all. The case thus raised and disposed of, but barely confronted, the basic question of the nature of sexual harassment's harm—specifically of whether the employee in and at work, or only the employee's work, attracts the law's equality protection. It also raises the question of the line between the injury and its damages.

One might say that a quid pro quo statement is by definition a severe incident, making the workplace hostile. Perhaps courts will take this view. But sexual threats by superiors are also arguably injuries of sex discrimination in themselves, whether or not work is affected.[49] It may make sense to treat undelivered-upon sexual threats by coworkers under hostile environment rules, but with workplace superiors as perpetrators, a sexual threat is effectively delivered upon when uttered. As a result of the supervisor's power, the threat surrounds the worker each and every day. As Judge Cudahy noted concurring in *Jansen*, the Seventh Circuit companion case to *Ellerth*, "quid pro quo is always a creature of power," presenting "the classic paradigm of powerful males forcing their wills on vulnerable females" whereby a "supervisor acts with actual or apparent authority when he promises employment goodies or threatens their withdrawal to extract sexual 'cooperation.'"[50] From the moment it is uttered by a supervisor, a quid pro quo statement imposes a sex-discriminatory condition of work. Such conditions are facially prohibited by Title VII's language. They are also what makes the loss of a job when a worker leaves be considered a constructive discharge rather than a voluntary quit. In *Ellerth*, by contrast, it is as if only the job interest, not the person in the job, is protected from sex discriminatory conditions. In life, workers are harassed when harassed, not only when the consequences of that harassment further mature. In *Ellerth*, the Court did not explain why women workers should have to wait for the sword to fall, or fall on it themselves, before having a legal claim for sex discrimination.

In this light, the *Ellerth* ruling reflects a lapse in measuring sexual harassment as an injury on equality terms. It fails to grasp that sexual harassment law protects not only one's work (the quo) but also a person's equality in and at work. The same lapse is visible in the Court's differential liability rules that favor liability for sexual harassment that creates "tangible employment loss." Both *Faragher* and *Ellerth* make employers responsible for losses of this kind regardless of whether the victim reports, while requiring reports when the incident creates no tangible employment loss. This distinction is inadequate if it is not only a person's work but a person's equality at work, analogously not only their grades but their learning process in education, that civil rights laws exist to protect. *Ellerth* may also be read as reflecting the moral view that sexual threats in themselves are not bad enough to be illegal until they are delivered upon through employment losses. The statutory question, however, is whether such threats, executed or not, discriminate against an individual in terms or conditions of employment on the basis of sex. Is there any doubt that quid pro quo threats do? A quid pro quo threat, from the moment uttered, is arguably a facially discriminatory "term" of employment as well as a discriminatory "condition," severe by definition. After *Ellerth*, the statement of a supervisor that "I haven't forgotten your review, it's on my desk," while patting his crotch, is either a single incident sufficiently severe to constitute a hostile environment or it is now legally nothing.[51] One wonders if a noose hanging over an African American's workstation now must be used before it is actionable, or if a company is still liable for the fact that it is there.[52]

In the last quarter of the twentieth century, it was notably women's public accusations of sexual misdeeds by politically powerful men, not primarily cases in court, that seismically rocked public consciousness, although they would have been unlikely without the backdrop of liability for sexual harassment. The Thomas-Hill hearings of 1991 and the Clinton-Lewinsky affair of 1998 provided a field day for moralists of all stripes and decisively shaped sexual harassment thinking and adjudication. In both situations, men with power among men were challenged by other powerful men for sexual misuse of their power relative to women who had less power—far less—than they did. In neither circumstance did the affected woman sue or say that she had been sexually harassed. In both situations, the facts may or may not qualify as sexual harassment under law. In Professor Hill's case, the alleged abuse may or may not have constituted an illegally hostile environment when it happened because hostile environment law barely existed. In Ms. Lewinsky's case, the sex was apparently welcome, although the difference in power between the parties was extreme. In neither case was the man held liable for what he was said to have done. Yet both cases produced firestorms that consumed first the right in defense of Judge Thomas, then the left in defense of President Clinton, in a rethinking of whether sexual harassment—formally charged in neither instance—should be actionable. As sympathy for the exposed men surged across the political spectrum, moral outrage that their so-called private lives could be interrogated fed a resurgent defense of the sexual as such. Critique of inequality in sex was submerged, drowned.[53] The fallout is not over.

Had it not been for the development of sexual harassment law, it seems fair to say that Professor Anita Hill's testimony, exploding national and global consciousness on the issue, would unlikely have happened. Yet the closest controlling case to hers—the breakthrough case of Sandra Bundy holding that sexually hostile working environments were actionable as sex discrimination—may well have been too fragile, isolated, and recent to have reliably helped Professor Hill when it was handed down around the time of the events to which she testified in the hearings.[54] Without her testimony before the Senate and the nation, Bill Clinton may not have been elected, as women enraged at Professor Hill's treatment by the Senate may have supplied his margin of victory. Without sexual harassment law, the impeachment of President Clinton, and the events surrounding it, would also not have unfolded as they did. It all began with Paula Jones's 1994 allegations of sexual harassment and proceeded fueled by, among other things, a heightened sensitivity to the place of extreme social inequality in sex that the law against sexual harassment focused, although most women continue to have sexual relations with men who have more power in society than they do.

When Paula Jones accused Bill Clinton of sexually harassing her,[55] and the Supreme Court allowed her case to proceed while he was in office,[56] the rules of power suddenly no longer outranked the rule of law, as they have since time immemorial. Droit du seigneur died, at least momentarily. Men could no longer rely on the informal (meaning real) power system safeguarded by traditional morality to get them out of the rules for treatment of women that the formal (meaning legal) power system of equality law prescribed. Panic set in. What used to be called indecent exposure by one's ultimate workplace superior, coupled with a demand for oral sex and a guarded threat to keep it all quiet—Ms. Jones's allegations—was allowed to proceed toward trial in a case brought by the woman subordinate subjected to it. The alleged perpetrator was no longer just a charming roué. He was a potential violator of human rights. The fact that he was the

President of the United States did not exempt him. This represented real change.

What Professor Hill's allegations contributed to national consciousness on the subject of sexual harassment, the dismissal of Paula Jones's case for legal insufficiency[57] went a long way toward undermining. Given that what happened to Professor Hill was publicly perceived as sexual harassment, and what happened to Paula Jones was legally deemed not to be, it is worth observing that the acts that Paula Jones alleged—including penile exposure, physical contact, and threats—were arguably both more severe and more certainly within then-existing legal standards for sexual harassment than were the acts that Professor Hill alleged at the time that they occurred.

Under existing precedent, Paula Jones's case should have been permitted to go to trial on her quid pro quo allegations at the least, and probably on her hostile environment claims as well. The record documented that other women (specifically Gennifer Flowers) who had sex with Governor Clinton had received employment benefits.[58] This supported the issue of material fact as to whether Paula Jones was denied a job benefit as a result of her failure to have the sex Mr. Clinton proposed. Of the quid pro quo, I observed in 1979, "men with power to affect women's careers allow sexual factors to make a difference. So the threats are serious: those who do not comply are disadvantaged in favor of those who do."[59] Paula Jones allegedly did not receive a job benefit because she did not submit to sex, as evidenced by the fact that other women of record in the case did receive job benefits when they did. Although courts are not as clear as they might be on this question, one district court in dicta suggested that, under similar circumstances, if a woman plaintiff's employer "rewarded others in the office for their response to his action, she may indeed have faced an implied quid pro quo situation."[60] Supposing *Ellerth* must be satisfied, the failure to give the benefit "completes" the quid pro quo.

Although Paula Jones said sexual touching was forced on her, its accomplishment a forced submission, she did not submit to the particular sex act of fellatio demanded. She did, for a time, submit to the silence allegedly demanded of her: "You're a smart girl. Let's keep this between ourselves."[61] This submission may bring her circumstances in line with other submission cases in which quid pro quo has been authoritatively found.[62] Jones's case also did not present the contraindicating factors commonly used to deny a finding of quid pro quo in otherwise similar cases. Unlike in those cases, in her case there were threats at the time of the request;[63] she could reasonably have believed that he had the power to affect her job conditions;[64] and she took the implications of threat seriously.[65] Moreover, the trial court's conclusion to the contrary, Ms. Jones did allege that adverse employment consequences flowed from her rejection of Bill Clinton's sexual advances: less challenging work assignments, a moved and less favorable work location, work by herself, an unpleasant working environment, and no work at all.[66] Such conditions have been found to be tangible enough to support a quid pro quo claim in other sexual harassment cases.[67] Finally, Mr. Clinton's requirement that Ms. Jones keep silent about his actions denied her access to a grievance process without fear of reprisals, an employment detriment in itself. A jury should have been permitted to judge the credibility of her factual allegations on these quid pro quo issues.

Arguably, Paula Jones also had a case for a hostile environment as a matter of law. Her version of the central incident included a superior's unwelcome touching of a subordinate's intimate body parts coupled with an attempted kiss, indecent exposure, and an unwelcome sexual demand or proposition. The term "harassment" may connote to some a continuing course of conduct, as when the Third Circuit held that hostile work environments must be "pervasive and regular."[68] However, the U.S. Supreme Court's formulation of the hostile environment sexual harassment claim has squarely recognized in the disjunctive the "severe or pervasive" harassment that makes an abusive working environment actionable. This leaves room for a single incident of severe harassment alone to be enough.[69] The Court's subsequent dictum that "isolated incidents (unless extremely serious) will not amount to discriminatory changes in the terms or conditions of employment,"[70] while raising the bar on the severity of actionable isolated incidents, served further to underline the possibility that isolated incidents can be actionable in themselves if serious enough. Hundreds of acts of sexual assault were alleged in *Meritor*; two on one occasion were alleged in *Brzonkala*, where the Fourth Circuit held that "the rapes themselves created a hostile environment" for the plaintiff at school.[71] Awaiting authoritative clarification, some lower courts have thought single incidents of harassment per se insufficient to constitute hostile working environments.[72] Others have affirmed that a single discriminatory act can be enough, if it is sufficiently severe.[73] The question is, how severe is severe enough?

In *Clinton v. Jones*, Judge Susan Weber Wright found that the alleged incident, if true, "was certainly boorish and offensive" but not "one of those exceptional cases in which a single incident of sexual harassment, such as an assault, was deemed sufficient to state a claim of hostile work environment sexual harassment."[74] It is as if Judge Wright, rather than assessing whether the acts were unequal on the basis of sex, assimilated sexual harassment back to tort or criminal standards. As with criminal law, the injury in *Jones* was not assessed in light of the relative power of the parties. As with tort law, its gravamen was moral outrage rather than employment equality. The moralism of this framing resonates with cases brought as both sexual harassment and intentional infliction of emotional distress or substantive due process together. In those cases, in analytic bleed-through, courts often hold that sexual incidents, while deplorable, are not outrageous and shocking enough to qualify as these torts.[75] Similarly, instead of measuring the severity of Paula Jones's allegations by sex equality standards—asking whether the challenged activity was gendered unequal or whether it was part of the context of subordination of women as a sex or whether men in that workplace had to work under similar conditions or whether sex equality at work could be achieved if such acts were tolerated—Judge Wright seems to have asked whether the acts were bad.

It was the wrong question, and took place in the context of a wider and equally legally irrelevant social discussion of whether Ms. Jones and her supporters were bad. Liberal moralists in particular contended that if Clinton was bad in whatever he did to Jones, the motives of his accusers were also bad in making or pursuing the claim, so it all cancelled out. Liberal moralists focused on whether Jones was in the grip of the evil right in claiming to have been discriminated against. Conservative moralists tended to focus on how bad Clinton was rather than on whether the acts he was accused of were sex-discriminatory. In the motives morass, whether or not a woman had been discriminated against, whether or not sexual harassment—inequality on the basis of sex—had occurred, seemed not to matter much to either side. The impeachment debates foregrounded Monica Lewinsky, who did not claim forced sex and raised moral but not legal issues of equality, rather than Paula Jones, who did raise legal issues of inequality and did claim a form of forced sex. In this context, in the recurrent reflex of judges who morally decry acts while ensuring nothing will be done about them, on Judge Wright's moral scale—not a transparent one but clearly not calibrated to zero tolerance—the incident with Paula Jones became not bad enough.[76]

One virtually unnoticed case makes vividly clear that *Clinton v. Jones* may be confined to its facts and turned on the power of a powerful man rather than on legal standards applied to factual allegations. In 2001, the Eighth Circuit affirmed two rulings by Judge Susan Webber Wright in the sexual harassment case that Sherry Moring brought under Section 1983 against the Arkansas Department of Correction for the behavior of her supervisor, Gary Smith.[77] Smith had engaged her in a conversation of a sexual nature while they were on a business trip, then appeared uninvited at her hotel room door barely clothed, sat on her bed, touched her thigh, and attempted to kiss her. She asked him to leave and resisted his advance, pushed him back, leaned to the side to avoid him, and locked the door when he left. He also said she "owed" him for her position. Ms. Moring spoke thereafter of the incident often, avoided him, was under stress at her job, and was visibly upset over the incident. She testified that she was afraid and considered his behavior abusive and threatening. Judge Wright denied a defense motion for judgment as a matter of law and a motion for a new trial for abuse of discretion. On appeal, the Eighth Circuit affirmed that a reasonable jury could find that the conduct would not have been directed at a male employee and that it was objectively hostile or abusive. The behavior was sex-based and sufficient to create a hostile working environment as a matter of law. The panel observed that "we are unaware of any rule of law holding that a single incident can never be sufficiently severe to be hostile-work-environment sexual harassment."[78]

Same judge, same statute, same state, same legal doctrine, same appellate circuit. But who ever heard of Mr. Smith? More similar facts are hard to imagine, except that Clinton's sexual aggression was alleged to have been more severe, and no evidence of similar exploits by Mr. Smith were noted. No one accused Ms. Moring of being trailer trash or a tool of the right. She got a jury trial and no national press. She won.

Which is not to say that *Clinton v. Jones* did not have substantial effects. If, in the wake of the Hill-Thomas fiasco, sexual harassment was transformed from a backroom joke into a weapon of politics as usual, after the Clinton-Jones-Lewinsky debacle, a cadre of liberal moralists seems to have decided that sex pressured by power of position is just sex,[79] not sexual exploitation or discrimination. In this respect, the discussion reverted to square one, to the time before sexual harassment was recognized as a legal claim. These critics, like their forebears who resisted sexual harassment's being recognized as sex discrimination at all, and on many of the same grounds, never seem to have considered that their position might imply a critique of sex. Rather, they argued in essence that since sexual harassment and sex are indistinguishable, the world should be made safe for sexual harassment. This missed the now rather obvious point that the sex they defend, sex that merges with sexual harassment as if that is all the sex there is, is unequal.

Epitomized by the slogan "All sex is harassment,"[80] the view seems to be that since women and men are gender unequals, all sex between them must, if sexual harassment law is right, be sex discrimination. Sexual harassment law is criticized in the name of sex; sex is not interrogated for an inequality that it and sexual harassment might share. If sex must be equal to be nondiscriminatory, they suggest, voices rising, the end of sex is at hand. Passing over the fact that there are no sex equality laws applicable anywhere in civil society except the islands of workplace and school, their point is not to try to equalize the sexes in the name of sexual mutuality and intimacy, or to provide equality rights that would promote equality in sexual relations. It is, instead, to try to make the world safe for sexual harassment by putting the political genie back into the personal bottle, de-exposing sexual exploitation by making it just another sexual practice, thus once again private, concealed, apolitical, and legally exempt.[81] The alternative of producing real sexual equality—the point of sexual harassment law—seems never to have crossed their minds.

Although Clarence Thomas was appointed to the Supreme Court, Anita Hill galvanized and inspired women. Seeing that their treatment was at least as egregious as hers, women swelled the numbers of complaints to the EEOC by coming forward by the thousands.[82] Whether women whose treatment is as egregious as Paula Jones's, who might well interpret the dismissal of her case as the reimposition of the old moral hierarchy of who counts and who does not, will stop resisting, turn their backs on the courts, and return to silent subordination and despair remains to be seen.

The next twenty-five years could go one of two ways. The last twenty-five could be historicized as a "sex panic," sexual harassment law trivialized and distorted and invalidated into a hysteria and a witch hunt, sexual harassment itself diagnosed epiphenomenally for why it was spoken about rather than why it became possible finally to speak of it. Like all sexual harassment unremedied, prostitution could become ever more explicitly the model and mold for women's lives, women's life chances depending ever more entirely on their relation to power among men. Another possibility is that sexual harassment law becomes more meaningful in the domains to which it applies and extends to hierarchies other than work and school—perhaps to relationships like cleric-congregant, doctor-patient, lawyer-client, even to spouses and domestic partners and between parents and children. It may become more possible to address situations where the sex is the work. Understanding sexuality as a system may become standard intellectual equipment, its laws of motion seen as being as determinative, and as taken for granted, as, say, economics. Those who report sexual abuse might no longer be targeted for destruction. Inequality may be eroticized less. If so, sexual harassment law will have been a tool in the liberation of women and a material forerunner—clear of today's sentimentality and denial—of a real equality-based sexual morality.

17

Disputing Male Sovereignty

On *United States v. Morrison*

In 2000, in *United States v. Morrison*,[1] The Violence Against Women Act (VAWA)[2] civil remedy provision making gender-motivated violence federally actionable became one of only two federal laws against discrimination to that date to be invalidated by the United States Supreme Court since Reconstruction.[3] In passing the VAWA, Congress sought to remedy well-documented inadequacies in existing laws against domestic violence and sexual assault—acts of which women are the principal victims and men the principal perpetrators—by providing a federal civil cause of action for sex discrimination that victims could use directly against perpetrators in state or federal court. Congress passed the statute under the authority of both the Commerce Clause[4] and the Enforcement Clause of the Fourteenth Amendment.[5] In a one-two punch, the 5-to-4 *Morrison* majority held that neither clause constitutionally authorized the VAWA.[6] Congress's commerce power, the Court said, reaches only those private acts that are "economic in nature,"[7] which violence against women, despite its impact on interstate commerce, was deemed not to be.[8] Congress's equality power, the Court ruled, is limited to addressing state acts, a limit the VAWA, in reaching what were termed private actors and private acts, was found to transgress.[9]

On its most obvious level, *Morrison* represented a high-water mark of this Court's specific notion of federalism. Shield and sword, this sweeping doctrine and sensibility protects states as sovereign both in dominating their traditional legal domains and in avoiding accountability for their acts.[10] In *Morrison*, this doctrine exceeded its previous limits to invalidate a federal law passed to fill a void the states had left in an area of their traditional prerogatives. When it has commanded a majority, this sensibility has damaged equality rights in particular, including by defining state responsibility for equality violations extremely narrowly.[11] *Morrison* went further still by preventing the federal government from legislating equality rights in an area that states have inadequately protected.

First published 114 *Harvard Law Review* 135 (2000).

But there may be a yet more direct relation between the denial of equality and the Court's new view of the formal doctrine of federalism. On a deeper level of law and politics, and seen against a historical backdrop of the use of federalism to deny racial equality and enforce white supremacy, *Morrison* can be seen to employ ostensibly gender-neutral tools to achieve a substantive victory for the socially unequal institution of male dominance. Read substantively, *Morrison* is not an abstract application of neutral institutional priorities but a concrete refusal to allow Congress to redress violence against women—a problem of substantive sex inequality that the Court declined to see as one of economic salience or national dimension. In *Morrison*, the Court revived and deployed against women as such the odious "states' rights" doctrine, the principal legal argument couched in institutional abstraction for the substantive maintenance of slavery that was used to deny equality rights on racial grounds well into the twentieth century. Combined with the Court's evolving equal protection jurisprudence—the "intent" requirement, which has made it increasingly difficult to hold states responsible for equal protection violations committed by state actors[12]—*Morrison* leaves women who are denied the effective equal protection of state criminal laws against battering and rape without adequate legal recourse.

In this wider perspective, the Supreme Court, having already kept women from holding states to effective standards of sex equality protection in its equality jurisprudence, moved in *Morrison* to preclude Congress from helping to fill the gap the Court had left. Doubly shut out, violated women were, in essence, told by the *Morrison* majority—a majority that did not mention them once—that this legal system not only need not, but by virtue of its structural design may not, where gender-based violence is concerned, deliver meaningful equal protection of the laws to them.

I. Background

The *Morrison* majority did not contest what Congress had found during its four years of hearings on the VAWA: violence against women is a sex-based abuse that the states have long failed adequately to address. "Violence against women," a phrase used by the women's movement since the 1970s, became in the name of the VAWA a shorthand for "gender-motivated violence," the legal term of art encompassing violent acts directed against men as well as women that are based on gender, the social meaning of sex. In passing the VAWA in 1994, Congress intended to put the ability to address sex-based violence into the hands of its survivors, in order more effectively to remedy and stop violence against them.

Crucially, for the first time in United States history, the VAWA established "zero tolerance" for sex-based violence as a matter of public policy when it provided that "[a]ll persons within the United States shall have the right to be free from crimes of violence motivated by gender."[13] By contrast, existing laws against violence that is based on sex, by omission as well as by pattern of practice, seem to embody a margin of toleration, project an aura of lassitude, exude a sense in enforcement that some aggression against women by men is inevitable. Legal institutional processes of enforcement are so imprinted with denial of sexual abuse—both its normality and effective impunity, especially when committed by men with power among men—that it is as if the laws do not mean what they say. The VAWA openly repudiated such systemically discriminatory habits.

Congress further perceived that the body of law that had pervasively and dramatically failed women subjected to violence by men needed not only a national floor of effectiveness, a uniform standard below which it could not fall, but also a conceptual overhaul from the ground up. Law defined the crime of rape long before women were permitted to vote or to serve on juries. Members of the group more likely to perpetrate sexual assault have written its legal rules, excluding from that process those more likely to be victimized by it. To be effective as well as democratic, the VAWA could not simply federalize preexisting criminal or tort law.

In a new departure, the VAWA's civil rights remedy, written with women's direct participation, placed violence against women within the law of sex discrimination, recognizing that violence against women is gender-based: it happens because those who do it, and those who have it done to them, are members of social groups defined by their sex. The VAWA was the first legislation anywhere to recognize that rape may be an act of sex inequality, its injury a violation of human status on the basis of membership in a gender group. Locating acts of gender-based violence under the rubric of civil rights, identifying the group grounds of a socially based injury, freed survivors from the acontextualized and stigmatic standards of prior criminal and tort law applied to these acts—laws enacted and interpreted when women had no public voice. After an extensive and detailed empirical investigation, Congress produced legislation against battering and rape that began to fit the facts of violence against women for the first time.

Because it was civil, Section 13981 of the VAWA by design placed the power of the state in the hands of those victimized by sex-based violence. It made perpetrators directly accountable to survivors, potentially intervening in the balance of power between the sexes by empowering rather than protecting the victims of sex-based violence. The civil remedy allowed survivors to initiate and control their own litigation against sex-based violation instead of leaving them at the mercy of police or prosecutorial discretion. Moving beyond incarceration as an outcome—which often accomplishes little beyond the brutalization (much of it sexual) of perpetrators, promoting brutality rather than change—the VAWA's civil remedy offered injunctive relief and damages: levers, resources, and authoritative findings to value and restore survivors and to potentially alter perpetrators' behavior.

In all these respects, the Violence Against Women Act took a historic stand and hopeful step toward free and safe lives for women as equal citizens of this nation. Like most legislation, it also bore the marks of compromise. It did not address all sex-based violence, but only those acts that met a particular mental requirement: those that could be proven to be gender-motivated, meaning wholly or partially produced by gender "animus."[14] How the mental element would have been interpreted—for instance, the extent to which a perpetrator's thoughts could exonerate his acts, or his thoughts would have been inferred from his acts—was not clear. Whether a mental element was even appropriate is questionable. In fact, the animus requirement was added only because the Judicial Conference conditioned its withdrawal of opposition to the bill on its insertion.[15] In practice, it would have excluded many victims of rape and battering from seeking relief in court: not because the acts against them were not violent, not because their injury was not inflicted because they were women, and not because adequate relief had already been provided, but solely because evidence of the mental element, uniquely elusive of proof and under defendants' control, would foreseeably be unavailable in many cases. Thus were many women, through action required by judges even before the law was passed, purposefully kept from access to relief for violence committed against them because they were women. In addition, because its reach was further limited to acts already recognized as felonies under state or federal law,[16] the VAWA was constrained in advance by the very laws it was passed to supersede.[17] In thus building deference to federalism in, cutting many violated women out, it foreshadowed rather than precluded its demise.

Christy Brzonkala's case, which became *United States v. Morrison*,[18] typified the congressional findings on sexual assault both in the facts of her assault and in her institution's responses to it. In 1994, Ms. Brzonkala, while a student at Virginia Polytechnic Institute, was allegedly gang-raped by two varsity football players at her school, Antonio Morrison and James

Crawford.[19] Within half an hour of meeting her, after she twice said "no" to their proposals of sex, the men, by her account, took turns pinning her down and forcibly penetrating her vaginally. After raping her, Mr. Morrison said to her: "you better not have any fucking diseases." Within months of the rape, Mr. Morrison announced publicly that he "like[d] to get girls drunk and fuck the shit out of them." As often happens, the two men received social support for what they had done. Mr. Crawford, Ms. Brzonkala later learned, was told by another male student athlete that he "should have killed the bitch."[20] Although the crime was reported to the police and a grand jury investigated it, no indictment issued.[21]

The school held two rounds of hearings, replete—as is reasonably common in such settings—with unequal treatment of Ms. Brzonkala compared with the accused perpetrators.[22] Relying on the school officials' assurances that they believed her, Ms. Brzonkala put herself in the hands of the institution and followed their advice, even as they did not always fulfill their promises to her and the perpetrators had their own lawyers. In both hearings, Mr. Morrison testified that he had had sexual contact with Ms. Brzonkala although she had twice told him "no." He was found to have sexually assaulted her. His sentence to a two-semester suspension was upheld on internal appeal. After the second de novo hearing—held as if the first hearing had not happened but, the school maintained, only to cover a procedural technicality—the charges were, without notice or explanation to Ms. Brzonkala, changed from "sexual assault" to "using abusive language." Then, again without notice to Ms. Brzonkala, Mr. Morrison's punishment was set aside—a fact she learned in a newspaper—and he was welcomed back to the campus on a full athletic scholarship. Unable to continue with her education under these circumstances, becoming suicidal and depressed as many raped women do, Ms. Brzonkala withdrew from school[23] and sued the perpetrators under the Violence Against Women Act.[24]

Like Christy Brzonkala, most rape victims are women or girls.[25] There are many of them. One in four women in America reports having been raped,[26] with 44 percent reporting having been subjected to completed or attempted rape at least once in their lives.[27] Almost one in ten women between the ages of fifteen and forty-four who has had sexual intercourse reports that her first act of sexual intercourse was "not voluntary."[28] These figures count women ever raped, not rapes. Like Christy Brzonkala, many young women are raped while they are at a college or university. In one large probability sample, eighty-three women in every thousand attending college or university in a six-month period in 1987 reported being raped.[29]

Again like Christy Brzonkala, most rape victims share a relational context, or some degree of acquaintance, with their rapists. The law's marital rape exclusion, once firmly ubiquitous and recently largely eroded but not entirely extinguished,[30] is only the most explicit example in criminal law of the latitude for force in sex that is often given to an accused rapist according to the degree of intimacy he has, or has had, with his victim. Only approximately half of the states in the United States completely abolished the marital rape exemption by the late 1990s.[31] Among the other half, special exemptions from prosecution existed if the parties were not living apart, were not legally separated, or had not filed for divorce or an order of protection. Some states exempt husbands from prosecution for first-degree rape; some require the wife to report the rape within a short period of time. Another group exempts husbands who rape wives under the age of consent or wives with physical or mental disabilities.[32] Congress had these statutes squarely in view in providing that the VAWA applied to acts "that would constitute a felony . . . but for the relationship between the person who takes such action and the individual against whom such action is taken."[33]

Unlike the rapes of Christy Brzonkala, most sexual assaults remain entirely unreported. This is because the victims anticipate, with reason, that the authorities will not believe them or that they will be revictimized in the legal process. Sexual-abuse survivors dread the legal system.[34] Women are routinely disbelieved, humiliated, harassed, and shunned as a result of reporting sexual assault to officials. The police practice of "unfounding," in which police decide that a rape report is without foundation, resembles Virginia Polytechnic's treatment of Ms. Brzonkala's allegations in changing Mr. Morrison's conviction from sexual assault to verbal insult.[35] Many women who bring rape charges feel violated by their encounter with the justice system: "The second rape is exemplified most dramatically when the survivor is strong enough, brave enough, and even naive enough to believe that if she decides to prosecute her offender, justice will be done. It is a rape more devastating and despoiling than the first."[36]

Most rape, like Christy Brzonkala's, is unremedied.[37] Most reported rapes are not prosecuted. Most prosecuted rapes do not result in convictions. Sentences for rapes are often short. The vast majority of rapists are never held to account for their acts in any way.[38]

The most atypical feature of Christy Brzonkala's rapes is that they were interracial—she is white and the men accused of raping her are African American—and the assailants went unpunished. Most rapes occur within rather than across racial groups,[39] even as the American legal system has often had an exaggeratedly punitive reaction to accusations of rape of white women by Black men.[40] The more typical pattern is that Black men are stereotyped as sexual predators and found to have raped white women whether they did or not.[41] When it granted two African American men impunity for having raped a white woman, the *Morrison* case became exceptional in its race-neutral application of misogyny's standard rules.

In receiving no relief through the criminal justice system, Christy Brzonkala was typical of most victims of rape. Social attitudes toward rape victims may have improved subtly beginning in the 1970s,[42] but rape law reform efforts in the United States in the 1970s and 1980s produced little or no detectable improvement in reporting, arrest, or conviction rates,[43] although the seriousness with which the system treats simple as opposed to aggravated rape may have improved slightly.[44] It was this entrenched lack of progress that the VAWA sought to address,[45] this tide that Christy Brzonkala was swimming against, this system that Chief Justice Rehnquist evoked for the *Morrison* Court when he wrote, in denying her access to a remedy, "[i]f the allegations here are true, no civilized system of justice could fail to provide her a remedy."[46]

II. The Decision

Chief Justice Rehnquist, writing for the majority in an opinion joined by Justices O'Connor, Scalia, Kennedy, and Thomas, cast violence against women as noneconomic, in the language of commerce, and as local, in the language of federalism, hence constitutionally inappropriate for federal legislation. Justice Souter and Justice Breyer, in separate dissents, powerfully contested the majority's Commerce Clause ruling;[47] only Justice Breyer, in brief but deft terms, doubted its Fourteenth Amendment holding.[48] The Court neither questioned the congressional finding that violence against women is a major social problem inadequately addressed by state authorities nor took up the issue whether the states' record in addressing gender-based violence constitutes sex discrimination by Fourteenth Amendment standards. The majority expressed repeated concern for the fate of other laws deemed local in nature and for the governmental balance between state and federal powers if the VAWA was upheld. For the fate of violated women if it was invalidated, no concern at all was expressed.

A. Of Economy and Locality

The *Morrison* majority found gender-motivated crimes of violence beyond Congress's power to regulate under the Commerce Clause because such acts, in its view, were not "economic in nature"[49] and lacked "commercial character."[50] The Court also held that to legislate federally against gender-based assault would violate the "distinction between what is truly national and what is truly local,"[51] exceeding the constitutional bounds on the federal legislative power and disturbing federal-state comity.

With respect to the Court, there is no economy in nature. The Court's economic essentialism devalued women's material activity and contributions and erased the documented financial losses caused by women's violation. Its narrow notion of the economic served specifically to evade the massive congressional record evidencing the impact of gender-based violence on women's economic opportunities, including lost work, lost productivity, lost mobility, and medical and other costs and expenses.[52] Justice Souter strongly protested the "devaluation" of Congress's conclusions that gender-based violence affected commerce in the majority's embrace of a narrowly categorical approach toward what was commerce and what was not.[53]

Stripping violence against women of its amply evidenced economic impact also provided a pretext for not applying the empirical test for regulation of commerce established in 1964 in the *Heart of Atlanta Motel* case: whether the activity involves commerce in "more States than one"[54] and "has a real and substantial relation to the national interest."[55] That satisfied, Congress was also allowed to legislate to right "a moral and social wrong"[56]—in *Heart of Atlanta Motel*, it was racial discrimination in public accommodation—that did not need to be confined to the commercial.[57] The combined evils the VAWA sought to address are strikingly similar. As Justice Souter observed, gender-based violence operates much like racial discrimination in its substantial effect on interstate commerce.[58] Although public accommodations may initially seem more inherently commercial, violence against women has a price as well as a toll, visible once women are seen as active participants in the marketplace. The economic effect of dropping out of school, as Christy Brzonkala did because of her rape, is a case in point.

But violence against women remained, to the *Morrison* Court, noneconomic in essence no matter its economic costs or consequences. The ideologically gendered lenses through which the majority viewed the factual record becomes apparent when comparing the facts of sex-based violence with the facts of *Wickard v. Filburn*,[59] a 1942 case that both Justices Souter and Breyer discussed in their dissents.[60] In *Wickard*, growing wheat at home for home consumption, an activity purposefully outside the stream of commerce and determinedly domestic, was found subject to regulation under the Commerce Clause because, when aggregated, it produced a substantial economic effect.[61] The *Morrison* Court expressly declined to aggregate the documented effects of violence against women into a national impact because it did not see them as economic effects. It rejected what the Court called "the but-for causal chain" in which "every attenuated effect" of violent crime on interstate commerce would have, in the Court's view, permitted Congress "to regulate any crime as long as the nationwide aggregated impact of that crime has substantial effects on employment, production, transit, or consumption."[62]

As a logically prior matter, it was unclear why, if substantiality of effect on commerce was what mattered, the Court confined aggregation to activity considered commercial, yet, if the commercial nature of the activity were what mattered, why its effects need to be aggregated when they are direct.[63] The same logical slip was visible in *Lopez*: "[t]he possession of a gun in a local school zone is in no sense an economic activity that might, through repetition elsewhere, substantially affect any sort of interstate commerce."[64] If an activity is in no sense economic, no amount of repetition makes it so. If, however, its location in the stream of commerce is recognized, the act itself is economic, without regard to aggregate impact. Why impact can change some noneconomic acts into economic ones is a mystery, as Justice Thomas seemed to imply in his concurrence in *Morrison*.[65] Moreover, in *Wickard*, home wheat subtracted from the market. Beyond being simply noncommercial, it replaced what might have been commerce. Precisely by not being in the stream of commerce, home wheat had a direct effect on commerce even without aggregation. There is nothing "attenuated" about the economic impact of rapes that keep women from working or studying, or of battering that keeps women on welfare. Congress found not only that violence against women had a cumulative effect on the national economy, but also that gender-based violence, act by act, individual by individual, disrupts women's lives as producers and consumers in the national marketplace. But women's productive activity was so marginalized by the Court that home-bound growers and eaters of wheat were more imaginably engaged in economic activity than were women removed from active roles in the national economy by sex-based violence. The VAWA record, a record that only had to reasonably support Congress's actions, showed both direct and extended economic impact. The *Morrison* Court saw neither.

Converging with the Court's rejection of the national impact of violence against women in its discussion of the Commerce Clause was the repeated description of sex-based violence as "local" in the Court's discussion of federalism. The fact that violence against women, to the extent it has been legally addressed, has historically been a crime addressed by each locality was used as a reason to refuse to face its society-wide uniformity and national scale. When Justice Souter contested the Court's "step toward recapturing the prior mistakes of the pre-1937 Courts to Commerce Clause review,"[66] specifically referring to its invalidations of federal laws that tempered the abuses of industrialization, he attributed the Court's revival of this long discredited jurisprudence to its interest in the new federalism.[67] Since its 1995 decision in *Lopez* cast doubt on half a century of Commerce Clause jurisprudence,[68] the Court has expressed recurring concern that federal enactments may endanger traditional state legislative preserves and disrupt federal-state relations. The VAWA heightened those fears. Even before it became law, the VAWA's supposed "potential to create needless friction and duplication among the state and federal systems" was publicly attacked by Chief Justice Rehnquist.[69] The *Morrison* majority expressed concern about the Court's future ability to limit congressional power in areas "where States historically have been sovereign"[70] if the VAWA was upheld.

How a federal law that duplicated no state law in theory, design, or remedy, a law with federalism-friendly concurrent jurisdiction[71] that provided merely a supplementary civil option while leaving state criminal remedies in place, threatened to compete with state law was not clarified. How it threatened the states, thirty-six of which supported the provision in the Supreme Court,[72] was also not addressed. However, the Court's slippery slope federalism fears, suggested by its repeated mention of family law,[73] had some basis. Discrimination against women in areas of traditional state regulation is hardly confined to violence. State court awards in divorce cases, for example, on average disadvantage women substantially on dissolution of marriage.[74] What both the decision below by the Fourth Circuit (whose concern for states' rights felt visceral) and the Supreme Court missed was the complicity of the federal courts in this problem. Largely because of the Court's requirement that official discrimination under the Fourteenth Amendment be intentional,[75] little effective constitutional sex equality oversight of state law exists beyond now rare instances of facial discrimination. The result for women has been to leave vast chasms of gender inequality unredressed in areas that "ha[ve] always been"[76] state law.[77] For women, the Fourteenth Amendment's "brooding omnipresence"[78] has been more brooding than present. In its power to interpret the Constitution, the Court has the means to address this problem without invading the prerogatives of states.

Is it any wonder that women seeking sex equality, having been abandoned by states and the federal judiciary alike, would turn to Congress? Divorcing women have no more interest in a federal remedy or forum as such than violated women do; it is the discrimination encountered in some legal forums that impels women to seek justice in others. The Court's federalism discussion, denying them this access, was afflicted by a nominalism similar to that on display in its discussion of commerce. By example, how a rape becomes "purely intrastate"[79] challenges the imagination. A new and compelling case for reconsidering the federal balance was presented by enfranchised mobilized women challenging violence against women as inequality. Women's change in status from silent chattel to full citizen called for questioning systemic norms and substantive law alike.[80] When long ignored, urgent, and pervasive injury, predicated on historic exclusion of a subordinated group from the legal system, reaches the Court for the first time, as it did for violated women in *Morrison*, surely it is inadequate to respond that the laws on the subject have been this way for some time.

Short of such reconsideration, the *Morrison* Court might have found the limit it desired on the commerce rationale in the VAWA's equality purpose by drawing on the Commerce Clause's history in upholding legislation for social equality. The VAWA did not have to be justified under *either* the Commerce Clause *or* the Fourteenth Amendment. A rationale crafted by combining the two could have provided both the basis and the desired limiting construction consistent with the precedents and purposes of both clauses—the Commerce Clause enabling Congress to reach private acts substantially affecting the economy across the nation and the equality clause confining this particular rationale for exercise of legislative authority to equality questions recognized within Section 1. On just such a theory, Justice Douglas, concurring in *Heart of Atlanta Motel*, traced the "dual bases" in commerce and equality of the public accommodations legislation upheld there,[81] observing that, "[i]n determining the reach of an exertion of legislative power, it is customary to read various granted powers together."[82] The VAWA record presented both bases at least as strongly. Justice Goldberg, also concurring in *Heart of Atlanta Motel*, predicated Title II's constitutionality on both the Commerce Clause and Section 5 of the Fourteenth Amendment,[83] as had Congress.[84] The combined rationale could have allayed the Court's expressed worry that if Congress could regulate gender-based murder on grounds of its impact on commerce, it could regulate all murder on the same grounds. The *Heart of Atlanta Motel* majority also could have worried, but did not, that Congress could, on a commerce rationale, prohibit all denials of public accommodation at motels or restaurants. On the combined analysis, a VAWA rationale could, for cases that raise both grounds, have stopped Congress's reach into state law's domains where its federal equality concern ended. Had the VAWA been upheld on both grounds together, the Court's dreaded slope would not slip far.

Instead, the *Morrison* majority revived a long-discredited tradition of striking down socially progressive legislation, a tradition that, in Justice Souter's words, "comes with the pedigree of near-tragedy."[85] This tradition's application to violence against women—something no legal system has ever effectively addressed—comes closer to post-tragedy. Under the majority's approach, Justice Souter predicted a standardless interregnum in commerce cases like the one in obscenity law between *Redrup* and *Miller*,[86] when every sexually explicit book or film was potentially susceptible to Supreme Court review case by case. Strikingly supporting this parallel is the utter indifference to violence against women exhibited in both areas of law. In both, it took violence against women in the facts, and ignoring it in law, to push an already questionable doctrinal structure into breakdown mode. Sex-based violence in reality may raise issues that legal doctrines did not have in mind but elide at their peril.

Under every doctrine it deployed, the Court minimized and domesticated violence against women. Under the Commerce Clause, it had no national impact. Under the rubric of federalism, it was local. Under Section 5 of the Fourteenth Amendment as well, the Court distinguished the VAWA from civil rights laws it found properly limited to localities.[87] But unlike in those cases, violence against women and ineffectual law enforcement against it were found across the country. Moreover, Reconstruction legislation against the Ku Klux Klan and kindred terrorist organizations, legislation that the VAWA more closely parallels, applied nationwide even though most racist terrorism at the time was confined to the South. Gender-based terrorism today is unconfined to any locality. No legal precedent requires a remedy to a nationwide problem be legislated state-by-state—precisely where *Morrison* leaves violated women.

The Court, in its ruling under the Commerce Clause, failed to grasp the gendered structure of violence against women and impunity for it, as well as its devastating and discriminatory material consequences on both the social and legal level. The Fourth Circuit[88] and the *Morrison* majority alike, preoccupied with what upholding the VAWA might do to the federal-state relationship, said nothing about what invalidating the VAWA would do to the male-female relationship. The Court's insistence that violence against women is inherently and intrinsically nonmaterial and nonnational constituted nothing less than a failure to evaluate the traditional division of legislative prerogatives in light of the unprecedented factual record of systemic gender-based inequality before the Court.

B. Of Public and Private

If its Commerce Clause ruling was doctrinally uncompelled as well as lacking in vision, *Morrison* did most damage to women in the long run in its ruling on state action. Stressing understandings of the Fourteenth Amendment contemporaneous with its passage, the *Morrison* Court reiterated that the Amendment historically "erects no shield against merely private conduct," but prohibits only acts of states.[89] The VAWA record—like that in the *Civil Rights Cases*, according to the Court, in that both showed "[t]here were state laws on the books bespeaking equality of treatment, but in the administration of these laws there was discrimination"[90]—was found an insufficient basis in state action to permit a federal remedy. The Court viewed the VAWA's civil remedy as insufficiently "corrective" of state breaches of equality rights, as legislation the *Civil Rights Cases* permitted under Section 5 had to be, or inadequately "prophylactic" to such violations.[91] Faulting the VAWA for visiting no consequences on state officials and for applying "uniformly throughout the Nation," the Court found that the provision lacked "congruence and proportionality between the injury to be prevented or remedied and the means adopted to that end."[92] That is, the fit between the predicate legislative facts of state treatment of gender-based violence and the VAWA's statutory civil remedy was not as close as recent Section 5 cases were said to require.[93]

The *Morrison* majority leaves the impression that history and precedent dictate that all statutes arising under the Fourteenth Amendment do or must address state action. This issue was not as closed as the Court claims, a claim that also obscured the prior question of what is deemed public and private: the question of how state action is defined. As under the Commerce Clause, both history and precedent on this point favored upholding the VAWA, implying that another explanation is needed for the Court's failure to do so.

1. History. Justice Breyer, in dissent, asked the right question: "[w]hy can Congress not provide a remedy against private actors?"[94] The Congress that passed the Fourteenth Amendment clearly intended thereby to ensure the constitutionality of legislation designed to reach racist atrocities committed by one citizen against another that the states were not addressing.[95] Although the text of the Fourteenth Amendment addresses states, Congress incontestably intended to create authority for federal legislation against private as well as state acts that deprived citizens of equal rights on a racial basis.[96] On this point, the *Civil Rights Cases* are closer to having been wrong the day they were decided—and ripe for being overruled today—than to being respectable for contemporaneity and longevity.

One member of the Congressional Committee on Reconstruction in hearings on the Third Enforcement Act in 1871 put the state action point this way:

> The fourteenth amendment of the Constitution also has vested in the Congress of the United States the power, by proper legislation, to prevent any State from depriving any citizen of the United States of the enjoyment of life, liberty, and property. But it is said that this deprivation . . . is not done by the State but by the citizens of the State. But surely, if the fact is as your committee believe and assert it to be, that the State is powerless to prevent such murders and felonies . . . from being daily and hourly committed in every part of the designated States, and if, added to that, comes the inability of the State to punish the crimes after they are committed, then the State has, by its neglect or want of power, deprived the citizens of the United States of protection in the enjoyment of life, liberty, and property as fully and completely as if it had passed a legislative act to the same effect.[97]

The act under consideration, called the Ku Klux Klan Act, and titled "An *Act to enforce the Provisions of the Fourteenth Amendment* to the Constitution of the United States, and for Other Purposes,"[98] provided civil remedies in law or equity for a range of acts undertaken by anyone, official or not, with the goal of denying a citizen the equal protection of the laws. In this Congressman's view, expressed at the time, the failure of states to protect citizens' civil rights "by . . . neglect or want of power" gave Congress authority to legislate to protect those rights.[99]

The testimony in the congressional hearings on the Fourteenth Amendment and its enforcement acts provides a striking parallel to the hearings on the VAWA. In both instances, privately executed but socially systematic terrorism with official impunity was documented to be directed against victims on a group basis. In both, witnesses spoke of many of the same specific acts of sexual and physical violence that had long gone unaddressed due to systematic bias in state law enforcement. Jacobus tenBroek, writing of the hearings that led to and surrounded the passage of the Fourteenth Amendment, could have been describing the VAWA hearings when he wrote: "Witness after witness spoke of beatings and woundings, burnings and killings, as well as deprivations of property and earnings and interference with family relations—and the impossibility of redress or protection except through the United States Army and the Freedmen's Bureau."[100] Except that, for women, the Army has yet to intervene and there still is no Freedwomen's Bureau.

The specific acts targeted by the VAWA were known to occur at the time the Fourteenth Amendment was passed. One contemporaneous account would have fit right into the VAWA hearings in its implicit parallel between race and sex and explicit comprehension that impunity for perpetrators is built into the legal system:

> If he comes home in the dead of the night, and because his wretched slave is asleep, or his supper is not ready at an impossible hour, or, being ready, is not cooked to his liking . . . he should beat and kick and pound his slave, why, of course nobody interferes—it is only a man licking his wife, and he is drunk he is not to blame, and the laws of domicile, the home-and-the-castle and so on, are so sacred that even a policeman may not interfere.[101]

But women were disenfranchised, their voices unheeded or unheard.

The connection between racist and sexist terrorism provides not only a conceptual and historical analogy, but also in many instances a single converged factual reality. A substantial amount of the Ku Klux Klan's violence, the basis for the Third Enforcement Act that became Section 1985(3),[102] was sexual violence that was also racially biased,[103] like some of the violence against women that formed the basis for Section 13981.[104] Klan violence during Reconstruction, like much gender-based violence today, was often highly sexualized, including eroticized whipping, oral rape, genital mutilation, and other forms of sexual torture.[105] "Sex was a central feature of the terror of Reconstruction, a salient marker of the tremendous upheaval witnessed during those years in relations of race, gender, and power."[106] Not only was the VAWA's mental element, "animus," taken from judicial interpretations of Section 1985(3) in race cases;[107] fused sex-and-race–based violence was expressly actionable under Section 13981 through the VAWA's definition of gender animus as motivating the acts "in whole or in part."[108] Not until the VAWA was the gender-based dimension of intimate violence called by its name under federal law, but it was unremedied violence that in fact combined sex and race that provided much of the impetus for the Fourteenth Amendment in the first place.

2. *Precedent.* Because nonstate actors inflict most of the inequality in society but states are legally designated as the primary violators and guard-

ians of social rights, the question whether federal legislation can reach "private" inequality implicates at once the depth of equality guarantees and the scope of the federal legislative power. Further, sex equality issues will often push the boundaries of the law because those issues were only recently and by interpretation recognized as part of the equality canon, and because so few avenues for women's rights exist. Despite the lack of consideration of sex equality in the constitutional design, Section 5 precedents had left a clear window open for upholding the VAWA, a window the *Morrison* Court not only closed but failed to acknowledge was open. Prior to *Morrison*, the Court had not precluded federal sex equality claims against nonstate actors and had permitted remedial uses of federal authority where states were not promoting equality effectively. Supporting the former on the latter theory was available as well: the Court had not ruled that private acts of sex discrimination could not be made civilly actionable under the Fourteenth Amendment's Section 5 authority when a record showed that those rights were not already being adequately protected by authorities on the basis of sex. In *Morrison*, the Court did.[109]

As a federal civil rights statute, the VAWA civil remedy raised two doctrinal questions: does the Fourteenth Amendment authorize congressional prohibition of inequality between nonstate actors, and does Section 5 empower Congress to legislate against discrimination based on sex as well as race? Given that nonstate actors commit most sex-based discrimination, the questions are intertwined as a practical matter. To invalidate Section 13981, the *Morrison* Court revitalized two post-Reconstruction rulings hostile to race and sex equality rights, the *Civil Rights Cases*[110] and *United States v. Harris*,[111] cases that had largely limited congressional exercise of Section 5 to official violations.[112]

The *Morrison* majority gave these cases particular weight because they were contemporaneous with the enactment of the Fourteenth Amendment.[113] But, as shown above, the Fourteenth Amendment's contemporaries disagreed among themselves. In 1871, a federal court upholding one of the enforcement acts ruled that the Fourteenth Amendment gave Congress the power to protect citizens' rights "against unfriendly or insufficient state legislation" because denial of equal protection of the laws "includes inaction as well as action."[114] Pointedly for the VAWA, that same court found that because "it would be unseemly for congress to interfere directly with state enactments, and as it cannot compel the activity of state officials, the only appropriate legislation it can make is that which will operate directly on offenders and offenses. . . ."[115] Although the Fourteenth Amendment incontestably authorized federal legislation against discriminatory state enactments, direct actions against nonstate perpetrators of discrimination, this analysis suggested, intrude less on states, hence on the values of federalism, than claims against state actors do. The VAWA was precisely legislation operating directly against offenders and offenses, not states.

Taking a similar view of the scope of Section 5, the Supreme Court in *United States v. Guest*[116] in 1966 upheld the constitutionality of a criminal federal civil rights statute[117] as applied to a conspiracy by six private individuals.[118] The defendants' only link with the state was one aspect of their conspiracy: their alleged plan to cause the arrest of "Negroes" by falsely reporting criminal acts.[119] No more official act or actor was required. Concurring in *Guest*, Justice Brennan wrote of the power of Congress to legislate equality:

> Viewed in its proper perspective, § 5 of the Fourteenth Amendment appears as a positive grant of legislative power, authorizing Congress to exercise its discretion in fashioning remedies to achieve civil and political equality for all citizens. No one would deny that Congress could enact legislation directing state officials to provide Negroes with equal access to state schools, parks and other facilities owned or operated by the State. Nor could it be denied that Congress has the power to punish state officers who, in excess of their authority and in violation of state law, conspire to threaten, harass and murder Negroes for attempting to use these facilities. And I can find no principle of federalism nor word of the Constitution that denies Congress power to determine that in order adequately to protect the right to equal utilization of state facilities, it is also appropriate to punish other individuals—not state officers themselves and not acting in concert with state officers—who engage in the same brutal conduct for the same misguided purpose.[120]

Three Justices concurring in *Guest* came to the conclusion that a majority of the Court had left "no doubt that the specific language of § 5 empowers the Congress to enact laws punishing all conspiracies—with or without state action—that interfere with Fourteenth Amendment rights."[121] It was almost as though (if rape is sex discrimination and sex discrimination violates the Fourteenth Amendment) a fraternity gang-rape was considered state action by virtue of the perpetrators' plan to avoid apprehension by the police or to lie to the authorities if caught. The *Guest* Court also expressly left open "the question of what kinds of other and broader legislation Congress might constitutionally enact under § 5 . . . to implement that Clause."[122]

To further recapitulate the history of this question, the *Civil Rights*

Cases' invalidation of the public accommodations provision of the Civil Rights Act of 1875 for exceeding Section 5 authority by reaching private activity was effectively if not doctrinally reversed in *Heart of Atlanta Motel* when the Court upheld under the Commerce Clause the prohibition on discrimination in public accommodations of the Civil Rights Act of 1964.[123] Formally, the *Civil Rights Cases* were distinguished; practically, nothing remained of their result. More of their vitality was vitiated when *Jones v. Alfred H. Mayer Co.*[124] held that private racial discrimination in housing could be constitutionally actionable under 42 United States Code Section 1982 on the authority of the Thirteenth Amendment. Since discrimination in private real estate transactions is in no sense slavery or involuntary servitude, that case makes most sense when read as giving Congress authority to legislate against private discrimination on the theory that it can attack directly what Congress could reasonably see as the current social, political, and economic consequences of prior official inequality. A woman is entitled to the same freedom from sex-based violence a man has. A woman should get the same state protection from violation that a man can get. To adapt the language of *Jones*, if Congress cannot say that the Fourteenth Amendment "means at least this much," the Fourteenth Amendment "made a promise the nation cannot keep."[125]

Ignoring *Guest* and out of step with civil rights precedents including the *Jones* methodology, invalidating a reasonable Section 5 response to centuries of official state deprivation of equal protection of the laws for women, *Morrison* thus came as a startling throwback to a line of authority identified with bulwarks of racism that had been progressively eroded, undermined, sidestepped, or repudiated by the Court since the 1960s. Nor did the *Morrison* majority explain why the Commerce Clause and the Thirteenth Amendment need not be confined to state action but the Fourteenth Amendment must be, or why a wheat grower not taking part in commerce is commerce but states' not acting is not state action. Granting the textual distinctions, the fact that constitutional provisions such as the Commerce Clause and the Thirteenth Amendment had not previously been held to apply to unofficial action did not stop later courts from so applying them for the first time in appropriate cases.

The VAWA's closest precursor, Section 1985(3), which prohibits conspiracies to deprive of civil rights, was not even mentioned in *Morrison*. Section 1985(3) prohibits purely private conspiracies as well as those committed under color of law.[126] Initially, in terms reminiscent of *Morrison*, the Court, citing the *Civil Rights Cases*, held Section 1985(3) to be limited to state actors because the first section of the Fourteenth Amendment was so limited.[127] Overruling this decision twenty years later, the Court in *Griffin v. Breckenridge* upheld a Section 1985(3) action against purely private actors in part under the Thirteenth Amendment.[128] To pass constitutional muster, the *Griffin* Court required Section 1985(3) plaintiffs to show that "some racial, or perhaps otherwise class-based, invidiously discriminatory animus [lay] behind the conspirators' action"[129]—language made statutory in the VAWA's "animus" requirement. Some lower courts have held this animus requirement under Section 1985(3) satisfied by sex-based behavior.[130] The *Griffin* Court further suggested that the Fourteenth Amendment might provide an additional source of congressional power to enact 1985(3).[131] The Court subsequently held in *United Brotherhood of Carpenters, Local 610 v. Scott*[132] that private conspiracies under Section 1985(3) must be "aimed at interfering with rights" that are "protected against private, as well as official, encroachment."[133]

The Supreme Court has yet to rule on whether sex-based conspiracies are actionable under Section 1985(3) and, if so, whether they must involve state acts or actors. The Court came closest to the question in *Bray v. Alexandria Women's Health Clinic*,[134] finding only that animus against women seeking abortions was not sex-based[135] and that the right to travel, protected against private interference, was not properly implicated.[136] The Court did not reach the question whether the acts of the conspirators—private entities planning violently to disrupt abortion clinics—would have had to be involved with a state for their activities to be actionable. The Court's analysis, while not encouraging on this point,[137] did not close the door either. After *Bray*, the Eleventh Circuit held, in an en banc opinion in a case against a public employer (that accordingly did not require ruling on the private action question either), that Section 5 of the Fourteenth Amendment gives Congress ample authority to include women in the protection of Section 1985(3) "at least where conspiracies to discriminate against them through action under color of state law are involved."[138] At least. Incoherent, distinguishable, or ominous after *Morrison* is the fact that the criminal conspiracy statute with identical wording to that of civil 1985(3) was found beyond Congress's power to enact in *United States v. Harris*[139] because it reached private actors. *Harris* was one of the two cases resurrected in *Morrison* to invalidate the VAWA.

Thus, before *Morrison*—and contrary to the *Morrison* majority's suggestion and the Fourth Circuit's bald statement—it was not settled that "wholly private acts of gender-motivated violence can never violate the Equal Protection Clause."[140] More accurately, Congress's clear intent to reach nonstate acts of discrimination under its Section 5 authority, battered and restricted by *Harris* and the *Civil Rights Cases* in the past, potentially survived.[141] Before *Morrison*, whether legislation enabling such claims could be predicated on the Fourteenth Amendment had not been decided. *Morrison*, other than by invoking cases largely repudiated, never addressed why the VAWA civil remedy could not constitutionally reach gender-motivated violence by nonstate actors under equality principles. All this further shows the need for an explanation of the Court's decision that is more than doctrinal.

From early on, the relation between Section 1 and Section 5 of the Fourteenth Amendment has also been contested along the cleavage of separation of powers, raising questions concerning the scope, breadth, and bases of equality rights and their implications for intergovernmental relations through the question of what institution takes priority in providing the answers. Specifically disputed has been how close a legislative record used to pass legislation under Section 5 must come to the judicial standard for a violation of Section 1, and which body, the Court or Congress, decides when the record has fallen short. One view has been that Congress has the authority to legislate to prevent and redress inequality, and courts may uphold under Section 5 legislation that reaches beyond acts courts would be required to prohibit under Section 1 if states were sued for engaging in them on the same factual record. To illustrate one aspect of the issue, states may or may not be susceptible to suit under the Fourteenth Amendment for the underinclusiveness of discrimination laws that fail to guarantee lesbian and gay rights,[142] but Congress may well be able to pass federal legislation guaranteeing those rights under its Section 5 powers on an appropriate record of harm, even though the Court has not yet ruled on whether sexual orientation discrimination is prohibited by the Fourteenth Amendment. On this reading, under the Fourteenth Amendment, the federal legislative power to create equality in society is broader than the judicial power to destroy inequality under law—at least where the Supreme Court has not ruled at all or has not ruled to the contrary.

Thus the majority in *Katzenbach v. Morgan*[143] held that "[a] construction of § 5 that would require a judicial determination that the enforcement of the state law precluded by Congress violated the Amendment, as a condition of sustaining the congressional enactment, would depreciate both congressional resourcefulness and congressional responsibility for implementing the Amendment."[144] This interpretation was found to be within the long tradition dating from *M'Culloch v. Maryland*[145] of appropriate legislation under the Necessary and Proper Clause, language the Fourteenth Amendment adapted.[146] The opposing view, articulated in Justice

Harlan's dissent in *Katzenbach v. Morgan* for example, has contended that an infringement of the Equal Protection Clause is a necessary predicate for valid exercise of Section 5 powers and whether an equal protection violation has occurred is a judicial question.[147] Justice Harlan pointed in particular to the lack of factual data supporting the congressional conclusion of discrimination on which the legislation in that case was predicated[148]—a problem the VAWA record did not have. On the other side of the question, Justice Brennan, concurring in *Guest*, rejected what he called "reduc[ing] the legislative power to enforce the provisions of the [Fourteenth] Amendment to that of the judiciary,"[149] a view he found also rejected by the *Guest* majority.

The Court comprehensively revisited these issues most recently in *City of Boerne v. Flores*,[150] which addressed a congressional attempt to overrule a First Amendment decision of the Supreme Court. Although *Boerne* therefore posed a question without parallel in the circumstances of the VAWA, its map of the terrain could have supported that provision. In *Boerne*, the Court invalidated the Religious Freedom Restoration Act (RFRA) because, according to the Court, Congress exercised its Section 5 authority to try to change the meaning of the Free Exercise Clause of the First Amendment, not to enforce it. The *Morrison* majority did not claim that the VAWA changed the meaning of Fourteenth Amendment equality. Indeed, the equality theory embodied in the VAWA—that violence against women violates sex equality rights—had been previously embraced by the Court in numerous settings and was not rejected in *Morrison*. The Court has interpreted various federal civil rights statutes against discrimination to apply to gender-based violence. For example, under the rubric of sexual harassment, Title VII's and IX's prohibitions on sex discrimination have been applied to rape and other instances of sexual aggression at work and school seemingly without offending state sovereignty or impermissibly altering the meaning of the Commerce Clause or the Spending Clause.[151] In a ruling that straddled Title VII and the Fourteenth Amendment, the Court held that rapeability constituted a woman's "very womanhood," such that women could be excluded from certain jobs on the basis of their sex.[152] Apparently, vulnerability to rape is sex-based, even recognized as sex itself under equality law. Further, although the theory was deprivation of liberty without due process rather than equal protection, a state court judge who had sexually assaulted women litigants and court employees was permitted to be prosecuted under 18 United States Code Section 242,[153] suggesting at least that the federal legislative power may extend to sexual violence without impermissibly altering the meaning of constitutional liberty or trampling states' rights. And sexual harassment has been consistently recognized as actionable against states directly under the Fourteenth Amendment,[154] although the Supreme Court has yet to rule on this theory. These rulings bring gender-based violence clearly within the Court's existing Section 1 equality jurisprudence.

The VAWA was thus not an alteration of the Fourteenth Amendment's substantive provisions of the kind *Boerne* prohibited. It could readily have been upheld as a measure to "remedy or prevent unconstitutional actions,"[155] precisely the kind of legislation the *Boerne* Court and even *The Civil Rights Cases* allowed. *Boerne* specifically held that "[l]egislation which deters or remedies constitutional violations can fall within the sweep of Congress' enforcement power even if in the process it prohibits conduct which is not itself unconstitutional and intrudes into 'legislative spheres of autonomy previously reserved to the States.'"[156] Further unlike RFRA and the Gun Free School Zone Act invalidated in *Lopez*, the VAWA did not displace other laws, and unlike the ADA provision invalidated in *Kimel v. Florida Board of Regents*,[157] it did not empower individuals to sue states. The VAWA provided an optional civil remedy in an area in which states had been unwilling or unable to act effectively, on an equality theory the Court has essentially accepted in many related contexts. Allowing women to do for themselves what the states, under state laws, had failed to do for them was precisely remedial in *Boerne*'s sense. Congress did not, in passing the VAWA, arrogate to itself the power to decide what violated the Fourteenth Amendment; it enforced it.

Granted, evidence like that amassed in the VAWA's legislative record has yet to be used to support a judicial finding of sex discrimination by a state under the Fourteenth Amendment. Little such litigation has been brought, most of it that has on records involving state agents' maltreatment of individuals and with mixed success.[158] But the question whether Congress's VAWA record would be sufficient to support a finding of intentional discrimination by Fourteenth Amendment standards was not addressed in *Morrison*.[159] One of the few distinctions between the opinions of the Fourth Circuit and the Supreme Court in *Morrison* was the Fourth Circuit's expressed view that the VAWA record did not show intentional discrimination under Section 1 standards;[160] of this, the Supreme Court said nothing.[161] Given that *Boerne* made much of the difference between what "alters" the substance of the Fourteenth Amendment and what does not, such that the scope of Section 5 since *Boerne* and *Kimel* turns largely on the scope the Supreme Court gives to Section 1, this omission is notable.

The states' record of failure on violence against women may or may not meet the Court's requirements for discrimination under the Fourteenth Amendment, although it should. The Court described the VAWA record as documenting "[an array of erroneous] discriminatory stereotypes [that] often result in insufficient investigation and prosecution of gender-motivated crime, inappropriate focus on the behavior and credibility of the victims of that crime, and unacceptably lenient punishments for those who are actually convicted of gender-motivated violence."[162] *Morrison* does not at all foreclose the possibility that litigation could be won against states based on evidence like that amassed by state after state in studying gender bias in their courts and collected in the VAWA hearings. The statement by the Supreme Court majority in *United States v. Virginia* that states may not use sex-based categorizations "to create or perpetuate the legal, social, and economic inferiority of women"[163] strongly suggests that it would.[164] At the same time, the fact that there is any question that the practices documented in the VAWA congressional record might be inconsistent with equal protection standards says a lot about those standards.

Boerne permitted remedial measures so long as the means and ends were congruent.[165] The Court's suggestion in *Morrison* that the VAWA would have been more precisely congruent with its aims if it had permitted suits against states[166] would not only have invited likely invalidation under the Court's recent federalism jurisprudence, markedly hostile to suits against states, as *Kimel* showed; it misunderstood the VAWA's aim. Suing states would not remedy the discriminatory harm of the sexual assault itself, only the compounded discrimination of the state's failure adequately to address it. The simple truth is that the sex-discriminatory harm of violence against women cannot be remedied without providing direct actions that women harmed by men across the society can use themselves. No state has the access, resources, motivation, or facilities to address a problem on this scale. No law that does not reach private action will be truly remedial, that is, congruent with this problem. In the VAWA, by going directly to the sex-discriminatory harm of sexual assault, Congress chose what harm to address—one the states concededly are not addressing—making a choice that is squarely within the province of a legislature.

Of all members of the Court, Justice O'Connor's position in *Morrison* was most in doubt. She had joined Justice Blackmun's dissent in *Carpenters* in rejecting a state action requirement for Section 1985(3) and its observation that "certain class traits, such as race, religion, sex, and national origin, per se meet [the] requirement"[167] of defining classes of persons "in danger of not receiving equal protection of the laws from local authorities."[168] Although *Carpenters* was a statutory opinion, its authors plainly did not think that their interpretation of Congress's intent in passing Section 1985(3) made it unconstitutional, implying that Section 1985(3) both reaches private acts and arises under the Fourteenth, not the Thirteenth, Amendment. That opinion even recognized that *Harris* would invalidate the statute as interpreted—which placed *Harris*, not the statute, on thin ice.[169] While Section 1985(3) is thus not likely to be subjected to the sword of federalism any time soon, Justice O'Connor's *Carpenters* views may explain the omission of any mention of that section from the majority opinion in *Morrison*. It is difficult to grasp how sex discrimination could be constitutionally prohibited by Congress under a Fourteenth Amendment legislative power that is not confined to state action without permitting the VAWA to be upheld.

Writing for herself, Justice O'Connor also dissented in *Bray*, making clear that Section 1985(3) could constitutionally have its own standard for "animus" going to sex; it did not have to conform to the Fourteenth Amendment intent standard that applies to discriminatory state action.[170] *Bray* involved unofficial actors and actions. Justice O'Connor's opinion in *Davis v. Monroe County School Board*[171] for a majority that included the *Morrison* dissenters permitted schoolchildren sexually harassed by other schoolchildren to sue school districts for sex discrimination, much to the outrage of the other members of *Morrison*'s new federalist majority. She expressed sensitivity to the realities of gender-based domestic violence in the abortion context in *Planned Parenthood v. Casey*.[172] All this implied that she might have supported the VAWA. Her plurality opinion in *City of Richmond v. J. A. Croson*,[173] suggesting that Congress may have broader authority to remedy society-wide discrimination than states have in the exercise of their police powers, favorably citing *Katzenbach v. Morgan*—"the power to 'enforce' may at times include the power to define situations which Congress determines threaten principles of equality and to adopt prophylactic rules to deal with these situations"[174]—deepens the mystery of her decisive vote striking down Section 13981.

Any remaining doubt that Congress is empowered to legislate against sex-based violence by nonstate actors could have been resolved on the basis of international agreements the United States has made. Half a century of adjudication having provided adequate constitutional authority under other clauses for various human rights to be legislated federally, Congress's authority to pass laws pursuant to the treaty power has been seldom used and even more rarely questioned since 1920. However, a ratified international treaty can provide Congress with a recognized independent source of authority to enact legislation. In the authoritative *Missouri v. Holland*,[175] a challenge to the Migratory Bird Treaty of 1916, the Supreme Court held that even if Congress could not have enacted the legislation under its enumerated powers, an international treaty provided a valid basis for exercise of the federal legislative power under the Necessary and Proper Clause.[176] Thus certain subjects that under domestic law may be exclusively within state authority can be brought under federal legislative authority pursuant to validly enacted international treaties.[177]

The International Covenant on Civil and Political Rights (ICCPR), ratified by the United States in 1992,[178] supports congressional use of the legislative power to address violence against women in society and under law. The ICCPR obligates State Parties "to respect and to ensure to all individuals within its territory the rights recognized in the present Covenant, without distinction of any kind, such as . . . sex."[179] Its protections are not limited to official violations. Article 3 obligates governments to "undertake to ensure the equal right of men and women to the enjoyment of all civil and political rights" in the covenant.[180] The guaranteed rights violated by violence against women with official impunity include the rights to life, liberty and security of the person, dignity, and equality and the right to be free from torture.[181] Article 26 specifically provides for equal protection of the law without discrimination on the basis of sex, including "equal and effective protection against discrimination."[182] That gender-based violence constitutes sex discrimination is as accepted internationally[183] as it was uncontested by the *Morrison* Court. The United States executive branch rightly presented the VAWA to the UN Human Rights Committee, established by the ICCPR to monitor its implementation,[184] as legislation in compliance with its ICCPR obligations.[185] The ICCPR, as a treaty and in substance, at minimum expands the federal legislative power to permit passage of the VAWA. At maximum, it obligates it. Under domestic and international law alike, the Court's decision to invalidate the VAWA civil remedy, by turns strained, anomalous, and illogical (even in areas that might themselves be so described), calls for further explanation.

3. Theory. The controversy over the scope of the Section 5 power to legislate equality is as much about where the line between public and private is drawn as about which part of the government will draw it. Historically, those forces who wanted to prevent racial equality and maintain white supremacy opposed laws against racial discrimination in society, so they opposed the recognition of the power to pass laws that would guarantee equality by those bodies that would pass them. Transparently, states' keeping the power to legislate citizen-to-citizen equality in their hands, rather than permitting the federal government to give that power to harmed individuals to enforce themselves, was the formal vehicle through which equality rights could continue to be denied. White supremacy may be more visible behind the precedents of the past, federalism their foil, than male supremacy is behind the same fig leaf today. Whatever the reason, none of the *Morrison* opinions considers the impact on the possibilities for addressing women's inequality by law of the majority's choice of where to draw the public/private line—or exhibits any awareness that they are creating, not just retracing, that line.

The Fourth Circuit drew the same line between public and private domains as the *Morrison* majority, although in more ideological and less temperate terms.[186] With deep historical resonance, the Fourth Circuit began its ruling sonorously: "We the People, distrustful of power, and believing that government limited and dispersed protects freedom best, provided that our federal government would be one of enumerated powers, and that all power unenumerated would be reserved to the several States and to ourselves."[187] Strikingly, these judges, writing in their judicial capacity, felt it appropriate to identify themselves as speaking in their personal capacity: as "we the People" and "ourselves," those to whom power is reserved that is not otherwise granted to others over them. One senses that it was not Christy Brzonkala with whom they were identifying. To state the obvious, women were not the "we the People" who decided to arrange the government along the lines described. Women had no voice in designing the doctrines or institutions that the Court wielded in *Morrison* to exclude them from access to court. Women never configured the geography of federalism so the "private" was the domain of the "local," for instance. These arrangements were made before women were even permitted to vote. Women, too, distrust power, but the power they have learned to distrust includes that of men being states and men like "ourselves," along with the other forms that dominance takes. The Fourth Circuit's preamble speaks in the voice of men who trust their own power but not the power of other men over them. But it is principally men's power over women that the VAWA civil remedy redresses.

The experience of subordinated groups has not necessarily taught that government "limited and dispersed protects freedom best." This system has protected their inequality, hence their *lack* of freedom. The experience of African Americans has been that states protect their freedom least; only the federal government has been any match for the power of the states to discriminate. More generally, it has been the freedom of those with power in society whose power is protected in the name of freedom by the federal system the Fourth Circuit evoked and, in so doing, enforced. This is not to say that states are the sole source of the maldistribution of power in society and its enforcement by law, only that they have not effectively changed it and have often obstructed change in it. As a result, making the states the sole avenue for seeking equality can be, and has been, a means of preventing equality from being effectively achieved through law. Actually, because the state at any level is far from the exclusive fountainhead of male power, confining constitutional sex equality initiatives to a narrow conception of state action is one way to guarantee that sex inequality will continue.

Violence against women, the Fourth Circuit decided, is wholly within state authority yet not embraced by state action, just as "family law [is] an area of law that clearly rests at the heart of the traditional authority of the States,"[188] yet what goes on in the family is "purely private."[189] The Fourth Circuit wanted to have it both ways: the sphere of violence against women is for the states when the federal legislative power is involved but not of the states when equality is invoked. On the VAWA record showing, what states do in the vision of the federal system that the Fourth Circuit and the *Morrison* majority defended is monopolize the power to address violence against women in order to do little about it. It would seem that states must exclusively occupy this territory so that inequality within it will continue.[190] But the Constitution is already involved in family law in the interest of equality. The *Morrison* and *Brzonkala* courts' conception of family law as an inviolable preserve of the states blinkers rulings like *Loving v. Virginia*[191] and *Palmore v. Sidoti*,[192] not to mention *Orr v. Orr*[193] and *Kirchberg v. Feenstra*,[194] all of which assert the preeminence of constitutional equality over state family statutory and case law. These decisions, although not per se providing precedent for the VAWA under Section 5, underline the affirmative nature of the decision in *Morrison* to permit unredressed violence against women in the name of what is called the private. The VAWA would hardly have been the first invasion by the Constitution in the name of equality into a state legal regime denominated private. The public, the law, the federal Constitution, the Fourteenth Amendment, are already there.

The *Morrison* majority does not simply respect a preexisting line between what is private and what is public. It draws that line by abandoning women wherever violence against them takes place. *Morrison* effectively defines the private as the location where effective redress for sex-based violence is unavailable, ignoring the destruction of women's freedom and equality in private by ratifying the lack of public limits on male violence. The private is thus constructed of public impunity. The jealous guarding of this specific line between public and private acts, under which exercise of state power is accountable to public authority but exercise of so-called private power is not, thus becomes one of the central public means of maintaining a system in which male power over women remains effectively without limit.[195] Christy Brzonkala was away at school when she was raped, paying to attend a public educational institution. She was gang-raped by men she had barely met in a room not her own. Public officials effectively condoned her violation through public legal processes. In what sense was her rape private?

At this juncture, one might well ask: why limit equality rights to the narrowest of official violations if not to ensure that the private remains unequal? *Morrison* is an official national decision that what men do to women in private will be beyond the reach of a public authority. Officially limiting equality rights to state acts while defining state acts extremely narrowly, thus keeping the so-called private a sphere of impunity for violence against women, *is a public act*. In dividing public from private along its chosen line—the identical line chosen by the Fourth Circuit, if with less overt venom—the Supreme Court failed to recognize the extent of the public's complicity in promoting violence against women in private by creating, and in constitutionally entrenching, a public standard of impunity for it.

Obscuring the affirmative nature of the abdication in *Morrison*, as the majority does, in turn obscures the involvement of the state in impunity for male dominance and its collaboration with the occurrence of violence against women society-wide. Although there are many explanations for violence against women, few think it would take place to the degree it does if it were not largely and predictably exempt from effective recourse. What is true for violence against women intimates is true for most violence against women: it is "a relatively low-risk behavior for a perpetrator in terms of identification or sanctions."[196] Certainly, few perpetrators have reason to think they will ever have to answer to the woman herself for how they treat her. Given that it is in so-called private—this private that is everywhere—that men most often violate women, the decision that intervention in the private is per se off limits to public authority, and that systematic state nonintervention in the private is not a state act, is a public decision by the highest Court of the nation to support male power, i.e., sex inequality, in the most violent ways in which it is socially exercised.

Practices of inequality occupy various positions in relation to state action, calling for flexible approaches if equality is to be achieved. The *Morrison* Court quoted *Shelley v. Kraemer*[197] for the proposition that the Constitution does not cover purely private acts.[198] But racially restrictive housing covenants are ineffective pieces of paper if they are not enforceable at law. Withdrawing legal backing from them eliminates their ability to enforce inequality. Violence against women, by contrast, is self-enforcing. It is effective *unless* addressed by law. In defining freedom from sex-based violence as a federal civil right, Congress recognized what the Supreme Court denied: the problem pervades the nation's civil society and state inseparably, so could only be effectively addressed by an instrument that distinguished neither between one state and another nor between narrowly official and other acts in determining what creates an inequality problem and what does not.

Congress recognized that an effective remedy to the inequality problem of violence against women, a problem primarily of aggression by one sex against the other, called for an approach that fit the contours of the problem. Most violence against women is engaged in by nonstate actors, people who are not public officials or acting with what is recognized as state authority. But they do act with the virtually total assurance that, as statistics confirm, their acts will be officially tolerated, they themselves will be officially invisible, and their victims will be officially silenced. That is, their acts will be kept private by exclusion from public recognition or public redress. They are state-exempt acts. They are done with near-total impunity. Sex discrimination through sexual violence, so long as it is publicly unredressed, will be a fact of public life that is no less of public concern when committed in so-called private—quite the contrary. Violated women are abandoned alone there. Discriminatory abdication by public authority makes private acts public.

The U.S. government is constructed to be sensitive to the dominance of some men over other men by formal institutional means. It is not created to be wary of the dominance of men over women, especially not by means seen as informal or noninstitutionalized. In this light, the Fourth Circuit's opening formulation presents the question: whose freedom is protected by the structural distribution of institutional power that court defends, and whose power does that court distrust? To put not too fine a point on it, one wonders why the Fourth Circuit and Supreme Court majorities, not doctrinally required to reach this result, made sure that women do not have equal rights against unofficial gender-based aggression. What was really at stake? In connection with the Fourth Circuit's opinion, it is also worth pondering why ensuring that nothing effective is done about violence against women is a systemic value worthy of rhetorically refighting the Civil War. Presumably, inflicting violence against women with official impunity was not one of "our fundamental liberties"[199] that the division between state and federal governmental powers was originally adopted to protect. Or was it?

III. Disputing Male Sovereignty

To the ear of violated women, the same obligato in two different keys plays beneath the *Morrison* majority opinion: keep her at home. In the *Morrison* Court's view, to address violence against women federally was to make a category mistake: to treat the local as if it were national, the noneconomic as if it were economic, the private as if it were public. The VAWA just felt wrong to them. These conventional reflexes were by no means universally shared, just as the outcome was by no means doctrinally preordained, the dissenters made clear. Justice Souter could not see why wheat and corn are national but women are not, or why wheat grown for consumption "right on the farm" was reachable under the commerce power but domestic violence was not.[200] Justice Breyer queried why drugs for home consumption and home fireplaces were federally regulable but violence against women in the home was not.[201]

Given that the VAWA civil remedy could readily have been upheld on precedent, why did the Supreme Court majority prevent violated women from pursuing accountability for bigoted violence against them? The answer may lie less with the imperatives of institutional forces the majority invoked than with the gender relations that impel those forces. The institutional doctrines on which the majority relied to invalidate Section 13981 are observably built on underlying social arrangements of male power. That is, the "traditional" allocation to state authorities of the governmental response to men's violence against women, an allocation respectfully invoked by majority and dissenters alike,[202] is built on nothing more than that: a historical tradition of men (men who had power among men) dividing up power among themselves under conditions in which women had no authoritative say and over which no substantive sex equality principles reigned or, since *Morrison*, yet reign. What "has always been,"[203] whether addressed from a gray stone building in Washington, D.C., or a red brick building upstate, is nothing more than that: two "spheres" from which women "ha[ve] always been" excluded, and in which they are not yet at home.

Categorical formalism may have become newly attractive in service of this particular federalism,[204] but what explains the attraction of this particular federalism? Do its categories cover substance with form? If so, what substance? Analyzing substantively the abstract institutional commitments in the name of which the VAWA civil remedy was invalidated requires asking what this federalism is concretely about, specifically whose interests its dynamics are constructed to favor. Could it be that men keep their power over women by keeping it local and private? Is male dominance served by ensuring that men keep control of certain things, including the terms of their relations with women, at close range? If so, federalism is an abstract institutional arrangement embodying judgments of those concerns that men want to control closely, and those over which they are willing to share control with other men farther removed. The VAWA squarely confronted this gentlemen's agreement by creating an entitlement to an equality for women that has not "always been." On this analysis, gender may be driving this federalism, explaining as sexual politics a result that otherwise eludes satisfactory explanation. On this reading, *Morrison* is not just another case in the march of the new federalism. It may be its bottom line.

Put another way, doctrine required the Court to confront, under the Commerce Clause, whether the economy is hurt by violence against women, and, under the Fourteenth Amendment, whether the states are hurt by the VAWA. (The answers were, respectively: yes, but that does not make it economic; and yes, whether they think so or not.) But no doctrine required the Court even to ask whether women as such are hurt by invalidating this law against violence against women. Leaving the answer to the political branches, as Justice Breyer advocated,[205] would at long last have saved a provision like this one, but is no answer when a doctrine like federalism, built in women's silence and on women's exclusion, and the constitutional standards for what is and is not economic, which do not value women's material contributions, can set the terms under which Congress's decision is authoritatively judged. This is not to say that the Court correctly assessed the VAWA's constitutionality under existing federalism, commerce, or equality doctrines. It did not. It is to observe that no doctrine—not federalism, not commerce, not yet equality—requires that women's interest in living as equals free from gender-based violence be judicially accorded the same level of constitutional priority as the states' interests in their traditional sphere of action or localities' interests in their economic autonomy. Nothing in the design of the system exposes the gender bias built into the history and tradition of the Constitution's structure and doctrines. Nothing requires that women's interests as such be given any consideration at all.

One way to describe the process of change in women's legal status from chattel to citizen is as a process of leaving home. The closer to home women's injuries are addressed, the less power and fewer rights women seem to have; the farther away from home the forum, the more power and rights women have gained—and with them freedom of action, resources, and access to a larger world. In experiential terms, women are least equal at home, in private; they have had the most equality in public, far from home. It is in the private, man's sovereign castle, where most women remain for a lifetime, where women are most likely to be battered and sexually assaulted, and where they have no recourse because the private, by definition, is inviolable and recourse means intervention. For physically and sexually violated women, going public with their injuries has meant seeking accountability and relief from higher sovereigns, men who have power over the men who abused them because they are above, removed from, hence less likely to be controlled by those abusers. This process has meant encountering systemic barriers to access at each higher level—pressures, it is said, that have nothing to do with gender but simply reflect the way the system works. Systemically, the preferred jurisdiction of resolution is always the closest to the abuser. In effect, at each level, women are told to go back where he rules. One way to describe this dynamic is to observe that men often respect other men's terrain as sovereign in exchange for those other men's respect for their own sovereignty on their own terrain. As a result of such balances that men with power strike among themselves, represented in the shape of public institutions, men have the most freedom at home, and women gain correspondingly greater equality, hence freedom, the farther away from home they go.

"Why is it that women do not dispute male sovereignty?" Simone de Beauvoir once asked.[206] Battered and raped women *have* disputed their various male sovereigns. Their advances in human status can be tracked in space and time up an ascending jurisdictional ladder. After failing for centuries to stop domestic violence and marital rape in their own families, women sought relief outside the family in the legal system. First, they moved out from the home, where they had had no rights except by grace, to acquire recognition of harms done to them as women under local and state law. Achieving enforcement of state laws against domestic battering was a major step.[207] Applying state rape laws to rape in marriages was another step up.[208] When the law of sexual assault continued to fail women, a partial remedy for some rapes was found under civil rights laws in the form of claims for sexual harassment,[209] achieving some national recognition for these injuries. Increasingly, international remedies are sought by women claiming a human right not to be violated because they are women.[210] Thus, Bosnian women sought relief from genocidal rape not in their own postgenocidal legal system, but in another country, far from home, under international law.[211] With the VAWA, women disputed male sovereignty itself.

As each jurisdiction fails them, and when they can, women seek accountability and relief in superior forums, disputing male sovereigns by appealing to higher male sovereigns. And at each level, women confront jurisdictional and systemic barriers as they are told in various terms that they do not belong there and should go back home where they belong.

Men have long fought over who has power over whom and what, battles of which institutions and doctrines like federalism and separation of powers are results. The women they victimize have no stake in whether their injuries are addressed by state or federal governments, by the Court or by Congress. What women do have a stake in, so long as men perpetrate violence against them on the basis of sex, is in having those injuries addressed: in effective and equal enforcement of laws against the acts that injure them. This concrete and urgent need, not any position on men's turf battles and not a desire for positive symbolism, produced the VAWA. It is in light of this concrete and urgent need that the *Morrison* outcome is most vicious. *Morrison* sent women back home, to their violators. Its constitutional message to violated women is: only the states can take your equality rights away, and only the states can give them back to you. If the states could have given women equality, they would have, and there would have been no VAWA because there would have been no need for one.

As post-Reconstruction courts obstructed racial equality, so the *Morrison* Court obstructed sex equality, and by the same means. The Court did not even do what it could. It reduced women claiming the most basic rights of citizenship to standing on ever narrower and shakier ground, ground now all but disappeared. Not one member of the Supreme Court argued that the rights the VAWA civil remedy gave women were constitutional under the Constitution's equality guarantee. Justice Breyer came closest in the part of his dissent that Justices Ginsburg and Souter declined to join. Perhaps the Constitution cannot be retrofitted adequately to address sex-based violations. An Equal Rights Amendment designed to promote equality of the sexes horizontally in society as well as vertically under law could.[212] International law could also provide new ground for violated women to stand on.[213] Recognition of Congress's expanded role pursuant to the treaty power would revitalize and update the discussion, once active concerning slavery and segregation,[214] of international law's contribution to the governmental balance by bringing higher sovereigns into the picture.

After *Morrison*, the time may have arrived to deploy international treaties, which have expanded their recognition of human rights, to enhance the constitutional basis for legislating domestic human rights for women federally.

United States v. Morrison closed a crucial avenue of access to equality under law and dealt a devastating blow to the development of women's human rights against sex-based violence. *Morrison* was a major battle in women's civil war: a battle at once over the structure of the union and the status of the sexes in civil society. It addressed ground zero for citizenship—physical security—and ground zero for women's human status—sexual inviolability.[215] At stake was nothing less than whether women are full citizens and full human beings: equals. The VAWA civil remedy stood for the principle that a woman could not, with impunity, be assaulted anywhere in this nation simply because she is a woman. It put the power to dispute male sovereignty in women's hands. The *Morrison* majority decided that the union could not permit that and be the same union it was. The ruling thus raised, as no case before it has, the question whether the structure of a nation organized to preclude relief for the violation of one half of its people by the other should survive.

18

Unequal Sex

A Sex Equality Approach to Sexual Assault

Sexual assault is sex-based violation. This analysis is supported by the data and experience on sexual assault that have emerged since 1970.[1] Among humans, sexual abuse is systematically inflicted by and on people who are socially gendered unequal to one another. The gendered inferiority attributed to sexual victims, and used to target them, and the gendered superiority attached to sexual prowess, along with the erotization of subordination and dominance, are socially imbricated with established and inculcated notions and roles of masculinity and femininity respectively. A prominent observable regularity is that men more often perpetrate, women are more often victimized. Even more of the variance is explained by the observation that sexual atrocities are inflicted on those who have less social power by those who have more, among whom gender is the most significant cleavage of stratification.

In light of the evidence, human sexual aggression is best understood as social—attitudinal and ideological, role-bound and identity-defined—not natural. Causally speaking, nothing makes inevitable its high prevalence and incidence in everyday life,[2] or in wars or genocides, except social rank orderings, advantage-seeking, inculcation, conformity (including to peer behavior and pressure, standards of prior generations, orders, media representations, and the like). These forces plainly make the behavior attractive and possible by some people against certain others, producing social incentives for perpetrators to attack and pressures for victims to be ignored under many different conditions.[3] Sexual perpetrators and victims are largely socially constructed males and females respectively—gendered in part by societies that impel and excuse both their relative hierarchical positions and the violative acts that express and define those positions by attributing both to men's and women's natures or physical bodies.

In this light, as explanation for sexual aggression, appeals to biology prove

Talk to New York Academy of Science, Conference on Understanding and Managing Sexually Coercive Individuals, June 8, 2002, Washington, D.C. First published, *Sexual Coercion: Understanding and Management* 265 (Robert Prentky, Eric Janus, and Michael Seto, eds., 2003).

both too little and too much. In the first place, not all women are victims and not all men are aggressors, and not only women are victims and not only men are aggressors. That sexual assault is propelled, indeed motivated, by social hierarchy rather than factors or forces of nature is evidenced by the fact of biologically female sexual aggressors[4] (if few, showing how powerful socialization is), as well as by the many biologically male victims and the child victims of both sexes,[5] not to mention postmenopausal women victims and same-sex victims of both sexes,[6] against all of whom sexual assault is a reproductive and, one suspects, evolutionary dead end.

Further evidence for a social over a biological explanation is the numbers of men who do not sexually aggress who have nothing wrong with them physically and the participation of race and class hierarchy in designating "appropriate" victims of sexual assault.[7] In genocides, in which women of the group to be destroyed are systematically raped by men of the group intending to destroy them, nothing biological has changed from a prior nongenocidal era. What has changed is that a political decision is made to destroy another racial or ethnic or religious group and the realization that rape is a highly effective tool to that end.[8] Nor do wars change men's biology; they do change the conditions of access, permission, and motivation for raping both women and men. In other words, sexual assault is based on social and political inequality not on biological distinction.

Embodied in the ideology of the naturalness of sexual assault (whether it takes the form of religious fundamentalism, fascism, sociobiology, or other) is necessarily the view that gender hierarchy—male supremacy and female inferiority—of which sexual aggression is a cardinal manifestation, is also natural. If the sexes are biologically different but not biologically superior and subordinate, sexual aggression is socially not biologically impelled—an act not of difference but of dominance, not of sexual dimorphism but of gender hierarchy. Put another way, because women are not men's sexual inferiors in nature, but are so ranked in societies in which sexual abuse of women in particular flourishes with social support, enforcing and expressing that inferiority, and because the sex roles and stereotypes that become realities gender sexual assault unequally and indelibly, and because gender is the social form sex takes, sexual abuse is properly analyzed as an act of sex inequality.

This realization is increasingly reflected by diverse legal authorities. The Supreme Court of Canada recognized in a 1993 rape case that "[s]exual assault is in the vast majority of cases gender based. It . . . constitutes a denial of any concept of equality for women."[9] International authorities including the General Assembly of the United Nations, the Committee on the Elimination of All Forms of Discrimination Against Women, the Organization of American States, the Beijing Conference, and the Council of Europe have all defined and condemned sexual violence as a gender-based function of unequal social power between the sexes.[10] The law against sexual harassment in the United States, which makes sexual incursions in employment and education civilly actionable as sex discrimination, construes sexual assault in certain settings as gender-based inequality.[11] The U.S. Supreme Court once found that women are raped because they are women, calling the capacity to be raped a result of the victim's "very womanhood."[12] In the Violence Against Women Act of 1994, rape was made civilly actionable as sex discrimination when the violence was "because of" or "on the basis of gender," including "animus based on the victim's gender."[13] Presumably, Congress was not making a biological fact into a federal case nor standing against nature when it legislated the United States' first zero tolerance standard for sex-based violence. Even the Supreme Court that invalidated the VAWA on other grounds did not question the legislative conclusion that sexual assault is describable as a practice of discrimination on the basis of sex.[14]

The growing consciousness of this reality is reflected virtually not at all in the criminal law of rape in the United States. Although sexual assault is always sexual and often physically violent, the awareness that rape is not so much an act of violence or sex as it is an act of sex inequality—specifically of sex eroticized by the dominance that inequality embodies and permits, of which physical violence is only one expression—is barely traceable in U.S. criminal law. Remarkably, given that criminal statutes are mostly state law, the equalization of which the Fourteenth Amendment was passed to guarantee, the well-documented sex inequalities in the criminal law of rape, from its design to most aspects of its state administration,[15] have remained almost entirely free of equal protection scrutiny, except for those rare rape statutes that differentiate between men and women on their face.[16] Surely the legal tolerance of sexual assault[17] is not a fact of nature. It is a fact of sex inequality in human societies, supported by ideologies that explain and exonerate systemic abuses of women by appeals to biological fiat. And if the U.S. criminal law of rape does not meet a sex equality standard, as contended here, it must also be said that it has not been legally subjected to one.

In fundamental aspects of its doctrine, the U.S. rape law can be seen to presuppose and enforce inequality between women and men in sex. A central instance is the legal standard for consent to sex, which does not hold contested sexual interactions to a standard of sexual equality. That is, when the law of rape finds consent to sex, it does not look to see if the parties were social equals in any sense, nor does it require mutuality or positive choice in sex,[18] far less simultaneity of desire. The doctrine of consent in the law of forcible rape envisions instead unilateral initiation (the stereotyped acted/acted-upon model of male dominant sex)[19] followed by accession or not by persons tacitly presumed equal. Consent is usually proven by the acted-upon's not saying no; it can, however, even famously include saying no.[20]

A lot of not-yes-saying passes for consent to sex.[21] The accession to proceeding known as legal consent that makes sex not rape can, in addition to an express no that becomes a legal yes, include resigned silent passive dissociated acquiescence in acts one despairs at stopping; fraud or pretense producing compliance in intercourse for false reasons[22] or with persons who are not who they say they are; multiplicity triggered by terror or programming (so that the person who accedes to the sex is just one inhabitant of the body with whom sex is had);[23] and fear of abuse short of death or maiming or severe bodily injury (such as loss of one's job or not being able to graduate from high school, including in jurisdictions that do not consider rape itself a form of severe bodily injury) resulting in letting sex happen.[24]

Outside settings of war and genocide, and those exceptions are recent and slight, little to no legal attention is paid to whether the parties enter sexual intercourse as social equals. Not even known hierarchies of boss/worker, teacher/student, doctor/patient, cleric/congregant, or lawyer/client formally register in the doctrine of the criminal law of rape. This law is indifferent to whether the sexual transactions in which assault is claimed occurred at (what contract law calls) arm's length. People who could not sign a binding contract, under conditions of overreaching under which it would not be enforced, can have sex and the law is none the wiser. In popular culture, where no one (man or woman) describes a magical moment of sexual intimacy or connection or eroticism as "consensual," the term consent is nonetheless used as if it actually means choice, mutuality, and desire. This is a fiction. Within its legal ambit, consent can include sex that is wanted, but it can also include sex that is not at all wanted and is forced by inequality.

Usually, consent is a club used as a defense by a man at the point a woman says he raped her or, in what amounts to the same thing, when she says that her prostitution was not freely chosen. Consent is more attributed than exercised. As is by now well known, if sexual intercourse took place, particularly if the woman had had sex before, if the parties knew each other, or lived together, or if the man paid, consent tends to be presumed or found.[25] Whether receipt of money makes sex wanted, or whether knowing a man or living in the same household with him means one wants to have sex with him, is not asked because whether a person wants to have sex is not all consent legally means. Whether she (or, in some instances, he) tolerated it, or could have appeared to the defendant to have gone along with it, is included.

This is to say one simple thing: consent to sex is not the same as wanting it. That a woman has reasons for giving up and letting sex happen that have nothing whatever to do with desire to have sex and everything to do with social gender hierarchy—all the way from saving one's job or future to placating a physically or emotionally abusive man—is irrelevant to the criminal law. No doubt many people think it should be. It fails to meet an equality standard, however. An equality standard, such as the one applied in the civil law that recognizes that sexual harassment is sex discrimination, requires that sex be welcome.[26] For the criminal law to change to this standard would require that sex be wanted for it not to be assaultive.

Awareness of social hierarchy is absent in the criminal law of rape's treatment of force as well. In this area of law, forms of force typically correlated with male sex and gender—such as the economic dominion of employers, dominance in the patriarchal family, authority of teachers and religious leaders, state office of policemen and prison guards, and the credibility any man has (some have much more than others based on race and class and age), not to mention the clout of male approval and the masculine ability to affirm and confirm feminine identity—are not regarded as forms of force at all. But they are. Whether or not men occupy these roles, these forms of power are socially male in that they are not equally available for women to assert over men. Socially speaking, women in general are neither socialized to these forms of power nor, as women, commonly authorized, entitled, socially positioned, or permitted to exercise them. That there are exceptions confirms the rule as well as further highlights its social determinants.

Of all the forms that power can take, the criminal law of rape's doctrine of force, similarly, registers only physical overpowering.[27] Some courts have begun to consider that a variety of factors can constitute force, such as Pennsylvania's embodiment of "moral, psychological or intellectual force used to compel a person to engage in sexual intercourse against that person's will" in its definition of "forcible compulsion." It also includes "the extent to which the accused may have been in a position of authority, domination or custodial control over the victim," together with age, mental and physical conditions, and the atmosphere and physical setting.[28] What even this standard, which is not the norm, does not expressly include is attention to inequalities including sex and race (as is well known, racism targets women of specific racial groups for sexual incursions and in the United States often accords greater credibility to white people than to African Americans), and other major social inequalities. Even consideration of physical force under standard approaches typically shows little sensitivity to the physical factors of height and weight, which on average stack the deck in favor of men over women.[29]

Only extreme physical force, preferably including weapons other than the penis, is usually credible enough to meet the criminal law's standard for enough force for sex to look like rape. Depending on how well the parties know each other, the amount and type of force required to prove that the sex was physically forced escalates.[30] While resistance requirements have been largely modified or abolished, it is as if they have not if a woman's calculation not to fight because she would rather be raped than dead, for example—an assessment some women make every day—means that the sexual acts are legally determined not to have been forced.

Typically, the only vulnerability recognized by the rape law as tantamount to an inequality is age,[31] in most places for underage girls only (in some for boys as well). The law of statutory rape makes all sex rape below an age line or outside certain age differentials below a certain age. While simplifying the administration of justice, this rule (along with a similar result of strict prohibitions on sex between teachers and students) confuses people by defining as rape some sex that some people want to have. It also presumptively authorizes all sex above the age line whether it was wanted or not, unless proven nonconsensual by standards that take no inequalities into account. Other inequalities, such as disparities of access and trust, that often go with age but do not end with the age of majority, are also neglected above and below the line.

If the rape law worked, there would be no need for statutory rape laws. Abuse of power, access, trust, and exploitation of vulnerabilities to pressure people into sex that is not wanted for its own sake would be illegal. Age would be one powerful inequality to be taken into account. Instead, the only inequality the law will countenance is youth, whether statutory rape laws are justified as making consent irrelevant or force unnecessary or both (the law is oddly indifferent to the actual rationale). Young age or age differential below a certain age is thus ossified into an absolute rule. This segregates out some of the most sympathetic cases for relative structural powerlessness in sexual interactions and leaves the rest of the victims—including in most states underage boys who have sex with women over the age of majority—unprotected, their inequalities uncounted. By cushioning its excesses, this helps keep male dominance as a social system in place. One also suspects that debates over shifting the age of consent are driven more by what legislators (mainly men) want in a female sex object than by what sex women want in their lives when.

Sex is relational; so is sexual assault. In unequal societies, what makes sexual assault sexual as well as possible is the hierarchy of relation between the parties. Rape is thus a crime of sexualized dominance on the basis of sex (which often includes sex and age, sex and race, sex and class variously combined and pyramided) that is legally unrecognized as such. Inequality, its central dynamic, is flat-out ignored by the criminal law. Far from promoting equality between women and men, the criminal law tacitly assumes that such equality already exists. On the surface, it shows total lack of interest in whether equality is there or not.[32] In other words, the law has refused to make criminal exactly what this crime *is*. This misfit between the law's concept of sexual assault and the reality of it produces legal standards that cannot see abuse in the real world and encourage neglect or worse by legal actors of the dynamics that make the abuse happen. This in turn serves as state collaboration in sexual assault and accordingly in the inequality of the sexes.

In this view, until inequality is directly addressed by the law of sexual assault, nothing adequate will be done about it. You cannot solve a problem you do not name. For the same reason, legal reform through consent alone or force alone, while improvements, will intrinsically fall short unless the concepts are fundamentally recast in terms of inequality. Requiring affirmative consent, as some states do,[33] for example, is an improvement over existing law, but can be polluted by inequality. No means no is a big improvement over no meaning yes, but until equality exists, not even yes can reliably mean yes. Yes can be coerced. It can be the outcome of forced choices, precluded options, constrained alternatives, as well as adaptive preferences conditioned by inequalities. This may be why states that require affirmative consent also require that it be freely chosen. But whether evaluations of the facts of individual cases adequately include the experiences of inequalities that make choice unfree—such as having been sexually abused in childhood, as are a third to a half of girls in the U.S.,[34] not to mention having one's first sexual intercourse being forced, as it is documented to be for up to a third of all girls in the world[35]—remains to be seen.

The problem with consent-only approaches to rape law reform is that sex under conditions of inequality can look consensual when it is not wanted—at times because women know that sex that women want is the sex men want from women. Men in positions of power over women can thus secure sex that looks, even is, consensual without that sex ever being wanted, without it being freely chosen far less desired. Consent, in other words, has never been legally coextensive with freedom. Even if it was in law, if the conditions for the exercise of freedom in life are not ensured—meaning actual conditions of equality, or a standard sensitive to inequalities between the parties so long as conditions of inequality exist—an autonomy approach to consent will not alone solve this problem in real life. Autonomy in sex cannot exist without equality of the sexes. Similarly, force approaches alone cannot address the problem of sexual assault in real life unless forms of force other than the physical, including all of those that enforce inequalities, are expressly recognized.

The question therefore framed is: what would a rape law look like that understood sexual assault as a practice of inequality? In brief, it would recognize that rape is a physical attack of a sexual nature under coercive conditions,[36] and inequalities are coercive conditions. The law of sexual assault could make it a crime to take advantage of a relation of inequality (including access or trust) to force sex on a person who does not want it. If force were defined to include inequalities of power, meaning social hierarchies, and consent were replaced with a welcomeness standard, the law of rape would begin to approximate the reality of forced and unwanted sex. Force could be defined so that it is sensitive to the vulnerabilities social hierarchies concretely create: age (middle over young and old); family (husband over wife, parents over children, older children over younger children); race (in the U.S., white over people of color); authority (educational, medical, legal, religious among them); law (police and prison guards over citizens and inmates); illegal statuses such as those created by the law of immigration, homosexuality, and prostitution; and economics (poverty, and employers over employees).

Gender too is a social hierarchy (masculine over feminine), ringed with stereotype, enforced by socialization to subordinate and superior identification as well as by physical force. Socially, it is largely fused with sex (male and female). The idea here is not to prohibit sexual contact between hierarchical unequals per se but to legally interpret sex that a hierarchical subordinate says was unwanted in the context of the forms of force that animate the hierarchy between the parties. To counter a claim that sex was forced by inequality, a defendant could (among other defenses) prove the sex was wanted—affirmatively and freely wanted—despite the inequality, and was not forced by the socially entrenched forms of power that distinguish the parties.[37] The assumption that money provides or shows consent to sex would be replaced by the assumption that money is a form of force in sex. On a social level, inequalities could also be reduced, of course. A recognition in law that sex is made an inequality in society through gender hierarchy, and sexual assault is a central practice and expression of that inequality, would go a long way toward ending its considerable social and legal impunity and toward making sexual assault obsolete.

If society is structured to promote, even encourage, sexual assault, and the law against it evades the forces driving it so that there is nothing effective to stop it, no wonder it happens. An approach designed to rectify this situation could underlie new statutes, provide a set of common-law rules for interpreting existing statutes, or sketch a set of equality standards for assessing the Fourteenth Amendment constitutionality of existing state practices or conformity of national laws and practices with international obligations. As a priority, new civil rights laws—sex equality laws—could be passed for all victims of sexual assault to use. Civil laws potentially offer accountability to survivors, a forum with dignity and control by them, the stigma of bigotry for perpetrators, a possibility of reparations, and the potential for social transformation by empowering survivors. This is not to say that perpetrators do not deserve incarceration, rather to say that jail has not tended to change their behavior, indeed has often entrenched and escalated it. Civil rights laws offer the prospect of redistributing power, altering the inequalities that give rise to the abuse.

This framework for analysis provides principles of direction that are adaptable to diverse cultural settings and varying structures of existing law. The approach would embody in law the sexual equality that people often say they want in their laws and in their relationships, should anyone act on it.

part two

sexuality, inequality, and speech

SECTION A. ▪ THEORY AND PRACTICE

19

Sex, Lies, and Psychotherapy

Reading the nine articles in Jeffrey Masson's *A Dark Science*, drawn from nineteenth-century French and German medical journals, is a lot like reading pornography. You feel you have come upon a secret codebook that you were not meant to see but that has both obscured and determined your life. The sexual atrocities advanced here by doctors as promoting mental health during the nineteenth century might be beyond belief were they not also practiced during the Inquisition as liturgical justice, by the Third Reich as racial purity and medical experimentation, by the juntas of Latin America and Greece to maintain political power, and today by pornographers in the United States and worldwide as sexual entertainment. Women should study these medical articles for the same reasons they should study pornography: to see what is behind how they are seen and treated and to find out what men really think of them.

Behind psychotherapy's guise of treatment, just as surely as beneath pornography's protestations of liberation, lies the sexual sadism that is at the core of misogyny, here in its medical form: women's bodies are dirty, women's minds are polluted by their bodies, women's sexuality is diseased, sex is evil because sex is women, women are evil because women are sex. Because men have social power over women—power as lawyers and employers and fathers and priests and teachers and policemen and pimps and writers and policymakers as well as doctors (our bodies in their hands)—what men think of women is what is done.

Like pornography, these articles trade in half-truths. As lawyer Gerry Spence puts it, "The real weaponry . . . is the half-truth. It's like a half brick . . . you can throw a half brick twice as far as a whole brick."[1] The resulting accounts have all the credibility of truth and all the clout of lies. Both in pornography and in these psychiatric accounts, it is very difficult to separate the simulated from the actual—what did *not* happen that the text says did, from what *did* happen that the text says did not. The diag-

First published as an introduction to *A Dark Science: Women, Sexuality, and Psychiatry in the Nineteenth Century* xi–xvii (Jeffrey Moussaieff Masson and Marianne Loring, trans., 1986).

noses are not true because the doctors' notion of their etiology, in which mind is diseased because body is diseased because body is female, is not true. The dead-meat-causes-flies approach to mental distress is not true. That anything was wrong with these women and girls—beyond perhaps having symptoms of venereal infection due to (undiagnosed) sexual assault—may also be untrue. The doctors' claims of healing by their savage methods are also, doubtless, not true.

But, as with pornography, what these men write about doing to these women *is* true. They did slice off these women's clitorises; they did cut into them and remove their ovaries; they did cut into them and not remove their ovaries but said they did; they did tie them to their beds and listen to their struggles and screams; they did rape them with red-hot irons. The acts that psychiatry calls treatment, pornography (in its one demystification) calls sex. In both, the acts are presented as being for her own good and ultimately consensual, the victim grateful in the end.

And, as with pornography, what these men say they thought, they thought. They thought that personality is genetically determined, that women and children lie about sexual abuse, that a woman's mind is sexed because her body is sexed, that a woman's qualities can be read by whether the look on her face is arousing. Thus, a woman's distress over what may well have been violation is attributed to moral defect and baseness of character,[2] to "precocious perversions,"[3] and diagnosed from "her somewhat erotic facial expression."[4]

Originally a challenger of this nineteenth-century tradition, Freud at first believed that adult women who told him they were sexually abused as children were telling the truth. When he revised his view and decided that the women were not describing actual events, he became tradition's heir. The standard clinical practice, rooted prior to Freud (but previously thought to be based on his work) had been to analyze reports of childhood sexual abuse as mentally telling but empirically false. Jeffrey Masson has argued that Freud changed his mind for reasons that were ultimately obscure but appeared far more personal, ideological, and professionally pressured than clinically based. In *The Assault on Truth*, Masson revealingly traces the documentary trail Freud left of his decision to disbelieve his patients, raising anew the possibility—never abandoned by many women—that Freud's patients and millions of anguished women since were simply recounting something that happened to them: something sexual they did not want that hurt them in a way they could not get over.

Either such events happened or they did not. It is a study in comparative credibility that even after Freud changed his mind on the subject, and even after his reasons for doing so were revealed as dubious, the fact that Freud had *once* believed these women apparently gave them more credibility than much else has before or since. In a brief moment of institutional free fall, the psychoanalytic establishment found itself confronting the possibility that the women had been telling the truth all along. If its rabid reaction to this possibility is any measure, psychoanalysis *must* believe not only that Freud was an objective scientist and right but also that childhood sexual abuse did not happen (at least not to Freud's patients) and does not happen now (at least not very often). Masson's book was more than iconoclastic; it threatened the ground on which psychoanalysis stands: more than Freud's credibility, women's lack of it. Finally, the truth about women's lives did not matter to Freud. And neither the truth about women's lives nor the truth about Freud now appears to matter to the Freudians.

When Freud changed his mind and declared that women were not telling the truth about what had happened to them, he attributed their accounts to "fantasy." This was regarded as a theoretical breakthrough. What we—those of us who believe that women and children do not secretly desire and imagine sexual abuse—now know is that "fantasy" in the psychoanalytic sense is not what women, in reality, imagine or desire any more than "fantasy" in the pornographic sense is. Both psychoanalytic and the pornographic "fantasy" worlds are what men imagine women imagine and desire, because they are what men (raised on pornography) imagine and desire about women. As one doctor put it, pre-Freud: "Hysterics [meaning women] and children with a lively imagination"[5] falsely allege sexual abuse. Once one realizes that the abuse is real, it is the doctors' elaborate alibis for the perpetrators, and their fantastical theoretical reconstructions of the victim's accounts, that require the "lively imagination." The fantasy theory is the fantasy.

The doctors say that the victims imagine sexual abuse, which is fantasy, not real, and that their sexuality caused it. In fact, it is the doctors who, because of *their* sexuality, imagine that sexual abuse is a fantasy when it is real. The acts these scientific texts recount, like the acts committed against Freud's patients in their childhoods, are no less real and no less harmful than the acts committed against women and children in and because of pornography. Indeed, they are the same acts. Today, pornography is legitimized in the same way psychoanalysis is legitimized: it is all in *her* mind. Psychoanalysis, of which these articles are precursors, has been used to legitimize pornography, calling it fantasy; and pornography has been used to legitimize psychoanalysis, to show what women really are. Pornography presents itself as the answer to Freud's famous query: *this* is what women want.

Perhaps the process of theory-building occurred like this: Men heard accounts of child abuse, felt aroused by the account, and attributed their arousal to the child who is now a woman. Freud's contribution was the formal theory of fantasy and the unconscious. (The unconscious is where you put what you do not want to own up to; the analyst is supposed to be an expert on it.) Perhaps men respond sexually when women give an account of sexual violation, in the same way that men respond to pornography, which is (among other things) an account of the sexual violation of a woman. Seen in this way, therapy—and court testimony in sexual abuse cases—functions as a kind of live oral pornography. Psychoanalysis attributes the connection between the experience of abuse (hers) and the experience of arousal (his) to the fantasy of the girl child. When he hears it, he is aroused, so *she* must be aroused. When he does it, he likes it, so it cannot be abusive to her. Because he wants to do it, she must want it done.

This peculiar process, definitely psychosexual and in need of analysis, did not originate with Freud, these readings show. Freud and his contemporaries appear to have shared a mass sexual hallucination that became a theory that became a practice that became a scientific truth because men wanted it that way. They would no doubt protest that what they did was not "sexual," just as genital assault on a child with a waxing brush was, according to Fournier, a mere "*simulation of rape*,"[6] and sexual murders are, to some today, violence, not sex.

Consider the lengths to which Dr. Milne, the psychiatrist in the twentieth-century case of Peter Sutcliffe, tried for the brutal rapes and murders of thirteen women, goes to insist that the killings are not sexual.[7] The fact that Sutcliffe systematically killed first prostitutes ("Prostitutes should be exterminated. . . . They corrupt men."), then just any woman because she was a woman ("I realized she wasn't a prostitute but at that time I wasn't bothered. I just wanted to kill a woman."), apparently indicated nothing sexual about the killings to Dr. Milne. There was no suggestion, he testified, that Sutcliffe's habit of stabbing his victims through the same hole over and over "had a specific sexual symbolism." Mr. Ognall, the prosecutor, pressed him: "You take the view . . . there is no underlying sexual component in his attacks?" Dr. Milne: "In simple terms, although his victims were female and it might be thought to provide the suggestion that he must be a sexual killer, I am of the opinion that he is not primarily a sexual killer." Mr. Ognall then held up a seven-inch sharpened screwdriver that had been used to attack Josephine Whitaker. "There is absolutely no doubt that this wicked agent was introduced deep into the vagina with almost no injury to the external parts. That indicates the most fiendish cruelty deliberately done for sexual satisfaction. Do you agree?" Dr. Milne: "It may be a most vicious and foul thing to do, but not necessarily for sexual satisfaction." Mr. Ognall reminded the jury of how Sutcliffe had stabbed Jacqueline Hill through the breast. "Unless I'm very naïve . . . that betrays a specific, clear sexual element in his killing." Dr. Milne: "If you interpret it that way, it does suggest that there may be a possible sexual component. . . ." He still did not think that Sutcliffe was a sexual sadist. Mr. Ognall described the killing of Helen Rytka, whom Sutcliffe had hit with a hammer. When she was near death, he had had sex with her. "Could you think of anything more obscenely abnormal?" Dr. Milne: "I entirely agree with you, but still think that this was a use of sexual behavior for entirely the wrong reason—to avoid detection, quieten her and get away. . . . *It was what the girl expected.*" It is a wonder that Dr. Milne did not consider Sutcliffe's acts to be therapy.

Just as Sutcliffe did what he did as sex, Dr. Zambaco, practicing medicine in nineteenth-century Europe,[8] may have enjoyed the genital mutilation by burning he performed on the two little girls he "treated" for masturbation. He may also have enjoyed writing what he wrote about them, as many of his male readers may enjoy reading it—sexually. Is Zambaco the soul of a scientist playing at pornographer, or the soul of a pornographer playing at science? Alas, there may be no such distinction. In a precise parallel to Sade's classic of pornography, *120 Days of Sodom*, Zambaco's sexual sadism moves from observation and examination through treatment, including aversive conditioning and restraints, to surgery and cauterization, just as Sade's moves from objectification and molestation through rape, battery, bondage, and discipline, to maiming and burning. Unlike Sade, Zambaco's sadomasochistic march toward death, the ultimate erotic act—death is death whether in pornography or in medicine—was stopped because his charges were removed from his care. Both men used children. Both men did what they wrote. Sade had to buy or steal the access for which Dr. Zambaco was presumably paid.

The motion beneath Zambaco's account is the motion beneath many an exalted text: the motion of erection. Pornography was the exclusive possession of the elite until mass media democratized it. In the nineteenth century, men were looking at pornography, writing theology; looking at pornography, writing literature; looking at pornography, writing laws and designing our political institutions. Who is to say they were not also looking at pornography and writing and practicing science and medicine?

The world of Freudian psychology, in which everyday objects are infused with sexual meanings, resembles the world of pornography, in which everyday life is transformed into an erotic spectacle for men and a chamber of horrors for women. In the nineteenth-century texts, when women and children refuse to confirm their abusers' beliefs that they are secretly having a wonderful time, it is said that they lie, congenitally. The early psychoanalytic belief in "the mendacious dispositions of prematurely perverted children"[9] seems to be grounded in a belief that children lie about sex. In these documents, as in much law today, mothers—women—are said to instigate the lies or inflate fragments of stories into full accusations.[10] Women lie about sex for money, we are often told, and habitually use children to do it. In these articles, as in pornography, children are used like women, so to speak smell like women, in powerlessness, in sex.

Now as then, courtrooms have often served as settings for dramas of credibility on questions of sexual abuse. To counter the child's likely lies, Auguste Motet in the nineteenth century can be observed urging a legal methodology that simply assumes the child lies, then inventing facts and designing a psychological construction of the child's facts that is far more bizarre than the child's[11]—which at least came from someone who was there. Without skipping a beat since the nineteenth century, public defenders in sexual assault cases today are still taught in training courses that when a child "tells a credible story . . . [t]he theory of defense is that there was no abuse, and that the child, without appreciating the consequences, has adopted and incorporated the suspicions of one or more adults. . . . The *unspoken* theory of defense may be that . . . while the defendant may be guilty of indecent assault and battery, he's not a rapist."[12] If the defendant did the acts but did not force himself on the child, there was sex but no abuse; that is, the child wanted it. Defense lawyers are instructed to phrase questions to undermine what the child said happened: "These things which you say happened"; to show how easily led and eager to please the child is: "Mummy was mad and kept asking what happened even when you said nothing. . . . Finally you said yes, and she was happy . . . "; to suggest that the story was manipulated or coached by the prosecutor: "You came to court . . . sat in that chair and practiced your story. . . . They told you when your answers were wrong and told you the right answers"; and to establish that the child got words like "penis" from an adult: "Mummy told you that a ding-dong is a penis. . . . Some parts of the story were hard to tell. . . . Mummy helped you with those words too." Always Mummy. Defense lawyers are instructed to "attack the assumption that the child could only know about sex as a result of first-hand experience": "Establish that she has seen her brother's penis, anybody other than your client's; that the family gets cable TV; that a friend was molested . . . that she has seen

Hustler or a similar magazine or book." Exposure of a child to pornography, which can be a part of or a form of sexual assault, thus becomes a defense to a charge of sexual assault. When children accuse adults of sexual abuse, whether or not a picture was taken, both the media and the defense lawyers often impugn the credibility of children because they are children. They take the view that abusive acts are not violations because the acts are sex. Where do you suppose they got an idea like that?

Reading that nineteenth-century children could have their genitals burned with irons for masturbating and nineteenth-century women could be eviscerated because they were upset, one could conceive a certain gratitude to Freud for getting the psychiatrists' hands off women's bodies, directing their attention elsewhere. But the theory of women's minds he put in the doctors' hands is cut from the same cloth. It is just as a priori, hierarchical, asocial, sexualized, gendered, medicalized—and also damaging in its own way. Many scientists of the psyche continue to this day to deny the simple reality of sexual abuse and its formative role in fracturing women's minds, something that surely calls out to be healed as well as stopped. Trained to ignore systematic sexual abuse, healers of the mind seem seldom to have noticed the striking psychological similarities between its survivors and survivors of other horrors and systems of torture. For survivors of sexual abuse, as has been said of survivors of Hiroshima, "all feelings [cease] to be on the surface because one [can]not exist and at the same time live with such feelings of abhorrence, disgust, and terror."[13] Survivors of sexual abuse, like survivors of the Holocaust, picture a world that is "characterized by . . . the destruction of the basic landmarks on which the world of human beings in our civilization is based, i.e. basic trust in human worth, basic confidence, basic hope."[14] With sexually abused girls, who grow up to become more than a third of all women,[15] the simple reality of the experience is denied or considered victim-precipitated. The Holocaust and Hiroshima are not considered not to have occurred because their survivors exhibit these sequelae. But because the trauma of sexual torture induces attitudes and behaviors that in women are considered exaggerated expressions of femininity—such as passivity, dependence, fearfulness, fawning, masochism, and promiscuity—the sexual abuse of women is essentially seen not to have happened, because of its impact on its victims.

Sexual abuse of women, like other mass persecutions, happens to each victim as a member of a group. Yet, unlike most other persecutions, it happens to each victim in utter isolation. Like other political atrocities, sexual abuse is a collective experience; all women are targeted for it and live with the terror of this knowledge on some level. But unlike other political atrocities, each act of violation is experienced alone. Unlike any other catastrophe, natural or political, it is often attributed to the secret desire of the victim and the affection of the perpetrator. Although a politics of the experience of sexual abuse has begun to emerge, its inner world, with its effect on all women whether or not it happens to them, is as yet a silent one, its psychology unwritten. Some psychologists are now working with individual victims of rape, battery, sexual harassment, pornography, and prostitution, as well as incest and other childhood sexual abuse, with existing psychological tools. The exposure of the foundations of contemporary psychology in the nineteenth-century writings suggests, however, that a full recognition of the reality of sexual abuse calls for a new paradigm of the psyche.[16]

Women and girls had to be treated in certain ways for nineteenth-century medical texts to have been written. And because these texts were written, women and girls will be treated in certain ways. These articles are authoritative instructions on method, procedure, and technique. If she cries, tie her down. If she screams, burn her. She wants it; it will make her well. Like pornography, the approaches and procedures recounted and recommended and eroticized have been done, and will be done, to countless other women and girls *because of these texts.* To step into these pages is to step into a world the pornographers have made and discover that you are in your doctor's office and the "image" is you. No, the patient did not orgasm while having her clitoris sliced off without anesthesia. No, she was not sexually aroused by the pain or by being sexually examined in front of an audience of male doctors. No, she did not combine abstinence with nymphomania. But yes, Dr. Braun did examine her sexually in front of a crowd of giggling medical spectators; yes, he did slice off her clitoris;[17] and, yes, I think he did fantasize about her sexuality and call it diagnosis. These articles, as writer John Stoltenberg said of pornography, "lie about women but tell the truth about men."[18]

20

Liberalism and the Death of Feminism

Once there was a women's movement. I first heard about it in January, 1970, from the liberated issue of *Rat*, which Robin Morgan and a collective of intrepid women made by taking over the underground newspaper they worked on. From liberated *Rat*, one learned that something that excluded women from equal participation, that denigrated women's voice, that silenced women's contribution, that did not take women seriously, that patronized women—no matter what else that something did or didn't do—had to be publicly repudiated at minimum, and at best taken over and transformed.[1] I heard no one say at the time that feminists had censored *Rat*, although no doubt some people thought so. Liberated *Rat* was speech.

Then, there was a women's movement that criticized as socially based—not natural or God-given—acts like rape as male violence against women, as a form of sexual terrorism. It criticized war as ejaculatory politics. It criticized marriage and the family as institutional crucibles of male privilege, and the vaginal orgasm as a mass hysterical survival response. It criticized definitions of merit as implicitly sex-biased, class-biased, and race-biased. It even criticized misogyny in fairy tales.

When this movement criticized rape, it meant rapists and the point of view that saw rape as sex. When it criticized prostitution, it meant pimps and johns and the point of view that women are born to sell sex. When it criticized incest, it meant those who inflicted it, and the made children's vulnerability and enforced silence sexy. When it criticized battery, it meant batterers, and the notion that violence expressed the intensity of love. Nobody thought that in criticizing these ideas and practices, the movement was criticizing their victims.

It also criticized sacred concepts like choice from the standpoint of women's existence, women's reality. It was a movement that knew that when material conditions preclude 99 percent of your options, it is not

Talk at conference, "The Sexual Liberals and the Attack on Feminism," New York University Law School, New York, New York, 6 April 1987. First published in *The Sexual Liberals and the Attack on Feminism* 3 (Dorchen Leidholdt and Janice G. Raymond, eds., 1990).

meaningful to call the remaining 1 percent—what you are doing—your choice. This movement was not taken in by concepts like consent. It knew that when force is a normalized part of sex, when no is taken to mean yes, when fear and despair produce acquiescence and acquiescence is taken to mean consent, consent is not a meaningful concept.

This movement also criticized concepts that it claimed and transformed, like equality. It knew not only that the way equality had been defined was premised on a meaningless symmetry, an empty equivalence, but also that it was defined according to a male standard. It knew the limits of being told you could be either the same as men or different from men. If you were the same as men, you were equal to their standards; if you were different from men, you were different from their standards. This movement said that if that was equality, we didn't want it. We also had a better idea for what the end of inequality would look like.

This movement criticized the ruling concept of freedom, especially sexual freedom, and unpacked and unmasked it as a cover for the freedom to abuse. When people with power defended their oppression of women as freedom, this movement knew it was the thrill of their power they were defending. This was a movement that was critical of the freedom to oppress, not one that thought women would be free when we had more of it.

Some intrepid spirits even criticized love, saying that it was a lust for self-annihilation that bound women to their oppression. And, eventually and at great cost, some criticized sex, including the institution of sexual intercourse as a strategy and practice in subordination.

Implicit in all these criticisms was a criticism of abstraction as a strategy in male hegemony. This was a movement that always wanted to know where the women were, substantively. Where was *women's* "choice"? Where was *women's* "consent"? Where was equality as *women* define it? What did freedom for *women* mean? As we criticized male reality in this movement that was, we always looked for the prick in the piece. We found that abstractions were a cover-up for the gendered reality that was really going on. On this basis, this movement produced a systematic, relentless, deeply materially based and empirically rigorous critique of the male-dominated reality of women's lives and the glossy abstractions that made it seem not male-dominated. It uncovered, in this process, deep connections between race, class, and sexual oppression, and pursued them not as an afterthought, not as a footnote, not as a list, but because they were essential. This was a movement that said that every issue was a women's issue and every place was a woman's place.

This was also a movement that demonstrated against the Miss America

Pageant and *Snuff* and understood the connection between the two. It understood that sexual objectification as use and sexual objectification as abuse are two facets of the same problem, that the logic of both is making a person into a sexual thing. Miss America is the foreplay, turning a woman into a thing. *Snuff* is the consummation, turning that thing into a corpse.

This was a movement that defaced objectifying posters. It marched, it petitioned, it organized, it hexed Wall Street and levitated the Pentagon, it sued, it used whatever it could get its hands on. In the words of Monique Wittig, failing that, it invented.

Why did we do all of this? We did it, I think, because we were a movement that valued women. Women mattered. We were not defensive about it. When women were hurt, this movement defended them. Individually and in groups, it organized and started shelters and groups of and for all women: raped women, battered women, incest survivors, prostituted women. We did this not because those women were thought "bad" by society or considered outlaws or shunned. We did it because what was done to them was a systematic act of power against each one of us, although they were taking the brunt of it. This was not a sentimental identification. We knew that whatever could be done to them could be, was being, would be done to us. We *were* them, also.

This was a movement that took women's side in everything. Of everything, it asked the question: "Is it good for women?" Each woman was all women in some way. Any woman who was violated was our priority. It was a deeply collectivist movement. In this movement, when we said "women, we," it had content. It didn't mean that we all had to be the same in order to be part of this common condition. That, in fact, was the genius, one of the unique contributions, of this movement: it premised unity as much on diversity as on commonality. It did not assume that commonality meant sameness.

This was a movement in which people understood the need to act with courage in everyday life, that feminism was not a better deal or a riskless guarantee but a discipline born of a hostile reality. To say that the personal was political meant, among other things, that what we do every day matters. It meant you become what you do not resist. The personal and everyday was understood to be part of the political order we organized to change, part of our political agenda. To see the personal as the political did not mean that what turns you on grounds the policies you promote.

We also felt a responsibility to all women. We opposed women's invisibility, insisted on women's dignity, questioned everything that advanced itself at women's expense. Most of all, this movement believed in change.

It intended to transform language, community, the life of the spirit and the body and the mind, the definition of physicality and intelligence, the meaning of left and right, right and wrong, and the shape and nature of power.

It was not all roses, this movement that we had. But it did mean to change the face of this earth. It knew that this was necessary. It knew that we did not yet have what we need and believed that we could get it.

I learned everything I know from this movement.

Then something happened. Or started to happen. Or maybe it had been happening all along and some of us had overlooked it. The first time I noticed it was with the Equal Rights Amendment. We were told that we could and should have this constitutional amendment because sex equality under law was not really going to do very much, would not really change anything, surely nothing basic. What the movement had identified as the pervasive, basic oppression and exploitation of women by men became transformed into an evil called "sex-based classifications by law."[2] That, suddenly, was what sex equality had to change. Under this notion of sex equality, we were given the choice of being the same as men—the left's option for us—or different from men—the right's version. We were told that the left's choice was clearly better and the only route to true equality. So-called gender neutrality—ignoring what is distinctively done to women and ignoring who is doing it—became termed the feminist position. I heard no one challenge the fact that, under this approach to ERA, either way it was the male standard, either way it was not what the movement had in mind by equality. The ERA strategy based on this analysis was, apparently, that sex equality can be made nonthreatening to the hierarchical status quo and still be real. This approach never identified male supremacy as what we had to contend with. It presented the extraordinary spectacle of feminists ardently denying that sex equality would make much difference while urgently seeking it.

Then this started to connect with what was going on with abortion. While the women's movement had criticized the line between public and private and had identified the private as a primary sphere of the subordination of women, *Roe v. Wade*[3] had decriminalized access to abortion as a right to privacy. A movement that knew that the private was a cover for our public condition was suddenly being told—and saying—that the abortion right was our right *to* that same privacy. If you forgot what this movement knew, this seemed like a good thing, just as being the same as men seemed like a good thing. Men, especially straight white ones, live in a kind of gender-neutral universe, which is a lot better than the sex-specific universe women live in. Men have privacy. Maybe if women had some, things would be better. Then *Harris v. McRae*[4] came along and denied public funding for all women who cannot pay for abortions, playing out the logic of the private as we had known it all along. If you can't pay for it, you can't get it—or there are other ways to get it, which are not what rights look like. A coat hanger is not a right. The logic was that the government, the public, had no duty to fund publicly what the government was supposed to keep out of, the private. It is not that decriminalization wasn't an improvement over jail. It is that getting a right to abortion as a privacy right without addressing the sex inequality of and in the private sphere is to assume that sexual equality already exists.

These suspicions about the male supremacist nature of the privacy right were furthered by another thing some of us noticed. That was that the freedom of the penis to engage in anal penetration in the name of privacy had become a priority issue for women under the banner of "gay and lesbian rights," without connecting a critique of homophobia with a critique of misogyny. Nothing in the sodomy cases criticized gender, far less gender inequality.

If these suspicions are pursued into sex discrimination law, further difficulties emerge, for example, in *Sears v. EEOC*, a garden-variety sex discrimination case.[5] There we see a drastic disparity between women and men in some of the better-paying jobs at Sears over a long time, a massive statistical disparity, and the Equal Employment Opportunity Commission suing them. A woman—a feminist—testified that this was necessarily evidence of discrimination by Sears because women want the same things from employment that men want, like money.[6] Another woman—a feminist—testified that this is not necessarily evidence of discrimination by Sears because women want different things from employment than men do. The gender difference is consistent with this statistical disparity because women choose jobs that pay less because they are women.[7]

So you have a large pile of men at the top and a large pile of women at the bottom and the question is, Which of the two theories best explains that: the theory that says women are the same as men or the theory that says women are different from men? Obviously the latter theory does, especially if you believe that women do what they want to do and are free to want anything. Even then, the women's movement was fairly clear that Sears's position, even in the mouth of a feminist, justified an oppressive status quo that kept some women on the bottom, and it was perverse to do this in the name of feminism.

Then it became a good day to go back to bed (if bed is a safe and consoling place for you) the day that some feminist groups said that guaranteeing maternity leave to women is a form of sex discrimination, and a statute that does this violates Title VII of the Civil Rights Act of 1964. No feminist group that filed a brief in the Supreme Court case on the subject said that it was sex discrimination *not* to give women maternity leave. No one said that if Title VII required maternity leave be *denied* to women, *that* would be unconstitutional sex discrimination. Nobody said squarely that if all the people hurt by this deprivation are women, *that* makes it discrimination on the basis of sex. The Supreme Court figured this out all by itself. The Supreme Court, in a decision by Justice Thurgood Marshall, a Black man, said essentially that granting maternity leaves by law is not sex discrimination, it is sex equality.[8] Women getting what they need to work is what sex equality means. Once he did it, some feminist groups cheered and took credit for what they had opposed.

Then came the debate over sadomasochism. If it had escaped one before, it was hard to miss this breakdown in what the women's movement had meant. It changed the ability to say the word "we" in discussions of sexuality, including of sexual abuse, and have it mean anything. It seems to me that the advocacy of sadomasochism as women's first love, women's final destiny, what we would all do if we really did what we wanted, is based on the absence of a critique of why women *would* experience sexuality in exactly the way in which it has been shoved down our throats since day one: top down. Actually, women have largely rejected the politics of sadomasochism. But the residue of its defense has been destructive nonetheless. In discussions of sexuality, women don't say "women" anymore, but "speaking only for myself, I. . . ." The debate over sadomasochism made "women, we" taboo in the sexual area. It began in a moral morass and left us, politically, with an individualistic analysis of sexuality, undermining a collectivity that was never based on conformity, but on resistance to conformity.

Everything some of us had started to notice exploded in the discussion on pornography. As many of you know, Andrea Dworkin and I conceived and designed a law based on the politics of the women's movement that we thought we were part of and fielded it with others who were under the same illusion. It is a sex equality law, a civil rights law, a law that says that sexual subordination of women through pictures and words, this sexual traffic in women, violates women's civil rights.[9]

This was done in feminist terms: as if women mattered; because we value women; because it was not enough only to criticize oppression, and it was not enough only to engage in guerrilla activities of resistance, although they are crucial. We wanted to change the norm. To change the norm, we looked for something we could use. We took whatever we could get our hands on, and when it wasn't there, we invented. We invented a sex equality law against pornography on women's terms.

To no one's surprise (especially ours) it was opposed by many people. It was opposed by conservatives who discovered that they disliked sex equality a lot more than they disliked pornography. It was opposed by liberals, who discovered that they liked speech—i.e., sex, i.e., women being used—a great deal more than they liked sex equality. Then came the opposition from a quarter that labeled itself feminist: from FACT, the Feminist Anti-Censorship Task Force. At this point, for me, the women's movement that we had known came to an end.

In an act of extraordinary horizontal hostility, FACT filed a brief against the ordinance in court as part of a media-based legal attack on it.[10] They did what they could to prevent from existing, to keep out of women's hands, this law, written in women's blood, in women's tears, in women's pain, in women's experience, out of women's silence, this law to make acts against women actionable—acts like coercion, force, assault, trafficking in our flesh. Pornography, they said, *is* sex equality. Women should just have better access to it. Using the debased model of equality-as-sameness that the women's movement we used to know was predicated on criticizing, they argued that pornography must not be actionable by its victims because, among other reasons, "the range of feminist imagination and expression in the realm of sexuality has barely begun to find voice. Women need the freedom and socially recognized space to appropriate for themselves the robustness of what traditionally has been male language." Men have it; FACT women want it. Thus, "even pornography which is problematic for women can be experienced as affirming of women's desires and of women's *equality*" (emphasis added). This is a subquote from Ellen Willis in the brief: "Pornography can be psychic assault,"—get it, that rape only happened in your head—"but for women, as for men, it can also be a source of erotic pleasure. . . . A woman who enjoys pornography, even if that means enjoying a rape fantasy, is, in a sense, a rebel." From what is she rebelling? Their answer: "Insisting on an aspect of her sexuality that has been defined as a male preserve."[11] Now who can't tell the difference between rape and sex? Rape has been a male preserve. But to insist on being defined by what one has been forced to be defined by is, to say the least, a limited notion of freedom. If feminism aspires to inhabit rapist preserves, I am part of some other movement.

Equality in the FACT brief means equal access to pornography by women. That is, equal access by women to the population of women who must be treated in the ways that the ordinance makes actionable, so that pornography of them can be available. The FACT brief further objects that the ordinance "makes socially invisible women who find sexually explicit images of women in positions of display or penetrated by objects to be erotic, liberating, or educational."[12] In other words, an entire population of women must continue to be treated in the ways the ordinance makes actionable so that this other population of women can experience its eroticism, liberation, or education at their expense.

The FACT brief was critical of the politics of the ordinance for implying that in a society of sex inequality—where sex is what women *have* to sell, sex is what we are, sex is what we are valued for, we are born sex, we die sex—whoever does not recognize all that as a choice is demeaning prostitutes and oppressing women. It said that when the ordinance told courts that they could not use all the excuses they have always used to disbelieve women when we say we are sexually coerced, that it was not respecting women's consent. This was a movement that understood that the choice to be beaten by one man for economic survival was not a real choice, despite the appearance of consent a marriage contract might provide. It was not considered demeaning or oppressive to battered women to do everything possible to help them leave. Yet now we are supposed to believe, in the name of feminism, that the choice to be sexually used by hundreds of men for economic survival must be affirmed as a real choice, and if the woman signs a model release there is no coercion there.[13]

You might be wondering what the FACT response was to all the knowledge, data, understanding, and experience of women's sexual victimization presented in support of the ordinance—to all the women who wanted to use the law, the women who had the courage to speak out so it could exist, who put their lives, their reputations, and, yes, their honor on the line for it. Mostly, FACT did not mention them. They were beneath their notice. Coerced women, assaulted women, subordinated women became "some women." In fact, the FACT brief did what pornography does: it made harm to women invisible by making it sex. It made harm to women into ideas about sex, just like the right-wing male judge did who found the ordinance unconstitutional. Bottom line, the FACT brief was a pure address to the penis. And you know, it worked. Women's equality, in the decision that invalidated the ordinance as a prohibition on ideas, became one "point of view" on sex.[14] Doing something about acts of inequality became the regulation of a point of view. FACT does not deserve all the credit for this, because their power came from fronting for male supremacy. Nor do they deserve all the blame. That belongs with the pornographers, their legitimate media cohorts, and the ACLU. But as an up-front antifeminist vehicle in the name of feminism, FACT made it possible for that right-wing judge to write, as he struck down the ordinance: "Feminists have entered this case as amici on both sides."[15] Yes: Linda Marchiano, the woman who was coerced into the pornography film *Deep Throat*, and Dorothy Stratten, who was in *Playboy* and murdered by her pimp, rape crisis centers, community groups representing working-class neighborhoods and communities of color—they filed on one side. FACT, an elite group mostly of academics and lawyers, filed on the other.

The Black movement has Uncle Toms and Oreo cookies. The labor movement has scabs. The women's movement has FACT.

What is the difference between the women's movement we had and the one we have now, if it can be called a movement? One way to describe the difference is liberalism. Where feminism was collective, liberalism is individualistic. We have been reduced to that. Where feminism is socially based and critical, liberalism is naturalistic, attributing the product of women's oppression to women's natural sexuality, making it "ours." Where feminism criticizes the ways in which women have been socially determined in an attempt to change that determination, liberalism is voluntaristic, meaning it acts as if we have choices that we do not have. Where feminism is based on material reality, liberalism is based on some ideal realm in the head. And where feminism is relentlessly political, about power and powerlessness, the best that can be mustered by this nouveau movement is a watered-down form of moralism: this is good, this is bad, no analysis of power or powerlessness at all. In other words, members of groups, like women, who have no choice but to live life as members of groups are taken as if they are unique individuals. Their social characteristics are then reduced to natural characteristics. Preclusion of choices becomes expression of free will. Material reality is turned into ideas about reality. And concrete positions of power and powerlessness are transformed into mere relative value judgments about which reasonable people can form different but equally valid preferences. Women's experience of abuse becomes a "point of view."

The way this gets itself up in law is as gender neutrality, consent, privacy, and speech. Gender neutrality means that you cannot take gender into account, you cannot recognize, as we once knew we had to, that neutrality enforces a nonneutral status quo. Consent means that whatever you are forced to do is attributed to your free will. Privacy protects the sphere of women's intimate oppression. Speech protects sexual violence against women and sexual use of women because they are male forms of self-expression. Under the First Amendment, only those who already have speech have protected speech. Women are more likely to *be* men's speech. No one who does not already have these rights guaranteed them socially gets them legally.

What has been achieved for women through these politics of liberalism? The ERA has been lost. Abortion funding has been lost. Nothing very significant has been accomplished with rape law reform. The Supreme Court is fashioning some progressive law on sex discrimination largely on its own. You know, it is an incredible insult when the state does sex equality better than the women's movement does it. We would have *lost* statutory maternity leave if this feminism had its way. And pornography has been saved.

Liberalism makes these results necessary, in part because it cannot see sexual misogyny. This is because misogyny *is* sexual. To be clear, it is sexual on the left, it is sexual on the right, it is sexual to liberals, and it is sexual to conservatives. Sexuality, as socially organized, is deeply misogynistic. To male dominance, of which liberalism is the current ruling ideology, the sexual misogyny that is fundamental to all these problems cannot be seen as a sex equality issue because its sexuality is premised on sex *in*equality. Equality law cannot apply to sexuality because equality is not sexy and inequality is. Equality cannot apply to sexuality because sexuality occurs in private and nothing is supposed to interfere in the private, however unequal it is. And equality cannot be more important than speech because sexual expression is sex and unequal sex is something men want to say.

There are more women in this room than it took Bolsheviks to topple the czar. We may have a women's movement to get back. Perhaps you will think of ways—we know many, the ordinance is one, and more are waiting to be discovered—to mobilize women's sex-based physical and economic insecurity, women's vulnerability and desperation, not to be defeated by women's sex-based personal indignity, women's boredom, and women's despair. Think about how to change women's fear, so that fear is no longer the most rational emotion we feel, how to transform women's invisibility and exhaustion and silence and self-hate. If we loosed all of that, what could stand against it? Also, think about how, against all odds, against history, against all the evidence, we can create—invent—a sex-based hope.

21

Does Sexuality Have a History?

It definitely does, if history is what historians do. This history—as defined by Freud and his successors, who see sexuality as a fundamental motive force in history; as pursued by Foucault and his followers, who see sexuality as socially created out of disciplinary power and discourses of knowledge—has been the history of pleasure and seeking it, of repression and derepressing it. The history these historians of sexuality write is the history of desire: of the impelled, compelled, wanting, grasping, taking, mounting, penetrating, thrusting, consummating. It is a history of some people's ecstasy and its prohibition or permission. It is a history of the active, the striving. It is what Nietzsche called a "monumental" history[1] (envision here the Washington Monument), an orgasming, ejaculating history of getting some.

This version of sexuality's past includes most but not all of what goes under the rubric "history of sexuality." Taken to a partial pinnacle in the collections *Pleasure and Danger*[2] and *The Powers of Desire*,[3] it also animates sexology-inspired retrofit versions of gay and lesbian history and the history of prostitution.[4] It is the history of what makes historians feel sexy. In it, prostitutes are "agents." In law, agent means someone whose strings are being pulled by someone else. Historians of sexuality mean someone who is actively choosing, pulling their own strings. Prostitutes are the freest of those who choose; you can tell because they make such a stigmatized choice. Why those who become prostitutes are always those with the fewest choices is not part of this history—maybe because facing this is not sexy. Even some gay male historians seem to need to know that a woman is being bought and sold for sex, out there somewhere, or being a man loses its meaning. This same spirit lives in the historical analysis of rape law as "surplus repression" and incest and sexual abuse of children as "intergenerational sex." It motivates the argument that pornography is an institution of sexual equality and the only historical problem is that women are com-

Talk, University of Michigan Institute for the Humanities, 12 September 1990, University of Michigan, Ann Arbor, MI. First published, 30 *Michigan Quarterly Review* 1 (1991).

paratively deprived of access to using women the way men use women. Particularly in the defenses of sadomasochism historical and current,[5] we are told that hierarchy is equality and slavery is freedom, maxims that everywhere but sex are recognized as an Orwellian mind-fuck but pass in this area as profound and daring.

This history of sexuality has certain imperatives. Here are just a few. First, sex is good and more sex is better. You need to know this to understand that when Foucault says that to say yes to sex is to not say no to power,[6] he is not criticizing sex. In this history, to sexualize something, like power, is to exonerate it, to urge its free expression. The norm is teleological and goal-oriented, such that as more sex occurs, history progresses. Second, sex is pleasure. It follows from the history of sexuality as the history of pleasure that it cannot be the history of oppression—except insofar as it is a history of resistance to the oppression of pleasure and getting it, a history of overcoming denials of pleasure being gotten. Third, this sexuality, to have a history, must go through changes. It must come in periods: how desire is defined, how pleasure is got, who does what to whom, how pleasure is restrained, how these restraints are dangerously and heroically broken out of. Sexuality must behave in this way or history is not had, at least not in the genealogical sense. One example is Foucault's analysis that sexuality was invented in the nineteenth century. Then it turns out it also existed in classical Greece, but never mind. The sexuality he serves us is the rise and deployment of the desiring subject, sexuality as the life and times of desiring man in bondage and being disciplined and loving every minute of it, and loving his struggle to get out of it even more.[7] The upshot is that when desiring man gets more or sees more or feels better or worse about what he gets or sees (and seeing sex is a form of getting it), history is made. A new day dawns. A new period is ushered in. The earth moves.

It actually helps this project of historicizing this sexuality that so much of sexuality is relational, happens between people and hence dies with them, so all these people are dead. There is no one around to tell the historians of sexuality that their account of how it was is not what happened to them. This makes it so much more indeterminate, so beautifully subject to endlessly varied interpretation, so Rorschach-like. Here we have the perfect academic subject. Now we can all have an erotic experience of the text and get tenure too.

Against this backdrop, my question is, what does any of this have to do with reality, or even realit*ies*? What, in particular, does this history of this sexuality, even sexualit*ies*, have to do with what people practice, or practiced, as sex?

This is a difficult question. What really happens in sex is largely hidden. Consider heterosexual intercourse, the dominant form of sexual practice. Mostly, people do not do it in public. Whatever intimacy sometimes goes along with it tends to be ephemeral. Pornography could be considered a nonephemeral presentation of what actually happens in sex. This is true of the most abusive pornography and of written pornography, but to make photographic pornography out of conventional heterosexual intercourse, one has to have sex so everything shows, so that the camera can see it. Generally people have sex so that if you look at them, you don't see much. And most of the essence of what goes on is not subject to external observation.

Looking for sex as practiced in history, one might look for reproduction, which might be regarded as hard evidence that sex took place in the past. But reproduction has only an occasional relation to what people practice as sex. Boys masturbating in circles seeing who can ejaculate the farthest, men putting money in slots to salivate over women in glass boxes with nothing on—that all of this is even about practicing up for reproduction is not very persuasive. Technically, one would only have to have had intercourse two or three times in their lifetime, a few more for good measure, to produce most of the current world's population. Practices of sexual abuse leave tracks on soft tissue and bones; physical anthropologists might be able to do *something* with that. But neither that nor its tracks on the spirit is spoken of, so leaves no trace. Once one considers what people actually do as sex, it becomes clear that a great deal of its reality is inaccessible to history. This seems especially true for sexual abuse, because its victims have not been permitted to speak, far less write their own history. How can a history of what is practiced as sex be written when those who have been used and abused through it have had no way of telling what happened to them? They can hardly tell it now, and they are all around.

How do we face these problems and give sexuality a history? History's answer—at least for the most part—has been so much the worse for facing these problems. The alternative is to write about what can be gotten at, basing it on what evidence exists, which is painted on vases; forget about what is not there, who and what are excluded, who is not permitted to paint on vases. Act as if what is at hand is all there is. Forget about what is not there, not known, maybe even not knowable. In other words, the silence of the silenced is filled by the speech of those who have it and the fact of the silence is forgotten in this clamorous discourse about sexuality, which then becomes its history.

This raises the question, What *is* known about what is practiced as sex? Can it be learned with live people? Some real answers to this question are emerging, largely as a result of the contemporary movement for the liberation of women. Most of it is new information. One thing that has been learned is that sex, as practiced, includes abuse, of women and children principally. They are abused in sex, in the course of the practice of sex, in order for (primarily) men to get the pleasure that defines sex. There is a lot of this abuse, but the point here is not its numbers but its impact on the possible experience of sex and its meaning for the relationship of sexual practice to how social life is lived over historical time.

We have this information because the women's movement has, it seems for the first time in history, created conditions under which the speech of those who have been abused and fetishized—those who have mainly not painted on vases, centrally women—has been validated and legitimized. The best study, by Diana Russell,[8] provides the first real information on the incidence of sexual abuse. Her interviewers, ethnically matched with the women they interviewed, went to 930 San Francisco households selected at random in a probability sample and asked the women about their experiences of sexual assault. In a revolutionary methodological procedure, what the women said was believed, written down, and treated as though it were data. Among the findings were that 44 percent of all women had been victims of rape or attempted rape at least once in their lives, and a great many more than once. Abuse of women of color was found to be more frequent than the average for all women. Thirty-eight percent of young girls had been sexually molested or violated or abused in some way by some person in authority or a family member, usually someone older, close and trusted, before they reached the age of majority. These figures dwarf any reported rates of these crimes. It appears from this that about a tenth of rapes are reported. Women are most often sexually abused by men they know or with whom they are close, from their own ethnic and racial groups. If all the sexual harassment, violation, abuse, intrusion, being yelled at on the street, being subjected to flashers, obscene phone calls is added up, only 7.5 percent of women reported experiencing none of it, ever.[9]

Have histories of sexuality seriously considered that something like this might have been going on before now? If not, how would it change sexuality's histories if it were? What creative methodologies might be devised to expose this in the past, its victims likely having taken it to their graves? How would the record read differently, in light of it? How is the absence of a trace of something to be analyzed? One would think that these possible facts might be at least as significant as Foucault's "hysterization of women's bodies"[10] (which he never really analyzes) in how sexuality, is, note the militaristic term, deployed? If sexuality is practiced *against* women in the process of men's pursuit of pleasure, isn't that significant? Once one knows that one has been kept from knowing this information by stigmatizing assaulted women so that the violation was a shameful fact about her that never went away instead of a shameful fact about what was done to her such that no one rested until it was made right; once one knows this information for the first time, wouldn't one's analysis of the past have to change?

Take as the primary historical impulse, not forgetting what happened. It is likely that whatever pleasure existed in the past has been amply documented in all this elegiac writing. This leads to a hypothesis about women's experience of sexuality historically, once sexual abuse is included within it. While ideologies about sex and sexuality ebb and flow, and the ways they attach to gender and map onto to women's status alter, actual practices of sex change little. The sexualization of aggression or the eroticization of power and the fusion of that with gender, such that the one who is the target or object of sexuality is the subordinate, usually a female, effeminized if a man or boy, are relatively constant. That hierarchy is always done through gender in some way, even if it is playing with gender or reversing gender or same-gendering, it is still using gender for sex. Gender hierarchy is either being played with or played out. The hypothesis would be that the practice of misogyny as sex has been there all along. Even if practiced more virulently here and now, it could be found in history, lying there like a snake coiled on a cold day. The implicit argument is: if the history of sexuality is measured by a standard of sexual equality, defined here as the absence of a norm of sexual force, variation may not be the most prominent feature of the historical landscape. The timelessness of the picture highlights how analyses requiring variation swallow and presuppose inequality.

For making such suggestions, feminists have been called ahistorical. We disrespect the profound and fascinating variations in the ways men impose sex on women to emphasize that however they do it, they do it. And they do it to us. If that has not changed enough to fit their definition of what a history has to look like, I submit that is not our fault.

So what *has* changed? If it has to change to make a history, what is different? If the landscape has to have edges the way a field has to have walls for us to get our minds around it, one needs to ask, what would a change be? This is not to dispute all the changes historians have found in the landscape of sexuality. It is to say that underneath all of these hills and valleys, ebbs and flows, there is this bedrock, this tide of the supremacy of men and the subordination of women. By this standard—under which equality would be a change—what *has* changed?

In the modern period, there have been some changes for the worse, away from equality. Women are expected to like sexual force better and better, partially as a product of the movement for sexual liberation. Freedom for women's sexuality becomes freedom for male sexual aggression. During this period, it appears that the actual level of sexual abuse to which women are subjected may have escalated. Age cohorts show a greater likelihood of rape for women maturing during the sixties than the thirties.[11] The FBI statistics (the FBI is always the last to know) show increases as well.[12] There are some indications of a drop in the age of the average rapist, which would dramatically increase the pool of men that women might legitimately take as a security risk. One used to be able to feel safe with thirteen- or fourteen-year-old boys. This cannot be assumed anymore, when five- or six-year-old boys are raping babies.[13]

It is my sense that more and more children are being sexually assaulted, including boys. The studies show a figure of 2 to 14 percent of boys are sexually abused as children.[14] I think it is higher. There are lots of reasons boys do not report. They include the shame and stigma of being treated like a girl—as such not a problem for girls, who are treated as who they are. For boys, there is a drop in status; raped men also experience this. There is the tendency of girls, as they grow up, to face as abuse their experiences of sexual abuse as children. Whatever they experienced as children, by the time of their late twenties, thirties, or forties, they tend to remember it, and feel it was not all right with them. Even if it felt like sex, even if that is all they have ever known as sex, it was abuse. Some boys go through the same process, in part through having learned it from women. Some boys make the abuse into sex. However they experienced it at the time, as adult men, it becomes a liberating, a loving education, what they wanted. Once abuse is sexualized, hence is not abuse, it is not reported as such.[15]

Another change is the explosion in the pornography industry. Social life is increasingly saturated with it and its sexualized misogyny. More information is available on the dynamic of pornography: the more pornography one consumes, the more violent and aggressive it needs to be to produce a sexual response.[16] Pornography increasingly desensitizes its consumers to abuse, as it sexualizes increasingly intense violation. This makes more and more force necessary for sexual arousal. Looking for what makes things move, if we know there is more sexual abuse, perhaps one explanation might be the one thing that is documented to make people experience abuse as sex.[17] That is, there is a connection between these changes.

Now go back to the histories of sexuality. These histories, on the whole, do not theorize gender. For example, Foucault in his second volume, *The Use of Pleasure*, brackets male dominance, the subjugation of women, and the prohibition of incest at the outset as essentially outside history. This is because "the extent and constancy of these phenomena in their various forms are well known."[18] Having gotten the flat and unbounded out of the way, he can proceed with sexuality and its history. Gone with them is the role of misogyny in sexuality and the place of rape, sexual harassment, forced prostitution, and pornography—sexual practices from objectification to murder. These practices are not unique to the contemporary period. What do they mean for the historians' precious sexuality?

Suppose the usual assumption that sexual abuse is exceptional and cabined off and means nothing for what people generally practice as sex is reversed? I would argue that sexuality is the set of practices that inscribes gender as unequal in social life. On this level, sexual abuse and its frequency reveal and participate in a common structural reality with everyday sexual practice.[19] The erotic sexualizes power differentials; the experience of hierarchy is the experience of sex under unequal conditions. The historical task would be to explore and map this location and to capture it as a dynamic, one that happens through gender. Then one would see how much racism, genocide, homophobia, and class exploitation could be explained. This would not be a history of who gets pleasure and how, but a history of who uses whom for pleasure and how they get away with it.

Sources that help this project include a book by Eva Keuls, *The Reign of the Phallus*, which gives a rather different interpretation of classical Greece and those vases.[20] German scholar Klaus Theweleit's brilliant study, *Männerphantasien*, analyzes the deployment of male sexuality in and as fascism culminating in Nazism.[21] The analysis and the materials are so rich, perceptive, and evocative, one almost forgives his Freudianism. An English historian, Sheila Jeffreys, has written *The Spinster and Her Enemies* on the suppression of the early feminist critiques of the use of sex for the subjection of women in England before and after the First World War.[22] Jeffreys's *Anticlimax* traces the development of sexology as the science of the suppression of women's attempts to resist exploitation through intercourse from the Second World War to today.[23] Stephen Heath, also English, has written *The Sexual Fix* on the rise of the drivenness of male sexuality, of sexuality as an imperative. He traces the thrust to getting some and offers a stunning gendered analysis of Charcot's clinic as a sexual spectacle and of the spectralization process, making sexuality a looked-at thing.[24] Thomas Laqueur, in *Making Sex*, historically traces how models of sexual difference have been predicated on views of the body and the place of nature in sexuality and reproduction. While it could use a tighter grasp on male dominance, gender ideology is effectively disconnected from known biology;[25] in his history, destiny is closer to making anatomy than the other way around. Jeffrey Masson's *The Assault on Truth* gives an historical account of Freud's rejection of his original belief that his patients were sexually assaulted when they said they were—giving rise to his theories of fantasy, the unconscious, and repression. It seems Freud could not hold onto the belief that all those men could actually have hurt all those children.[26]

The project building here, rather than a monumental history, is a critical history: in Nietzsche's terms, the history of those who suffer and are in need of liberation.[27] Especially for women, but not for women alone, such a history would rely on not forgetting what you know and refusing to forget what you cannot know. It would reject the posture of dominance in making the history that feels good. It would be an insubordinate history. Its task would be to give sexuality a history so that women may have a future.

22

Speaking Truth to Power

On the morning of October 7, 1991, much of the world was suddenly riveted to, debating over, galvanized around a set of converged concerns—sexual harassment, pornography, racism—that many of us had been trying to get taken seriously for over fifteen years. Snatches of conversation floating by on the street, altercations unavoidably overheard between the couple at the next table, steamy tones wafting up from the other side of the hot tub, grating voices dominating the planes' airspace were all engaged with the allegations of Anita Hill against Clarence Thomas in his consideration for a position as justice of the Supreme Court. While I went through bends from going from margin to mainstream so quickly, the mountain of national consciousness moved as the fitness for office of a Supreme Court justice was measured by his sexual maltreatment of one woman.

The media made this moment possible, but those hearings were less mediated than almost any event one has not seen in person. Usually, the media necessarily presents a highly selective reality, and what people can think is based on it. In this case, reactions were based on seeing the event with one's own eyes through that transfixed camera that gawked, unmoving, through virtually the whole thing. By contrast, the William Kennedy Smith rape trial of around the same time was presented in the more usual way. Reactions to that trial, while telling, were less of a referendum on women's status; no national teach-in on rape accompanied it, either.

Both confrontations were agonies of public and private speech, the language of sexual abuse colliding with the language of public discourse, the distance between the two measured by the word "credibility." The more refined versions sounded like "he spoke of some things he had seen in pornographic magazines,"[1] the rawer ones, "Who put a pubic hair on my Coke."[2] More speakable words were, "He spoke about his sexual prowess,"[3] which, when pushed, became the less speakable "Long Dong

Speech, Boalt Hall Law School, University of California at Berkeley, 5 November 1991, and University of New Mexico, 30 January 1992. Some parts were published in *Only Words* (1993).

Silver."[4] The long breath of the woman passing a point of no return preceded "He spoke of the pleasure he gave women . . . ,"[5] followed by the pause and drop in her voice before she spoke even the clinical words "through oral sex."[6] Patricia Bowman's composure broke on the sexually graphic language thrust at her on cross-examination, particularly on the details of Mr. Smith's states of arousal, until she managed to say to his lawyer, in direct address, what women have wanted to say to rape defense lawyers forever: "Your client raped me."[7]

There were the big words and the little words: little words like "lie," big words like "mendacity," halfway-in-between words like "fantasy." On one side of each case, there was the woman's spoken voice uttering the sound of abuse, the moment in which silence breaks on the unspeakability of the experience, the crack in the voice of the powerless, the echo of the unheard. On the other side there was the rearticulation of disbelief, the reaffirmation of silence of "Nothing happened," the attempt to push the uncomfortable and insubordinate reality back underground or into some pathological dismissible shape. In the Hill/Thomas confrontation, we heard the fancy language of professional high concept: words like "erotomania"[8] and "burden of proof,"[9] words that seem to convey so much to so few but actually say so little to so many, words that aim to frame the process, that purport to compress a complex reality but squeeze the life out of women, words that cost a lot of money to learn to use as your own, that magnify what is not there until they swamp a public discourse that takes for granted that nothing real is being said anyway.

So, how does saying things in public change them? In particular, what happens when the powerless and the powerful speak about sexual abuse in public? Since the public order was not designed to hear the truth of the sexual abuse of women, what happens around and beneath and beyond the coast-to-coast shock wave when you put the real language of sexual abuse in a Senate hearing on network television? How much of what makes sexual abuse possible lies in the dead-certain belief that it will never enter the public order, will never become part of anyone's Supreme Court confirmation hearing? Did this event change that? How much is sexual abuse supported by the equally dead-certain belief that if it ever does enter the public order, it will be shoved back into the silence from which it came under glossy public phrases like "the most intimate parts of my private life" or "the sanctity of my bedroom"?[10] How much of the media's standards of what they call taste works to cover up the realities of men's abuse of women, making that reality publicly unspeakable, making it more possible for that abuse to continue in private, even as defenses of pornography, including by the same media, are couched in terms of the necessity of free public speech, especially about sex? In other words, how much does the public defense of the sexual abuse of women through speech—the defense of pornography—contribute to the sexual abuse of women in private, including through sexual harassment in all of its words? Did this confrontation change that?

Is there a connection between Patricia Bowman's desire not to be paraded as a sexual spectacle of abuse in public—not to become a raped woman for the rest of her life when she still had that chance—and the press's asserted right to use her as its speech, its claim of the public's right to access her sexual violation by name? What do we make of the suggestion that it is women like her, not men like Smith, who make rape shameful? Is there a connection between sexual harassment and acquaintance rape in the view that women sexually belong to men and the media's opinion that women's sexual violation belongs to them? Is a common sense of male sexual entitlement to women as a class at work here that also extends to pornography and its defense? What does women's treatment when they speak about sexual abuse in public do to their ability to do so? What are, in other words, the sexual politics of this process, and what effect did the Hill/Thomas hearings and the Kennedy Smith trial have on these dynamics?

I believe Anita Hill and Patricia Bowman. What happens when they speak their truth to male power?

Because it was not tried in a court, Anita Hill's experience did not have a strictly legal frame. These are the facts as I understand them.[11] Anita Hill, a lawyer now law professor, accused Clarence Thomas, a former employer of hers at the EEOC among other places, of acts amounting to hostile environment sexual harassment eight to ten years before the hearings. The treatment she alleged included pressure for dates, not taking no for an answer, sexual assessments of her appearance, and vile pornographic comments. She stuck out the job but eventually arranged to move to another job. She told him she did not like it but did not complain officially. Over time, she kept her professional connection with him. When he was presented for confirmation for the Supreme Court, the FBI asked her about him in a routine investigation. She gave them the outlines of her experience. She asked them to investigate, to tell Judge Thomas and the other senators on the committee about what she said, but otherwise to keep it confidential. It was leaked to the press. Senator John Danforth, in not his most prescient comment, said, "This isn't going to be a big story."[12]

Professor Hill, when called to the Senate hearing that was investigating her allegations, testified with dignity, clarity, and simplicity. Her version of events was corroborated in part by friends she had told contemporaneously and over time, and by an unrebutted affidavit by another woman who recounted unwanted sexual pressure by the same man under similar circumstances.[13]

The nominee, who said he did not bother to listen to this testimony against him,[14] denied all sexual improprieties both "categorically" and "uncategorically."[15] He was angry, vehement, and belligerent. He attacked the process as a "high-tech lynching," invoking to a committee composed exclusively of white men, the true history of the use of amorphous allegations of sexual misconduct against Black men like him. The fact that Professor Hill is a Black woman was a new twist on this history. Sexual treatment of African American women has not traditionally provided the pretext for lynchings. Judge Thomas's invocation of race as a defense was aptly characterized by Kimberlé Crenshaw as an affirmative action defense to a sexual harassment charge.[16]

Judge Thomas refused to discuss what he called his privacy: "I am not here to put my private life on display for prurient interest or other reasons. I will not allow this committee or anyone else to probe into my private life. . . . I will not provide the rope for my own lynching or for further humiliation. I am not going to engage in discussions nor will I submit to roving questions of what goes on in the most intimate parts of my private life or the sanctity of my bedroom. These are the most intimate parts of my privacy and they will remain just that, private."[17] To this, Senator Joseph Biden replied, "Thank you, judge, you will not be asked to."[18] Supporting testimony for Judge Thomas went to whether Judge Thomas *could* have done what he was accused by Professor Hill of doing, not to whether he *did*.

The Senate debated, voted, and confirmed him 52–48.[19] The opponents of Judge Thomas's nomination needed nine more votes than they had originally. They got six of them.

I saw the Hill/Thomas hearings on live feed deep inside NBC, mostly on the set because whenever someone in Washington went to the bathroom, Tom Brokaw had to go on the air, and I went on with him. As a result of being in dialogue with what felt like the entire country at the time, these events live in my head in dialogue form. So here is an interview with myself on the nine most frequently asked questions from that dialogue.

Question one: Senator Arlen Specter observed that Professor Hill's story was inconsistent, that she kept changing it. Is this unusual?

Speaking of Senator Specter, I hope he pays for his abominable treatment of Professor Hill. She gave additional details when pressed. The reality she described was consistent throughout. Usually, when sexually abused women are asked more, they tell more; different questions elicit different details. It is also common to forget certain parts of traumatic events, but when put through the account again and again, it is relived, and more details sometimes surface in memory. Professor Hill said she initially described the incidents to her "level of comfort."[20] Later, she went past that. Her reticence seems a characterological self-containment, one expression of self-respect. She was not asking for pity or trying to put her troubles onto others. She also did not want those words in her mouth.

Women do not want to become pornography. Patricia Bowman had the same instinct. When the sexual abuse is in our mouths, that is what we become, because that is one thing pornography is: women performing men's sexually abusive scripts. Senator Grassley said, "It was an offensive story."[21] Deborah Norville said she "left feeling dirty somehow."[22] President Bush said he "felt unclean watching it."[23] The offensiveness, the dirt, the uncleanliness sticks to the woman, the woman of color especially. Eleanor Holmes Norton said the account made her uncomfortable.[24] Even among those who believed her, few people seemed as unsettled by the reality of what Anita Hill told about as they were by her telling it.

The revulsion stuck to *her*. I received one letter asking, "How could she lower herself to saying those things in public?" There was no letter asking, "How could he have lowered himself to say those things to her in private?" Judge Thomas said that once these allegations are made, they stick to him indelibly.[25] The fact of the matter is, once these things are said by a woman, they stick to *her* indelibly. Patricia Bowman will always be the woman who was fucked by a Kennedy, most invisible not behind the blue dot but behind those underpants of hers from that night that the defense paraded on national television.

Question two: All right, suppose it did happen the way Anita Hill said it happened. Why didn't she leave?

The real answer is probably lack of another opportunity as good. Most women are employed at men's will and pleasure. When they are sexually harassed, they are more likely to be damaged in their employment if they leave and sue than if they stick it out. If they fight openly, they are likely to be blackballed, blacklisted, regarded as troublemakers and liars, and not hired. The same question is asked of battered women. Both have a right to be where they are, to stand their ground. But there are also differences. Women are guaranteed equality at work, not in marriage. Wives have a legal right not to be battered but not to be married to that particular man. Anita Hill had a legal right to *that particular* job without being sexually harassed in it. So, one, she had a right to that job without discrimination. Maybe she did not leave because she had a right to stay. Two, she got him to stop. Why should she leave? Three, she did leave.

Third question: But if it happened, wouldn't she have said so long before? Why did she wait ten years to complain?

Patricia Bowman complained right away; look at the good it did her. Data suggest that a lot more incidents of sexual harassment happen that are not reported than are reported that did not happen. Besides, the law was unclear at the time. Hostile environment sexual harassment was not reliably illegal yet. The D.C. Circuit thought so in one case from around then,[26] but one could not be at all sure which way the courts would go until 1986, when the Supreme Court first held it actionable.[27]

Besides, what relief could she have gotten from a court if she *had* complained back then and won? No damages; they were not statutorily available. (The Civil Rights Act of 1991, providing for damages in discrimination cases, passed after these hearings after being stalled for years. It may be just one of the lasting effects of what Anita Hill did.) No back pay; because she stuck it out, she had not lost significant work time. Legally, the best she could have gotten was an injunction ordering him to stop and help getting another position. She got both on her own. She lawyered it for herself as effectively as any lawyer who had sued and settled for ever could have, and at less cost on every dimension.

She probably also thought, as most women do, that she would not be believed. Was she wrong? Even if she imagined she might be believed, maybe she thought nothing would change as a result. Was she wrong? Many of the women who testified for Judge Thomas used as a credential that they had been sexually harassed by other men. No one said to them: tell us his name. Would they have? Presumably the women and maybe the harassers are still in the federal bureaucracy. Most women do not complain because they do not trust the legal system not to hurt them worse than they have been hurt already. They feel they will be punished for telling the truth. Are they wrong?

Anyway, she did complain when she knew other women's lives were on the line, facing this man making decisions about all of our lives for decades. When someone behaved as though she might know something important enough to *ask* her, she told them. When it would have been perjury not to give a truthful answer, she reported it.

Remember that there was no culture of reporting sexual harassment at the time. Back before there was a law against sexual harassment, few women complained, but that did not mean they were not sexually harassed. In situations like this, where the law recognizes something in the abstract, but often not in reality, the question is not why it takes so long for women to complain but why they ever complain at all.

Question four: But look, what Anita Hill said Clarence Thomas said to her are these "foul," "universally crude and obscene things," (this is the Alan Simpson voice),[28] so how could she keep talking to him?

Eleven professional calls in seven years is not what I call intimate. She is entitled to maintain a professional relationship with this man. These senators, with their delicate sensibilities, are lucky not to have to live women's lives. If women refused to talk with every man who ever said vile sexual things to us, we would be talking mostly to women and unemployed.

Question five: How could Clarence Thomas be the man he seems to be and have done something like this?

What was he supposed to seem like? A little green man from Mars? They are your ordinary everyday "decent" men we all know and love, our bosses, our judges, our doctors. Men are very different with women than they are with men. Specifically, men's public reputation among men and their private realities with women can make them seem like two different people if they ever converge. A lot of women thought serial killer Ted Bundy was a great guy too. As Andrea Dworkin put it, next time you defend a bank robber, bring in the ten banks he didn't rob. Courts tend to have a tighter sense of relevance than the Senate did, but the testimony of three other women who were said to have told of similar attacks on them by Smith were excluded from his trial,[29] so even the three other banks he maybe *did* rob may be inadmissible. The better question is, how many women does it take to make one claim against a man stick over his denial?

Question six: Well, if I was going to seduce a woman, what she said Thomas did sure is not the way I would do it. And if Kennedy Smith did only what *he* said he did, he's a cad and a lout, but that doesn't make him a rapist.

My job is not to write successful seduction scripts for men. It is to talk about what men do, and men *do* say and do these kinds of things. Anita Hill felt that Thomas wanted to bring her down.[30] That was, for him, the sex; he got pleasure from it. He wanted to be able to say exactly these things to exactly this kind of woman. If so, he got out if it what he wanted sexually. You know, questions like this suggest that people believe the man did it but do not care or think it should matter. Reducing rape and sexual harassment to bad manners suggests that even more.

Seven: OK, OK, we hear what you think about her and him. Let's look at the Senate's process. What do you think about how the Committee handled it?

Now I have a question for you: Why didn't the Democrats ask Clarence Thomas about his use of pornography from 1981 to 1983? Was a decision made to respect this man's right to use pornography, no matter how vicious? We're talking about sex with animals, rape scenes. A lot of people who have been investigated would love to be able to limit the investigation. Why was he allowed to? "Privacy" and "pornography" became code for each other. Whenever anyone went near the pornography question, down came the gavel and Senator Biden reminded us that we were not going to inquire into *that*. It did not have to happen that way. I want to know how that happened and why.[31]

One possibility is there was an agreement: the Republicans traded not asking her about something for the Democrats' not asking him about this. If so, it was a bad deal. Anita Hill was not being considered for a seat on the Supreme Court and appeared ready to deal with whatever came. Another possibility is, perhaps the Democrats were intimidated by Judge Thomas, bullied by him. The result is, we do not know if pornography is part of his private life or not. This is a complicated question, but does it invade your privacy to be asked about something that is not in it?

Whatever the reason, they failed to ask about his pornography use, the exclusion of experts on the question—in the Hill/Thomas hearings as well as in the Kennedy Smith trial—meant that information was left out that would have helped make sense of the evidence. Pornography of women having sex with animals was, at that time, available mainly only in so-called adult or sex shows, along with peepshows where live women under glass are paid money by men to perform sexually. In those places were booths, their walls wet with ejaculate, where loops of tape present women having sex with animals over and over and over again. *Long Dong Silver* was also in the loops at the time.[32] This stuff was not available in nice clean home video. One had to go to these places or spend a great deal of money for one's own film. If Judge Thomas saw this material then, he was unlikely to have seen it in the intimacy of his bedroom. A pornography store is not a bedroom. If this is right, this pornography was consumed in public, not in private. But we will probably never know, because he was not asked.

On the racial intimidation theory, maybe the Senators heard Judge Thomas's speech as a withdrawal speech: Enough is enough. Push me on this, I will withdraw. The Senators with Black constituencies in particular did not want to look responsible for that and be called racist. On this analysis, Judge Thomas was seen to represent race, Anita Hill sex, which avoided the rather pertinent facts that Judge Thomas is a man, like all the members of the Committee, and Anita Hill is Black, unlike any of them. They seemed not to get that a Black woman has sex *and* race and so does a Black man. Didn't it matter to their constituencies how their treatment of *her* looked?

A final theory to explain the committee's respecting of Thomas's limits is male bonding: the glass house effect. The Senators did not want to be called to account themselves beyond those limits—a fundamental rule of male politics being that the penis gets to do what the penis wants to do, and one is not permitted to expose it doing so. People said of Professor Hill that hell hath no fury like a woman scorned, but I think that hell hath no fury like a man exposed. On that analysis, this man made it very clear where the penis drew the line, and the fourteen men on the committee respected it viscerally, sympathetically, in a same-pain sense. (I think I saw Senator Ted Kennedy smoothe his tie whenever the word masturbation was mentioned.)

If Thomas had been asked about his pornography use, he could have said yes, no, or I refuse to answer. Yes: but I was between marriages and desperate and had no woman at hand to use so I had to use anonymous women. No: and then he could have been cross-examined, perhaps based on whatever the FBI had unearthed. They knew what was on Robert Bork's video card. If he said no, they could have said, "On such and such a night did you not go the Graffiti at northeast and whatever and rent *Big Mamma* et cetera?" A "no" could have left open a possible perjury charge, ticking like a time bomb, until the *Washington Post* got energetic. Where *did* the press go after his confirmation?

The pornography question was relevant beyond cavil. The effects of consumption of exactly this kind of pornography on attitudes and behaviors toward women, including legal attitudes toward rape and women's equality, are well-documented.[33] American women had a right to know. Nominees prior to Clarence Thomas have not been confronted with the Anita Hills in their lives, so we do not know how many judges would fail this test. Just as men like Clarence Thomas have become judges, men like William Kennedy Smith have become doctors without ever having to go to a public room and be asked questions as a question like, "Was pornography part of your medical training?"[34] of their fitness to hold women's bodies in their hands.

The Hill/Thomas determination turned on credibility. I think many people believe he asked her out; many believe he sexually pressured her;

many probably believe he commented on her appearance. Those who did not believe her, did not believe her account of the pornography. The pornography became the key evidence she was lying and at the same time was the one thing they refused to ask him about. The Committee proceeded as if the only way they could get to the bottom of the factual dispute between the two was to destroy her credibility and see if it could recover. In fact, they could have pursued independently the facts on which her credibility had supposedly foundered. Ask the FBI. Ask his first wife.[35]

Eight: So he was confirmed. What do you think the long-term implications will be?

Clarence Thomas was put on the Supreme Court, but something major moved. Professor Hill let out genies that will not go back into their bottles. One African American woman stopped the U.S. Senate for a week. Patricia Bowman's trial would likely not have made a ripple if this had not preceded it. Women are raped every day, even by scions of famous families, and their trials are not seen as worth much public notice. Male sexual compartmentalization skipped a beat. Reality got loose. Many occupants of public office have to have perpetrated sexual abuse, but they are never called to account. Professor Hill had the goods and, when asked, brought them out where it counted. Sexual impunity will never feel or be quite as perfect again.

A large percentage of Americans, men as well as women, white as well as Black, were outraged when the Senate initially refused to hear her testimony, believed her, and were shocked and discouraged when Clarence Thomas was confirmed anyway. The wall of misogyny was hit by many who had denied it was there. To say the same thing another way, a reality of pornography surfaced in normal political speech. It is easy to deny how deeply women are hated, and how the ways women are despised are sexual. How Professor Hill was treated is how women who go public about sexual abuse are treated. This time it was on national television. Women, in particular, saw it up close. What was said about her is what is said about them: she's a liar, she's a whore. A liar because it did not happen; a whore because it did, but she wanted it. As Patricia Williams put it, she was said to be "consciously lying, but fantasizing truth."[36] (Consistency has never been male supremacy's strong point.) Women's training as women is in forgetting what happens to us, not noticing what happens to other women, and in denying there is any connection between the two. Misogyny cannot be ended until the fact that it is there is faced. With Thomas's confirmation, many women did.

Anita Hill spoke truth to power. Sometimes, power took her truth on board. There was Senator Biden examining John Doggett, puncturing his leap of "faith or ego" that Professor Hill must have been interested in him.[37] There was Senator Heflin's dumbfounded articulateness that Judge Thomas did not even listen to Professor Hill's testimony.[38] There was Senator Byrd's moving explanation of why he changed his mind. This old Southern gentleman "did not see the knotted brow of satanic revenge or hear the voice tremulous with passion" that would have led him to think Anita Hill was lying.[39] He saw the face of a human being and it was a Black woman's face. We heard Senator Kennedy; actually, we did not hear Senator Kennedy quite a lot of the time. But when he finally spoke, he criticized Judge Thomas incisively for invoking one form of oppression to excuse another.[40] Senator Biden, in the floor debate, perceptively formulated how even Anita Hill's believability had been turned against her: "She is credible, therefore believe her, or she is credible, therefore she is crazy." Then he demolished the challenges to her mental condition.[41] Barbara Mikulski told "the women watching this, do not lose heart, [for] we will lose ground."[42] In truth-telling, they rose to Anita Hill's standard.

Last question: Are there any questions about the Hill/Thomas episode that you don't have answers to?

There are. First, why did Professor Hill have more credibility before she started talking? At the stage at which the Senate and the country were incensed because it looked as though the Committee wasn't even going to listen to her, her credibility was at its height. Why are disembodied allegations more credible than real women are? Second, why was it not said that what Thomas did to Hill was protected speech? Where were the critics of political correctness at the office? Where were the libertarians and their bedfellows, the civil libertarians? Third, why were people so gripped by this? Was it just because the man had so much power? Granted, it was tremendous drama, high stakes, real suspense—great television, as they say. But equally gripping things happen in women's lives every day. The answer must lie in part with the nerve of sexualized racism that made this morality play a kind of prime-time pornography.

Finally, and this goes for Patricia Bowman's trial also, what does it take for people to believe that something happened? Many legal cases come down to whether a key witness is believed, but it is only in cases of sexual abuse that it is thought that this makes the whole claim inherently problematic. Does it have to have happened to you? Or, if it does happen to you, are you trying so hard to live it down in your own head that you do not believe it then either? With sexual abuse, both victims and perpetrators have a stake in disbelief: the survivors, that they are not surrounded by this, that it could *not* happen again; the perpetrators, that it is known that they could do this anytime they want.

Women learned, or relearned, that powerlessness means not being believed no matter how much sense you make or how much evidence you have. It means losing whether you are believed or not. And power means being believed no matter how little sense you make or evidence you have and winning whether or not you are believed. Even as they were displayed in high relief in the Hill/Thomas confrontation, something shifted under these equations. Remember the old philosophical puzzle; if a tree falls in the forest, and no one is around to hear it, does it make a sound? From the standpoint of the tree, the answer has always been yes. For women, abused for centuries, with no one around but their abusers saying no tree fell, power starts when their truth makes a sound. Anita Hill's did.

23

Mediating Reality

Two unimaginable things to the men who designed our governmental institutions were the mass media and women speaking in public. The dominance of the media over public discourse and the presence of women's voices in that discourse were equally unthinkable to them. In their context, men's sexual treatment of women in particular was relegated to the disreputable back room of politics by whispering campaign. Once women could vote and moved into the public sphere, including as journalists and lawyers, men's treatment of women, including through sex, began to occupy a more open place in politics. The extent to which women are citizens might even be tracked by how men's sexual use of women is discussed in public, specifically by whether it is trivialized or recognized as significant, not only in discussions of law and policy but also in elections for public office and contests over the legitimate exercise of public authority. The place in public discussion of men's sexual treatment of women can be observed to be a sensitive indicator of women's entitlement to occupy public space. When women speak in public in a media that is mass, how the governmental institutions are changed that the founders *did* imagine is a question seldom asked.

The media, which is not monolithic but does share certain common features, does not simply appropriate something from one part of the world and place it in another. Although realism, not fiction or fantasy, is its business, the mass media is not a simple conduit, a neutral transmission belt for reality. It transforms what it conveys. It selects, necessarily; its specific stance is that of an onlooker, spectator, watcher, or bystander, on sexual matters, voyeur. By norms of realism, to misrepresent reality is to twist and spread it in a way that is inaccurate to its source. By this standard, it seems to me that the media often makes violence, including sexual violence, unreal, falsifying its reality.

The consequences can be traced in reports on schoolhouse massacres in

Keynote, Journalism and Women Symposium (JAWS) fall camp, 12 September, 1998, Grand Teton National Park, WY.

Arkansas and Oregon where the first reaction of schoolchildren seeing their peers shooting at them was that it was not real. They had seen this kind of thing in moving pictures, leading them to experience it as not real even when it was actually happening to them.[1] What does this suggest for the reality status of what they see in the media? If it was not real to them when it was actually happening to them because it seemed like media, what they see in the media cannot be very real to them either. Children who fired assault rifles at their teachers and schoolmates said things like, "I didn't really think anyone was going to get hurt."[2] Before there was the media to dissociate reality this way, people said it was like a bad dream.

Under traditional norms of public discourse—the same ones that have excluded women as such from public voice—sexual use and abuse is not to be openly discussed. Today, it can be discussed some, but preferably without conveying that it is abusive, without admitting that it is sexual to the perpetrator, and obscuring that it is usual. The media seldom presents sexual abuse in the context of its actual severity, proportions, motive, and place in the unequal social status of the sexes. Specific incidents are often airbrushed while being treated as unusual and inexplicably exceptional, as if this is the first time anything like this has ever happened in the history of the world: news. Criticized for such de-realization, editors often respond that anything more gritty would shock and unsettle readers. One wonders who they think their readers are. Neither perpetrators nor victims are likely to be very surprised. Added up, they make a huge audience.

Pornography, that most mass of media, even as it seems to contradict this point, proves it in a way. Pornography in moving pictures presents sexual use and abuse in public, but typically as if the abuse (which is often real) is unreal, and always as if the sex (which is usually unreal in the sense of being mutually pleasurable for the people involved) is real. Editors who fear that the realities of sexual abuse will shock the public if disclosed are apparently not thinking of this very public disclosure of sex, which has more consumers than *Time* and *Newsweek* combined, whom one imagines are very unshocked. Sex, including sexual abuse, clearly *does* belong in public or it would not be in pornography. In both pornography and the mainstream media, sexual abuse is seldom presented so that the consumer feels what the person being used in the materials is feeling. Similarly, the mainstream press often sensationalizes reports of sexual atrocities so that they, too, become entertainment. Most users do not experience the materials as conveying abuse as long as they are enjoying themselves. (Sadists experience abuse of others as entertainment; a common undercurrent of this theme runs through both outlets to varying degrees.) At the same time, the norms of distinction between pornography, where sex is open, and the mainstream media where "we don't do that"—a distinction observed in degree of explicitness but otherwise more in ideology than practice—help keep the reality of sexual abuse, both in specific cases and in general, from being acknowledged in public, where accountability lives.

The norms that tend to censor coverage of sexual exploitation and abuse from the mainstream media, particularly from national outlets, put specific pressures on women in the media. When stories of sexual use of women by powerful men are reported, the pressure is to convey that these matters are properly private and trivial. While it polices a public/private line that permits abuse and sexual overreaching to go on in so-called private with little fear that it will be exposed as part of a man's public life, having women do this serves to keep norms that support male dominance from looking like male dominance. In the public mind, as a result of all these distancing and dissociating mechanisms, it becomes as if sexual use and abuse is not quite real. When so much of public consciousness is formed by the media, not seeing sexual abuse represented in public as it actually happens makes it seem to each sexually abused person as if they are the only one to whom it ever has happened.

Although there are exceptions, the media's standard story on issues of sexual abuse, which is substituted for reality, is as follows. On battering, it is women do it too, and if it was that bad, they would leave. On sexual harassment, it is that anything anyone takes amiss can be it and it is just sex. On child sexual abuse, it is that kids make it up, their mothers manipulate them into saying it, and children cannot tell reality from fantasy anyway. On rape, it is that women make it up, the data on its prevalence are invented, and some amount of it is inevitable. On prostitution, it is that women in prostitution like it. On ritual abuse, it is that it is so bizarre, who can believe it? On pornography, it is that it is harmless, the studies are manipulated, only right-wing nuts care about it, most of it is not violent, and some women like it too. These story lines become the reality backdrop for law and policy, the taken-for-granted assumptions that anyone who wants to do anything about the problem has to counter.

This party line of reality as mediated makes it impossible for people to know what is happening to women. As a partial antidote—from the people who brought you battering before the FBI would admit that it existed, now said to be the most frequently occurring crime; from the people who found sexual harassment lying around in public before there had been a single study documenting its existence; from the people who documented the harm of pornography that has been said for decades was not there and could not be substantiated; from the people who figured out that HIV was sexually transmitted a full year before that possibility even surfaced in public—here is some reality, un-mediated.

Children, in large numbers, boys as well as girls, are routinely sexually abused. Only a fraction of the acts is ever reported to anyone. The effects are massive and long-lasting. About a third of people who are sexually abused as children do not remember a particular act of abuse at any particular point in time.[3] If the torture is extreme and early, it can produce, as a survival strategy, a self fractured into multiple selves,[4] which is then used to convince authorities that the person is crazy rather than injured. Rape is an everyday occurrence. The data on its prevalence—the 44 percent of women being raped or subjected to attempted rape at some point in their lives[5] that, when mentioned in public, is thought so shocking—measures how many women are ever raped, not how many rapes occur. Most women in prostitution say they loathe it. They are being pimped, tortured, and want to leave but are trapped without alternatives. By psychological measures, they are traumatized worse than soldiers who fought in Vietnam,[6] and that war is over. Survivors of ritual abuse describe a parallel universe in which sexual torture, often of very young children, is organized and engaged in by political or religious cults. Prosecutors usually do not mention it for fear of disbelief; they charge child abuse instead, so a public record of it never gets made. Connected to all of this is pornography, a mass-mediated form of sexual abuse. All these abusive acts just mentioned and more can be found in it, and it contributes to making men into the people who want to do, and do, all of these acts of abuse. Pornography mass-produces sexual abuse.

Although there is little serious question that all these violations commonly happen, much reporting on them veers between sensationalism and suppression, making each story seem unreal as the media lurches between sexploitation and denial. The sensationalism is to attract an audience for the spectacle. The denial is to keep people from getting upset enough to take it seriously. One recurring trope, of which "Even Presidents have private lives" is the latest rendition, keeps the public/private line firmly in place. In this latest instance, the "private life" being referred to is sexual attacks on government employees and sexual relationships with workplace subordinates in public office buildings. People are supposed to be titillated or scandalized by these reports but not to connect these so-called private realities with things that matter, like the exercise of public power or the creation of public policies.

As President Bill Clinton is coming under scrutiny in the Paula Jones case, in which he is accused of sexual aggression against a state employee when he was Governor, and the facts about his possible sexual relationship with Monica Lewinsky, a young woman about half his age who worked as an intern in the White House, are beginning to come to light, the traditional norms of discussion of men's sexual treatment of women are being challenged and defended. The public façade is visibly ruptured. None of what is being said would be possible without women speaking in public, beginning with the women involved. This moment has also been prepared by women journalists covering everything from White House politics to the Supreme Court to terrorism. It has been prepared specifically by Enid Nemy's reporting on sexual harassment and Claire Safran's early analysis of it; indeed, the beginnings of public consciousness of the subject can be dated from Safran's article in *Redbook* and Nemy's article in *The New York Times*.[7] Women who have fought for space in newsrooms and reporting beats[8] and managed to get off the Style page, carry women with them in public. Without Nina Totenberg's landmark reporting on the Hill/Thomas story, sexual harassment would not be taken as seriously as it is in national politics. Without Judy Klemesrud's reporting of antipornography feminism,[9] that work would likely have disappeared in public. Few distinguish themselves reporting on pornography, it being perceived as a career-breaker. Cynthia McFadden's coverage of the O.J. Simpson trial and Christiane Amanpour's reporting of the genocide in Bosnia changed the way those events were seen around the world, making battering and genocidal rape more not less real and contributing to how states acted. Where would we be without Linda Greenhouse's legal lucidity, Maureen Dowd's antic political edge, Barbara Walters's grace and pointed presence of mind, Katie Couric's accessibility and bounce, Oprah Winfrey's credibility and perceptiveness, and the women producers behind the scenes at shops like *60 Minutes* and *20/20*, and so many more who *have* put the reality of women's lives on the map?

What women in the media can do, and sometimes win the fight to do, is place their stories of men's sexual mistreatment of women in real context. Sexual abuse is an everyday event—common, systematic, nonexceptional. Talk about it as if you know what you are talking about. Women in the press have been abused just as vast numbers of women in every profession have. Report and analyze events as if you live in the world we know we live in, in which sexual use, manipulation, and abuse can be believed to happen because they do happen. Talk about it as if it hurts and as if it matters because it does hurt and it does matter.

Remember that men, including many men who control the mass media, commonly use pornography. In Minneapolis, some women reporters covered the hearings on the civil rights law against pornography to which survivors of abuse through pornography came and testified. One reporter said to me of the stories she wrote, "I have never been so censored in my life." Pornography's well-documented role in sexual violation, instead of being systematically denied, could be considered in answering the press's frequent, agonized, and crucial question about specific sexual violations: how could this happen? How would this approach change how stories are reported? Apart from changes in demeanor and tone, it directs attention behind the story—for instance, behind teenage pregnancy, anorexia, heterosexually transmitted HIV—to sexual abuse. When nice boys kill, look for ritual torture, pornography. Look for multiplicity in the mother of a murdered little girl who competed in beauty pageants, in which sexual abuse is rampant. Remember that not only women are sexually violated: men violate other men sexually a lot more often than they say. It can explain a lot, including their fear of other men and certain events in international politics. Many of these men were together in prisoner of war camps and other aversive all-male settings like religious schools. Their abuse may explain their often extreme heterosexual posturing: they want to "be a man" so that what happened to them before will never happen to them again. Sexually abused men are women's allies; they just may not know it yet.

This perspective also frames a dual-track way of listening to the public acts of public men. Consider Bill Clinton's 1998 State of the Union address. His possible sexual relationship with a young woman intern had just broken in the press. Those attuned to men's sexual mistreatment of women are used to listening to public men speak publicly while knowing what they do sexually to women. You should hear prostituted women talk about the prominent johns in their books this way. As the men drone on in their public speech, what he does to her plays alongside it on track two in their heads. Remarkably, the whole country seemed to listen to President Clinton's State of the Union address that way; women in the media reported his address out of that same dual consciousness. Clinton says, "Save Social Security first!" and everyone is wondering what he really did to or with Monica Lewinsky. The first thing the commentators say is that the President did not mention the breaking scandal. The point is, what he did sexually registered in how he was heard talking about Social Security. As a moralistic point, this would be irrelevant, even abusive. As a point of sexual politics—understanding that how women are treated sexually matters, sex is a sphere of power, and personal and political are rarely as compartmentalized as many men prefer to think—it could not be more politically pertinent.

Many public men do and have done the equivalent of what it is said President Clinton did to Paula Jones, where the allegations involve unwanted sex, and with Monica Lewinsky, where they involve wanted sex with a subordinate. Traditionally, following its norms, the media has known but said nothing about both kinds of sexual infractions. A straight white man being lowered by, or to, sex is not a pretty picture. Whether Bill Clinton should resign depends on whether his ability to govern can survive being made into sex in public. Welcome to women's lives, Bill, and to Black men's and gay men's as well. Now that you are sex, do you have any authority left?

Either for your resignation speech, or to save you from having to make it, here is what you should do. Apologize to Monica Lewinsky in public for manipulating her vulnerability on the basis of age, sex, and status, for using your power relative to her and pretending that it was personal. Apologize for repudiating whatever was real between the two of you when the going got tough and for ruining her life in a way that you should have been able to foresee and cared about enough not to do. Her name will be the punch line of dirty jokes for longer than her lifetime. Then apologize, in public, to Hillary for breaking a promise you probably made to her that you would never do this again, and for making her a liar for you in public. How could you do that? She did not sign on for that kind of public humiliation and to be made to look like a fool. Then I want you to apologize to Chelsea, in public, for diddling with a girl only three years older than she is now. And then demand that the press stop running full body shots of her for the first time.

Next, apologize to Kathleen Willey for jumping her and calling her a liar when she said so, and then to Paula Jones for the same thing, and for not even remembering who she was, which I do believe. And then, I want you to apologize to all of the women you ever did this to. Since life is short and airtime is precious, "You know who you are" will have to do. Say you are sorry for doing this to them because of your sexual power needs. And then I want you to apologize—on your knees would not be too much—to the women of America for using women like Kleenex, and for betraying our belief that you were worth our votes, because we did elect you. Give meaning to the term "abuse of power," so that ever after it will mean the exploitative use of public power for private, sexual gain.

That is not why we gave it to you. Then I want you to work hard for women to prove to us that your personal limits will not be the limits of our politics in your hands.

Then, Bill, as your legacy for the next century, you can take credit for putting men's sexual use and abuse of women in private on the public agenda as relevant to fitness for office. Take credit for transforming the public sphere into a place where this way that men keep women down and out is finally aired in order to be ended. To follow through, set up a national Truth and Reconciliation Commission with branches in every city and town where men can go to tell, in public, all they have ever done to use and abuse a woman, where it will be up to the survivors, or their survivors, whether or not to give them amnesty. The men of America can go through the growth experience of public accountability that you are going through now.

Maybe this is what men are afraid of when they exclude women from public speech: having to face the women they have used and lied to, lied about, and left out. Maybe that is why they define this kind of talk as off-limits in public, so they can own the public and the private too. The real rules have been that they can do anything to a woman in private, and not talk about it in public, so if it escapes into the public they are entitled to lie about it, because it should not be there in the first place. So its reality has been the unrepresentable. They are nervous that women will not play by these rules, and a public record of their sexual use and abuse of women will undermine their ability to hold and exercise power as they have. If they give women a microphone or a byline, they are afraid that their sexual use and abuse of women will become a public issue. If women live up to their fears, and represent reality as we know and find it, and the use of public political power for private sexual profit is opened to public scrutiny, maybe by the end of the next millennium the private will be a place of sexual equality, politics will no longer be sexual, and sex will no longer be political.

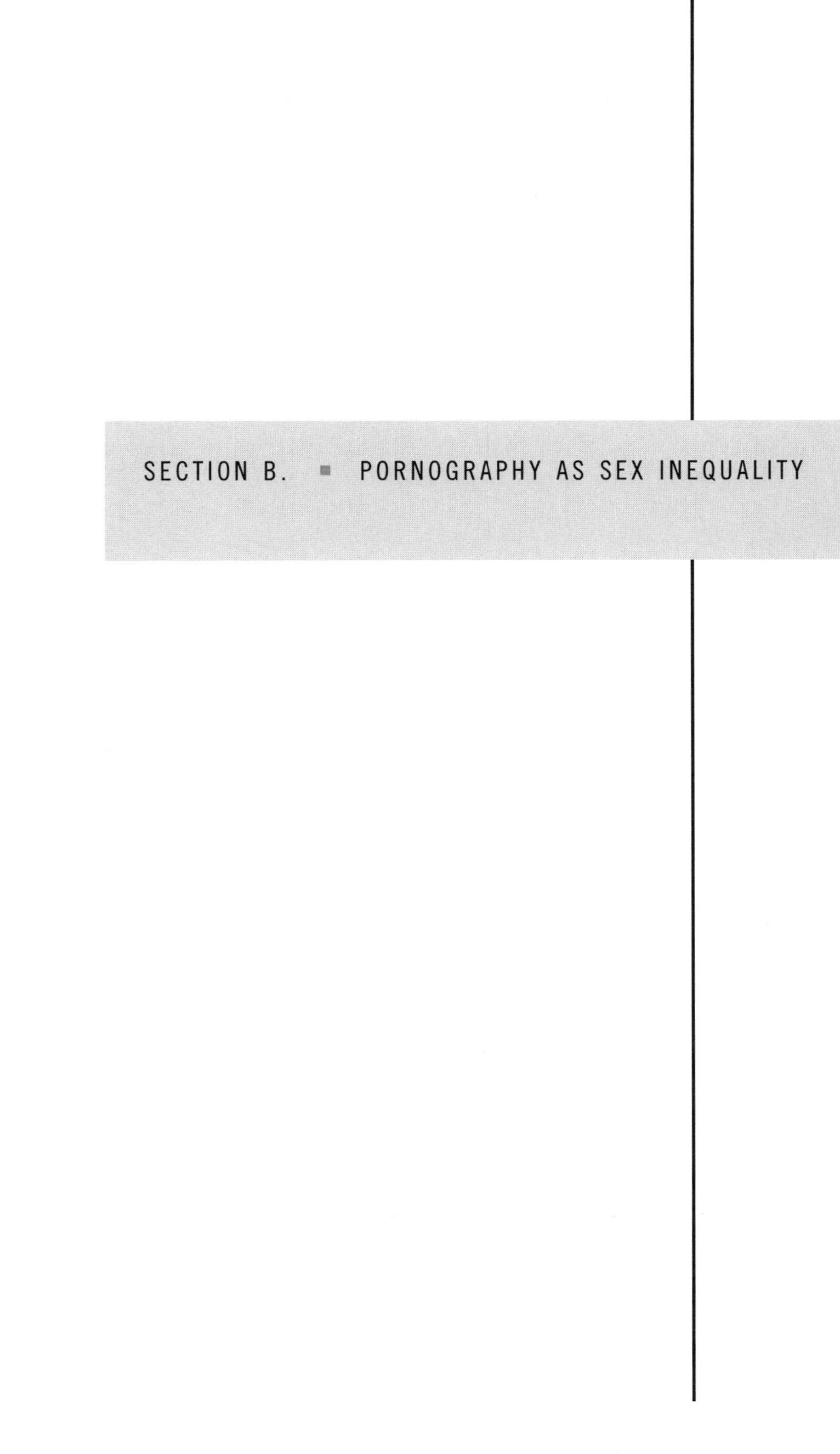

SECTION B. ▪ PORNOGRAPHY AS SEX INEQUALITY

24

Civil Rights Against Pornography

Over time, the United States government has tried various approaches to the problem of pornography. In 1970, the President's Commission on Obscenity and Pornography concluded that, although pornography may outrage sensibilities and offend taste and morals, it was harmless.[1] In the face of these findings, the Supreme Court nonetheless decided that when materials violate community standards, appeal to the prurient interest, are patently offensive, and are otherwise worthless, they may be prohibited as obscenity.[2] State and local legislatures have tried, among other maneuvers, confining obscenity by zoning it,[3] defining it as a moral nuisance,[4] hiding it behind opaque covers in secret rooms,[5] or by paying the pornographers to get out of town.[6]

Despite these attempts, the pornography industry has flourished. Obscenity law may be part of the reason. In order to find that something appeals to the prurient interest, a finder of fact must admit to arousal by the material. The more violent the material, the less likely this becomes, because people do not tend to want to admit publicly that they are sexually aroused by violent materials. Similarly, to be patently offended by materials, it is necessary to not be desensitized to them. People are neither aroused nor offended by materials to which they are desensitized, so that the more pornography one sees, the less offensive it becomes. Taken together, the tests of prurient interest and patent offensiveness have a built-in bind. Finders of fact are required to admit both that the materials arouse them sexually and that the materials offend them patently. That which turns them on, they must also reject as revolting. That pornography, as opposed to seedy literature, is the last thing obscenity law has been used to address, may make some sense in this light.

An even more fundamental problem is that pornography is so profitable—sexually to its users and financially to its pushers—that it effectively sets community standards. The more pornography exists in a community,

Testimony, Attorney General's Commission on Pornography, July 25, 1985, Chicago, IL. First published as "Pornography as Sex Discrimination," *4 Law and Inequality: A Journal of Theory and Practice* 38 (1986).

the more likely it becomes that community standards will de facto come to correspond to it. As Edward Donnerstein's data show,[7] consumer preferences escalate toward the more violent materials—a dynamic that means that new markets, hence greater profits, are created through creating community standards that tolerate more and more violating materials.

Primarily, though, pornography has been allowed to flourish because its real harm—the violation of women and children that is essential to its making and inevitable through its use—has been legally and socially obscured. This harm could be overlooked because the pornographers, who are pimps, take people who are already socially powerless—the poor, the young, the innocent, the used and used up, the desperate, the female—and deepen their invisibility and their silence. Through pornography, their subjection is made sexually enjoyable, sexually enjoyed, sex itself. Women and children who are made to perform for pornography are also made to act as if they are enjoying themselves.[8] The pornography made this way is then forced on women and children who are forced to act it out, that is, to correspond to the way the pornography uses and presents the women and children in it. It then becomes possible to point to what many of those in and outside of it have little choice but to do—the world pornography has made—and say that it expresses their nature because it corresponds to reality. This process has succeeded in making the victims of pornography so invisible as victims that through years of inquiry, including the 1970 commission, the only harm this government could see was sex it disapproved of seeing, rather than its most powerless citizens being hurt. Pornography has made its victims so silent that until the hearings on the proposed civil rights antipornography ordinance in Minneapolis in December of 1983, no official body had heard them scream, far less speak.[9]

The United States Supreme Court recently admitted that obscenity doctrine had missed something, someone actually, for whose injuries the law had been inadequate. When it recognized in the *Ferber*[10] case (over the opposition of the ACLU)[11] that child pornography is a form of child abuse, and some members of the Court became particularly clear that whether or not the materials are obscene is beside that point,[12] the Court found that pornography made using children could be criminally banned consistent with the First Amendment. Andrea Dworkin and I, with many others, have been working to expose the specific atrocities to women that have also been hidden, and for which existing law is equally inadequate. These abuses were documented in Minneapolis in December 1983, for the first time.[13] The abuses that were spoken in public include coercion to perform for pornography,[14] the pervasive forcing of pornography on individuals,[15] assaults directly caused by specific pornography,[16] and the targeting for rape,[17] battery,[18] sexual harassment,[19] sexual abuse as children,[20] forced prostitution,[21] and the civil denigration and inferiority characteristic of the second-class civil status endemic to this traffic in female sexual slavery.[22]

Pornography makes women what Andrea Dworkin has called "the sexual disappeared of this society."[23] Because these injuries are disproportionally inflicted on women, because they are inflicted on everyone who is victimized by them on the basis of their sex, because virtually nothing is being done about it, and because women matter, we proposed a new approach: that pornography be civilly actionable by its victims as sex discrimination and recognized as a violation of human rights.

I first want to discuss the harm of pornography, then the appropriateness of our civil rights approach to that harm, and finally, briefly, the First Amendment issues, beginning with an analysis of the evidence showing how the ordinances respond to the injuries in a way that existing law does not.

The harm of pornography begins with the women in it. In pornography, women are seen being bound, battered, tortured, humiliated, and sometimes killed, or merely taken and used. For every act in the visual materials, a woman actually had to be tied or cut or burned or gagged or whipped or chained, hung from a meat hook or from trees by ropes (as in *Penthouse*, December 1984), urinated on or defecated on, forced to eat excrement, penetrated by eels or rats or knives or pistols, raped deep in the throat with penises, smeared with blood, mud, feces, and ejaculate.[24] Or merely—and this includes the glossy legitimate men's entertainment magazines—taken through every available orifice or posed, presented, displayed as though that were her fondest wish in life. Penis-into-vagina intercourse is a minority theme.

Pornography sexualizes women's inequality. It makes the inequality of women sexy. It sexualizes, most broadly speaking, dominance and submission. Every kind of woman is used, each one's particular inequalities exploited as deemed sexually exciting.

Asian women are bound so they are not recognizably human, so inert they could be dead. Black women play plantation, struggling against their bonds. Jewish women orgasm in reenactments of Auschwitz. Pregnant women and nursing mothers are accessible, displayed. Women are splayed across hoods of cars, trussed like dead prey. Amputees and other disabled or ill women's injuries or wounds or stumps are proffered as sexual fetishes. Retarded girls are gratifyingly compliant. Adult women are infantilized as children, children are adult women, interchangeably fusing vulnerability with the sluttish eagerness said to be natural to women of all ages, beginning at age one. So-called lesbians, actually women sexually arranged with other women to be watched and used, are bought and sold with the rest.

Because the profit from these mass violations counts and women do not, because these materials are valued and women are not, because the pornographers have credibility and rights and powerful friends to front for their interests and women do not, the products of these acts are protected and women are not. So these things are done so that pornography can be made of them. Everyone who has been looking high and low for a "direct causal link" between pornography and harm might consider this one: it takes harming some women to make it.

The pornography industry is largely an industry of organized crime in which overt force is standard practice. Yet the question persists, are these women there because they like it? Pimps are known for their violence, yet the question persists, are these women there as an expression of freedom? In a society where women's opportunities are so limited that prostitution is many women's best economic option, even when explicit violence is not used, as often it is,[25] the compulsion of poverty, drugs, homelessness, foreclosed alternatives, and fear of retribution for noncooperation can be force enough.[26]

Every act that is exacted from the women in the pornography, who are typically made to act as though they are enjoying themselves, is acted out on yet more women integral to the pornography's consumption. Women and children on whom it is acted out often are given no choice about seeing the pornography or performing the sex. They are held down while the pornography is held up, turned over as the pages are turned over. Pornography is forced on them to destroy their self-respect and resistance to sexual aggression, to pressure or terrorize them into compliance, to instruct and season them for exact replication of the scripts and postures and scenes, or as a sex act in itself. In these many ways, the testimony shows, rapes are thereby stimulated, inspired, fantasized, planned, and actualized.[27]

The evidence is consistent from social studies,[28] clinicians who work with victims and perpetrators,[29] battered women's shelters,[30] rape crisis centers,[31] groups of former and current prostitutes,[32] incest survivors and their therapists,[33] court cases,[34] and police.[35] The most direct evidence, typically given the low value of those who provide it, comes from the victims themselves, used on one end of pornography or the other. This evidence, together with the laboratory tests in controlled experiments on what are termed nonpredisposed normals (usually men) and recent correlational results, supports the conclusion that exposure to pornography increases attitudes and behaviors of aggression and discrimination by men against women.[36] Depending upon how explicit the aggression in the pornography is, and how much of it is consumed under what conditions, the resulting harms vary but only in degree assuming that administering electric shocks is behavior, and that not seeing an account of a rape as an account of a rape is discrimination.[37]

Sex and violence are inextricably interwoven in the harm of pornography. They are interwoven in the material itself. Pornography makes sex into a violation and makes rape and torture and intrusion into sex. The sex and the violence are interwoven on every other level of the pornography's social existence as well. Over time and exposure, many viewers respond sexually to violence against women whether it is sexualized or not.[38] It therefore *is* sex, behaviorally speaking. Violence is used to coerce women into performing for materials that show violence, but violence is also used to coerce women to perform for materials that are sexually explicit, are subordinating, but do *not* show the violence it took to make them.[39] In these instances, the violence that is recognized as violence occurs off-screen, except perhaps for the bruises the makeup fails to cover. Women are also forcibly compelled to consume pornography until they acquiesce without further complaint or resistance in sex that violates their personal dignity, their desires, their bodies, not to mention their sexual preferences, without the need for further violence.

Pornography is an icon of male supremacy, the fusion of those twin icons, sex and speech. So legitimized, it neither appears nor needs to be violent all the time. Subjection is always violating, but it is not always violent; even less often is it perceived as such.

Further effects of exposure to pornography include the trivialization and objectification of women, increased acceptance of rape myths, desensitization to sexual force, and spontaneous rape-fantasy generation.[40] These are the so-called attitudes, so far from being generally considered violence that they are not even considered behavior. Sexual arousal does not desensitize so long as the materials escalate; no one seems sure whether it is an attitude or a behavior. The group results are clear. The only thing not yet predictable (although some of the researchers are working on the question) is which individual woman will be next on which individual man's list and for what specific expression of his escalated misogyny. We know that such acts will occur. We know that these materials, through the arousal they *do* cause, will contribute to these acts of misogyny, causally to many. We know that the more pornography is consumed in the society, the less harmful these acts will socially be perceived as being. We know that many such acts will typically occur in contexts traditionally regarded as intimate—in marriages and families, on dates, among acquaintances, on the job, in churches, schools, doctors' offices, prostitution—giving the aura of consent. Rarely between strangers. Most often between women and men.

On the basis of this evidence, we have concluded that pornography, not alone but crucially, institutionalizes a subhuman, victimized, second-class status for women in particular. If a person can be denigrated, and doing that is defended and legalized as freedom; if one can be tortured and the enjoyment of watching it is considered entertainment protected by the Constitution; if the pleasure that other people derive from one's pain is measure of one's social worth, one is not worth much, socially speaking. Legally speaking, tolerance of such practices is inconsistent with any serious mandate of equality and with the reasons speech is protected. The civil rights approach to pornography takes the position that this remains true even when the means employed are words and pictures, the enjoyment and pleasure gained are sexual and economic, and the victims exploited and violated are women.

Based on empirical investigation of the materials actually available now in this country that do this harm, the civil rights law defines pornography as the graphic sexually explicit subordination of women through pictures and words that also includes women being sexually used and abused, for example being dehumanized as sexual objects who enjoy pain, humiliation or rape, bound, mutilated, bruised, dismembered, in postures of servility or submission or display, or penetrated by objects or animals. Men, children, or transsexuals, all of whom are sometimes violated in these same ways in and through pornography, can sue for similar treatment.[41]

"Sexually explicit" is an existing term in common legal and popular use. It means explicitly showing sex. Adults generally know what sex is from their everyday experience. Indeed, until the term was used in this proposed law, it was difficult to find an adult who had any problem knowing what sex meant. Explicit means express, the opposite of implicit or implied or inchoate or suggested. "Sexually explicit," in law, is typically used to clarify the meaning of other descriptors for what can be regulated that are considered ambiguous or problematic, like "prurient."[42] It usually refers to the "X" in X-Rated, the line between what is shown on network television and written in mainstream newspapers, and what is not.

A subordinate is the opposite of an equal. The term "subordination" in the ordinance refers to an active practice of making a person unequal or placing a person in an unequal position. The verb "to subordinate" refers to the active processes of enforcement of second-class status. Teacher/student, employer/employee, guard/prisoner are fixed relationships of categorically unequal status. The idea of the law of sex equality in general is that man/woman not be such a relationship. Subordination has long been used to analyze race relations under white supremacy. Again, the only problem in identifying it appears to arise when it is applied to the situation of women in pornography. This seems to be a problem of the pervasiveness of the subordination of women, specifically of the sexualization of women's subordination, so that a woman being subordinated comes to be perceived as who women are and what sex is. This invisibility produces more harm, not less. As the difficulty of seeing the harm increases, so also can its severity.

Subordination can include objectification: making a person into a thing. It can include hierarchy: having made a person into a thing, making them less, lower. It can include forced submission: after making a person a thing and lower and less, they better do what they are told to do. At its extreme, subordination includes violence. All are fundamental to, and typical in, pornography.[43]

To be pornography, materials must be graphic and sexually explicit and subordinate women and also include at least one of the concrete list of particulars in the ordinance's definition. If the materials fit this definition, they do this harm. Just the fact that such materials exist does not make them actionable, however. Only alleged victims of specific activities of coercion into pornography, of forcing pornography on a person, of assault caused by specific pornography, and of trafficking—production, sale, exhibition, or distribution of provable subordination—can sue. Some people believe that most if not all of these acts are already illegal. To the extent they are on paper, they are not in reality, and nothing even on paper, civil or criminal, effectively reaches the materials through these harms. No existing law adequately reaches the materials that are the incentive, the actualization, and the realization of these harms. So long as the materials are protected and profitable, it will be effectively impossible to reach the acts it took to make them. The legal protections for pornography are an incentive to molest and rape and run.

To insist on limiting enforcement to existing criminal laws while leaving such materials untouched requires that the acts already be done before anything can be done about them. It also provides an incentive for murder in that, the more likely it is that the perpetrator will be criminally prosecuted, the greater incentive there is to do away with the evidence: another prostitute OD'd in an alley, so what? Conveniently, murdering women and children on camera creates snuff films,[44] a very profitable form of pornography that also ensures that the victim is not a witness. This is just one reason it is important that women other than those in pornography can also bring claims.

In theory, some of these materials could be reached by other legal approaches. Much of it invades privacy, but suits for media invasions of privacy through the media have not been helpful to the women who have sought relief for use of their sexual images without their permission.[45] Calling an injury what it is, is important to effectively addressing it. Lynching is assault or murder but was not effectively addressed by law until it was legally called a civil rights violation on the basis of race. Sexual harassment involves torts and batteries and assaults, but it was not until sexual harassment was recognized as sex discrimination that something began to be done about it by law. Existing law exists, and so does pornography, with its entire range of abuse. To rely on existing law to address pornography's harms is to be complacent in the face of human suffering, the legal status quo having permitted the social status quo.

The law of the First Amendment has been part of that status quo. The First Amendment is often spoken of in absolute terms but it does recognize exceptions. Speech interests are sometimes outweighed by other interests. The most common one is harm. Pornography as defined in the civil rights ordinance undermines sex equality—a compelling state interest and a legitimate concern of government—by harming people, differentially women. Compared with existing exceptions and counterbalances to the First Amendment, the harm that this law permits to be actionable meets a higher standard than any of them has met or has been required to meet.

This ordinance is not an obscenity law, but obscenity, on no showing of harm at all, is considered not speech, hence unprotected by the First Amendment. This is not a libel law, but it does recognize, as libel law does, that words can do harm. On this ground, laws against libel and invasions of privacy, both only words, are constitutionally permitted in some tension with the First Amendment. This is not a group libel law. Unlike with group libel, a criminal law, under the civil rights ordinance against pornography, the people who are hurt by the materials could use it themselves, proving a direct rather than presumed connection between their status and treatment and the materials it covers. And group libel laws are, if tenuously, constitutional. Women are not children. But on the basis of an assumption (not evidence) that children do not meaningfully choose to be in pornography and are hurt by being paraded having sex in public, criminal bans on the production and distribution of child pornography are constitutional. Although the sex equality law against pornography does not arise strictly under any prior recognized theory, each of these displays concerns, sensitivities, and policies that provide the reason that the First Amendment has been outweighed. Those same concerns, sensitivities, and policies, the ordinance shares.

Expressive values have been permitted to be qualified when the people hurt are real and the interests harmed matter: in the interests of unwilling viewers, captive audiences, young children, beleaguered neighborhoods (that means property values), for comfort and convenience, and to avoid that recently discovered atrocity, "visual blight."[46] If speech interests can become comparatively less valued for constitutional purposes when the materials are false, obscene, indecent, lewd, racist, provocative, dangerous, coercive, threatening, intrusive, inconvenient, or inaesthetic, they should be able to be civilly actionable when they can be proven to be coerced, assaultive, and sex-discriminatory.

Coercion, force, assault, and trafficking are not ideas. Coercion is not a fantasy, force is not a representation, assault is not a symbol, and trafficking subordination is not mere advocacy. Pornography is at the center of a cycle of abuse that cannot be reached or stopped without reaching and stopping the pornography that is its incentive, product, stimulus, and realization.

So far, the courts that have looked at this law have found it unconstitutional. Judge Sarah Evans Barker, accepting the legislative findings of harm,[47] opined that most women seem able to avoid being coerced into pornography and, since the law was not the same as any prior law, held it unconstitutional.[48] Perhaps most women can avoid sexual harassment; perhaps most people can even avoid murder. There are still laws against them. Judge Frank Easterbrook of the Seventh Circuit affirmed Barker's opinion. He, too, accepted that pornography does harm, but said that the more harm, the more protection. That kind of harm is the price of a free market in ideas even if it leads to genocide.[49]

I used to think the Supreme Court case on this ordinance would be the *Plessy v. Ferguson* of the pornography issue: women can be treated as inferiors because they are different.[50] That appears to have been optimistic. We may be facing something more like the *Dred Scott*[51] of this issue, the abolitionist issue: an institution under which some people can be bought and sold to others defines the meaning of their freedom under the Constitution, and they are not permitted access to court for redress against it.[52]

The bottom line of the resistance to this ordinance is that people who matter enjoy pornography. That is why they defend it. That is also why there is so much distortion of the civil rights approach: not that it would misfire, but that it would work as intended.

The fact that some people like pornography does not mean it does not hurt other people. As in any instance of a conflict of rights, the side one takes is a choice. So long as pornography exists as it does now, women and children will be used and abused to make it, as they are now, and it will be used to abuse them, as it is now. The question is whether we are willing to wait for each act of victimization that we know will occur to occur, relying on existing law to clean up after the pornographers—one mind, one body, one devastated life at a time—never noticing the gender of the bodies, never noticing that the victimization is centrally actualized through pictures and words, never noticing that we encounter the pornography in the attitudes of police, in the values of laws, on juries, in courts every time we try to prove that a woman has been sexually hurt. It tells us how much women are worth that something few people have much good to say about is more important than we are.

I hope that judges will see this law in court someday, in a real case in which a real woman who has been hurt is fighting for her life against real pornographers who are fighting to keep her, meaning all women, subjected in the name of freedom. Perhaps those courts will recognize that, even in law, things are sometimes done for the first time.

25

Pornography as Defamation and Discrimination

What matters for a legal system is what words *do*, not what they *say*. . . .
—Edward J. Bloustein[1]

Late one night a few years back, during a referendum campaign in Cambridge, Massachusetts, on the civil rights ordinance against pornography that Andrea Dworkin and I conceived,[2] a photocopied hand written leaflet was placed on cars and telephone poles in several neighborhoods. Over the scrawled black swastika the size of the whole page, it said: "Help STOP man hating, anti sex lezzie kike cunts from deciding what we can read!" This tiny triumph of economy of abuse referred to the supposed political attitudes, religious heritage, sexuality, and gender of the ordinance's proponents, and made the further quaint assumption that consuming pornography is just reading.

While the referendum organizers absorbed this and pondered what to do, to our astonishment the police decided that a crime had been committed and confiscated most of the leaflets before morning. Massachusetts has a law against group defamation.[3] Freedom of speech in Massachusetts appears to have survived the existence of this law and this instance of its enforcement. The Cambridge ordinance did not survive its detractors, however, who defended pornography in the name of a freedom of speech that would also have precluded this law.

In discussing this little masterpiece of vilification, one encounters widely differing responses to its elements. Part of the reason, I have come to think, is that real atrocities provide the vocabulary of experience that animates the concept of group defamation, and some of the situations it refers to are real to people, and some are not. Some are seen as threatening as well as offensive; others are regarded as perhaps insulting but comparatively innocuous. The comparatively more real situations are the Holocaust

Lecture, Distinguished Lecturer Series, 16 February 1990, Boston University School of Law, Boston, MA. First published, 71 *Boston University Law Review* 793 (1991).

against the Jews under Germany's Third Reich, the genocide of Native Americans, the slavery and segregation of Blacks in the United States and South Africa, and the internment and atomic bombing of the Japanese during World War II. The verbal and visual terms of vilification and denigration that mark these events, when reiterated in the words and symbols that were used to inflict them, bring their traumas alive anew as well as reinscribe and revivify a prejudice that did not begin or end with them. These experiences are not mere examples for application of the doctrine of group defamation. They are its life, its blood; it exists, and is legal to the extent that it is, because they happened.

In discussions of these epithets and in international instruments resolving to eradicate their doctrines,[4] the role of these words in systematically reducing, violating, and killing people because of who they are is recognized. Even when a law against group defamation is rejected as censorship, the defamatory words, and the ideas and attitudes they animate and actualize, are conceded to have justified, legitimated, and potentiated the devastation. The words are understood to construct social reality. The epithets from the leaflet that refer to race and religion, and sometimes those that refer to sexual orientation, are often granted to be not only offensive but also dangerous; the prejudices they express, mobilize, propagate, and imprint are seen as false and are condemned.

In the same discussions, one encounters the sense that the reality these terms represent is not happening here and now, at least not the way it was "there" and "then." These events, it seems, are largely regarded as essentially over, lurking only in the isolated unpleasant or insensitive remark or in the occasional bizarre but impotent incident, like Magic Marker leaflets published by Xerox and distributed by hand by night. Nothing large or systematic or cumulative is happening. In the view of most interlocutors, the formative experiences of group libel live on in discourse principally as analogy or memory, at most casting a shadow across the future in a tenuous causality. At the same time, how to explain these past events is a cause for anguished questioning: How could these atrocities have been allowed to happen? What could people have been thinking? How could they have not known or have looked the other way? How could the law have become so perverted as to legalize them? Implicit is that here and now these past outrages would be recognized for what they were at the time. "We" would have seen through them, spoken out against them, stood up to them, done something to stop them.

Here and now, there is something virtually never included in the lexicon of group defamation. People are being callously dehumanized, horribly brutalized, and sometimes killed. Verbal, visual, and physical atrocities are committed, demeaning an entire group because of a condition of birth, targeting them for physical atrocities that *are being done.* This case is distinctive in a number of ways, including the fact that a lot of money is being made from the defamatory materials, and that the connections between the material and specific physical abuses are far better documented than in any other instance.[5] Yet the atrocity is not acknowledged but is widely denied. Its ideas are neither widely identified as false nor generally condemned. On the contrary, the materials are rather widely celebrated, alternately defended as freedom itself and as the price "we" must pay for freedom. Not only is this permitted to happen, but it is defended by many as a measure of principle itself. I refer to the "cunts" of the leaflet: to pornography and the situation of women.

Part of the problem in this case is the lack of recognition that there is such a thing as the condition of women to which this body of materials could contribute. In reality, the status and treatment of women has certain regularities across time and space, making gender a group experience of inequality on the basis of sex. Traditionally, women have been disenfranchised, excluded from public life and denied an effective voice in public rules, denied even the use of their own names. Women are still commonly relegated to the least compensated and most degraded occupations. Their forced dependency is exploited and venerated as woman's role; their work is devalued because they are doing it, as women are devalued through the devaluation of the work they do. Women remain reproductively colonized, subjected to systematic physical and sexual insecurity and violation, and blamed for it. Women are commonly raped, battered, sexually harassed, sexually abused as children, forced into motherhood and prostitution, depersonalized, denigrated, and objectified—then told this is fun and equal by the left and just and natural by the right. Women's abilities and contributions continue to be suppressed, their achievements denied and marginalized and, when valued, appropriated, and their children stolen.

In the present as well, women are used, abused, bought, sold, and silenced.[6] The level of victimization of women varies within and across cultures; in the contemporary United States, for example, women of color are hardest hit.[7] But no woman is exempt from this condition from the moment of her birth to the moment of her death, in the eyes of the law, or the memory of her children.

This condition is imposed—sometimes in more covert forms of socialization, pressure, and inculcation to passivity and femininity, sometimes in the more overt forms of poverty and sexual violence. In the United States, the average woman does not yet have an income that is two-thirds that of the average man. Forty-four percent of American women report rape or attempted rape at least once in their lives. Thirty-eight percent report having been sexually abused as children. Between a quarter and a third are battered in their homes. Eighty-five percent have been, or will be, sexually harassed in the workplace, 35 percent of them physically. Most prostitutes are female.[8] These facts are uncontested and incontestable; yet they are not really acknowledged or faced. Mostly this reality is elided because neither women nor men like thinking about it, and because men like living it, or at least benefit from it. So its victims go under without a trace. Life and letters are unchanged. Law and politics go on as usual. Virtually nothing is done about any of it anywhere.

Pornography has a central role in actualizing this system of subordination in the contemporary West, beginning with the conditions of its production. Women in pornography are bound, battered, tortured, harassed, raped, and sometimes killed; or, in the glossy "men's entertainment" magazines, merely humiliated, molested, objectified, and used. In all pornography, women are prostituted. This is done because it means sexual pleasure to pornography's consumers and profits to its providers, largely organized crime. But to those who are exploited, it means being bound, battered, tortured, harassed, raped, and sometimes killed, or merely humiliated, molested, objectified, and used. It is done because someone who has more power than they do, someone who matters, someone with rights, a full human being and a full citizen, gets pleasure from seeing it, or doing it, or seeing it as a form of doing it.[9] In order to produce what the consumer wants to see, it must first be done to someone, usually a woman, a woman with few real choices. Because he wants to see it done, it is done to her.

To understand how pornography works, one must know what is there. In the hundreds and hundreds of magazines, pictures, films, videocassettes, and so-called books now available across America in outlets from adult stores to corner groceries, women's legs are splayed in postures of sexual submission, display, and access. We are named after men's insults to parts of our bodies and mated with animals. We are hung like meat. Children are presented as adult women; adult women are presented as children, fusing the vulnerability of a child with the sluttish eagerness to be fucked said to be natural to the female of every age. Racial hatred is sexualized; racial stereotypes are made into sexual fetishes. Asian women are presented so passive they cannot be said to be alive, bound so they are not recognizably human, hanging from trees and light fixtures and clothes hooks in closets. Black women are presented as animalistic bitches, bruised and bleeding, struggling against their bonds. Jewish women orgasm in reenactments of actual death camp tortures. In so-called lesbian pornography, women do what men imagine women do when men are not around, so men can watch. Pregnant women, nursing mothers, amputees, other disabled or ill women, and retarded girls, their conditions fetishized, are used for sexual excitement. In the pornography of sadism and masochism, better termed assault and battery, women are bound, burned, whipped, pierced, flayed, and tortured. In some pornography called snuff, women or children are tortured to death, murdered to make a sex film. The material features incest, forced sex, sexual mutilation, humiliation, beatings, bondage, and sexual torture, in which the dominance and exploitation are directed primarily against women.[10]

Hearings held by the Minneapolis City Council when our antipornography ordinance was introduced there documented the harms of pornography's making and use in proceedings a member of the city's Civil Rights Commission likened to the Nuremberg Trials.[11] The studies of researchers and clinicians documented the same reality women documented from life: pornography increases attitudes and behaviors of aggression and other discrimination by men against women. Women told how pornography was used to break their self-esteem, train them into sexual submission, season them to forced sex, intimidate them out of job opportunities, blackmail them into prostitution and keep them there, terrorize and humiliate them into sexual compliance, and silence their dissent. They told of being used to make pornography under coercion, of the force that gave them no choice about viewing the pornography or performing the sex. They told how pornography stimulates and condones rape, battery, sexual harassment, sexual abuse of children, and forced prostitution. Those not expressly coerced into pornography were there for the same reasons prostitutes are in prostitution: poverty, sexual abuse as children, homelessness, hopelessness, drug addiction, and desperation. Those who say women are in pornography by choice should explain why women who have the fewest choices are in it the most.

In the Minneapolis hearings, and the public events surrounding them, women and men spoke in public about the devastating impact of pornography on their lives. Women spoke of being coerced into sex so that pornography could be made of it.[12] They spoke of being raped in a way that was patterned on specific pornography that was read and referred to during the rape, or repeated like a mantra throughout the rape, of being turned over as the pages were turned over.[13] They spoke of living or working in neighborhoods or job sites saturated with pornography.[14] A young man spoke of growing up gay, learning from heterosexual pornography that to be loved by a man meant to accept his violence, and, as a result, accepting the destructive brutality of his first male lover.[15] Another young man spoke of his struggle to reject the thrill of sexual dominance he had learned from pornography and to find a way of loving a woman that was not part of it.[16] A young woman spoke of her father using pornography on her mother and, to silence her protest against her mother's screams, threatening to enact the scenes on the daughter if she told anyone.[17] Another young woman spoke of the escalating use of pornography in her marriage, violating her physical integrity, unraveling her self-respect and belief in her future, and destroying any possibility of intimacy. And she spoke of finding the strength to leave.[18] Another young woman spoke of being gang-raped by hunters who looked up from their pornography at her and said: "There's a live one."[19] Former prostitutes spoke of being made to watch pornography and then duplicate the acts exactly, usually starting when they were children.[20] Many spoke of the self-revulsion, the erosion of intimacy, the unbearable indignity,[21] the shattered self, and the shame, anger, anguish, outrage, and despair they felt at living in a country where their torture is enjoyed,[22] and their screams are heard only as the "speech" of their abusers. They spoke of the silence, and out of the silence, that pornography had imposed on them.

Of those who could not speak for themselves, therapists told of battered women tied in front of video sets and forced to watch, and then participate in, acts of sexual brutality.[23] Psychologists who worked with survivors of incest spoke of the role of pornography in sexual tortures involving sex with dogs and electric shocks.[24] Another study showed correlations between increases in the rate of reported rape and increases in the consumption figures of an index of major men's entertainment magazines.[25] Laboratory experiments showed that pornography that portrays sexual aggression as pleasurable for the victim—as so much pornography does—increases the acceptance of the use of coercion in sexual relations.[26] They showed that this acceptance of coercive sexuality appears related to sexual aggression, and that exposure to violent pornography increases men's punishing behavior toward women in the laboratory.[27] Pornography increases men's perception that women want rape and are not injured by rape, that women are worthless, trivial, nonhuman, objectlike, and unequal to men.

The testimony, taken as a whole, revealed that the more pornography men see, the more abusive and violent they want it to be. The more abusive and violent it becomes, the more they enjoy it and the more aroused they get. The more abusive and violent it becomes, the less harm they see in what they are seeing or doing. And the more they do what is in it.

Evidence of the harm of pornography has only become stronger over time. When explicit sex and express violence against women are combined, particularly when rape is portrayed as pleasurable or positive for the victim, the risk of violence against women increases as a result of exposure. It is uncontroversial that exposure to such materials increases aggression against women in laboratory settings, increases attitudes that are related to violence against women in the real world, and increases self-reported likelihood to rape. As a result of exposure, a significant percentage of men, many not otherwise predisposed, as well as the 25 to 35 percent who report some proclivity to rape a woman, come to believe that violence against women is acceptable.[28] Materials that combine sex with aggression also have perceptual effects that desensitize consumers to rape trauma and to sexual violence. In one study, simulated juries who had been exposed to such material were less able than real juries to perceive that an account of a rape was an account of a rape, through which the victim was harmed.[29]

Some of the most advanced research in this area studied the effects of materials that degrade and dehumanize women without showing violence, as that term is defined in the research.[30] Exposure to significant (but not naturalistically unrealistic) amounts of such material has been shown to lower men's inhibitions on aggression against women, increase their acceptance of women's sexual servitude, increase men's sexual callousness toward women, decrease the desire of both sexes to have female children, increase men's reported willingness to rape, and increase men's belief in male dominance in intimate relationships. For high-frequency consumers, these materials also increase self-reported sexually aggressive behavior.[31]

Men who use pornography often believe that they do not think or do these things. But the evidence shows that the use of pornography makes it difficult to impossible for men to tell when sex is forced, that rape is rape, and that women are human. Pornography makes men hostile and aggressive toward women, and it makes women silent.[32] While these effects are not invariant or always immediate, and do not affect all men to the same degree, there is no reason to think they are not acted upon and every reason and much evidence to think that they are—if not right then, then sometime; if not violently, then through some other kind of discrimination.

On the basis of this evidence and analysis, at the request of localities, Andrea Dworkin and I designed a law—the ordinance whose advocates were libeled in the leaflet mentioned—that recognizes pornography as a practice of sex discrimination. This law defines pornography as graphic sexually explicit pictures or words that subordinate women and also include one or more of a number of specified scenarios that typify pornography.[33] Four practices are actionable: coercion into pornography, forcing pornography on a person, assault due to specific pornography, and trafficking in pornography.[34] We did not claim that sexual atrocities never happen without pornography. We said that sometimes they do, but when they are proven to have happened because of pornography, it should be possible to do something about it by law. We did not claim that sexual abuse is all that happens because of pornography. We said that no matter what else happens, that does. Pornography is thus not so much a prognostication or representation of a status acted out elsewhere, but an integral dynamic in that second-class citizenship that is sex-based sexual abuse, hence a civil rights violation.

In this light, pornography, through its production and distribution, is revealed as a traffic in sexual slavery. Through its consumption, it further institutionalizes a subhuman, victimized, second-class status for women by conditioning men's orgasm to sexual inequality. When men use pornography, they experience in their bodies, not just their minds, that one-sided sex—sex between a person (them) and a thing (it)—is sex, that sexual use is sex, sexual abuse is sex, sexual domination is sex. This becomes the sexuality that they then demand, practice, purchase, and live out in their everyday social relations with others. Pornography works by making sexism sexy. As a primal experience of gender hierarchy, pornography is a major way in which sexism is enjoyed and practiced as well as learned. It is one way that male supremacy is spread and made socially real. Through the use of pornography for masturbation—what the leaflet was pleased to call reading—power and powerlessness are experienced and inculcated as sexual excitement and release. Inequality between women and men is what is sexy about pornography—the more unequal the sexier. In other words, pornography makes sexuality into a key dynamic in gender inequality by viscerally defining gender through the experience of hierarchical sexuality. On the way, it exploits inequalities of race, class, age, religion, sexual identity, and disability by sexualizing them through gender.

Seen in this way, pornography is at once a concrete practice and an ideological statement. The concrete practices are discriminatory; the ideological statements are defamatory as well. Construed as defamation in the conventional sense, pornography says that women are a lower form of human life defined by their availability for sexual use. Women are dehumanized through the conditioning of male sexuality to their use and abuse, which sexualizes, hence lowers, women across the culture, not only in express sexual interactions. Pornography makes women a public sexual spectacle and common sexual property, works to lower the public standard of their perception and treatment, terrorizes and humiliates women, and also at times offends their sensibilities. Like group libel's historic atrocities, pornography's effects are known but denied or blinked at while being acted out. The abusive acts are presumptively illegal but pervasively permitted, decried in public and savored in private.

When pornography's reality is examined against the terms of group defamation as a legal theory, some of the theory fits, but much of it does not. Pornography does purvey an ideology about all women; too, pornography of women and men of color sexualizes racism. It is in this sense defamatory. But its ideological impact, the prejudice it engenders, while very real, is only one of its effects and is not the one on which the civil rights approach most centrally focuses. The deepest injury of pornography is not what it says but what it does.

The damage of pornography neither begins nor ends in its mental content. For example, the text above says what it says but does not do what it does: it is possible to say what pornography says without doing what it does. Although all discriminatory practices say as well as do, coercion is not an idea; force is not an argument; assault is not advocacy, nor is trafficking a discourse. On a deeper level, pornography provides direct sexual stimulation, the experience of which is sex, not just the idea of sex. In the arena of legal regulation, no adequate analogy to this exists,[35] and no reply in kind is available. Pornography is not an argument about why bigotry is right, nor even a base appeal to bigoted interests; its pleasure is a reinforcer for bigotry that makes it feel natural.

The conditions of the production of pornography further distinguish it from the rest of group defamation. Nobody has to violate or use a person to make most anti-Semitic propaganda. Nobody has to pose for a lynching, i.e., be lynched, to create most Klan hate literature. Most cities do not offer businesses where one can go and pay to abuse a Jew or a Black, unless she is a woman and the abuse is sex. When a live human being is not used, and the materials are not sex, it makes some sense to discuss the materials as representations or images and to focus on their consequences as the effects of ideas. Their idea content is a substantial vehicle for the harm they do. But, except in a realm of abstraction divorced from reality (where most academics seem to prefer to reside), it covers up reality to discuss pornography in these terms. Both pornography and hate literatures are hateful; both propagate invidious group stereotypes; both promote and often instigate violence; both dehumanize. But pornography—because it is also an industry, because its dynamic is sexual, and also for the visual forms because the camera requires live fodder—is not only often predicated on abuse and eventuates in abuse; it *is* abusive. It does not only lay the groundwork or provide a persuasive basis or impelling rationalization, however destructive or immediate, for consequent acts. It is a kind of act.

For this reason, pornography is most appropriately addressed through what it does, as discrimination, not defamation. Defamation and discrimination emerge from distinct theoretical and political traditions. The idea of group defamation, like the idea of obscenity, is that group defamation expresses a harmful idea about a group; discrimination, even when it expresses an attitude, as it always does, is always recognized as an act. Defamation is a tort principally addressed to reputational harm to individuals; only derivatively and uncomfortably is it applied to groups. Discrimination is first and always a group-based concept, even when applied one person at a time. The law of defamation since *New York Times v. Sullivan*[36] has been explicitly circumscribed by First Amendment safeguards because state laws against individual libel, and group libel even more so, have been thought to potentially compromise freedom of expression. But discrimination that takes a verbal form has never—not until pornography was challenged as sex discrimination—been regarded as protected by the First Amendment.[37]

Discrimination is commonly accomplished through words: "you're fired," "it was essential that the understudy to my Administrative Assistant be a man,"[38] "whites only,"[39] "[m]ale help wanted,"[40] "did you get any over the weekend?,"[41] "sleep with me and I'll give you an 'A,'"[42] and "walk more femininely, talk more femininely, dress more femininely, wear makeup, have [your] hair styled, and wear jewelry."[43] Nearly every time a refusal to hire or promote or accommodate is based on a prohibited group ground, some verbal act either constitutes the discrimination or proves it. When words are not the discriminatory act itself, as harassing comments are for example,[44] they prove that the treatment is based on a prohibited group ground. In the discrimination context, verbal expressions can be actionable per se or evidence of actionable practices, not protected speech; they are smoking guns, not political opinion. No sexual harassment defendant to my knowledge has claimed his sexually harassing remarks were protected expression. Not yet.

Not even clearly symbolic conduct such as crossburning has been considered protected by the First Amendment,[45] even though, unlike pornography, it is pure expression. Crossburning inflicts its harm through its meaning as an act that promotes racial inequality through its message and impact, engendering terror and effectuating segregation.[46] Its damage to equality rights is not only symbolic but also real. Crossburning does not so much harm a group's reputation as it effectuates terror, intimidation, and harassment on a group basis. The First Amendment frame on the issue, taken alone, would be more likely to see what is said than what is done. When the traditions of defamation and discrimination confront each other, the First Amendment question is how equality can exist without free expression, while the Fourteenth Amendment question is how expression can be free without equality.

Defamation and discrimination address differently imagined harms. Defamation law addresses harm to group reputation; discrimination law addresses harm to group status and treatment. But to the degree status is a matter of reputation, reputation a matter of status, and treatment a matter of both, they overlap significantly.[47] Whether the treatment is verbal, symbolic, or physical, being treated as a second-class citizen certainly furthers the second-class reputation of the group of which one is a member. Segregated lunch counters or toilets or water fountains were not challenged as defamatory symbolic expression, nor defended because of what they said—that is, as symbolic speech or as expressions of political opinion—although they were arguably both expressive and political. Racial segregation in education was not regarded as protected speech to the extent it required verbal forms, such as laws and directives, to create and sustain it. Nor was it regarded as actionable defamation against African Americans, although a substantial part of its harm was the message of inferiority it conveyed, as well as its negative impact on the self-concept of Black children.[48] Yet the harm of segregation and other racist practices is at least as much what it says as what it does. As with crossburning, what it says is indistinguishable from what it does. Considered this way, pornography can be said to do substantial reputational damage to women, but its harm does not end there. Accordingly, the civil rights approach to pornography does not center on its defamatory aspects any more than the civil rights approach to segregation centered on its defamatory aspects, although they are present in both cases.

Pornography is propaganda, an expression of male ideology, a hate literature, an argument for sexual fascism. It conveys ideas just as any systematic social practice does. It is also, like most group defamation, often immoral, tasteless, ugly, and boring. But none of this is what pornography distinctively is, how it distinctively works, or what is most harmful about it. Was the evil of the Holocaust what it *said* about Jews? If the tortures at Dachau had been required to make anti-Semitic propaganda, would its harm be considered ideological only? If lampshades made of women's skin were sold beside the road, would the law address this practice through its impact on women's self-image or public reputation? The trade would offend, but would its legal harm be reduced to its offensiveness, as opposed to addressing what it took to make them?

The theory of group defamation does not adequately encompass the reality of pornography. One has to wonder whether it adequately encompasses the reality of group defamation either. For instance, building on the individual libel model, some laws of group defamation require that the statements be proven false or permit truth as a defense.[49] While much of what pornography says about women is a pack of lies, for the visual materials at least, it actually has to happen to be made, and in that sense is empirically true. Much group defamation contains a similar mix of lies with imposed realities. The stereotypes defamation presents begin false and remain largely false, but to the extent the stereotypes are imposed on a group, they will accurately describe at least some of its members sometimes. As when the world is made into pornography, success in forcing the world to correspond to a defamatory image makes defamation both more true and arguably more, not less, damaging. But where truth is a defense, the material is, for that reason, legally regarded as less defamatory or not defamatory at all.[50] Also, do we really want hearings on African American penis size or the bathing habits of Jews?

As another example, the law of group libel generally restricts the promotion of hatred, or hatred and contempt.[51] Hatred is an extreme feeling of negative animus that can express itself verbally or physically.[52] Discrimination law begins with an assumption of human status and focuses on deviations in treatment from that standard. If a man chains his dog in his backyard, only a few people would say that the dog's civil rights are violated. If a man chains a woman in his basement, more will. It does not matter if he loves or hates her. What matters is how he treats her and what that treatment and its permissibility say about what a woman socially is.[53] Perhaps, in terms of human rights, such treatment can be considered hateful regardless of his subjectivity. But the bottom line of discrimination, I think, is less do they hate and more will they kill. Hatred rationalizes and impels genocide, certainly, but so do colder things like self-interest, sense of superiority, or fun, and more banal things like indifference or system. In the case of women and men, love deals at least as much death, and so do hotter things, like pleasure and passion. The fact that pornography so often presents itself as love, indeed resembles much of what passes for it under male dominance, makes construing it as hate literature a challenging exercise. The concept of discrimination, by distinction, aims not at what is felt by perpetrator or victim or what is said as such, but at what is done, including through words.

Defamation and discrimination law also diverge in the mental requirements for the "willfulness" or knowledge of falsity required in many group defamation statutes.[54] Sincere sex bigots, which the consumption of pornography creates, would presumably not be covered under such defamation standards. Discrimination, although many parts of the law require a showing of group-based intent or motive, need not always be intended or meant to be discriminatory.[55] In reality, both in situations of group defamation and pornography, having one's humanity recognized enough to have it willfully degraded can be an improvement over its erasure by unconscious bigots.

This analysis suggests that an equality theory may remedy some of the same inadequacies for group defamation that it has for pornography. A discrimination theory of defamation would center on its harm to subordinate groups.[56] Group libel is an equality issue when its promotion undermines the social equality of a target group that is traditionally and systematically disadvantaged. Group defamation promotes the disadvantage of disadvantaged groups. Group-based enmity, ill will, intolerance, and prejudice are the attitudinal engines of the exclusion, denigration, and subordination that comprise social inequality. Without bigotry, social systems of enforced separation and apartheid would be unnecessary, impossible, and unthinkable. Stereotyping and stigmatization of historically disadvantaged groups through group hate propaganda shape their social image and reputation, arguably controlling the opportunities of individual members more powerfully than their individual abilities do.[57] It is impossible for an individual to receive equality of opportunity when surrounded by an atmosphere of group hatred or contempt.

In this light, group defamation can be seen as a specific kind of discriminatory practice, a verbal form inequality takes. Anti-Semitism promotes the inequality of Jews on the basis of religion and ethnicity. White supremacy promotes inequality on the basis of race, color, and sometimes ethnic origin. Group defamation in this sense is not the mere expression of anti-Semitic or white supremacist opinion but a practice of discrimination similar to sexual harassment and other discriminatory acts that take verbal form. It is arguably an integral link in systemic discrimination that keeps target groups in subordinated positions through the promotion of terror, intolerance, degradation, segregation, exclusion, vilification, violence, and genocide. The nature of the practice can be seen and proven by the damage it does, from immediate psychic wounding to consequent physical aggression.[58] Where advocacy of genocide is part of group defamation,[59] an equality approach to its regulation would observe that to be liquidated because of the group you belong to is the ultimate inequality.

Thus, any nation that has a constitutional guarantee of equality can potentially defend on equality grounds a group defamation statute that is challenged as a violation of freedom of expression.[60] A law against group defamation promotes equality and opposes inequality. It would violate any constitutional equality provision in existence for a legislature to pass a law authorizing the promotion of hatred on the basis of sex, race, religion, and national origin. It follows that governmental action against promoting group hate is protected under constitutional equality provisions. Just as governmental action to promote group hatred would violate a constitutional equality provision, governmental action to prohibit group hatred promotes constitution-based equality.[61]

Once laws against group defamation can be supported as well as challenged on a constitutional level, the tension between equality and speech would be resolved by whatever standards constitutional conflicts are accommodated. Typically, the courts would decide whether the group libel provision burdened expression significantly or at all, and whether its regulation promoted equality as unintrusively as possible, and in a way a legislature could have found effective.[62] The balancing would be done however balancing is done, but it would be two constitutional rights in the balance, not just one constitutional right against a nice idea or good manners or political sensitivity or standards of civility. In a constitutional tradition like the United States, the harms are comparatively trivialized when considered as defamation, the state interest obscured, disabling the constitutional defense of such laws against First Amendment attack. When the equality interest is recognized, focusing on lived consequences rather than message content, practices like lynching, crossburning, and pornography are revealed as expressive forms inequality takes, and the constitutional balance shifts.

Analyzing group defamation in equality terms recasts many well-worn issues in the free-expression debate. Perhaps the most startling concerns the dogma that there is no such thing as a false idea for purposes of constitutional analysis of speech.[63] When equality is recognized as a constitutional value and mandate, the idea that some people are inferior to others on the basis of group membership is authoritatively rejected as the basis for public policy. It is a false idea. This does not mean that ideas to the contrary cannot be expressed. It should mean, however, that group-based social inferiority cannot be imposed through any means, including expressive ones.[64] Because society is made of language, distinguishing talk about inferiority from verbal imposition of inferiority may be complicated at the edges but is nonetheless often very clear.[65] At the very least, such practices would not be constitutionally insulated from regulation on the ground that the ideas they express cannot be regarded as false. And attempts to address such practices should not be considered invalid because, in taking a position in favor of equality, they assume that the idea of human equality is true. There is no requirement that the state remain neutral when inequality is practiced—quite the contrary. Expressive means of practicing inequality have never been recognized as exceptions to this rule.[66]

In the United States, the receptivity of the law of free speech to an equality theory of group defamation can be partially assessed from courts' responses to the sex discrimination ordinance against pornography. The U.S. Court of Appeals for the Seventh Circuit in *American Booksellers Association v. Hudnut* found that the ordinance violated the First Amendment guarantee of freedom of speech.[67] The court reached this conclusion in spite of its agreement that pornography contributed materially to rape and other sexual violence, was a form of subordination in itself, and was partly responsible for second-class citizenship in various forms, including economic ones.[68] In some passages, the court conceded that pornography is an active practice.[69] Yet protecting pornography was held to be more important than avoiding or remedying its harms. Indeed, the court held that pornography's importance as speech can be measured by its effectiveness in doing the harm that it does.[70]

The civil rights law against pornography was held to be a form of discrimination on the basis of "viewpoint" because it was not neutral on the subject of sex-based exploitation and abuse.[71] By this standard, every discriminatory practice and every antidiscrimination law expresses a point of view. Acts express ideas; yet they are legally restricted and do not have to be proven expressionless first. Segregation expresses the view that Blacks are inferior to whites; rulings against segregation express the contrary view. Segregation is not therefore protected speech, nor are rulings against it considered "thought control."[72] Affirmative action plans and antidiscrimination policies are not regarded as discrimination on the basis of viewpoint, although they prohibit the view that Blacks are inferior to whites from being expressed by discriminating against them, including by telling them "you're fired" for the wrong reasons. This remains true even though deinstitutionalizing segregation does a great deal to undermine the point of view it expresses, just as making pornography actionable as sex discrimination would delegitimize the ideas the practice advances. Under the ordinance, misogynist attitudes toward women and sexuality can be expressed; they just cannot be practiced in certain ways, such as when verbal and visual subordination based on sex are trafficked. What the *Hudnut* court missed is both that acts speak and that speech acts.[73]

As an illustration of the convergence of expression with action, consider lynching.[74] Lynching has a vocabulary and a message. It is a vehicle for the communication of an ideology. It expresses a clear point of view about African Americans, one that is difficult to express as effectively any other way. One point of lynching is that other Black people see the body. The idea expressed by hanging the body in public is that all Black people belong in a subordinate position and should stay there or they will be horribly brutalized, maimed, and murdered. Another point of lynching is that white people see the body. Its display teaches them that they are superior and deserve to live: this was done for them. In the past, photographs were sometimes taken of lynchings and made available for sale for those who missed seeing the real thing.[75] Compare such a photograph, or the recent one of a Black man hanging lynched from a tree sent out by Klanwatch in an envelope with a warning that it is highly disturbing,[76] with a 1984 *Penthouse* spread in which Asian women were bound, trussed, and hanging from trees.[77] One cannot tell if they are alive or dead. In both cases, individuals are tied up and hung from trees, often with genitals displayed. In both cases, they are people of color. In both cases, sexual humiliation was involved. But when the victim is a man, the photograph is seen to document an atrocity against him and an entire people. I doubt many masturbate to it. Because the victim in *Penthouse* is a woman, the photograph is considered entertainment, experienced as sex, called speech, and protected as a constitutional right.

If Black people were lynched in order to make photographs of lynchings on a multi-billion-dollar-a-year scale, would that make them protected speech? The issue here is not whether the acts of lynching are formally illegal or not. As with the acts surrounding pornography, on paper lynchings were illegal, while in reality they mostly were not, until a specific law—a civil rights law—was passed against them. The issue is also not whether lynchings or sexual atrocities can be visually documented. The issue is, rather, given the fact that someone must be lynched to make a picture of a lynching, what is more important, the picture or the person? If it takes a lynching to show a lynching, what is the social difference, really, between seeing a lynching and seeing a picture of one? What would it say about the seriousness with which society regards lynching if lynching were illegal but pictures of lynchings were affirmatively protected and constituted a highly profitable, visible, and pervasive industry, defended as a form of freedom and a constitutional right? What would it say about the seriousness and effectiveness of laws against lynching if people paid good money to see one, and the law looked the other way, so long as photographs of it were mass-produced? What would it mean if the courts held that because lynching effectively expresses a point of view about African Americans, it is an "idea" whose mass expression, over and over and over again, thousands of pictures of it every year, is protected speech? What would it say about one's status in the community that the society permits one to be hanged from trees and calls it entertainment—that is, protects it for those who enjoy it, rather than prohibits it for those it harms?

Actually, *Hudnut* does not rule on the Indianapolis ordinance at all, but on some imaginary group defamation ordinance directed toward what pornography says. By turning harmful practices into bad thoughts and acts into ideas about acts, *Hudnut* does rule on hate speech regulation, which, unlike the Indianapolis ordinance, *does* turn on point of view. Under antihate laws, love is not racially defamatory; hate is. After reducing discriminatory acts to defamatory ideas, the *Hudnut* court held that no amount of harm from group-based speech can justify legal action by its victims.[78] This is simply legally wrong. Courts are supposed to measure value against harm, not by harm. A doctrinally correct approach to the ordinance would have balanced the harms of such materials against their value, if any,[79] or might even have considered the value of the materials irrelevant so long as they are proven to do injury that states can legitimately regulate. The harm of pornography, as made actionable by the ordinance, is not done through viewpoint, even though it is done in part through content. Pornography is identified in part through its content, but regulated through its acts, the acts the ordinance makes actionable. It must be faced that the *Hudnut* approach is fatal for regulating racial defamation, no matter how much harm it does.

Just as courts have often protected the group defamation of the past,[80] when the Supreme Court summarily affirmed *Hudnut*, protecting and defending pornography became the official state position in the United States. So now an entire class of women can be discriminated against so that others can have what they call freedom of speech: freedom meaning free access to women's bodies, free use of women's lives; speech meaning women's bodies as a medium for others' expression. As African Americans, men as well as women, once were white men's property under the Constitution, women are now men's "speech" because our pain, humiliation, torture, use, and second-class status is something they want to say. That they cannot say it without doing it does not matter.

Now that U.S. law has adopted the point of view of the pornographers on women's rights as its basis for state policy in this area, holding that the pornography is more important than the women they know it harms, one might ask the questions that are asked of the classic experiences of group defamation: Why the silence? Why the complicity? How can "we" let this go on? How can it be officially permitted? How can the law be so twisted as to collaborate in it? What are people thinking? Don't they know? Don't they see? Don't they care? Perhaps the lack of explanation for the success of past campaigns of group defamation is connected with the lack of recognition of present ones. Why have most people not heard all this before? Why have those who have seen the pornography not seen it in this way? Now that they know, why will most people find satisfying reasons to do nothing about it?

26

Pornography Left and Right

In a telling convergence between left and right, when Rush Limbaugh, a conservative commentator, said that I say "all sex is rape," he was repeating a lie that *Playboy*, a glossy men's sex magazine with liberal politics and literary pretensions, has been pushing for years.[1] This is a lie, rather than a mistake, on the assumption that they both read my work, which may be giving them too much.[2] That those whose politics conventionally divide them are united on this point reveals the common nerve struck by questioning the presumptive equality of men and women in sex.

With issues other than sexuality, it has been possible to ask whether sex equality has been achieved without being slandered. In other areas of social life, poverty, physical coercion, socialization to passivity, and sexual abuse from cradle to grave are not seen to support freedom, consent, and choice. But to argue that these same forces may create something other than equality in sexual relations is to call forth an escalating litany of increasingly defamatory names.[3]

To say that I—and others who analyze sexual abuse as part of gender inequality—say all sex is rape is a political libel, a false statement of fact that destroys repute in a community in which sex is the secular religion. Focusing an amorphous, visceral misogyny in sound bite, spit-out, get-her form, it targets hatred by harnessing the fantasy that men are deprived of sex and are about to be deprived of more sex. Sexual energy is thus mobilized and displaced onto those who would supposedly deprive men of sex as men are supposedly deprived of rape. For allegedly *saying* this, or what is said to amount to this, women are vilified, shunned, unemployed, unpublished, scorned, trivialized, stigmatized, marginalized, threatened, ignored, personally hated by people we have never met, and unread. All this for what we *do* say: sexuality occurs in a context of gender inequality, a fact no hate propagandist has yet tried to rebut.

Address, conference on "Laws and Nature: Shaping Sex, Preference, and Family," Brown University, 6 February 1993, and Lecture, Sumner Canary Memorial Lectureship, Case Western Reserve University School of Law, 25 March 1993, Cleveland. First published as Book Review, 30 *Harvard Civil-Rights Civil-Liberties Law Review* 143 (1995).

The line between those who wield this libel and those against whom it is wielded cuts across left and right. It divides those who want to maintain and advance under male supremacy from those who want to end it. It draws a line of sexual politics.

The same line divides the real sides in the pornography debate. Much of the left and right together, prominently including liberals, civil libertarians, and libertarians, occupy the pro-pornography side. On the other side are those for whom sexual abuse is real and matters, those who oppose inequality based on sex even in sexual relations. This alignment was visible, for example, in the sudden unity between the Moral Majority and some liberals in support of the U.S. obscenity approach to pornography,[4] a remarkable (if wholly unremarked) left-right consensus occasioned by the law Andrea Dworkin and I conceived to recognize pornography as a form of sex discrimination by allowing civil actions by victims who can prove harm.[5] The real threat to male dominance posed by this law propelled the liberals into the arms of the conservatives.[6] The right has always supported obscenity law; it embodies their concept of the pornography problem. The left has always criticized it as moralistic, antisex, homophobic, vague, overbroad, a "chilling" criminal sanction for expression of unpopular ideas, and a device for right-wing repression—indeed, as everything the same forces have said, falsely, of our proposed law. Once our proposal became a live possibility, this same obscenity law the liberals had long excoriated suddenly looked good. Now, anything that needed to be done about pornography could be done by obscenity law. Given a law that, unlike obscenity law, would actually be effective against the pornography industry, liberals woke up to the fact that U.S. obscenity law has done nothing against the industry and never will. Perhaps they noticed that the pornography industry, unstemmed by the prosecutorial efforts of three conservative administrations, has quadrupled in size since the U.S. Supreme Court announced its obscenity test in 1973.[7] Perhaps they noticed that obscenity doctrine is unworkable and unrealistic.[8] Perhaps they realized that no criminal law will ever be effective against a business that can be run from jail. The right likes how much obscenity law says, the left likes how little it does, so everyone is satisfied except those who want the pornographers, and the harm they do, stopped.

Another charge generated in the struggle over this proposed ordinance is that Andrea Dworkin and I are in bed with the right.[9] This fabrication, with the requisite sexual innuendo, emanated from liberals who defend pornography on the identical First Amendment ground conservatives do. Its sole function is to scare liberals off—which frankly does not take much. The right knows better than to embrace the sex equality the ordinance advances and they oppose. In fact, individual legislators on left and right have both supported and opposed the equality approach to pornography, but only one individual of the scores we have worked with closely identifies as conservative.[10] One person is not a wing or an organization. This lie would be easier to survive if it were true. If civil rights laws against pornography had the right's resources, money, access, votes, and power behind them anywhere, they would have been in place for over a decade.

Together with politicians, journalists, and pornographers, judges left and right in the United States have also taken a single position on the sex discrimination law against pornography for the same reason: to make injury through pornography civilly actionable as sex discrimination violates the First Amendment.[11] This convergence is not publicly decried as an unholy alliance or an abandonment of marginalized and powerless groups by the left. It is hailed as an objective reading of the law. In other words, when people converge without regard to left and right to support this law, their convergence is stigmatized as "strange bedfellows,"[12] sinister and unprincipled, and attributed by liberals to the right. When forces align across left and right to oppose the measure, to silence violated women and to bury recognition of their human rights, that is seen by the left as a victory for the left, and moreover bipartisan, so it must be correct.

Only if one assumes that left and right relevantly diverge is it remarkable to find them together. The assumption that the political spectrum is defined by these polarities dates from the French Revolution.[13] The left/right distinction, even as it makes increasingly little sense of many political cleavages, is nonetheless still taken as almost a natural fact, like north and south, and academic points are made by showing when extremes converge. But if left and right are not relevantly defined by distinction, their convergence is unremarkable.

Through the lens of a systemic analysis of sex inequality, left and right alignments in conventional politics share a deep, common, grounded bond, a common misogyny, a common sexualization of inequality that makes sexual abuse visible only as sex and invisible as abuse, inequality, or politics. This analysis exposes a new politics; recognizing these realities reconfigures political geography.[14] Left and right become two modes in one system: male dominance. In this perspective, women as such do not inhabit the same political terrain men do. They live in a flatter world of male authority characterized by possession, exclusion, diminution, violation, marginalization, stigmatization, and foreclosure of opportunities on the basis of sex packaged in a variety of distracting political guises. Whatever difference left and right can and do make at times, the politics of neither left nor right addresses the deep structure of women's condition or defines what must be done to change it.

This perspective illuminates the unremarkable (and widely unremarked) left-right convergence in two recent books on the subject of pornography: on the left, Edward de Grazia, *Girls Lean Back Everywhere: The Law of Obscenity and the Assault on Genius*,[15] and on the right, Judge Richard Posner, *Sex and Reason*.[16] Both treatments postdate the recent public exposure of pornography's concrete harms. Neither is part of the academic cottage industry that has sprung up to exploit the attention to the topic created by this exposure, rushing to capitalize on the breaking of women's silence while doing everything volumes of words can do to reimpose it. Rather, these two books are products of two authentic lifetime commitments.

De Grazia is a lawyer practicing at the line between pornography and art. Judge Posner is a theorist of the legal applications of means-ends rationality, centering on but not confined to economics. Both writers have a legal project as well as theoretical and political agendas that include pornography but are not limited to it. De Grazia locates on the left, which shows how little class politics it takes to be there in the United States; Judge Posner locates on the right, in the forefront of libertarian conservatism. De Grazia is a modern liberal. Judge Posner correctly terms himself a classic liberal,[17] pursuing a diminished role for government and expansive liberties for those who can take them. That this characterization defines the right of the existing spectrum, yet also exactly describes the position of de Grazia and much of the left on the question of pornography, makes the point. On pornography, left and right are two cogs in a single machine, meshing to crush women.

Focusing on his treatment of pornography is fairer to de Grazia, whose whole book is about it, than to Posner, who sets it within a sustained theory of sexuality, with one chapter on pornography and connections made throughout the text. The books are not comparable in other ways as well. De Grazia's book requires a lot of analysis to get at what he is saying; his position emerges more from his exercise of editorial prerogatives than from what he says in his own voice. Indeed, almost the entire book consists of selections from the work of others. Posner, in contrast, says what he thinks directly; he even writes his own book. Posner's is more open to, and worthy of, theoretical engagement; de Grazia's is narrowly legal by comparison. De Grazia's parade of actual historical materials, and the need to search out his argument like the murderer in a murder mystery, makes his book more difficult to analyze, if more fun.

De Grazia presents his argument substantially through exhibits, relying on choice and placement to convey his message. Interpretation of what he is doing is required to get at what he is saying. He traces a history of censorship of erotic materials from engravings through printed books, to photographs, films, and videos, to the beginnings of computers, in a presentation that unfolds like a documentary film. It is made of bits and cuts, including interviews he did, other people's briefs, magazine articles, transcripts, parts of the materials at issue, and so on. And on. The author, as well as much about his sources, is largely concealed this way. The materials are placed in a uniform format beginning with the source's name. To find out when and where it was said, you have to dig around in the back.

The book is organized to showcase de Grazia's one smart moment: his defense of William Burroughs's *Naked Lunch*[18] and Henry Miller's *Tropic of Cancer*.[19] The argument is: if material has value, it cannot be obscene. From this it follows that nothing can be done about it.[20] The reader can get bogged down in the parade of materials, fascinating in themselves, and think that de Grazia is not saying anything, but it is all strategized to convince the reader of this argument.

Although he never puts it this way, de Grazia clearly believes that censorship harms the censored. Authoritatively telling people that there are things they cannot say, or punishing them for saying them, destroys them. When the government restricts art and literature—genius for short—wives and publishers flee, reputations crash, health fades, friends and houses vanish. Writers cannot write, contemplate suicide, commit suicide.[21] Censorship causes death. One person, after losing a Supreme Court case, "went into clothing."[22] Certainly the effects of silencing are real and serious, and the causal link between censoring art and harm to artists is real even if it is only proven through experience. If only de Grazia took the harms of pornography—its silencing and other devastating consequences for women, which include murder—even a fraction as seriously, and viewed that causal and experiential connection half as sympathetically.

Judge Posner is a more self-conscious theorist. His views on the larger issues of sexuality and politics underlie many common social attitudes, laws, and policies. His book argues that the ends of sexuality are determined genetically through evolutionary biology,[23] and that these ends are pursued rationally to maximize fitness through social organization and behavior, particularly economics. He interprets regularities of women's sexual status and treatment as expressions of such biological imperatives pursued economically.[24] His analysis of pornography is situated within this larger theoretical edifice.

Sex and Reason is oddly reminiscent of Frederick Engels's combination of largely unquestioned biologism with economic determinism,[25] leaving this reader with a similarly unsatisfied sense that most of the important questions about women and men and their society were resolved before the curtain went up. The natural base posited for sexuality does most of the explanatory work. For Posner, the biology comes first, then the "theory of sexuality" proper. Biology is not a theory to him in this context; it is a fact. But to locate sexuality in nature, and to see nature as fixed, is not *prior to* a theory of sexuality; it *is* a theory of sexuality. It takes the theoretical position that sexuality is determined in nature. This should be justified as such, not bracketed at the outset.

Posner characterizes the opposing view as the social constructionist position of, among others, radical feminists who are "strong believers in the plasticity of human nature."[26] As someone who might be so described, I do not believe that human nature is plastic so much as that, with regard to the inequality of women and men, there is no such thing as human nature except socially speaking. It is not that human nature plays a more or less determinative role, not that I would put different things in that box, but rather that to posit a human nature and its contents is to both make and refer to a social determination. Nature has no such box. Or, if anything is in it, it is not sex inequality.

The point of human nature theories—Posner's is not the most rigid among them but is also no exception—is to attribute a fixed bottom line, an unchangeability that we must live within and keep in view, a baseline to which all discussion must refer and that no choice or policy can alter. These theories set limits, telling us that "there have always been"[27] certain things, as if this necessarily points to biology and no further explanation is needed, certainly not a social one. This assumption, even if not justified, as it is not in his text, does not in itself make such theories false. But the variability of sexual facts across and within cultures and times, as well as the fact that the particular limits thus asserted reinscribe the unequal gendered social status quo, tends to undermine their claim to being prior to society.

Put another way, theories that attempt to explain in terms of human nature what are actually facts of women's inequality to men—say, rape or prostitution or sexual harassment or pornography—are first and last theories of what women must put up with. These theories cannot see the degree to which they rationalize social inequality as natural because they think that they are scrutinizing sex difference. They do not see that to do this, to assume socially situated gender behavior is natural, is to assume that gender *inequality* is natural. They cannot prove it is natural, because it has never been found outside a social context. So they assume, because it has seemingly never not existed, it must be natural. In other words, they assume that the socially *inferior* status of women is, at least in part, an expression of the biology of gender dimorphism. The assumption this entails—that women are, at least in part, biologically inferior to men—explains the insult of such theories to women's human status.

Posner says we do not have to buy his biology to buy his economics.[28] Formally, this is true because his economics provides the means in a means-ends analysis. But without nature to set its particular ends, his theory would be radically incomplete.

As the empirical content of his construct of human nature, Judge Posner adopts many social beliefs about women and sexuality common on the Right but also pervasive across political lines. One is that men have a stronger sex drive than women.[29] That sex is a drive is assumed; that pleasure and reproduction drive men's drivenness is treated as a natural fact. Socially compulsive and compulsory masculinity is not considered as a competing explanation. Given no weight in this calculus, as is common for those who explain male sexual aggression with appeals to nature, is the clitoral orgasm, which, once it gets going, goes on for weeks, and no man can keep up with it, to no end of the frustration of some. (This underlies the often nasty edge to the query "Did you come?," when it means, "Aren't you done yet? I am.") This does not figure in Judge Posner's relative sex-drive calculation, although its existence is recognized widely, including in societies that aim to control and own women through clitoridectomy.[30]

Posner believes that sexual preferences are largely genetically fixed.[31] He also uses terms like "highly sexed"[32] to describe individuals, as if he is observing a fact of an individual's genetic or characterological endowment with no discussion of its potential social determinants, such as the relationship of childhood sexual abuse to promiscuity.[33] The judge concedes that what people experience as the erotic varies historically, across cultures, and sometimes changes over the lifetime of an individual. He knows this is odd from a genetic point of view.[34] It is an embarrassment to a genetic theory of sexual scripts that, for example, the back of a woman's neck routinely produces erections in Japan and a flat nothing in the United States.[35] (Will racial theories of genetic sexual scripts try to solve this?)

The slighting of the social determinants of sexuality is most visible in his treatment of the determinants of homosexuality. In Posner's view, social determinants create "occasional" or "opportunistic" homosexuals; biology creates "real" ones.[36] Why homosexuality calls for explanation, while heterosexuality, with all its abuses, does not, is unexplored. The biological approach to the explanation of homosexuality minimizes the social facts of sexuality under conditions of gender inequality: women are abused, despised, objectified, and targeted sexually through presumptively exclusive sexual use by men, who are socially defined as sexual aggressors and actors, not to be acted upon or aggressed against, at least not as adults. Many women resent the indignity of being sexually defined, which, given the social equation of sexuality with heterosexuality, becomes resentment at being heterosexually defined. They want to be human. Being lesbian can be a stand against this treatment and for women's equality and humanity, often an intentional and conscious one, in a way an evolutionary explanation for sexual preference elides. Given an opportunity, they choose women, which does not make their sexual preference any less real. Posner alludes to this in passing[37] (as he does to nearly every piece of evidence or argument against his positions) but here only to divide lesbians between real ones whose sexuality is biological and less real ones whose sexuality comes from their lives.

This division subordinates women's experience to a social Darwinism.[38] It is also circular: sexual preference can be argued to be biological because only what biology is said to produce counts as "real" sexual preference. As it minimizes lesbianism as a choice for sexual equality, form of political resistance, and affirmation of women, his approach also ensures that no amount of evidence to the contrary can falsify the hypothesis that sexual preference is biological. By denigrating as "not the real thing" a sexual behavior and identity that is often admittedly socially and politically produced—how, again, does lesbianism protect the gene pool?[39]—compelling evidence that sexual preference itself is social, not biological for everyone, can be dismissed.

Missing here, as well as elsewhere in Judge Posner's analysis, is the social fact of male dominance—both as explanation and as something to be explained. Applied to homosexuality among men, the biological analysis misses the possibility that male homosexuality might be an instance of some men's extending to sexuality the higher social value placed on men in every other respect. Maybe some male homosexuality involves overconforming heterosexuality in the sense of affirming male dominance, including over other men. At the same time, maybe some gay men want more equality in sex and resist the fixed preferences and gender roles of heterosexuality and hate being made to be a man—meaning in part a sexual aggressor against women—by social force.[40] Are the latter not "real" gay men?

Most theorists of sexuality leave sexual abuse out of their theories. To his credit, Judge Posner does not. This does not mean, however, that his sociobiological theory explains it adequately. For example, what survival value child sexual abuse contributes is not discussed.[41] Pursuing Judge Posner's sources does reveal a line of literature on how girls feel about rape that suggests some of the hazards of the sociobiological approach. This research purports to demonstrate that girls raped before puberty are not as traumatized by it as those raped after, because the sacred gene pool is unsullied.[42] Emotions, it would seem, are biologically determined too. Are women most traumatized by rape mid-month, not too upset during their periods? It is tempting to suggest that rape-murder of women after menopause would be less traumatic for the victims because their contribution to the gene pool is over, but someone might test it.[43]

The same tradition has investigated visual cues to sexual arousal, thought to attract men more than women, in studies to which Judge Posner repeatedly refers.[44] The idea is that men are hard-wired to respond to pornography. It is hormonal, evolutionary by now. Although this work cannot measure any reality that is not also social, because there is no context outside society, indeed outside male dominant societies, in which this phenomenon has been documented to occur, these studies give a patina of science and inevitability to the same observations pornographers rely on and exploit to make bank deposits. As *Penthouse* pornographer Robert Guccione puts what this science seeks to make into a fact of nature: "Men traditionally are voyeurs. Women traditionally are exhibitionists."[45] Relax and enjoy this happy complementarity because there is nothing you can do about it but study it. Unconsidered is that men might be sexually conditioned to arousal through visual possession and intrusion in sex-unequal societies in which pornography plays a powerful role—which then may even have hormonal or evolutionary consequences. In this research, if something has physical effects, it has physical causes. Similarly, it is not considered that the unupset raped little girls might be terrorized into silence, lacking in words, dissociated, split, or telling researchers what they can stand to tell them or think they want to hear.[46]

The same sociobiological researchers Judge Posner cites, in other studies he did not use, find that women differentially respond positively to visual cues for dominance, such as pictures of Lamborghinis and Brooks Brothers suits.[47] What a surprise: visual subordination triggers men sexually, and visual cues to dominance (in which no one is actually dominated) attract women. This is equality? When men go about looking like Lamborghinis, women will doubtless find them irresistible. And when women go around raping either Lamborghinis or inhabitants of Brooks Brothers suits, these researchers will have my undivided attention.

Studies suggesting that men rape because of their biology are not used to urge the decriminalization of rape, although that has arguably been largely accomplished anyway.[48] No one suggests that since men are evolutionarily more aggressive, they are hard-wired to murder, and that laws against murder should therefore be eliminated. Nor do those who believe in biological theories, including Judge Posner, generally support biological intervention against these abuses. Exonerating abuse on biological grounds has been mostly confined to pornography.

Once the adaptational telos is established, Judge Posner's economic analysis kicks in. Rational man pursues choices for sex. As one reviewer of Posner's book put it: "It is not too far wrong to characterize the theory he offers as one of men's rational, if fervent, search for places to ejaculate."[49] Being a man in the sense of socially becoming a member of a dominant gender class is not among the ends that Posner's sexual man rationally seeks. In a reverse of de Beauvoir,[50] for Posner, one is born, one does not become, a man. What amounts to male power is always already there in the genetic endowment. His biology of sexuality—men acting, women acted upon; men raping, women getting raped; men buying and selling, women being bought and sold—is male dominance by another name. His fixed sexual preferences of men for women, of women for men, are compulsory heterosexuality by another name. His objectification of women through visual cues as the essence of heterosexual excitement is pornography by another name. Male dominance, in other words, is essential. Sex inequality in society is not what Judge Posner sets out to explain because, as a system of social force, he does not seem to know it is there. It is remarkable that one can still attribute what is, in fact, male dominance to the genes and be taken as making a serious contribution to policy and scholarship.[51]

Both Posner and de Grazia embody their main theses on pornography in the ways they write. Judge Posner's graceful writing style ranges flexibly from the familiar to the elevated but is profoundly non–sexually explicit. The closest to vernacular he comes is to say that a boy will sometimes "do okay"[52] in a sexual pinch for men who are otherwise heterosexual. He refers to sexual partners in sexual intercourse as "the penetrator" and "the penetrated," or to the penetrated as "the insertee."[53] In an obscenity case on which Judge Posner sat as a Seventh Circuit judge, his opinion for the panel observes that "the least unprintable of the descriptions reads as follows: 'Magazine entitled, Let's F. . . . ' "[54] Edward de Grazia, by contrast, includes in his book many materials that have been litigated for obscenity, which also seem selected for the purpose of clustering at a line between pornography and not.[55] Judge Posner is reasonable sexual man. Edward de Grazia is as sexually explicit as mainstream publishing permits, attempting, including by moving the reader sexually, to open the mainstream to more pornography.

As for women, Judge Posner discusses them but little, while de Grazia hides everything he can behind a woman, including his title and jacket cover. When Jane Heap, prosecuted for obscenity for selling *Ulysses*, said "Girls lean back everywhere . . ." in its defense, she meant that women do everywhere what was challenged as obscene about the book.[56] De Grazia's cover shows a woman with her hand slightly over her mouth, suggesting that censorship of pornography is about shutting women up (especially women with well-manicured nails). De Grazia may not know it, because awareness of sexual abuse seems not to enter his world, but this gesture is common among adult women who begin to speak about being sexually abused as children, particularly when their abuse included oral penetration. Fronting women like this is a favorite strategy of the left when they defend pornography.[57]

Each author is gender-neutral in his way. Posner elides most social inequality behind biological determination or market forces. De Grazia makes women's place in a tradition of sex in literature seem equal, even egalitarian—obscuring entirely the role of sexual abuse in pornography, and of pornography in sexual abuse. Each makes it seem impossible that pornography is harmful to women in particular.

Judge Posner *is* persuaded, by contrast, that children are harmed by being sexually used to make child pornography.[58] That he had to carefully scrutinize research to reach this conclusion is a little chilling. Edward de Grazia openly wars against existing laws against child pornography in his footnotes, arguing essentially that it should be protected speech—or, at least, that high-quality child pornography should be.[59] If Judge Posner's book is preoccupied with male homosexuality,[60] Edward de Grazia's shows recurrent interest in sex between adults and children.[61]

Judge Posner interprets rape, intercourse, and masturbation as fungible in terms of the benefits men get from them.[62] Rape, he says, is "a substitute for consensual sex rather than an expression of hostility to women."[63] For this, he has probably never been called antimale, or even antisex. This may be because he does not explore the possibility that misogyny is an aphrodisiac of male supremacy—that hostility to women may be common to some sex and rape. The observation that "most rapists want to have sex, not to make a statement about, or contribute to, the subordination of women"[64] is seen to be enough to distinguish the sex from the subordination. Unconsidered is that the experience of subordinating women may be much of what the rapist gets *sexually* out of rape. Wanting to have sex without being faced with a human being,[65] seeing women as sexual objects—which Posner says "in moments of sexual excitement even egalitarian men" do[66]—is not seen as having anything to do with rape, as being hostile, subordinating, or even dehumanizing.

In a parallel split, Posner argues that pornography is erotic not ideological, distinguishing between its "aphrodisiacal effect," meaning its sexual arousal value, and its "ideological effect," meaning its denigrating and rape-promoting potential.[67] As he puts this, "the audience for pornography is interested in sexual stimulation, not in sexual politics."[68] Again, what is sexually stimulating embodies or reveals no politics. Apparently, it can only be what the perpetrator consciously intends it to be. Again, the possibility that the sexual politics of pornography, meaning its power disparities, may be precisely what is sexually stimulating about it, the possibility that the dehumanization of women makes pornography sexy (and helps create a sexuality of dehumanizing women), is not considered. He misses the feminist point: the politics of rape and pornography *are* their sexuality. Posner seems to be of the view that to be "morally indifferent" to sex,[69] and hence rational about its analysis, one must ignore its politics. A politics is not a morality. An analysis of power dynamics in power terms is no more morally based, and no less rationally descriptive of a rational system, than is an analysis of market forces in market terms.

From their books, one gets the impression that Richard Posner has not seen much pornography and that Edward de Grazia bathes in it nightly. From such seemingly divergent experiential backgrounds, they converge on *ignorance of its contents* as the principled state of mind in which to consider what, if anything, should be done about it. The premium on ignorance—de Grazia's seems studied, Posner's actual—pervades their legal work on the subject as well as these two books. In what other area of law is ignorance of what one is regulating the most principled approach to its regulation? Judge Posner, for example, wrote a decision overturning on appeal a conviction of *Hustler* for invading a woman's privacy—a woman whose situation might have led him to think more deeply about the women in the materials than he appears to have done in this book.[70] Robin Douglass won at trial her claim that *Hustler* had published nude pictures of her without her authorization. She lost on appeal not because the panel thought she had no privacy to lose—a miracle, this, as she had apparently consented to be in *Playboy*—but because the jury had been shown a "best of *Hustler*" selection. Judge Posner thought this may have inflamed them against the magazine. What pornographers actually do, in this case the context in which they did what they did to the plaintiff, if known, will make people think badly of pornographers. With pornography, reality produces bias, not realism. Only ignorance of it can produce the requisite rationality. At least Judge Posner recognized, for all the good it did Robin Douglass, that pornography does something—something that not even a properly instructed jury can be relied upon rationally to control.

When expedient, Edward de Grazia's legal work also places a premium on ignorance of pornography. He, too, tells us not to look when thinking about what to do—at least, sometimes. In *Mishkin v. New York*, which adjudicated whether sadomasochistic verbal and visual pornography written by formula with covers showing "scantily clad women being whipped, beaten, tortured, or abused"[71] could be obscene, de Grazia represented an array of illustrious publishers in an amicus brief[72] arguing that these materials must be protected as speech. None of the publishers had seen the materials, so they said. Their argument was, what was in them did not matter; what mattered was that something of some value somewhere, from which these materials were indistinguishable, would be hurt someday if anything was done about the materials at issue. (Their side lost in this case.) The materials in *Mishkin* are unambiguously pornography, in contrast with most of de Grazia's book, which does not excerpt the *Mishkin* materials. Nor is his view that ignorance makes principle, so convenient when the materials show overt violence, applicable in all cases. In his brief in *Oakes*, a case on the boundaries of child pornography, de Grazia described the photos and specifically referred the Court to them as exhibits in the trial record.[73] It is an invitation to look. With photographs of the defendant's "partially nude and physically mature 14-year-old stepdaughter" wearing only bikini pants and a long red scarf[74] and prominently displaying her breasts[75]—photographs de Grazia calls "child nudes" and that the young woman had tried to destroy[76]—content suddenly matters. Violent sexual materials should be protected in spite of their content, but other sexual materials, including those of children, should be protected because of it.

In their policy positions and ways of writing, then, Posner and de Grazia exemplify the two complementary strategies through which pornography historically has been protected. The conservative strategy is to cover it up. The liberal strategy is to parade it. While sometimes appearing to clash, the approaches are in effect perfectly complementary. Keeping it out of public view ensures that those who want it can have it, unaccountable to anyone. But the more it is seen, the more it is normalized, the more women's status and treatment comes to correspond to it, the more its harm merges into the appearance of women's nature and becomes invisible, and the more consumers are hooked on it. If it is covered up, the harm will not be seen; if it is made public enough, the harm will not be seen either. Both strategies allow the harm to be done while protecting pornography from the perception that anyone is being hurt by it.

Centrally, both authors argue that pornography should be protected because it has value, or more precisely, when it has value.[77] But when, according to them, doesn't it? As a measure of value, Posner proposes that what is valuable is what an artist does.[78] Artists do art; whatever they do cannot be pornography. (This would be news to artists like Anaïs Nin who made pornography on purpose, knowing exactly what they were doing—and, in her case, why they were doing it (money), how it differed from art ("no poetry"), "murdered" writers, and destroyed sex).[79] That work has artistic ambition is Posner's fallback position. He also allows value to be measured, in part, economically: what someone will pay for is valuable.[80] To de Grazia, too, pornography should be protected if it has value. What is valuable to him is what anyone sees value in. Anyone.[81] Entertainment is valuable. Sexual arousal confers value. In the value argument, Judge Posner holds down the high end, the elite end, de Grazia the low end, the democratic end. In pornography, left and right come to this: male desire confers value; they are just the desires of different men. What men want is valuable, and what men value, they get. This, in a nutshell, is their constitutional argument.

That materials are valuable because men value them is, actually, close to axiomatic in the world of case law as well. The Seventh Circuit decision in *American Booksellers Ass'n v. Hudnut*,[82] written by Frank Easterbrook, another economic-libertarian judge, illustrates. (Judge Posner did not sit on this case.) It held that Indianapolis's civil rights law against pornography violated the First Amendment. Merely quoting the query "If a woman is harmed, why should it matter that the work has other value?" was treated as invalidating to the civil rights approach.[83] The invisibility of the women harmed in and through pornography was so total, their insignificance so complete, their human status so nonexistent, that asking why the product of their abuse was more valuable than they were, was taken as a rhetorical question. It is a question that has yet to be answered.

The *Hudnut* decision went further: it took harm to women as a measure of the power, hence value, of pornography as speech.[84] De Grazia would doubtless find this position congenial, although it turns existing First Amendment law on its head and goes far beyond anything suggested by Judge Posner. For instance, Judge Posner did not suggest that *Hustler*'s use of Robin Douglass was more valuable than her privacy was, or that the speech value of using women the way *Hustler* did was more important than the woman who was used without her permission.

Much of the left and right see pornography as what Posner calls a "victimless crime,"[85] like witchcraft or heresy.[86] He is clear that in situations in which an "adult model is physically injured," suppression of materials made under these circumstances would be warranted.[87] De Grazia does not give even this ground. But it is unclear whether Posner has considered the fact that physical injury to women can produce an artistic product. What if materials are harmful *and* aesthetic, the artistic snuff film with the wonderful camera angles, the original visual stylization? Or, when a woman is forced to have sex for pornography by a gun at her head that is not fired?[88] If the resulting materials show no aggression, does this qualify as Posner's "physical injury," justifying doing something about the resulting materials?

At this point, one wonders why coercion into pornography is not a good example of market failure. The victims bear the cost; the consumers get the benefits at an artificially low price; the producers reap inflated profits at the victims' expense. If coerced women were compensated for their injuries, if the real cost of production were paid, we would see if the pornography industry would survive. Judge Posner's failure to apply the kind of economic thinking he pioneered is puzzling.

But this is the author who writes that "[p]rostitution is itself a consensual activity."[89] If child abuse plus abductions and homelessness and poverty and forced drug addiction and physical assault and stigma and no police protection and being bought and sold and treated as a leper in society and being so vulnerable that anything anyone will pay to do to you can be done to you is consent, prostitution is consensual.[90] All of this and more are what it takes to get women into pornography. This kind of abuse supplies the missing link Judge Posner sought in one of his First Amendment decisions between "blood sport," which is illegal although expressive, and erotic dancing, which, according to him, is protected speech.[91] Pornography and prostitution, including erotic dancing, are blood sports of male supremacy. Edward de Grazia refers with a sneer to women who are violated through pornography as "victims,"[92] in quotes, then parades all two women he can find saying what a wonderful time they had with it. This is the pimp's line; it is good for business.

Given their lack of grasp of violence against women, it is not surprising that both men misstate the research on the harm of pornography, if not to the same degree. Social studies, laboratory data, and testimony from real perpetrators and real victims all support the conclusion that men's exposure to pornography makes women's lives more violent, dangerous, and unequal.[93] The connection varies in strength depending upon factors like the violence of the material, length of exposure, and predisposing factors, but in a population of exposed normal men, it is never not there. And no population of real consumers is controlled as the experimental groups, by ethical fiat of the funders of the experiments, are controlled—by eliminating those who will most certainly act on the materials. Yet Posner repeatedly entertains, without embracing, the disproved catharsis hypothesis[94] and mistakenly writes as though the data on this question were in equipoise, or close.[95] This is noteworthy because Posner seldom gets anything descriptively wrong.

De Grazia, for his part, mouths the press lie that the *Final Report*[96] of the Attorney General's Commission on Pornography, which calmly reviewed the research to date and concluded that it substantiated these effects of exposure, is wild, exaggerated, and unsupported. In fact, it is cautious and measured. That Judge Posner even leans toward exonerating the harmful effects of pornography,[97] when the research he can usually read so well clearly establishes the opposite, testifies to the success of the public relations campaign to cast doubt on the existence of pornography's harms by distorting the research findings and discrediting the commission.[98] Neither writer can grasp the concrete damage done to women through pornography, which has been documented in testimony and has even been conceded by the courts—including, prominently, the *Hudnut* court in a clear statement de Grazia edits out.[99]

It is with their evaluation of feminist work against pornography that any daylight between de Grazia and Posner disappears: they become indistinguishable. Excerpted and affirmed, Posner becomes a part of de Grazia's book.[100] Now who is in bed with the right? Posner wrongly assumes that feminist work against pornography attacks the literary canon.[101] De Grazia wrongly assumes that it attacks all the works he has long defended. Common reflex is the ignorant assumption that a new civil rights definition of pornography[102] must pose the same problems as the old criminal definition of obscenity,[103] as if a test of material harm is the same as a test of moral content. Neither seems to have a grip *even on the words* of the new definition.[104] Neither intimates awareness of the common legal and social usage of the term "sexually explicit."[105] Neither grasps the fact that, under the civil rights ordinance, subordination must be proved as fact, not merely asserted as content.[106] Together or separately, these simple definitional requirements exclude virtually all the examples either attempts to use to invalidate it. Civil rights work against pornography does not belong in de Grazia's history of the abuses of obscenity law at all, except as a critique of that tradition.[107]

While both authors confuse the literary canon with the civil rights statutory definition, de Grazia makes an affirmative strategy out of conflating literature attacked for obscenity with pornography, in order to protect both. It is, in fact, unclear whether there is some pornography he would restrict and only defends the kind of writing typically published by Grove Press, which he has so often represented.[108] He does move from defending literature from false accusations of being pornography toward using literature as a means of defending pornography itself. In so doing, he moves from denying an unreal harm to denying a real one.

The two authors also converge in complaining that the civil rights approach to pornography does not take the "value" of the materials into account, as obscenity law does. Because obscenity law criminalizes sexual materials defined as morally bad, it makes sense to allow their value—moral good—to outweigh it. The civil rights law, by contrast, defines pornography in terms of the sex discrimination—the real harm—it does. It makes pornography civilly actionable when coercion, force, assault, defamation, or trafficking in sex-based subordination are proven.[109] To offset the value of the materials against their harms, as both writers urge, would mean concretely that when Linda "Lovelace" proves she was coerced into the film *Deep Throat,*[110] a court should weigh its literary worth against her injuries before granting relief, perhaps even before allowing her to go to trial. When a young girl is gang-raped by her brother and his friends, who hold up and read from pornography magazines and force her to imitate the poses exactly,[111] the value of those magazines, say in promoting anticlericalism, should be weighed against her assault. When a Native American woman is gang-raped by white men who repeatedly refer to the video game *Custer's Revenge,*[112] when a prostituted woman is raped by a man who insists she likes it because he saw it in a movie he mentions,[113] the value of the video game (a historical satire?) and the movie (a critique of fascism?) should be weighed against these women's rapes before anything can be done about the materials shown to cause them. When women prove that due to pornography trafficked in their jurisdiction, they are harassed at work, battered in their homes, disrespected in school, and endangered on the street,[114] the literary, artistic, political, or scientific value of the materials would have to be balanced against the women's equality they have been proven to destroy.

There is something monstrous in balancing "value" against harm, things against people, this on which left and right speak as one. It is not only balancing the value of human rights against the value of products that violate them. It is not only balancing rape, murder, sale, molestation, and use against pleasure and profits, or even aesthetics and politics. It is not only writing off the lives and dignity of human beings as if that were a respectable argument in a legal and academic debate. It is not even that this position that elevates the rights of pimps and predators over their victims and targets is supposedly part of current law. It is prior: when injury to women and children can be balanced against the "value" of pornography, women and children do not have human status—even though, pace de Grazia, women stand up everywhere.

27

From Silence to Silence

Violence Against Women in America

In many forums, sexual abuse has been unspeakable until recently, which is why it was rarely spoken about. Its victims were usually not believed, were blamed and punished for telling about what was done to them, and were told they wanted it or provoked it or fantasized it. Little good public information existed on how common it was, so it could not be understood in social context. Each victim felt alone. Perpetrators were seldom held accountable. Abuse flourished in this silence.

This silence was broken by the women's movement. Women's activism produced rape crisis centers, battered women's shelters, organizations of prostituted women against prostitution, incest survivor support groups, research, publications, legislative and policy changes, lawsuits. Now we know of the sexual atrocities inflicted on massive numbers of women and children. This reality was uncovered not by imagining that women's lives or men's behavior are worse than they are, but by listening to survivors of these atrocities and believing them.

Now, for the first time in almost a quarter of a century of this work, there is a very real danger that the sexually violated are being resubmerged in the silence of disbelief, blame, ignorance, denial, stigma, shame, and impunity. Sexual violence is on the way to becoming unspeakable again—this time in the name of freedom of speech. In retrospect, this began in earnest in the public treatment of women's resistance to pornography, and expanded into sexual harassment, child abuse, and rape.

Starting in the mid-1970s, women began speaking out about the aggression and denigration it takes to make pornography and the violence and discrimination that results from its use. They said that this assault was not a discussion but terrorism. While they received overwhelming grass-roots support, these women were publicly reviled, ridiculed, harassed, fired, denied promotion, evicted, unpublished, hounded, threatened, and assailed with an almost hysterical fury. They were demonized. The por-

Speech, National Press Club, 22 November 1993.

nographers led the charge. Women who spoke against pornography were made into pornography. If pornography does no harm to women, as pornographers say, why do they make pornography out of women they are trying to destroy?

The mainstream was not far behind, following up the sexual slander with book reviews full of misquotes and outrageous mischaracterizations, fabricated accounts based on false facts, planted stories getting tremendous currency, set-up interviews held under false pretenses, stories that represented the movement accurately that were killed, and routine refusals to run retractions or corrective letters. The means varied but the end was the same: to plant these women on a pike—not our heads, which still do not symbolize who we are, but up our genitals—as a warning to anyone who dared dissent from the culturally dominant view that pornography must be protected as speech.

More than anyone, this has been done to feminist writer Andrea Dworkin. The vaunted protection for "ideas that offend" does not apply to hers. Against her, the organs of speech have moved with virtually total unanimity to create personal contempt and hostility, to prevent publication of her work, to destroy what of her writing manages to see the light of day, and to bury the writer alive. This is how dissenters are treated in this country when the powerful feel implicated in what writers say.

This dynamic can be illustrated through one concrete instance. A *New York Times* blackout on factual articles covering antipornography feminist activism began in 1978 following publication of an article by Judy Klemesrud on a conference on pornography at NYU.[1] The article was accurate, respectful, and balanced. After it ran, managing editor Abe Rosenthal told Klemesrud that there would be no more coverage of feminist work against pornography in the *Times* because it was bad for the First Amendment.[2] One editorial and one op-ed piece came out shortly after, attacking the antipornography feminist position, targeting Andrea Dworkin's speech at NYU.[3]

Mr. Rosenthal, reached at his office last week, denied saying this to Klemesrud and recalls no conversation with her on this topic. He confirmed that he does not favor movements against pornography but stated that "the connection between what I think and whether we cover it does not exist." He also said there is no relation between editorial opinion and news policy.

In fact, the coverage evaporated. For the next five years, silence fell in the national newspaper of record. A point of view was effectively shut out, with minor exceptions, by disappearing reports of its activism. This ended, perhaps by mistake, in 1983 when a stringer sent in a story from Minneapolis over a weekend. It described hearings on a law against pornography that Andrea Dworkin and I drafted at the City Council's request. The article said that it was a civil rights bill, a sex equality law that people who were injured through pornography could use for relief.[4] Other than one follow-up article when the bill passed,[5] that was the first and last time this legislative approach was accurately presented by that paper until 1991 in the Sunday magazine.[6]

Meanwhile, Judy Klemesrud hung in. In summer 1985, she wrote a story on Andrea Dworkin and John Stoltenberg's work against pornography and their life together. It ran, by careful plan, on the Style page[7] when Abe Rosenthal was on vacation.

In this and other forums, women's accounts of the role of pornography in acts of forced sex against them are edited out while ink by the barrel proclaims that no causal link exists. Facts on the role of pornography in rape, murder, and sexual harassment are routinely cut out of national coverage, appearing, if at all, in local reports. Escalating rates of sexual abuse are regularly reported with puzzled alarm, while on other pages the lack of relation between pornography and sexual abuse is stated as fact, although women's experience and research overwhelmingly document their connection.

Explaining this requires no conspiracy theories. In early June 1986, when women had been working against pornography for over a decade and for civil rights laws against it for three years, the Attorney General's Commission on Pornography was about to issue its *Final Report*, telling the truth about the harms of pornography in a restrained, workmanlike summary of the scholarly literature. To deal with this threat, a group of mainly print publishers, pornographers and not, called the Media Coalition, whose goal is to protect sexually explicit materials, hired Gray & Company, a PR firm. The strategy Gray & Company proposed, in a document leaked to us, lays out a campaign "to discredit" the commission and other organizations and individuals, including those it describes as "self-styled anti-pornography crusaders."[8] The plan stressed the need to say that no empirical evidence supports the conclusion that pornography harms women. Following the rule writer Renata Adler identified in her study of libel,[9] once the false story was reported, all that was reported was more and more of the same false story. This PR campaign was projected to cost upwards of a million dollars, which, according to Susan Trento, was largely paid for by *Playboy* and *Penthouse*.[10] Along with the lie that women who oppose pornography are allied with the right, which it also recommended using, this distortion of empirical fact became conventional wisdom worldwide overnight.

Part of the impact of this discrediting campaign can be traced in one example. Just prior to his execution, Ted Bundy spoke powerfully of the role of pornography in making him a serial killer of women. The public did not then get panels of experts discussing the extensive empirical support for his analysis or local police officers confirming that they regularly find pornography with raped and dead women or even mention of Bundy's own earlier consistent account of his own development.[11] There was none of the depth and detail Eugene Roberts has said is the mandate of journalism.[12] Instead, we got a major and virtually unanimous damage-control sneer of ridicule and disparagement of Bundy claiming "Porn-made-me-do-it", reducing his account to a last-minute attempt at self-exoneration when it was neither last-minute nor self-exonerating. All this was premised on the fact that the man Bundy chose to discuss his life with on videotape was a religious conservative.

In this frantic all-stops-out attempt to contain the risk that pornography would look bad, Ted Bundy became at best the exceptional, predisposed individual. The point of view that men are not born serial murderers and pornography is part of what makes some of them that way was simply excluded from the discussion. So the incongruity of defaming those who make this argument as arguing that sexual violence is inherent in being male could also go on—no contradiction marked.

On November 1, 1993, another convicted sex murderer's death penalty case was argued before the U.S. Supreme Court.[13] Whether this man, Thomas Schiro, will be executed turns in part on evidence, accepted by the courts, that his years of consumption of sadomasochistic pornography and snuff films made him unable to tell right from wrong. Since there was not a single discussion of this issue in a mainstream outlet, nobody pointed out the bind the Court of Appeals for the Seventh Circuit had gotten itself into here. In previously striking down the antipornography civil rights law, the Seventh Circuit had recognized that pornography promotes rape but said the pornography had to be protected. Was it now going to exonerate the rapes, and in Schiro's case the murder, that the pornography produced as well? That the question seemed self-answering did not address its implications, in turn, for the pornographers' protection from accountability for its harms.

As pornography was treated in media discourse, sexual harassment, child abuse, and rape followed. With Professor Anita Hill's testimony against Clarence Thomas, which included her account of the role of pornography in her sexual harassment, the stigma that had formerly attached to resistance to pornography began to spread to resistance to sexual harassment. For most who did not believe Professor Hill, it was what she said about pornography that they did not believe. Once the issues converged, history had to be revised to make the fight against sexual harassment appear as an attempt to restrict speech rather than the struggle for equality and against sexual aggression that it has always been.

One experience involving this convergence says it all. I was asked by the *New York Times* to write an op-ed piece on a court victory of Lois Robinson, a woman who was sexually harassed through pornography. The piece was killed, although an editor fought for it. We were told the quotations from the abuse itself were "too graphic," unfit to print, although every word of the abuse had been previously published in the judge's decision in the federal reporter.[14] That *Times* readers cannot be told what was done to Lois Robinson, even as doing the same abuse, we are told by the same people, is legally protected speech—is rather hard to take. Once the evidence is eliminated from public view, it becomes easy to say the abuse is exaggerated and its targets should stop whining.

All this has cleared the way for the return, ever louder, of the view that children invent, exaggerate, fantasize, or are manipulated into saying that sexual things were done to them that were not. Once the children are terrorized into silence, or will say anything to relieve the adult pressure on them, they are said to "recant." A "false memory syndrome" (I call it the "false syndrome syndrome") is invented to stigmatize by phony diagnosis the children who speak of what was done to them. All this exemplifies in spades Susan Faludi's observation that we get five minutes of serious consideration followed by five years of backlash.[15]

In this there is no left and right, only an increasingly fast track from pornography to the mainstream, as recent discussion of rape vividly shows. Women's human status sinks lower in public daily. For years, *Playboy* had spread the lie that Andrea Dworkin says all sexual intercourse is forced in order to trivialize her analysis of the role of supremacist sexuality in rape; this distortion was then recycled endlessly in mainstream forums. Then, within a year or so, the lie was updated: now *I* say all sex is rape. In the blink of an eye, it flew from Rush Limbaugh[16] and *Playboy*[17] to the *Yale Law Journal*, if corrected in the latter.[18] Within months, the parallel defense of date rape as just a bad night flashed from *Playboy* to the *National Review* to a lousy student paper elevated to the cover of the *New York Times Sunday Magazine*,[19] in what might be called a new trend in rape coverage: "just shut up" journalism.

There is no left and right in the funding consequences either. When it comes to the pornography issue, all the big money goes to one side: the pro-pornography side. Meantime, the Council on Foundations has yet to present information on women's organized resistance to the harms of pornography at its annual plenary sessions.

In all these issues, those who point out that women are being victimized are said to victimize women. Those who resist the reduction of women to sex are said to reduce women to sex. Subordinating women harms no one when pornographers do it, but when feminists see women being subordinated and say so, they are harming women. Words do nothing except when feminists use them. Go figure.

The result is to surround victims with disbelief and contempt, chill reporting, create a hostile environment for adjudicating complaints, and stigmatize efforts for change. For example, one has to go as far as Sweden or the Philippines these days to find legislators with enough courage to face the intimidation and threats that are now standard for anyone who proposes consideration of the civil rights approach to pornography—even though the American people want something done. This happens through the process described, which creates the context that defines what counts as credible in families, on street corners, in the academy, in jury rooms, and determines the social standard for reasonableness in and out of court.

It is time to face the role of public rape in silencing women. Public rape begins in pornography, with women literally being raped in public. It extends to mainstream reports of sexual assaults that make victims into sexual spectacles, exploited as entertainment. Awareness of it encompasses my Bosnian client's stand that her name could be used in the complaint but not in a press release. She was not saying she wanted to prosecute in secret or to preserve her privacy; she wanted dignity in public. She wanted what all women who go public want: they want back what the rapist has taken away from them, not more of the same taken away. One of the most important reasons women say they do not report their rapes is fear of the press. Public rape also encompasses a recent review in *The Nation* of a scholarly book arguing against the harms of pornography. The review opens with a putative rape of the author—me.[20]

Then, in a vicious turn of the screw, the fact that any of this is publicly spoken is said to prove that there is no silence, there is nothing more to say. Breaking the barrier proves no barrier is there. If we never saw Solzhenitsyn's writings, would that mean he was not censored? Given what it has taken to get even this much out, imagine how much—both of women's speech and untold atrocities—we still know nothing about.

Political dissent is being suppressed by manipulating the norms of the free press. This censorship in order to protect freedom of speech belongs in the same ashcan as destroying villages in order to save them.

I have not mentioned the reasons for the vested interest in this suppression, but the known ones include sex, money, other forms of power, ambition, approval, and at least some ignorance. Nor have I spoken of those who see this for what it is and do not cave in to it, beginning with the reporters who report the story they find rather than the story they are told to find. They know who they are. They also know the costs. They also know that, in this area in particular, they are the exceptions.

Speech about violence against women in America is not free. It can cost your reputation, your ability to survive, and a lot more. The press could make it less expensive. When sexual abuse can be freely spoken about, it can be stopped.

28

Vindication and Resistance

Like a Trojan horse, each new communication technology—the printing press, the camera, the moving picture, the tape recorder, the telephone, the television, the video recorder, the VCR, cable, and, now, the computer—has brought more pornography with it. As pornography has proliferated with each new tool, what had been a more elite possession and obsession is progressively democratized, spreading ever wider the sexual abuse required for its making and promoted through its use.[1] Ever more women and children have had to be used ever more abusively in ever more social sites and human relationships to feed the appetite that each development stimulates and profits from filling. Ever more women have had to live out ever more of their lives in environments pornography has made. As pornography saturates social life, it becomes more visible and legitimate, hence less visible as pornography. The abuse intensifies and deepens, becoming ever more intrusive, hidden, unaccountable, leaving fewer islands of respite. And the pornography acquires the social and legal status of its latest technological vehicle, appearing not as pornography but as books, photographs, films, videotapes, television programs, and images in cyberspace.

Pornography on computer networks is the latest wave in this tide. Pornography in cyberspace is pornography in society—just broader, deeper, worse, and more of it. Pornography is a technologically sophisticated traffic in women; electronically communicated pornography traffics women in a yet more sophisticated form. But as new technologies open new avenues for exploitation, they can also open new avenues for resistance. As pornography comes ever more into the open, crossing new boundaries, opening new markets and pioneering new harms, it also opens itself to new scrutiny.

Carnegie Mellon's landmark study of pornography in cyberspace is also the first massive study of the consumption of pornography in a natural

First published, 83 *Georgetown Law Journal* 1849 (1995).

setting. Access to those using pornography was made possible by the same expanded access that computer networks provide to pornography itself. As pornography invades offices, homes, and schools through upscale computer technology, and the age of the average consumer potentially drops below its already dropping level, the Carnegie Mellon study signals that the possibilities for exposing pornography are keeping pace with its takeover of public and private spaces. The pornographers are clearly betting that they can survive the light. For those who are hoping they cannot, this new technology, like each one before it, merely raises in a new domain the same questions pornography has always raised: What will it take for pornography to be seen for what it is? What will it take to stop it?

Like each new technology before it, computer networks shift and focus the social and legal issues raised by pornography in specific ways. Like pornography everywhere else, before and after it becomes Carnegie Mellon's "images" for study in cyberspace, it is women's lives. Women resisted being made into pornography, being sexually violated in public for the pleasure and profit of others, long before the materials made using them hit computer screens. And while resistance to pornography from the standpoint of the women in it has centered on visual materials, real women have often posed for the words as well, in the sense that the men who wrote them often did what they wrote about. The Marquis de Sade, a seminal pornographer, was jailed for sexual atrocities he committed against women, acts that included the same rape and torture his pornography celebrates.[2] One wonders how far most pornographers' imagination has extended beyond their experience.

Something is done when women are used to make pornography, and then something is done again and again to those same women whenever their violation—their body, face, name, whatever of identity and dignity can be stolen and sold as sex—is sexually enjoyed, in whatever medium. Most pornography, if circulated in a working environment, would be actionable as sexual harassment.[3] The damage done would be clear if the materials were nonsexual libel or the people involved were understood to be people rather than prostitutes or sex or "some women" who are "like that." For insisting that a woman is violated every time she is sexually trafficked without her permission, by word or celluloid or databyte, for insisting that each act of sexual consumption predicated on the unfree use of a person damages that person, those who oppose pornography's harms have essentially been accused of witchcraft or, at least, of a voodoo sensibility. Pornography in the marketplace of life where there are no equality laws—in the world of books, photographs, films, videos, phone sex, and cable television everywhere but work and school—has fallen into a reality warp. Harmless fantasy, it is called.

Consider this instance. In 1995, Michigan undergraduate Jake Baker sent verbal snuff pornography using a woman undergraduate's name and physical description over the Internet.[4] Verbal pornographers have always had the tools visual pornographers are only beginning to develop that allow them to make pornography, including women presented being killed, without actually doing it to real women. Still they use real women, presumably for sexual reasons. Jake Baker did not first commit the rape, torture, and murder he wrote about doing as sex. Because he "fantasized" time, place, and manner of execution into the ether of e-mail, he was arrested and jailed before he could try. He did use the identity of a woman he had seen to make pornography of her subjected to those acts, and then pimped her by name on the bulletin board alt.sex.stories, if experience is any guide, for men to masturbate over. With its estimated 270,000 consumers, he had, for a pornographer manqué, unprecedented access to spreading his harm. And the FBI had unprecedented access to him.

Federal authorities investigated and prosecuted Jake Baker for interstate transmission of a threat. He was not prosecuted for fantasizing. He was prosecuted for *doing* something, an act that embodied a clear notion of what else he was *going to do*. A threat is an act in itself, the nature of which is a promise of further action. The fact he was prosecuted makes clear that a man's threat is more credible than a woman's complaint. What he said he was going to do was more credible than everything all the women who have ever said they *were* used in pornography against their will have said that men *did* do to them. A trial would be based on what "he said"; no "she said" involved. And even though names are only words, making pornography of a real person's name was seen as part of doing real harm to that person.[5] In this textual world, suddenly, if only momentarily, this injury became visible, real. It took putting pornography in cyberspace to produce this.

What makes VR (virtual reality) more real than RL (real life)? Why is sexual violation in cyberspace taken more seriously, seen as real, when the same pornography elsewhere in social life has been widely passed off as harmless?[6] Why did it take the Internet to make the harm of coerced pornography real enough to produce an indictment for an *act* against a woman in it for the first time? How long will it last? What is—and will be—the legal and social relation between telecommunicated pornography on computer networks—the Internet, Usenet, World Wide Web, commercial and personal bulletin boards—and the rest of social life? The Carnegie Mellon study provides a rich context of data and analysis in which to begin to consider these questions. The study also raises new possibilities for resistance by documenting, with unprecedented scientific precision and definitiveness, who is using whom, where, when, and how.

That pornography on computers is part of real life, not apart from it, is made indelibly clear by the Carnegie Mellon study. The content, consumers, and patterns documented in this study are the same as those long observed in the pornography industry and in its tracks through the rest of society.[7] The research team documents beyond question the simplest and most obvious, if some of the most contested, facts. Overwhelmingly, it is men who use pornography—98.9 percent of these consumers, to be exact.[8] Even many of the women who use it, Carnegie Mellon found, are paid by pornographers to be there, in order to give men the impression, while online, that women enjoy women being violated.[9] Women are disproportionately used in violating ways in pornography. More than 99 percent of all the bestiality pictures studied on the "Amateur Action" bulletin board, for instance, present women having sex with animals,[10] in spite of the fact that nearly 50 percent of the pornography studied has men in it.[11] The more violating the act, the more women have it committed against them.

Moreover, the more violating the material, the more it is wanted, out of proportion to supply. Sex with children is 6.9 percent by supply, 15.6 percent by demand.[12] The demand to see vaginal sex (not to be assumed harmless) approaches the vanishing point (6.9 percent by supply, 4.6 percent by demand),[13] while the demand for women vaginally penetrated by animals on the "Amateur Action" bulletin board approaches 50 percent of all visual bestiality material.[14] When a woman is marketed being intensively physically harmed, consumer demand doubles; fellatio gets a lukewarm response, but downloads double for "choking."[15] Amateur Action BBS, which distributes the most materials in which physical harm is shown being inflicted on women, is the market leader.[16] The Carnegie Mellon study disproves allegations that those who oppose the pornography industry have distorted its largely benign reality through "the use of highly selected examples."[17] By focusing on pornography *as used*, the Carnegie Mellon results also counter the view that "most commercial pornography . . . is not violent."[18]

Pornography is a huge amount of the activity on the Internet. As it aspires to be a universal network to unite the world, pornography takes up much of the Internet's collective brain. Over 80 percent of all pictures available on the Usenet are pornography.[19] Three-quarters of the total space occupied by the visual boards, the lion's share of multimedia activity, is pornography.[20] The pornography bulletin boards, although a small percentage of the BBS overall, are disproportionately accessed. Use of the most violent and dehumanizing materials is not only the most frequent;[21] it is also geographically widespread. The research team documents consumption of such materials by men in at least 2,000 cities in all fifty states of the U.S., most Canadian provinces, where it is more clearly illegal, and thirty-nine foreign countries and territories.[22] When men make new communities,[23] they bring their pornography with them. They bond through it. Computer networks are not only metaphors for society; they track it and happen within it.

Why it was necessary to log on to see what has been just down the street all along is an interesting question. The greatest achievement of the Carnegie Mellon study lies in the fact it noticed what is there. Simply treating the content of pornography as a serious database for detailed empirical measurement is almost unprecedented. Apparently the shift in frame from books and videos to cyberspace has had the effect of revealing to simple empirical documentation that what is done to women in pornography is not a fact of nature or an act of liberation or a private peccadillo to be respectfully skirted but an ongoing social atrocity. The significance of this recognition, implicit in the entire study, cannot be overstated. The study's refusal to back off from the findings represented by the its use of at least some concrete descriptive categories and many illustrative quotations is equally remarkable. The political epistemology of this moment is that cyberspace seems to have made possible a clarity of perspective, a reframing of this form of violence against women, a getting out of society in order to get into it, that no mental trip to Mars and back has previously accomplished.

However, computer networks do not, as the research team suggests, market unusually abusive materials and thus "redefin[e] the pornographic landscape."[24] They reveal it. The study expresses occasional skepticism about the fit between pornography in cyberspace and pornography in the rest of the world. It states that the most abusive pornography (e.g., bestiality and torture) and child pornography are much easier to get online than otherwise.[25] This confuses what is acknowledged as being acceptable with what is actually accepted in the sense of being widely available and used. Abusive pornography using adult women is readily available, and anyone who wants child pornography can get it with a little effort. Computer networks *are* contributing significantly to abuse of women and children by facilitating access to such pornography, expanding its reach. However, the fact that these materials become more readily available, while they remain illegal, even highly illegal, does not mean that they are not, in fact, otherwise already there. Electronic communication makes more visible to scrutiny a reality that was already pervasive.

Some viewers may also be skeptical that the individuals presented as children in computer pornography are really children. More likely, pornographers are using children when they say they are not. This will become much more common after the U.S. Supreme Court's recent ruling in *X-Citement Video*, which held that, if pornographers do not know that the children they use are children, the pornography made using them is legal.[26] This accomplishes an effective drop in the age of consent for use in child pornography to age of physical maturation—for some girls, ten or eleven years old—a change that pornographers, including those on computer networks, can be predicted to exploit fully. In fact, the research team documents extensive use of children for sex in this forum.[27]

One feature of much computer network pornography that appears to distinguish it from the rest of the pornography market is that it is distributed free of charge. Actually, much child pornography is traded as well as sold.[28] A primary form of the profit in pornography is sexual, pure and simple. Meantime, with computer networks now being used for trafficking, community standards in yet another rapidly expanding elite are created that are toxic to women's humanity and potentiating to male dominance, which has to be good for business. And the pornographers of organized crime are at work, with some of the best technical minds money can buy, figuring out how to make money pimping women in cyberspace.[29]

Each new technology raises anew the question of the adequacy of existing legal approaches. Cyberspace makes vivid, if it was not already, the inefficacy of current obscenity law, which coexists with this exploding market in human abuse, as it has with every other means of sexual trafficking. Just as the harms pornography does are no different online than anywhere else, the legal approach taken to them need be no different. It need only be effective, as it nowhere is. Computer networks present a newly democratic, yet newly elite, mass form of pornography becoming less elite by the minute, just as pornography always has. In whatever form pornography exists, its harms remain harms to the equality of women; it is through addressing these harms that pornography can be confronted. Civil rights legislation designed to remedy pornography's harms at their point of impact is well suited to this task online as everywhere else.[30]

Computer technology does pose newly complex issues of anonymity and privacy. Unidentified speech has always presented dangers of harassment and reputational destruction but never before on this scale.[31] Privacy has always been fragile, but never before has it been possible, undetected, to find out what a person is reading while they are reading it. Technical problems of proving liability and measuring damages also exist, although now that the pornographers are figuring out how to get paid for pornography in cyberspace, many of these problems will be solved, as the transactions will leave a trace. Once a legal approach through actual harms is taken, accountability for pornography on computer networks poses no new conceptual problems, only practical problems of delivery.[32] The legal problem is, women hurt by pornography have no rights against it anywhere. If circulating pornography in this new, still legitimate, forum reframes the same old abuse to alter that impunity, this new technology will be the first to be revolutionary.

The Carnegie Mellon research team has had the vision to see, the technical acumen to capture, and the courage to expose what is there. Beyond further information to be analyzed and organizing opportunities to be pursued, the question the study poses for pornography in cyberspace is the same that pornography poses everywhere else: whether anything will be done about it.

The Roar on the Other Side of Silence

If we had a keen vision and feeling of all ordinary human life . . . we should die of that roar which lies on the other side of silence. As it is, the quickest of us walk about well wadded with stupidity.

—George Eliot, *Middlemarch*

Women spoke in public for the first time in history of the harms done to them through pornography in the hearings on the antipornography civil rights ordinance in Minneapolis, Minnesota, on December 12 and 13, 1983. Their first-person accounts of violation through pornography stand against the pervasive sexual violation of women and children that is allowed to be done in private and is not allowed to be criticized in public. Their publication, which came almost fifteen years[1] after the hearings were held, ended the exclusion from the public record of the information they contain on the way pornography works in social reality. Ended was the censorship of these facts and voices from a debate on the social and cultural role of pornography that has gone on as if it could go on without them.

Until these hearings took place, pornography and its apologists had largely set the terms of public discussion over pornography's role in social life. Public, available, effectively legal, pornography has stature: it is visible, credible, and legitimated. At the same time, its influence and damaging effects are denied as nonexistent, indeterminate, or merely academic, contrary to all the evidence. Its victims have had no stature at all. The hearings changed the terms of this discussion by opening a space to speak for the real authorities on pornography: the casualties of its making and use. Against a background of claims that the victims and the harms done to them do not exist, cannot be believed, and should not be given a legal hearing, the harms of pornography were exposed and took shape as po-

First published as an introduction to *In Harm's Way: The Pornography Civil Rights Hearings* 3 (Catharine A. MacKinnon and Andrea Dworkin, eds., 1997).

tential legal injuries. These hearings were the moment when the voices of those victimized through pornography broke the public surface. Their publication gave the public unmediated and unrestricted access to this direct evidence for the first time. The authority of their experience made the harm of pornography undeniable: it harmed them.

In late 1983, legislators in Minneapolis initiated this process[2] by employing Andrea Dworkin and me to write a law for the city that we had conceived on pornography as a civil and human rights violation. Other jurisdictions followed, including Indianapolis, Los Angeles County, and the Commonwealth of Massachusetts,[3] each seeking to adapt the civil rights approach to local concerns. All these proposed laws recognized the concrete violations of civil rights done through pornography as practices of sex discrimination[4] and gave the survivors access to civil court for relief through a law they could use themselves. The hearings that resulted from the introduction of the legislation gave pornography's survivors a forum, an audience, and a concrete opportunity to affect their world. Grasping the real chance that rights might be given to them, seeing that their participation could make a difference to the conditions of their lives, these women and men became prepared to run the risks of this political expression. The consequences anticipated at that time included public humiliation and shame, shunning and ostracism, loss of employment, threats, harassment, and physical assault.

The act of introducing the antipornography civil rights ordinances into the legislative arena gave pornography's victims back some measure of the dignity and hope that the pornography, with its pervasive social and legal support, takes away. The ordinances, in formulating pornography's harms as human rights deprivations, captured a denigrated reality of women's experience in a legal form that affirmed that to be treated in these ways violates a human being; it does not simply reveal and define what a woman is. As ending these violations and holding their perpetrators accountable became imaginable for the first time, and women participated directly in making the rules that govern their lives, the disgrace of being socially female—fit only for sexual use, unfit for human life—was exposed as a pimp's invention. In these hearings, women were citizens.

The first-person testimony, contextualized by expert witnesses as representative rather than unique or isolated, documented the material harm pornography does in the real world, showing the view that pornography is harmless fantasy to be as false as it is clichéd. Women used for sex so that pornography can be made of them against their will—from Linda "Lovelace"[5] forced to fellate men so *Deep Throat* could be made to a young girl sold as sex to *Hustler*'s "Beaverhunt"[6] to Valerie Harper's face on another woman's naked body on a T-shirt[7]—refute the assumption promoted by the pornography industry that all women are in pornography because they want to be there. The information provided by these witnesses also underlines the simplest fact of the visual materials: to be made, the acts in them had to be *done to someone*. In the hearings, a few who have escaped the sex factories describe the forms of force required.

There, woman after woman used by consumers of pornography recounts its causal role in her sexual violation by a man close to her. A husband forces pornography on his wife and uses it to pressure her into sex acts she does not want.[8] A father threatens his children with pornography so they will keep silent about what he shows them is being done, audibly, to their mother at night.[9] A brother holds up pornography magazines as his friends gang-rape his sister, making her assume the poses in the materials, turning her as they turn the pages.[10] A woman's boyfriend becomes aroused by watching other women being used in pornography and forces sexual access on her.[11] A young gay man inflicts the abusive sex learned through using pornography on his male lover, who tolerates it because he learned from pornography that a man's violence is the price of his love.[12]

Although intimate settings provide privileged access for these acts, such violations occur throughout social life. White male motorists, spewing racist bile, rape a Native American woman at a highway rest stop in reenactment of a pornographic video game.[13] Working men plaster women's crotches on the walls of workplaces.[14] Therapists force pornography on clients.[15] Pimps use pornography to train and trap child prostitutes.[16] Men who buy and use women and children for sex bring pornography to show those prostituted what the men want them to do.[17] Pornography is made of prostituted children to threaten them with exposure to keep them in prostitution.[18] Serial sexual murderers use pornography to prepare and impel them to rape and kill.[19]

Grounded in these realities, the ordinance that produced and resulted from the hearings provides civil access to court to prove the abuse and the role of pornography in it in each such situation. The ordinance, with local variations, provides a cause of action to individuals who are coerced into pornography, forced to consume pornography, defamed by being used in pornography without consent, assaulted due to specific pornography, or subordinated as a member of a sex-based group through traffic in pornography as legally defined.[20] The chance to prove in court the harmful role of pornography in each situation is what pornography's victims have sought. This, to date, is what they have been denied.

The opponents of the civil rights laws against pornography were amply represented in these hearings. They did not openly defend pornography as such,[21] or address the harms the witnesses documented even to deny them. They treated the survivors as if they were not there or do not matter. That those victimized by pornography are lying or expendable is the upshot of the First Amendment defense of pornography that the opponents do present, proceeding as if the "speech" of violation matters over the violation of the violated. Some opponents adopt the view that any factual disputes over the harm of pornography should not be resolved in court—in other words, whatever harm may exist can be debated endlessly but the harm can never be stopped. As the Massachusetts hearing shows, the issue of whether pornography is harmful mattered to pornography's defenders only as long as it was considered impossible to demonstrate that harm. Once it was judicially established that pornography does the harms made actionable in this law—as it was established in the litigation on the ordinance in 1985[22]—the ordinance's opponents lose interest in the question.

Addressed not at all by the opposition in the hearings is whether or not the practices of pornography made actionable by the ordinance are properly conceptualized as sex-based discrimination. Like the conclusion that pornography causes harm, the conclusion on the nature of that harm is based on evidence, on fact; the hearings provide those facts. As an analytic matter, although many people are shown to be victimized, actually and potentially, if even one woman, man, or child is victimized *because of their sex*—as a member of a group defined by sex—that person is discriminated against on the basis of sex; those who testified to their experiences in the hearings incontestably and without dispute were hurt as members of their gender. Their specifically, differentially, and uncontestedly sex-based injuries ground the state's compelling interest in equality that the ordinance vindicates.

The hearings show the ordinance in practice: it produced them. The hearings also present case after case of precisely the kinds of evidence the ordinance would introduce into court if it were enacted into law. These are the people who need to use it, who have nothing to use without it. The hearings empowered individuals to speak in public, provided a forum for them to confront their abusers, to prove their violations, and to secure accountability and relief, as the ordinance would in court. The hearings present witnesses to acts of abuse and injury—acts, not ideas, like those acts the ordinance would redress in court. In the hearings, an industry of exploitation and violence that produced these acts connected inextricably with them, as it would also have to be in civil court proceedings. The hearings challenged the same concentration of nongovernmental power that the ordinance would challenge in court, empowering the government no more than the hearings did. The hearings simply used the legislative process for the ends to which it is given to citizens to use, just as the ordinance would use the civil judicial process for its designed purposes: to resolve conflict and rectify injury. As the ordinance would in court, the hearings brought pornography out of a half lit underground into the public light of day. The hearings freed speech that was previously suppressed. So would the ordinance. Neither the hearings nor the ordinance have anything in common with censorship.[23]

Until the publication of the hearings, the public discussion of pornography was impoverished and deprived by often inaccurate or incomplete reports of victims' accounts and experts' views.[24] Media reports of victims' testimony at the time of the hearings themselves were often cursory, distorted, or nonexistent. Some reports by journalists covering the Minneapolis hearings were rewritten by editors to conform the testimony to the story of pornography's harmlessness that they wanted told.[25] Of this process, one Minneapolis reporter assigned to cover those hearings told me, in reference to the reports she filed, "I have never been so censored in my life." Thus weakened, the victim testimony became easier to stigmatize as emotional and to dismiss as exceptional. Its representativeness has been further undermined by selective or misleading reports of expert testimony on scientific studies. This body of scholarship predicted that the precise kinds of consequences *will* happen from exposure to pornography that the survivors in the hearings reported *did* happen in their own experience. The two kinds of evidence converged to document the same harm in two different ways.

The hearings contributed additional neglected or otherwise inaccessible information to the public discussion over the civil rights ordinance against pornography. For example, the allegation that opposing points of view were excluded from the hearings by the bills' proponents[26] is refuted by the hearings on their face. Opponent after opponent of the civil rights of women, mostly liberals, testified ad nauseam. The hearings also went some distance toward refuting the ubiquitous fabrication that locates the engine of the civil rights antipornography ordinances in an "unusual coalition of radical feminists and conservative women politicians."[27] This invention originated in a false report in the *New York Times* that Charlee Hoyt, one of the bill's original sponsors in Minneapolis, opposed the Equal Rights Amendment. The *Times* published a correction affirming Hoyt's constant support of ERA, but the lie about the ordinance's alliance with the right stuck, always changing ground but always growing.[28] The same *Times* article stated that the Indianapolis ordinance was passed with "the support of the Rev. Greg Dixon, a former Moral Majority official," who "packed Council hearings to lobby for passage of the proposed ordinance."[29] Neither Rev. Dixon nor his followers appear to have spoken at the Indianapolis hearings. Enough votes for passage (the bill passed 24 to 5) existed prior to the meeting at which these individuals sat in the audience. No one has said that Rev. Dixon or his group had any other contact with the process. Thus it was that the outcome of a legislative vote came to be attributed to the presence of some people who came to watch as other peoples cast it.

Taint through innuendo has substituted for fact and analysis in much reporting and discussion of the ordinance. As the hearings document, of all the sponsors of the bill in all the cities in which it was introduced, only one—Beulah Coughenour of Indianapolis—was conservative. Work on one bill with an independent individual is hardly an alliance with a political wing.[30] Exactly what is sinister about women uniting with woman across conventional political lines against a form of abuse whose politics are sexual has remained unspecified by the critics.

The hearings correct such widely distorted facts simply by showing the sponsors and supporters of the ordinance in action, illustrating its progressive politics. In them, the ordinance's two original sponsors in Minneapolis appear: Van White, a liberal Democratic African American man, and Charlee Hoyt, a liberal Republican white woman. (Sharon Sayles Belton, the Democratic African American woman later mayor of Minneapolis, sponsored the reintroduced ordinance after the first veto.) The grassroots groups who inspired the Minneapolis ordinance by requesting help in their fight against pornographers' invasion of their neighborhoods testified in support of it. These same groups later supported the Indianapolis ordinance when it was challenged in court.[31] Battered women's groups, rape crisis center workers and advocates, organizations of survivors of sexual abuse in childhood, and groups of former prostitutes presented unanimous evidence from their experience in favor of the ordinance. They, too, supported it against later legal challenge.[32] Members of the large, ethnically diverse Los Angeles County Commission on Women that sponsored and supported the ordinance chaired the hearings there.

The progression of hearings reveals that opposition to the ordinance became better organized over time, its strategy refined. In the Los Angeles hearing on April 22, 1985, in which the pro-pimp lobby remained, as always, centered in the American Civil Liberties Union, the woman card was first played. There, tiny, noisy elite who defended pornography professionally contrasted with survivor after survivor whom they talked past and disregarded—a division of a few women from all women subsequently magnified by a gleeful press. Women's material interest in pornography was presented as divided: if it hurts some women, other women love it, and stopping it hurts women more.[33] Women against women subsequently became the pornographers' tactic of choice—as if women's oppression by pornography had been argued to be biological, as if biological females saying they were not hurt by it undercut that case. This choice of strategy was revealed in the orchestration of the ordinance referendum battle in Cambridge, Massachusetts, in November 1985, in which the ordinance narrowly lost, and even more graphically in the Boston, Massachusetts, hearing of March 1992. In Boston, speaking almost entirely through female mouthpieces, the corporate interests of the entertainment industry came out of the woodwork to weigh in on the side of the pornography industry, arraying abstraction after evasion after obfuscation after self-interested, profit-oriented rationalization against survivors' simple, direct accounts of the role of pornography in their abuse.[34] Much of the media persistently positioned women against women in their coverage, employing the pornographers' strategy in the way they reported events and framed issues for public discussion. Corrective letters showing wide solidarity among women on the ordinance were routinely not published.[35]

The hearings on the civil rights antipornography ordinances took place in public and on the record. The witnesses, unless they said otherwise, were fully identified to the governmental bodies before whom they testified. Some of the consequences of testifying for them show why it took so long and was so hard to make this information public, and prefigured the onslaught that followed. Some of those who spoke in Minneapolis were hounded and punished for what they said. One woman's testimony was published by *Penthouse Forum* without her knowledge or permission, selling her assault for sexual use. A copy of *Penthouse*'s pages with her testimony, with "We're going to get you, squaw" scrawled across it in red appeared in her mailbox. A dead rabbit appeared there a few days later; she was telephoned repeatedly by a man who appeared to be watching her in her home. Another witness was subsequently telephoned night after night at her unlisted telephone number: "The calls are not simply harassing phone calls. It is like someone is reading something out of the pornography books . . . we can't get away from it."[36] These are techniques of terror.

By bringing forward festering human pain that had been denied, the hearings unleashed an explosion of reports by women and men desperate for help. A local organizing group formed after the Minneapolis hearing was deluged with them. Women told "about the time their boyfriend urinated on them while using pornography depicting 'golden showers.'"[37] Rape victims reported that "their attacker took pictures during the rape and that she's afraid he is going to sell and distribute them."[38] The group reported that "we have received a call from a man in Fort Collins, Colorado, terrified because a group of men were holding him captive and making pornography with him. He has called and sent us the pornography in hopes that it could be used as evidence, that the whip lashes would prove that he was forced."[39] Some groups held more hearings. The National Organization for Women held hearings on pornography across the nation.[40]

The Minneapolis hearings, circulated in photocopied transcript hand to hand, had a substantial impact on consciousness, politics, scholarship, theory, and policy.[41] At the federal level, the first explosion of publicity surrounding the Minneapolis hearings revived a long-moribund proposal for a new national commission on pornography. Attorney General William French Smith created the Attorney General's Commission on Obscenity and Pornography and selected its members. The prior Commission on Obscenity and Pornography in 1970, appointed by President Nixon, had exonerated "obscenity" and "erotica" of a role in "crime," looking at no violent materials and looking only for violent effects.[42] The President's Commission heard from not a single direct victim—offended moralists are not victims—and considered only evidence from "experts," meaning academics, on the question of harm. Understanding that asking the wrong questions of the wrong people might have produced the wrong answers, the Attorney General's Commission took extensive testimony from scores of survivors of real abuse and investigated the effects of violent as well as nonviolent sexual materials. In other words, it investigated what those on the receiving end were in a position to know about the materials that are actually made and marketed by the pornography industry and consumed by its users. This commission was later dubbed "the Meese Commission" by a hostile press to discredit it by association with an almost universally despised man who did announce the inquiry's formation but did not originate it and did virtually nothing with its results.

The *Final Report* of the Attorney General's Commission, which repeatedly footnoted the Minneapolis hearings, substantially adopted the civil rights approach in its approach, findings, and recommendations. The report included an entire chapter on harm to "performers"—of all survivors the most ignored and, when noticed, blamed. It found that "the harms at which the ordinance is aimed are real and the need for a remedy for those harms is pressing."[43] It concluded that "civil and other remedies ought to be available to those who have been in some way injured in the process of producing these materials."[44] It endorsed a limited concept of civil remedies.[45] It found that the civil rights approach "is the only legal tool suggested to the Commission which is specifically designed to provide direct relief to the victims of the injuries so exhaustively documented in our hearings throughout the country."[46] The Commission also agreed that pornography, as made actionable in the ordinance, "constitutes a practice of discrimination on the basis of sex."[47] In an embrace of the ordinance's specific causes of action as well as its approach, the Commission recommended that Congress "consider legislation affording protection to those individuals whose civil rights have been violated by the production or distribution of pornography. . . . At a minimum, claims could be provided against trafficking, coercion, forced viewing, defamation, and assault, reaching the industry as necessary to remedy these abuses."[48] Unable to find constitutional a legal definition of pornography that did not duplicate the existing obscenity definition, the Commission nonetheless found itself "in substantial agreement with the motivations behind the ordinance, and with the goals it represents."[49]

Not long after the hearings and the release of the Commission's Report, parts of the ordinance were introduced as bills in Congress. Senator Arlen Specter introduced a version of the ordinance's coercion provision as the Pornography Victims' Protection Act, making the coercion of an adult or the use of a child to make pornography civilly actionable.[50] Senator Mitch McConnell introduced a rendition of the ordinance's assault provision as the Pornography Victims' Compensation Act, creating a civil action for assault or murder caused by pornography.[51] Most stunningly, Congress in 1994 adopted the Violence Against Women Act, providing a federal civil remedy for gender-based acts of violence such as rape and battering.[52] In so doing, Congress made legally real its understanding that sexual violation is a practice of sex discrimination, the legal approach that the antipornography civil rights ordinance pioneered in legislative form.

More broadly, the exposure of pornography's harms moved the ground under social theory across a wide range of issues. The place of sex in speech, including literature and art, and its role in social action was thrown open to reconsideration, historically and in the present. The implications of visual and verbal presentation and representation for the creation and distribution of social power—the relation between the way people are imaged and imagined to the ways they are treated—are being rethought. The buying and selling of human flesh in the form of pornography has given scholarship on slavery and human trafficking, including demand for it, a new dimension. More has been learned about the place of sexuality in ideology and the importance of sexual pleasure to the exercise of dominant power. The hearings remain fertile ground for analyzing the role of visceral commitment to inferiority in practical systems of discrimination and of the role of denial of inequality in maintaining that inequality. The cultural legitimation of sexual force, including permission for and exoneration of rape and use of prostitutes and transformation of sexual abuse into sexual pleasure and identity, was newly interrogated. New human rights theories are being built to respond to the human rights violations unearthed. As events that were hidden came to light, the formerly unseen appeared to determine more and more of the seen. The repercussions for theory, the requisite changes in thinking on all levels of society, have just begun.

For those who survived pornography, the hearings were like coming up for air. Then the water closed over their heads once again. The ordinance is not law anywhere. Mayor Donald Fraser of Minneapolis vetoed it twice after passage by two different city councils. Minneapolis dithered and did nothing. The Indianapolis ordinance was declared unconstitutional by the Court of Appeals for the Seventh Circuit in a decision that inverted First Amendment law, saying that the harm of pornography only proved the importance of protecting it as speech, and reduced equality rights, by comparison, to a constitutional nullity.[53] The U.S. Supreme Court summarily affirmed this result on a divided vote without hearing arguments, reading briefs, or issuing an opinion,[54] using a now largely obsolete legal device for upholding a ruling without expressing a view on its reasoning.[55] Although the Seventh Circuit decision is wrong in law,[56] and the summary affirmance of it need not necessarily bind subsequent courts, the ordinance passed in Bellingham, Washington, by public referendum was invalidated by a federal court citing the Indianapolis decision as controlling.[57] The Los Angeles ordinance was narrowly defeated, 3 to 2, in a vote delayed in order to be as inconspicuous as possible. The Massachusetts ordinance was maneuvered behind the scenes out of coming to a vote at all. Senators Specter and McConnell compromised their bills fundamentally.[58] Neither bill—for all the purported political expediency of their sponsors in gutting them—passed or even made it out of committee.

The victims have been betrayed. To adapt George Eliot's words, "that roar which lies on the other side of silence"[59] about sexual violation in the ordinary lives of women was heard in the hearings. Society learned what is being done to the victims and decided to turn away, close its mind, and, "well wadded with stupidity,"[60] go back to masturbating to the violation of their human rights. The debate over pornography that was reconfigured by the survivors' testimony to make harm to women indispensable to the discussion has increasingly regressed to its old right/left, morality/freedom rut, making sexual violence against women once again irrelevant and invisible.[61] Politicians are too cowed by the media even to introduce the bill. Truth be told, for survivor and expert both, it has become even more difficult than it was before to speak out against pornography as those in the hearings did. The consequences are not merely feared but known to include professional shunning and blacklisting, attacks on employment and publishing and professional credibility, deprivation of research and grant funding, public demonization, litigation and threats of litigation, death threats, and physical assault.[62] The holy rage of the pornographers at being publicly exposed, given legal form through ACLU lawyers at every bend in the road and accompanied by a relentless beat of media lies, has made aggression against pornography's critics normative and routine, fighting back unseemly, seemingly impossible. In this atmosphere, few stand up and say what they know. The silencing is intentional, and it is effective.

In the establishment today, support or at least tolerance for pornography, if slightly shaken, remains an article of faith among liberals and libertarians alike. The liberal establishment is its chief bastion but the right is actively complicit, its moralistic decency crusades and useless obscenity laws protecting pornography while pretending to stop it, contributing its share of judicial and other misogynists to the ranks of pornography's defenders, forever defending private concentrations of power and mistaking money for speech. The concerted attacks on anyone who dares to give even a respectful hearing to the critique of pornography from this point of view have been reminiscent of the left's vicious treatment of so-called premature antifascists during the period of the Hitler-Stalin pact, or of those who questioned Stalin, including after the Moscow Trials.

Against this united front, many a well-placed and secure professional, upon taking a seemingly obvious position against exploitation and abuse, or upon simply describing what is in the pornography or in the research on its effects, has been startled to be screamed at by formerly rational colleagues, savaged by hostile mail (sometimes widely electronically disseminated), defamed by attacks on professional competence, subjected to false rumors, ostracized instead of respected, libeled in and out of pornography, sued for speech by those who say they oppose suits for speech, and investigated by journalists and committees—not to mention receiving blandishments of money from pornographers, eviction from homes, and threats against families. Most fold. With intellectuals intimidated, what chance do prostituted women and raped children have?

In the defense of pornography against the ordinance—the first effective threat to its existence—the outline of a distinctive power bloc became discernible in the shadows of American politics. Cutting across left and right, uniting sectors of journalism, entertainment, and publishing with organized crime, sprawling into parts of the academy and the legal profession, this configuration has emerged to act as a concerted political force. Driven by sex and money, its power is largely hidden and institutionally without limits. Most of those who could credibly criticize it either become part of it or collaborate through silence. No political or legal organ is yet designed or equipped to counter it. Existing structural restraints on excess power—such as the government's checks and balances—are not designed to counter social combinations like this one. In western democracies, only governmental power is formally controlled, as if the government is the only entity that can cohere power or abuse it. Private in the sense of nongovernmental in origin, this bloc uses government (such as First Amendment adjudications) as just one tool, wielding less visibly against dissenters a clout similar to the government's clout during the McCarthy era.

Politicians who live and die by spin and image grovel before this machine. Law has been largely impotent in the face of it and lacks the will and resources to resist it. Indeed, law has largely been created by it, the reality perceptions entrenched through the machine's distinctively deployed weapons of sex, money, and reputation having become largely indelible and impervious to contrary proof. Academic institutions are often found cowering before it and have ceded to it much of their role of credentialing the intelligentsia. Its concerted power defines what is taken as reality and aims to destroy those who challenge or deviate. Political scientists have yet to analyze it. Almost no one stands up to it. Those who testified in these hearings did.

One incident exposed the workings of this machine accidentally. In 1986, a leaked memo from the public relations firm of Gray & Company proposed a press campaign for the Media Coalition, the group of trade publishers and distributors, including some pornographers, that is substantially funded by *Penthouse*[63] and was behind the litigation against the ordinance in Indianapolis and Bellingham. Gray & Company proposed to "discredit the Commission on Pornography" and stop "self-styled anti-pornography crusaders" from creating "a climate of public hostility toward selected publications."[64] They got the contract, which budgeted about a million dollars to pursue their recommended lines of attack. As reflected in the press this campaign produced, this planned onslaught focused on two items of disinformation contained in the proposal. The first is that there is no evidence that pornography does harm. In their euphemistic PR language, "there is no factual or scientific basis for the exaggerated and unfounded allegations that sexually-oriented content in contemporary media is in any way a cause of violent or criminal behavior."[65] The second is that the campaign to stop pornography "is being orchestrated by a group of religious extremists."[66] The mainstream media slavishly published *as news* the spewings of the groups fronting this strategy, establishing both lies as conventional wisdom.

As a result, the false statement that scientific evidence on the harmful effects of exposure to pornography is mixed or inconclusive is now repeated like a mantra, even in court. It has become the official story, the baseline, the preestablished position against which others are evaluated, the standard against which deviations must defend themselves, the commonsense view that needs no source and has none, the canard that individuals widely believe as if they had done the research themselves. Few read the scholarly literature or believe they need to. No amount of evidence to the contrary—and evidence to the contrary is all there is—is credible against the simple reassertion of what was believed, without evidence, to begin with. Associating all work against pornography with widely reviled extremists of the religious and political right, similarly without regard for the lack of factual basis for this guilt by association, is similarly impervious to contrary proof and produces a self-righteous witch-hunt mentality. Individuals strategically singled out as threatening to the financial health of Gray & Company's "selected publications" are also used in pornography,[67] this cabal's ultimate weapon. Such attack-pornography potently and pervasively targets sexualized hostility at pornography's critics and destroys their status as credible speakers who have anything of value to say. The effect of lowering the human status of the critics is discounted under norms of public discourse that hold that what is done in pornography occurs offstage in some twilight zone—coming from nowhere, meaning nothing, doing nothing, going no place.

If this cabal acts in planned and organized ways at times, usually its common misogyny and attachment to pornography are themselves the conspiracy. The legitimate media act in their own perceived self-interest when they defend pornography, making common cause with mass sexual exploitation by calling pornography "speech." They seem to think that any restraint on pornography is a restraint on journalism. Their mistaken view that mainstream media and pornography are indistinguishable—the ordinance's definition of pornography distinguishes them, as does every pornography outlet in the world—pervasively distorts factual and legal reporting.[68] The resulting tilt is inescapable and uncorrectable; other than one's own experience to the contrary, which this process makes marginal, readers have no access to other information. That mainstream journalists tend to see their own power at stake in the legal treatment of pornography is particularly worth noting because they are not pornographers.

Sometimes the ax being ground is closer to home, as it was for journalists to whom Linda "Lovelace" was pimped when she was in captivity.[69] Those who used her sexually have a specific stake in not believing that she was coerced to perform for the pornography film *Deep Throat.* They remain at large, mostly unidentified and writing. How often pornographer-manipulated news stories are concretely bought and planted can only be imagined, but how difficult can privileged access be for the pornographers and their point of view, given that they are often dealing with their own customers? Under these conditions, with access to information owned and controlled for content, with sex and money as potent motivators, the availability of unmediated original materials such as the hearings—documents against the deluge—is as precious as it is rare.

The antipornography civil rights hearings are the samizdat of a resistance to a sexual fascism of everyday life—a regime so pervasive, so ordinary, so normalized, so established, so condoned, that there is no underground from which to fight it or into which to get away from it. The hearings are the only primary source on the way pornography concretely works in everyday life that has seen the public light of day. And they may be the last. Every day the pornography industry gets bigger and penetrates more deeply and more broadly into social life, conditioning mass sexual responses to make fortunes for men and to end lives and life chances for women and children. Pornography's up-front surrogates swallow more public space daily, shaping standards of literature and art. The age of first pornography consumption is young and probably dropping, and the age of the average rapist is ever younger.[70] The acceptable level of sexual force climbs ever higher; women's real status drops ever lower. No law is effective against the industry, the materials, or the acts. Because the aggressors have won, it is hard to believe them wrong. When women can assert human rights against them, through a law the victims can use themselves, women will have a right to a place in the world.[71]

Notes

Index

Notes

Introduction: Realizing Law

The theory sketched here was presented at Harvard Law School on November 20, 2000, in delivering, "Disputing Male Sovereignty," infra at 206, in dialogue with Akhil Amar for the annual Supreme Court issue of the *Harvard Law Review.* The comments of Kent Harvey, Cass Sunstein, Lisa Cardyn, John Stoltenberg, Charlotte Croson, and Marc Spindelman helped clarify it immeasurably.

1. "The Path of the Law," 10 *Harvard Law Review* 457, 465 (1897).
2. See "Toward a New Theory of Equality," infra at 44.
3. See "Reflections on Sex Equality Under Law," infra at 116, as well as "Sex, Lies, and Psychotherapy," infra at 251, for historical and psychosocial context, and "Unequal Sex: A Sex Equality Approach to Sexual Assault," infra at 240, for an alternative.
4. See "Civil Rights Against Pornography," infra at 299, "Pornography as Defamation and Discrimination," infra at 309, "Pornography Left and Right," infra at 327.
5. See "Prostitution and Civil Rights," infra at 151.
6. See "From Practice to Theory, or What Is a White Woman Anyway?" infra at 22, "Keeping It Real: On Anti-'Essentialism,'" infra at 84, and "Pornography as Defamation and Discrimination," infra at 309.
7. See "Speaking Truth to Power," infra at 277, and "Mediating Reality," infra at 289.
8. See "The Logic of Experience: The Development of Sexual Harassment Law," infra at 162.
9. See "Speaking Truth to Power," infra at 277.
10. See "Beyond Moralism: Directions in Sexual Harassment Law," infra at 184.
11. See "Toward a New Theory of Equality," infra at 44, "Reflections on Sex Equality Under Law," infra at 160, and "Accountability for Sexual Harassment," infra at 180. The main progress in this area has registered in Canada, as discussed more fully in *Women's World, Men's States*, the companion collection to come from Harvard University Press.
12. See "Civil Rights Against Pornography," infra at 299, and "The Roar on the Other Side of Silence," infra at 359. For a discussion of the distinction between morality and harm, see "Beyond Moralism: Directions in Sexual Harassment Law," infra at 184.

13. See "Liberalism and the Death of Feminism," infra at 259, and "Pornography Left and Right," infra at 327.

14. See "Disputing Male Sovereignty: On *United States v. Morrison*," infra at 206.

15. See "Unequal Sex: A Sex Equality Approach to Sexual Assault," infra at 240, in particular the discussion of the Akayesu case.

16. "Beyond Moralism: Directions in Sexual Harassment Law," infra at 184, and "The Logic of Experience: The Development of Sexual Harassment Law," infra at 162, address this question, as does "Disputing Male Sovereignty," and "The Power to Change," infra at 103. The existing situation is analyzed in "Law in the Everyday Life of Women," infra at 32, the reasons for the failure to change it in "Unthinking ERA Thinking," infra at 13.

17. This theory is central to all my work, from *Sexual Harassment of Working Women* (1979) through *Feminism Unmodified* (1987), to *Toward a Feminist Theory of the State* (1989), *Only Words* (1993), and *Sex Equality* (2001).

18. See "Toward a New Theory of Equality," infra at 44. "What *Brown v. Board of Education,* Should Have Said," infra at 72, embodies this approach in a mock judicial opinion on the subject of racism.

19. A great many published and unpublished pieces were eliminated for length.

20. On the latter, see "Of Mice and Men: A Fragment on Animal Rights," infra at 91.

21. This is Harold Lasswell's definition of politics. See Harold D. Lasswell and Abraham Kaplan, *Power and Society: A Framework for Political Inquiry* (1950).

22. See Bush v. Gore, 531 U.S. 98 (2000).

23. See United States v. Morrison, 529 U.S. 598 (2000).

24. See Lawrence v. Texas, 539 U.S. 558 (2003).

25. See "Disputing Male Sovereignty," infra at 206, for fuller explication of this point.

26. Nevada Dept. of Human Resources v. Hibbs, 538 U.S. 721 (2003).

27. See, e.g., Grutter v. Bollinger, 539 U.S. 306 (2003).

28. See, e.g., Virginia v. Black, 538 U.S. 343 (2003).

29. This theme is articulated, and this approach exemplified, in "'Freedom from Unreal Loyalties': On Fidelity in Constitutional Interpretation," infra at 65.

30. Herbert Wechsler, "Toward Neutral Principles of Constitutional Law," 73 *Harvard Law Review* 1 (1959).

31. Id.

32. Catharine A. MacKinnon, *Toward a Feminist Theory of the State* (1989) addresses this thesis in philosophical terms.

33. For further discussion, see Catharine A. MacKinnon, *Sex Equality*, Chapter 1 (2001).

34. This is variously shown throughout "Pornography Left and Right," infra at 345.

35. On how gay and lesbian issues are substantively sex equality issues, see Catharine A. MacKinnon, *Sex Equality*, Chapter 7 (2001).

36. For discussion of abortion in sex equality terms, see "Reflections on Sex Equality Under Law," infra at 116.

37. For discussion of the compulsion trope, in which judges so deeply regret to do what they are saying they have to do, see "Law's Story as Reality and Politics," infra at 58.

38. See Lochner v. New York, 198 U.S. 45 (1905).

39. The latter proposition is argued in Catharine A. MacKinnon, *Toward a Feminist Theory of the State* (1989).

40. This approach to equality interpretation was argued to, and is embraced by, the Supreme Court of Canada under the Charter of Rights and Freedoms equality guarantee in Andrews v. Law Society of British Columbia, [1989] 1 S.C.R. 143, although not all subsequent decisions of that Court have fully sustained that commitment to substance.

41. Analogies too can be substantive, but they can also abstract parallels into unreality and obscure substantive connections. To continue with the Morrison example, federalism is also a white supremacist institution. But no state's rights federalism appeal has invalidated the federal laws against racially discriminatory violence. Substantively, as a matter of interpretation of legal outcomes, this suggests that group-based violence like that of the Ku Klux Klan may not now occupy the same place in the reality of white racism in the United States that sexual violence still does in sexism. Thus, race-based violence laws have been constitutional where sex-based violence laws are not yet, whether or not they should be. Much violence, however, is both.

42. For the way he uses this phrase, see Alexander M. Bickel, *The Morality of Consent* 3 (1975).

1. Unthinking ERA Thinking

This book review of Jane Mansbridge, *Why We Lost the ERA* (1986) was first published in "Unthinking ERA Thinking," 54 *University of Chicago Law Review* 759 (1987).

1. Facts from a conversation with Mary Eberts (Toronto, April 13, 1987) and from Penney Kome, *The Taking of Twenty-Eight: Women Challenge the Constitution*, 97–105 (1983). This comparison is instructive because nothing, cross-culturally, is quite like women's equality. The comparison is not based on the notion that Canada is exactly like the United States or that the constitutional situations were the same. The resulting Canadian language also provides a useful standard of comparison. Equality Rights under Section 15 of the Canadian Charter of Rights and Freedoms provides:

> (1) Every individual is equal before and under the law and has the right to the equal protection and equal benefit of the law without discrimination and, in particular, without discrimination based on race, national or ethnic origin, colour, religion, sex, age or mental or physical disability. (2) Subsection (1) does not preclude any law, program or activity that has as its object the ame-

> lioration of conditions of disadvantaged individuals or groups including those that are disadvantaged because of race, national or ethnic origin, colour, religion, sex, age or mental or physical disability.

Section 28 provides that sex equality rights cannot be overridden by a legislature or Parliament:

> Notwithstanding anything in this Charter, the rights and freedoms referred to in it are guaranteed equally to male and female persons.

2. Mansbridge recounts polls in which a majority of both sexes favored the ERA. Jane J. Mansbridge, *Why We Lost the ERA* 16–19 (1986). Throughout, while she carefully compares the results of various wordings of poll questions, Mansbridge takes poll results as true expressions of people's opinions on the questions they are asked. When it comes to sex, people lie a lot. They also say one thing and do another—like say they are for the ERA and then vote against it. Accepting poll results at face value—methodology and wording aside—may be an occupational hazard of the political scientist, but a deeper order of skepticism seems warranted.

3. For example, Harris v. McRae, 448 U.S. 297 (1980), holds that public funding of medically necessary abortions for indigent women is not constitutionally compelled.

4. For further discussion, see Catharine A. MacKinnon, "Feminism, Marxism, Method and the State: Toward Feminist Jurisprudence," 8 *Signs: Journal of Women in Culture and Society* 635 (1983) (discussing the law of rape). See also American Booksellers Ass'n, Inc. v. Hudnut, 771 F.2d 323 (7th Cir. 1985), *aff'd*, 106 S.Ct. 1172 (1986), which holds unconstitutional a law making pornography actionable as a civil rights violation when women are coerced into it, when it is forced on them, when they are assaulted because of it, and when they are subordinated through trafficking in it. This ruling wraps the male point of view in the First Amendment, labeling "viewpoint discrimination" a law that makes pornographers and others liable for sex-discriminatory acts.

5. Mansbridge, x.

6. Id. 2, 122, 132, 178–186, 132.

7. This kind of thinking is evident in Mansbridge's characterization of ERA staffers: "They differed from the rest of the American population in one major respect—they believed in, and wanted to bring about, major changes in the roles of men and women in America" (p. 121).

8. One particularly startling example of this failure to take inequality of power seriously is Mansbridge's analysis that a difference between pro-ERA and STOP ERA forces was that STOP ERA only had to stop something while pro-ERA had to do something (p. 122). The real difference is that STOP ERA had all the power of male supremacy as wind at its back.

9. See Andrea Dworkin, *Right-wing Women* (1983), for a cogent feminist analysis of the appeal of the Right to women as women under male dominance. Mansbridge briefly displays a peculiar but not unique opposition to calling the victimized "victims."

Equating feminist opposition to violence against women with right-wing protectionism, Mansbridge couples "blame the victim" with "kill the messenger" when she criticizes the National Organization for Women (NOW) for contending that the victimization of women, as evidenced by data on violence against women, substantiated the need for a sex equality law:

> The protectionist position led both men and women to expect women to be passive victims. *Victims they became.* As the NOW "Position Paper on the Registration and Drafting of Women in 1980" pointed out, in America in the 1980s, "One rape occurs every five minutes. One out of every four American married women is a victim of wife beating. . . . When the word *protection* is used, we know it costs women a great deal." In rejecting protectionism, feminists urged women to stand on their own feet and wield power in their own right (p. 69) (emphasis added; footnote omitted).

It is impossible to tell from these remarks whether Mansbridge thinks NOW was exemplifying protectionism or opposing it, whether NOW got Sam Ervin and Phyllis Schlafly into their agenda or whether Ervin and Schlafly got NOW into theirs, far less whether the ERA would address rape or battery. The most bizarre feature underlying this analysis, however, is the notion that *criticizing* the victimization of women *makes women into victims*, as if women speaking of rape data makes men rape women.

10. See, e.g., Barbara A. Brown, Thomas I. Emerson, Gail Falk, and Ann E. Freedman, "The Equal Rights Amendment: A Constitutional Basis for Equal Rights for Women," 80 *Yale Law Journal* 893 (1971) (stating that ERA would make sex a prohibited legal classification).

11. See cases collected in David Cole, "Strategies of Difference: Litigating for Women's Rights in a Man's World," 2 *Law and Inequality: Journal of Theory and Practice* 33, 34 n.4 (1984).

12. Mansbridge suggests that the approach of Brown, Emerson, Falk, and Freedman was explicitly accepted by feminist lawyers and implicitly accepted by ERA activists (p. 128).

13. Mansbridge, 141.

14. This is discussed more fully in "Difference and Dominance: On Sex Discrimination," in Catharine A. MacKinnon, *Feminism Unmodified: Discourses on Life and Law* 32–46 (1987).

15. Mansbridge, ix.

16. Harris v. McRae, 448 U.S. 297 (1980) (upholding denial of federal funding for abortions against challenges based primarily on the right to privacy and secondarily on discrimination based on indigency).

17. Mansbridge, 124–125.

18. Pauline Bart has characterized "pregnant persons" as, in their view, a third sex. Pauline Bart, "In the Best Interests of the Sperm: The Pregnancy of Judge Sorkow," in *The Sexual Liberals and the Attack on Feminism* (Dorchen Leidholdt and Janice G. Raymond, eds., 1990).

19. See Geduldig v. Aiello, 417 U.S. 484 (1974) (equal protection); General Electric Co. v. Gilbert, 429 U.S. 125 (1976) (same ruling under Title VII).

20. Pregnancy Discrimination Act, 42 U.S.C. §2000e(k) (1978) (abortion exception).

21. For further discussion, see MacKinnon, "Privacy v. Equality: Beyond *Roe v. Wade*," *Feminism Unmodified* 93.

22. Rumor has it that even organized crime knows, and opposed ERA because it wanted to make abortion illegal again, having made a lot of money from it and having used it to control their prostitutes.

23. Mansbridge, 118.

24. Other analytic and informational lacunae exist as well. For example, in the discussion of discrimination in auto insurance, Mansbridge buys the insurance-lobby line that sex discrimination benefits women when she assumes that sex-based auto insurance rates are to women's financial advantage (pp. 41, 151, and accompanying notes). NOW documented in 1982, however, that sex-based auto insurance rates for women overcharged women by 30 percent. Because men, on average, drive more miles than women, see NOW advertisement, *New York Times* (East Coast edition, June 3, 1982), unisex rates—sex-declassified, the conventional ERA solution—are even *less* of a solution, because under them, women pay auto insurance at the rate at which men need it. Thus, unisex rates are immensely profitable for insurance companies and costly for women. See Pennsylvania NOW v. State Farm Mutual Auto Insurance Co., No. R86–9–6 (1987) (challenging unisex auto rates as sex discriminatory). Further, Mansbridge suggests that Title VII was eliminating sex discrimination in pensions and thereby made ERA unnecessary in this context. But she does not mention that both of the major Supreme Court cases on this issue—in a break with the usual practice—refused to give retroactive relief, leaving in place existing plans that had been found to have discriminated against women. Compare Title VII cases where women were harmed and denied retroactive relief, Arizona Governing Committee v. Norris, 463 U.S. 1073 (1983), and Los Angeles Dep't of Water & Power v. Manhart, 435 U.S. 702 (1978), with Title VII cases where men were harmed and granted retroactive relief, Fitzpatrick v. Bitzer, 427 U.S. 445 (1976).

The discussion of pornography contains egregious factual errors, although they may not be Mansbridge's fault. The footnote on the pornography ordinances Andrea Dworkin and I conceived and drafted states that we "tried to read [those who opposed our ordinance] out of the feminist movement" (p. 309 n.16). We did point out that pimps are not feminists nor is defending them, which is not the same. Contrary to Mansbridge's implication, we only "pressed" (id.) municipalities to pass our ordinance when and where expressly requested. Our law does not allow women to sue "on a tort basis" (id.) but on a sex discrimination basis. It is said our legislation "was explicitly not gender neutral; it addressed itself only to men's oppression of women" (id.). However, the legislation expressly provides that men who can show harm may also sue. The ordinance is expressly sex-specific in its identification of a sex-specific harm, and expressly gender-neutral in its overall design. I am told, however, that this paragraph was edited by the publisher without Mansbridge's knowledge or permission and does not reflect her views on the ordinance.

25. These harms were documented in *Public Hearings on Ordinances to Add Pornography as Discrimination Against Women, Gov't Operations Committee of the Minneapolis City Council* (Dec. 12–13, 1983) (statements by researchers, clinicians, scholars, victims, and other citizens documenting and debating pornography's harms to women), later published in Catharine A. MacKinnon & Andrea Dworkin, eds., *In Harm's Way: The Pornography Civil Rights Hearings* (1997).

26. Furnco Construction Corp. v. Waters, 438 U.S. 567 (1978) (ruling defendant need merely "articulate" a legitimate, nondiscriminatory reason for a hiring decision to defeat a prima facie case); Texas Dept. of Community Affairs v. Burdine, 450 U.S. 248 (1981) (ruling plaintiff must prove by a preponderance of the evidence that the defendant's proffered reason was merely a pretext for discrimination).

27. Personnel Administrator of Mass. v. Feeney, 442 U.S. 256 (1979) requires that sex discrimination be intentional to violate the equal protection clause.

28. American Booksellers Ass'n, Inc. v. Hudnut, 771 F.2d 323 (7th Cir. 1985), *aff'd* 475 U.S. 1001 (1986), makes women speech.

29. S. J. Res. 21, 68th Cong., 1st Sess. (Dec. 10, 1923), in 65 Cong. Rec. 150 (Dec. 3, 1923–Jan. 15, 1924) (Senator Curtis); H.J. Res. 75, 68th Cong., 1st Sess. (Dec. 13, 1923), in 65 Cong. Rec. 285 (Dec. 3, 1923–Jan. 15, 1924) (Representative Anthony).

30. Proposed Equal Rights Amendment New Form, 79th Cong., 2d Sess. (Feb. 2, 1944), in 90 Cong. Rec. 1039 (Jan. 10–Feb. 8, 1944) (referring to the 1943 revision).

2. From Practice to Theory, Or What Is a White Woman Anyway?

This address to the conference on Women of Color and the Law, 9 February 1991, Yale Law School, New Haven, Connecticut, was first published in 4 *Yale Journal of Law and Feminism* 13 (1991). This paper benefited from the comments of members of the Collective on Women of Color and the Law at Yale Law School.

1. The whole quotation is "Black feminists speak as women because we are women and do not need others to speak for us."

2. I detail this argument further in Catharine A. MacKinnon, "Reflections on Sex Equality Under Law," 100 *Yale Law Journal* 1281 (1991).

3. Meritor Sav. Bank v. Vinson, 477 U.S. 57 (1986).

4. California Fed. Sav. & Loan Ass'n v. Guerra, 479 U.S. 272 (1987).

5. Richard Rorty, "Feminism and Pragmatism," 30 *Michigan Quarterly Review* 231, 234 (1991) ("MacKinnon's central point, as I read her, is that 'a woman' is not yet the name of a way of being human—not yet the name of a moral identity, but, at most, the name of a disability.").

6. Elizabeth V. Spelman, *Inessential Woman: Problems Of Exclusion In Feminist Thought*, 158–159 (1988).

7. "[O]ne can be excited *about* ideas without changing at all. [O]ne can think *about* ideas, talk *about* ideas, without changing at all. [P]eople are willing to think

about many things. What people refuse to do, or are not permitted to do, or resist doing, is to change the way they think." Andrea Dworkin, *Woman Hating*, 202 (1974).

8. Spelman, *Inessential Woman*, 164–166, 174, 186. Spelman defines "essentialism" largely in terms of central tenets of radical feminism, without being clear whether the experience "as a woman" she identifies in radical feminism is a social or a biological construct. Having done this, it becomes easy to conclude that the "woman" of feminism is a distilled projection of the personal lives of a few comparatively powerful biological females, rather than a congealed synthesis of the lived social situation of women as a class, historically and worldwide.

9. Spelman implies that "differences" ought not be valorized or used as a theoretical construct, id. at 174, but others, building on her work and that of Carol Gilligan, *In a Different Voice* (1982), do.

10. The philosophical term "essentialism" is sometimes wrongly applied to socially based theories that observe and analyze empirical commonalities in women's condition. See e.g., Angela P. Harris, "Race and Essentialism in Feminist Legal Theory," 42 *Stanford Law Review* 581, 590–601 (1990). One can also take an essentialist approach to race or class. In other words, a theory does not become "essentialist" to the degree it discusses gender as such nor is it saved from "essentialism" to the degree it incorporates race or class.

11. Simone de Beauvoir, *The Second Sex*, 64 (H. M. Parshley, editor and translator, 1971).

12. Susan Brownmiller, *Against Our Will: Men, Women, and Rape*, 4, 6 (1976).

13. I am thinking in particular of Spelman, *Inessential Woman*, and Marlee Kline, "Race, Racism, and Feminist Legal Theory," 12 *Harvard Women's Law Journal* 115 (1989), although this analysis also applies to others who have made the same argument, such as Harris, "Race and Essentialism." Among its other problems, much of this work tends to make invisible the women of color who were and are instrumental in defining and creating feminism as a movement of women in the world, as well as a movement of mind.

14. This is by contrast with the massive feminist literature on the problem of class, which I discuss and summarize as a foundational problem for feminist theory in *Toward a Feminist Theory of the State* (1989). Harris in "Race and Essentialism" discusses race but does nothing with either class or sexual orientation except invoke them as clubs against others. See, for example, id. at 588, n.26 and accompanying text.

15. LeRoi Jones, "Black Dada Nihilismus," *The Dead Lecturer*, 61, 63 (1964).

16. "I became a rapist. To refine my technique and *modus operandi*, I started out by practicing on black girls in the ghetto . . . and when I considered myself smooth enough, I crossed the tracks and sought out white prey." Eldridge Cleaver, *Soul on Ice*, 14 (1968). "[R]aping the white girl" as an activity for Black men is described as one of "the funky facts of life," in a racist context in which the white girl's white-girlness is sexualized—that is, made a site of lust, hatred and hostility—for the Black man through the history of lynching. Id. at 14–15.

17. Helmut Newton, *White Women* (1976).

18. Ntozake Shange, *Three Pieces*, 48 (1981).

19. In 1989, the median income of white women was approximately one-fourth less

than that of Black men; in 1990 it was one-fifth less. U.S. Bureau of the Census, *Current Population Rep., Ser. P-60, No. 174, Money Income of Households, Families, and Persons in the United States: 1990*, 104–105 (tbl. 24) (1991).

20. This is an insight of Dorothy Teer.

21. Andrea Dworkin, *Pornography: Men Possessing Women*, 215–216 (1981).

22. "Thus, to know what the contemporary Jew is, we must ask the Christian conscience. And we must ask, not 'What is a Jew?' but '*What have you made of the Jews?*' The Jew is one whom other men consider a Jew: that is the simple truth from which we must start. In this sense . . . it is the anti-Semite who *makes* the Jew." Jean-Paul Sartre, *Anti-Semite and Jew*, 69 (George J. Becker trans., 1948).

23. Robin Morgan, *Going Too Far*, 169 (1978).

24. Personal communication with Andrea Dworkin. See also Andrea Dworkin, *Mercy*, 232, 304–307 (1991).

25. Perhaps a similar dynamic is at work in the attraction among some lesbians for identifying with "gay rights" and not, or and not also, "women's rights," negating the roots of the oppression of both lesbians and gay men in male dominance.

3. Law in the Everyday Life of Women

This essay was first published in *Law in Everyday Life* 109 (Austin Sarat and Thomas R. Kearns eds., 1993).

1. See the evocative treatment by Austin Sarat, "'The Law Is All Over': Power, Resistance, and the Legal Ideology of the Welfare Poor," 2 *Yale Journal of Law and the Humanities* 343 (1990).

2. I learned this from working with women in prison in the United States and Canada, specifically at Niantic, Connecticut, and Kingston, Ontario.

3. Rita J. Simon and Jean Landis, *The Crimes Women Commit the Punishments They Receive* (1991).

4. There are striking exceptions like Wanrow v. State of Washington, 88 Wash. 2d 221, 559 P.2d 548 (1977).

5. EEOC v. Sears, 839 F.2d 302 (7th Cir. 1988).

6. Rabidue v. Osceola Refining, 548 F. Supp. 419 (E. D. Mich. 1984); but compare Robinson v. Jacksonville Shipyards, 760 F. Supp. 1486 (D. Fla. 1991).

7. Roe v. Wade, 410 U.S. 113 (1973) (abortion decriminalized); Webster v. Reproductive Health Services, 492 U.S. 490, 518, 529 (1989) (*Roe*'s decriminalization of abortion questioned). See also Planned Parenthood v. Casey, 505 U.S. 833 (1992) (*Roe*'s fundamental holding affirmed).

8. Of course, this would only be effective for the defendant permitted to testify in his own defense, a relatively recent development.

9. People v. Mayberry, 15 Cal. 3d 143, 542 P.2d 1337 (1975); Pappajohn v. The Queen, 11 D.L.R. 3d 1 (1980); DPP v. Morgan, 2411 E.R. 347 (1975).

10. Diana E. H. Russell, *Sexual Exploitation*, 36 (1984). ("[O]nly about 1 in 10 nonmarital rapes in the Russell sample were ever reported to the police.")

11. The Florida Star v. B.J.F., 491 U.S. 524 (1989).

12. See generally, *Senate Judiciary Committee, The Response to Rape: Detours on the Road to Equal Justice*, May 1993.

13. This is documented in Catharine A. MacKinnon, "Reflections on Sex Equality Under Law," 100 *Yale Law Journal* 1281, 1301 n.94 (1991).

14. See Laurie Nsiah-Jefferson, "Reproductive Laws, Women of Color and Low-Income Women," 11 *Women's Rights Law Reporter* 15 (1989).

15. Andrea Dworkin said this in many public speeches in 1982 and 1984. The analysis behind it was originally developed in her *Pornography: Men Possessing Women*, 70–100 (1979).

16. Hudnut v. American Booksellers Ass'n., Inc., 771 F.2d 323 (7th Cir. 1985).

17. See Dailey v. Dailey, 635 S.W.2d 391 (Tenn. Ct. App. 1982); Jacobson v. Jacobson, 314 N.W.2d 78 (N.D. 1981); L. v. D., 630 S.W.2d 240 (Mo. Ct. App. 1982); Constant A. v. Paul C.A., 496 A.2d 1 (Pa. Super. Ct. 1985). But cf. S.N.E. v. R.L.B., 699 P.2d 875 (Alaska 1985); Stroman v. Williams, 353 S.E.2d 704 (S.C. App. Ct. 1987). See also Roe v. Roe, 324 S.E.2d 691 (Va. 1985).

18. See Comment, "The Emerging Constitutional Protection of the Putative Father's Parental Rights," 70 *Michigan Law Review* 1581 (1972); Phyllis Chesler, *Mothers on Trial* (1989).

19. Harris v. McRae, 448 U.S. 297 (1980).

20. Roberson v. Rochester Folding Box Co., 171 N.Y. 538 (1902); Cooley, *Torts*, 4th ed. sec. 135 (1932). See also Samuel D. Warren and Louis D. Brandeis, "The Right to Privacy," 4 *Harvard Law Review* 193 (1890); Samuel Hofstadter and George Horowitz, *The Right to Privacy*, 1–2 (1964).

21. Andrea Dworkin, "A Battered Wife Survives," *Letters from a War Zone*, 100 (1988).

22. On the structural level, see, e.g., Harris v. McRae, 448 U.S. 297 (1980); Deshaney v. Winnebago County Dep't. of Social Services, 489 U.S. 189 (1989). For further discussion, see Catharine A. MacKinnon, *Toward a Feminist Theory of the State*, chap. 10 (1989). For an attempt to reconstruct the privacy right, see Anita Allen, *Uneasy Access: Privacy for Women in a Free Society* (1988).

23. U.S. Equal Employment Opportunity Commission, *Job Patterns for Minorities and Women in Private Industry 1986*, (1988) (occupational segregation by race and sex); Kevin L. Phillips, *The Politics of Rich and Poor*, 202–203 (1990).

24. Russell, *Sexual Exploitation*, 50.

25. Harold Lentzner and Marshall DeBerry, *Intimate Victims: A Study of Violence Among Friends and Relatives* (Bureau of Justice Statistics, U.S. Dept. of Justice, 1980).

26. For further critique of the obscenity definition and detailed citations, see Catharine A. MacKinnon, *Feminism Unmodified: Discourses on Life and Law*, 152–154 (1987).

27. For a vivid analysis of this point, see Patricia J. Williams, "On Being the Object of Property," 14 *Signs: Journal of Women in Culture and Society* 5, 5–24 (1988).

4. Toward a New Theory of Equality

This talk was delivered at the Institute for Advanced Study, Berlin, on July 12, 1994. A modified version was delivered to the Seventh East/West Conference Honolulu, Hawaii, January 9–21, 1995. It is published for the first time here.

1. United Nations, *The World's Women 1970–1990, Trends and Statistics* (1991).
2. See Edward H. Levi, *An Introduction to Legal Reasoning* 2–3 (1948).
3. Book V iii 1131a, 1131b, 112–116 (W. Ross trans., 1925).
4. Id. at 113.
5. Reed v. Reed, 404 U.S. 71 (1971).
6. Barbier v. Connolly, 113 U.S. 27, 30–32 (1885).
7. Royster Guano Co. v. Virginia, 253 U.S. 412, 415 (1920). See also Hayes v. Missouri, 120 U.S. 68, 71 (1887).
8. 42 U.S.C. §2000e-2.
9. See Elizabeth V. Spelman, *Inessential Woman* 37–56 (1988).
10. Plessy v. Ferguson, 163 U.S. 537 (1896).
11. Georg Weippert, *Das Prinzip der Hierarchie*, 29 (1932).
12. "Der Gleichheitsgedanke in der volkischen Verfassungsordnung," 99 *Zeitschrift für die Gesamte Staatswissenschaft* 245, 260–267 (1939) ("Aus der volkischen Grundlage des heutigen deutschen Rechts folgt notwendig die Absonderung der artfremden Elemente, insbesondere der Juden, aus dem deutschen Volkskorper und ihre. . . . differentielle Behandlung," p. 267).
13. Prengel, "Gleichheit versus Differenz—eine falsche Alternative im feministischen Diskurs" in *Differenz und Gleichheit* 120, 121 (1990).
14. Regents of the University of California v. Bakke, 438 U.S. 265 (1978).
15. BVerfGE 23, 98, at 99.
16. Owen Fiss, "Groups and the Equal Protection Clause," 5 *Philosophy and Public Affairs* 107 (1976); Alan Freeman, "Legitimizing Racial Discrimination Through Antidiscrimination Law: A Critical Review of Supreme Court Doctrine," 62 *Minnesota Law Review* 1049 (1978); Kimberlé Crenshaw, "Race, Reform and Retrenchment: Transformation and Legitimation in Antidiscrimination Law," 101 *Harvard Law Review* 1331 (1988).
17. Aristotle, *Ethica Nichomachea*, 112 (J. L. Ackrill and J. O. Urmson, eds., W. Ross, trans., 1980).
18. John Cournos, *A Modern Plutarch*, 27 (1928) (quoting Anatole France).
19. The Nazi term was *Sonderbehandlung*.
20. See, e.g., Muller v. Oregon, 208 U.S. 412 (1908).
21. Aristotle, *The Politics*, 19 (Stephen Everson, ed., Benjamin Jowett, trans., 1988).
22. See Catharine A. MacKinnon, "Reflections on Sex Equality Under Law," 100 *Yale Law Journal* 1281 (1991); Catharine A. MacKinnon, *Toward a Feminist Theory of the State* (1989).
23. Richard Rorty, "Feminism and Pragmatism," in *The Tanner Lectures on Human Values: 1992*, 1, 7 (Grethe B. Peterson, ed., 1992).

24. David Cole, "Strategies of Difference: Litigating for Women's Rights in a Man's World," 2 *Law and Inequality* 33, 34, n.4 (1982).

25. Andrews v. Law Society of B.C., [1989] 1 S.C.R. 143.

26. 1 S.C.R. 143 at ¶10.

27. M. (K.) v. M. (H.), [1992] 3 S.C.R. 6.

28. Jane Doe v. Board of Commissioners, 126 C.C.C.3d 12 (1998).

29. R. v. Lavallée, 1 S.C.R. 852 (1990).

30. Daigle v. Tremblay, 2 S.C.R. 530 (1989).

31. Queen v. Sullivan and Lemay, [1991] 1 S.C.R. 489.

32. Queen v. Canadian Newspapers Co. [1988] 2 S.C.R. 122.

33. The Violence Against Women Act, Pub. L. No. 103–122, Title IV, 108 Stat. 1902 (1994).

34. Catharine A. MacKinnon, *Only Words* (1993).

35. R. v. Keegstra, [1990] 3 S.C.R. 697.

36. R. v. Butler, [1992] 1 S.C.R. 452. Elsewhere, German law opposes *Völksverhetzung* (hatred of peoples, or racial hatred), but more in reference to the value of dignity than equality. Eastern Europe and other emerging democracies define the systematic violation of women's equality through pornography as an emblem and spoil of long-sought freedom, revealing a one-sided notion of freedom predicated on the subordination of women. The European Parliament has recognized pornography as a systematic practice of sex discrimination, Comm. Civil Liberties and Intern. Aff. Res. 83–0121/93 at 4–7, U.N. Doc. A30259/93 (24 September 1993), but this insight has not been enacted as law anywhere or yet reached the European legal system.

37. American Booksellers Ass'n Inc. v. Hudnut, 771 F.2d 323 (7th Cir. 1985); R.A.V. v. City of St. Paul, Minn., 505 U.S. 377 (1992); Collin v. Smith, 578 F.2d 1197 (7th Cir. 1978).

5. Law's Stories as Reality and Politics

This essay was delivered as a reflection summing up a weekend conference of papers and discussion on Narrative and Rhetoric in the Law on February 11, 1995, at Yale Law School, New Haven, Connecticut. It was first published in the resulting volume, *Law's Stories: Narrative and Rhetoric in the Law* 232 (Peter Brooks and Paul Gewirtz, eds., 1996).

1. See Elaine Scarry, "Speech Acts in Criminal Cases," in *Law's Stories: Narrative and Rhetoric in the Law* 165, 166 (Peter Brooks and Paul Gewirtz eds. 1996) [hereinafter, *Law's Stories*].

2. David Rosen made this point concerning his own cases in David N. Rosen, "Rhetoric and Result in the Bobby Seale Trial," *Law's Stories* 110, 112.

3. Paul Gewirtz, "Victims and Voyeurs: Two Narrative Problems at the Criminal Trial," *Law's Stories* 135, 143.

4. Robert A. Ferguson, "Untold Stories in the Law," *Law's Stories* 84.

5. For an example, see Alan M. Dershowitz, "Life Is Not a Dramatic Narrative," *Law's Stories* 99, 100.

6. Catharine A. MacKinnon, *Feminism Unmodified*, 169 (1987). See generally Center for Women Policy Studies, *Violence Against Women as Bias-Motivated Hate Crime* (1991).

7. Each year, thousands of American women are killed in battering contexts by husbands or partners who have abused them. Evan Stark et al., *Wife Abuse in the Medical Setting, An Introduction for Health Personnel,* National Clearinghouse on Domestic Violence, Monograph Series no. 7, USGPO, 1981. See also generally Senate Judiciary Committee, *Violence Against Women: A Week in the Life of America* (October 1992); Ann Jones, *Next Time, She'll Be Dead: Battering and How to Stop It* (1994).

8. Jean-François Lyotard, "The Differend, the Referent, and the Proper Name," 4 *Diacritics* (Fall 1984).

9. Martha Minow's Verona story, in which, depending on one's religion, the identical facts are differentially but factually perfectly interpreted, appealingly illustrates this point. See Martha Minow, "Stories in Law," *Law's Stories*, 24–25.

10. To continue with Martha Minow's example, although everyone in the story saw a different story in the same facts, in fact there was only one reality: the presence of the Jews in Verona was threatened, and they *were* allowed to stay.

11. Daniel Farber and Martha Minow report this; Harlon Dalton and Richard Delgado exemplify it. See Daniel A. Farber and Suzanna Sherry, "Legal Storytelling and Constitutional Law"; Minow, "Stories in Law"; Harlon L. Dalton, "Storytelling on Its Own Terms," *Law's Stories.*

12. The comments of Louis Michael Seidman provide an excellent example of this. See Louis Michael Seidman, "Some Stories About Confessions and Confessions About Stories," *Law's Stories* 162.

13. For discussion of this point, see Harlan Dalton, *Law's Stories* 57.

14. See, e.g., Karin Obholzer, *Gespräche mit dem Wolfsmann* (1980).

15. See, e.g., Diana E.H. Russell, "The Incidence and Prevalence of Interfamilial and Extrafamilial Sexual Abuse of Female Children," 7 *Child Abuse and Neglect: The International Journal* 2 (1983).

16. Peter Brooks, "Storytelling Without Fear? Confession in Law and Literature," *Law's Stories* 114. Marion is the woman about whose entry into prostitution Rousseau fantasizes in his *Confessions*, the subject of Peter Brooks's essay, at 122 and following.

17. As an illustration, Janet Malcolm's sidebars preserve jurors' illusions, offering fact-finding by imagination. See Janet Malcolm, "The Side-Bar Conference," *Law's Stories* 106.

18. Malcolm seems to me to take this position at id. at 108 ("The juror, no less than the reader of a novel, needs to be protected from disbelief.").

19. For studies that document this, see Catharine A. MacKinnon, "Prostitution and Civil Rights," 1 *Michigan Journal of Gender and Law* 13, 27–28 (1993).

20. U.S. Merit Systems Protection Board, *Sexual Harassment in the Federal Workplace: Is It a Problem?* (1981).

21. Russell, "The Incidence and Prevalance," supra at note 15.

22. This discussion is briefly opened in John Hollander, "Legal Rhetoric," *Law's Stories* 182–183.

23. The example of a hypothetical Judge Calabresi is offered in Sanford Levinson, "The Rhetoric of the Judicial Opinion," *Law's Stories*, 194.

24. Collin v. Smith, 575 F.2d 1187, 1210 (1976).

25. One engaging and productive instance can be found in Hollander, "Legal Rhetoric," *Law's Stories*, 185, of "It takes two to tango."

6. "Freedom from Unreal Loyalties": On Fidelity in Constitutional Interpretation

This essay began as a comment on the papers of Ronald Dworkin and Jack Balkin at a conference on Fidelity in Constitutional Interpretation, September 20–21, 1996 at Fordham Law School, New York, New York. It was originally published in LXV *Fordham Law Review* 1773 (1997). The quotation "freedom from unreal loyalties" is from Virginia Woolf. In her *Three Guineas*, she explains how an organization of women that she imagines would both criticize and re-create institutions:

> By criticizing education they would help to create a civilized society which protects culture and intellectual liberty. By criticizing religion they would attempt to free the religious spirit from its present servitude and would help, if need be, to create a new religion based it might well be upon the New Testament, but, it might well be, very different from the religion now erected upon *that basis*. And in all this . . . they would be helped . . . by their position as outsiders, that freedom from unreal loyalties, that freedom from interested motives which are at present assured them by the State.

Virginia Woolf, *Three Guineas* (1938), reprinted in *A Room of One's Own and Three Guineas* 107, 234 (1984) (emphasis added).

In her view, insiders have the "interested motives," ones that outsiders are certain to encounter in their dealings with the State. A conversation with Jed Rubenfeld encouraged the shape of this talk; comments by Cass Sunstein and Martha Nussbaum helped clarify it. Representing my Bosnian and Croatian clients, survivors of the Serbian genocide, with Natalie Nenadic and Asja Armanda, has deepened my understanding of accountability.

1. This is how I translate Jean-Jacques Rousseau, *Du Contrat social* 153, 160 (1978) (1762) ("Qu'est-ce qui peut le rendre légitime?").

2. I am not condemning all moral theory by taking Ronald Dworkin's particular approach to it as all there is. This is a critique of the kind of moral theory he engages in, some features of which, while perhaps extreme in his work, exemplify tendencies common to much, if not all, moral philosophy.

3. Jack M. Balkin, "Agreements with Hell and Other Objects of Our Faith," 65 *Fordham Law Review* 1703, 1706 (1997).

4. Jack M. Balkin, Symposium, *Fidelity in Constitutional Theory*, Fordham University School of Law, 127 (Sept. 21, 1996) (transcript on file with the *Fordham Law Review*).

5. Scott v. Sandford, 60 U.S. 343, 404–412 (1856); see Patricia J. Williams, "On Being the Object of Property," 14 *Signs: Journal of Women in Culture and Society* 5, 5–6 (1988) (slave ancestors of Professor Williams).

6. Bradwell v. Illinois, 83 U.S. (16 Wall.) 130, 139–142 (1873) (Bradley, J., concurring).

7. Korematsu v. United States, 323 U.S. 214, 217–219 (1944); see, e.g., Charles R. Lawrence III & Mari J. Matsuda, *We Won't Go Back: Making the Case for Affirmative Action* xvi (1997) (internment of Professor Matsuda's Okinawan family members during World War II).

8. American Booksellers Ass'n, Inc. v. Hudnut, 771 F.2d 323 (7th Cir. 1985) (finding that pornography harms women but holding it protected speech), *aff'd*, 475 U.S. 1132 (1986) (summary affirmance).

9. Ronald Dworkin, *Freedom's Law: The Moral Reading of the American Constitution* 1–38 (1996).

10. See Woolf, *Three Guineas*, 234, on "unreal loyalties."

11. See Herbert Wechsler, "Toward Neutral Principles of Constitutional Law," 73 *Harvard Law Review* 1 (1959).

12. Plessy v. Ferguson, 163 U.S. 537, 559 (1896) (Harlan, J., dissenting); see Cass R. Sunstein, "The Anticaste Principle," 92 *Michigan Law Review* 2410 (1994).

13. This assumes, of course, that other requisites like state action are met, but also provides a basis for interrogating them.

14. Meritor Sav. Bank, FSB v. Vinson, 477 U.S. 57, 64–67 (1986) (sexual harassment is sex discrimination under Title VII); Bohen v. City of E. Chicago, 799 F.2d 1180, 1185 (7th Cir. 1986) (sexual harassment is sex discrimination under 42 U.S.C. §1983).

15. The subtext of this discussion is United States v. Lanier, 73 F.3d 1380 (6th Cir. 1996) (reversing sexual assault convictions of judge prosecuted under substantive due process liberty theory on grounds that such a right is not clearly defined for purposes of 18 U.S.C. §242). See *Brief Amicus Curiae for Vivian Forsythe-Archie and the National Coalition Against Sexual Assault*, United States v. Lanier, 116 S. Ct. 2522 (1996) (No. 95–1717) (granting cert.) (arguing that sexual assault by judge of litigants and employees violates well-defined sex equality rights).

16. Kurt Gödel, "On Formally Undecidable Propositions of Principia Mathematica and Related Systems I," in 1 *Kurt Gödel: Collected Works* 145, 145–195 (Solomon Feferman ed., 1986); see Ernest Nagel, James R. Newman, *Gödel's Proof* 26–36 (1958). Reading Nagel and Newman's chapter 3 on "Absolute Proofs of Consistency," paralleling "the Constitution" to "mathematics" and "constitutional interpretation" to "meta-mathematics," illustrates this point.

17. Ronald Dworkin, *Law's Empire* 228–238 (1986) (discussing law as chain novel).

18. Id. at 381 (stating the "abstract principle" of equality as he understands it); id. at 296 ("Government, we say, has an abstract responsibility to treat each citizen's fate as equally important").

19. On why the objective stance supports power, see Catharine A. MacKinnon, *Toward a Feminist Theory of the State* 162–163, 231–234 (1989).

20. Dworkin, *Freedom's Law*, 234.

21. Id. at 216–223, 233–239 (ballistic discussion of civil rights approach to pornography).

22. Balkin, Symposium, 1704, 1729.

23. See Dworkin, *Law's Empire* (discussing law as integrity).

7. What *Brown v. Board of Education* Should Have Said

Originally published in *What Brown v. Board of Education Should Have Said*, 143 (Balkin, J. M. ed., 2001). Jack Balkin's idea for this book, which began as a panel at the American Association of Law Schools Annual Meeting on January 9, 2000, Washington, D.C., was an exercise in counter-historical imagination. A bench of nine contemporary legal scholars each wrote an opinion as if they were on the U.S. Supreme Court at the time of *Brown*, using only sources they could have had access to at the time, saying what they thought the opinion should have said.

1. Brown, et al., Appellants, v. Board of Education of Topeka, Shawnee County, Kansas, et al., 98 F.Supp. 797 (D. Kan. 1951); Briggs, et al., Appellants, v. Elliott, et al., 103 F. Supp. 920 (E.D.S.C. 1952); Davis, et al., Appellants v. County School Board of Prince Edward County, Virginia, et al., 103 F.Supp. 337 (E.D. Va. 1952); Bolling, et al., Petitioners, v. Sharpe, et al., 347 U.S. 497 (1954); Gebhart, et al., Petitioners, v. Belton, et al., 91 A.2d 137 (Del. 1952).

2. Describing why he "got into the suit whole soul and body," Mr. Fleming, said: "[M]y point was that not only I and my children are craving light; the entire colored race is craving light. And the only way to reach the light is to start our children together in their infancy and they come up together." Record of Trial at 109–110, *Brown v. Board of Education of Topeka*, 98 F. Supp. 797 (D. Kan. 1951) (No. T-316).

3. "Plaintiffs" here refers to the original moving parties in these consolidated cases, Appellants in *Brown* (No. 1), *Briggs* (No. 2), and *Davis* (No. 4), and Respondents in *Belton* (No. 10).

4. Defendant Topeka School Board, having determined to integrate racially in the midst of the litigation, did not resist the claim of the *Brown* plaintiffs beyond trial, taking acquiescence in the plaintiffs' position far enough to have raised the question of mootness. See Transcript of Oral Argument of Robert L. Carter on Reargument, Dec. 8, 1953, at 1–4 (responding to questions by Justice Frankfurter on reargument). Topeka sought only gradualism in the relief ordered. Brief for the Board of Education, Topeka, Kansas, on Questions Propounded by the Court at 2. The State of Kansas, while not defending racial segregation as a policy and "grant[ing] that segregation may not be the ethical or political ideal," defended its statute permitting local choice of racial segregation before the Supreme Court on the ground that constitutional law "permits determination of state and local policy to be made on state and local levels." Brief for the State of Kansas on Reargument at 14, 56. We reject this argument from federalism. Equality in public schools is not an ethical or political matter alone, but one that has been made a matter of constitutional right by the Fourteenth Amendment.

5. See Testimony of Dr. Kenneth Clark and Dr. David Krech in *Briggs*; Testimony

of Louisa Holt and Hugh Speer in *Brown*; Testimony of M. Brewster Smith and Isidor Chein in *Davis*.

6. This widely known but little acknowledged motivation for and function of segregation was alluded to obliquely by the American Jewish Congress in discussing the role of segregation statutes by quoting a Kentucky court's reference to "the general feeling everywhere prevailing [that] the Negro, while respected and protected in his place, is not and cannot be a fit associate for white girls." Brief of American Jewish Congress as Amicus Curiae at 13 (quoting Axton Fisher Tobacco Co. v. The Evening Post, 169 Ky. 64 (1916)). The missing persons in the Kentucky court's analysis—Black women in "the Negro," at least the entire Black community in "everywhere"—serve to highlight the subliminal obsession.

7. Brief of American Jewish Congress as Amicus Curiae at 14 argues that the enforced separation of races affirms "white dominance," and further that racial segregation of schools incorporates the doctrine of "white supremacy" into the provision of facilities for citizens, id. at 20.

8. The racial particulars have varied arbitrarily, see *Gong Lum v. Rice*, 275 U.S. 78 (1927) (permitting state to define race so as to send students of Chinese descent to schools for Black children), but what does not vary, in segregated systems, is the exclusion of Black children from schools principally for whites.

9. The disenfranchisement and exclusion of women as a group from public life and their often lower status in private life suggest that it is not entirely due to lesser numbers that so-called minority groups are discriminated against or can be kept unequal.

10. Treating "unlikes unalike" in the Aristotelian language could even have gone beyond "separate but equal" and supported unequal facilities—justified, for example, by lower performance, even if that lower performance was shown due to poor facilities. In reality, if not in doctrine, the *Plessy* rule accomplished exactly this.

11.

What happens to a dream deferred?
Does it dry up
Like a raisin in the sun?
Or fester like a sore—
And then run?
Does it stink like rotten meat?
Or crust and sugar over—
like a syrupy sweet?
Maybe it just sags
like a heavy load.
Or does it explode?

Langston Hughes, "Harlem [2]," *Montage of a Dream Deferred* (1951).

8. Keeping It Real: On Anti-"Essentialism"

This talk was originally delivered as a comment on the opening panel of the Critical Race Theory Conference held at Yale Law School, November 14, 1997, a panel on which Professor Kimberlé Crenshaw and Professor Mari Matsuda also delivered papers. It is dedicated to christi cunningham, who made it possible for me to say it. It was first published in *Critical Race Theory: Histories, Crossroads, Directions* (Jerome Culp, Angela P. Harris, and Francisco Valdes, eds., 2002).

1. Kimberlé Williams Crenshaw, "The First Decade: Critical Reflections, or 'A Foot in the Closing Door'"; Mari Matsuda, "Beyond and Not Beyond, Black and White: Deconstruction Has a Politics," in *Critical Race Theory: Histories, Crossroads, Directions*, (Jerome M. Culp, Angela P. Harris, and Francisco Valdes, eds., 2002).

2. Patricia J. Williams, *Alchemy of Race and Rights* (1991).

3. For an analysis of postmodernism that documents and expands on this point, see Catharine A. MacKinnon, "Points Against Postmodernism," 75 *Chicago-Kent Law Review* 687 (2000).

4. Aristotle's term that is translated "essence" is the Greek phrase "what it is to be." Thus, the essence of a house would be what it is to be a house—say, providing shelter or a place to live or a center for family life. So some characteristics would be central to a thing being what it is; others would be more peripheral. But, through changes, the "essence" of a thing is what inheres in it that makes it be what it is. See Aristotle, *Metaphysics VII, VIII*. See generally Martha Nussbaum, "Aristotle," in *Ancient Writers Greece and Rome*, 377–416 (T. James Luce, ed., 1982), and Martha Nussbaum, "Aristotle on Human Nature and the Foundations of Ethics," in J. E. J. Altham and Ross Harrison, *World, Mind, and Ethics: Essays on the Ethical Philosophy of Bernard Williams*, 86–131 (1995). Of relevance to the contemporary discussion is Aristotle's rejection of the idea that a universal, such as a Platonic form, is the essence of a thing. See *Metaphysics VII*, 13. Wittgenstein's treatment of the notion of "essential" focuses on the notion of what things have in common that are called by a common name, and the difficulties of doing so. See Ludwig Wittgenstein, *Philosophical Investigations*, 2nd ed., ¶66, ¶67 (G. E. M. Anscombe trans., 1972). Thus, in challenging readers to exhaustively define "games," he said, "What is common to them all? . . . If you look at them you will not see something that is common to all, but similarities, relationships, and a whole series of them at that. To repeat: don't think, but look! . . . And the result of this examination is: we see a complicated network of similarities overlapping and criss-crossing; sometimes overall similarities, sometimes similarities of detail"; id., ¶66.

5. Elizabeth Spelman, *Inessential Woman*, 158 (1988).

6. For further discussion, see Catharine A. MacKinnon, "From Practice to Theory, Or What Is a White Woman Anyway?" 4 *Yale Journal of Law and Feminism* 113 (1991), discussing Susan Brownmiller and Simone de Beauvoir.

7. Angela P. Harris, "Race and Essentialism in Feminist Legal Theory," 42 *Stanford Law Review* 581, 585 (1990). As of 1995, this article was the most widely cited article in law published in 1990. Fred R. Shapiro, "The Most-Cited Law Review Articles Revisited," 71 *Chicago-Kent Law Review* 751, 777 (1995) (142 citations). Using the same method as Shapiro, I found that as of January 2, 1998, the Harris article had been referenced in 191 articles, 180 of them law journals.

8. For analysis, see e. christi cunningham, "Unmaddening: A Response to Angela Harris," 4 *Yale Journal of Law and Feminism* 155, 158 (1991).

9. See Spelman, *Inessential Woman*, 165.

10. Id., 13.

11. See Harris, "Race and Essentialism," 588.

12. The issues discussed here are not confined to individuals, nor are they personal. However, research in 1999 disclosed more than one hundred law review articles falsely referring to my work as "essentialist," usually based solely on citation to Professor Harris's 1990 article. Only a handful even hesitantly questioned the label, and fewer still discussed my work itself. Representative examples from this flood of defamation include Katharine T. Bartlett, "Feminist Legal Methods," 103 *Harvard Law Review* 829, 874 (1990) ("A theory that purports to isolate gender as a basis for oppression obscures [factors other than gender that victimize women] and even reinforces other forms of oppression," citing Angela Harris for "mak[ing] this point specifically about MacKinnon"); Kathryn Abrams, "Title VII and the Complex Female Subject," 92 *Michigan Law Review* 2479, 2485 (1994) ("My use of the term *antiessentialism* . . . is more consistent with that of Angela Harris, who targets from the standpoint of black feminists what she described as the 'essentialism' of Catharine MacKinnon"); Linda C. McClain, "'Atomistic Man' Revisited: Liberalism, Connection, and Feminist Jurisprudence," 65 *Southern California Law Review* 1171, 1186 (1992), but compare Linda C. McClain, "Toward a Formative Project of Security, Freedom, and Equality," 85 *Cornell Law Review* 1221 (2000) (using MacKinnon's work itself to respond to Harris's charges); Thomas Ross, "Despair and Redemption in the Feminist Nomos," 69 *Indiana Law Review* 101, 105 (1993); Eric Blumenson, "Mapping the Limits of Skepticism in Law and Morals," 74 *Texas Law Review* 523, 557 (1996); Note, "The Myth of Context in Politics and Law," 110 *Harvard Law Review* 1292, 1295 (1997) ("As Harris argues, . . . essentialism may be identified in the writings of Catharine MacKinnon"); Kathryn Abrams, "Sex Wars Redux: Agency and Coercion in Feminist Legal Theory," 95 *Columbia Law Review* 304, 335, 336 (1995) (noting "Catharine MacKinnon is frequently taken to be the paradigmatic dominance feminist" and stating that "[d]ominance theory shares a central flaw of the 'essentialist' feminisms Harris critiques"); Nancy C. Staudt, "Taxing Housework," 84 *Georgetown Law Journal* 1571, 1573 (1996) ("Commentators who take an essentialist approach to women's subordination tend to make sex based generalizations about all women, regardless of the race, class, and sexuality differences among women," citing Harris's article for "discussing the marginalizing effects of Catharine MacKinnon's . . . theories of sexual difference"); Susan H. Williams, "A Feminist Reassessment of Civil Society," 72 *Indiana Law Journal* 417, 428 (1997) ("Feminists of color have been pointing out with increasing frequency that the view of women as simply the victims of society, shaped rather than shaping, has the effect of systematically excluding them," citing only Harris "discussing the work of Catharine MacKinnon"); Daniel R. Ortiz, "Categorical Community," 51 *Stanford Law Review* 769, 801 (1999); Zanita E. Fenton, "Domestic Violence in Black and White: Racialized Gender Stereotypes in Gender Violence," 8 *Columbia Journal of Gender and Law* 1, 17, 52 (1998); Peter A. Alces and Cynthia V. Ward, "Defending Truth Beyond All Reason: The Radical Assault on Truth in American Law" (book review), 78 *Texas Law Review* 493, 528 (1999) (citing Harris's article as a "widely respected example" of critical race theory

and a "well-known critique of feminist essentialism" that "focuses specifically on 'gender essentialism' in the work of Catharine MacKinnon"); Jody Armour, "Critical Race Feminism: Old Wine in a New Bottle or New Legal Genre?" (book review), 7 *Southern California Review of Law and Women's Studies* 431, 434 (1998) (quoting Professor Adrien Wing's book criticizing "prominent white feminist Catharine MacKinnon . . . for using white women as the epitome of all women" and citing the Harris article); Kathryn Abrams, "The New Jurisprudence of Sexual Harassment," 83 *Cornell Law Review* 1169, 1192, 1201 (1998) (referring to "MacKinnonesque essentialism," citing Harris's article), 1214; Jane Wong, "The Anti-Essentialism v. Essentialism Debate in Feminist Legal Theory: The Debate and Beyond," 5 *William and Mary Journal of Women and the Law* 273, 284 (1999).

13. Starting in the 1970s, within the women's movement sexuality was commonly discussed in political context as a social experience. When speaking and writing during that period of "sexuality as a social construct," I had not previously heard those words used to describe that common understanding. The movement I was part of pioneered this theory.

14. Catharine A. MacKinnon, "Feminism, Marxism, Method, and the State: Toward Feminist Jurisprudence," 8 *Signs: Journal of Women in Culture and Society* 635, 639 (1983). This passage is quoted in Harris, "Race and Essentialism," 592. Another example is: "The particularities become facets of the collective understanding within which differences constitute rather than undermine collectivity" (Catharine A. MacKinnon, *Toward a Feminist Theory of the State*, 86 (1990)).

15. See cunningham, "Unmaddening," 164–167. Professor cunningham documents how "Harris often repeats MacKinnon's ideas when she describes Black women's experiences of dominance."

16. After this talk was delivered, Professor Sallyanne Payton, as part of an online discussion that followed, said:

> I was not at the CRT meeting . . . I do happen to know what MacKinnon thinks, however, and I would be greatly surprised if she did not say what she thinks. Here is what she thinks, filtered through my way of talking.
>
> The charge of "essentialism" as leveled against much of feminist writing is fair and accurate. That is, many white feminists seem to think there is something inherent about being female that accounts for women's attitudes and behaviors, crossculturally, and lots of them take Western white women as the normative representatives of true womanhood in the sense of true-to-nature womanhood, the rest of us being deficient or substandard or odd or whatever. The racist dimension of this stems from the fact that a great many white feminists seem to regard Western white male-female relations as prototypical of male-female relations, which conveniently reinforces the Western white male as the representative of the most advanced manhood: if male-female relations in non-Western cultures don't look like those in (middle-class) Western society, it is only because the non-Western men are not as advanced as the Western men.

It has been a long time since I have participated in feminist discourse, but I seem to remember that in the early days (1970s into early 1980s) this is how almost all the white feminists thought: they were interested in their relationships with their men, who were the powerful men. If the rest of us were not having their experience, it was because our men, being inferior, had not achieved power. So we had nothing to say: if our men ever achieved power in the sense in which white men had power, we would have the same kinds of experiences the white women were having. The actual experiences of women of color were therefore material for footnotes and asides: they were not central, not emblematic. White women controlled the discussion, which was about themselves. We spent years fighting this kind of thinking, with only mixed success.

The refreshing aspect of MacKinnon's approach is that she does not think this way. She did not start with the situation of the privileged white woman even though she was one; she started with the situation of the most powerless women in the system, and built her theory on what she saw as the relationship between male desire and opportunity where women were unprotected. The situation of the more privileged she then saw as the consequence of their relative sheltering from the full force of male domination. In MacKinnon's world the least privileged woman (frequently a woman of color) therefore becomes emblematic; the more privileged woman is revealed to be a beneficiary of protection, and the typical white feminist a victim of the delusion that the status of middle-class white women is something more than an artifact of male protection for some specially favored women, a protection that is strenuously maintained. This line of thought . . . moves the middle-class white women off of center stage and it forces the middle-class white men to look at the sexually gritty sides of themselves and the society that they have built. It moves the experience of women of color to center stage and it accounts for our experience in a way that is theoretically coherent. In MacKinnon's work, the experience of women of color is in the text, not in the footnotes.

No one's work is above criticism, but I think it cannot plausibly be argued that MacKinnon's feminism is essentialist. It actually comes closest to being essentialist in its treatment of men, not women, whose situation depends centrally on context and the particular cultural ways in which protections and vulnerabilities are constructed. I think that MacKinnon is sensitive on this point, not only because unexamined racism is a sin of which she is unwilling to stand accused inaccurately, but also because she thinks that people who believe that her feminism is essentialist and therefore racist do not avail themselves of the powerful critique of male dominance that might be analytically useful to them in anti-racist thinking.

This text is on file with the author.

17. See Harris, "Race and Essentialism," 598.

18. Id., 592, 595, 596. Compare cunningham, "Unmaddening," 163–164: "MacKinnon's inclusive definition of women is evident . . . Black women cannot be a nuance of women because Black women are women [in her work;] we are often the model. MacKinnon does not marginalize Black women, nor does she make us into something more than women, because MacKinnon considers Black women to be women."

19. Saying this is not to say that the only problems of women of color are worse versions of white women's problems. Nor do I "define" Black women as "different"; see Harris, "Race and Essentialism," 595. I reject "differences" definitions explicitly and implicitly. And Professor Harris is incorrect to suggest that "feminism unmodified" refers to women without particularities. It clearly refers to a politics of women unmodified by preexisting politics, like liberalism or socialism.

20. See Harris, "Race and Essentialism," 592–594, 603. See cunningham, "Unmaddening," 160–161: "MacKinnon does not relegate Black women to footnotes and brackets. Her theory is explicitly about us." How footnotes that document, credit, and elaborate, become "guilty" is unclear. See Harris, "Race and Essentialism," 603.

21. See Harris, "Race and Essentialism," 594. Compare cunningham, "Unmaddening," 161–163.

22. See, for example, Martha Minow, "The Supreme Court 1986 Term Forward: Justice Engendered," 101 *Harvard Law Review* 10, 63 (1987): "Some, for example, have expressly argued that sexism is more fundamental than racism," citing as the first of three sources Catharine A. MacKinnon, *Feminism Unmodified: Discourses on Life and Law* 166–168 (1987). I never made any such statement or adopted any such approach, there or anywhere, expressly or otherwise. Moreover, extensive evidence that this is not my view—including drawing on African American women's experiences and writings, discussions of racism throughout, a central focus on class, and a pervasive combined analysis of race and ethnicity with sex, much of which is readily accessible through the indices of my published books—had to be ignored. It is a lot to overlook.

Published in 1979, *Sexual Harassment of Working Women: A Case of Sex Discrimination*, for example, explicitly builds the concept of sexual harassment itself on the experiences of Black women in particular. See, for example, pp. 33, 65 (Paulette Barnes); pp. 30, 73–74 (Maxine Munford); p. 60 (Diane Williams); p. 61 (Margaret Miller); p. 34 (referring to Pamela Price); see also pp. 42, 48, 52, 78–80, 84 (Carmita Wood). Nor is these women's ethnicity submerged in their gender. Why it was Black women who had what it took to bring all the early sexual-harassment cases is analyzed in terms of their race, sex, and class particularities: p. 53 ("Of all women, [black women] are most vulnerable to sexual harassment, both because of the image of black women as the most sexually accessible and because they are the most economically at risk"). Other Black women's voices analyzing women's condition are either quoted—see, for example, p. 176 (an anonymous Black woman); p. 273 (Pauli Murray); and p. 23 (Ntozake Shange)—or their insights are otherwise drawn on (see p. 275 [Toni Morrison]). Race and racism are discussed throughout, legally and socially, as a parallel to or contrast with sex and sexism: p. 129 ("The analogy [between the histories of sex and race distinctions] should not be allowed to obscure the distinctive content and dynamics of sex and race"); specified within sex and outside of it: p. 176 ("The generality of 'women' and 'men' must be qualified by recognizing the distinctive effect of race"); and in interaction with and overlapping with sex: p. 30 ("Sexual harassment can be both a sexist way to express racism and a racist way to express sexism"). For additional examples, see p. 14 ("Black women are much more likely to be poor than white women"); pp. 17–18, 23, 30–31, 88–90, 97–98, 118–119, 127–141, 169, 173, 176–177, 189–190, 203, 210, 215 (Helen Hacker's work on Black people as a group and women as a group); p. 247 ("Presumably, black women are doubly burdened"); p. 257 (noting that the filing of an amicus brief in a case by Organization of Black Activist Women "is of special interest since both the perpetrator and victim were black"); p. 267 (noting the history of scientific racism); p. 273 (noting scholarship in Black women's feminism); pp. 273–274 (noting scholarship on the parallel between race and sex); p. 274 (noting cases that point to the parallel between race and sex); and p. 274 (analyzing an article comparing racism and sexism). These are just some selected instances.

Feminism Unmodified, published in 1987, follows the same pattern. It criticizes nonreporting of the race of rape victims: pp. 81–82 ("The invisibility of women of color is such that if you do not say that a woman is of color, it is assumed that her race is nonexistent—therefore, oddly, white"). It locates women of color as active agents in their own cultures and in resisting white male domination: p. 69 ("What women like Julia Martinez might make equality mean, no white man invented"). It speaks of women of color's specific rates of rape (p. 82), death from illegal abortion (p. 25), and abuse in pornography (pp. 199–200). It refers to voices, work, insights, and experiences of women including LaDoris Cordell, Pamela Price, Mechelle Vinson, Vanessa Williams, Gayatri Spivak, Beth Brant, and many others. It speaks about race in relation to sex (p. 2 ["We urgently need to comprehend the emerging pattern in which gender, while a distinct inequality, also contributes to the social embodiment and expression of race and class inequalities, at the same time as race and class are deeply imbedded in gender. For example, the sexualization of racial and ethnic attributes like skin color or stereotypes is no less a dynamic within racism for being done through gender"]) and on its own terms; about women of color as women and as women of color throughout. See, for example, pp. 7, 9, 25, 42, 44, 56, 63–67, 76, 81–82, 89, 101, 164–168, 178, 193–194, 199–200, 202, 208–209, 211, 220, 238 (explaining why "Black" is capitalized in the book and "white" is not), 248, 256, 302–303, 305.

The same is true of *Toward a Feminist Theory of the State*, published in 1989. The introduction states: "All women possess ethnic (and other definitive) particularities that mark their femaleness; at the same time their femaleness marks their particularities and constitutes one. Such a recognition, far from undermining the feminist project, comprises, defines, and sets standards for it. It also does not reduce race to sex. Rather, it suggests that comprehension and change in racial inequality are essential to comprehension and change in sex inequality, with implications that link comprehending and changing sexism to comprehending and changing racism" (p. xii). Again, race and racism and its impact on men and women and theorizing their condition are discussed throughout (see, for example, pp. xi–xiii, 6, 26, 55, 63, 110, 125, 136, 138, 154, 172–

173, 181, 204, 245, 288). In addition, the words and work, among others, of Johnnie Tillmon, Zora Neale Hurston, Harriet Jacobs, Alice Walker, and Audre Lorde are used to define the condition of women as such.

At the conference at which the remarks in the text above were delivered, the paragraph preceding this endnote (minus its footnotes) was spoken virtually as it appears here. After the panel, Professor Harris thanked me for the critique of her work, said it was fair and right, and expressed her appreciation for the attention to what she had said back then because my work had been important to her. Professor Crenshaw (who was sitting next to me when Professor Harris said this) and I both admired the courage and forthrightness of this statement.

23. On April 7, 1990, shortly after Professor Harris's article was published, Karen E. Davis wrote to her, analyzing many of the issues raised in the foregoing paragraphs:

> I have always read Catharine MacKinnon's work as deeply anti-essentialist. It is deconstructive in the Derridean sense, except that she considers power while he doesn't. It is genealogical in the Foucauldian sense, except that she considers gender while he doesn't. MacKinnon's analysis of male power includes an analysis of its "essentialism" or "phallogicentrism," although she does not use these terms in her critiques of metaphysics, objectivity, liberalism, and "theory." I believe you introduce essentialism into Catharine MacKinnon's work that isn't there.
>
> In fact, I see in your writing a pervasive use of moral essentialism typical of that which pervades feminist theory. Throughout your article, power and powerlessness are understood in terms of guilt and innocence, good and bad. The most obvious example of this is where you attribute to MacKinnon the view that Black men are not as bad as white men, "although they are still bad, being men" [Harris, "Race and Essentialism," 596, n. 17]. The quote you cite, however, supports only MacKinnon's point that Black men are not as powerful as white men. Nowhere in her work does MacKinnon conflate powerful—bad, and powerless—good, as many strains of feminism are wont to do. Rather, she explicitly rejects the moralism and naturalism contained in the views that men abuse women because they are bad or naturally rapacious, and that "women might be congenitally nicer" [MacKinnon, *Feminism Unmodified*, 219].
>
> While you say MacKinnon violates the particularities of the experiences of women of color, the standard against which you measure her work is not embodied experience but a formulation of five attributes of gender essentialism as abstracted from Elizabeth Spelman, a white feminist. You define gender essentialism as 'The notion that there is a monolithic "women's experience' that can be described independent of other facets of experience like race, class, and sexual orientation" [Harris, "Race and Essentialism," 588]. But nothing you quote in MacKinnon's writings in any way supports your premise that

MacKinnon does this. In fact, the things you quote directly support the opposite reading. Your idea that she "postpones the demands of black women until the arrival of a 'general theory of social inequality'" [Harris, "Race and Essentialism," 593] is based incongruously on her statement that such a theory is prefigured in connections between race, sex and class: "gender in this country appears partly to comprise the meaning of, as well as bisect, race and class, even as race and class specificities make up, as well as cross-cut gender" [quoted in Harris, "Race and Essentialism," 593]. To accuse MacKinnon of a "colorblind" approach here is to miss her critiques of objectivity, of abstraction, and of the principles of neutrality in law. The whole point of her *Signs* articles is that a commitment in feminism to not submerging particularity into universals is a methodological departure from all previous theories.

You go on here to suggest parenthetically that MacKinnon is not committed to the effort such a theory will take, "(presumably that is someone else's work)." This not only belies her work but is gratuitously insulting. MacKinnon does not claim to present a finished thing but rather a contribution to a larger project which she sees as necessarily collaborative. To this end, her footnotes are not just lists, but an engaged intertextuality with shared and ongoing concerns.

The point where you come close to having to acknowledge her engagement with issues of race and class, you provide MacKinnon's theory with the appellation "nuanced," suggesting that nuance is essentialism's empty gesture toward engaging particularity. While this critique may be true of liberal feminism, it is not true of MacKinnon's radicalism. In her preface to *Toward a Feminist Theory of the State*, MacKinnon is herself quite critical of liberal feminism's response to the challenge of diversity: "to proliferate 'feminisms' (a white racist feminism?) in the face of women's diversity is the latest attempt of liberal pluralism to evade the challenge women's reality poses to theory, simply because the theoretical forms those realities demand have yet to be created" [MacKinnon, *Feminist Theory*, xii]. And yes, MacKinnon counts herself among the feminists who will be creating such a theory.

The other times you are close to being forced to acknowledge MacKinnon's attention to race and class, you castigate her for relegating these concerns to footnotes. You mention MacKinnon's use of footnotes about ten times without analyzing their function in her text. Do you have a meta-theory of footnotes in the same way you have a meta-theory of nuance or of essentialism? You seem to be banking on a tacit universal agreement ("we") that footnotes are always marginal and dismissive. Instead of outlining a textual examination of the structure of footnotes in MacKinnon's writing, you rely on the convention that footnotes are the place of empty gestures. Yet even a cursory textual analysis of MacKinnon's style would suggest that her footnotes are an essential element of a multitiered structure of argument. . . .

Toward a Feminist Theory of the State appeared last August, shortly after you presented your paper, but well in advance of the time you published it. In the preface to this book, MacKinnon specifically addresses methodological questions of essentialism and totalization that you and others have raised about her work (see especially, pp. xi–xii on racial particularity). It may well be that the bulk of your criticisms were preempted by MacKinnon's attention to them, so that all that was left of the substance of your critique is nuance and footnotes.

Your article speculates about why essentialism is so appealing to feminists and so easy to fall into, but does not consider essentialism as a strategy of hegemony, as MacKinnon does. MacKinnon's analysis of male power casts essentialism as a deliberate strategy of consolidating and authorizing political power. Essentialism is built into our language, our metaphysics, and our jurisprudence so that social inequality appears based on natural differences. Neutrality principles in discrimination law, for instance, systematically reinforce existing social inequalities. MacKinnon's insight forces a reexamination of Aristotle, from whom the doctrine derives that equality means treating likes alike and unlikes unalike [see MacKinnon, *Feminism Unmodified*, 37].

In your section "Beyond Essentialism" you credit to Martha Minow the realization that difference and identity are not inherent but are always relational [Harris, "Race and Essentialism," 610]. This echoes MacKinnon's analysis in the first *Signs* article that both women and men are socially constructed through political relations of sexual objectification. You attribute to Joan Williams the idea that "sameness" and "difference" must be supplanted by "a deeper understanding of gender as a system of power relations" [quoted in Harris, "Race and Essentialism," 612]. This insight is precisely MacKinnon's argument in "Difference and Dominance: On Sex Discrimination" [*Feminism Unmodified*, 32]. In fact, MacKinnon articulates these ideas as early as 1979 in *Sexual Harassment of Working Women*, particularly in the sections "What Is Sex?" (pp. 149–157), and "Two Theories of Sex Discrimination" (pp. 106–126). Only the effacement of MacKinnon's contribution to feminist jurisprudence makes possible this truly puzzling circularity in your article in which her text is measured up against the substance of her theories and found wanting. (On file with the author).

After delivering the talk printed here, I learned that Professor Ann Scales had written the following in a draft of her article, "Disappearing Medusa: The Fate of Feminist Legal Theory," 20 *Harvard Women's Law Journal* 34 (1997), but decided not to publish this passage in that format on that occasion:

The anti-essentialism literature asserted three primary criticisms, directed primarily (and too generally) at feminism. First, that feminism, in describing the metaphenomenon of gender, treats the experience of privileged white women as if it were the experience of all women. Thus, feminism engages in

> false universalization. Second, feminism assumes gender as a meta-phenomenon, as the primary oppression, to which all other oppressive situations endured by women are merely "additive." Thus, feminism is reductionist. Third, feminism, in its definition of gender as a condition of systematic sexual oppression, cannot adequately explain the survival of women, particularly women of color. Thus, feminism denigrates the creativity and agency of women, forever relegating women to the category of "victim" and actually impeding progress. Though I proudly identify myself as a radical feminist, I have no theoretical problem, by and large, with the anti-essentialism critique. I think it was initially overbroad, and initially misdirected, insofar as it targeted Professor MacKinnon. She has never posited a necessarily universal anything, never asserted that gender was the beginning or end of the story, and always celebrated the infinite forms of women's resistance, particularly by putting in context the dangers thereof. The overbreadth was in not distinguishing very carefully between radical feminism and "cultural" feminism, which relies on some inherent female point of view as a result of biology or otherwise. ("Disappearing Medusa: The Fate of Feminist Legal Theory" [draft], January 25, 1997, 14–16, on file with the author).

Another account of these issues is provided by Elizabeth Rapaport, "Generalizing Gender: Reason and Essence in the Thought of Catharine MacKinnon," in *A Mind of One's Own* 127 (Louise Antony and Charlotte Witt, eds., 1993).

24. See Angela Harris, "Categorical Rhetoric and Critical Social Theory: Review of Catharine A. MacKinnon, *Toward a Feminist Theory of the State*," 26–27 (unpublished draft circulated on February 23, 1990). The published version of the review does not include this passage. It says that the book "seems in tension with itself" because it sometimes "seems to want to transcend categorical discourse" and "repeatedly calls for a feminist analysis that is historical, contextual, and concerned with contradiction and paradox." Angela Harris, "Categorical Discourse and Dominance Theory," 5 *Berkeley Women's Law Journal* 181, 181–183 (1990). In fact, my book never "calls for" analysis "concerned with contradiction and paradox." It does engage in an analysis that is historical, contextual, and attentive to the diverse realities of power.

25. See Anne C. Dailey, "Feminism's Return to Liberalism," 102 *Yale Law Journal* 1265, 1271 (1993): "As a result of the anti-essentialism critique, 'asking the woman question' assumes a new meaning; the focus of feminist inquiry shifts from the difference between men and women to the differences among women themselves." That is, divide and conquer.

26. See, for example, Nancy Fraser and Linda J. Nicholson, "Social Criticism Without Philosophy," in *Feminism/Postmodernism* 31 (Linda J. Nicholson ed., 1990), who claim that Catharine MacKinnon has "constructed a quasi-metanarrative" around sexuality, which itself is said to be "associated with a biological or quasibiological need and is construed as functionally necessary to the reproduction of society" and "is not the sort of thing, then, whose historical origins need be investigated." The conflation

of the sexuality I analyze with biology is in the minds of these writers. See also Catharine A. MacKinnon, "Does Sexuality Have a History?" 30 *Michigan Quarterly Review* 1 (1991), delivered on September 12, 1990, considering sexuality's history. See infra at .

27. See generally Mari J. Matsuda, Charles R. Lawrence III, Richard Delgado, and Kimberlé W. Crenshaw, *Words That Wound: Critical Race Theory, Assaultive Speech, and the First Amendment* (1993), and in particular the lucid analysis by Kimberlé Crenshaw. See also Sumi K. Cho, "Converging Stereotypes in Racialized Sexual Harassment: Where the Model Minority Meets Suzie Wong," in *Critical Race Feminism*, (Adrien K. Wing, ed., 1997), 203. By contrast with these works, it is my impression that most of those who adopt the anti-"essentialism" line criticized in this paper defend pornography and oppose measures to address the harms to civil rights done through it.

28. See MacKinnon, *Toward a Feminist Theory of the State* 215–234.

29. This analysis is developed more fully in Catharine A. MacKinnon, *Sex Equality* (2001).

30. See, for example, Judith Butler, *Gender Trouble: Feminism and the Subversion of Identity* (1990). The concept of "gender identity" in such work appears to derive from Dr. Robert Stoller's 1964 article on transsexuality. See Robert J. Stoller, "A Contribution to the Study of Gender Identity," 45 *International Journal Psycho-analysis* 220 (1964).

9. Of Mice and Men: A Fragment on Animal Rights

Special thanks go to Ryan Goodman, Cass Sunstein, Lisa Cardyn, Kent Harvey, and most of all to Carol Adams for their helpful comments, and to the University of Michigan law library staff as always for their resourceful and responsive research assistance. This talk was originally published in *Animal Rights* 263 Cass Sunstein and Martha Nussbaum, eds., Oxford, 2004).

1. Recognizing that human beings are also animals, and the linguistic invidiousness that elides this fact of commonality, I sometimes here, for simplicity of communication, term nonhuman animals "animals," while feeling that this usage gives ground I do not want to concede.

2. One analysis and documentation of male dominance is Catharine A. MacKinnon, *Sex Equality* (2001).

3. For discussion of this standard approach to equality, and a book full of examples of the problem discussed in this paragraph in the case of women, see MacKinnon, *Sex Equality*.

4. Bradwell v. Illinois, 83 U.S. 130, 142 (1872).

5. See, e.g., Mark Thomas Connelly, *The Response to Prostitution in the Progressive Era* (1980); David J. Pivar, *Purity Crusade: Sexual Morality and Social Control, 1868–1900* (1973).

6. Carolyn Merchant, *The Death of Nature: Women, Ecology, and the Scientific Revolution* (1980), and Josephine Donovan, "Animal Rights and Feminist Theory," 15 *Signs: Journal of Women in Culture and Society* 350 (1990), reprinted in *Beyond Animal*

Rights: A Feminist Caring Ethic for the Treatment of Animals (Josephine Donovan and Carol J. Adams, eds., 1996), and Carol Adams, *Neither Man Nor Beast: Feminism and the Defense of Animals* (1994) have theorized this question.

7. James Boswell, I *Boswell's Life of Johnson* 266 (Mowbray Morris, ed., 1922).

8. See Lea Vandervelde, "The Legal Ways of Seduction," 48 *Stanford Law Review* 817 (1996).

9. See Joan Dunayer, "Sexist Words, Speciesist Roots," in *Animals and Women: Feminist Theoretical Explorations* 11 (Carol J. Adams and Josephine Donovan, eds., 1995).

10. The parallels are documented and analyzed in Carol Adams, *The Pornography of Meat* (2003).

11. This may have begun with Fourier, to whom the insight is often credited, who said something somewhat different: "As a general proposition: *Social progress and changes of historical period are brought about as a result of the progress of women toward liberty; and the decline of social orders is brought about as a result of the diminution of the liberty of women.* . . . To sum up, *the extension of the privileges of women is the basic principle of all social progress.*" Charles Fourier, *The Theory of the Four Movements* 132 (Gareth Stedman Jones and Ian Patterson, eds., 1996) (italics in original). (The first edition published in the United States was in 1857.) He was making an empirical causal observation that the condition of woman causes social progress and decline, not drawing the moral conclusion that one can tell if one's era is virtuous by how women are treated. Closer to the usual interpretation, Fourier also said that "the best countries have always been those which allowed women the most freedom." p. 130.

12. 109 Cong. Rec. 8915 (88th Cong. 1st Sess. 1963). Probably Senator Randolph was referring to Emerson's statement, "Women are the civilizers. 'Tis difficult to define. What is civilization? I call it the power of a good woman." "Address at the Woman's Rights Convention, 20 September 1855," in 2 *The Later Lectures of Ralph Waldo Emerson, 1843–1871* 15, 20 (Ronald A. Bosco and Joel Myerson, eds., 2001), which is something else again.

13. Mahatma Gandhi quoted in Christopher C. Eck and Robert E. Bovett, "Oregon Dog Control Law and Due Process," 4 *Animal Law* 95, 95 (1998).

14. As James Rachels puts it, "If the animal subjects are not sufficiently like us to provide a model, the experiments may be pointless. (That is why Harlow and Suomi went to such lengths in stressing the similarities between humans and rhesus monkeys.)" James Rachels, *Created from Animals: The Moral Implications of Darwinism*, 220 (1990). Harlow and Suomi designed horrific aversive experiments in an unsuccessful attempt to create psychopathology in monkeys by depriving infant monkeys of loving mothers. They did, however, succeed in creating monstrous mothers through isolation and rape by a machine. See Harry Harlow and Stephen J. Suomi, "Depressive Behavior in Young Monkeys Subjected to Vertical Chamber Confinement," 80 *Journal of Comparative and Physiological Psychology* 11 (1972). As Rachels points out, if monkeys are sufficiently similar to people to make the experiments applicable to humans, ethical problems arise in using the monkeys, but if the monkeys are sufficiently different from people to make

the experiment ethical, the results are less useful in their application to humans. Rachels does not analyze the common mother-blaming theory of child psychopathology the experiments sought to test—an antifemale notion directed equally at humans and nonhuman animals—or the misogyny of an experimental methodology that would, in an attempt to create a bad mother, place female monkeys in an isolation chamber for up to eighteen months after birth, so all they felt was fear, and then impregnate them with a device they called a "rape rack." With their multilayered sexism, these are experiments in the perpetuation of abuse.

15. Elizabeth Anderson productively explores answers in, "Animal Rights and the Value of Nonhuman Life," in *Animal Rights* 277 (Cass Sunstein and Martha Nussbaum, eds., 2004).

16. Deep ecology makes a similar point on the existence of animals on their own terms. See Bill Devall and George Sessions, *Deep Ecology: Living as if Nature Mattered* (1985); Alan Drengson and Yuichi Inoue, eds., *The Deep Ecology Movement: An Introduction* (1995); George Sessions, ed., *Deep Ecology for the Twenty-First Century* (1995). However, deep ecology has been criticized as lacking awareness of gender issues. See Val Plumwood, *Feminism and the Mastery of Nature* (1993); Joni Seager, *Earth Follies: Coming to Feminist Terms with the Global Environmental Crisis* (1993) ("Despite its surface overtures to feminists, the transformation of deep ecology into an environmental force has been characterized by deeply misogynistic proclivities. . . . Despite their putative tilt toward feminism, deep ecologists are unwilling to include gender analysis in their analytical tool kit." p. 230).

17. Alice Walker puts it: "The animals of the world exist for their own reasons. They were not made for humans any more than black people were made for whites or women for men." Alice Walker, Preface to Marjorie Spiegel, *The Dreaded Comparison: Human and Animal Slavery*, 10 (1988).

18. "When I see something that looks racist, I ask, 'Where is the patriarchy in this?' When I see something that looks sexist, 'Where is the heterosexism in this?'" Mari J. Matsuda, "Standing Beside My Sister, Facing the Enemy: Legal Theory out of Coalition," in Mari J. Matsuda, *Where Is Your Body? And Other Essays on Race, Gender and the Law* 61, 64–65 (1996).

19. It figures little to not at all in the following large surveys. Gary L. Francione, *Animals, Property, and the Law* (1995); Pamela D. Frasch, et al., eds., *Animal Law* (2000); Keith Tester, *Animals and Society: The Humanity of Animal Rights* (1991); Emily Stewart Leavitt, *Animals and Their Legal Rights: A Survey of American Laws from 1641 to 1990* (1990); Daniel S. Moretti, *Animal Rights and the Law* (1984).

20. See, for example, Wisconsin Statutes, making "sexual gratification" a class A misdemeanor for anyone who "commits an act of sexual gratification involving his or her sex organ and the sex organ, mouth or anus of an animal." §944.17(2)(c).

21. 76 Utah Criminal Code §76–9–301.8, Chapter 9 is "Offenses Against Public Order and Decency," of which Part 3 is "Cruelty to Animals."

22. People in Colonial times apparently abhorred intercourse with animals because

they thought it could produce progeny. On the race and gender axes, bestiality for white men was considered like interracial sex for white women, both in their unnaturalness and in forfeiting of moral superiority and privileged status for the dominant group member. See Kirsten Fischer, *Suspect Relations: Sex, Race, and Resistance in Colonial North Carolina* 147–148, 156–157 (2002).

23. One of the more thorough and enthusiastic investigations of the subject of sexual contact of humans with animals, Midas Dekkers, *Dearest Pet: On Bestiality*, 71 (Paul Vincent, trans., 2000), contains the following observation: "[T]hose wishing to have sexual intercourse with chickens—which have no vagina—use the communal exit of all the waste channels, the cloaca. What is large enough for an egg is large enough for a penis. Nevertheless this usually proves fatal to the chicken, if for no other reason than because the height of pleasure is achieved only by decapitating the creature just before ejaculation in order to intensify the convulsions of its sphincter." He also reports what a man who has sex with female pigs claims are their sounds and other expressions of desire for his predations. See Dekkers, 72–73.

24. It is often said that Hitler was a vegetarian, but some people say he ate sausages and squab and the notion he was a vegetarian is Nazi propaganda. It is also said that he was gentle and kind and solicitous to his dogs. Some men who abuse other people also abuse animals. See Carol J. Adams, "Woman-Battering and Harm to Animals," in Adams and Donovan, *Animals and Women*, 55.

25. People v. Thomason, 84 Cal. App. 4th 1064, 1068 (Ct. App. 2d 2000).

26. 18 U.S.C. §48.

27. Id.

28. 145 Cong. Rec. H10, 268 (daily ed. Oct. 19, 1999) (statement of Representative Scott).

29. Id.

30. A.B. 1853, sec. 2, Amending Section 597 of the Penal Code at 597 (g) (1). The first conviction is a misdemeanor. The second is a felony. There is an exception for a serious constitutionally protected purpose.

31. A.B. 1853, sec. 1 (a), Amended in Assembly March 20, 2000.

32. The First Amendment double standard posed by those who oppose statutes against the harms of pornography but do not oppose laws against hunter harassment is explored by Maria Comninou, "Speech, Pornography, and Hunting," in Adams and Donovan, *Animals and Women*, 126–148.

33. People v. Thomason, 84 Cal. App. 4th 1064 (2002).

34. 84 Cal. App. 4th at 1067.

35. "It does not include conduct committed against a human being to which the human being has given his or her consent." A.B. 1853, sec. 1 (a).

36. Cal. Penal Code §599b (West 1999).

37. Canada prohibits as obscene "any publication a dominant characteristic of which is the undue exploitation of sex, or of sex and . . . crime, horror, cruelty [or] violence." 163 (8) Criminal Code (Canada).

38. Carol Adams, "Vegetarianism: The Inedible Complex," 4 *Second Wave* 36 (1976); Carol J. Adams, *The Sexual Politics of Meat: A Feminist-Vegetarian Critical Theory* (1990).

39. This question is implicit in Cass R. Sunstein, "Standing for Animals (With Notes on Animal Rights)," 47 *UCLA Law Review* 1333 (June 2000).

40. For an argument that, rather than ethology, what is needed is an anthropology of animals that acknowledges them as subjects, see Barbara Noske, *Beyond Boundaries: Humans and Animals* (1997).

41. See, e.g., Amelia Kinkade, *Straight from the Horse's Mouth* (2001). One description is contained in the portrayal of Elizabeth in Jane Smiley, *Horse Heaven* (2000).

42. See Steve Wise, "Animal Rights, One Step at a Time," in *Animal Rights*, 19 supra, n15.

43. This of course refers to Jeremy Bentham's famous repudiation of reason and speech as the basis for animal rights and invocation of suffering as its basis. See Jeremy Bentham, Chapter XVII n.122 *Introduction to the Principles of Morals and Legislation* (1907 (1823) (1780)): "It may come one day to be recognized, that the number of the legs, the villosity of the skin, or the termination of the *os sacrum*, are reasons equally insufficient for abandoning a sensitive being to the same fate. What else is it that should trace the insuperable line? Is it the faculty of reason, or, perhaps, the faculty of discourse? But a full-grown horse or dog is beyond comparison a more rational, as well as a more conversable animal, than an infant of a day, or a week, or even a month old. But suppose the case were otherwise, what would it avail? the question is not, Can they *reason?* nor, Can they *talk?* but, Can they *suffer?*"

44. That they do is analyzed and documented in Jeffrey Moussaieff Masson and Susan McCarthy, *When Elephants Weep: The Emotional Lives of Animals* (1995).

45. John Steinbeck, *Of Mice and Men* (1937).

46. For an analysis of protectionism, see Suzanne Kappelar, "Speciesism, Racism, Nationalism . . . or the Power of Scientific Subjectivity," in Adams and Donovan, *Animals and Women*, 320, 322.

10. The Power to Change

This piece was published first in *Sisterhood is Forever: The Women's Anthology for a New Millennium* 447–455 (Robin Morgan, ed., Washington Square Press, 2003).

1. The federal ERA as proposed in recent times reads: "Equality of rights under the law shall not be denied or abridged by the United States or any State on account of sex."

2. See *In Harm's Way: The Pornography Civil Rights Hearings* (Catharine A. MacKinnon and Andrea Dworkin, eds., 1997).

3. In 2000, for the first time, more women than men applied to law school. The American Bar Association estimates female enrollment in the law-school class of 2004 to be 49 percent. See "Law Schools' New Female Face," Ted Gest, *U.S. News & World Report* (April 9, 2001).

11. Sexual Harassment: The First Five Years

Originally published as "Introduction," *Sexual Harassment: A Symposium Issue*, 10 *Capitol University Law Review* 1 (1981).

1. To my knowledge, this is true in the North American legal tradition.

2. Barnes v. Costle, 561 F.2d 983 (D.C. Cir. 1977); Tomkins v. Public Serv. Elec. & Gas Co., 422 F. Supp. 553 (D.N.J. 1976); Miller v. Bank of America, 600 F.2d 211 (9th Cir. 1979), *rev'd and remanded,* 568 F.2d 1044 (3d Cir. 1977); Alexander v. Yale University, 459 F. Supp. 1 (D. Conn. 1977); Alexander v. Yale University, 631 F.2d 178 (2nd Cir. 1980). On sexual harassment in education, see Phyllis Crocker and Anne Simon, "Sexual Harassment in Education," 10 *Capital University Law Review* 541 (1981).

3. Bundy v. Jackson, No. 79–1693, slip. op. at 21 (D.C. Cir., Jan. 12, 1981); Continental Can Co. Inc. v. Minnesota, 297 N.W.2d 241 (Minn. 1980); E.E.O.C. Guidelines on Sexual Harassment, 29 CFR 1604.11(a)(3); Caldwell v. Hodgeman, Civ. No. 36573, Memorandum Decision (D. Mass., April 6, 1981). Gender-based byplay as a discriminatory condition of work is recognized as actionable sexual harassment in Wilson v. Northwest Publications, Inc.:

> What appears most significant in this case and what does not appear in *Continental Can Company, Inc.* is the fact that Mlynarczyk was intimidated by her male co-workers because of her sex. This had little to do with sexual advances or propositioning in the sense discussed in those cases. There was never any physical touching in a sexual sense. Instead, comments were made to, and actions taken against, Mlynarczyk that were intended to degrade, demean or offend her because she was a woman. According to Moeller, they were the type of things a man would not say to another man. The physical abuses—the throwing of paper towels, paper clips, and the spraying of alcohol—were physical abuses against a physically weaker person. Walking by a person and saying "Horseshit" is purely an act of disdain. Standing around a woman and chanting "Fuck you, fuck you" is pure abuse. Placing a piece of Ku Klux Klan literature on Mlynarczyk's desk was also an act of intimidation.

Report of Hearing Examiner of Human Rights May 10, 1979 (144479); *aff'd.,* Minnesota Supreme Court (March 30, 1981).

4. EEOC v. Sage Realty, 521 F. Supp. 263 (S.D.N.Y. 1981) (see also 87 F.R.D. 365 [S.D.N.Y. 1980]).

5. Barnes v. Costle, 561 F.2d 983, 1001 (D.C. Cir. 1977). "We are not here concerned with racial epithets or confusing union authorization cards, which serve no one's interest, but with social patterns that to some extent are normal and expectable" (MacKinnon, J., concurring). Racial epithets probably serve the interest of racists no less than coercive sexual advances—often what might be called sexual epithets—serve the interests of sexists. Sexual harassment as a concept challenges precisely "the common attitude that sexual demands [in student-teacher relations] are an ambiguous

and even trivial problem, merely a complicitous game between the powerful and ambitious, in which nothing important is suffered by the victim or gained by the victimizer." Erika Munk, "A Case of Sexual Abuse," *The Village Voice* XXIV, 45 (October 22, 1979). The problem is moving the perceived line between normal practices and victimization in the first place.

6. Neely v. American Fidelity Assurance Co., 17 FEP Cases 482 (W.D. Okla. 1978).

7. It is much like not comprehending Blacks protesting relegation to the back of the bus on the ground that they got where they were going, or giving protesters of lunch-counter segregation a hot dog as a remedy. After strenuous and costly effort (see, e.g., Crocker and Simon's account of the Alexander v. Yale litigation "Sexual Harassment in Education," 10 *Capital University Law Review* at 551), the legal system has become somewhat more responsive. Bundy v. Jackson, No. 79–1693 slip op. at 21 (D.C. Cir., January 12, 1981) (constant unsolicited and unreciprocated sexual attention is sex discrimination in employment, even though no formal index of the job is disturbed); E.E.O.C. Guidelines on Sexual Harassment, 29 CFR 1604.11(a)(3) (prohibiting sexual advances that create an intimidating, hostile, or offensive working environment).

8. This is the upshot of Texas Department of Community Affairs v. Burdine, 450 U.S. 248 (1981), sealing the implications of Furnco Construction Co. v. Waters, 438 U.S. 567 (1978), and Board of Trustees of Keene State College v. Sweeney, 439 U.S. 24 (1979). Once the defendant "articulates lawful reasons for the action" on rebuttal, the plaintiff is returned to the status quo prior to her prima facie case—i.e., to the (hidden) presumption of a prior nondiscriminatory social universe, 450 U.S. at 258. This is not to say that courts should hold defendants liable on merely a prima facie showing. Rather allocations of burden of proof should give the plaintiff some benefit of the Congressional recognition that discrimination against women exists, as a context within which to evaluate claims and weigh evidence. *Burdine*, to the contrary, has the effect of assessing each claim within the context of a presumption that the merit system generally works. This is a very substantive rule on an apparently technical point. Each plaintiff is prevented from having her evidence heard in the context of the findings that have prompted Congressional action in the sex discrimination area—that women have often not been advanced according to ability.

9. See Crocker and Simon, "Sexual Harassment in Education," 10 *Capitol University Law Review* at 544.

10. Tomkins v. Public Serv. Elec. Gas Co., 568 F.2d 1044 (3rd Cir. 1977) (consent order) and Bundy v. Jackson, No. 79–1693 slip op. at 22ff (D.C. Cir., Jan. 12, 1981) (injunction).

11. See Joan Vermeulen, "Employer Liability Under Title VII for Sexual Harassment by Supervisory Employees," 10 *Capital University Law Review* 499 (1981); Jan Leventer, "Sexual Harassment and Title VII: EEOC Guidelines, Conditions Litigation, and the United States Supreme Court," 10 *Capital University Law Review* 481 (1981).

12. Heelan v. Johns-Manville Corp., 451 F. Supp. 251 (D. Colo. 1978) (finding for the plaintiff at trial, discussing credibility in detail); Alexander v. Yale, "Memorandum of Decision," Civil No. N-77–277 (D. Conn., July 3, 1977) (finding against the plaintiff

at trial, making no reference to credibility or explicitly weighing evidence, stating only: "On the basis of all the evidence the court finds that the alleged incident of sexual proposition did not occur . . ." (Judge Ellen B. Burns) at 3.

13. Compare the opinions denying motions to dismiss in, for example, Munford v. James T. Barnes & Co., 441 F. Supp. 459 (E.D. Mich. 1977) and Alexander v. Yale University, 459 F. Supp. 1 (D. Conn. 1977), with the losses at trial in both. Munford v. James T. Barnes & Co., "Judgment of District Court After Trial," (E.D. Mich. S.D., April 20, 1978) and Alexander v. Yale University, "Memorandum of Decision" and "Judgment," Civil No. N-77–277 (D. Conn., July 3, 1979). Both plaintiffs were Black women.

14. Teamsters v. U.S., 431 U.S. 324, 335–336, n.15 (1977). When a rule or practice is differentially applied to an individual on a prohibited basis, disparate treatment occurs. McDonnell-Douglas v. Greene, 411 U.S. 792 (1973); Albermarle Paper v. Moody, 422 U.S. 405 (1975). When an action or policy is neutral on its face but adversely affects members of the plaintiff's group on a prohibited basis, disparate impact arises. Griggs v. Duke Power, 401 U.S. 424 (1971).

15. A similar argument was made in Price v. Yale, "Plaintiff's Post-Trial Memorandum," (March 9, 1979) at 4. Anne E. Simon helped clarify this point. The issue this formulation leaves open is whether there is also social hierarchy between men and women.

16. One consequence of the incoherence of the treatment/impact distinction has been its collapse in practice. Disparate treatment plaintiffs seem effectively to need to make what amounts to a disparate impact showing to prove that their treatment is sex-based (see, e.g., Kyriazi v. Western Electric Co., 461 F. Supp. 894 (D.N.J. 1978)) unless available atrocities are unusually explicit. (See, e.g., David v. Passman, 99 S. Ct. 2264 (1979) ("[O]n account of the unusually heavy work load in my Washington office, diversity of the job, I concluded that it was essential that the understudy to my Administrative Assistant be a man," at 2269, n.3). In light of the group showing needed to situate an individual claim, it is particularly disabling to confine a discrimination plaintiff to her facts alone. See Crocker and Simon, "Sexual Harassment in Education," 10 *Capitol University Law Review* at n.39 and text. Disparate impact cases need exemplarily abused individual plaintiffs, no matter how compelling the statistical disparity.

17. Teamsters v. U.S., 421 U.S. 324, 335 n.15 (1977); Washington v. Davis, 426 U.S. 229 (1976); Personnel Administrator of Mass. v. Feeney, 99 S. Ct. 228 (1979).

18. Reed v. Reed, 404 U.S. 71 (1971); Frontiero v. Richardson, 411 U.S. 677 (1973); Craig v. Boren, 429 U.S. 190 (1976).

19. Examples where this is relatively clear include: Muller v. Oregon, 208 U.S. 412 (1908); Philips v. Martin-Marietta, 400 U.S. 542 (1971); Diaz v. Pan American World Airlines, Inc., 311 F. Supp. 559 (S.D. Fla. 1970); Diaz v. Pan American World Airways, Inc., 442 F.2d 385 (5th Cir. 1971) *cert. denied*, 404 U.S. 950 (1971); Geduldig v. Aiello, 417 U.S. 484 (1974); Gilbert v. General Electric, 429 U.S. 125 (1976). It is instructive to compare Geduldig v. Aiello with Michael M. v. Superior Court of Sonoma County, 450 U.S. 464 (1981). *Michael M.* challenged a statutory rape law as sex discrimination.

The Supreme Court found the sexes "not similarly situated" toward the risks of intercourse (primarily pregnancy) so that the statute rationally related gender to a valid state interest in preventing teenage pregnancy. In *Geduldig*, a sex discrimination challenge to the exclusion of pregnancy disabilities from a state employee insurance plan, pregnancy was found not a sex-based distinction, its exclusion not sex discrimination, because some women as well as all men are "non-pregnant persons." 417 U.S. at 496–497, n.20. In *Michael M.*, because "only women may become pregnant" (450 U.S. at 471), risk of pregnancy was a sex-based distinction. In *Geduldig*, because men as well as women are nonpregnant, risk of pregnancy was not a sex-based distinction. In both cases, the state's purpose in making the distinction was found valid; both turned upon pregnancy as a characteristic of gender. In *Michael M.* it was sexually based. In *Geduldig* it was not. This is not only inconsistent; it is, if anything, reversed. Not all statutorily underage girls are even "potentially pregnant," since many have not reached puberty; not all underage girls who have intercourse conceive (the plaintiff in *Michael M.*, for example); not all (or even most) unwed mothers are underage; male sterility is not a defense; and not all underage children at risk of intercourse are girls. By contrast, as a matter of rational fit between gender, the characteristic, and its application, all "persons" at risk of noncoverage for pregnancy disabilities are women and all who would receive benefits would be both pregnant and female. *Michael M.* suggests a possible need perceived by the Court for sympathetic "rational basis" law in advance of its resolution of the sex discrimination challenge to the male-only draft. Goldberg v. Rostker, 453 U.S. 57 (1981). In its implication for sexual harassment law, the *Michael M.* case (together with Dothard v. Rawlinson, 433 U.S. 321 (1977) (women's rapability grounded a BFOQ for prison guard contact positions in all-male prisons), strengthens the notion that women's and men's sexuality make the sexes "not similarly situated" with regard to sexual intercourse. Doing this on a purportedly biological ground, such as pregnancy potential in *Michael M.* and "her very womanhood" (sexuality as gender itself) in *Dothard*, suggests that nothing that makes this true can be changed. The same holding on a social ground could indict the context that makes women's sexuality a vulnerability or pregnancy a disability (instead of an ability). Arguably, the practice of coercive male sexual initiation toward women, particularly those perceived as vulnerable, targets young girls, even more than it does all women. This, together with women's lack of access to meaningful consent, which may vary with age (as well as economic resources and other factors), would criticize the social context of gender inequality that situates women and men nonsimilarly in the sexual arena. Such an argument would produce a very different conception of the injury of rape upon which to support a sex-specific statutory prohibition than the ones used by either the legislature or the Court in this case.

20. The social creation of biological differences is considered in City of Los Angeles, Department of Water and Power v. Manhart, 98 S. Ct. 1370, 1376 n.17 (1978).

21. The first case to decide that gay sexual harassment is sex discrimination is Wright v. Methodist Youth, 511 F. Supp. 307 (N.D. Ill. 1981). The EEOC Guidelines do not directly address this issue but do not preclude this result. While recognizing

that same-sex discrimination can be sex-based, this is not exactly a gay rights ruling. It protects a man's right to be free from homosexuality, not to prefer it.

22. For discussion of this conflict, see Susan Rae Peterson, "Coercion and Rape: The State as a Male Protection Racket," in Mary Vetterling-Braggin, Frederick Elliston, Jane English, *Feminism and Philosophy* (1977); Janet Rifkin, "Toward a Theory of Law and Patriarchy," 3 *Harvard Women's Law Journal* 83, 83–92 (1980).

23. See Alexander Bickel, *The Morality of Consent*, 133 (1975).

24. Herbert Wechsler, "Toward Neutral Principles of Constitutional Law," 73 *Harvard Law Review* 1 (1959).

25. Andrea Dworkin, *Woman Hating*, 202 (1974).

12. Reflections on Sex Equality Under Law

This article was first published as "Reflections on Sex Equality Under Law," 100 *Yale Law Journal* 1281 (1991). It benefited greatly from readings by Alex Aleinikoff, Susanne Baer, Karen E. Davis, Andrea Dworkin, Owen Fiss, Kent Harvey, Yale Kamisar, Rick Lempert, Janice Raymond, Deborah Rhode, Kim Scheppele, Ted Shaw, Anne E. Simon, Cass Sunstein, Peter Westen, and James B. White. The law librarians at Michigan, especially Barbara Vaccaro and her staff, supported the research persistently and creatively. Rita Rendell supported everything with tremendous resourcefulness and competence. The argument on sexual assault as a form of sex discrimination was largely shaped in discussions with Andrea Dworkin over the years. More recently it was focused in collaboration with Elizabeth Shilton and other colleagues at the Women's Legal Education and Action Fund (LEAF) in litigation in Canada. Cass Sunstein thought I should write my argument on abortion for years and never neglected an opportunity to bring it up. The approach to reproductive control as a sex equality issue has also grown with colleagues at LEAF through cases and legislative testimony. I have tried to footnote distinctive language by others and to highlight arguments focused and formulated by LEAF's submissions. These attempts will necessarily fall short of giving adequate credit to a collective process. Discussions about reproductive rights with Christine Boyle, Christie Jefferson, Helena Orton, and Lynn Smith were formative. This aspect of the work owes the most to Mary Eberts. Her brilliant insights, depth of mind, breadth of knowledge, incisive yet tactful legal formulations, and her courage and tenacity in bearing witness to the truth of women's lives in court, are written all over these pages.

1. In the United States, many men were also excluded from the official founding process. African American men and women were considered property. Indigenous peoples were to be subdued and exterminated rather than consulted. Non–property owners were not qualified to participate in most states. Charles Beard, *An Economic Interpretation of the Constitution of the United States* 64–72 (1913) (state-by-state property requirements for delegates to Constitutional Convention).

2. *Adams Family Correspondence* 370, 382 (L. Butterfield, ed., 1963) (original manuscript dated 1776).

3. Being beneath notice takes many forms, but often looks much like this English example from a century after the U.S. founding: "I pass over many sections punishing particular acts of violence to the person, and in particular the whole series of offenses relating to the abduction of women, rape, and other such crimes. Their history possesses no special interest and does not illustrate either our political or our social history." James Stephen, 3 *History of the Criminal Law of England* 117–118 (1883).

4. Thomas Hobbes, *Leviathan* 80–82 (Blackwell's Political Texts ed., 1946) (1651) (In the state of nature, "[n]ature hath made men so equal [that] when all is reckoned together, the difference between man, and man, is not so considerable. . . . For as to the strength of body, the weakest has strength enough to kill the strongest . . .").

5. John Locke, *The Second Treatise Of Civil Government* 49–50 (Thomas Peardon ed. 1952) (6th ed. 1764).

6. Jean-Jacques Rousseau, *The Social Contract And Discourses* 210 (George Cole trans. 1950) (1762). Lorenne Clark called my attention to this quotation.

7. Barbara Babcock, Ann Freedman, Eleanor Norton, Susan Ross, *Sex Discrimination and the Law* 592–599 (1975). See generally Susan Okin, *Women in Western Political Thought* (1980). For an insightful critique of the meaning of contractarianism for women, see Carole Pateman, *The Sexual Contract* 7–8 (1988).

8. The enumeration clause reads: "Representatives and direct Taxes shall be apportioned among the several States which may be included within this Union, according to their respective Numbers, which shall be determined by adding to the whole Number of free Persons, including those bound to Service for a Term of Years, and excluding Indians not taxed, three fifths of all other Persons." (U.S. Const. art. I, §2, cl. 3.)

Modern historical accounts document that apportionment was based on census data for the entire white population. See, e.g., Michael Balinski, H. Peyton Young, *Fair Representation* 7 (1982). Laurence Schmeckebier, *Congressional Apportionment* 109 (1941), shows that "free white females including heads of families" and "all other free persons" were counted for apportionment purposes.

9. See for example, the otherwise interesting treatment of this concept in Bruce Ackerman, "The Storrs Lectures: Discovering the Constitution," 93 *Yale Law Journal* 1013, 1032–1043 (1984). My point also mirrors Ackerman's in the sense that constitutional interpretation is about who "we, the people" are taken to be.

10. This characterization would have insulted those who fought for a larger principle, but the insult is done by history, not by this description of it.

11. The explicit language of section 2 of the Fourteenth Amendment limits the prohibition on denial or abridgement of the right to vote in federal elections to "male inhabitants" who are over twenty-one and citizens. The Senate Committee on the Right of Women to Vote reported to the Senate that "the right of female suffrage is inferentially denied by the second section of the fourteenth amendment. . . . It is evident, from this provision, that females are not regarded as belonging to the voting population of a State." S. Rep. No. 21, 42d Cong., 2d Sess. 4 (1872), reprinted in Alfred Avins, *The Reconstruction Amendments' Debates* 571, 572 (2d ed. 1974). For a contemporaneous discussion of failed attempts to strike "male" from the Fourteenth Amendment,

see Elizabeth Cady Stanton, Susan B. Anthony, Matilda Gage, 2 *History Of Woman Suffrage* 90–151 (1882).

In debates on the ratification of the Fourteenth Amendment, congressional repudiations of the notion that it would guarantee women's rights centered on suffrage, with little consideration of whether Section 1 would grant women equal protection of the laws in areas other than the vote. In the exchanges, Senator Howard claimed that Madison would have granted suffrage to the "whole negro population as a class." Senator Johnson asked whether Madison would have included women, given that he used the term "persons." Senator Howard responded, "I believe Mr. Madison was old enough and wise enough to take it for granted there was such a thing as the law of nature which has a certain influence even in political affairs, and that by that law women and children were not regarded as the equals of men." *Cong. Globe*, 39th Cong., 1st Sess. 2767 (1866). Another exchange occurred on the question of whether the Fourteenth Amendment could be used to invalidate laws that distinguished on the basis of sex and marital status. Senator Hale asked if the Amendment would affect the common legal distinction between the property rights of married women on the one hand and those of unmarried women and men on the other. Senator Stevens replied, "When a distinction is made between two married people or two *femmes sole*, then it is unequal legislation; but where all of the same class are dealt with in the same way then there is no pretense of inequality." Senator Hale noted the fallacy in this reasonable-classification model: "[I]f that means you shall extend to one married woman the same protection you extend to another, and not the same you extend to unmarried women or men, then by parity of reasoning it will be sufficient if you extend to one negro the same rights you do to another, but not those you extend to a white man." *Cong. Globe*, 39th Cong., 1st Sess. 1064 (1866). Generally, those who spoke in favor of including women under the Fourteenth Amendment confined themselves to suffrage under section 2 and lost. Those few who imagined section 1 could apply to women seemed to be using that possibility as a rhetorical device to defeat the Amendment altogether. Once again, women were largely beneath notice. A paradoxical result is that, because few seriously contemplated that "equal protection of the laws" might apply to sex, the record contains surprisingly little direct repudiation of the notion.

12. It was not effectively delivered to Black men either and has not been to this day. See generally Derrick Bell, *And We Are Not Saved* (1987) (analyzing why racial equality has eluded Black Americans).

13. U.S. Constitutional Amendment XIX.

14. 110 *Cong. Rec.* 2577 (1964).

15. Later Congresses, with considerable supporting evidence, have shown that they are serious about combating sex discrimination under Title VII. See, e.g., H.R. Rep. No. 899, 92d Cong., 2d Sess., reprinted in 1972 U.S. Code *Cong. and Admin. News* 2137 (report accompanying Equal Employment Opportunity Act of 1972).

16. 110 *Cong. Rec.* 2578–2580 (1964) (comments of Rep. Martha Griffiths [D-Mich.]).

17. Reed v. Reed, 404 U.S. 71 (1971).

18. H.R.J. Res. 208, 92d Cong., 1st Sess., 117 *Cong. Rec.* 35, 326 (1971). For an illuminating history of the ERA, see Deborah Rhode, *Justice And Gender* 63–80 (1989).

19. Men who are not white have similar records in countries they run, but it remains to be seen what men of color would do with power in countries like the United States in which they have been kept subordinate on the basis of race. Some pivotal moments of progress in the law of sex equality have been produced by American judges who are Black men. See, e.g., Barnes v. Costle, 561 F.2d 983 (D.C. Cir. 1977) (Robinson, J.) (recognizing sexual harassment as sex discrimination by Court of Appeals for the first time); Priest v. Rotary, 98 F.R.D. 755 (N.D. Cal. 1983) (Henderson, J.) (excluding victim's sexual history from sexual harassment trials); California Fed. Sav. and Loan v. Guerra, 479 U.S. 272 (1987) (Marshall, J.) (holding state initiative mandating unpaid pregnancy leave consistent with Title VII).

20. See, e.g., Bradwell v. Illinois, 83 U.S. 130 (1872) (upholding exclusion of women from practice of law).

21. See, e.g. Rhode, *Justice and Gender* (women's legal equality initiatives analyzed in context of social movements); Patricia J. Williams, "On Being the Object of Property," 14 *Signs: Journal of Women in Culture and Society* 5 (1988).

22. See generally Catharine A. MacKinnon, *Toward a Feminist Theory of the State* (1989).

23. Examples include works by Andrea Dworkin: *Our Blood* (1976), *Pornography: Men Possessing Women* (1981), *Ice and Fire* (1986), *Intercourse* (1987), *Letters from a War Zone* (1988), and *Mercy* (1990); by Kate Millett: *Sexual Politics* (1970) and *The Basement: Meditations on a Human Sacrifice* (1979); by Toni Morrison: *The Bluest Eye* (1970) and *Beloved* (1987); and works edited by Barbara Smith, *But Some of Us Are Brave* (1982) (with Gloria Hull and Patricia Scott) and *Home Girls: A Black Feminist Anthology* (1983). This is a vast literature to which no selection begins to do justice.

24. Muller v. Oregon, 208 U.S. 412 (1908), which permitted hours restrictions in the workplace for women only, accompanied by demeaning rhetoric, was the formative trauma, the negative benchmark.

25. It was not only the lawyers. A significant segment of the women's movement made a version of this argument as well. Susan Brownmiller's *Against Our Will: Men, Women, and Rape* (1976) was widely adopted as the basis for gender-neutralizing rape statutes in the name of treating rape as a crime of violence and not of sex.

26. See, e.g., Barbara Brown, Thomas Emerson, Gail Falk, Ann Freedman, "The Equal Rights Amendment: A Constitutional Basis for Equal Rights for Women," 80 *Yale Law Journal* 871 (1971).

27. Aristotle, *Ethica Nichomachea* bk. V.3, 1131a, 1131b (W. Ross, trans., 1925) (Things that are alike should be treated alike, while things that are unalike should be treated unalike in proportion to their unalikeness). Without explicit reference to Aristotle, this approach was adopted very early in cases under the Fourteenth Amendment. In a challenge to a municipal ordinance prohibiting washing and ironing in public laundries during certain hours, the Supreme Court found that "[i]t is not legislation discriminating against any one. All persons engaged in the same business within it are treated alike. . . . Class legislation . . . is prohibited, but legislation which . . . affects alike

all persons similarly situated, is not within the amendment." Barbier v. Connolly, 113 U.S. 27, 30–32 (1885). In another case decided soon after, the Court found that state laws that differed in the number of peremptory challenges allowed to jurors in capital cases did not violate the Fourteenth Amendment: "It [the Fourteenth Amendment] merely requires that all persons subjected to such legislation [in each state] shall be treated alike, under like circumstances and conditions. . . ." Hayes v. Missouri, 120 U.S. 68, 71 (1887). These cases paved the way for the formulation that remains fundamentally unchanged and unchallenged to this day. See, e.g., Reed v. Reed, 404 U.S. 71, 76 (1971) (citing Royster Guano Co. v. Virginia, 253 U.S. 412, 415 [1920]).

28. See, e.g., Royster Guano, 253 U.S. at 415 ("[T]he classification must be reasonable, not arbitrary, and must rest upon some ground of difference having a fair and substantial relation to the object of the legislation, so that all persons similarly circumstanced shall be treated alike."); Joseph Tussman, Jacobus tenBroek, "The Equal Protection of the Laws," 37 *California Law Review* 341, 344 (1949).

29. General Elec. Co. v. Gilbert, 429 U.S. 125 (1976), is a pinnacle example of this approach.

30. Actually, this concept of equality *was* used with perfect logic by a Nazi author to justify hierarchy under the Third Reich: "Equality can only mean relative equality, where an equal is treated equally and an unequal is treated unequally." ("*Gleichheit kann nur verhältnismäßige Gleichheit bedeuten, wo Gleiches gleich, Ungleiches ungleich behandelt wird.*") G. Weippert, *Das Prinzip der Hierarchie*, cited in Prengel, "*Gleichheit versus Differenz—eine falsche Alternative im feministischen Diskurs*," in *Differenz und Gleichheit* 120, 121 (1990) (translated by author with Susanne Baer). (In German, one word, *Gleichheit*, means both equality and sameness or identity, so the second clause could as well be translated: "where like is treated alike and unlike unalike.") The fascist implications of this approach—which readily rationalizes treating Jews one way and Aryans another—are embodied in a legend over the entrance to an extermination camp: *Jedem das Seine*, translatable as, "To everyone what he deserves" or "To each their own." See Prengel, above, at 121.

31. For a superb analysis of the status and treatment of women in ancient Greece, see Eva Keuls, *The Reign of the Phallus* (1985), especially at 6, 30, 98, 108–109 (even women who were not slaves were virtually chattel) and 99, 187–203, 299, 327 (prostitution flourished). For discussion of Aristotle's treatment of slavery and the status of women, see Elizabeth Spelman, *Inessential Woman* 37–56 (1988).

32. See Twiss Butler, "Pregnancy and Sex Equality: A 'Unique Problem for Women?'" 1–4 (Mar. 25, 1990) (unpublished paper presented at Twenty-first National Conference on Women and the Law, on file with author) (criticizing exclusion of these issues together with military combat and homosexual rights from ERA's strategy).

33. An early and innovative sex discrimination casebook, Babcock, et al., *Sex Discrimination and the Law*, above at 975–990, for example, discussed abortion prohibitions on the premise that they revealed sex discrimination in *society* and the law's response to it. The *law* against sex discrimination as such was not discussed in terms of its possible application to abortion. Legally, the line this drew was exactly accurate.

In early litigation on abortion rights, sex equality claims were sometimes included among the initial grounds for women's right to abortion, but were dropped. One of the first initiatives against criminal abortion laws, colloquially called *Women v. Connecticut*, for example, contained an allegation that the abortion prohibition discriminated against women on the basis of sex. See Abele v. Markle, 452 F.2d 1121, 1123 (2d Cir. 1971) (discussing plaintiffs' initial claims). This claim does not seem to have been pursued at later stages in the litigation. A three-judge district court eventually declared Connecticut's antiabortion laws to be unconstitutional on other grounds. Abele v. Markle, 342 F. Supp. 800 (D. Conn. 1972), *vacated for reconsideration of mootness*, 410 U.S. 951, *on remand*, 369 F.Supp. 807 (D. Conn. 1973) (finding case not moot and reaffirming constitutional holding).

In Roe v. Wade, the first amended complaint pleaded an equal protection violation, but this did not, apparently, refer to sex discrimination, and was not pursued. First Amended Complaint at IV, ¶ 5, Roe v. Wade, 314 F.Supp. 1217 (N.D. Tex. 1970) (No. CA-3–3690-B) (on file with author), *aff'd in part and rev'd in part,* 410 U.S. 113 (1973). One amicus brief in *Roe* at the Supreme Court level squarely argued that the criminal abortion statutes at issue "violate the most basic Constitutional rights of women" because women bear "the disproportionate share of the de jure and de facto burdens and penalties of pregnancy, child birth and child rearing. Thus any statute which denies a woman the right to determine whether she will bear those burdens denies her the equal protection of the laws." Brief Amicus Curiae on Behalf of New Women Lawyers, Women's Health and Abortion Project, Inc., National Abortion Action Coalition at 6, Roe v. Wade, 410 U.S. 113 (1973) (No. 70–18) (on file with author). This brief assumed that while sexual intercourse was equal, its consequences were not: "Man and woman have equal responsibility for the act of sexual intercourse. Should the woman accidentally become pregnant against her will, however, she endures in many instances the entire burden or 'punishment.'" Id. at 26. "And it is not sufficient to say that the woman 'chose' to have sexual intercourse, for she did not choose to become pregnant." Id. at 31.

In Harris v. McRae, the Medicaid abortion-funding case, only one amicus brief mentioned sex discrimination, and that was to point out that since women are *socially* discriminated against on the basis of sex, denying them abortions is an additional hardship. Brief Amicus Curiae for NOW, et. al. at 44, Harris v. McRae, 448 U.S. 297 (1980) (No. 79–1268) (on file with author). This brief did not make the *legal* argument that when the state does not pay for abortions, an act that hurts only women, they are denied equal protection of the laws on the basis of sex.

Most recently, in the litigation in Webster v. Reproductive Health Services, although several briefs discussed the importance of abortion for women's *social* equality, only one argued that denial of legal abortion constitutes sex discrimination in violation of equality *law*. Brief for the National Coalition Against Domestic Violence as Amicus Curiae Supporting Appellees at 5–25, Webster v. Reproductive Health Servs., 109 S.Ct. 3040 (1989) (No. 88–605) (on file with author) [hereinafter NCADV's *Webster* Brief].

34. Andrea Dworkin and I discuss this theme in our *Pornography and Civil Rights* 11 (1988).

35. Slaughter-House Cases, 83 U.S. (16 Wall.) 36, 81 (1873) (Miller, J., for the Court) ("We doubt very much whether any action of a State not directed by way of discrimination against the negroes as a class, or on account of their race, will ever be held to come within the purview of this provision [fifth section of the Fourteenth Amendment]. It is so clearly a provision for that race and that emergency, that a strong case would be necessary for its application to any other").

36. Loving v. Virginia, 388 U.S. 1, 7 (1967) (invalidating antimiscegenation statutes as institutionalization of "White Supremacy"); Brown v. Board of Educ., 347 U.S. 483 (1954) (holding racially segregated public educational system inherently unequal); Swann v. Board of Educ., 402 U.S. 1 (1971) (stating that neutrality may not be enough to overcome segregated school system; "affirmative action" may be required); Fullilove v. Klutznick, 448 U.S. 448 (1980) (upholding guarantee of federal funds for local public works projects to minority businesses). These results have been almost totally vitiated in Washington v. Davis, 426 U.S. 229 (1976) (requiring proof of intent in constitutional discrimination cases), Regents of the University of California v. Bakke, 438 U.S. 265 (1978) (invalidating, in part, affirmative action plan for disadvantaged groups in higher education in action by white man), and City of Richmond v. J. A. Croson Co., 488 U.S. 469 (1989) (invalidating city contract preferences for minority businesses).

37. Plessy v. Ferguson, 163 U.S. 537, 551–552 (1896).

38. See *Brown*, 347 U.S. at 494 n.11 (citing Kenneth Clark, *Effect of Prejudice and Discrimination in Personality Development* (1950)). I deduce this conclusion from the *Brown* result, which mandates the same treatment, in the form of integration, for Black and white schoolchildren and from the Court's failure to conclude that Black children were "different" based on their "different" response to segregation. That is, unlike *Plessy*, the fact that segregation made Blacks feel inferior was not evidence that they were, but a measure of harm. They could only be harmed by being treated as inferior if they had already entered liberal humanity, or potentially could. This is not the same as saying that the *Brown* Court saw Blacks as equal to whites.

39. Some African Americans have long questioned integration as the only or best strategy for equality, a questioning that has not gone away. Commentators have recently noted, for example, that historically Black colleges and universities, although they enroll only 17 percent of all Black college students, graduate 34 percent of all Black college graduates. Page, "A Black Anti-integration Backlash," *Chicago Tribune*, 3 (Feb. 19, 1989); Jordan, "Is Desegregation Working for Blacks?," *Boston Globe*, 89 (July 1, 1990).

40. City of Richmond v. J. A. Croson Co., 488 U.S. 469 (1989), is a stunning example of pouring new politics (here conservative) into old doctrinal bottles (here liberal). The decision reverses the result of earlier precedents while leaving the doctrine arguably undisturbed.

41. Even the relevance of the so-called differences to the ends in view is often obscure. In Regents of the University of California v. Bakke, 438 U.S. 265 (1978), for example, the admission tests that were used to assess qualifications for medical school were *presumed* valid, rather than validated. There was no inquiry into whether the test

scores, which were racially disparate, were relevant to the goal of providing skilled doctors.

42. This argument is elaborated and documented in Chapter 12 of my *Toward a Feminist Theory of the State* (discussing sameness and difference as traditional equality theory).

43. Kimberlé Crenshaw, "Demarginalizing the Intersection of Race and Sex: A Black Feminist Critique of Antidiscrimination Doctrine, Feminist Theory and Antiracist Politics," 1989 *University of Chicago Legal Forum* 139, 141–150; Judy Scales-Trent, "Black Women and the Constitution: Finding Our Place, Asserting Our Rights," 24 *Harvard Civil Rights-Civil Liberties Law Review* 9 (1989); Note, "Conceptualizing Black Women's Employment Experiences," 98 *Yale Law Journal* 1457 (1989); P. Smith, "Justice Denied: Black Women and the Search for Equality Under Title VII" (1990) (M.A. thesis, Yale University, on file with author); see also Mari Matsuda, "When the First Quail Calls: Multiple Consciousness as Jurisprudential Method," 11 *Women's Rights Law Reporter* 7 (1989).

44. DeGraffenreid v. General Motors Assembly Div., 413 F.Supp. 142 (E.D. Mo. 1976), *aff'd in part and rev'd in part*, 558 F.2d 480 (8th Cir. 1977); Jeffries v. Harris County Community Action Ass'n, 425 F.Supp. 1208 (S.D. Tex. 1977), *aff'd in part and vacated in part*, 615 F.2d 1025 (5th Cir. 1980); see also Judge v. Marsh, 649 F.Supp. 770 (D.D.C. 1986) (holding Title VII plaintiff must pick one primary category of protected discrimination that is directed against a group sharing another protected characteristic).

45. Fortunately, this is not now the leading legal view. Hicks v. Gates Rubber Co., 833 F.2d 1406, 1416 (10th Cir. 1987) (holding, in Title VII case brought by Black woman, evidence of racial and sexual harassment may be "aggregated"); Jeffries v. Harris County Community Action Ass'n, 615 F.2d 1025, 1032 (5th Cir. 1980) (holding that Black woman may plead combined race and sex discrimination under Title VII). While this recognition is an improvement, if the law protected people, not categories, from historic subordination, not misclassification, this solution would not have been necessary.

46. Partial exceptions are legal initiatives in the areas of sexual harassment, comparable worth, and pornography. Of these, only sexual harassment has succeeded in the courts to date. See, e.g., Meritor Sav. Bank v. Vinson, 477 U.S. 57 (1986) (holding sexual harassment actionable as sex discrimination); AFSCME v. Washington, 578 F.Supp. 846 (W.D. Wash. 1983) (permitting comparable worth as equality claim), *rev'd*, 770 F.2d 1401 (9th Cir. 1985). In American Booksellers Association v. Hudnut, 771 F.2d 323 (7th Cir. 1985), *aff'd*, 475 U.S. 1001 (1986), an ordinance making pornography actionable as sex discrimination on an equality theory relying on neither sameness nor difference was invalidated on First Amendment grounds.

47. Bradwell v. Illinois, 83 U.S. 130 (1872) (ruling that privileges or immunities clause does not compel women's admission to bar); *In re* Mabel P. French, (1905) 37 N.B.R. 359.

48. Reed v. Reed 404 U.S. 71 (1971). As I use this term, the male standard is also white and upper-class to a considerable extent, as evidenced by the fact that poor

women of color do least well under it. That this standard, as applied to the situations being examined, is not ultimately about race and/or class, but gender is suggested by its social meaning content and by the fact that women of the dominant race and/or class do not tend to do well under it either. It is accessible, to a degree, to men regardless of race or class, although it greatly helps men to be white and/or rich. It is also sex-specific for men of color. Finally, it is of some interest that, as in *Reed*, the policies invalidated in most constitutional cases of sex discrimination brought by women involve preferences for men and detriments to women that lack express race or class specificity.

49. A current example is Price Waterhouse v. Hopkins, in which Ann Hopkins was made partner in an accounting firm for meeting the male standard, a victory against holding her to a "femininity" standard. 490 U.S. 228 (1989) (finding sex discrimination through stereotyping played role in denial of partnership), *on remand*, 737 F. Supp. 1202 (D.D.C. 1990) (granting relief including making plaintiff a partner). The victory lies in the recognition of women's merits when they meet the male standard. The limits lie in the failure to recognize that the standard is a male one.

50. David Cole, "Strategies of Difference: Litigating for Women's Rights in a Man's World," 2 *Law and Inequality* 33, 34 n.4 (1984) (collecting cases).

51. See Catharine A. MacKinnon, "Unthinking ERA Thinking", infra at 13, for further discussion.

52. See, e.g., Califano v. Webster, 430 U.S. 313 (1977) (holding provision of Social Security Act allowing women to eliminate more low-earning years than men in calculating their retirement benefits compensates them for past discrimination).

53. Kahn v. Shevin, 416 U.S. 351 (1974) (upholding statute giving $500 tax exemption to widows but not widowers); Schlesinger v. Ballard, 419 U.S. 498 (1975) (upholding statutory scheme giving women naval officers longer to be promoted than men before being discharged for lack of promotion).

54. See generally Carol Gilligan, *In A Different Voice* (1982).

55. State of Washington v. Wanrow, 88 Wash. 2d 221, 559 P.2d 548 (1977); Ibn-Tamas v. United States, 407 A.2d 626, 634 (D.C. 1979); State v. Kelly, 97 N.J. 178, 200, 478 A.2d 364, 375 (1984); State v. Norman, 89 N.C. App. 384, 394, 366 S.E.2d 586, 592 (1988). *But cf.* State v. Thomas, 66 Ohio St. 2d 518, 423 N.E.2d 137 (1981) (holding expert evidence on battered women's syndrome inadmissible). See generally Lenore Walker, *The Battered Woman Syndrome* (1984).

56. See, e.g., New York v. Liberta, 64 N.Y.2d 152, 474 N.E.2d 567 (1984), *cert. denied*, 471 U.S. 1020 (1985); Warren v. State, 255 Ga. 151, 336 S.E.2d 221 (1985). These laws typically apply, however, only to women who are separated from their husbands rather than to the day-in, day-out rape experienced by many while *in* a marriage; they often also have express cohabitant exceptions. See generally Diana E. H. Russell, *Rape in Marriage* (1990). This area is changing rapidly. See Annotation, "Criminal Responsibility of Husband for Rape, or Assault to Commit Rape, on Wife," 24 *A.L.R.* 4th 105 (1983).

57. See *Fed. R. Evid.* 412.

58. Roe v. Wade, 410 U.S. 113 (1973).

59. See, e.g., Cal. Civ. Proc. Code §340.1 (West Supp. 1990); Petersen v. Bruen, 792 P.2d 18 (Nev. 1990); Jones v. Jones, 242 N.J. Super. 195, 576 A.2d 316 (1990); Hammer v. Hammer, 142 Wis. 2d 257, 418 N.W.2d 23 (Wis. Ct. App. 1987); see also Melissa Salten, "Statutes of Limitations in Civil Incest Suits: Preserving the Victim's Remedy," 7 *Harvard Women's Law Journal* 189 (1984).

60. See, e.g., Phyllis Chesler, *Mothers on Trial* (1986); Martha Fineman, "Dominant Discourse, Professional Language and Legal Change in Child Custody Decision-making," 101 *Harvard Law Review* 727 (1988).

61. See, e.g., Thurman v. City of Torrington, 595 F.Supp. 1521 (D. Conn. 1984) (ruling on motion to dismiss, that failure of police as a matter of policy to protect women complaining of violence by intimate males violates equal protection); Leslie Bender, "Feminist (Re)Torts: Thoughts on the Liability Crisis, Mass Torts, Power, and Responsibilities," 1990 *Duke Law Journal* 848. Recent legal scholarship has expanded on *Thurman*'s implicit recognition that police nonenforcement of laws against domestic violence is discrimination against women as a matter of law. Note, "Battered Women and the Equal Protection Clause: Will the Constitution Help Them When the Police Won't?" 95 *Yale Law Journal* 788 (1986); Case Comment, "Gender Based Discrimination in Police Reluctance to Respond to Domestic Assault Complaints," 75 *Georgetown Law Journal* 667 (1986).

62. Clare Dalton, "An Essay in the Deconstruction of Contract Doctrine," 94 *Yale Law Journal* 997, 1000–1003 (1985); Mary Joe Frug, "Re-reading Contracts: A Feminist Analysis of a Contracts Casebook," 34 *American University Law Review* 1065 (1985).

63. Exceptions include Catharine A. MacKinnon, *Sexual Harassment of Working Women* (1979); Christine Littleton, "Reconstructing Sexual Equality," 75 *California Law Review* 1279 (1987). There has been far deeper and more extensive criticism of the law of racial equality, although it stops short of challenging the "similarly situated" requirement as such. See, e.g., Alan Freeman, "Legitimizing Racial Discrimination Through Antidiscrimination Law: A Critical Review of Supreme Court Doctrine," 62 *Minnesota Law Review* 1049 (1978); Charles Lawrence, "The Id, the Ego, and Equal Protection: Reckoning with Unconscious Racism," 39 *Stanford Law Review* 317 (1987); texts cited note 180.

64. Vinson v. Taylor, 753 F.2d 141 (D.C. Cir. 1985), *aff'd sub. nom.* Meritor Sav. Bank v. Vinson, 477 U.S. 57 (1986); California Fed. Sav. and Loan Ass'n v. Guerra, 479 U.S. 272 (1987); Pregnancy Discrimination Act of 1978, 42 U.S.C. §2000e(k) (1982).

65. Meaning, all those who are pregnant, hence discriminated against, are of one sex, even though some of those who are not pregnant, hence not discriminated against, are also of that same sex. Note that this is no different from most cases of sex discrimination, in which not all women may be discriminated against by a policy or practice, but all or most of those who are, are women.

66. Although these changes occurred first under Title VII, and thus were statutory not constitutional, it is under the Constitution that the "similarly situated" test was

developed and has persisted most strongly. Pregnancy discrimination has not been recognized as sex discrimination under the Fourteenth Amendment, Geduldig v. Aiello, 417 U.S. 484 (1974), but sexual harassment has, see, e.g., King v. Board of Regents, 898 F.2d 533, 537 (7th Cir. 1990) (ruling environmental sexual harassment violates equal protection if it is intentional); Trautvetter v. Quick, 916 F.2d 1140, 1151 (7th Cir. 1990) (holding intentional sexual harassment violates equal protection guarantee if claimant shows discrimination was because of her status as a female and not because of characteristics of her gender that are personal to her).

67. This approach has been challenged in Canada. In Andrews v. Law Society of British Columbia, [1989] 1 S.C.R. 143, the Supreme Court of Canada, interpreting the new equality provision of the Canadian Charter of Rights and Freedoms (the Canadian constitution) unanimously rejected the "similarly situated" test as "seriously deficient" for producing equality, id. at 166, and adopted the approach based on substantive historical disadvantage advanced here. In so doing, that Court noted that "the similarly situated test would have justified the formalistic separate but equal doctrine of Plessy v. Ferguson." Id.; see also Regina v. Turpin, [1989] 1 S.C.R. 1296.

68. *U.S. Equal Employment Opportunity Comm'n, Job Patterns For Minorities And Women In Private Industry–1986* at 1 (1988) (occupational distribution by race and sex); *Comparable Worth: New Directions For Research* 3 (Heidi Hartmann, ed., 1985); *Comparable Worth, Pay Equity, And Public Policy* 32–39 (Rita Mae Kelly, Jane Bayes, eds., 1988).

69. Bradwell v. Illinois, 83 U.S. 130, 141 (1872).

70. Id. at 142; cf. Plessy v. Ferguson, 163 U.S. 537, 551 (1896).

71. Lemons v. Denver, 17 Fair Empl. Prac. Cas. (BNA) No. 906 (Apr. 17, 1978), *aff'd*, 620 F.2d 228 (10th Cir.), *cert. denied*, 449 U.S. 888 (1980).

72. AFSCME v. Washington, 770 F.2d 1401, 1408 (9th Cir. 1985).

73. Rostker v. Goldberg, 453 U.S. 57, 72 (1982) (holding women "not similarly situated" for purposes of draft registration because Congress has excluded women from combat).

74. EEOC v. Sears, 628 F.Supp.1264, 1305 (N.D. Ill. 1986), *aff'd*, 839 F.2d 302 (7th Cir. 1988).

75. *EEOC v. Sears* is the cardinal example. Mary Becker makes this connection in "From *Muller v. Oregon* to Fetal Vulnerability Policies," 53 *University of Chicago Law Review* 1219 (1986).

76. See, e.g., EEOC v. Sears, 839 F.2d 302, 313 (7th Cir. 1988).

77. See, e.g., Price Waterhouse v. Hopkins, 490 U.S. 228 (1989).

78. See notes 104–107 and accompanying text.

79. A lucid analysis of sexual assault of men by men is provided by Darieck Scott, "Between Men and Women/Between Men and Men: Male Rape and Straight Man's Law," (unpublished paper, 1991) (on file with author).

80. This description has the developed West primarily, but not exclusively, in mind. In other cultures, the specific means differ but the ends of sexualized inferiority, use, and control are the same. Veiling and stripping both provide parallel examples, as does

female genital mutilation. See Lilian Sanderson, *Female Genital Mutilation, Excision and Infibulation: A Bibliography* (1986).

As to women's economic inequality in the United States, one finds that from the 1950s to the 1970s, the ratio of Black women's earnings to Black men's has narrowed from slightly over half to 75 percent. For whites, it has widened. In 1955, white women earned two-thirds of men's earnings. In the mid-1960s through 1980, they earned less than 60 percent. In 1982, white women's earnings were 62 percent of white men's, the highest since 1958. Among women, the gap between Blacks and whites narrowed considerably from 1955, when Black women earned about half of what white women earned, to 1982, when the difference was less than 10 percent. Rita Simon, Jean Landis, *The Crimes Women Commit, the Punishments They Receive* 35–37 (1991). Even as this paltry progress was made in women's income relative to men's, men's average income dropped. And as women's share of employment has increased, so has their share of poverty. While men who are poor tend to be unemployed, women who are poor tend to be working full time—many at marginal jobs after divorce. Kevin Phillips, *The Politics of Rich and Poor* 202–203 (1990).

81. The Women's Legal Education and Action Fund of Canada advanced this description as the meaning of substantive inequality, a concretely based definition to be preferred to abstract differentiation. See Factum of the Women's Legal Education and Action Fund of Canada (LEAF) paras. 49–53, at 21–23, Andrews v. Law Society of British Columbia, [1989] 1 S.C.R. 143 (Nos. 19955, 19956). In *Andrews*, the Supreme Court of Canada adopted an interpretation of constitutional equality consistent with this substantive approach.

82. Richard Rorty, "Feminism and Pragmatism" in *The Tanner Lectures on Human Values: 1992* 1, 7 (Grethe B. Peterson, ed., 1992) ("MacKinnon's central point, as I read her, is that 'a woman' is not yet the name of a way of being human. . . ."). Elizabeth Spelman misses this concrete meaning of the phrase "as a woman" in her critique of its use in feminism. See generally Spelman, *Inessential Woman*.

83. Andrea Dworkin provides a superb analysis of the joint role of sexual abuse and deprivation of reproductive control in women's politics in Andrea Dworkin, *Right-wing Women* (1983).

84. They also leave out of account a good deal of racial subordination.

85. Reed v. Reed, 404 U.S. 71 (1971).

86. Craig v. Boren, 429 U.S. 190 (1976).

87. Menachem Amir, *Forcible Rape* 44 (1971), finds that 90 percent of rapes are intraracial. The rapist is a stranger in only 17 percent of all incidents, but in 55 percent of those reported to police. Diana E. H. Russell, *Sexual Exploitation* 96–97 (1984); see also Russell, *Rape in Marriage* 66–67. A recent study for the Department of Justice shows that in rapes with one offender, seven of every ten white victims were raped by a white offender, and eight of every ten Black victims were raped by a Black offender. Caroline Harlow, *Female Victims of Violent Crime* 10 (1991).

88. Andrea Dworkin, *Intercourse* 129 (1987) ("Consent in this world of fear is so passive that the woman consenting could be dead and sometimes is."); Susan Estrich,

Real Rape 29–41 (1987) (originally through resistance requirement, passive submission amounts to consent in law of rape); see also State v. Alston, 310 N.C. 399, 312 S.E.2d 470 (1984) (woman's passivity supports finding of insufficient force for rape conviction). There is a division of authority in U.S. criminal cases on the question whether sexual assault of a dead body can constitute rape.

89. See MacKinnon, *Toward a Feminist Theory of the State* 171–183.

90. While women may actually *have* abortions for many reasons, the formulation in the text, which owes much to Elizabeth Shilton, is a systemic point about why abortions are permitted. Consider this pungent juxtaposition:

Juli Loesch, a self-styled "pro-life feminist" associated with Operation Rescue, says, "the idea [of abortion] is that a man can use a woman, vacuum her out, and she's ready to be used again[.]" A NOW chapter advises feminists involved with anti-choice men to "[c]ontrol his access to your body. 'Just say no' to more sex[.]" Pro- and anti-choice women meet on common ground.

Judith Baer, "Book Review," 52 *Journal of Politics* 1012 (1990); see also Dworkin, *Right-wing Women* 138–139.

91. "Compulsory sterilization for eugenic reasons was legal in Puerto Rico during the years 1937 to 1960. . . . The total number of people undergoing compulsory sterilization for such reasons in this period has not been estimated." Harriet Presser, *Sterilization and Fertility Decline in Puerto Rico*, 6 n.2 (1973); see also 1937 P.R. Laws 267 (repealed 1960) (providing for involuntary sterilization under variety of circumstances); Madrigal v. Quilligan, No. CV 75–2057, slip op. (C.D. Cal. 1978) (unpublished) (refusing to recognize or remedy sterilization of Chicanas at U.S.C. Los Angeles County Medical Center, allegedly without their knowledge or informed consent *aff'd*, 639 F.2d 789 (9th Cir. 1981, cited in I. Velez "The Nonconsenting Sterilization of Mexican Women in Los Angeles," in *Twice a Minority: Mexican American Women* 235, 242–246, 248 n.4 (Margarita Melville ed., 1980). The experiences of the individual plaintiffs in *Madrigal* are further discussed in Hernandez, "Chicanas and the Issue of Involuntary Sterilization: Reforms Needed to Protect Informed Consent," 3 *Chicano Law Review* 3, 4–9 (1976). Thirty-nine percent of married women are currently sterilized in Puerto Rico, some voluntarily. Dep't Of Int'l Economic and Social Affairs, *Recent Levels and Trends of Contraceptive Use as Assessed in 1983* at 32 (1984). Ramírez de Arellano and Seipp explain that "[w]hile it is difficult to prove that the choice made by thousands of Puerto Rican women [to be sterilized] was not voluntary, it can nevertheless be argued that this choice was conditioned and constrained by the surrounding social framework. Medical authority, eugenist ideology, *machismo*, restricted employment opportunities, and the lack of other birth control alternatives were all factors that limited women's options." Annette Ramírez de Arellano, Conrad Seipp, *Colonialism, Catholicism, and Contraception* 144 (1983) (footnote omitted).

92. *In re* A.C., 533 A.2d 611 (D.C. 1987) (ordering cesarean section for terminally ill pregnant woman), *reh'g granted and judgment vacated*, 539 A.2d 203 (D.C. 1988), *on reh'g*, 573 A.2d 1235 (D.C. 1990); Jefferson v. Griffin Spalding County Hosp. Auth., 247 Ga. 86, 274 S.E.2d 457 (1981) (ordering pregnant woman to submit to cesarean

section); *In re* Jamaica Hosp., 128 Misc. 2d 1006, 491 N.Y.S.2d 898 (N.Y. Sup. Ct. 1985) (ordering forced blood transfusion to pregnant woman to save her life or that of unborn child); Raleigh Fitkin-Paul Morgan Memorial Hosp. v. Anderson, 42 N.J. 421, 201 A.2d 537, (same) *cert. denied*, 337 U.S. 985 (1964).

93. See cases cited note 127.

94. Bureaucratic burdens on abortions enacted by state legislatures include, in addition to prohibitions on public funding, prohibitions on abortions in public facilities, prohibitions on abortion counseling by public employees, elaborate viability determination provisions, parental-consent and-notification requirements for minor girls, and licensing and other regulation of abortion facilities. Greenberg, "State Abortion Laws and the Webster Decision," *State Legis. Rep.*, Aug. 1989, at 7–9.

95. The following argument was developed in collaboration with colleagues at LEAF and argued in interventions before the Supreme Court of Canada, including in the Factum of The Women's Legal Education and Action Fund (LEAF), The Queen v. Canadian Newspapers Co., [1988] 2 S.C.R. 122 (No. 19298) (on file with author).

96. Russell, *Sexual Exploitation* 35.

97. The following percentages of women report being victimized at least once by rape or attempted rape: white (non-Jewish), 45 percent; Jewish, 50 percent; Black, 44 percent; Latina, 30 percent; Asian, 17 percent; Filipina, 17 percent; Native American, 55 percent; other, 28 percent. Note that these figures refer to the proportions of women victimized and say nothing of the number of times they were victimized. Russell, *Sexual Exploitation* 84; see also Gail-Elizabeth Wyatt, "The Sexual Abuse of Afro-American and White-American Women in Childhood," 9 *Child Abuse and Neglect* 507 (1985) (57 percent of African American women and 67 percent of white American women report at least one incident of sexual abuse before age eighteen).

98. Diana Russell made this calculation on her database at my request.

99. Margaret Gordon and Stephanie Riger, *The Female Fear* (1989).

100. Brownmiller, *Against Our Will* 15; Peggy Sanday, "The Socio-Cultural Context of Rape: A Cross-Cultural Study," 37 *Journal of Social Issues* 5 (1981).

101. Diaba Scully, *Understanding Sexual Violence* 47–50, 59–92 (1990) (rape as "normal deviance" for men); John Stoltenberg, *Refusing to Be a Man* 15 (1989) (rape central to masculinity); James Check, Neil Malamuth, "An Empirical Assessment of Some Feminist Hypotheses About Rape," 8 *International Journal of Women's Studies* 414 (1985) (rape and forced sex widespread and largely acceptable).

102. Russell, *Rape in Marriage* 64–68; see also Peggy Sanday, *Fraternity Gang Rape* (1990).

103. Neil Malamuth, "Rape Proclivity Among Males," 37 *Journal of Social Issues* 138 (1981); Neil Malamuth, James Check, "The Effects of Mass Media Exposure on Acceptance of Violence Against Women: A Field Experiment," 15 *Journal of Research in Personality* 436 (1981); Neil Malamuth, "Aggression Against Women: Cultural and Individual Causes," in *Pornography And Sexual Aggression* 22–23 (Neil Malamuth and Edward Donnerstein, eds., 1984); Neil Malamuth, James Check, "The Effects of Aggressive Pornography on Beliefs in Rape Myths: Individual Differences," 19 *Journal of*

Research in Personality 299 (1985); James Check, Ted Guloien, "Reported Proclivity for Coercive Sex Following Repeated Exposure to Sexually Violent Pornography, Nonviolent Dehumanizing Pornography, and Erotica," in *Pornography: Research Advances and Policy Considerations* (1989); see also Daniel Linz, "Exposure to Sexually Explicit Materials and Attitudes Toward Rape: A Comparison of Study Results," 26 *Journal of Sex Research* 50 (1989); Diana E. H. Russell, "Pornography and Rape: A Causal Model," 9 *Political Psychology* 41, 43–45 (1988). Pornography is also implicated in the domestic battering of women. Evelyn Sommers, James Check, "An Empirical Investigation of the Role of Pornography in the Verbal and Physical Abuse of Women," 2 *Violence and Victims* 189 (1987).

104. Estrich, *Real Rape* 15–20 (1987) (summary of legal system's response to rape). In Oakland, California, recently, after disclosure that one in four reported rapes and attempted rapes in 1989 were "unfounded" by the Oakland Police, an investigation revealed that 79 of the 112 alleged rapes reviewed did in fact occur. Police conceded that some victims, many of whom were "cocaine users, prostitutes, or acquainted with their assailants," were never interviewed by investigators after the initial report. "Prosecution Seen as Unlikely in 228 Rape Cases in Oakland," *New York Times*, B10 (Nov. 13, 1990).

105. S. Smithyman, "The Undetected Rapist" (1978) (Ph.D. dissertation, Claremont Graduate School, on file with author).

106. MacKinnon, *Toward a Feminist Theory of the State* 171–183.

107. D.P.P. v. Morgan, [1975] 2 W.L.R. 913, 2 All E.R. 347; Pappajohn v. The Queen, [1980] 111 D.L.R.3d 1; People v. Mayberry, 15 Cal. 3d 143, 542 P.2d 1337, 125 Cal. Rptr. 745 (1975).

108. Reporting rates may be higher for interracial rape of white women because white women may perceive they are more likely to be believed in such cases. Gary LaFree, "Male Power and Female Victimization: Toward a Theory of Interracial Rape," 88 *American Journal of Sociology* 311 (1982). In one study, Black men also appear to be slightly overrepresented in the stranger rape category. Russell, *Sexual Exploitation* 98–99. That the white male attention to this comparatively rare pattern in rape is a deadly obsession is supported by the fact that almost 90 percent of those executed for rape from 1930 to 1980 were Black men convicted for the rape of white women. Jack Greenberg, "Capital Punishment as a System," 91 *Yale Law Journal* 908, 912 (1982).

109. Michael M. v. Superior Court of Sonoma County, 450 U.S. 464 (1981). Justice Blackmun wrote separately, adding a fifth vote to uphold the statute, but did not mention biology as a reason. He pointed out the tension between the plurality's recognition of sex equality issues in teenage pregnancy and their failure to see the same issues in the abortion context. Id. at 481–483 (Blackmun, J., concurring in the judgment).

110. Russell, *Sexual Exploitation* 184–185, 215–231; Diana E. H. Russell, *The Secret Trauma* 217, 222 (1986). Note that the majority of perpetrators in all cases of sexual abuse of girls have been found to be nonstranger nonrelatives, id. at 219, like the situation in the *Michael M.* case.

111. Dothard v. Rawlinson, 433 U.S. 321, 336 (1977) (using women's capacity to be raped, termed their "very womanhood," to justify state regulation disqualifying female employees from contact positions in men's prison). Male gender, then, constituted a bona fide occupational qualification (BFOQ) for the job. Thus does sexual assault define gender as such.

112. See generally Judicial Council Advisory Comm. on Gender Bias in the Courts, *Achieving Equal Justice for Women and Men in the Courts* (Draft Report 1990) (California); New Jersey Supreme Court Task Force on Women in the Courts, *The First Year Report of the New Jersey Supreme Court Task Force on Women in the Courts* (1984); New Jersey Supreme Court Task Force on Women in the Courts, *The Second Report of the New Jersey Task Force on Women in the Courts* (1986); "Report of the New York Task Force on Women in the Courts," 15 *Fordham Urban Law Journal* 11 (1986–1987); see also Lynne Schafran, "Documenting Gender Bias in the Courts: The Task Force Approach," 70 *Judicature* 280 (1987). The California report documents that women victims, witnesses, and expert witnesses were generally perceived as less credible than men, and women lawyers as less competent. Judicial Council Advisory Comm. on Gender Bias in the Courts, above, tab 4, at 59, 61. It also shows that legal areas that disproportionately affect women and children, such as family law, are allocated fewer court resources. Id. tab 5, at 82–93.

113. Recently cited in testimony by NOW before the Senate Judiciary Committee are the following cases, which could be picked virtually at random from a newspaper. In 1982, a Wisconsin judge called a five-year-old victim "an unusually sexually promiscuous young lady." In 1987, another Wisconsin judge sentenced a defendant to only ninety days in jail for four felony sexual assault convictions involving two fifteen-year-old girls. In that case, the judge commented favorably on the defendant's appearance and personality at sentencing, stating he "could have had the pick of the flock; unfortunately he spread it around." In 1986, a Pennsylvania judge declared a defendant not guilty of attempted rape and aggravated assault despite a police witness to the attack, stating: "This was an unattractive girl and you are a good-looking fellow. You did something . . . stupid." Women and Violence: Hearing Before the Senate Comm. on the Judiciary on Legislation to Reduce the Growing Problem of Violent Crime Against Women, 101st Cong., 2d Sess. 66–67 (1990) (Statement of NOW Legal Defense and Education Fund).

114. Most narrowly, state action traditionally is interpreted to include state criminal statutes and their interpretation, as well as acts of government officials such as police. Of the many legal nuances and constraints to the state action doctrine, see generally Laurence Tribe, *American Constitutional Law* 1688–1720 (2d ed. 1988), this facet of the argument raises none of them.

115. A pioneering attempt to advance this argument, in spite of its lack of questioning of equal protection doctrine and its acceptance of some biological arguments, is Vivian Berger, "Man's Trial, Woman's Tribulation: Rape in the Courtroom," 77 *Columbia Law Review* 1 (1977) (use of sexual conduct or reputation evidence to show consent violates Fourteenth Amendment sex equality). Supportive related arguments

include Comment, "Rape in Illinois: A Denial of Equal Protection," 8 *John Marshall Journal of Practice and Procedure* 457 (1975) (contending that disparate evidentiary rules treating rape of vagina less favorably than forced anal or oral sex constitutes sex discrimination against women in violation of equal protection clause of Illinois Constitution); Robin West, "Equality Theory, Marital Rape, and the Promise of the Fourteenth Amendment," 42 *Florida Law Review* 45 (1990) (theorizing exclusion of married women from coverage by rape law as denial of equal protection).

116. "Section 261.5 defines unlawful sexual intercourse as 'an act of sexual intercourse accomplished with a female not the wife of the perpetrator, when the female is under the age of 18 years.' The statute thus makes men alone criminally liable for the act of sexual intercourse." Michael M. v. Superior Court, 450 U.S. 464, 464 (1981). Note that the statute does not mention men.

117. Meritor Sav. Bank v. Vinson, 477 U.S. 57 (1986).

118. It is also arguable that men who are raped (usually by men) are raped *as* men, as well as feminized in the process. Thus rape of men by men, and its unfavorable treatment by law, could also be seen as sex discrimination.

119. Barnes v. Costle, 561 F.2d 983, 990 (D.C. Cir. 1977) (holding that "[b]ut for her womanhood" plaintiff would not have been sexually harassed); cf. Orr v. Orr, 440 U.S. 268, 295 (1979) (Rehnquist, J., dissenting) (contending that "but for his sex" test should be used to deny standing to man challenging law precluding alimony awards to men).

120. This argument would support the results, and likely a stronger statutory exclusion, in cases like People v. Blackburn, 56 Cal. App. 3d 685, 128 Cal. Rptr. 864 (1976) (upholding constitutionality of rape shield statute against fair-trial attack), and People v. McKenna, 196 Colo. 367, 585 P.2d 275 (1978) (upholding rape shield statute against separation of powers and Sixth Amendment confrontation attack). The Women's Legal Education and Action Fund of Canada argues in Seaboyer v. The Queen and Gayme v. The Queen, No. 20835 (Can. S.Ct. filed June 1, 1988, and Oct. 26, 1988, and consolidated for argument) that Canada's statutory sexual history exclusion is supported by the sex equality guarantee of The Canadian Charter of Rights and Freedoms. Such an argument would also be relevant to cases like People v. Lucas, 160 Mich. App. 692, 408 N.W.2d 431 (1987), *cert. granted*, 111 S.Ct. 507 (1990) (No. 90–149) (challenging constitutionality of Michigan rape shield statute that permits judge to determine relevance of sexual history evidence in camera for purposes of admissibility).

121. This argument could potentially produce a different result in Florida Star v. B.J.F., 109 S.Ct. 2603 (1989).

122. See 136 *Cong. Rec.* S8263 (daily ed. June 19, 1990) (Violence Against Women Act) (creating federal civil cause of action for violation of civil rights through sexual assault or domestic battering when based on gender). Section 5 of the Fourteenth Amendment gives Congress authority to implement the amendment's guarantees through legislation. Not entirely settled is the scope of this power as regards both private (as opposed to state) action and grounds for discrimination other than sex.

Such a law fits within the very restrictive reading of the Civil Rights Cases, 109 U.S. 3, 25 (1883) ("If the laws themselves make any unjust discrimination, . . . Congress has full power to afford a remedy under that amendment and in accordance with it"). In Katzenbach v. Morgan, 384 U.S. 641 (1966), the Court stated, "Correctly viewed, § 5 is a positive grant of legislative power authorizing Congress to exercise its discretion in determining whether and what legislation is needed to secure the guarantees of the Fourteenth Amendment." Id. at 651. Such authority would seem particularly clear where, as in the Violence Against Women Act, no conflict with state law is involved.

Most of the litigation examining the congressional authority to remedy equality violations between private parties has centered on interpreting congressional intent in situations of ambiguity as to whether a state party was envisioned or purely private conduct was also meant to be (or could be) reached. See Griffin v. Breckenridge, 403 U.S. 88 (1971) (holding Congress had authority to reach private conspiracies with section 1985(3) under Thirteenth Amendment and right to travel); Collins v. Hardyman, 341 U.S. 651 (1951) (holding predecessor to section 1985(3) reached conspiracies under color of state law only). Further, whether private conspiracies on bases other than race could constitutionally be reached under section 1985(3) has been left open by the Supreme Court. United Bhd. of Carpenters & Joiners v. Scott, 463 U.S. 825, 836–839 (1983); *Griffin*, 403 U.S. at 102 n.9. Recent cases have interpreted section 1985(3) to apply to sex-based conspiracies. New York State Nat'l Org. for Women v. Terry, 886 F.2d 1339, 1358–1359 (2d Cir. 1989); see also National Org. for Women v. Operation Rescue, 914 F.2d 582, 584–586 (4th Cir. 1990) (ruling gender-based animus satisfies purposive discrimination requirement for purposes of section 1985(3) claim). Thus, the constitutionality of new legislation expressly forbidding sex discrimination between two private parties in an area traditionally covered by state criminal law under the authority of section 5 of the Fourteenth Amendment would present a new, but not wholly uncharted, issue. See, e.g., Fitzpatrick v. Bitzer, 427 U.S. 445 (1976) (finding Congress has authority under section 5 of Fourteenth Amendment to prohibit sex discrimination in employment, including against states). Its resolution would likely turn on the extent to which the Court was persuaded that the injuries covered implicated Fourteenth Amendment equality values, and on the legislative record. There is no direct precedent in its way.

123. Factum of the Intervenor Women's Legal Education and Action Fund para. 18, at 10, Sullivan and Lemay v. Regina, No. 21494 (Can. Sup. Ct. filed Feb. 22, 1989) (decision pending) (on file with author) [hereinafter LEAF's *Sullivan and Lemay* Factum].

124. Andrea Dworkin, *Our Blood* 100 (1976).

125. In the original case treating a fetus as a woman's body part, Oliver Wendell Holmes held in 1884 that a child could not recover for prenatal injuries because it was just a part of the mother at the time the injuries were sustained. Thus was the unity between the fetus and the pregnant woman affirmed as both of their harms were obscured. Dietrich v. Inhabitants of Northampton, 138 Mass. 14 (1884).

126. Roe v. Wade, 410 U.S. 113 (1973).

127. Cases creating fetal rights and attributing personhood to the fetus are en-

countered in the context of allowing wrongful death actions on behalf of stillborn fetuses, see, e.g., Commonwealth v. Cass, 392 Mass. 799, 467 N.E.2d 1324 (1984) (holding viable fetus is person for purposes of vehicular homicide statute); Vaillancourt v. Medical Center Hosp. of Vt., 139 Vt. 138, 425 A.2d 92 (1980) (finding statutory wrongful death liability exists for negligently caused death of viable fetus); of awarding custody of the fetus to others than the mother for purposes of forcing surgery, see, e.g., Jefferson v. Griffin Spalding County Hosp. Auth., 247 Ga. 86, 274 S.E.2d 457 (1981) (per curiam) (awarding temporary custody of fetus to Department of Human Resources and ordering woman who objected to cesarean section to submit to surgery); and of prosecuting mothers for neglect for supplying harmful substances to their fetuses, see, e.g., *In re* Smith, 128 Misc. 2d 976, 492 N.Y.S. 2d 331 (N.Y. Fam. Ct. 1985) (holding fetus is person for purposes of New York Family Court Act and can be considered neglected child on basis of mother's drinking and failure to obtain prenatal care during pregnancy). For a discussion of the attempts to develop fetal legal rights and personhood and how this intrudes upon the rights of pregnant women, see Janet Gallagher, "Prenatal Invasions and Interventions: What's Wrong with Fetal Rights," 10 *Harvard Women's Law Journal* 9 (1987); Note, "The Creation of Fetal Rights: Conflicts with Women's Constitutional Rights to Liberty, Privacy, and Equal Protection," 95 *Yale Law Journal* 599 (1986). For a sex equality argument in the Canadian context opposing apprehension of a fetus by government for purposes of forcing a cesarean section, see Memorandum of Argument of the Women's Legal Education and Action Fund (Intervenor), Re Baby R., [1988] 30 B.C.L.R.2d 237 (S.Ct.) (No. A872582).

128. One interpretation of Freud suggests another reason: men might identify with the fetus as the embodiment of the penis, making abortion a symbolic castration. Freud thought that the baby was a penis to the woman and that women wanted penises. Sigmund Freud, "Some Psychical Consequences of the Anatomical Distinction Between the Sexes," in 19 *Standard Edition of the Complete Psychological Works of Sigmund Freud* 256 (James Strachey trans., 1923–1925) ("the equation 'penis-child'"). Luce Irigaray summarizes this aspect of Freud's analysis as follows: "*The desire to obtain the penis from the father is replaced by the desire to have a child*, this latter becoming, in an equivalence that Freud analyzes, *the penis substitute*." Luce Irigaray, *This Sex Which Is Not One* 41 (1985) (emphasis in original). If penis envy is regarded as a male construct, attributed to women and introjected by men, the baby, and prenatally the fetus, becomes a penis to men.

Reenvisioned as an insight into male psychology, and given that a woman's pregnancy and subsequent child are sometimes seen as proof of a man's potency, there may be something to the Freudian observation. Then again, the way the fetus can overtake the female may be better described as metaphysical. It would not be the first time that something less real that increases male power became invested with reality while something fully real that does not increase male power became deprived of it. In the end, as Kim Scheppele pointed out to me in the abortion context, the male capacity for abstraction may be more powerful than men's capacity for identification with anyone who is not them.

129. See, e.g., *In re* A.C., 533 A.2d 611 (D.C. 1987) (denying motion to stay trial

court's order authorizing hospital to deliver fetus by cesarean section from terminally ill woman without her consent), *reh'g granted and judgment vacated*, 539 A.2d 203 (D.C. 1988) (vacating judgment denying stay following operation and death of woman and fetus), *on reh'g*, 573 A.2d 1235 (D.C. 1990) (requiring informed consent of woman or substituted judgment to perform cesarean under such circumstances); Minn. Stat. Ann. §626.556.1 (West 1990) (mandatory reporting and involuntary civil commitment of women who abuse drugs during pregnancy). But cf. Re Baby R., [1988] 30 B.C.L.R.2d 237 (S.Ct.); Re A. (in utero), (1990) 75 O.R.2d 82 (holding parens patriae jurisdiction inadequate to force mother to have hospital birth because of impossibility of protecting child without forcing mother to undergo restraint and medical procedures against her will, possibly leading to "abuse of pregnant mothers"); Re F. (in utero), [1988] 2 W.L.R. 1288, 2 All E.R. 193 (ruling unborn child cannot be ward of court because of difficulties enforcing order against mother). See also *In re* Troy D., 215 Cal. App. 3d 889, 263 Cal. Rptr. 869 (1990) (declaring child born under influence of drugs due to mother's drug use while pregnant dependent of juvenile court, court stating that it would reject dependence petition in case of unborn fetus).

130. Factum of The Women's Legal Education and Action Fund (LEAF) para. 3, at 1, Borowski v. Attorney General for Canada, [1989] 1 S.C.R. 342 (No. 20411) (on file with author) [hereinafter LEAF's *Borowski* Factum]; Rosalind Petchesky, "Fetal Images: The Power of Visual Culture in the Politics of Reproduction," 13 *Feminist Studies* 263 (1987).

131. For further discussion of this as male, see MacKinnon, *Toward a Feminist Theory of the State* 162–163.

132. From this perspective, killing the fetus on-screen produces fetal snuff pornography.

133. Mary Eberts, Oral Argument in *Borowski v. Attorney General for Canada* before the Supreme Court of Canada (Oct. 4, 1988).

134. See, e.g., Griswold v. Connecticut, 381 U.S. 479 (1965); Eisenstadt v. Baird, 405 U.S. 438 (1972); Roe v. Wade, 410 U.S. 113 (1973). Some early privacy cases in tort protected women from intrusive outsiders. See, e.g., Demay v. Roberts, 46 Mich. 160, 9 N.W. 146 (1881) (doctor invaded woman's privacy by bringing young man into her home while she was giving birth); see also Melvin v. Reid, 112 Cal. App. 285, 297 P. 91 (1931) (publication of film of former prostitute held impermissibly invasive). See generally Anita Allen, *Uneasy Access* (1988).

135. Webster v. Reproductive Health Servs., 109 S.Ct. 3040 (1989); Deshaney v. Winnebago County Dep't of Social Servs., 489 U.S. 189 (1989); Harris v. McRae, 448 U.S. 297 (1980).

136. This is discussed further in MacKinnon, *Toward a Feminist Theory of the State* 184–194. See also a concurrence to the European Commission of Human Rights decision affirming the West German abortion decision requiring criminal restrictions on abortion in certain circumstances: "We are aware that the reality behind these traditional views [of abortion] is that the scope of protection of private life has depended on the outlook which has been formed mainly by men, although it may have been

shared by women as well." Brüggemann and Scheuten v. Federal Republic of Germany, 3 E.H.R.R. 244, 256 (1977) (Opsahl, concurring, with Nørgaard and Kellberg).

137. California Fed. Sav. & Loan Ass'n v. Guerra, 479 U.S. 272 (1987).

138. Anne Helton, Judith McFarlane, Elizabeth Anderson, "Battered and Pregnant: A Prevalence Study," 77 *American Journal of Public Health* 1337 (1987); Richard Gelles, *Family Violence* 126–134 (2d ed. 1987); Richard Gelles, *The Violent Home* 145–147 (1972); Elaine Hilberman, Kit Munson, "Sixty Battered Women," 2 *Victimology* 460, 462 (1977–1978); John Gayford, "Wife Battering: A Preliminary Survey of 100 Cases," 1 *British Medical Journal* 194 (1975). One researcher found that, of the wives in his sample who were assaulted, 23 percent were attacked while pregnant. Other researchers have recorded a range of 9 percent to 50 percent of battered women assaulted while pregnant. Lewis Okun, *Woman Abuse*, 51–52 (1986) (summarizing studies).

139. Andrea Dworkin, *Pornography: Men Possessing Women* 218–223 (1981).

140. In an extreme instance of conditioning women's employment opportunities on the possibility of childbearing, the Johnson Controls Corporation's "fetal protection policy" excluded all "fertile" women from work where their exposure to lead in battery manufacture might affect a fetus through the placenta in the first weeks after conception. UAW v. Johnson Controls, 886 F.2d 871 (7th Cir. 1989), *cert. granted*, 110 S.Ct. 1522 (1990) (No. 89–1215).

141. Having children has been documented as a leading cause of poverty among women in Canada. Canadian Advisory Council on the Status of Women, *Women and Labour Market Poverty* 7–35 (1990).

142. Compare Buck v. Bell, 274 U.S. 200 (1927) (allowing mentally incompetent woman to be sterilized) with Skinner v. Oklahoma, 316 U.S. 535 (1942) (disallowing sterilization of male prisoner).

143. See Thornburgh v. American College of Obstetricians & Gynecologists, 476 U.S. 747 (1986) (striking down provisions requiring doctors to report basis for non-viability conclusion as means of assuring any potentially viable fetus be born alive and mandating second doctor's presence at any abortion where fetus might be born alive); Webster v. Reproductive Health Servs., 109 S. Ct. 3040, 3061 (O'Connor, J., concurring), 3076 (Blackmun, J., concurring in part and dissenting in part) (1989); Colautti v. Franklin, 439 U.S. 379 (1979) (invalidating statute criminalizing doctors for neglect of viability, or possible viability, of fetus as void for vagueness).

144. See LEAF's *Sullivan and Lemay* Factum, paras. 19–24, at 11–14.

145. A case like UAW v. Johnson Controls, 886 F.2d 871 (7th Cir. 1989), *cert. granted*, 110 S.Ct. 1522 (1990) (No. 89–1215), collapses this distinction. See above note 140. For an incisive analysis of the sex equality issues involved in "fetal vulnerability" policies, see Becker, "From Muller v. Oregon."

146. See above note 127.

147. This is the insight of Judith Jarvis Thompson's celebrated hypothetical. Thompson, "A Defense of Abortion," 1 *Philosophy and Public Affairs* 47 (1971); see also Donald Regan, "Rewriting *Roe v. Wade*," 77 *Michigan Law Review* 1569 (1979).

148. Mary Eberts created this characterization.

149. J. Katz, "Maternal-Fetal Conflicts," 45–48 (Apr. 25, 1990) (unpublished manuscript on file with author).

150. On this issue, consideration of sex inequality would add a dimension to the perceptive analysis of comparative abortion laws provided by Mary Ann Glendon in her *Abortion and Divorce in Western Law* (1987).

151. Adrienne Rich, *Of Woman Born* 64 (1976) ("The child that I carry for nine months can be defined *neither* as me nor as not-me") (emphasis in original). Lynn Smith suggested stating Rich's definition in the affirmative.

152. The analysis of Sylvia Law gets no further than this in its consideration of gender in the abortion context, although it does consider the social consequences for women of being deprived of the abortion right in the context of a legal sex discrimination argument. Sylvia Law, "Rethinking Sex and the Constitution," 132 *University of Pennsylvania Law Review* 955, 1016–1028 (1984).

153. This is emphatically *not* to permit individual determinations of the balance of power in particular relationships as a predicate to granting a right to abort. The analysis here is of a political reality—women's subordinate status in society—that permeates, conditions, and transcends individuals and relationships. Laurence Tribe correctly points out that predicating the abortion right on individual determinations would be an invasion of privacy under existing law. Laurence Tribe, *Abortion: The Clash of Absolutes* 92–99 (1990); see also Massachusetts v. Secretary of Health & Human Servs., 899 F.2d 53 (1st Cir. 1990) (state has no compelling interest in intruding into consultation between woman and her physician).

154. The consequences of this argument for abortion for sex selection purposes are not entirely clear to me but suggest that such practices should not be permitted. Selective abortion of female fetuses by state policy or encouraged or pressured by private entities would surely constitute sex discrimination—both against the woman's choice to bear a female child and, through her, against the gendered fetus. If fetal gender can be known for purposes of elimination, it should be able to be recognized for purposes of preservation. Most selectively aborted fetuses are female, in societies that denigrate and devalue women, see, e.g., "India Makes Sure of Baby Boys," *New Scientist*, 8 (Dec. 25, 1986–Jan. 1, 1987), and may also practice female infanticide and dowry murder, for example. The question is, should this recognition extend to official blocking of decisions by women to abort female fetuses? One state in India has restricted the practice of abortions for sex selection by law. Lakshmi Lingam, "New Reproductive Technologies in India: A Print Media Analysis," 3 *Issues in Reproductive and Genetic Engineering* 13, 18–19 (1990) (citing position taken by Indian Forum Against Sex Determination and Sex Pre-Selection, a nationwide umbrella organization in India); Weisman, "No More Guarantees of a Son's Birth," *New York Times*, A1 (July 20, 1988). In addition to other costs, aborting female fetuses may further erode women's power as women make up less and less of the population. On the one hand, it is difficult to say why the reason for the abortion decision should matter until those who prescribe what matters live with the consequences the way the mother does, or until women can make such decisions in a context of equality. At the same time, in a context of mass

abortions of female fetuses, the pressures on women to destroy potential female offspring are tremendous and oppressive unless restrictions exist. While under conditions of sex inequality monitoring women's reasons for deciding to abort is worrying, the decision is not a free one, even absent governmental intervention, where a male life is valued and a female life is not.

155. Andrea Dworkin made this observation in a conversation with me.

156. See NCADV's *Webster* Brief, at 2. The same reality was highlighted by LEAF in Memorandum of Facts and Law Submitted by the Intervenor, The Women's Legal Education and Action Fund para. 58, at 16, Tremblay v. Daigle, [1989] 2 S.C.R. 530 (No. 21553), in which it was noted that Ms. Daigle stated Mr. Tremblay's violence against her contributed to her decision to abort.

157. Rebecca Dobash, Russell Dobash, *Violence Against Wives* 14–20 (1979); Lenore Walker, *The Battered Woman* 19–20 (1979); Evan Stark, Anne Flitcraft, William Frazier, "Medicine and Patriarchal Violence: The Social Construction of a Private Event," 9 *International Journal of Health Services* 461–493 (1979). See generally Bureau of Justice Statistics, U.S. Dep't of Justice, *Intimate Victims: A Study of Violence Among Friends and Relatives* (1980).

158. Carol Gilligan's discussion of women's abortion decisions, which include examples of such pressures, concludes that women reason morally in a way that is "different" from men. The discussion here suggests that sex inequality forces women to reason more relationally (inter alia) than men are required to do; specifically, women are forced to take men's views into account in a way that reflects the fact that men have social power that women do not have. Gilligan, *In a Different Voice* 106–127. For an evocative discussion of factors involved for women who confront abortions, see Magda Denes, *In Necessity and Sorrow* 91–127 (1976).

159. This argument is made under the sex equality provision of the Canadian Charter of Rights and Freedoms in LEAF's *Sullivan and Lemay* Factum, paras. 11–27, at 8–15.

160. This is not to say that *Roe* should necessarily have been argued on sex equality grounds. Sex equality law was in its infancy at the time. But then privacy law barely existed either. It is to say that the real constitutional issue raised by criminal abortion statutes like that in *Roe* is sex equality and that it should be recognized as such. Guido Calabresi, *Ideals, Beliefs, Attitudes, and the Law* 87–114 (1985); Tribe, *Abortion* 105; Ruth Bader Ginsburg, "Some Thoughts on Autonomy and Equality in Relation to *Roe v. Wade*," 63 *North Carolina Law Review* 375 (1985); Frederick Schauer, "Easy Cases," 58 *Southern California Law Review* 399, 431 n.83 (1985); David Strauss, "Discriminatory Intent and the Taming of *Brown*," 56 *University of Chicago Law Review* 935, 990–998 (1989); Frances Olsen, "The Supreme Court, 1988 Term—Foreword: Unraveling Compromise," 103 *Harvard Law Review* 105 (1989); Cass Sunstein, "Why the Unconstitutional Conditions Doctrine Is an Anachronism (With Particular Reference to Religion, Speech, and Abortion)," 70 *Boston University Law Review* 593, 616–620 (1990). The preamble to the East German Law on the Interruption of Pregnancy states that "[e]qual rights [*Gleichberechtigung*] of the woman in education and the profes-

sions, marriage, and the family requires that the woman herself can decide about pregnancy and whether to carry it to term." *Gesetz über die Unterbrechung der Schwangerschaft*, GBl.I der DDR 89 (1972) (translated by author with Susanne Baer).

161. If ways are found for men to gestate fetuses, this would change. Extrauterine gestation would raise additional issues.

162. Medicaid funding for abortion has been upheld under a sex equality rubric in Doe v. Maher, 40 Conn. Supp. 394, 515 A.2d 134 (Conn. Super. Ct. 1986) (holding restriction of abortion funding to life-threatening situations violates, inter alia, state equal rights amendment). But cf. Fischer v. Department of Pub. Welfare, 85 Pa. Commw. 215, 482 A.2d 1137 (1984) (holding restriction of abortion funding to life-threatening situations does not violate state equal rights amendment). The more usual theory is not sex equality, but equal protection for indigent women, see, e.g., Committee to Defend Reproductive Rights v. Myers, 29 Cal. 3d 252, 625 P.2d 779 (1981), or privacy.

163. See Harris v. McRae, 448 U.S. 297 (1980) (upholding Hyde Amendment restrictions on government funding of Medicaid abortions).

164. Guam recently passed an initiative to recriminalize all abortion "after implantation of a fertilized ovum" unless two doctors declare the mother's life or health to be at risk should she continue the pregnancy. The law criminalizes soliciting abortions, having them, and performing them. See Guam Soc'y of Obstetricians & Gynecologists v. Ada, No. 90–00013, 1990 LEXIS 11910, at 3–4 (D. Guam, Aug. 23, 1990) (quoting statute).

165. Mississippi Univ. for Women v. Hogan, 458 U.S. 718, 724 n.9 (1982); Personnel Adm'r of Mass. v. Feeney, 442 U.S. 256, 273 (1979); Craig v. Boren, 429 U.S. 190, 197 (1976). The related argument could also be made that such statutes do not bear a rational relation to a valid state purpose under Reed v. Reed, 404 U.S. 71, 76 (1971).

166. Disparate treatment cases under Title VII and disparate impact cases under the Equal Protection Clause require a showing of intent or purpose to discriminate before the behavior will be regarded as discriminatory. Facial cases under the Equal Protection Clause do not. Sexual harassment is treated as if facial in the sense that no showing of purpose or intent to discriminate has been generally required even though the cases are not argued as Title VII disparate impact cases and otherwise better fit the differential treatment model. See, e.g., Katz v. Dole, 709 F.2d 251, 256 (4th Cir. 1983) (holding intent not specifically required as element of Title VII sexual harassment case). But see Huebschen v. Department of Health and Social Servs., 716 F.2d 1167, 1171 (7th Cir. 1983) (holding intent required in equal protection sexual harassment case); Bohen v. City of E. Chicago, 799 F.2d 1180 (7th Cir. 1986) (same).

167. Washington v. Davis, 426 U.S. 229, 242 (1976). I oppose the intent requirement, as it focuses on mental state not consequences, on perpetrators not victims, and on individuals not members of groups. It requires perpetrators to know what they are doing and why. While some discrimination happens intentionally in this sense, most of it does not.

168. *Feeney*, 442 U.S. at 274–275; see also New York State Nat'l Org. for Women v. Terry, 886 F.2d 1339, 1359 (2d Cir. 1989) ("[B]ecause defendants' conspiracy [under section 1985(3)] is focused entirely on women seeking abortions, their activities reveal an attitude or animus based on gender").

169. Geduldig v. Aiello, 417 U.S. 484, 496 n.20 (1974).

170. General Elec. Co. v. Gilbert, 429 U.S. 125 (1976).

171. Pregnancy Discrimination Act of 1978, 42 U.S.C. §2000e(k).

172. The Pregnancy Discrimination Act provides an express exception for abortion: "This subsection shall not require an employer to pay for health insurance benefits for abortion, except where the life of the mother would be endangered if the fetus were carried to term, or except where medical complications have arisen from abortion. . . ." Id.

173. See above notes 68–77 and accompanying text.

174. Newport News Shipbuilding & Drydock Co. v. EEOC, 462 U.S. 669 (1983). Justice Rehnquist, author of *Gilbert* for the Court, dissented in *Newport News*, arguing that the majority had there in effect overruled *Gilbert*. Id. at 686 (Rehnquist, J., dissenting); see also Nashville Gas Co. v. Satty, 434 U.S. 136, 141–142 (1977) (distinguishing *Gilbert*; policy of denying accumulated seniority to pregnant women violates Title VII, imposing on women a burden men do not suffer).

175. California Fed. Sav. & Loan Ass'n v. Guerra, 479 U.S. 272 (1987).

176. Id. at 289.

177. Harris v. McRae, 448 U.S. 297 (1980), could have provided this occasion, but the sex equality argument was not made.

178. Cates and Rochat estimate that the death-to-case rate for illegal abortions is approximately eight times greater than for legal abortions. Willard Cates, Roger Rochat, "Illegal Abortions in the United States: 1972–1974," 8 *Family Planning Perspectives* 86, 92 (1976); see also Nancy Binkin, Julian Gold, Willard Cates, "Illegal Abortion Deaths in the United States: Why Are They Still Occurring?" 14 *Family Planning Perspectives* 163, 165–166 (1982) (pointing to lack of funding, lack of providers or access to them, desire for privacy, fear, and ignorance as factors in illegal abortion deaths since 1974). The death rate from illegal abortions for women of color in New York City prior to the legalization of abortion was found to be substantially higher than that for white women. Julian Gold, Erhardt, Jacobziner and Nelson, "Therapeutic Abortions in New York City: A 20-Year Review," 55 *American Journal of Public Health* 964, 965 (1965).

179. LEAF's *Borowski* Factum, para. 54, at 17.

180. Useful texts urging an approach consistent with the one advanced here are Owen Fiss, "Groups and the Equal Protection Clause," 5 *Philosophy and Public Affairs* 107 (1976), and David Strauss, "The Myth of Colorblindness," 1986 *Supreme Court Review* 99 (1986).

181. For an illustration of this last category of gendered law, see American Booksellers Ass'n v. Hudnut, 771 F.2d 323 (7th Cir. 1985), summarily affirmed, 475 U.S. 1001 (1986).

182. For an example in the racial context, consider the recent case upholding em-

ployment practices that one dissenting Justice aptly described as "bear[ing] an unsettling resemblance to aspects of a plantation economy." Wards Cove Packing Co. v. Atonio, 490 U.S. 642, 664 n.4 (1989) (Stevens, J., dissenting). Justice Stevens and the three justices who joined him in his dissent indicated that the facts did not exactly fit either Title VII's "disparate treatment" or its "disparate impact" model. See id. at 673–678 (citing International Bhd. of Teamsters v. United States, 431 U.S. 324, 339–340 n.20 (1977)). These two theories of discrimination find rough constitutional parallels in equal protection's distinction between facial classifications and facially neutral classifications invidiously applied. If a segregated workplace does not fit either of the two leading legal models for discrimination, perhaps a more responsive model should be created. The Court, in creating the models in *Teamsters* originally, stated they were not mutually exclusive and did not say they were exhaustive. Teamsters, 431 U.S. at 335–336 n.15; see also Wards Cove, 490 U.S. at 668 n.13. For an illuminating discussion of the more realistic Canadian concept of systemic discrimination, see Action Travail des Femmes v. C.N.R., [1987] 1 S.C.R. 114 (Dickson, C.J.).

183. This is properly rejected under current law and social conditions. See, e.g., Planned Parenthood v. Danforth, 428 U.S. 52, 69–71 (1976) (states cannot constitutionally give spouse veto power over woman's first-trimester abortion decision); Wolfe v. Schroering, 541 F.2d 523, 525–526 (6th Cir. 1976) (expanding *Danforth* to second trimester); Poe v. Gerstein, 517 F.2d 787, 794–796 (5th Cir. 1975) (man's right outweighed), affirmed, Gerstein v. Coe, 428 U.S. 901 (1976); Doe v. Rampton, 366 F.Supp. 189, 193 (C.D. Utah 1973) (individual right of woman cannot be burdened by veto); Conn v. Conn, 526 N.E.2d 958 (Ind.) (refusal to reconsider *Danforth*'s ruling that putative fathers may not interfere with women's abortion decisions), cert. denied, 488 U.S. 955 (1988); Tremblay v. Daigle, [1989] 2 S.C.R. 530 (no legal basis for putative father blocking abortion); Paton v. United Kingdom, 3 E.H.R.R. 408 (1980) (right to respect for family life does not give putative father right to be consulted on, or to make applications about, wife's intended abortion).

184. Morgenthaler v. The Queen, [1988] 1 S.C.R. 30, 172 (Wilson, J., concurring).

185. Webster v. Reproductive Health Servs., 109 S.Ct. 3040, 3058–3064 (1989) (O'Connor, J., concurring in part and concurring in judgment).

186. Id. See also Justice O'Connor's decision in Hodgson v. Minnesota, 110 S.Ct. 2926, 2950 (1990), stressing the dilemma of the neglected or abused girl seeking an abortion and the inadequacy of the state's procedures for addressing her need not to be required to notify her parents.

13. Prostitution and Civil Rights

This address was given to the *Michigan Journal of Gender & Law* Symposium, "Prostitution: From Academia to Activism," October 31, 1992, University of Michigan Law School, Ann Arbor, Michigan. It was first published in 1 *Michigan Journal of Gender and Law* 13 (1993). Comments by Dorchen Leidholdt and Margaret Baldwin were especially helpful. The assistance of the ever resourceful University of Michigan Law Library and Rita Rendell are gratefully acknowledged. This article is for Evelina.

1. This discussion focuses on prostituted women and girls as the paradigm, while remembering that there is also a substantial sex trade in boys, transsexuals, and men.

2. See generally Symposium Issue, 1 *Michigan Journal of Gender and Law* (1993); Evelina Giobbe, "Juvenile Prostitution: Profile of Recruitment," in *Child Trauma I: Issues And Research* 117 (Ann W. Burgess ed., 1992); Evelina Giobbe, "Prostitution: Buying the Right to Rape," *Rape and Sexual Assault III: A Research Handbook* 143 (Ann W. Burgess ed., 1991); and citations throughout this article.

3. See Andrea Dworkin, *Letters from a War Zone: Writings 1976–1989* 229 (1989).

4. See generally Kathleen Barry, *Female Sexual Slavery* (1979).

5. Elizabeth Fry Society of Toronto, *Streetwork Outreach with Adult Female Street Prostitutes* 13 (May 1987) ("Approximately 90 percent of the women contacted indicated they wished to stop working on the streets at some point, but felt unable or unclear about how to even begin this process.").

6. Some think there is a separate civil right to family. Women face losing their children if it is found they are prostitutes. I have never heard of a man losing his children because he was found to be a trick or a pimp.

7. In the standard posturing of the advocates of decriminalization, harm is recognized to result only from criminal laws against prostitution, seldom from prostitution itself.

8. See generally People v. Superior Court of Alameda County, 562 P.2d 1315 (Cal. 1977).

9. See generally American Booksellers Ass'n v. Hudnut, 771 F.2d 323 (7th Cir. 1985), *aff'd*, 475 U.S. 1001 (1986).

10. William Blackstone, 1 *Commentaries* *442.

11. See generally John Stoltenberg, "Male Sexuality: Why Ownership Is Sexy," 1 *Michigan Journal of Gender and Law* 59 (1993).

12. State v. DeVall, 302 So. 2d 909, 910 (La. 1974) (quoting La. Rev. Stat. Ann. § 14:82 (West 1986)).

13. DeVall, 302 So. 2d at 913. See also City of Minneapolis v. Buschette, 240 N.W.2d 500, 505 (Minn. 1976) (holding that arresting chiefly female violators of prostitution law is a rational way to meet the objective of controlling prostitution). This position has not changed significantly with elevated scrutiny. See, e.g., State v. Sandoval, 649 P.2d 485, 487 (N.M. Ct. App. 1982) (ruling that there is no arbitrary enforcement of prostitution statute under state equal rights amendment); Bolser v. Washington State Liquor Control Bd., 580 P.2d 629, 633 (Wash. 1978) (holding that male and female dancers are equally covered by restrictions on topless dancing, resulting in no violation of state equal rights amendment).

14. But cf. Fluker v. State, 282 S.E.2d 112, 113 (Ga. 1981) (applying Michael M. v. Superior Court of Sonoma County, 450 U.S. 464 (1981)) (upholding a sex-specific pandering statute based on U.S. Supreme Court recognition of biological differences between the sexes when upholding a statutory rape law). Another strategy for preserving sex-specific prostitution statutes, a two-wrongs-make-a-right rationale, was exhibited in Morgan v. City of Detroit, 389 F.2d 922, 928 (E.D. Mich. 1975) (a prostitution statute allegedly selectively enforced against women was found not to ground an

equal protection claim because the second section of the challenged ordinance against pimping applied only to males). Compare Plas v. State, 598 P.2d 966, 968 (Alaska 1979) (striking a sex-specific prohibition but finding it severable).

15. I am told by women police officers that they loathe being decoys, although some of their work has resulted in spectacular arrests of pillars of the community. No woman should be forced to present herself as available for sexual use, whether as a prostitute or as a police officer ordered to pose as a prostitute as part of her employment.

16. United States v. Moses, 339 A.2d 46, 55 (D.C. 1975). Another reason offered for not using women police decoys is that, due to past sex discrimination, there are few or no women to use. See People v. Burton, 432 N.Y.S.2d 312, 315 (City Ct. of Buffalo 1980).

17. People v. Superior Court of Alameda County, 562 P.2d 1315, 1321 (Cal. 1977).

18. People v. Nelson, 427 N.Y.S.2d 194, 195 (City Ct. of Syracuse 1980).

19. Janice Toner, a former prostitute, argued that the money she made as a prostitute was not income to her because she was merely a conduit to her husband/pimp, who beat and threatened to kill her and their children. The tax court rejected the argument, although her husband was convicted of assault in a separate case. Toner v. Commissioner, 60 T.C.M. (CCH) 1016, 1019 (1990). The court found that Toner did not show that her husband's abuse was causally connected to her earning of an income from prostitution and characterized her as an active, voluntary participant in some aspects of the prostitution business. Id. at 1021.

20. State v. Tookes, 699 P.2d 983, 984 (Haw. 1985) (finding no denial of due process when civilian police agent had sex with woman for money before arresting her for prostitution).

21. See *Superior Court of Alemeda County*, 562 P.2d at 1320–1323. When both prostitute and customer are male, anecdotal evidence suggests that it is more typical to arrest both. Some cases alleging sex-differential enforcement fail for lack of showing of discriminatory intent. See, e.g., People v. Adams, 597 N.E.2d 574, 585 (Ill. 1992); United States v. Wilson, 342 A.2d 27, 31 (D.C. Ct. App. 1975). Others fail for lack of proof that men in comparable circumstances are treated differently. See, e.g., United States v. Cozart, 321 A.2d 342, 344 (D.C. Ct. App. 1974) (finding that male homosexual prosecuted for solicitation to sodomy failed to prove equal protection violation based on unequal enforcement because "[t]here is no indication in the record . . . as to whether lesbian solicitation was known to the police"); State v. Gaither, 224 S.E.2d 378, 380 (Ga. 1976) (finding no evidence that male prostitutes exist in detectable numbers); Young v. State, 446 N.E.2d 624, 626 n.4 (Ind. Ct. App. 1983); Commonwealth v. King, 372 N.E.2d 196, 205 (Sup. Jud. Ct. Mass. 1977) (finding no evidence that male prostitutes are not prosecuted); City of Minneapolis v. Buschette, 240 N.W.2d 500, 504 (Minn. 1976).

22. See *Superior Court of Alameda County*, 562 P.2d at 1323. See also Morgan v. City of Detroit, 389 F. Supp. 922, 928 (E.D. Mich. 1975).

23. One court rejected this decisively in the 1920s: "Men caught with women in

an act of prostitution are equally guilty, and should be arrested and held for trial with the women. The law is clear, and the duty of the police is to act in pursuance of the law. The practical application of the law as heretofore enforced is an unjust discrimination against women in the matter of an offense which, in its very nature, if completed, requires the participation of men. . . . As long as the law is upon the statute books, it must be impartially administered without sex discrimination." People v. Edwards, 180 N.Y.S. 631, 635 (Ct. Gen. Sess. 1920). In 1980, the City Court of Syracuse, endorsing this reasoning, further rejected the dodge arguing that prostitute and patron are "not similarly situated" for equal protection purposes because they violate separate sections of the penal code. That court found that "the only significant difference in the proscribed behavior is that the prostitute sells sex and the patron buys it. Neither gender nor solicitation is a differentiating factor." People v. Nelson, 427 N.Y.S.2d 194, 197 (City Court of Syracuse 1980) (finding no evidence of intent to discriminate, therefore no discrimination shown). One court upheld a gender-neutral prostitution law from equal protection attack by pointing out that "[w]hat would be prostitution for a female would be equally prohibited and punished as lewdness for a male." State v. Price, 237 N.W.2d 813, 815 (Iowa 1976), appeal dismissed, 426 U.S. 916 (1976). It was apparently inconceivable that a male could be a prostitute. Most courts that have considered sex-differential enforcement challenges on equal protection grounds have relied, for rejecting them, on the distinction in statutes under which prostitutes and patrons fall. See, e.g., Matter of Dora P., 418 N.Y.S.2d 597, 604 (N.Y. App. Div. 1979) (prostitution and patronizing a prostitute are discrete crimes making differential treatment of women and men under them not discriminatory); Commonwealth v. King, 372 N.E.2d 196 (Sup. Jud. Ct. Mass. 1977) (finding that the lack of a statute against patronage does not violate equal protection rights of prostitutes). See also Garrett v. United States, 339 A.2d 372 (D.C. Ct. App. 1975) (holding that a state's failure to require corroboration in prostitution cases, although requiring it in homosexuality cases, is not unconstitutional sex discrimination because it is not based on gender). A ray of reality is provided by one recent ruling holding that women's equality rights were violated when female performers, and not male patrons, were selectively prosecuted for sexual activity at a private club. However, it was important to the ruling that the sexes were "similarly situated" because the women and the men could have been charged under the same statutory provision. See generally State v. McCollum, 464 N.W.2d 44 (Wis. Ct. App. 1990).

24. See *Superior Court of Alameda County*, 562 P.2d at 1323.

25. See Reynolds v. McNichols, 488 F.2d 1378, 1383 (10th Cir. 1973) (finding no equal protection violation in arresting only the prostitute when she is regarded as "the potential source" of venereal disease and the customer is not).

26. One significant departure from this line of cases, from the standpoint of equality analysis, is represented by the Seventh Circuit's invalidation of a strip-search policy for prostituted women only, which ignored "similarly situated males." This policy was found not to be validly based on gender and therefore in violation of the equal protection guarantee under current standards of scrutiny. Mary Beth G. v. City of Chicago,

723 F.2d 1263, 1273–1274 (7th Cir. 1983). See also White v. Fleming, 522 F.2d 730 (7th Cir. 1975) (finding that a statute prohibiting female, but not male, bar employees from sitting or standing at or behind the bar violates equal protection).

27. As Margaret Baldwin has stressed, part of the complexity of this situation is that jail sometimes provides comparative safety for the women, and the criminal status of prostitution provides some barrier to recruitment and validation for the women's sense of violation. These concerns might be met without making women criminals.

28. For a vivid description of the inequality between pimp and prostitute, see Dorchen Leidholdt, "Prostitution: A Violation of Women's Human Rights," 1 *Cardozo Women's L.J.* 133 (1993).

29. U.S. Const. amend. XIII. § 1 ("Neither slavery nor involuntary servitude, except as a punishment for crime whereof the party shall have been duly convicted, shall exist within the United States, or any place subject to their jurisdiction."). See also Robertson v. Baldwin, 165 U.S. 275, 282 (1897) (Justice Brown said that "involuntary servitude" was added to "slavery" to cover the peonage of Mexicans and the trade in Chinese labor); Butler v. Perry, 240 U.S. 328, 332 (1916) ("[T]he term involuntary servitude was intended to cover those forms of compulsory labor akin to African slavery which in practical operation would tend to produce like undesirable results."). See generally Howard D. Hamilton, "The Legislative and Judicial History of the Thirteenth Amendment," 9 *Nat'l B.J.* 7 (1951) (an illuminating history of the early years of the Thirteenth Amendment).

30. See Bailey v. Alabama, 219 U.S. 219, 241 (1911) ("[T]he words involuntary servitude have a 'larger meaning than slavery'") (quoting The Slaughter-House Cases, 83 U.S. (16 Wall.) 36, 69 (1872)). Also the Ninth Circuit has stated: "[Y]esterday's slave may be today's migrant worker or domestic servant. Today's involuntary servitor is not always black; he or she may just as well be Asian, Hispanic, or a member of some other minority group. Also, the methods of subjugating people's wills have changed from blatant slavery to more subtle, if equally effective, forms of coercion." United States v. Mussry, 726 F.2d 1448, 1451–1452 (9th Cir. 1984) (citation and footnotes omitted), *cert. denied*, 469 U.S. 855 (1984).

31. See Vednita Nelson, "Prostitution: Where Racism and Sexism Intersect," 1 *Michigan Journal of Gender and Law* 81, 84, 85 (1993).

32. Prosecutions under the Thirteenth Amendment are typically brought under 18 U.S.C. section 1584 (1988), which makes it a crime knowingly and willfully to hold or sell another person "to involuntary servitude," and 18 U.S.C. section 241 (1988), which prohibits conspiracy to interfere with an individual's Thirteenth Amendment right to be free from "involuntary servitude."

33. Hamilton, above note 29, at 7.

34. See, e.g., United States v. Ancarola, 1 F. 676, 683 (C.C.S.D.N.Y. 1880) (considering the case of an eleven-year-old Italian boy held in involuntary servitude by a padrone due to his youth and dependence, which left him incapable of choosing alternatives).

35. United States v. Kozminski, 487 U.S. 931, 949–950 (1988). For an analysis of

combined psychological and economic coercion, see United States v. Shackney, 333 F.2d 475 (2d Cir. 1964).

36. Kozminski, 487 U.S. at 952.

37. See Kozminski, 487 U.S. at 952 (mental retardation); United States v. King, 840 F.2d 1276 (6th Cir.), cert. denied, 488 U.S. 894 (1988) (children); United States v. Mussry, 726 F.2d 1448, 1450 (9th Cir.), cert. denied, 469 U.S. 855 (1984) (non–English speaking, passports withheld, paid little money for services); Bernal v. United States, 241 F. 339, 341 (5th Cir. 1917), cert. denied, 245 U.S. 672 (1918) (alienage, no means of support, "did not know her way about town"); *Ancarola*, 1 F. at 676 (child).

38. No cases of involuntary servitude involve wealthy or solvent victims. For examples where the poverty of the victims is emphasized as both a precondition of the servitude and a product of it, see Kozminski, 487 U.S. at 935 ("Molitoris was living on the streets of Ann Arbor, Michigan, in the early 1970s when Ike Kozminski brought him to work . . ."); United States v. Warren, 772 F.2d 827, 832 (11th Cir. 1985), cert. denied, 475 U.S. 1022 (1986) ("Gaston could not leave because he had no money. . . . These accounts . . . revealed an operation where individuals were picked up under false pretenses, delivered to a labor camp to work long hours for little or no pay, and kept in the fields by poverty, alcohol, threats, and acts of violence.") (citations omitted); *Mussry*, 726 F.2d at 1450 (poor Indonesians paid little for services); United States v. Booker, 655 F.2d 562, 566 (4th Cir. 1981) (finding that migrant labor camp, into which laborers were abducted, fits vision of forced labor under statutes that protected "persons without property and without skills save those in tending the fields. With little education, little money and little hope . . ."); Pierce v. United States, 146 F.2d 84, 84 (5th Cir. 1944), cert. denied, 324 U.S. 873 (1945) (women who could not pay their own fines were released when pimp paid their fines, then forced them to work at his roadhouse); *Bernal*, 241 F. at 341 (low-paid woman fraudulently induced by promise of better pay to go to brothel where "[s]he had no money").

39. See generally Mussry, 726 F.2d 1448.

40. *Mussry*, 726 F.2d at 1450, 1453.

41. Kozminski, 487 U.S. at 952 (O'Connor, J., for the plurality); id., at 956 (Brennan, J., concurring).

42. Case of Mary Clark, 1 Blackf. 122 (Ind. 1821). See generally Hamilton, above note 29.

43. See, e.g., Mussry, 726 F.2d 1448. The later ruling by the Supreme Court in Kozminski, 487 U.S. 931, restricting *Mussry* doctrines does not cut back on this aspect of the courts' customary approach to this issue.

44. United States v. King, 840 F.2d 1276, 1281 (6th Cir. 1988), cert. denied, 488 U.S. 894 (1988) (finding a conspiracy to deprive children living in a religious commune of rights under Thirteenth Amendment, in part because of a belief by the children that they "had no viable alternative but to perform service for the defendants"). When physical force is also present, *Kozminski* poses no barrier to prosecution. Id. at 1281.

45. United States v. Bibbs, 564 F.2d 1165, 1168 (5th Cir. 1977), cert. denied, 435 U.S. 1007 (1978).

46. Hamilton, above note 29, at 7.

47. This term was apparently used originally to parallel and distinguish prostitution of all women, including women of color, from slavery of Africans as such. *Traite des Noires*, trade in Blacks, referred to slavery of African people; in 1905, *Traite des Blanches*, trade in whites, was used at an international conference to refer to sexual sale and purchase of women and children. Marlene D. Beckman, "The White Slave Traffic Act: The Historical Impact of a Criminal Law Policy on Women," 72 *Georgetown Law Journal* 1111 n.2 (1984) (citing V. Bullough, *Prostitution: An Illustrated History* 245 (1978)); Kathleen Barry, above note 4, at 32 (1979). The British government translated the latter term as "White Slave Traffic or Trade," then shortened it to white slavery. Beckman, above at 1111 n.2 (quoting Bullough, at 245). Whatever its initial intent, the appellation "had immediate appeal to racists who could and did conclude that the efforts were against an international traffic in *white* women," although women of all colors were exploited in prostitution. Barry, above note 4, at 32. Kathleen Barry further observes that the 1921 substitution of the term "Traffic in Women and Children" for white slavery worked to separate international trafficking in women from local prostitution, "thereby distracting attention from the continuing enslavement of women in local prostitution." Barry, above note 4, at 32–33. Recognizing prostitution as unconstitutional slavery would help restore attention to their indistinguishability in most significant respects.

48. Here I draw on Akhil Amar's and Daniel Widawsky's proposed working definition of slavery. Akhil Amar and Daniel Widawsky, "Child Abuse as Slavery: A Thirteenth Amendment Response to *DeShaney*," 105 *Harvard Law Review* 1359, 1365 (1992).

49. See generally Leidholdt, above note 28; Barry, above note 4, at 3–5; "Activities for the Advancement of Women: Equality, Development and Peace," U.N. ESCOR, 1st Sess., Provisional Agenda Item 12, at 7–8, U.N. Doc. E/1983/7 (1983).

50. For analogous situations, see Jaremillo v. Romero, 1 N.M. 190, 197–199 (1857) (involuntary servitude formally sanctioned by law). See also Taylor v. Georgia, 315 U.S. 25, 29–31 (1942) (striking down state laws that did not sanction involuntary servitude directly, but played a key role in it).

51. This raises a civil claim under 42 U.S.C. section 1983 (1981) and potential criminal prosecution under 18 U.S.C. section 242 (Supp. 1992).

52. "Activities for the Advancement of Women: Equality, Development and Peace," above note 49, at 8 (quoting testimony by three "collectives" of women prostitutes given to the Congress of Nice on September 8, 1981).

53. The Peonage Cases, 123 F. 671, 681 (M.D. Ala. 1903) (stating that the trier of fact "must consider the situation of the parties, the relative inferiority or inequality between the person contracting to perform the service and the person exercising the force or influence to compel its performance . . .").

54. See, e.g., Pierce v. United States, 146 F.2d 84 (5th Cir. 1944), cert. denied, 324 U.S. 873 (1945); Bernal v. United States, 241 F. 339 (5th Cir. 1917), cert. denied, 245 U.S. 672 (1918). See also United States v. Harris, 534 F.2d 207, 214 (10th Cir. 1975), cert. denied, 429 U.S. 941 (1976) (upholding conviction for involuntary servitude in prostitution context).

55. Pierce, 146 F.2d at 84.

56. Bernal, 241 F. at 341.

57. A grand jury in Austin, Texas, failed to indict a man for rape where the victim asked him to wear a condom. Apparently, the woman's request somehow implied her consent. Ross E. Milloy, "Furor over a Decision Not to Indict in a Rape Case," *New York Times*, Oct. 25, 1992, § 1 at 30. A second grand jury did indict the man for rape and he was later convicted in a jury trial. "Rapist Who Agreed to Use Condom Gets 40 Years," *New York Times*, May 15, 1993, § 1 at 6.

58. For data on rape in prostitution, see Leidholdt, above note 28, at 138; Mimi H. Silbert and Ayala M. Pines, "Occupational Hazards of Street Prostitutes," 8 *Criminal Justice and Behaviour* 395, 397 (1981) (70 percent of San Francisco street prostitutes reported rape by clients an average of 31 times); Council for Prostitution Alternatives, *1991 Annual Report* 4 (48 percent of prostitutes were raped by pimps an average of sixteen times a year, 79 percent by johns an average of thirty-three times a year). For data on beatings, see Silbert & Pines, above at 397 (65 percent of prostitutes beaten by customers); Council for Prostitution Alternatives, above at 4 (63 percent were beaten by pimps an average of fifty-eight times a year). For data on mortality, see *Pornography and Prostitution in Canada: Report of the Special Committee on Pornography and Prostitution, Volume II* 350 (1985) (finding that in Canada the mortality rate for prostituted women is forty times the national average); Leidholdt, above note 28, at 138 n.15 (the Justice Department estimates that a third of the over 4,000 women killed by serial murderers in 1982 were prostitutes).

59. See Mimi H. Silbert & Ayala M. Pines, "Entrance into Prostitution," 13 *Youth & Society* 471, 479 (1982) (60 percent of prostitutes were sexually abused in childhood); Leidholdt, above note 28, at 136 n.4 (quoting Mimi Silbert, *Sexual Assault of Prostitutes: Phase One* 40 (1980)) (66 percent of subjects are sexually assaulted by father or father figure); The Council for Prostitution Alternatives, *1991 Annual Report* 3 (85 percent of clients have histories of sexual abuse in childhood, 70 percent most frequently by their fathers).

60. See Cecilie Høigard and Liv Finstad, *Backstreets: Prostitution, Money, and Love* 76 (Katherine Hanson et al. trans., 1992) (average age of prostitutes interviewed in Norway began at 15½ years). Compare Leidholdt, above note 28, at 136 n.3 (citing Evelina Giobbe, founder of Minneapolis-based advocacy project, Women Hurt in Systems of Prostitution Engaged in Revolt (WHISPER)) (fourteen is the average age of women's entry into prostitution); Roberta Perkins, *Working Girls: Prostitutes, This Life and Social Control* 258 (1991) (finding in her Australian sample that almost half entered prostitution before age 20, and over 80 percent before age 25); Mimi H. Silbert and Ayala M. Pines, "Occupational Hazards of Street Prostitutes," 8 *Criminal Justice and Behaviour* 395, 396 (1981) (68 percent were sixteen years or younger when entered prostitution).

61. For a superb discussion of the "choice" illusion, see Leidholdt, above note 28, at 136–138.

62. For an argument that domestic battery of women is involuntary servitude, see Joyce E. McConnell, "Beyond Metaphor: Battered Woman, Involuntary Servitude, and the Thirteenth Amendment," 4 *Yale Journal of Law and Feminism* 207 (1992).

63. Bray v. Alexandria Women's Health Clinic, 122 L. Ed. 2d 34, 46, 47 n.2 (1993).

64. Evelina Giobbe, "Confronting the Liberal Lies About Prostitution," in *The Sexual Liberals and the Attack on Feminism* 67, 77 (Dorchen Leidholdt and Janice G. Raymond eds., 1990).

65. Leidholdt, above note 28, at 138–139.

66. See Andrea Dworkin and Catharine A. MacKinnon, *Pornography and Civil Rights: A New Day for Women's Equality* apps. A, B, & C (1988); Andrea Dworkin & Catharine A. MacKinnon, *In Harm's Way: The Pornography Civil Rights Hearings* (1997).

67. Fla. Stat. ch. 796.09 (1992) (providing a cause of action for those coerced into prostitution to sue their pimps for compensatory and punitive damages). *See* Margaret A. Baldwin, "Strategies of Connection: Prostitution and Feminist Politics," 1 *Michigan Journal of Gender and Law* 65, 70 (1993).

68. See Gayle Kirshenbaum, "A Potential Landmark for Female Human Rights," *Ms.*, Sept./Oct. 1991, at 13 (report on proposed U.N. Convention Against All Forms of Sexual Exploitation).

69. A proposed sexual exploitation convention would require states parties to adopt legislation to "hold liable" traffickers in pornography. International Convention to Eliminate All Forms of Sexual Exploitation, Sept. 1993, Art. 6(d).

14. The Logic of Experience: The Development of Sexual Harassment Law

This address was delivered to the Bicentennial Celebration for the Courts of the District of Columbia Circuit, 9 March 2001, Washington, D.C. It was first published in 90 *Georgetown Law Journal* 813 (2002). The research assistance and perceptive comments of Lisa Cardyn are gratefully acknowledged. Conversations with Kent Harvey were formative. The author participated in most of the cases discussed here. This essay is dedicated to the memory of my father, George E. MacKinnon, who served as Circuit Judge of the District of Columbia Circuit Court of Appeals from 1969 to 1995.

1. Oliver Wendell Holmes, *The Common Law* 167 (Mark DeWolfe Howe ed., 1963) (1881).

2. 413 F. Supp. 654 (D.D.C. 1976).

3. 561 F.2d 983 (D.C. Cir. 1977).

4. 641 F.2d 934 (D.C. Cir. 1981).

5. 753 F.2d 141 (D.C. Cir. 1985).

6. *Barnes*, 561 F.2d at 986–989.

7. Alexander v. Yale Univ., 459 F. Supp. 1 (D. Conn. 1977), *aff'd*, 631 F.2d 178 (2d Cir. 1980).

8. Woerner v. Brzeczek, 519 F. Supp. 517 (N.D. Ill. 1981).

9. 42 U.S.C. §2000e-2(a)(1) (1994).

10. See Franklin v. Gwinnett County Pub. Sch., 503 U.S. 60 (1992); Alexander, 631 F.2d at 180–184.

11. Reed v. Reed, 404 U.S. 71 (1971); Woerner, 519 F. Supp. at 519–522.

12. See generally Simeon E. Baldwin, *The History of the Common Law* (1906);

Derek Roebuck, *The Background of the Common Law* 2 (2d ed. 1990) (understanding the common law as a "creature of times and places, of economic forces and class interests, of battles for power between political factions and trials of wits between lawyers of great skill and inventiveness"); Oliver Wendell Holmes Jr., "The Path of the Law," 10 *Harvard Law Review* 457 (1897). Sir Frederick Pollock makes a similar point about law generally. See Frederick Pollock, *A First Book of Jurisprudence* chs. 1, 4 (6th ed. 1929); id. at 27 ("[T]he conception of law, many of its ideas, and much even of its form, are prior in history to the official intervention of the State . . .").

13. For discussion and documentation of this point, see Mathias Reimann, "Who Is Afraid of the Civil Law? Kontinentaleuropäisches Recht und Common Law im Spiegel der englischen Literatur seit 1500," 21 *Zeitschrift für Neuere Rechtsgeschichte* [ZNR] 357 (1999).

14. For some accounts of women's experiences of sexual harassment, see Martha J. Langelan, *Back Off! How to Confront and Stop Sexual Harassment and Harassers* (1993); and Celia Morris, *Bearing Witness: Sexual Harassment and Beyond—Everywoman's Story* (1994).

15. See, e.g., Norma Basch, *In the Eyes of the Law: Women, Marriage, and Property in Nineteenth-Century New York* 14–19, 27, 42–43, 48–49, 62, 68–69, 229–230 (1982); Reva B. Siegel, "The Rule of Love: Wife Beating as Prerogative and Privacy," 105 *Yale Law Journal* 2117 (1996); Carl Tobias, "Interspousal Tort Immunity in America," 23 *Georgia Law Review* 359 (1989); Lea VanderVelde, "The Legal Ways of Seduction," 48 *Stanford Law Review* 817 (1996); Sara L. Zeigler, "Wifely Duties: Marriage, Labor, and the Common Law in Nineteenth-Century America," 20 *Social Science History* 63 (1996); Cassandra M. DeLaMothe, Note, "*Liberta* Revisited: A Call to Repeal the Marital Exemption for All Sex Offenses in New York's Penal Law," 23 *Fordham Urban Law Journal* 857 (1996).

16. The insight may not have been original to Holmes, but surely was not his alone. Albert Alschuler notes that Holmes, in preparing his *Common Law* lectures, has been documented to have read Rudolph von Jhering, who said something strikingly similar. In addition, many Americans had said the same thing in substance, so that the pragmatic resistance to formalism and historicism embodied in the analysis were a common heritage at the time Holmes said it. See Albert W. Alschuler, *Law Without Values: The Life, Work, and Legacy of Justice Holmes* 92–103 (2000).

17. One prominent nineteenth-century women's rights newspaper regularly exposed the fallacy behind coverture's strictures. See "Justice to Women," *Woman's Journal*, Apr. 8, 1876, at 115, 115 ("The legal fiction which ignores every wife as one of the two heads of the family is jealously maintained . . . [and] gives rise to infinite injustice."); "Married Women and Law," *Woman's Journal*, July 13, 1878, at 222, 222 ("The old theory that Woman lost all her identity when she entered the bonds of matrimony has lost much of its patronage . . ."); "Ownership of Wives," *Woman's Journal*, Aug. 28, 1875, at 276, 276 ("The idea of the ownership of wives by their husbands still lingers, and causes more mischief and brutality than any other relic of barbarism.").

18. See, e.g., Tomkins v. Pub. Serv. Elec. & Gas Co., 422 F. Supp. 553 (D.N.J. 1976); Miller v. Bank of Am., 418 F. Supp. 233, 236 (N.D. Cal. 1976); Corne v. Bausch & Lomb, Inc., 390 F. Supp. 161 (D. Ariz. 1975); Barnes v. Train, 13 Fair Empl. Prac. Cas. (BNA) 123 (D.D.C. Aug. 9, 1974).

19. See generally Jack Greenberg, *Crusaders in the Courts: How a Dedicated Band of Lawyers Fought for the Civil Rights Revolution* (1994); Richard Kluger, *Simple Justice: The History of Brown v. Board of Education and Black America's Struggle for Equality* (1975).

20. On the history of the Black civil rights movement, see generally Taylor Branch, *Parting the Waters: America in the King Years, 1954–63* (1988); and Taylor Branch, *Pillar of Fire: America in the King Years, 1963–65* (1998).

21. The history of the modern women's movement is chronicled in Ruth Rosen, *The World Split Open: How the Modern Women's Movement Changed America* (2000).

22. See id. at 143–226.

23. See Catharine A. MacKinnon, *Sexual Harassment of Working Women* 164–174 (1979). That no state tort law on these facts existed for sexual harassment law to supercede or displace also meant that the creation of the federal cause of action created no concern among the guardians of federalism. After federal courts recognized sexual harassment under federal law, states began to prohibit it as well, usually under state sex discrimination prohibitions. For a useful analysis of the development of federal common law, including its potential to complement rather than conflict with state law and to work with rather than against state tort claims, see Martha A. Field, "Sources of Law: The Scope of Federal Common Law," 99 *Harvard Law Review* 881 (1986). The classic discussion is Henry J. Friendly, "In Praise of Erie—and of the New Federal Common Law," 39 *New York University Law Review* 383 (1964).

24. See, e.g., Angela Davis, "Reflections on the Black Woman's Role in the Community of Slaves," *Black Scholar*, Dec. 1971, at 2, 12–14.

25. See Lisa Cardyn, "Sexualized Racism/Gendered Violence: Outraging the Body Politic in the Reconstruction South," 100 *Michigan Law Review* 675 (2002).

26. The groups were Working Women United, at Cornell University, and Alliance Against Sexual Coercion, in the Boston area. The article was Claire Safron, "What Men Do to Women on the Job," *Redbook*, Nov. 1976, at 149.

27. See Barnes v. Costle, 561 F.2d 983 (D.C. Cir. 1977); Williams v. Saxbe, 413 F. Supp. 654 (D.D.C. 1976).

28. Williams, 413 F. Supp. at 655–657.

29. Id. at 657–658.

30. Id. at 662.

31. See Williams v. Bell, 587 F.2d 1240 (D.C. Cir. 1978).

32. See, e.g., Tomkins v. Pub. Serv. Elec. & Gas Co., 422 F. Supp. 553, 556–557 (D.N.J. 1976); Miller v. Bank of Am., 418 F. Supp. 233, 236 (N.D. Cal. 1976); Corne v. Bausch & Lomb, Inc., 390 F. Supp. 161, 163–164 (D. Ariz. 1975).

33. See Tomkins, 422 F. Supp. at 556; Corne, 390 F. Supp. at 163.

34. Barnes v. Costle, 561 F.2d 983, 989 (D.C. Cir. 1977).

35. Id. at 990 n.55.

36. 510 U.S. 17 (1993).

37. Id. at 25 (Ginsburg, J., concurring).

38. 523 U.S. 75, 80 (1998).

39. Tomkins v. Pub. Serv. Elec. & Gas Co., 568 F.2d 1044, 1047 (3d Cir. 1977).

40. Id. (citation omitted) (quoting Appellees' Brief at 8) (rejecting this argument urged by appellees).

41. Tomkins v. Pub. Serv. Elec. & Gas Co., 422 F. Supp. 553, 556 (D.N.J. 1976).

42. Barnes v. Costle, 561 F.2d 983, 990 n.55 (D.C. Cir. 1977) (distinguishing the "bisexual superior" whose "insistence upon sexual favors would not constitute gender discrimination because it would apply to male and female employees alike").

43. Williams v. Saxbe, 413 F. Supp. 654, 659 n.6 (D.D.C. 1976).

44. Barnes, 561 F.2d at 990.

45. See Miller v. Bank of Am., 600 F.2d 211 (9th Cir. 1979); Corne v. Bausch & Lomb, Inc., 562 F.2d 55 (9th Cir. 1977) (vacating the district court); Tomkins v. Pub. Serv. Elec. & Gas Co., 568 F.2d 1044 (3d Cir. 1977).

46. The group basis of the individual claim was a point missed by the *Barnes* concurrence, which treated sexual harassment as a tort for purposes of employer liability. See Barnes, 561 F.2d at 995–1001 (MacKinnon, J., concurring).

47. See Barnes, 561 F.2d at 994.

48. See Nichols v. Frank, 42 F.3d 503, 511 (9th Cir. 1994) (emphasis omitted); see also Farpella-Crosby v. Horizon Health Care, 97 F.3d 803, 806 n.2 (5th Cir. 1996) (deeming heterosexual sexual harassment "unquestionably based on gender").

49. Since *Barnes*, in those few cases in which defendants have attempted to make the so-called bisexuality of an alleged perpetrator a defense, courts have often concluded that the abuse was unequally distributed by sex. See, e.g., Steiner v. Showboat Operating Co., 25 F.3d 1459, 1464 (9th Cir. 1994) ("And while his abuse of men in no way related to their gender, his abuse of female employees . . . centered on the fact that they were females"); Kopp v. Samaritan Health Sys., Inc., 13 F.3d 264, 269 (8th Cir. 1993) ("On this record, a fact-finder could conclude that Albaghdadi's treatment of women is worse than his treatment of men"); Chiapuzio v. BLT Operating Corp., 826 F. Supp. 1334, 1337 (D. Wyo. 1993) ("This Court would not so much characterize Bell as a bisexual harasser, but simply as an 'equal-opportunity' harasser whose remarks were gender-driven").

50. Oncale v. Sundowner Offshore Servs., Inc., 523 U.S. 75, 80 (1998) ("We have never held that workplace harassment, even harassment between men and women, is automatically discrimination because of sex merely because the words used have sexual content or connotations").

51. Bundy v. Jackson, 641 F.2d 934, 943 (D.C. Cir. 1981) (emphasis omitted) (internal quotation marks omitted). Apparently unbeknownst to the *Bundy* court, the district court in Brown v. City of Guthrie, 22 Fair Empl. Prac. Cas. (BNA) 1627 (W.D. Okla. May 30, 1980), in language that tracks the EEOC guidelines, previously held that

"sexual harassment that permeates the workplace thereby creating an intimidating, hostile, or offensive working environment should be deemed an impermissible condition of employment." Id. at 1632. That case itself, however, involved a constructive discharge. See id. at 1631.

52. See 42 U.S.C. §1981a (1994) (providing compensatory and punitive damages for discrimination).

53. Bundy v. Jackson, 19 Fair Empl. Prac. Cas. (BNA) 828, 831 (D.D.C. Apr. 25, 1979) (internal quotation marks omitted).

54. Bundy, 641 F.2d at 944.

55. 477 U.S. 57 (1986).

56. Id. at 64 (alteration in original) (quoting 42 U.S.C. § 2000e-2(a)(1)). A similar trajectory, if longer and more complex, can be traced on the employer liability issue, although there the D.C. Circuit's *Vinson* wisdom was less fully embraced by the Supreme Court in its opinions in Faragher v. City of Boca Raton, 524 U.S. 775 (1998), and Burlington Industries, Inc. v. Ellerth, 524 U.S. 742 (1998)—promoting equality less securely as a result. In its attention to tort standards for liability, *Faragher* may be seen as the heir more of the *Barnes* concurrence than of the majority. The employer liability issue also marks the largest deviation from D.C. Circuit holdings, which, however, thankfully included the Supreme Court's rejection of the D.C. Circuit's panel opinion in Gary v. Long, 59 F.3d 1391 (D.C. Cir. 1995). See Faragher, 524 U.S. at 793–794 (1998) (criticizing that court and others for having "typically held, or assumed, that conduct similar to the subject of [Faragher's] complaint falls outside the scope of employment").

57. Vinson v. Taylor, 753 F.2d 141, 146 n.36 (D.C. Cir. 1985) (citations omitted).

58. Id. at 150.

59. Meritor, 477 U.S. at 69, 72–73.

60. Faragher, 524 U.S. at 802–805; Ellerth, 524 U.S. at 764–766. The EEOC Enforcement Guidance may mitigate this effect somewhat. See EEOC Enforcement Guidance: Vicarious Employer Liability for Unlawful Harassment by Supervisors, EEOC Compl. Man. (BNA) N:4075 (June 18, 1999).

61. See generally Janine Benedet, "Hostile Environment Sexual Harassment Claims and the Unwelcome Influence of Rape Law," 3 *Michigan Journal of Gender and Law* 125, 165–167 (1995); Louise F. Fitzgerald and Suzanne Swan, "Why Didn't She Just Report Him? The Psychological and Legal Implications of Women's Responses to Sexual Harassment," 51 *Journal of Social Issues* 117, 120–123 (1995).

62. Unsuccessful prior attempts were Tomkins v. Public Service Electric & Gas Co., 422 F. Supp. 553 (D.N.J. 1976); Miller v. Bank of America, 418 F. Supp. 233 (N.D. Cal. 1976); Corne v. Bausch & Lomb, Inc., 390 F. Supp. 161 (D. Ariz. 1975); and, of course Barnes v. Train, 13 Fair Empl. Prac. Cas. (BNA) 123 (D.D.C. Aug. 9, 1974).

63. Barnes v. Costle, 561 F.2d 983, 989 n.49 (D.C. Cir. 1977). The sentence continued "but from the fact that he imposed upon her tenure in her then position a condition which ostensibly he would not have fastened upon a male employee." Id.

64. See Holmes, above note 1, at 4–5, 10–11, 37; Oliver Wendell Holmes, "Law in Science and Science in Law," 12 *Harvard Law Review* 443, 450–452 (1899).

65. This is not to imply that sexual harassment cases are disparate treatment cases or that disparate treatment straitjackets should be applied to them more stringently than they have been. Far from it—sexual harassment cases illustrate how the disparate treatment–disparate impact division, in concept and proof, does not adequately encompass much discrimination as it is socially practiced.

66. As discussed earlier in this essay, an instance of this test was articulated by Justice Ruth Bader Ginsburg, concurring in *Harris*, and embraced by the majority in *Oncale*. "The critical issue, Title VII's text indicates, is whether members of one sex are exposed to disadvantageous terms or conditions of employment to which members of the other sex are not exposed." Oncale v. Sundowner Offshore Servs., Inc., 523 U.S. 75, 80 (1998) (quoting Harris v. Forklift Systems, Inc., 510 U.S. 17, 25 (1993) (Ginsburg, J., concurring)) (internal quotation marks omitted). Exactly what in Title VII's text so indicates is unclear. Nothing in Title VII's text indicates that the term "discrimination" is so limited. Both sexes are routinely exposed to pornography at work without vitiating its discriminatory effect on women, for example. See, e.g., Robinson v. Jacksonville Shipyards, 760 F. Supp. 1486, 1523 (M.D. Fla. 1991). Certainly, when one sex is exposed to disadvantageous terms or conditions of employment and the other sex is not, discrimination has unquestionably occurred. Whether this is always "the critical issue" under Title VII, or even whether it is always necessary, is less clear. Perhaps the answer here is that one sex can be differentially exposed to disadvantage in conditions because of sex, even if both sexes are exposed to the same condition.

67. See Oncale, 523 U.S. at 78–82.

68. Rogers v. EEOC, 454 F.2d 234 (5th Cir. 1971).

69. See, e.g., Bolden v. PRC Inc., 43 F.3d 545 (10th Cir. 1994); Snell v. Suffolk County, 782 F.2d 1094 (2d Cir. 1986); Walker v. Ford Motor Co., 684 F.2d 1355 (11th Cir. 1982); Harris v. Int'l Paper Co., 765 F. Supp. 1509 (D. Me. 1991).

70. For a few instances, see Torres v. Pisano, 116 F.3d 625 (2d Cir. 1997); Watkins v. Bowden, 105 F.3d 1344 (11th Cir. 1997); and Hicks v. Gates Rubber Co., 833 F.2d 1406 (10th Cir. 1987).

71. Examples of gendered terms as evidence of sex stereotyping as discrimination are abundant, for example, in Price Waterhouse v. Hopkins, 490 U.S. 228 (1989). Quoting from the record before Judge Gesell in the D.C. district court, the Court noted, "One partner described her as 'macho'; another suggested that she 'overcompensated for being a woman'; a third advised her to take 'a course at charm school.'" Id. at 235 (citations omitted); see also Nadine Taub, "Keeping Women in Their Place: Stereotyping Per Se as a Form of Employment Discrimination," 21 *Boston College Law Review* 345 (1980) (providing more examples).

72. See McKinney v. Dole, 765 F.2d 1129, 1138–1139 (D.C. Cir. 1985). Cases routinely hold accordingly. See, e.g., Hall v. Gus Constr. Co., 842 F.2d 1010, 1014 (8th Cir. 1988) ("[O]ther courts of appeals have held that the predicate acts underlying a sexual harassment claim need not be clearly sexual in nature. . . . [N]one of our pre-

vious cases hold that the offensive conduct must have explicit sexual overtones"); Cline v. Gen. Elec. Capital Auto Lease, Inc., 757 F. Supp. 923, 931–933 (N.D. Ill. 1991) (finding what it calls gender harassment to be based on sex as a form of sexual harassment of plaintiff "because she was a woman"); Accardi v. Superior Court, 21 Cal. Rptr. 2d 292, 293 (Ct. App. 1993) (finding "[s]exual harassment does not necessarily involve sexual conduct. . . . [W]e hold that sexual harassment occurs when an employer creates a hostile environment for an employee because of that employee's sex").

73. 510 U.S. 17 (1993).

74. Id. at 19 (internal quotation marks omitted).

75. Oncale v. Sundowner Offshore Servs., Inc., 523 U.S. 75, 80 (1998).

76. See Nichols v. Azteca Rest. Enters., Inc., 256 F.3d 864 (9th Cir. 2001).

77. See, e.g., Davis v. Monroe County Bd. of Educ., 526 U.S. 629 (1999) (holding schools liable to students for peer harassment under Title IX when authorities are deliberately indifferent to known acts and harasser is under the school's disciplinary authority); United States v. Virginia, 518 U.S. 515 (1996) (stating that sex-based "classifications may not be used, as they once were, to create or perpetuate the legal, social, and economic inferiority of women" (citation omitted); see also Planned Parenthood v. Casey, 505 U.S. 833, 892–895 (1992) (plurality opinion) (rejecting spousal notification requirement because of abuse of wives by some husbands as undue burden on right to abortion).

78. See, e.g., General Recommendation No. 19, Convention on the Elimination of All Forms of Discrimination Against Women (CEDAW), 11th Sess., Agenda Item 7, at 2, U.N. Doc. CEDAW/C/1992/L.1/Add. 15 (1992).

79. Although to date less prominent, other cogent D.C. Circuit sexual harassment decisions also belong in this tradition, including Judge Harry Edwards's decision in King v. Palmer, 778 F.2d 878, 881 (D.C. Cir. 1985) (holding that unlawful sex discrimination occurs whenever sex is a substantial factor in the promotion of one employee over coworkers); and Judge John Pratt's decision in Broderick v. Ruder, 685 F. Supp. 1269, 1280 (D.D.C. 1988) (holding that exchange of consensual sexual relations for tangible employment benefits can and did create sexually hostile working environment for other workers).

80. Fukuoka Chiho Sainbansho, 783 Hanrei Taimuzu 60 (Fukuoka Dist. Ct., Apr. 16, 1992).

81. Vishaka v. State of Rajasthan, (1997) 6 S.C.C. 241.

82. C. Pén. art. 222–233 Titre II; C. Trav. art. L. 122–146 (criminal provision; equality not mentioned).

83. *Prevention of Sexual Harassment Law*, 1998, S.H. 166 (predicating civil and criminal provisions on equality and dignity).

84. The D.C. Circuit handed down its decision in Bundy v. Jackson, 641 F.2d 934 (D.C. Cir. 1981), on January 12, 1981; the district court opinion in the case, 19 Fair Empl. Prac. Cas. (BNA) 828 (D.D.C. Apr. 25, 1979), is dated April 25, 1979. In her testimony before the Senate Judiciary Committee, Anita Hill described being sexually harassed at various points in 1981, when she was employed at the Department of Education, and throughout the fall and winter months of 1982, after she had transferred

to the EEOC. See Nomination of Judge Clarence Thomas to Be Associate Justice of the Supreme Court of the United States: Hearings Before the Senate Comm. on the Judiciary, 102d Cong., 1st Sess., pt. 4, at 36–41 (1991) (testimony of Anita F. Hill).

85. See Jones v. Clinton, 990 F. Supp. 657 (E.D. Ark. 1998).

86. See EEOC, Trends in Harassment Charges Filed with the EEOC During the 1980s and 1990s, at http://www.eeoc.gov/stats/harassment.html.

87. Holmes, "The Path of Law" at 466.

88. See *Prevention of Sexual Harassment Law*, 1998, S.H. 166.

89. Baldwin, *History* at 17.

90. Id. at 11 (defining the Anglo-American common law as "a history of public custom").

91. Holmes, "The Path of Law" at 472.

15. On Accountability for Sexual Harassment

This analysis was published in its original form by the American Bar Association as "New Developments in Sexual Harassment Law," 7 *Perspectives* 8 (Fall 1998).

1. Barnes v. Costle, 561 F.2d 983 (D.C. Cir. 1977); Meritor Savings Bank, FSB v. Vinson, 477 U.S. 57 (1986).

2. Alexander v. Yale University, 631 F.2d 178 (2d Cir. 1980); Franklin v. Gwinnett County Public Schools, 503 U.S. 60 (1992).

3. 524 U.S. 775 (1998).

4. 524 U.S. 742 (1998).

5. 524 U.S. 274 (1998).

6. Does v. Covington County Sch. Bd., 969 F. Supp. 1264 (M.D. Ala. 1970); Pell v. Trustees of Columbia University, No. 97 Civ. 0193(55), 1998 WL 19989, at *14 (S.D.N.Y. Jan. 21, 1998) ("[t]here is no question that plaintiff has pled a prima facie case of quid pro [quo] harassment. Hausman was plaintiff's thesis advisor and in that capacity had supervisory authority over plaintiff."); Lawrence v. Central Connecticut State University, 1997 WL 527356 (D. Conn. 1997); Mary M. v. North Lawrence Community School Corp., 131 F.3d 1220 (7th Cir. 1997); Patricia H. v. Berkeley Unified School Dist., 830 F. Supp. 1288 (N.D. Cal. 1993) ("[t]he very severity of the molestation, and the grave disparity in age and power between the girls and Hamilton, suggests that a reasonable student, having experienced such an assault, would be intimidated and fearful of Hamilton's presence at her school, so much so that her fear would interfere with her ability to learn, and to enjoy all aspects of her education fully, even though the alleged molestations were isolated in time and occurred outside of the school setting"); Marsh v. Dallas Independent School Dist., 1997 WL 118416 (N.D. Tex. 1997); Doe v. Berkeley County School Dist., 989 F. Supp. 768 (D.S.C. 1997); Deborah O. v. Lake Central School Corp., No. 94–3804, 1995 WL 431414 (unreported), 61 F.3d 905 (7th Cir. 1995) (per curiam) (table); Davis ex rel. Doe v. DeKalb County School Dist., 996 F. Supp. 1478 (N.D. Ga. 1998); Rosa H. v. San Elizario Independent School Dist., 106 F.3d 648 (5th Cir. 1997); Kracunas v. Iona College, 119 F.3d 80, 89 (2d Cir. 1997) ("he exploited his professorial authority by asking Kracunas to come with him to

his office to retrieve reading material and then harassing her"); Smith v. Metropolitan School Dist. of Perry Twp., 128 F.3d 1014 (7th Cir. 1997) ("This occurred in his office in the school building during the class period in which she was assigned as his student assistant. . . . Throughout the school year, the two had sex about twice a week, always (except for two occasions) on school premises"); Wentz v. Park County School Dist. No. 16, 968 F.2d 22, 1992 WL 149914, at **1 (10th Cir. 1992) (unpublished) (male teacher allegedly entered male former student's room, "told Rodman what he was doing was 'educational,' and proceeded to sexually assault Rodman"); Seneway v. Canon McMillan School Dist., 969 F. Supp. 325 (W.D. Pa. 1997). See also Micari v. Mann, 481 N.Y.S.2d 967, 972 (Sup. Ct. 1984) (in state tort action, "defendant, a person with a distinguished reputation as an acting teacher, abused the relationship which he, as a teacher with overpowering influence over his students, possessed").

7. Catharine A. MacKinnon, "The Logic of Experience: Reflections on the Development of Sexual Harassment Law," 90 *Georgetown Law Journal* 813, 821 n.45 (2002) (collecting cases).

8. *Gebser*, 524 U.S. at 290–291.

9. *Meritor*, 477 U.S. at 60, 68; Nichols v. Frank, 42 F.3d 503 (9th Cir. 1994); Karibian v. Columbia University, 14 F.3d 773 (2d Cir. 1994); Thoreson v. Penthouse Int'l. Magazine, Ltd., 563 N.Y.S.2d 968 (N.Y. Sup. Ct. 1990); Gilardi v. Schroeder, 672 F. Supp. 1043 (N.D. Ill. 1986); Moylan v. Maries Co., 792 F.2d 746 (8th Cir. 1986); Chamberlin v. 101 Realty, 915 F.2d 777 (1st Cir. 1990); Phillips v. Smalley Maintenance Servs., 711 F.2d 1524 (11th Cir. 1983); Showalter v. Allison Reed Group, 56 FEP Cases 989 (D.R.I. 1991); Cummings v. Walsh Constr. Co., 561 F. Supp. 872 (S.D. Ga. 1983); Westmoreland Coal Co. v. West Virginia Human Rights Comm'n, 382 S.E.2d 562 (W. Va. 1989).

10. Keppler v. Hinsdale Twp. H.S. Dist. 86, 715 F. Supp. 862 (N.D. Ill. 1989); Babcock v. Frank, 729 F. Supp. 279 (S.D.N.Y. 1990); Boddy v. Dean, 821 F.2d 346 (6th Cir. 1987); Prichard v. Ledford, 55 FEP Cases 755 (E.D. Tenn. 1990); Shrout v. Black Clawson Co., 689 F. Supp. 774 (S.D. Ohio 1988); Williams v. Civiletti, 487 F. Supp. 1387 (D.D.C. 1980).

11. Wilson v. Wayne Co., 856 F. Supp. 1254, 1261 (M.D. Tenn. 1994) (so holding and reviewing cases); Grant v. Lone Star Co., 21 F.3d 649 (5th Cir. 1994); Miller v. Maxwell's International, Inc., 991 F.2d 583 (9th Cir. 1991); Czupih v. Card Pak Inc., 916 F. Supp. 687 (N.D. Ohio 1996); Johnson v. Northern Indiana Public Service Co., 844 F. Supp. 466 (N.D. Ind. 1994); Lowry v. Clark, 843 F. Supp. 228 (E.D. Ky. 1994).

16. Beyond Moralism: Directions in Sexual Harassment Law

Originally published as the afterword to *Directions in Sexual Harassment Law* (Catharine A. MacKinnon and Reva B. Siegel, eds., 2003) (*Directions*). Insightful readings by Kent Harvey, Cass Sunstein, Marc Spindelman, and John Stoltenberg improved this essay. The resourceful and creative research and technical assistance of Kristal Otto, Jennifer Thornton, and Jane Yoon are gratefully acknowledged.

1. Places in which sexual harassment occurs but is generally not actionable include

doctors' and lawyers' offices, religious settings, and on the street. See Nan D. Stein, *Classrooms and Courtrooms: Facing Sexual Harassment in K–12 Schools* (1999); Cynthia Grant Bowman, "Street Harassment and the Informal Ghettoization of Women," 106 *Harvard Law Review* 517 (1993).

2. Louise Fitzgerald et al., "Why Didn't She Just Report Him?," 51 *Journal of Social Issues* 117 (1995).

3. U.S. Merit Systems Protection Board, *Sexual Harassment in the Federal Workplace: Trends, Progress, Continuing Challenges* 14 (1995) (42 percent of women federal employees studied in 1980, 42 percent in 1987, 44 percent in 1994 reported experiencing sexual harassment).

4. See generally Ian Shapiro, *Democratic Justice* (1999), for creative ideas on this subject.

5. This being the language of Title VII, 42 U.S.C. §2000e-2 (West 1994).

6. Even the assessment of punitive damages is not simply based on a judgment of moral reprehensibility, but involves a more precise assessment that an employer was malicious or recklessly indifferent in knowingly violating federal law. See, e.g., Kolstad v. American Dental Association, 527 U.S. 526 (1999) (rejecting requirement that employer conduct must be "egregious" and clarifying malice and reckless indifference to federal law as punitive damages test under 42 U.S.C. §1981a(b)(1)); EEOC v. Wal-Mart Stores, Inc., 187 F.3d 1241, 1244 (10th Cir. 1999) (holding that punitive damages are available under Title VII where employer engaged in intentional discrimination with malice or reckless indifference to federally protected rights, citing *Kolstad*).

7. See Diana E. H. Russell, *The Secret Trauma: Incest in the Lives of Girls and Women* 61 (1986) ("Thirty-eight percent (357) of the 930 women reported at least one experience of incestuous and/or extra familial sexual abuse before reaching the age of eighteen years"). Similarly, because rape is inconsistent with the conventional idea of marriage and ought not happen by its moral rules, rape in marriage has traditionally been exempted from coverage by the rape law. And, where rape in marriage can be formally charged, actual rapes in marriage are not recognized as having occurred in case after case.

8. The invalidation in 2000 of the civil remedy provision of the Violence Against Women Act because it reached the "private" is just one of countless examples. See United States v. Morrison, 529 U.S. 598 (2000).

9. See General Recommendation No 19, Convention on the Elimination of All Forms of Discrimination Against Women (CEDAW), 11th Sess., Agenda Item 7, U.N. Doc. CEDAW/C/1992/L.1/Add. 15 (1992), including at ¶¶23 and 24, and under necessary measures, §1(a). See also Europe's binding directive, Directive 2002/73/EC Amending the 1976 Directive on Equal Treatment of Men and Women, art. 1.

10. Nichols v. Frank, 42 F.3d 503, 511 (9th Cir. 1994); Farpella-Crosby v. Horizon Health Care, 97 F.3d 803, 806 n.2 (5th Cir. 1996) (deeming heterosexual sexual harassment "unquestionably based on gender").

11. See Catharine A. MacKinnon, *Sexual Harassment of Working Women: A Case of Sex Discrimination* 164–174 (1979); Corne v. Bausch & Lomb Inc., 390 F. Supp. 161, 162–163 (D. Ariz. 1975).

12. See Kate Millett, *Sexual Politics* (1970).

13. See Abigail Saguy, "French and American Lawyers Define Sexual Harassment," in *Directions* 602.

14. See Yukiko Tsunoda, "Sexual Harassment in Japan," in *Directions* 618.

15. See Martha Nussbaum, "The Modesty of Mrs. Bajaj: India's Problematic Route to Sexual Harassment Law," in *Directions* 633.

16. Presumably, too, if traditional morality actually opposed abuse through sex because it was sexual, rape laws would be effective and sexual harassment would have been recognized as a legal claim long before it was.

17. In one study of almost 650 federal opinions from 1986 to 1995, physical harassment of a "sexual nature" is found to have a lower win rate at trial than does physical harassment of a "nonsexual nature," a differential that climbs to 24.4 percent on appeal, where 46.2 percent of sexual cases are won compared with 70.6 percent of nonsexual cases involving physical contact. Ann Juliano and Stewart J. Schwab, "The Sweep of Sexual Harassment Cases," 86 *Cornell Law Review* 548, 596 App. A (2001). Oral comments about individuals that are nonsexual similarly showed a slightly higher win rate at trial than did oral comments about individuals that are sexual, while the win rate on appeal for the nonsexual comments is over 10 percent higher. Id. It is only through the conflation of group-based comments with nonsexual behaviors that the authors are able to suggest that they found that courts have not acknowledged harassment premised upon nonsexual behavior. See, e.g., id. at 555. Their data document the opposite. Less favorable work assignments do show a slightly lower win rate (55.9 percent) than do the more sexualized forms of abuse, but requests for dates, regarded by the authors as sexual, is lower still (53.0 percent). Actually, most cases for less favorable work assignments are properly litigated as sex discrimination per se or under labor agreements; virtually no sexual harassment cases claim such behavior alone. The meaningfulness of data that separates such factors is thus questionable. Some individual judges, seeming to miss the doctrinal reality that the term "sexual" in equality law refers to sexuality and gender alike, do wrongly believe that gender-based but nonsexual harassment is not covered by Title VII. An illustration is Williams v. General Motors Corp., 187 F.3d 553, 569 (6th Cir. 1999) (Ryan, J., dissenting).

18. Examples of sex stereotyping as discrimination are abundant in Price Waterhouse v. Hopkins, 490 U.S. 228 (1989), which also held that direct evidence shifted the burden of disproving discrimination to the defendant. The D.C. District Court opinion by Judge Gesell notes that, despite considerable positive feedback, "[t]here were clear signs . . . that some of the partners reacted negatively to Hopkins' personality because she was a woman. One partner described her as 'macho' . . . ; another suggested that she 'overcompensated for being a woman' . . . ; a third advised her to take 'a course at charm school.'" 490 U.S. at 235. See also Robinson v. Jacksonville Shipyards, 760 F. Supp. 1486 (M.D. Fla. 1991); Nichols v. Azteca Restaurant Ent., 256 F.3d 864 (9th Cir. 2001) (holding gay sexual harassment to be sex stereotyping hence sex discrimination); Nadine Taub, "Keeping Women in Their Place: Stereotyping as a Form of

Employment Discrimination," 21 *Boston College Law Review* 345 (1980); 2 *EEOC Compliance Manual* §615.6 (October 1981) (distinguishing sexual harassment from nonsexual sex-based harassment, affirming the latter is illegal).

19. For further discussion, see Catharine A. MacKinnon, "Feminism, Marxism, Method and the State: An Agenda for Theory," 7 *Signs: Journal of Women in Culture and Society* 515 (1982); Catharine A. MacKinnon, "Feminism, Marxism, Method and the State: Toward Feminist Jurisprudence," 8 *Signs: Journal of Women in Culture and Society* 635 (1983).

20. The leading case is McKinney v. Dole, 765 F.2d 1129, 1138–1139 (D.C. Cir. 1985). The obviousness of this position animated the U.S. Supreme Court decision in *Harris.* See Harris v. Forklift Systems, Inc., 510 U.S. 17 (1993) (reversing a lower court ruling, No. 3:89–0557, 1990 U.S. Dist. LEXIS 20115 at *5–*7, that found comments including "You're a dumb ass woman" not actionable as sexual harassment). The Court also could not have been more clear that sexual desire, at least, is not requisite for a sexual harassment claim than it was in *Oncale*, "harassing conduct need not be motivated by sexual desire to support an inference of discrimination on the basis of sex." Oncale v. Sundowner Offshore Services, Inc., 523 U.S. 75, 80 (1998). On the clear coverage of gender-based but not sexual forms of harassment under sexual harassment law, see Hall v. Gus Construction Co., 842 F.2d 1010, 1014 (8th Cir. 1988) ("[O]ther courts of appeals have held that the predicate acts underlying a sexual harassment claim need not be clearly sexual in nature. . . . [N]one of our previous cases hold that the offensive conduct must have explicit sexual overtones"); Hicks v. Gates Rubber Co., 833 F.2d 1406, 1414 (10th Cir. 1987); Cline v. General Electric Capital Auto Lease, Inc., 757 F. Supp. 923, 931–932 (N.D. Ill. 1991) (finding what it calls gender harassment to be based on sex as a form of sexual harassment of plaintiff "because she was a woman"); Accardi v. Superior Court of California, 21 Cal. Rptr. 2d 292, 293 (Cal. Ct. App. 1993) (finding "[s]exual harassment does not necessarily involve sexual conduct. . . . [W]e hold that sexual harassment occurs when an employer creates a hostile environment for an employee because of that employee's sex"). Cases so hold in the First Circuit, Lipsett v. University of Puerto Rico, 864 F.2d 881, 905 (1st Cir. 1988); Eleventh Circuit, Henson v. City of Dundee, 682 F.2d 897, 904 (11th Cir. 1982); Third Circuit, Andrews v. City of Philadelphia, 895 F.2d 1469, 1485 (3d Cir. 1990); and Sixth Circuit, Williams v. General Motors Corp., 187 F.3d 553, 565 (6th Cir. 1999) ("conduct underlying a sexual harassment claim need not be overtly sexual in nature . . . harassing behavior that is not sexually explicit but is directed at women and motivated by discriminatory animus against women satisfies the 'based on sex' requirement"). See also EEOC Decision No. 71–2725, 1973 EEOC Dec. (CCH) 6290 (June 30, 1971).

21. Vicki Schultz, "Reconceptualizing Sexual Harassment," 107 *Yale Law Journal* 1683 (1998), advances the contrary view, arguing that sexual harassment law's focus on sexual forms of harassment has fostered neglect of gender-based but not sexual forms. At once minimizing the clarity of precedents that squarely and repeatedly hold both actionable, while missing the considerable abuse that *is* sexual that courts permit,

the article, in its zeal to recoup the sexual and expand legal attention to gendered but not sexual abuse, becomes what it criticizes, as gender is disaggregated from sex. It also becomes a purported authority for the proposition it opposes, that gender harassment is not widely recognized as sexual harassment.

Some cases cited by Schultz as excluding nonsexual but sex-based acts actually include them. Boarman v. Sullivan, 769 F. Supp. 904 (D. Md. 1991), for example, is cited as revealing Schultz's criticized "disaggregation of the sexual from the nonsexual." Id. at 1713–1714. The case found the acts alleged were insufficiently severe to constitute an abusive working environment. One alleged act was nonsexual ("on one occasion her supervisor remarked that a woman's film which she intended to show was stupid, and kept people from their work"); the other, however, was sexual (he "asked her to close his office door and remove all of her clothing"). 769 F. Supp. at 910. Whether or not the court was correct to find these acts insufficiently severe to be actionable, both sexual and nonsexual acts were so found. If the court was insensitive to gender, it was also insensitive to sex.

Similarly, Raley v. Board of St. Mary's County Commissioner, 752 F. Supp. 1272 (D. Md. 1990), is cited as authority for the proposition that "nonsexual forms of hostility escape judicial scrutiny altogether. . . . Harmful acts of hazing and harassment frequently fall between the cracks of legal analysis altogether." Schultz, 107 *Yale Law Journal* at 1721. The *Raley* assignment of clerical work outside the plaintiff's job description, unsatisfactory job evaluations, and a letter of reprimand are cited as examples of nonsexual acts that neither rose to the level of hostile environment nor constituted disparate treatment. Id. at 1721 n.182. Wholly apart from their nonsexual nature, such actions may or may not be based on sex, and they may or may not constitute harassment by a variety of other measures. But incidents of *sexual* touching of the plaintiff were also found by the *Raley* court to be "isolated," hence insufficiently severe or pervasive to be actionable. 752 F. Supp. at 1280, unremarked by Schultz. No doubt much harassment is not caught by courts, but the fault may be something Schultz shares with the cases she criticizes: not seeing sexual abuse that is there.

Some cases cited by Schultz in support of the proposition that "[m]any other cases have held expressly that conduct that is not sexual in nature does not—and cannot—constitute hostile work environment sexual harassment," Schultz, 107 *Yale Law Journal* at 1718, the core thesis of the article, do not so hold. In Holmes v. Razo, No. 94 C 50405, 1995 U.S. Dist. LEXIS 10599 (N.D. Ill. July 18, 1995), for example, in response to the defendant's argument that the allegations do "not allege behavior of a sexual nature," the court finds, referring to plaintiff's allegation of pressure for dates, that "there is no deficiency in the sexual content of the discriminatory actions alleged in the complaint," id. at *18. That particular facts are found adequately sexual for a sexual harassment claim does not necessarily mean that only sexual facts will be found adequate. Moreover, this ruling goes only to the plaintiff's quid pro quo claim. There is no way to tell which allegations—which include threats regarding scheduling conflicts that arose from plaintiff's pregnancy—made the hostile environment claim adequate. There is no express holding of the sort Schultz contends.

Some cases say the opposite of what they are cited for. Morrison v. Carleton Woolen Mills, Inc., 108 F.3d 429 (1st Cir. 1997), for example, cited for the proposition that "some courts have ruled against plaintiffs after trial on the ground that the challenged conduct is not sufficiently sexual to comprise a hostile work environment," Schultz, 107 *Yale Law Journal* at 1718, holds that frequency of discriminatory treatment (a "single, brief encounter," 108 F.3d at 439) rather than its nature as nonsexual or its gravity as insufficiently severe (plaintiff addressed as "girlie" and told to go see the "nursie," id. at 439), rendered the facts insufficient to be actionable. Strikingly, the plaintiff argued that she did not "need to show that management's conduct . . . was 'expressly sexual' in order to establish a sexually hostile work environment based on gender discrimination," id. at 441, and the court agreed: "We accept that many different forms of offensive behavior may be included within the definition of hostile environment sexual harassment. However, the overtones of such behavior must be, at the very least, sex-based, so as to be a recognizable form of sex discrimination." Id. Nonsexual-but-sex-based acts were thus not only not excluded from the actionably sex-based conduct; they were potentially included in it.

22. Such acts, when based on sex, have long been recognized as discriminatory. An early example is EEOC Decision No. 71–2725, 10 73 EEOC Dec. (CCH) 6290 (June 30, 1971), which found that refusal to instruct or assist or cooperate in work requiring team effort, if directed at an individual because of sex, constitutes sex discrimination. This is not to say that courts have always adequately sustained this (or any other) recognition of sex discrimination.

23. Many courts that miss gendered harassment that is not sexual also miss explicitly sexual forms of harassment. Courts routinely give short shrift to sexual acts at least as often or more often than to nonsexual gender-based abuse—including in cases Schultz, above note 21, cites to the contrary. Sometimes she misses that sexual acts are sexual. Missed, for example, is the *Harris* district court's minimization of specifically sexual acts, such as the employer's asking the plaintiff and other female employees to retrieve coins from his front pants pocket, and throwing objects on the ground for women to bend over and pick up as he watched. These acts were recognized by the district court as sexual but were not found to rise to the level of a hostile sexual environment; they were, instead, characterized in customary moral vocabulary as "annoying and insensitive" or "inane and adolescent," not sex-discriminatory. See Harris v. Forklift Systems, Inc., No. 3:89–0557, 1990 U.S. Dist. LEXIS 20115, at *16 (M.D. Tenn. Nov. 28, 1990). The fact that the acts were sexual did *not* give them any special legal status in this court's eyes. And when the *Harris* Supreme Court reversed, it reversed for both sexual and nonsexual harassment equally.

Similarly, in Reed v. Shepard, 939 F.2d 484 (7th Cir. 1991), violent sexist abuse such as chaining the plaintiff to a toilet and shoving her head into it was moralistically condemned as "repulsive" by the Seventh Circuit panel, id. at 486, but found nonactionable—not because it was seen to be nonsexual, but because Reed was seen as the kind of woman who did not mind such treatment, who even "relished reciprocating in kind." Id. This was because she told "dirty jokes." Id. at 487. The Seventh Circuit, which exonerated the defendants, and Schultz, above note 21, who is rightly critical of that court's dismissal of plaintiff's claims, alike miss the sexual nature of this abuse—which even the briefest acquaintance with, say, *Hustler* would reveal. The irony of using the *Reed* court's failure to find this abuse actionable as support for the critique of what Schultz terms the "sexual desire-dominance paradigm" of sexual harassment law, see Schultz, above note 21, at 1729–1730, is thus lost on her. Whether she would have been as critical of the court's failure to perceive the harassment if she had grasped the sexual nature of the abuse is an open question.

24. For a few instances, see Torres v. Pisano, 116 F.3d 625 (2d Cir. 1997), Watkins v. Bowden, 105 F.3d 1344 (11th Cir. 1997), and Hicks v. Gates Rubber Co., 833 F.2d 1406 (10th Cir. 1987).

25. Hostile environment sexual harassment law, initially drawing on a lone Fifth Circuit precedent that prohibited racially hostile environments, Rogers v. EEOC, 454 F.2d 234 (5th Cir. 1971), then became precedent for equality claims against racist bigotry in the working environment. The number of those claims then grew. Race cases include Snell v. Suffolk County, 782 F.2d 1094 (2d Cir. 1986); Harris v. International Paper Co., 765 F. Supp. 1509 (D. Me. 1991); Bolden v. PRC Inc., 43 F.3d 545 (10th Cir. 1994); Walker v. Ford Motor Co., 684 F.2d 1355 (11th Cir. 1982). Religion cases include Venters v. City of Delphi, 123 F.3d 956, 974–978 (7th Cir. 1997); Del Erdmann v. Tranquility, Inc., 155 F. Supp. 2d 1159–1164 (N.D. Cal. 2001).

26. Oncale v. Sundowner Offshore Services, Inc., 523 U.S. 75 (1998).

27. The leading authority for this proposition is the en banc ruling in Rene v. MGM Grand Hotel, Inc., 305 F.3d 1061 (9th Cir. 2002), *cert. denied*, 3002 WL 1446593, which held that a gay man, sexually harassed as gay, can sue for sex discrimination under Title VII. The plurality held that conduct of a sexual nature is conduct because of sex. A concurring opinion agreed for the reason that discrimination based on sexual orientation is a form of gender stereotyping. Other federal courts of appeals have ruled, in my view erroneously, to the contrary. See, e.g., Bibby v. Philadelphia Coca-Cola Bottling Co., 260 F.3d 257, 265 (3d Cir. 2001); Spearman v. Ford Motor Co., 231 F.3d 1080, 1084–1085 (7th Cir. 2000); Higgins v. New Balance Athletic Shoe, Inc., 194 F.3d 252, 259 (1st Cir. 1999); Simonton v. Runyon, 232 F.3d 33, 36 (2d Cir. 2000).

28. This argument is further developed in Catharine A. MacKinnon, *Sex Equality* 766–1056 (2001).

29. See Janet Halley, "Sexuality Harassment," in *Directions in Sexual Harassment Law* 182 (MacKinnon and Siegel, eds.).

30. See Marc Spindelman, "Discriminating Pleasures," in *Directions in Sexual Harassment Law* 201 (MacKinnon and Siegel, eds.).

31. See Stephen Schulhofer, *Unwanted Sex: The Culture of Intimidation and the Failure of Law* (1998).

32. Meritor Savings Bank v. Vinson, 477 U.S. 57 (1986).

33. One case that raises the issue is *Trautvetter*, but on appeal the majority held that Ms. Trautvetter's sexual harassment claim was not "based on sex" because the sexual relationship she had with her superior was "personal," rather than holding that it was unactionable because welcome. Trautvetter v. Quick, 916 F.2d 1140 (7th Cir.

1990). Others that notably find the challenged behavior unwelcomed include Carr v. Allison Gas Turbine Division General Motors Corp., 32 F.3d 1007 (7th Cir. 1994); Burns v. McGregor Electronic Industries, Inc., 989 F.2d 959 (8th Cir. 1993); Jenson v. Eveleth Taconite Co., 824 F. Supp. 847 (D. Minn. 1993); Cuesta v. Texas Department of Criminal Justice, 805 F. Supp. 451 (W.D. Tex. 1991). Cases finding the challenged behavior welcome include Reed v. Shepard, 939 F.2d 484 (7th Cir. 1991) and Balletti v. Sun Sentinal Co., 909 F. Supp. 1539 (S.D. Fla. 1995), that latter of which may have been inspired by homophobia.

34. See Harris at 20 (1993) ("[I]f the victim does not subjectively perceive the environment to be abusive, the conduct has not actually altered the conditions of the victim's employment, and there is not a Title VII violation").

35. One good example is Flockhart v. Iowa Beef Processors, Inc., 192 F. Supp. 2d 947, 967 (N.D. Ia. 2001), in which a harassed woman's occasional response to abuse by strong language "does not demonstrate that the conduct was not unwelcome," leaving the jury free to so conclude. Some courts have held that evidence that a woman "'engaged in behavior similar to that which she claimed was unwelcomed or offensive' is evidence that the behavior was not unwelcome." Beard v. Flying J., 266 F.3d 792, 798 (8th Cir. 2001) (quoting Scusa v. Nestle U.S.A. Co., 181 F.2d 958, 966 (8th Cir. 1999)). See, e.g., Burns v. McGregor Electronic Industries, Inc., 989 F.2d 959 (8th Cir. 1993) (holding that plaintiff's posing for nude pictures for magazine did not indicate that sexual advances at work were welcome); Gallagher v. Delaney, 139 F.3d 338, 346 (2d Cir. 1998) (holding that plaintiff's extramarital office affair did not permit court to find plaintiff was open to sexual advances). Some cases keep evidence of sexual activity outside the workplace out of workplace sexual harassment cases under Rule 412. See B.K.B. v. Maui Police Department, 276 F.3d 1091, 1106 (9th Cir. 2002) (remanding for new trial for failure of correctional instruction to dispel lurid prejudicial nonprobative testimony concerning victim's fantasies or autoerotic sexual practices in an attempt to establish that sexual harassment at work was not unwelcome). For further discussion, see Wolak v. Spucci, 217 F.3d 157, 160–161 (2d Cir. 2000) (holding that plaintiff's out-of-work viewing of pornography did not mean pornography at work did not alter her status at work, causing injury regardless of trauma inflicted by the images alone).

Of some concern are cases like Mosher v. Dollar Tree Stores, Inc., 240 F.3d 662, 668 (7th Cir. 2001), in which an employer was granted summary judgment for a long-term uncomplained-of live-in relationship with a supervisor that continued after she left her job, a relationship that the court thought "can only be reasonably described as consensual." The woman, described by the court as "a willing participant," said she was afraid, that the relationship was entirely involuntary, and she agreed to the sex only because she needed to keep her job. Id. Another is Stephens v. Rhem Manufacturing Co., 220 F.3d 882 (8th Cir. 2000), in which evidence of rumors of sexual affairs among company employees was excluded at trial under Rule 412, and the defendant's sexual behavior was found welcome to the plaintiff, although she argued that she tolerated it as long as she did only because the rumors led her to believe she had no recourse.

36. See Louise F. Fitzgerald, "Who Says? Legal and Psychological Constructions

of Women's Resistance to Sexual Harassment," in *Directions* 94.

37. Janine Benedet, "Hostile Environment Sexual Harassment Claims and the Unwelcome Influence of Rape Law," 3 *Michigan Journal of Gender and Law* 125 (1995). This proposal is an improvement over that of Susan Estrich, "Sex at Work," 43 *Stanford Law Review* 813 (1991), which recommends eliminating unwelcomeness from sexual harassment doctrine, apparently making it possible for a woman to sue for a sexual relationship she affirmatively wanted, whether or not it was forced by inequality. This is not to say that if a wanted sexual relationship ends badly and an employee is punished for it at work, the punishment cannot be sex-based.

38. For further discussion, see Catharine A. MacKinnon, *Feminism Unmodified* 146–162 (1987).

39. See Janine Benedet, "Pornography as Sexual Harassment in Canada," in *Directions in Sexual Harassment Law* 417 (MacKinnon and Siegel, eds.).

40. In addition to Frederick Schauer, "The Speeching of Sexual Harassment," 347; Jack M. Balkin, "Free Speech and Hostile Environments," 437; and Dorothy Roberts, "The Collective Injury of Sexual Harassment," 365, in *Directions in Sexual Harassment Law*, (MacKinnon and Siegel, eds.), see Catharine A. MacKinnon, *Sex Equality* 973–974 n.46, 1626–1651 (2001); Richard H. Fallon Jr., "Sexual Harassment, Content Neutrality, and the First Amendment Dog That Didn't Bark," *1994 Supreme Court Review* 1.

41. Grant v. Lone Star Co., 21 F.3d 649 (5th Cir. 1994); Miller v. Maxwell's International, Inc., 991 F.2d 583 (9th Cir. 1991); McBride v. Routh, 51 F. Supp. 2d 153 (D. Conn. 1999); Czupih v. Card Pak Inc., 916 F. Supp. 687 (N.D. Ohio 1996); Wilson v. Wayne County, 856 F. Supp. 1254, 1261 (M.D. Tenn. 1994); Johnson v. Northern Indiana Public Service Co., 844 F. Supp. 466 (N.D. Ind. 1994); Lowry v. Clark, 843 F. Supp. 228 (E.D. Ky. 1994). Immunities and other qualifications on personal and institutional responsibility to similar effect also operated under the Equal Protection Clause.

42. For discussion of this structure, see Gebser v. Lago Vista Independent School Dist., 524 U.S. 274, 285–293 (1998).

43. The essays of Deborah Rhode, "Sex in Schools: Who's Minding the Adults?," *Directions* 290, and David B. Oppenheimer, "Employer Liability for Sexual Harassment by Supervisors," *Directions* 272 analyze these rulings.

44. Compare Faragher v. City of Boca Raton, 524 U.S. 775 (1998) (holding employer vicariously liable for hostile environment created by supervisor but allowing employer to demonstrate that it reasonably acted to correct or prevent the harassment and that the plaintiff unreasonably failed to correct or prevent harm through channels offered by employer) and Burlington Industries, Inc. v. Ellerth, 524 U.S. 742 (1998) (same), with Gebser v. Lago Vista Independent School Dist., 524 U.S. 274 (1998) (holding that plaintiff, a female high school student who was sexually harassed by her teacher, may not recover damages against a school district where relevant school officials do not have actual notice and are not deliberately indifferent to teacher's misconduct), and Davis v. Monroe County Board of Education, 526 U.S. 629 (1999) (holding

schools liable to students for peer harassment under Title IX only where authorities are deliberately indifferent to acts reported to proper authority in control and harasser is under the school's disciplinary authority).

45. Burlington Industries, Inc. v. Ellerth, 524 U.S. 742 (1998).

46. 29 C.F.R. §1604.11(a) (2001) (emphasis added).

47. See, for example, Sparks v. Pilot Freight Carriers, Inc., 830 F.2d 1554, 1559 (11th Cir. 1987); Robinson v. City of Pittsburgh, 120 F.3d 1286, 1296–1297 (3d Cir. 1997); Jansen v. Packaging Corp. of America, 123 F.3d 490 (7th Cir. 1997). Nichols v. Frank, 42 F.3d 503, 513 (9th Cir. 1994), and Karibian v. Columbia University, 14 F.3d 773, 777–778 (2d Cir. 1994), found a quid pro quo where sexually harassed women submitted to sex in employment in exchange for job benefits. See also Cram v. Lamson & Sessions Co., 49 F.3d 466, 473 (8th Cir. 1995) (drawing elements of quid pro quo proof from EEOC Guidelines); Kauffman v. Allied Signal, Inc., 970 F.2d 178, 186 (6th Cir. 1992) (same). The Fourth Circuit had not ruled out the possibility that a threat alone was enough to make out a quid pro quo case. Reinhold v. Virginia, 135 F.3d 920, 933–934 n.3 (4th Cir. 1998).

48. 524 U.S. at 748.

49. Harris, 510 U.S. 17 (1993), holds that whether or not a worker is severely psychologically affected by sexual harassment, she can be deemed injured by it.

50. Jansen v. Packaging Corp. of America, 123 F.3d 490, 504 (7th Cir. 1997) (Cudahy, J., concurring).

51. The facts are from *Jansen*, 123 F.3d at 503, which settled before *Ellerth* was argued in the Supreme Court.

52. Facts are from Vance v. Southern Bell Telephone and Telegraph Co., 863 F.2d 1503 (11th Cir. 1989).

53. For further commentary, see Andrea Dworkin, "Dear Bill and Hillary," *Guardian* (London) (January 29, 1998).

54. The D.C. Circuit handed down its decision in Bundy v. Jackson, 641 F.2d 934 (D.C. Cir. 1981), on January 12, 1981; the district court opinion in the case, 19 Fair Empl. Prac. Dec. (CCH) 9154 (Apr. 25, 1979), is dated April 25, 1979. In her testimony before the Senate Judiciary Committee, Anita Hill described being sexually harassed at various points in 1981, when she was employed at the Department of Education, and throughout the fall and winter months of 1982, after she had transferred to the EEOC with Thomas. See *Nomination of Judge Clarence Thomas to Be Associate Justice of the Supreme Court of the United States: Hearing Before the Senate Committee on the Judiciary*, 102d Cong. 36–48 (1991).

55. Her claim was brought under section 1983, effectuating the Equal Protection Clause of the Constitution, which in sexual harassment cases has been interpreted the same as, and together with, Title VII. Presumably, she sued under section 1983 rather than (or also under) Title VII because the statute of limitations had run on her potential Title VII claim.

56. See Clinton v. Jones, 520 U.S. 681 (1997).

57. See Jones v. Clinton, 990 F. Supp. 657 (E.D. Ark. 1998).

58. Flowers Declaration, ¶¶1, 5, 6 (March 12, 1998), Civil Action No. LR-C-94–290, Jones v. Clinton, 990 F. Supp. 657 (E.D. Ark. 1998).

59. Catharine A. MacKinnon, *Sexual Harassment of Working Women: A Case of Sex Discrimination* 39 (1979).

60. Keppler v. Hinsdale Township High School District, 715 F. Supp. 862, 868 (N.D. Ill. 1989).

61. Jones Declaration, ¶17 (March 11, 1998), Civil Action No. LR-C-94–290, Jones v. Clinton, 990 F. Supp. 657 (E.D. Ark. 1998).

62. See, for example, Nichols v. Frank, 42 F.3d 503 (9th Cir. 1994), and Karibian v. Columbia University, 14 F.3d 773 (2d Cir. 1994).

63. See Sanders v. Casa View Baptist Church, 134 F.3d 331 (5th Cir. 1998).

64. See Bonenberger v. Plymouth Township, 132 F.3d 20 (3d Cir. 1997).

65. Highlander v. K.F.C. Nat'l Management Co., 805 F.2d 644 (6th Cir. 1986).

66. Jones Declaration, ¶32 (March 11, 1998), Civil Action No. LR-C-94–290, Jones v. Clinton, 990 F. Supp. 657 (E.D. Ark. 1998).

67. See Davis v. Palmer Dodge West, Inc., 977 F. Supp. 917 (S.D. Ind. 1997) (altering working conditions); Hawthorne v. St. Joseph's Carondelet Child Center, 982 F. Supp. 586 (N.D. Ill. 1997) (moved work location and working by herself); Reinhold v. Virginia, 135 F.3d 920 (4th Cir. 1998) (change in work assignments, less work, different duties). The place of these gender-based but not expressly sexual conditions in sexual harassment cases is also worth noting.

68. Andrews v. City of Philadelphia, 895 F.2d 1469, 1483 (3d Cir. 1990).

69. For part of its test, the Supreme Court cited an Eleventh Circuit case that had limited actionability to "pervasive" harassment, Meritor Savings Bank v. Vinson, 477 U.S. 57, 67 (1986) ("For sexual harassment to state a claim under Title VII, it must be sufficiently pervasive to alter the conditions of employment and create an abusive working environment") (quoting Henson v. City of Dundee, 682 F.2d 897, 904 (11th Cir. 1982)).

70. Faragher v. City of Boca Raton, 524 U.S. 775, 788 (1998).

71. Brzonkala v. Virginia Polytechnic Institute and State University, 132 F.3d 949, 959 (4th Cir. 1997) (holding claim could be founded on this showing of severity without any showing of pervasiveness).

72. Examples include Rush v. Scott Specialty Gases, 113 F.3d 476, 482 (3d Cir. 1997) (stating "isolated or single incidents of harassment are insufficient to constitute a hostile environment" but finding plaintiff's claim constituted a continuous pattern); Moylan v. Maries County, 729 F.2d 746, 749 (8th Cir. 1986) (holding prior to *Vinson* that "the plaintiff must show a practice or pattern of harassment against her or him; a single incident or isolated incidents generally will not be sufficient" in case in which plaintiff was raped); Rabidue v. Osceola Refining Co., 805 F.2d 611, 620 (6th Cir. 1986); Highlander v. K.F.C. Nat'l Management Co., 805 F.2d 644, 649–650 (6th Cir. 1986) (dismissing hostile environment claim as not subjectively perceived to alter working environment, reiterating frequency requirement); see also Waltman v. Int'l

Paper, 875 F.2d 468, 483 (5th Cir. 1989) (Jones, J., dissenting) ("a hostile environment cause of action is comprised of more than one alleged offense").

73. Authorities include Bohen v. City of East Chicago, Indiana, 799 F.2d 1180, 1186–1187 (7th Cir. 1986) (stating in sexual harassment case that "as a general matter, a single discriminatory act against one individual can amount to intentional discrimination for equal protection jurisprudence"); King v. Board of Regents, 898 F.2d 533, 537 (7th Cir. 1990) ("a single act can be enough"); Smith v. Sheahan, 189 F.3d 529, 533 (7th Cir. 1999) ("The Supreme Court has repeatedly said, using the disjunctive 'or,' that a claim of discrimination based on the infliction of a hostile working environment exists if the conduct is 'severe or pervasive'"); Tomka v. Seiler Corp., 66 F.3d 1295 (2d Cir. 1995); Brzonkala v. Virginia Polytechnic Institute, 132 F.3d 949 (4th Cir. 1997) (under Title IX); Lockard v. Pizza Hut, Inc., 162 F.3d 1062 (10th Cir. 1998); Vance v. Southern Bell Telephone & Telegraph Co., 863 F.2d 1503 (11th Cir. 1989) (holding noose hung over African American woman's work stations on two separate occasions sufficiently severe for hostile environment claim, reversing on grounds of incorrect application of *Henson* and *Meritor* the district court's judgment notwithstanding the verdict for the company).

74. 990 F. Supp. 657, 675 (E.D. Ark. 1998).

75. See, for example, Lillard v. Shelby County Board of Education, 76 F.3d 716, 726 (1996) ("[T]he incident in the hallway, while deplorable, simply is not of the outrageous and shocking character that is required for a substantive due process violation. Leventhal's rubbing of Little's stomach, accompanied by a remark that could reasonably be interpreted as suggestive, was wholly inappropriate, and, if proved, should have serious disciplinary consequences for Leventhal. But without more, it is not conduct that creates a constitutional claim"); Chancey v. Southwest Florida Water Management District, 1997 WL 158312, *11 (M.D. Fla. Mar. 17, 1997) (finding hostile environment sexual harassment sufficiently alleged to overcome summary judgment motion but also stating that "[t]he Court finds such behavior, while reprehensible, does not approach the extreme degree of outrageousness required to show intentional infliction of emotional distress"). See also Leibowitz v. Bank Leumi Trust Company, 152 A.D.2d 169, 181–182 (N.Y. App. Div. 1989), dismissing plaintiff's cause of action for intentional infliction of emotional distress and of "harassment" where it was "nothing more than component parts of her claim for wrongful discharge" under New York Labor Law 740 ("While we share in the indignation of our dissenting colleague over the use of the religious and ethnic slurs 'Hebe' and 'kike,' the particular conduct complained of in this case did not rise to such an extreme or outrageous level as to meet the threshold requirements for the tort. . . . Certainly, the use of any religious, ethnic or racial slur must be strongly disapproved and condemned. However, the fact that we view the alleged conduct as being deplorable and reprehensible does not necessarily lead to the conclusion that it arose to such a level that the law must provide a remedy").

76. One would think that if courts were antisex but insufficiently opposed to gender harassment, a case in which a plaintiff was called a "dumb bitch" and "shoved . . . so

hard that she fell backward and hit the floor, sustaining injuries from which she has yet to fully recover" would not be—as it was—found sufficiently severe to create a hostile environment, see Crisonino v. New York City Housing Authority, 985 F. Supp. 385, 388 (S.D.N.Y. 1997), while Paula Jones's allegations, nothing if not sexual, would not have been—as they were—dismissed as not severe enough.

77. Moring v. Arkansas Department of Correction, 243 F.3d 452 (8th Cir. 2001). The facts and law in the rest of this paragraph are drawn from this decision.

78. 243 F.3d at 456.

79. See, e.g., Jeffrey Toobin, *A Vast Conspiracy: The Real Story of the Sex Scandal That Nearly Brought Down the President* 172–176 (1999).

80. Id. at 174.

81. This is the agenda of the likes of Jeffrey Rosen. See his *The Unwanted Gaze: The Destruction of Privacy in America* (2000). That women have been subjected to centuries of unwanted gazes in what is defended as the private is not mentioned.

82. See EEOC, *Trends in Harassment Charges Filed with the EEOC During the 1980s and 1990s.* Available at http://www.eeoc.gov/stats/harassment.html.

17. Disputing Male Sovereignty: On *United States v. Morrow*

Originally published as "Disputing Male Sovereignty: On *United States v. Morrison,*" 114 *Harvard Law Review* 135 (2000). I was involved in formulating the Violence Against Women Act and also signed the Brief of Law Professors as Amici Curiae in Support of Petitioners, *Morrison,* 529 U.S. 598 (2000) (Nos. 99–5, 99–29), written by others. For their generous support and insights, I am grateful to Cass Sunstein, Laurence Tribe, Frank Michelman, Lisa Cardyn, Sally Goldfarb, and Burke Marshall, who dropped everything to comment on a draft of this article virtually overnight. These thoughts took their initial public form in a dialogue with Charles Fried and Diane Rosenfeld, from whom I learned a great deal. Lisa Cardyn, Victoria Brescoll, and the staff of the University of Michigan Law Library, in particular Barbara Vaccaro and Nancy Vettorello, provided superb research assistance for which they cannot be thanked enough. I also thank Victoria Nourse and Bonnie Campbell for their intelligent and stalwart commitment in this cause.

1. 529 U.S. 598 (2000).

2. Violence Against Women Act of 1994, Pub. L. No. 103–322, 108 Stat. 1941 (codified as amended at 42 U.S.C. §13981 (1994)).

3. In January 2000, the Supreme Court invalidated the Age Discrimination in Employment Act's provision authorizing suits against public employers for age discrimination as an invalid abrogation of Eleventh Amendment immunity in excess of Congress's powers under Section 5 of the Fourteenth Amendment. Kimel v. Fla. Bd. of Regents, 528 U.S. 62, 66 (2000).

4. U.S. Const. art. I, §8, cl. 3.

5. Id. amend. XIV, §5.

6. Morrison, 529 U.S. at 627.

7. Id. at 612.

8. Id. at 613–615.

9. Id. at 625.

10. See, e.g., Kimel, 528 U.S. at 66; Coll. Sav. Bank v. Fla. Prepaid Postsecondary Educ. Expense Bd., 527 U.S. 666, 691 (1999) (holding that the Trademark Remedy Clarification Act did not validly waive state sovereign immunity and that Florida did not constructively waive its immunity by engaging in interstate commerce); City of Boerne v. Flores, 521 U.S. 507, 532–536 (1997) (holding that the Religious Freedom Restoration Act of 1993 invaded state preserves in excess of Congress's enforcement power under §5 of the Fourteenth Amendment by changing the meaning the Supreme Court had given to the First Amendment); Seminole Tribe v. Florida, 517 U.S. 44, 47 (1996) (holding that Congress may not abrogate states' sovereign immunity from suit in federal court pursuant to the Indian Commerce Clause); United States v. Lopez, 514 U.S. 549, 567–568 (1995) (holding that the Gun-Free School Zones Act exceeded Congress's authority under the Commerce Clause); see also Garcia v. San Antonio Metro. Transit Auth., 469 U.S. 528, 579 (1985) (Powell, J., dissenting) (arguing that application of the Fair Labor Standards Act to state employees violated state sovereign immunity); id. at 588 (O'Connor, J., dissenting) ("It is insufficient, in assessing the validity of congressional regulation of a state pursuant to the commerce power, to ask only whether the same regulation would be valid if enforced against a private party. It remains relevant that a *State* is being regulated . . .").

11. See, e.g., Gebser v. Lago Vista Independent School District, 524 U.S. 274, 277 (1998) (holding that a student may not recover for teacher-student sexual harassment under Title IX of the Education Amendment Act, 20 U.S.C. §1681 (1994), enacted under the Spending Clause, unless a school district official with authority to act had actual notice and was deliberately indifferent).

12. See, e.g., Pers. Adm'r v. Feeney, 442 U.S. 256, 279 (1979) (confining the Fourteenth Amendment's equality protection to intentional state violations); Soto v. Flores, 103 F.3d 1056, 1067 (1st Cir. 1997) ("A domestic violence victim seeking to prove an equal protection violation must thus show that the relevant policymakers and actors were motivated, at least in part, by a discriminatory purpose"), *cert. denied*, 522 U.S. 819 (1997).

13. 42 U.S.C. §13981(b) (1994).

14. Under the VAWA, "the term 'crime of violence motivated by gender' means a crime of violence committed because of gender or on the basis of gender, and due, at least in part, to an animus based on the victim's gender. . . ." Id. §13981(d).

15. See Morrison, 529 U.S. at 636 n.10 (Souter, J., dissenting) (noting that the Judicial Conference withdrew its opposition after animus was added).

16. 42 U.S.C. §13981(d)(2)(A) (1994).

17. A Gender Violence Act introduced in Illinois did not have either of these drawbacks. After finding that "[e]xisting State and federal laws do not adequately prevent and remedy gender-related violence," the Illinois legislature proposed defining "sex discrimination" as "any of the following: (1) One or more acts of violence or

physical aggression on the basis of sex, gender, or sexuality[;] (2) A physical intrusion or physical invasion of a sexual nature under coercive conditions[;] (3) A threat of an act described in item (1) or (2)." H.B. 4407, 91st Gen. Assemb., Reg. Sess. (Ill. 2000).

18. The case was originally brought as Brzonkala v. Virginia Polytechnic Institute & State University, 935 F. Supp. 772 (W.D. Va. 1996); the district judge ruled against Ms. Brzonkala's claims. It retained this caption through the Fourth Circuit panel decision reversing, Brzonkala v. Va. Polytechnic Inst. & State Univ., 132 F.3d 949 (4th Cir. 1997), and the en banc decision reversing the panel, Brzonkala v. Va. Polytechnic Inst. & State Univ., 169 F.3d 920 (4th Cir. 1999), with Mr. Morrison and Mr. Crawford as joint defendants throughout. The Fourth Circuit remanded Ms. Brzonkala's Title IX claim against the University, leaving only the VAWA claim against Mr. Morrison and Mr. Crawford. See *Morrison*, 529 U.S. at 604. Both the United States and Ms. Brzonkala applied for certiorari. The Supreme Court consolidated the two cases under the caption United States v. Morrison (which was filed first) when it granted review. See United States v. Morrison, 527 U.S. 1068 (1999) (mem.). Thus did Christy Brzonkala become the United States and Virginia Polytechnic Institute become Mr. Morrison.

19. Brief for Petitioner at 3, Morrison, 529 U.S. 598 (2000) (Nos. 99–5, 99–29).

20. Id. at 3–4.

21. Office of the Commonwealth's Attorney for Montgomery County, News Release (April 10, 1996) (press release) (on file with the Harvard Law School Library) (announcing that the grand jury returned "no true bill" on the indictments of Mr. Morrison and Mr. Crawford for the alleged rape of Ms. Brzonkala); Jan Vertefeuille, "Players Are Not Indicted: Ex-Tech Student To Pursue Rape Claim in Federal Suit," *The Roanoke Times*, A1 (Apr. 11, 1996).

22. For example, the accused perpetrators received notice of hearings and access to affidavit materials but Ms. Brzonkala did not. Brief for Petitioner, note 19 above, at 5.

23. Id. at 4–6.

24. Brzonkala v. Va. Polytechnic Inst. & State Univ., 935 F. Supp. 772 (W.D. Va. 1996). For a more detailed account of Ms. Brzonkala's story, see Patrick Tracey, "Christy's Crusade," *Ms. Magazine*, 53 (Apr./May 2000). Brzonkala also sued Virginia Tech for violating Title IX, which prohibits sex discrimination by universities receiving federal funds. Brzonkala, 935 F. Supp. at 773. The Fourth Circuit remanded the Title IX claim, Brzonkala v. Va. Polytechnic Inst. & State Univ., 132 F.3d 949, 974 (4th Cir. 1997). According to Tracey, the claim settled for $75,000. Tracey, above, at 61.

25. The Bureau of Justice Statistics indicates that three percent of the rapes reported in 1996 in a survey of victims age twelve and over were rapes of men. Bureau of Justice Statistics, U.S. Dep't of Justice, *Crime Victimization in the United States, 1994* at 4 (1997).

26. Diana E.H. Russell, *Sexual Exploitation: Rape, Child Sexual Abuse, and Workplace Harassment* 35 (1984) (reporting that of 930 female residents of San Francisco, 24 percent reported having been raped at least once); see also Mary P. Koss, Lisa A. Goodman, Angela Browne, Louise F. Fitzgerald, Gwendolyn Puryear Keita & Nancy

Felipe Russo, *No Safe Haven: Male Violence Against Women at Home, at Work, and in the Community* 167–171 (1994) (collecting major studies on rape prevalence among college-age and adult women, almost half of the studies reporting rape rates greater than 20 percent); Majority Staff of Senate Comm. on the Judiciary, 102d Cong., *Violence Against Women: A Week in the Life of America* 3 (Comm. Print 1992) [hereinafter *Violence Against Women*] (estimating the number of women raped at least once to be between one in five and one in eight); "Women and Violence: Hearings on Legislation to Reduce the Growing Problem of Violent Crime Against Women Before the Senate Comm. on the Judiciary," 101st Cong. 33–42 (1990) [hereinafter "Hearings, Women and Violence"] (statement of Mary P. Koss on behalf of the American Psychological Association) (discussing factors that cause the National Crime Survey to underreport the true incidence of rape in the United States). Fourteen percent of women report having been raped by their husbands. Diana E.H. Russell, *Rape in Marriage* 57 (1990). African American women are generally considered to be subjected to the highest incidence of rape in the American population. Russell, *Sexual Exploitation*, above, at 82 (reporting on studies of rape completed as of 1984). However, a more recent study finds no significant ethnic disparity in the incidence of rape between Black and white women. Gail Elizabeth Wyatt, "The Sociocultural Context of African American and White American Women's Rape," 48 *Journal of Social Issues* 77, 85 (1992) [hereinafter Wyatt, "Sociocultural Context"]. Thirty-eight percent of girls report having been sexually abused before they reached the age of majority, most by men close to or with authority over them, the majority before the age of fourteen. Diana E.H. Russell, *The Secret Trauma: Incest in the Lives of Girls and Women* 60–62 (1986); see also Gail Elizabeth Wyatt, "The Sexual Abuse of Afro-American and White-American Women in Childhood," 9 *Child Abuse and Neglect* 507, 513 (1985) (finding that 57 percent of a sample of African American women and 67 percent of a sample of white women reported at least one incident of sexual abuse before age eighteen).

27. Russell, *Sexual Exploitation* at 49.

28. Joyce C. Abma, Anjani Chandra, William D. Mosher, Linda S. Peterson & Linda J. Piccinino, U.S. Dep't of Health & Human Servs., *Fertility, Family Planning, and Women's Health: New Data from the 1995 National Survey of Family Growth* 5 (1997). For those who first had intercourse under age fifteen, almost one in four report that it was "not voluntary." Id. at 32.

29. Mary P. Koss, Christine A. Gidycz & Nadine Wisniewski, "The Scope of Rape: Incidence and Prevalence of Sexual Aggression and Victimization in a National Sample of Higher Education Students," 55 *Journal of Consulting and Clinical Psychology* 162, 168 (1987).

30. Lalenya Weintraub Siegel, Note, "The Marital Rape Exemption: Evolution to Extinction," 43 *Cleveland State Law Review* 351, 352–353 (1995).

31. Id. at 377.

32. Id. at 367–369 (documenting partial marital exemptions in state laws).

33. 42 U.S.C. §13981(d)(2)(B) (1994).

34. See Lynda Lytle Holmstrom & Ann Wolbert Burgess, *The Victim of Rape:*

Institutional Reactions 2 (1978) (examining the experiences of victims in dealing with the justice system); Lee Madigan & Nancy C. Gamble, *The Second Rape* 7 (1991) (describing rape victims' perceptions of dealing with police and other authorities); Joyce E. Williams & Karen A. Holmes, *The Second Assault* 89–94 (1981) (reporting victims' evaluations of support services). African American women particularly dread the justice system's racism and its concomitant devaluation of their rape. See Wyatt, "Sociocultural Context," note 26 above, at 86; Jennifer Wriggins, Note, "Rape, Racism, and the Law," 6 *Harvard Women's Law Journal* 103, 121–123 (1983).

35. For a similar analysis, see Kimberly A. Lonsway & Louise F. Fitzgerald, "Rape Myths in Review," 18 *Psychology of Women Quarterly* 133, 135 (1994) (arguing that the rate of unfounding reveals more about police attitudes than about women's deceit).

36. Madigan and Gamble, note 34 above, at 7; see also "Violence Against Women: Victims of the System: Hearing on S. 15 Before the Senate Comm. on the Judiciary," 102d Cong. 137 (1991).

37. Russell, *Sexual Exploitation* at 36 (finding that, in a study of 930 women in San Francisco, only 9.5 percent of rapes were reported); Mary P. Koss, "The Hidden Rape Victim: Personality, Atittudinal, and Situational Characteristics," 9 *Psychology of Women Quarterly* 193, 206 (1985) (finding that, of 38 percent of university women whose experiences met the legal definition of rape or attempted rape, only 4 percent had reported the assaults to the police); Crystal S. Mills and Barbara J. Granoff, "Date and Acquaintance Rape Among a Sample of College Students," 37 *Social Work* 504, 506 (1992) (reporting that, among twenty student rape victims, none told police and only three told anyone); see also David P. Bryden & Sonja Lengnick, "Rape in the Criminal Justice System," 87 *J. Criminal Law and Criminology* 1194, 1220 n.170 (1997) (collecting studies with estimates ranging from 1 percent to 60 percent). Other studies describe the underenforcement of rape charges. See Majority Staff of Senate Comm. on the Judiciary, 103d Cong., *The Response to Rape: Detours on the Road to Equal Justice* iii (Comm. Print 1993) [hereinafter *The Response to Rape*] (concluding based on a survey of several jurisdictions that 98 percent of rape victims "never see their attacker caught, tried and imprisoned"); Joan McGregor, "Introduction to Symposium on Philosophical Issues in Rape Law," 11 *Law and Philosophy* 1, 2 (1992) (stating that the likelihood of a rape complaint's ending in conviction is estimated to be between 2 and 5 percent). In response to the problem of underreporting, the National Crime Victimization Survey was redesigned, and a new questionnaire was in wide use by 1992. Bureau of Justice Statistics, U.S. Dep't of Justice, *Violence Against Women: Estimates from the Redesigned Survey* 1 (1995). Yet in 1994, only 102,096 rapes were reported to authorities, and ultimately there were only an estimated 36,610 arrests for forcible rape. Fed. Bureau of Investigation, U.S. Dep't of Justice, *Crime in the United States* 1994, at 24 (1995).

38. *The Response to Rape*, note 37 above, at 7–8, 13. David P. Bryden and Sonja Lengnick summarize their thesis as follows:

> Although false reports of rape are no more common than of other crimes, justice system officials are highly skeptical of women who claim to have been raped by acquaintances. If the rape victim's conduct prior to the crime vio-

> lated traditional sex-role norms, police commonly disbelieve her report or blame her for the rape. Thus, officials deny justice to women who have engaged in nonmarital sex, or other 'improper' activities such as heavy drinking or hitchhiking. . . . [P]rosecutors are excessively reluctant to prosecute acquaintance rapists. When they do prosecute, the system puts the victim rather than the defendant on trial. Juries, motivated by the same biases as other participants in the system, often blame the victim and acquit the rapist.

Bryden and Lengnick, note 37 above, at 1195–1196. Bryden and Lengnick found substantial social science evidence to support these points, if often in qualified or nuanced form. The sole exception was the statement on false reporting, which was found difficult to substantiate empirically. Id. at 1208–1212, 1295–1298.

39. Menachem Amir, *Patterns in Forcible Rape* 44 (1971) (finding that 93 percent of rapes are intraracial); Bureau of Justice Statistics, U.S. Dep't of Justice, *Criminal Victimization in the United States 1992* at 61 (1994) (finding that approximately three-quarters of rapes are intraracial).

40. See Gary D. LaFree, *Rape and Criminal Justice: The Social Construction of Sexual Assault* 141 (1989) (noting that of 453 men executed for rape in the United States since 1930, 405 of them, or 89 percent, have been African American); Gary D. LaFree, "The Effect of Sexual Stratification by Race on Official Reactions to Rape," 45 *American Sociology Review* 842, 842 (1980) (finding that Black men accused of sexual assault of white women received more serious charges and longer sentences, were more likely to have their sentences carried out, and were more likely to serve time in state penitentiaries than white men accused of sexual assault); see also Dan T. Carter, *Scottsboro: A Tragedy of the American South* (rev. ed. 1980) (analyzing a notorious 1931 trial of nine African American young men accused dubiously of raping two white women); James Goodman, *Stories of Scottsboro* (1994) (same).

41. In this iconography, Black women are stereotyped as indiscriminately lustful and whorish, making raping them seem trivial or impossible. See Dorothy E. Roberts, "Rape, Violence, and Women's Autonomy," 69 *Chicago-Kent Law Review* 359, 364–369 (1993).

42. See Bryden and Lengnick, note 37 above, at 1383–1384.

43. See Ronet Bachman and Raymond Paternoster, "A Contemporary Look at the Effects of Rape Law Reform: How Far Have We Really Come?," 84 *Journal of Criminal Law and Criminology* 554, 565–573 (1993) (noting that, postreform, only very small increases in the rate of reporting rape, in the probability of imprisonment given arrest, and in the probability of conviction and imprisonment for acquaintance rape have occurred); Wallace D. Loh, "The Impact of Common Law and Reform Rape Statutes on Prosecution: An Empirical Study," 55 *Washington Law Review* 543, 591–614 (1980).

44. Julie Horney and Cassia Spohn, "The Influence of Blame and Believability Factors on the Processing of Simple Versus Aggravated Rape Cases," 34 *Criminology* 135, 152–53 (1996).

45. In addition, Congress sought to address domestic battering, which was also found to be sex-based, pervasive, and unremedied. See Morrison, 529 U.S. at 619;

Violence Against Women, note 26 above; "Hearings, Women and Violence," note 26 above, at 33–42 (statement of Mary P. Koss). For further support of these findings, see generally Ann Jones, *Next Time, She'll Be Dead: Battering and How to Stop It* (1994); *Out of the Darkness: Contemporary Perspectives on Family Violence* (Glenda Kaufman Kantor and Jana L. Jasinski, eds., 1997); Reva B. Siegel, "'The Rule of Love': Wife Beating as Prerogative and Privacy," 105 *Yale Law Journal* 2117, 2172–2173 (1996) (analyzing the "gender asymmetry of violence between intimates"); Evan Stark and Anne Flitcraft, "Violence Among Intimates: An Epidemiological Review," in *Handbook of Family Violence* 293 (Vincent B. Van Hasselt, Randall L. Morrison, Alan S. Bellack and Michel Hersen, eds., 1988); "Developments in the Law—Legal Responses to Domestic Violence," 106 *Harvard Law Review* 1498, 1501 (1993) (compiling data).

46. Morrison, 529 U.S. at 627.

47. Id. at 628–655 (Souter, J., dissenting); id. at 655–663 (Breyer, J., dissenting).

48. Id. at 663–666 (Breyer, J., dissenting).

49. Id. at 612.

50. Id. at 610 (quoting United States v. Lopez, 514 U.S. 549, 580 (1995) (Kennedy, J., concurring)).

51. Morrison, 529 U.S. at 617–618 (citing *Lopez*, 514 U.S. at 568; and NLRB v. Jones & Laughlin Steel Corp., 301 U.S. 1, 30 (1937) (internal quotation marks omitted)).

52. See id. at 628–638 (Souter, J., dissenting) (detailing congressional findings on the impact of violence against women on commerce). Medical costs of gender-based violence in terms of immediate relief, long-term utilization of health care, and insurance costs have only begun to be counted.

53. Id. at 636.

54. Heart of Atlanta Motel, Inc. v. United States, 379 U.S. 241, 254 (1964) (quoting Gibbons v. Ogden, 22 U.S. (9 Wheat.) 1, 194 (1824)).

55. Id. at 255.

56. Id. at 257.

57. Morrison, 529 U.S. at 637 (Souter, J., dissenting) (quoting *Heart of Atlanta Motel*, 379 U.S. at 257).

58. Id. at 635.

59. 317 U.S. 111 (1942).

60. Morrison, 529 U.S. at 634–641 (Souter, J., dissenting); id. at 776 (Breyer, J., dissenting).

61. Wickard, 317 U.S. at 128–129.

62. Morrison, 529 U.S. at 613–617.

63. My thanks to Larry Tribe for helping to clarify this feature of the problem.

64. United States v. Lopez, 514 U.S. 549, 567 (1995).

65. Morrison, 529 U.S. at 627 (Thomas, J., concurring).

66. Id. at 642 (Souter, J., dissenting).

67. Id. at 642–644.

68. Lopez, 514 U.S. at 567 (holding that Congress exceeded its authority in enacting a federal law prohibiting possession of a firearm in a school zone).

69. William H. Rehnquist, "Welcoming Remarks: National Conference of State-Federal Judicial Relationships," 78 *Virginia Law Review* 1657, 1660 (1992).

70. Morrison, 529 U.S. at 612 (quoting *Lopez*, 514 U.S. at 567 (internal quotation marks omitted)).

71. 42 U.S.C. §13981(e)(3) (1994).

72. Brief of the States of Arizona et al. as Amici Curiae in Support of Petitioners, Morrison, 529 U.S. 598 (2000) (Nos. 99–5, 99–29).

73. Morrison, 529 U.S. at 612, 615–616.

74. See Lenore J. Weitzman, *The Divorce Revolution: The Unexpected Social and Economic Consequences for Women and Children in America* 323 (1985) (noting that "[w]hile most divorced men find that their standard of living improves after divorce, most divorced women and the minor children in their households find that their standard of living plummets"); Saul D. Hoffman and Greg J. Duncan, "What Are the Economic Consequences of Divorce?," 25 *Demography* 641, 644 (1988) (noting that "[c]orrected estimates suggest a decline in economic status [for divorced women] of about one-third"); Richard R. Peterson, "A Re-Evaluation of the Economic Consequences of Divorce," 61 *American Sociology Review* 528, 532 (1996) (finding a 27 percent decline in women's standard of living postdivorce, and a 10 percent increase in men's); Jana B. Singer, "Alimony and Efficiency: The Gendered Costs and Benefits of the Economic Justification for Alimony," 82 *Georgetown Law Journal* 2423, 2426 n.14 (1994) (collecting studies showing that women in general compared with men in general are economically worse off after divorce); Cynthia Starnes, "Divorce and the Displaced Homemaker: A Discourse on Playing with Dolls, Partnership Buyouts and Dissociation Under No-Fault," 60 *University of Chicago Law Review* 67, 92–95 (1993) (discussing the documentation of gender bias against women in property division and child support awards by gender bias task forces).

75. See, e.g., Pers. Adm'r v. Feeney, 442 U.S. 256 (1979) (holding that Massachusetts did not discriminate against women by providing lifetime preferences to veterans); Washington v. Davis, 426 U.S. 229, 239 (1976) (noting that a law does not violate the Equal Protection Clause unless the purpose behind its enactment was to discriminate).

76. Morrison, 529 U.S. at 617.

77. See Catharine A. MacKinnon, *Sex Equality* chs. 6–7 (2001).

78. Katzenbach v. Morgan, 384 U.S. 641, 670 (1966) (Harlan, J., dissenting).

79. Morrison, 529 U.S. at 613–614.

80. Textual bases for this reconsideration include both the Fourteenth Amendment and the Nineteenth Amendment. A valuable analysis arguing that the VAWA can be grounded in the Citizenship Clause of the Fourteenth Amendment, because it was intended to eliminate class-based subordination by states, is made by Jennifer S. Hendricks, "Women and the Promise of Equal Citizenship," 8 *Texas Journal of Women and Law* 51, 86 (1998).

81. Heart of Atlanta Motel, Inc. v. United States, 379 U.S. 241, 284 (1964) (Douglas, J., concurring) (citing H.R. Rep. No. 914, at 20 (1963)).

82. Id. at 280.

83. Id. at 291–293 (Goldberg, J., concurring) (arguing that the primary purpose of

the Civil Rights Act of 1964 was "the vindication of human dignity and not mere economics").

84. Id. at 292 (citing hearings to indicate congressional intent to base Title II's constitutionality on dual rationales).

85. Morrison, 529 U.S. at 642 (Souter, J., dissenting).

86. Id. at 655 (citing Redrup v. New York, 386 U.S. 767 (1967); and Miller v. California, 413 U.S. 15 (1973)).

87. See Morrison, 529 U.S. at 626–627 (distinguishing *Morrison* from Katzenbach v. Morgan, 384 U.S. 641 (1966), and South Carolina v. Katzenbach, 383 U.S. 301 (1966)).

88. Brzonkala v. Va. Polytechnic & State Univ., 169 F.3d 820, 853 (4th Cir. 1999).

89. Morrison, 529 U.S. at 621 (quoting Shelley v. Kraemer, 334 U.S. 1, 13 (1948)).

90. Id. at 624–626. In the Civil Rights Cases, 109 U.S. 3, 9–10 (1883), the Supreme Court confined the power of Congress under the Fourteenth Amendment to "state action," holding unconstitutional the Civil Rights Act of 1875, which had made private racial discrimination in public accommodations illegal.

91. Id.

92. Id. (quoting Florida Prepaid Postsecondary Education Expenses Board v. College Savings Bank, 527 U.S. 627, 639 (1999)).

93. Id. (citing Florida Prepaid, 527 U.S. at 639; and City of Boerne v. Flores, 521 U.S. 507, 526 (1997)).

94. Justice Breyer did not answer the Section 5 question because he found the Commerce Clause to be an adequate basis for upholding the VAWA. Id. at 664 (Breyer, J., dissenting).

95. Eric Foner, *Reconstruction* 454–458 (1988).

96. Everette Swinney, *Suppressing the Ku Klux Klan: The Enforcement of the Reconstruction Amendments 1870–1877* 166 (1987); Jacobus tenBroek, *Equal Under Law* 203 (1966) ("The protection intended [by the Fourteenth Amendment] was not merely against state action").

97. H.R. Rep. No. 41–37, at 4 (1871) (statement of Rep. Butler).

98. Act of Apr. 20, 1871, ch. 22, 17 Stat. 13 (emphasis added).

99. For a solid historical demonstration that both the congressional framers of the Fourteenth Amendment and those who ratified it in the states comprehended that the Fourteenth Amendment was not confined to addressing state action, see Frank J. Scaturro, *The Supreme Court's Retreat from Reconstruction: A Distortion of Constitutional Jurisprudence* 85–89 (2000).

100. TenBroek, note 96 above, at 203–204.

101. "Killing No Murder," *Woodhull and Claflin's Weekly*, June 11, 1870, at 8.

102. Act of Apr. 20, 1871, ch. 22, §2, 17 Stat. 13, 13–14 (codified. at 42 U.S.C. §1985(3) (1994)).

103. See, e.g., Lisa Cardyn, "Sexualized Racism/Gendered Violence: Outraging the Body Politic in the Reconstruction South," ch. 5, at 18–20 (2000) (unpublished Ph.D. dissertation, Yale University) (on file with the Harvard Law School Library).

104. See, e.g., "Crimes of Violence Motivated by Gender: Hearing Before the Subcomm. on Civil and Constitutional Rights of the House Comm. on the Judiciary," 103d Cong. 10–11 (1993) (statement of Sally Goldfarb, senior staff attorney, NOW Legal Def. & Educ. Fund).

105. See Cardyn, note 103 above, at 28, 52–53, 59–60, 64–65.

106. Id. at 151.

107. For the Court's animus requirement under Section 1985(3), see Griffin v. Breckenridge, 403 U.S. 88, 103 (1971).

108. 42 U.S.C. §13891(d).

109. Morrison, 529 U.S. at 619–627.

110. 109 U.S. 3 (1883).

111. 106 U.S. 629 (1883).

112. Morrison, 529 U.S. at 621–622.

113. Id.

114. United States v. Hall, 26 F. Cas. 79, 81 (C.C.S.D. Ala. 1871) (No. 15,282).

115. Id.

116. 383 U.S. 745 (1966).

117. 18 U.S.C. §241 (1994 & Supp. II 1996).

118. Guest, 383 U.S. at 753–760.

119. Id. at 747 n.1, 757.

120. Id. at 784 (Brennan, J., concurring) (citations omitted).

121. Id. at 762 (Clark, J., concurring).

122. Guest, 383 U.S. at 755.

123. Heart of Atlanta Motel, Inc. v. United States, 379 U.S. 241, 261 (1964).

124. 392 U.S. 409 (1968).

125. Id. at 443 ("If Congress cannot say that being a free man means at least this much, then the Thirteenth Amendment made a promise the Nation cannot keep").

126. Griffin v. Breckenridge, 403 U.S. 88, 104–105 (1971).

127. Collins v. Hardyman, 341 U.S. 651, 658 (1951).

128. Griffin, 403 U.S. at 104–105.

129. Id. at 102.

130. See Lyes v. City of Riviera Beach, 166 F.3d 1332, 1339 (11th Cir. 1999) (en banc) ("Of the circuits that have squarely confronted and decided the issue, seven have held that women are a protected class of persons under §1985(3), and none have held that they are not. If both holdings and dicta are counted, eight of the circuits that have taken a position have said that women are a protected class under §1985(3); only two have said that they are not"); see also id. at 1338–1339.

131. Griffin, 403 U.S. at 107.

132. 463 U.S. 825 (1983).

133. Id. at 833.

134. 506 U.S. 263 (1993).

135. Id. at 274.

136. Id. at 277.

137. Id. at 274–278.

138. Lyes v. City of Riviera Beach, 166 F.3d 1332, 1340 (11th Cir. 1999) (en banc).

139. United States v. Harris, 106 U.S. 629, 644 (1883).

140. Brzonkala v. Va. Polytechnic Inst. & State Univ., 169 F.3d 820, 874 (4th Cir. 1999) (en banc).

141. Because Section 1985(3) is a separate statute that the Court has not discussed, its use against unofficial violations of sex equality rights under the Fourteenth Amendment is not conclusively precluded.

142. Canada has found its provincial human rights legislation unconstitutionally underinclusive, hence unequal, on precisely this ground. See Egan v. The Queen, [1995] 2 S.C.R. 513 (Can.); Vriend v. Alberta, [1998] 1 S.C.R. 493 (Can.).

143. 384 U.S. 641 (1966).

144. Id. at 648.

145. 17 U.S. (4 Wheat.) 316, 421 (1819).

146. Morgan, 384 U.S. at 650–651. See also Ex parte Virginia, 100 U.S. 339, 345–346 (1879); Strauder v. West Virginia, 100 U.S. 303, 311 (1879); United States v. Crosby, 25 F. Cas. 701 (C.C.D.S.C. 1871) (No. 14893); *Proceedings in the Ku Klux Trials, at Columbia, S.C. in the United States Circuit Court, November Term, 1871*, at 90 (1872); Swinney, note 96 above, at 166.

147. Morgan, 384 U.S. at 666 (Harlan, J., dissenting).

148. Id. at 669–671.

149. United States v. Guest, 383 U.S. 745, 783 (1966) (Brennan, J., concurring).

150. 521 U.S. 507 (1997).

151. Franklin v. Gwinnett, 503 U.S. 60 (1992); Meritor Sav. Bank v. Vinson, 477 U.S. 57 (1986).

152. Dothard v. Rawlinson, 433 U.S. 321, 336 (1977) (holding that capacity to be raped was a bona fide occupational qualification excluding women on the basis of sex from contact positions in male-only, high-security prisons).

153. United States v. Lanier, 520 U.S. 259 (1997). This provision "incorporates constitutional law by reference," id. at 259, because the statute requires willfully and under color of law "depriv[ing] a person of rights protected by the Constitution or laws of the United States," id. at 264. Judge Lanier was not allowed to claim immunity based on the fact that sexual assault had not been ruled on with sufficient particularity as prohibited by the liberty component of the Due Process Clause of the Fourteenth Amendment.

154. Annis v. County of Westchester, 36 F.3d 251 (2d Cir. 1994); Pontarelli v. Stone, 930 F.2d 104, 113 (1st Cir. 1991); Bohen v. City of East Chicago, 799 F.2d 1180, 1185 (7th Cir. 1986); Woerner v. Brzeczek, 519 F. Supp. 517, 519–20 (N.D. Ill. 1981).

155. Boerne, 521 U.S. at 508.

156. Id. at 518 (quoting Fitzpatrick v. Bitzer, 427 U.S. 445, 455 (1976)).

157. 120 S. Ct. 631 (2000).

158. The most active attempt to hold states responsible for equal protection vio-

lations in their treatment of violence against women has occurred in the context of police nonresponsiveness to domestic violence. In Thurman v. City of Torrington, 595 F. Supp. 1521 (D. Conn. 1984), Tracey Thurman was rendered paraplegic and nearly killed by her husband as the police ignored her many reports of his violence, and, in one instance, looked on as he kicked her in the head and ran away after stabbing her repeatedly with a knife. Id. at 1525–1526. She was awarded $2.3 million in her suit against the officers. See Amy Eppler, Note, "Battered Women and the Equal Protection Clause: Will the Constitution Help Them When the Police Won't?," 95 *Yale Law Journal* 788, 795 n.31 (1986). Attempts to assert battered women's rights to equal protection of the laws after *Thurman* have produced mixed results. The Supreme Court's decision in DeShaney v. Winnebago County Department of Social Services, 489 U.S. 189 (1989), recognized that "the State may not, of course, selectively deny its protective services to certain disfavored minorities without violating the Equal Protection Clause." Id. at 196 n.3. Courts have required showings that discrimination against women was intentional in police policies that provide less protection to victims of domestic violence than to victims of other types of violence. See Hynson v. City of Chester Legal Dep't, 864 F.2d 1026 (3d Cir. 1988). Compare Balistreri v. Pacifica Police Dep't, 901 F.2d 696 (9th Cir. 1988), and Watson v. City of Kansas City, 857 F.2d 690, 696–697 (10th Cir. 1988), with Soto v. Flores, 103 F.3d 1056 (1st Cir. 1997).

159. The Court's treatment of the facts in *Morrison* as sufficient to establish gender-biased "animus" for statutory purposes may be significant in light of its holding of "animus" as equivalent to Fourteenth Amendment intent in *Bray*.

160. Brzonkala v. Va. Polytechnic Inst. & State Univ., 169 F.3d 820, 852 (4th Cir. 1999) (en banc).

161. The Court noted, on its way to criticizing the VAWA's failure to confine itself to state action, that the VAWA "is not aimed at proscribing discrimination by officials which the Fourteenth Amendment might not itself proscribe." Morrison, 529 U.S. at 626. This observation may mean that, to the extent the VAWA is constitutional, it is redundant—that sex-discriminatory assault like that by Judge Lanier is already proscribed by the Fourteenth Amendment. Or it could mean that, to the degree it is not aimed at officials, the VAWA is not aimed beyond the Fourteenth Amendment's purview. That the VAWA remains constitutional as applied to state actors seems possible.

162. Id. at 620.

163. United States v. Virginia, 518 U.S. 515, 534 (1996).

164. For holdings that sex stereotyping is sex discrimination, see United States v. Virginia, 518 U.S. at 541; Price Waterhouse v. Hopkins, 490 U.S. 228, 250–251, 256 (1989); and Mississippi University for Women v. Hogan, 458 U.S. 718, 725 (1982).

165. City of Boerne v. Flores, 521 U.S. 507, 530 (1997).

166. Morrison, 529 U.S. at 625–626.

167. United Bhd. of Carpenters, Local 610 v. Scott, 463 U.S. 825, 853 (1983) (Blackmun, J., dissenting). For a contrasting reading of the authorities on the private action question, see Brzonkala v. Virginia Polytechnic Institute & State University, 169 F.3d 820, 869 n.26 (4th Cir. 1999) (en banc).

168. Carpenters, 463 U.S. at 853 (Blackmun, J., dissenting).

169. Id. at 848 n.11.

170. Bray v. Alexandria Women's Health Clinic, 506 U.S. 263, 345 (1993) (O'Connor, J., dissenting).

171. 526 U.S. 629 (1999).

172. 505 U.S. 833 (1992).

173. 488 U.S. 469 (1989).

174. Id. at 490. The *Croson* ruling was built on Fullilove v. Klutznick's holding that Section 5 would support a federal minority set-aside program based on congressional findings of society-wide discrimination. Fullilove v. Klutznick, 448 U.S. 448, 476–478 (1980).

175. 252 U.S. 416 (1920).

176. See id. at 432.

177. See id.; Neely v. Henkel, 180 U.S. 109, 121–122 (1901); United States v. Lue, 134 F.3d 79, 82–84 (2d Cir. 1998) (holding the Hostage Taking Act to be a valid exercise of congressional power under the Necessary and Proper Clause pursuant to an international treaty rather than unconstitutional under the Tenth Amendment); Louis Henkin, *Foreign Affairs and the United States Constitution* 191 and n.** (2d ed. 1996) (noting that many matters under the Tenth Amendment "are, one might say, left to the states subject to 'defeasance' if the United States should decide to make a treaty about them"); David M. Golove, "Treaty-Making and the Nation: The Historical Foundations of the Nationalist Conception of the Treaty Power," 98 *Michigan Law Review* 1075, 1099 (2000) ("Under the Necessary and Proper Clause, it is quite clear that Congress has the power to adopt legislation executing the provisions of any valid treaty").

178. International Covenant on Civil and Political Rights, 999 U.N.T.S. 171 (1966) [hereinafter ICCPR]. The United States ratified the ICCPR on September 8, 1992. U.S. Dep't of State, *Treaties in Force: A List of Treaties and Other International Agreements of the United States in Force on January 1, 1999* at 389 (1999).

179. ICCPR, note 178 above, art. 2(1), 999 U.N.T.S. at 173.

180. Id. art. 3, 999 U.N.T.S. at 174.

181. Id. arts. 6, 9, 10, 14, 7, 999 U.N.T.S. at 174–177.

182. Id. art. 26, 999 U.N.T.S. at 179.

183. See, e.g., Declaration on the Elimination of Violence Against Women, G.A. Res. 104, U.N. GAOR, 48th Sess., U.N. Doc. 1/49/104 (1993); U.N. GAOR, 48th Sess. 85th plen. mtg. at 5, U.N. Doc. A/48/PV.85 (1994) (adopting resolution).

184. ICCPR, note 178 above, arts. 28, 40, 999 U.N.T.S. at 179, 181–182.

185. Summary Record of the 1401st Meeting, U.N. Hum. Rts. Comm., 53rd Sess., U.N. Doc. CCPR/C/SR.1401 (1995).

186. For a perceptive analysis of "the private" in the VAWA setting, including its role in the Fourth Circuit opinion, see Sally F. Goldfarb, "Violence Against Women and the Persistence of Privacy," 61 *Ohio State Law Journal* 1, 45–85 (2000).

187. Brzonkala v. Va. Polytechnic Institute & State University 169 F.3d 820, 825–

826 (4th Cir. 1999) (en banc) (holding that the challenged section of the VAWA could not be upheld under the Commerce Clause and that the section was not a constitutionally legitimate exercise of Congress's power under the enforcement section of the Fourteenth Amendment).

188. Id. at 842.

189. Id. at 853.

190. One wonders about the fate of the federal Defense of Marriage Act, Pub. L. No. 104–199, 110 Stat. 2419 (1996) (codified at 1 U.S.C. §7, 28 U.S.C. §1738C (Supp. II 1996)), in this picture.

191. 388 U.S. 1 (1967) (striking down a Virginia miscegenation statute as an unconstitutional institutionalization of white supremacy under the Fourteenth Amendment).

192. 466 U.S. 409 (1984) (holding that fear of stigmatization was an unconstitutional reason to remove a child from the custody of his white mother after she remarried a Black man).

193. 440 U.S. 268 (1979) (striking down as sex discrimination under the Fourteenth Amendment an Alabama statutory scheme that provided that only husbands, and not wives, be required to pay alimony).

194. 450 U.S. 455 (1981) (holding unconstitutional under the Fourteenth Amendment a Louisiana statute giving a husband the unilateral right to dispose of marital property jointly held by him and his wife).

195. For critiques of the public-private line as promoting subordination of women to men, see Susan Moller Okin, "Gender, the Public and the Private," in *Political Theory Today* 67 (David Held. ed., 1991); and Carole Pateman, "Feminist Critiques of the Public/Private Dichotomy," in *Public and Private in Social Life* 281–303 (S. I. Benn & G. F. Gaus, eds., 1983).

196. Mary P. Koss, Lisa A. Goodman, Angela Browne, Louise F. Fitzgerald, Gwendolyn Puryear Keita & Nancy Felipe Russo, *No Safe Haven: Male Violence Against Women at Home, at Work, and in the Community* 41 (1994).

197. 334 U.S. 1 (1948).

198. *Morrison*, 529 U.S. at 621 ("[The Fourteenth] Amendment erects no shield against merely private conduct, however discriminatory or wrongful") (quoting *Shelley*, 334 U.S. at 13 and n.12).

199. Garcia v. San Antonio Metro. Transit Auth., 469 U.S. 528, 572 (1985) (Powell, J., dissenting).

200. *Morrison*, 529 U.S. at 643 (Souter, J., dissenting).

201. See id. at 657 (Breyer, J., dissenting).

202. *Morrison*, 529 U.S. at 611; see id. at 636 n.10 (Souter, J., dissenting).

203. *Morrison*, 529 U.S. at 618.

204. See id. at 640–645 (Souter, J., dissenting) (so asserting in addressing the majority's approach to commerce).

205. See id. at 659–662 (Breyer, J., dissenting).

206. Simone de Beauvoir, *The Second Sex* xxi (1974).

207. Bruno v. Codd, 396 N.Y.S.2d 974 (Sup. Ct. 1977), reversed, 407 N.Y.S.2d 165 (App. Div. 1978), affirmed, 393 N.E.2d 976 (N.Y. 1979).

208. See, e.g., People v. Liberta, 474 N.E.2d 567, 575, 578 (N.Y. 1984) (invalidating a state marital rape law as a violation of equal protection of the laws).

209. See Meritor Sav. Bank v. Vinson, 477 U.S. 57, 63–67 (1986) (holding that a claim of "hostile environmental" sexual harassment is a form of sex discrimination that is actionable under Title VII); Barnes v. Costle, 561 F.2d 983, 994 (D.C. Cir. 1977) (holding that a male superior violated the Equal Opportunity Act of 1972 when he abolished a female employee's job after she rejected his sexual advances).

210. Joan Fitzpatrick, "The Use of International Human Rights Norms to Combat Violence Against Women," in *Human Rights of Women*, 532 (Rebecca J. Cook, ed., 1994); see generally *United Nations World Conference on Human Rights: Vienna Declaration and Programme of Action*, U.N. Doc. A/CONF.157/23 (1993); *United Nations Fourth World Conference on Women: Beijing Declaration and Platform for Action*, U.N. Doc. A/CONF.177/20, ¶ ¶ 96, 112–141, 224 (1995).

211. See Kadic v. Karadzic, 70 F.3d 232, 236 (2d Cir. 1995) (recognizing jurisdiction over a nonstate actor for genocidal rape, among other atrocities, under the Alien Tort Act).

212. See, e.g., S. Afr. Const. ch. 2, § 9(4) (adopted May 8, 1996; amended Oct. 11, 1996).

213. Adoption of the Convention on the Elimination of All Forms of Discrimination Against Women, U.N. Doc. A/RES/34/180 (1979), would help.

214. See Golove, note 177 above, at 1077–1078, 1210–1238.

215. The latter is argued to be the case in Catharine A. MacKinnon, *Toward a Feminist Theory of the State* (1989).

18. Unequal Sex: A Sex Equality Approach to Sexual Assault

This address was given to the New York Academy of Science, Conference on Understanding and Managing Sexually Coercive Individuals, June 8, 2002, Washington, D.C. It was first published at 989 *Annals of the New York Academy of Science* 1 (2003) in a volume titled *Sexual Coercion: Understanding and Management* 265 (Robert Prentky, Eric Janus, and Michael Seto, eds., June, 2003). The research assistance and thoughts of Lisa Cardyn and Candice Aloisi are gratefully acknowledged. Stephen Schulhofer's work was exceptionally helpful.

1. Data is summarized in Catharine A. MacKinnon, *Sex Equality* 776–778 (2001).

2. See Mary P. Koss et al., *No Safe Haven: Male Violence Against Women at Home, at Work, and in the Community* 167–671 (1994) (analyzing major studies on rape prevalence done as of 1994, many showing approximately 20 percent of women subject to completed rape, some numbers lower, some higher); Diana E. H. Russell, *Sexual Exploitation: Rape, Child Sexual Abuse, and Workplace Harassment* 31, 35 (1984) (finding 9.5 percent of rapes reported and 24 percent of women experiencing rape in lifetime in large probability sample).

3. The work of Diana E. H. Russell, David Finkelhor, Peggy Reeves Sanday, Diana Scully, and many others converges on this conclusion.

4. Andrea J. Sedlak and Diane D. Broadhurst, U.S. Dep't of Health and Human Servs., *Executive Summary of the Third National Incidence Study of Child Abuse and Neglect* 14 (1996) found that 12 percent of all sexually abused children are abused by a female.

5. Before they reach the age of majority, 38 percent of girls report having been sexually abused, most by men close to them or in authority over them. The average age of first abuse is around ten. Diana E. H. Russell, "The Incidence and Prevalence of Intrafamilial and Extrafamilial Sexual Abuse of Female Children," in *Handbook on Sexual Abuse of Children* 19, 24 (Lenore E. Walker, ed., 1986); Diana E. H. Russell, *The Secret Trauma* 99–100 (1986); Gail E. Wyatt, "The Sexual Abuse of Afro-American and White American Women in Childhood," 9 *Child Abuse and Neglect* 507 (1985) (finding 57 percent of sample of African American women and 67 percent of white American women report at least one incident of sexual abuse before age eighteen).

6. Data on sexually assaulted men includes documentation showing that 6 percent of the rapes reported to a survey of victims age twelve and over in 1996 were rapes of men by men. See Bureau of Justice Statistics, 2001 National Crime Victimization Survey, *Bureau of Justice Statistics Bulletin*, Table 2, Table 38 (2001). Sexual abuse of boys has been found to be "common, underreported, underrecognized, and undertreated." William C. Holmes and Gail B. Slap, "Sexual Abuse of Boys: Definition, Prevalence, Correlates, Sequelae, and Management," 280 *JAMA: Journal of the American Medical Association* 1855, 1855 (1998).

7. African American women are generally considered to be subjected to a higher incidence of rape than white women in the American population. See Diana E. H. Russell, *Sexual Exploitation* 82 (1984) (reporting all studies to date). Professor Russell's study found that the highest percentage of women to be subjected to at least one rape or attempted rape were Native American women (55 percent), followed by Jewish women (50 percent), white non-Jewish women (45 percent), African American women (44 percent), Latinas (30 percent), Asian women (17 percent), Filipinas (17 percent), and other ethnicities (28 percent). See id. at 83–84. Note that these are figures for women ever raped or victimized by attempted rape, not the number of rapes. According to recent statistics, people from households with low incomes experienced higher violent crime victimization rates than people from wealthier households. For instance, people from households with annual incomes below $7,500 were twenty-six times as likely as those from households with incomes of $75,000 to be rape and sexual assault victims and have significantly higher rates of rape, sexual assault, and aggravated assault compared with people in all other income groups. See Bureau of Justice Statistics, *Criminal Victimization in the United States 2000*, Table 14 (2000).

8. See, e.g., Binaifer Nowrojee, *Shattered Lives: Sexual Violence During the Rwandan Genocide and Its Aftermath* 1–2 (1996).

9. R. v. Osolin [1993] 4 S.C.R. 595, 669 (Cory, J.).

10. The General Assembly of the United Nations in 1994 adopted a resolution condemning sexual violence that defined it as gender-based violence, G.A. Res. 48/

104, U.N. GAOR, 48th Sess., at art. 4, U.N. Doc. A/48/49 (1994); 33 I.L.M. 1049. General Recommendation No. 19, Committee on the Elimination of Discrimination Against Women, 11th Sess., U.N. Doc. CEDAW/C/1992/L.1/Add. 15 (1992). The most far-reaching international convention to date, the Convention of Belem do Para adopted by the Organization of American States in 1994, recognized in its preamble that violence against women "is . . . a manifestation of the historically unequal power relations between women and men." Convention of Belem do Para, 33 I.L.M. 1994. It declares that "every woman has the right to be free from violence in both the public and private spheres," id. at art. 3, and required in detail that states parties and societies take action "to protect the right of every woman to be free from violence," id. at art. 10. The Beijing Declaration and Platform of Action in 1995 expressly embraced the right of women "to have control over and decide freely and responsibly on matters related to their sexuality" as a human right, Beijing Declaration and Platform for Action of the United Nations Fourth World Conference on Women, U.N. Doc. A/CONF.177/20 (1995) at ¶96, and condemned violence against women as "a manifestation of the historically unequal power relations between men and women, which have led to domination over and discrimination against women by men," all expressly analyzed as social realities. Id. at ¶118. The Committee of Ministers of the Council of Europe recently "reaffirm[ed] that violence towards women is the result of an imbalance of power between men and women and is leading to serious discrimination against the female sex, both within society and within the family." Council of Europe, Committee of Ministers, Recommendation Rec(2002)5 of the Committee of Ministers to member states on the protection of women against violence (30 April 2002).

11. See Meritor Sav. Bank v. Vinson, 477 U.S. 57 (1986) (recognizing hostile environment sexual harassment on facts of repeated rape as sex discrimination in employment); Alexander v. Yale University, 631 F.2d 178 (2d Cir. 1980) (recognizing sexual harassment in education as prohibited under Title IX prohibition on sex discrimination); Franklin v. Gwinnet County Public Schools, 503 U.S. 50 (1992) (permitting damages for Title IX sexual harassment).

12. Dothard v. Rawlinson, 433 U.S. 321, 336 (1977) (permitting women to be excluded from contact positions in high-security prison employment on the basis of sex because of capacity to be raped). The Court may have been thinking of sexual biology, but the sexed reality was nonetheless observed.

13. 42 U.S.C. §13981 (1994).

14. See United States v. Morrison, 529 U.S. 598, 635–636 (2000).

15. Most sexual assaults remain unreported, unprosecuted, and unremedied. See, e.g., National Victim Center, Crime Victims Research and Treatment Center, *Rape in America* 5 (1992) (finding that 16 percent of rapes are reported); Staff of Senate Comm. on the Judiciary, 103rd Cong., *The Response to Rape: Detours on the Road to Equal Justice* iii (Comm. Print 1993) (drawing on data from several jurisdictions, concluding that 98 percent of rape victims "never see their attacker caught, tried and imprisoned.")

16. An example is Michael M. v. Superior Court of Sonoma County, 450 U.S. 464 (1981).

17. The manifest ineffectiveness of existing laws against sexual assault was amply demonstrated before the Congress that passed the Violence Against Women Act. See *Women and Violence: Hearings Before the Senate Comm. on the Judiciary*, 101 Cong. (1990). Estimates are that the likelihood of a rape complaint's ending in conviction is 2 to 5 percent of rapes. See Joan McGregor, "Introduction to Symposium on Philosophical Issues in Rape Law," 11 *Law and Philosophy* 1, 2 (1992).

18. The Antioch College Sexual Offense Prevention Policy (June 8, 1996), reproduced in MacKinnon, *Sex Equality* 836–837, does.

19. The model was recently pungently described by a female-to-male transsexed person and longtime advocate of S/M (sadism and masochism) in sex, when asked why he transsexed: "[r]unning the fuck is an integral part of maleness in our society." Patrick Califia, "Transman Seeks Sex Life: T 4 U," *Village Voice*, June 26–July 2, 2002.

20. See, e.g., Commonwealth v. Berkowitz, 609 A.2d 1338 (Pa. Super. Ct.), *aff'd* 641 A.2d 1161 (Pa. 1994). The Pennsylvania legislature attempted to address the problem after public outcry, see, e.g., 18 Pa. Cons. Stat. Ann. §3124.1, but it is unclear if they did. One better approach can be seen in R. v. Ewanchuk, [1999] 169 D.L.R. 4th 193 (Can.) (holding that consent is a purely subjective fact to be determined by trial judge by ascertaining complainant's state of mind toward sexual touching when it occurred and that consent out of fear is not freely given, hence ineffective).

21. Women are not alone in this. See, e.g., R. v. R.J.S. [1994] 123 Nfld & P.E.I.R. 317 (finding that erection may be sufficient evidence of consent to sex).

22. Examples are Boro v. Superior Court, 163 Cal. App. 3d 1224, 210 Cal. Rptr. 122 (1985), and People v. Ogunmola, 238 Cal. Rptr. 300 (Cal. Ct. App. 2d Dist. 1987), involving doctors and patients. In *Boro*, the patient, who had permitted sex in the guise of treatment, was found to have consented. In *Ogunmola*, two patients who consented to an examination but were penetrated by the doctor's penis instead were found not to have consented. California partially addressed the *Boro* situation by statute prohibiting sexual intercourse "procured by false or fraudulent representation or pretense that is made with the intent to create fear, and which does induce fear" with a spousal exception. Cal. Penal Code §266C. (The spousal exception was removed by amendment in 1994, see Cal. Penal Code §266C.) Recent developments in the law of rape by fraud are discussed in Patricia J. Falk, "Rape by Fraud and Rape by Coercion," 64 *Brooklyn Law Review* 39, 89–131 (1998). See also Jane E. Larson, "Women Understand So Little, They Call My Good Nature 'Deceit': A Feminist Rethinking of Seduction," 93 *Columbia Law Review* 374 (1993).

23. For general discussion of multiplicity, see Daniel Brown, Alan W. Scheflin, and D. Corydon Hammond et al., *Memory, Trauma Treatment, and the Law* (1998); for a brilliant treatment of the subject, see Harvey Schwartz, *Dialogues with Forgotten Voices* (2000). See also Carole Goettman, George B. Greaves, and Philip M. Coons, *Multiple Personality and Dissociation, 1791–1992, A Complete Bibliography* (1994), and Sabra Owens, *Criminal Responsibility and Multiple Personality Defendants* (American Bar Association, 1997).

24. See, e.g., State v. Thompson, 792 P.2d 1103 (Mont. 1990) (defendant high

school principal allegedly forced student to submit to sexual intercourse by threatening to prevent her from graduating from high school; court affirmed dismissal of sexual assault charges because of lack of physical force). The Supreme Court of Canada found a rape threat to be a threat of severe bodily harm in R. v. McCraw, [1991] 3 S.C.R. 72, a conclusion far from obvious to many courts in the world.

25. See Morrison Torrey, "When Will We Be Believed? Rape Myths and the Idea of a Fair Trial in Rape Prosecutions," 24 *University of California at Davis Law Review* 1013 (1991); Robin West, "Equality Theory, Marital Rape, and the Promise of the Fourteenth Amendment," 42 *University of Florida Law Review* 45, 66–70 (1990). See also Jaye Sitton, Comment, "Old Wine in New Bottles: The 'Marital' Rape Allowance," 72 *North Carolina Law Review* 261, 280–281 (1993) (describing extension of traditional marital rape law's doctrine of implied consent to cohabitants and "voluntary social companions").

26. For the standard's initial articulation, see Meritor Savings Bank v. Vinson, 477 U.S. 57, 69 (1986), a sexual harassment case distinguishing between the criminal law standard of "voluntary" sex and the civil equality standard of "unwelcome" sex. For further discussion, see MacKinnon, *Sex Equality* 977–989.

27. An excellent examination of this topic is Stephen Schulhofer, *Unwanted Sex: The Culture of Intimidation and the Failure of Law* (1998).

28. Commonwealth v. Rhodes, 510 A.2d 1217, 1226 (Pa. 1986).

29. See People v. Warren, 446 N.E.2d 591 (Ill. App. Ct. 1983) (finding of stranger-rape allegations that 6-foot-3-inch 185-pound defendant, "apart from picking up [5-foot-2-inch 100-pound woman] complainant and carrying her into and out of the woods" where he had sex with her, showed insufficient force, and faulting complainant for failing to resist). Analysis of the role of women's and men's different average height and weight in the context of potential rape can be found in Dothard v. Rawlinson, 433 U.S. 321 (1977) (holding that a particular minimum height/weight standard for prison guards at male-only prisons discriminated against women on the basis of sex).

30. My impression of marital rape cases where they are prosecuted is that the amount of force required for a conviction is often extreme, compared with what is required in stranger-rape cases in the same jurisdictions.

31. Some states have prohibitions similar to statutory rape for prison guards, e.g., Conn. Penal Code §53a–71.

32. One of the few legal discussions of this question took place in the *Michael M.* case, Michael M. v. Superior Court of Sonoma County, 450 U.S. 464 (1981), the Supreme Court justices, majority and dissenting alike, falling all over each other not to question whether women and men were equal in sex in the name of sexual egalitarianism.

33. See, e.g., State in the Interest of M.T.S., 609 A.2d 1266 (N.J. 1992).

34. Before they reach the age of majority, 38 percent of girls report having been sexually abused, most by men close to them or in authority over them. See Diana E. H. Russell, "The Incidence and Prevalence of Intrafamilial and Extrafamilial Sexual Abuse of Female Children," in *Handbook on Sexual Abuse of Children* 19, 24 (Lenore E.

Walker, ed., 1998) (also finding 16 percent of girls abused by a family member); Diana E. H. Russell, *The Secret Trauma* 99–100 (1986).

35. World Health Organization, *World Report on Violence and Health* 149 (Etienne G. Krug, et al., eds., Geneva 2002) (finding "up to one-third of adolescent girls report their first sexual experience as being forced").

36. This is a variant on the test in Prosecutor v. Akayesu, Case No. ICTR 96 4 T (1998), addressing rape in the Rwandan genocide. There, the coercive conditions were provided by the other jurisdictional requisites under the tribunal's statute, which include crimes against humanity and genocide. It is also enacted at Cal. Civ. Code 52.4(c)(2) as a civil claim for gender-based discrimination.

37. This arrangement could make a reconstructed definition of consent into an affirmative defense.

19. Sex, Lies, and Psychotherapy

Originally published in Jeffrey Moussaieff Masson, *A Dark Science: Women, Sexuality, and Psychiatry in the Nineteenth Century* xi–xvii (Jeffrey Moussaieff Masson and Marianne Loring trans., 1986), this essay was the preface to a compilation of translations of psychiatric publications from the nineteenth-century French and German that provide the professional context in which Freud practiced and theorized.

1. Gerry Spence, *Trial by Fire: The True Story of a Woman's Ordeal at the Hands of the Law* 374 (1986).

2. Masson, *A Dark Science* 162 (Schrenck-Notzing referring to case as potentially among those of "simulators, people who lie, hysterics, fantasy-liars, and those whose instinct toward dishonesty lies deeply rooted in their character, as a result of which they very often make false accusations").

3. Id. at 125 (Fournier).

4. Id. at 55 (Flechsig).

5. Id. at 157 (Schrenck-Notzing).

6. Id. at 110–111 (italics in original).

7. All the references to this case are from Gordon Burn, *". . . somebody's husband, somebody's son": The Story of Peter Sutcliffe* 253–257 (1984) (emphasis added).

8. Masson, *A Dark Science* 61–89.

9. Masson, *A Dark Science* 127 (Fournier).

10. See Phyllis Chesler, *Mothers on Trial* (1986).

11. Masson, *A Dark Science* 90–105.

12. All the quotations in this paragraph are from "Crossexamination of a Child," distributed by the Committee for Public Counsel of the Commonwealth of Massachusetts, appearing in duplicated materials prepared for the Bar Advocacy Program, Westford Regency Inn, Westford, Massachusetts, May 2, 1986 (emphasis in original).

13. William Niederland, "Post-traumatic Symptomology," in *Massive Psychic Trauma* 67 (Henry Krystal, ed., 1968), discussing Robert Lifton's theory of "psychological closure."

14. Gustav Bychowski, "Permanent Character Changes as an Aftereffect of Persecution," in *Massive Psychic Trauma* at 81.

15. Diana E. H. Russell, in *The Secret Trauma: Incest in the Lives of Women and Girls* 70 (1986), documents 43 percent of girls as victims of incestuous and/or extrafamilial sexual abuse involving sexual contact.

16. In this project, helpful sources include Phyllis Chesler, *Women and Madness* (1972); Alice Miller, *For Your Own Good: Hidden Cruelty in Child-Rearing and the Roots of Violence* (1983) and *Thou Shalt Not Be Aware: Society's Betrayal of the Child* (1984); and Klaus Theweleit, *Männerphantasien* (1977).

17. Masson, *A Dark Science* 128–138 ("The Amputation of the Clitoris and Labia Minora: A Contribution to the Treatment of Vaginismus").

18. John Stoltenberg, "The Forbidden Language of Sex," speech to American Writers' Congress (New York October 10, 1981), published in John Stoltenberg, "The Forbidden Language of Sex," in *Refusing to Be a Man* 107 (2000 edition) ("Pornography tells lies about women. But pornography tells the truth about men.") The insight refers to Andrea Dworkin, *Pornography: Men Possessing Women* (1981), who said that pornography tells lies about women.

20. Liberalism and the Death of Feminism

Delivered April 6, 1987, at a conference at New York University Law School titled "The Sexual Liberals and the Attack on Feminism." Published in *The Sexual Liberals and the Attack on Feminism* 3 (Dorchen Leidholdt and Janice G. Raymond eds., 1990).

1. For Robin Morgan's "Goodbye to All That," which appeared in that issue of the magazine, see *Going Too Far: The Personal Chronicle of a Radical Feminist* 121 (1978).

2. An example of this transformation is the analysis in Barbara Brown, Thomas Emerson, Gail Falk, Ann Freedman, "The Equal Rights Amendment: A Constitutional Basis for Equal Rights for Women," 80 *Yale Law Journal* 871 (1971).

3. Roe v. Wade, 410 U.S. 113 (1973).

4. Harris v. McRae, 448 U.S. 297 (1980).

5. EEOC v. Sears, Roebuck & Co., 839 F.2d 302 (7th Cir. 1988).

6. *Offer of Proof Concerning the Testimony of Dr. Rosalind Rosenberg* and *Written Rebuttal Testimony of Dr. Rosalind Rosenberg* before the United States District Court for the Northern District of Illinois in EEOC v. Sears, Roebuck & Co., 504 F. Supp. 241 (N.D. Ill. 1988).

7. *Written Testimony of Alice Kessler-Harris* before the United States District Court for the Northern District of Illinois in EEOC v. Sears, Roebuck & Co., 504 F. Supp 241 (N.D. Ill. 1988).

8. California Federal Savings & Loan. et al. v. Guerra, 479 US 272 (1987).

9. *An Ordinance for the City of Minneapolis*, Amending Title 7, Chapter 139 of the Minneapolis Code of Ordinances relating to Civil Rights, section 139.10 et seq., reprinted in Andrea Dworkin and Catharine A. MacKinnon, *Pornography and Civil Rights: A New Day for Women's Equality* (1988).

10. "Brief Amici Curiae of Feminist Anti-Censorship Task Force et al. in American Booksellers Association v. Hudnut," 21 *Journal of Law Reform* 69 (1988).

11. Id. at 121.

12. Id. at 129.

13. Id. at 122, 127–128, 130, 131.

14. American Booksellers v. Hudnut, 771 F.2d 323, 327 (7th Cir. 1985).

15. Id. at 324.

21. Does Sexuality Have a History?

Presented September 12, 1990, as a lecture sponsored by the University of Michigan Institute for the Humanities and the University of Michigan Law School, this essay was first published in *Discourses of Sexuality: From Aristotle to AIDS* 117 (Domna C. Stanton, ed., 1992) and at 30 *Michigan Quarterly Review* 1 (1991).

1. Friedrich Nietzsche, *The Advantages and Disadvantages of History for Life* 14–15 (Peter Preuss, trans., 1980).

2. *Pleasure and Danger: Exploring Female Sexuality* (Carole S. Vance, ed., 1984). There are exceptions to this characterization in the collection, notably the essay by Kate Millett on sex between adults and children. When she asks, "Adults can turn around and hit you at any moment. They can send you off to bed. Who wants a relationship with a lover who has this sort of authority?" it is clear she is in the wrong book.

3. *Powers of Desire: The Politics of Sexuality* (Ann Snitow, Christine Stansell, and Sharon Thompson, eds., 1983). Again, not all of the contributions fit this characterization.

4. See, for example, Jeffrey Weeks, *Sex, Politics and Society: The Regulation of Sexuality Since 1800* (1981); John D'Emilio, *Sexual Politics, Sexual Communities: The Making of the Homosexual Minority in the United States, 1940–1970* (1983); Judith R. Walkowitz, *Prostitution and Victorian Society* (1980) and "Male Vice and Female Virtue: Feminism and the Politics of Prostitution In Nineteenth-Century Britain," in *Powers of Desire* 419–438.

5. See, for example, George Bataille, *Death and Sensuality* (1962); Samois, *Coming to Power* (1982); Pat Califia, "Feminism and Sadomasochism," *Coevolution Quarterly*, 33, 33–40 (Spring 1982).

6. "We must not think that by saying yes to sex, one says no to power." Michel Foucault, *The History of Sexuality, Volume 1: An Introduction* 157 (Robert Hurley, trans., 1980). Indeed.

7. There seems to me a deep underlying continuity of sadomasochism in Foucault's work between his analysis both of torture and its replacement with disciplinary power, see Michel Foucault, *Discipline and Punish*, (Alan Sheridan trans., 1979), and his version of what sexuality, per se, is about.

8. Works from the study include Diana E. H. Russell, *Sexual Exploitation: Rape, Child Sexual Abuse, and Sexual Harassment* (1984), *Rape in Marriage* (1982), and *The Secret Trauma: Incestuous Abuse of Women and Girls* (1986).

9. Diana Russell did this calculation at my request on her database.

10. Foucault, *History of Sexuality* 1:104.

11. Russell, *Sexual Exploitation* 55–57. ("The tragic finding of this survey is an alarming increase in the true rape rate over the years.") It is true that women feel more able to report now, but this compares women reporting under the same conditions about being assaulted during different times. It is also possible that younger women are more likely to report rape than older women.

12. In 1987, the forcible rape total rose 15 percent over 1982 and 42 percent over 1977, according to the Justice Department. In 1989, it rose 7 percent over 1985 and 14 percent over 1980. From 1983 to 1987, the female forcible rape data rose 11 percent. *Uniform Crime Reports* (1987, 1988, 1989, 1990). Note these are *reported* rapes, those that are not "unfounded" by the police.

13. Elizabeth Holtzman, "Rape—The Silence Is Criminal," *New York Times*, sec. 1, 35 (May 5, 1989). Ms. Holtzman reports "startling increases in rape by teenagers" such that in New York City, in the two years before her article, saw a 27 percent increase in rape arrests of boys under eighteen and a 200 percent increase of boys under thirteen. No such trend has yet registered in federal crime statistics.

14. David Finkelhor, *Child Sexual Abuse: Theory and Research* (1984).

15. This is an impression, a sense influenced by discussions of the subject with Andrea Dworkin, not an interpretation for which evidence is yet available.

16. See citations at n6, p. 304 in my *Toward a Feminist Theory of the State* (1989).

17. Diana E. H. Russell, "Pornography and Rape: A Causal Model," 9 *Political Psychology* 41, 41–74 (1988).

18. Michel Foucault, *The Uses of Pleasure* 14 (Robert Hurley trans., 1985).

19. This is argued in more depth in Chapter 7, "Sexuality," in *Toward a Feminist Theory of the State* (1989).

20. Eva C. Keuls, *The Reign of the Phallus: Sexual Politics in Ancient Athens* (1985).

21. In English, it is Klaus Theweleit, *Male Fantasies, Volume 1: Women, Floods, Bodies, History* (Stephen Conway, trans., with Erica Carter and Chris Turner 1987).

22. Sheila Jeffreys, *The Spinster and Her Enemies: Feminism and Sexuality, 1880–1930* (1985).

23. Sheila Jeffreys, *Anticlimax: A Feminist Perspective on the Sexual Revolution* (1990).

24. Stephen Heath, *The Sexual Fix* (1982).

25. Thomas Laqueur, *Making Sex: Body and Gender from the Greeks to Freud* (1990).

26. Jeffrey Moussaieff Masson, *The Assault on Truth: Freud's Suppression of the Seduction Theory* (1984).

27. Critical history "belongs to the living man . . . so far as he suffers and is in need of liberation." Nietzsche, *History for Life* 14.

22. Speaking Truth to Power

This speech was given first at Boalt Hall Law School, the University of California at Berkeley, on November 5, 1991, and again at the University of New Mexico, on

January 30, 1992, under the title it bears here. Special thanks go to Ann Scales and Lauren Baldwin for arranging the New Mexico event. The piece is published here for the first time.

1. *The Complete Transcripts of the Clarence Thomas–Anita Hill Hearings, October 11, 12, 13, 23, 1991* (Anita Miller, ed., 1994) (Testimony of Anita F. Hill) ("He spoke about acts that he had seen in pornographic films involving such matters as women having sex with animals, and films showing group sex or rape scenes. He talked about pornographic materials depicting individuals with large penises, or large breasts involved in various sex acts").

2. Id. at 24 ("One of the oddest episodes I remember was an occasion in which Thomas was drinking a Coke in his office. He got up from the table, at which we were working, went over to his desk to get the Coke, looked at the can and asked, 'Who has put pubic hair on my Coke?'"). See also id. at 33.

3. Id. at 23 ("On several occasions Thomas told me graphically of his own sexual prowess").

4. Id. at 33 ("This was a reference to an individual who had a very large penis and he used the name that he had referred to in the pornographic material . . . The name that was referred to was Long John [sic] Silver").

5. Id. at 24 ("and he also spoke on some occasions of the pleasures he had given to women with oral sex").

6. Id.

7. Quoted in David Margolick, "Smith Lawyers Assail Accuser's Memory," *New York Times*, A16 (December 6, 1991).

8. For use of the word "erotomania" in press accounts, see Felicity Barringer, "The Thomas Nomination: Psychologists Try to Explain Why Thomas and Hill Offer Opposing Views," *New York Times*, A10 (October 14, 1991); Frank Rich, "Journal: Justice for None," *New York Times*, A31 (November 3, 1991); Andrew Rosenthal, "Psychiatry's Use in Thomas Battle Raises Ethics Issues," *New York Times*, sec. 1, p. 23 (October 20, 1991); Alessandra Stanley, "Ideas and Trends, Erotomania: A Rare Disorder Runs Riot in Men's Minds," *New York Times*, sec. 4, p. 2 (November 10, 1991); "How Memory May Figure In Thomas–Hill Debate: Experts Say They May be Lying to Themselves," *San Francisco Chronicle*, A1 (October 14, 1991) from *The New York Times*, quoting psychiatrist Johnathan H. Segal: "'Most patients treated for erotomania are young, single women whose scenario concerns an older male, often a boss,' Segal said. 'But that is also the most common relationship involved in cases of sexual harassment.'"

For further attacks on Professor Hill's mental state, see Statement of Sen. Strom Thurmond, 137 *Congressional Record* 14649 (October 15, 1991) ("I have been contacted by several psychiatrists, suggesting that it is entirely possible she [Professor Hill] is suffering from delusions. Perhaps she is living in a fantasy world"); "Letter of Elizabeth Brodie, M.D. to Sen. Biden," 137 *Congressional Record* 14676 (entered into the record by Sen. Alan Simpson). Senator Simpson had previously alluded to this letter saying "he was getting stuff over the transom . . . saying 'Watch out for this woman' but offered no further explanation." John E. Yang, "Sen. Simpson Shows Letters Faulting Hill," *The Washington Post*, A22 (October 16, 1991).

9. *Complete Transcripts* at 166 (Statement by Sen. Orrin Hatch) ("I also want to say that the burden of proof is certainly not on Judge Thomas. This is America. The burden of proof is on those who use statements that are stereotypical statements").

10. *Complete Transcripts* at 18 (Further Testimony of Hon. Clarence Thomas). See also id. at 149–150, 211 ("Senator, I will not get into any discussions that I might have about my personal life or my sex life with any person outside the workplace"; "I didn't want my personal life or allegations about my sexual habits or anything else broadcast in every living room in the United States").

11. Id. at 22–35 (Testimony of Anita F. Hill).

12. Quoted in Adam Clymer, "The Thomas Nomination; Delaying the Vote: How Senators Reached Accord," *New York Times*, B15 (October 10, 1991).

13. *Complete Transcripts* at app. A, 471–472 ("Letter and Affidavit from Sukari Hardnett, Former Special Assistant, EEOC, Washington D.C."). Letter from Sukari Hardnett also at 137 *Congressional Record* 26327 (October 15, 1991). See also testimony of Angela Wright, *Complete Transcripts* at 376–407 and testimony of Rose Jourdain, id. at 408–425.

14. *Complete Transcripts* at 120 (Further Testimony of Hon. Clarence Thomas).

15. Id. at 117, 121, 153 ("Senator, I would like to start by saying unequivocally, uncategorically that I deny each and every single allegation against me today that suggested in any way that I had conversations of a sexual nature or about pornographic material with Anita Hill, that I ever attempted to date her, that I ever had any personal sexual interest in her, or that I in any way ever harassed her."; "What I have said to you is categorical that any allegations that I engaged in any conduct involving sexual activity, pornographic movies, attempted to date her, any allegations, I deny"; "Senator, my response is that I categorically, unequivocally deny them.").

16. Kimberlé Crenshaw, "Whose Story is it Anyway? Feminist and Antiracist Appropriation of Anita Hill," in *Race–ing Justice, En–gendering Power: Essays on Anita Hill, Clarence Thomas, and the Construction of Social Reality* 421 (Toni Morrison, ed., 1992).

17. *Complete Transcripts* at 18 (Further Testimony of Hon. Clarence Thomas).

18. Id.

19. 137 *Congressional Record* 26354 (October 15, 1991).

20. *Complete Transcripts* at 40 (Testimony of Anita F. Hill) ("He [FBI agent] asked me to describe the incidents, and rather than decline to make any statement at all, I described them to my level of comfort").

21. My notes at the time recorded Senator Grassley uttering these words on a national television show in October 1991 in commentary on Anita Hill's testimony.

22. My notes at the time recorded Deborah Norville making this statement on her radio show in October 1991 in commentary on Anita Hill's testimony.

23. Quoted in Christopher Connell, "Bush Says His Heart 'Aches' for Thomas," *San Francisco Chronicle*, A1 (October 14, 1991).

24. "I'm too dark to blush, but it makes you so uncomfortable," Eleanor Holmes Norton, quoted in Peter G. Gosselin, "Dignity a Casualty of Hearing Subjects, Emotions Equal Bizarre Theater," *Los Angeles Daily News*, N16 (October 13, 1991).

25. *Complete Transcripts* at 155, 157, 158 (Further Testimony of Hon. Clarence Thomas) ("[I]n this country when it comes to sexual conduct we still have underlying racial attitudes about black men and their views of sex. And once you pin that on me, I can't get it off"; " . . . in the 19th and 20th centuries, the lynchings of black men, you will see that there is invariably or in many instances a relationship with sex—an accusation that that person cannot shake off. . . . I cannot shake off these accusations because they play to the worst stereotypes we have about black men in this country"; "I feel as though something has been lodged against me and painted on me and it will leave an indelible mark on me").

26. The D.C. Circuit handed down its decision in Bundy v. Jackson, 641 F.2d 934 (D.C. Cir. 1981), on January 12, 1981; the district court opinion in the case, 19 Fair Empl. Prac. Dec. (CCH) 9154 (Apr. 25, 1979), is dated April 25, 1979. In her testimony before the Senate Judiciary Committee, Anita Hill described being sexually harassed at various points in 1981, when she was employed at the Department of Education, and throughout the fall and winter months of 1982, after she had transferred to the EEOC with Thomas. See above, note 11.

27. Meritor Sav. Bank FSB v. Vinson, 477 U.S. 57 (1986).

28. *Complete Transcripts* at 257, Statement by Sen. Simpson ("So, here is this foul stack of stench").

29. See Martin Dyckman, "Smith Judge Gave Him Big Break," *St. Petersburg Times*, A27 (December 5, 1991); Ed Cafasso, "Prosecution is Dealt Setback as Judge Bans Other Assault Claims," *Boston Herald*, 1 (December 3, 1991) (discussing ruling barring "similar fact evidence" including in context of Smith case).

30. *Complete Transcripts* at 67 (Testimony of Anita F. Hill). In response to questions from Sen. Howell Heflin, Prof. Hill stated:

Ms. Hill: Well, it was almost as though he wanted me at a disadvantage, to put me at a disadvantage, so that I would concede to whatever his wishes were.

Sen. Heflin: Do you think that he got some pleasure out of seeing you ill at ease and vulnerable?

Ms. Hill: I think so, yes.

Sen. Heflin: Was this feeling more so than a feeling that he might be seeking some type of dating or social relationship with you?

Ms. Hill: I think it was a combination of factors. I think he wanted to see me vulnerable and that, if I were vulnerable, then he could extract from me whatever he wanted, whether it was sexual or otherwise, that I would be under his control.

Sen. Heflin: As a psychology major, what elements of human nature seem to go into that type of a situation?

Ms. Hill: Well, I can't say exactly. I can say that I felt he was using his power and authority over me, he was exerting a level of power and attempting to make sure that that power was exerted. I think it was the fact that I had said no to him that caused him to want to do this.

31. This is not hindsight. When asked by the Committee in advance, I suggested this line of questioning.

32. Joseph Gelmis, "The Demand is There; The Porn Film Isn't," *Newsday*, 19 (October 15, 1991) ("Long Dong Silver is reportedly the name of a character played by an anonymous actor in one or more 8–mm. film loops, running about 15 minutes each and shown a decade ago in peep–style vending machines. The film loops apparently bore the star's name"); Jesse Hamlin, "Tracking Down Long Dong Silver," *San Francisco Chronicle*, E2 (October 15, 1991) ("according to informed sources in the dirty picture world, Long Dong never made any full-length movies. In the 1970s, he appeared in a few untitled 8mm short films—loops, as they're called in the industry—that ran in peep-show arcades").

33. On attitudes toward women's equality, see Larry Baron and Murray A. Straus, "Sexual Stratification, Pornography, and Rape in the United States," in *Pornography and Sexual Aggression* 186 (Neil M. Malamuth and Edward Donnerstein, eds., 1984). On attitudes toward rape, see Daniel Linz, et al., "The Effects of Multiple Exposures to Filmed Violence Against Women," 34 *Journal of Communication* 130, 142 (Summer, 1984) (documenting that men exposed to filmed violence against women judged a rape victim to be less injured than did the control group); Dolf Zillman, "Effects of Prolonged Consumption of Pornography," in *Pornography: Research Advances and Policy Considerations* 127 (Dolf Zillman and Jennings Bryant, eds., 1989); Dolf Zillman and James B. Weaver, "Pornography and Men's Sexual Callousness Toward Women," in *Research Advances* 95; James V. P. Check and Ted H. Guloien, "Reported Proclivity for Coercive Sex Following Repeated Exposure to Sexually Violent Pornography, Nonviolent Dehumanizing Pornography, and Erotica," in *Research Advances* 159.

34. It was relatively usual in late the 1970s, early 1980s, to use pornography to train doctors. See "Letter of Michelle Harrison, M.D., December 9, 1983," in *In Harm's Way: The Pornography Civil Rights Hearings* 220 (Catharine A. MacKinnon and Andrea Dworkin, eds., 1997). It is less usual today.

35. The failure to investigate his use of pornography at least disproves the conspiracy theory that the establishment was out to do anything they could to destroy him. Apparently there are limits.

36. Patricia J. Williams, "A Rare Case Study of Muleheadedness and Men," in *Race–ing Justice* 169.

37. *Complete Transcripts* at 433 (Statement of Sen. Joseph Biden) ("It seems to me that is a true leap in faith or ego, one of the two").

38. *Complete Transcripts* at 120.

39. 137 *Congressional Record* 26278–26279 (October 15, 1991) (Statement of Sen. Robert Byrd).

40. Id. at 26289 (Statement of Sen. Edward Kennedy) ("The struggle for racial justice, in its truest sense, was meant to wipe out all forms of oppression. No one, least of all Judge Thomas, is entitled to invoke one form of oppression to excuse another. The deliberate provocative use of a term like lynching is not only wrong in fact; it is a gross misuse of America's most historic tragedy and pain to buy a political advantage.").

41. Id. at 26299 (Statement of Sen. Joseph Biden).

42. Id. at 26299 (Statement of Sen. Barbara Mikulski) ("To the women watching this, do not lose heart, but we will lose ground.").

23. Mediating Reality

This address keynoted the Journalism and Women Symposium (JAWS) fall Camp on September 12, 1998, in Grand Teton National Park, Wyoming. Many thanks to Sharon Walsh and Rita Henley Jenson for their support. The piece is published for the first time in this volume.

1. Shooting at Thurston H. S., Springfield, Oregon, May 21, 1998: "'I thought it was fake. I had never heard a gun go off,' [Stephanie] Quimby said. 'It was like a movie and you were there. I felt so calm. I knew it was real when I saw him point the gun at someone and heard a girl yell "Tressa!" I knew she wouldn't joke.'" Associated Press, "One Dead in Oregon School Shooting," (May 21, 1998); "Larissa Rybka, a 16-year-old sophomore, said Thursday morning was 'like a movie. It keeps playing over and over again. In slow motion.'" Bill Graves, Steve Carter, Jerry Boone and Jane Filips, "Whirlwind of Emotions Unleashed at Scene," *Portland Oregonian*, A20 (May 22, 1998); "When A. J. saw reports of the shooting on television, he said it seemed like a movie. Now, it will always be 'really real.'" Kate Taylor and Laura Trujillo, "Students Allowed Back in Repaired Cafeteria," *Portland Oregonian*, A1 (May 26, 1998). From a newspaper article on *Small Soldiers*, a children's movie about toy soldiers going to war, the director, Joe Dante said: "[T]his is fantasy violence. Kids know when it's not real." Marcus Hammond, age twelve, said: "I thought it was really hard to tell the special effects from the real action. . . ." Claudia Puig, "Unexpected Skirmishes," *USA Today*, 1E (July 10, 1998).

2. Shooting at Westside Middle School, Jonesboro, Arkansas, March 24, 1998: eleven-year-old shooter says "I thought we were going to shoot over their heads . . . We didn't think anybody was going to get hurt." Rick Bragg, "Two Boys Convicted in School Shooting," *Austin-American Statesman*, A1 (August 12, 1998).

3. Linda Meyer Williams, "Recall of Childhood Trauma: A Prospective Study of Women's Memories of Child Sexual Abuse," 62 *Journal of Consulting and Clinical Psychology* 1167 (1994) (finding 38 percent of women whose childhood rapes had been medically documented at the time were not recalled by victims seventeen years later).

4. See Harvey L. Schwartz, *Dialogues with Forgotten Voices: Relational Perspectives On Child Abuse Trauma And Treatment Of Dissociative Disorders* (2000).

5. Diana E. H. Russell, *Sexual Exploitation: Rape, Child Sexual Abuse and Workplace Harassment* 35 (1984).

6. See Melissa Farley, Isin Baral, Merab Kiremire and Ufuk Sezgin, "Prostitution in Five Countries: Violence and Post-traumatic Stress Disorder," 8 *Feminism and Psychology* 405 (1998).

7. Claire Safran, *Redbook Magazine* (November 1976); Enid Nemy, "Women Begin to Speak Out Against Sexual Harassment at Work," *New York Times*, 38 (August 19, 1975).

8. Nan Robertson, *The Girls in the Balcony: Women, Men, and the "New York Times"* (1992).

9. Judy Klemesrud, "Women, Pornography, Free Speech: A Fierce Debate at N.Y.U.," *New York Times*, D10 (December 4, 1978); "Joining Hands in the Fight Against Pornography," *New York Times*, B7 (August 26, 1985).

24. Civil Rights Against Pornography

This speech was given at the Seventh Annual Conference of the National Association of Women Judges, University of Minnesota Law School, May 1986. An earlier version was delivered to a hearing of the Attorney General's Commission on Pornography, July 25, 1985, Chicago, Illinois. The Charter of the Commission was "to determine the nature, extent, and impact on society of pornography in the United States and to make specific recommendations to the Attorney General concerning more effective ways in which the spread of pornography could be contained, consistent with constitutional guarantees." Attorney General's Commission on Pornography, *Final Report* 1957 (July 1986). It was originally published as "Pornography as Sex Discrimination" in 4 *Law and Inequality: A Journal of Theory and Practice* 38 (1986).

1. *The Report of the Commission on Obscenity and Pornography* (1970).

2. Miller v. California, 413 U.S. 15, 24 (1973).

3. Young v. American Mini Theatres, Inc., 427 U.S. 50 (1976). An example enunciated after this speech was delivered is City of Renton v. Playtime Theatres, Inc., 106 S. Ct. 925 (1986), which permitted a zoning scheme that banished adult theaters to industrial areas.

4. Brockett v. Spokane Arcades, Inc., 105 S. Ct. 2794 (1985).

5. Upper Midwest Booksellers Ass'n v. City of Minneapolis, 780 F.2d 1389 (8th Cir. 1985).

6. St. Paul, Minnesota, is an example.

7. A lucid presentation of Professor Donnerstein's data can be found in *In Harm's Way: The Pornography Civil Rights Hearings* 44–60 (Catharine A. MacKinnon and Andrea Dworkin, eds., 1997). See also Edward Donnerstein, "Pornography: Its Effect on Violence Against Women," in *Pornography and Sexual Aggression* 53 (Neil M. Malamuth and Edward Donnerstein, eds., 1984).

8. Linda Lovelace and Michael McGrady, *Ordeal* (1980); Michael A. Gershel, "Evaluating a Proposed Civil Rights Approach to Pornography: Legal Analysis as if Women Mattered," 11 *William Mitchell Law Review* 41, 55 (1985); Margaret Baldwin, "The Sexuality of Inequality: The Minneapolis Pornography Ordinance," 2 *Law and Inequality: A Journal of Theory and Practice* 629, 636–637 (1984).

9. *In Harm's Way* at 39–268; see Baldwin, 2 *Law and Inequality* 629; Catharine A. MacKinnon, "Pornography, Civil Rights, and Speech," 20 *Harvard Civil Rights-Civil Liberties Law Review* 1, 22–60 (1985).

10. New York v. Ferber, 458 U.S. 747 (1982).

11. *Brief on Behalf of American Booksellers Association, Association of American Publishers, Inc., Council for Periodical Distributors Associations, Freedom to Read Foundation, International Periodical Distributors Association, Inc., National Association of College Stores, Inc., American Civil Liberties Union, the Association of American University Presses, Inc., New York Civil Liberties Union and St. Martin's Press, Incorporated as Amici Curiae*, New York v. Ferber, 458 U.S. 747 (1982).

12. *Ferber*, 47 U.S. at 774–775, (concurring opinion, O'Connor, J.): "I write separately to stress that the Court does not hold that New York must except 'material with serious literary, scientific, or educational value,' from its statute. The Court merely holds that, even if the First Amendment shelters such material, New York's current statute is not sufficiently overbroad to support respondent's facial attack. The compelling interests identified in today's opinion suggest that the Constitution might in fact permit New York to ban knowing distribution of works depicting minors engaged in explicit sexual conduct, regardless of the social value of the depictions. For example, a 12-year-old child photographed while masturbating surely suffers the same psychological harm whether the community labels the photograph 'edifying' or 'tasteless.' The audience's appreciation of the depiction is simply irrelevant to New York's asserted interest in protecting children from psychological, emotional, and mental harm."

13. *In Harm's Way: The Pornography Civil Rights Hearings* (Catharine A. MacKinnon and Andrea Dworkin, eds., 1997).

14. Id. at 60–66.

15. Id. at 44–60.

16. Id. at 98–99.

17. Diana Russell later documented a rate of 16,000 rapes per million women that the victims attributed directly to pornography. Diana E. H. Russell, *The Impact of Pornography on Women* (testimony prepared for the Attorney General's Commission on Pornography Hearings, Houston, Texas, Sept. 11, 1985). See also MacKinnon, 20 *Harvard Civil Rights-Civil Liberties Law Review* at 12 n.20.

18. *In Harm's Way* at 170–171.

19. Id. at 104–107.

20. Id. at 99–100.

21. Id. at 44–60.

22. *In Harm's Way*, above note 7. Kathleen Barry describes the larger context in which women are trapped into selling their sexuality for survival in *Female Sexual Slavery* (1979). The Model Ordinance emerged from this work as a whole:

> MODEL ANTIPORNOGRAPHY CIVIL-RIGHTS ORDINANCE
> Section 1. STATEMENT OF POLICY
>
> 1. Pornography is a practice of sex discrimination. It exists in [place], threatening the health, safety, peace, welfare, and equality of citizens in our community. Existing laws are inadequate to solve these problems in [place].
>
> 2. Pornography is a systematic practice of exploitation and subordination

based on sex that differentially harms and disadvantages women. The harm of pornography includes dehumanization, psychic assault, sexual exploitation, forced sex, forced prostitution, physical injury, and social and sexual terrorism and inferiority presented as entertainment. The bigotry and contempt pornography promotes, with the acts of aggression it fosters, diminish opportunities for equality of rights in employment, education, property, public accommodations, and public services; create public and private harassment, persecution, and denigration; promote injury and degradation such as rape, battery, sexual abuse of children, and prostitution, and inhibit just enforcement of laws against these acts; expose individuals who appear in pornography against their will to contempt, ridicule, hatred, humiliation, and embarrassment and target such women in particular for abuse and physical aggression; demean the reputations and diminish the occupational opportunities of individuals and groups on the basis of sex; contribute significantly to restricting women in particular from full exercise of citizenship and participation in the life of the community; lower the human dignity, worth, and civil status of women and damage mutual respect between the sexes; and undermine women's equal exercise of rights to speech and action guaranteed to all citizens under the [Constitutions] and [laws] of [place].

Section 2. DEFINITIONS

1. 'Pornography' means the graphic sexually explicit subordination of women through pictures and/or words that also includes one or more of the following:

a. women are presented dehumanized as sexual objects, things or commodities; or

b. women are presented as sexual objects who enjoy humiliation or pain; or

c. women are presented as sexual objects experiencing sexual pleasure in rape, incest, or other sexual assault; or

d. women are presented as sexual objects tied up or cut up or mutilated or bruised or physically hurt; or

e. women are presented in postures or positions of sexual submission, servility, or display; or

f. women's body parts—including but not limited to vaginas, breasts, or buttocks—are exhibited such that women are reduced to those parts; or

g. women are presented being penetrated by objects or animals; or

h. women are presented in scenarios of degradation, humiliation, injury, torture, shown as filthy or inferior, bleeding, bruised or hurt in a context that makes these conditions sexual.

2. The use of men, children, or transsexuals in the place of women in (1) of this definition is also pornography for purposes of this law.

3. 'Person' shall include child or transsexual.

Section 3. CAUSES OF ACTION

1. *Coercion into pornography.* It is sex discrimination to coerce, intimidate,

or fraudulently induce (hereafter, 'coerce') any person into performing for pornography, which injury may date from any appearance or sale of any product(s) of such performance(s). The maker(s), seller(s), exhibitor(s) and/or distributor(s) of said pornography may be sued for damages and for an injunction, including to eliminate the product(s) of the performance(s) from the public view.

Proof of one or more of the following facts or conditions shall not, without more, preclude a finding of coercion:

a. that the person is a woman; or

b. that the person is or has been a prostitute; or

c. that the person has attained the age of majority; or

d. that the person is connected by blood or marriage to anyone involved in or related to the making of the pornography; or

e. that the person has previously had, or been thought to have had, sexual relations with anyone, including anyone involved in or related to the making of the pornography; or

f. that the person has previously posed for sexually explicit pictures with or for anyone, including anyone involved in or related to the making of the pornography; or

g. that anyone else, including a spouse or other relative, has given permission on the person's behalf; or

h. that the person actually consented to a use of a performance that is then changed into pornography; or

i. that the person knew that the purpose of the acts or events in question was to make pornography; or

j. that the person showed no resistance or appeared to cooperate actively in the photographic sessions or events that produced the pornography; or

k. that the person signed a contract, or made statements affirming a willingness to cooperate in the production of the pornography; or

l. that no physical force, threats, or weapons were used in the making of the pornography; or

m. that the person was paid or otherwise compensated.

2. *Forcing pornography on a person.* It is sex discrimination to force pornography on a person in any place of employment, education, home, or any public place. Complaints may be brought only against the perpetrator of the force and/or the entity or institution responsible for the force.

3. *Assault or physical attack due to pornography.* It is sex discrimination to assault, physically attack, or injure any person in a way that is directly caused by specific pornography. Complaints may be brought against the perpetrator of the assault or attack, and/or against the maker(s), distributor(s), seller(s), and/or exhibitor(s) of the specific pornography.

4. *Defamation through pornography.* It is sex discrimination to defame any person through the unauthorized use in pornography of their proper name,

image, and/or recognizable personal likeness. For purposes of this section, public figures shall be treated as private persons. Authorization once given can be revoked in writing any time prior to any publication.

5. *Trafficking in pornography.* It is sex discrimination to produce, sell, exhibit, or distribute pornography, including through private clubs.

a. Municipal, state, and federally funded public libraries or private and public university and college libraries in which pornography is available for study, including on open shelves but excluding special display presentations, shall not be construed to be trafficking in pornography.

b. Isolated passages or isolated parts shall not be the sole basis for complaints under this section.

c. Any woman may bring a complaint hereunder as a woman acting against the subordination of women. Any man, child, or transsexual who alleges injury by pornography in the way women are injured by it may also complain.

Section 4. DEFENSES

1. It shall not be a defense to a complaint under this law that the respondent did not know or intend that the materials at issue were pornography or sex discrimination.

2. No damages or compensation for losses shall be recoverable under Sec. 3(5) or other than against the perpetrator of the assault or attack in Sec. 3(3) unless the defendant knew or had reason to know that the materials were pornography.

3. In actions under Sec. 3(5) or other than against the perpetrator of the assault or attack in Sec. 3(3), no damages or compensation for losses shall be recoverable against maker(s) for pornography made, against distributor(s) for pornography distributed, against seller(s) for pornography sold, or against exhibitor(s) for pornography exhibited, prior to the effective date of this law.

Section 5. ENFORCEMENT

1. *Civil Action.* Any person who has a cause of action under this law may complain directly to a court of competent jurisdiction for relief.

2. *Damages.*

a. Any person who has a cause of action under this law, or their estate, may seek nominal, compensatory, and/or punitive damages without limitation, including for loss, pain, suffering, reduced enjoyment of life, and special damages, as well as for reasonable costs, including attorneys' fees and costs of investigation.

b. In claims under Sec. 3(5), or other than against the perpetrator of the assault or attack under Sec. 3(3), no damages or compensation for losses shall be recoverable against maker(s) for pornography made, against distributor(s) for pornography distributed, against seller(s) for pornography sold, or against exhibitor(s) for pornography exhibited, prior to the effective date of this law.

3. *Injunctions.* Any person who violates this law may be enjoined except that:

a. In actions under Sec. 3(5), and other than against the perpetrator of the assault or attack under Sec. 3(3), no temporary or permanent injunction shall issue prior to a final judicial determination that the challenged activities constitute a violation of this law.

b. No temporary or permanent injunction shall extend beyond such pornography that, having been described with reasonable specificity by said order(s), is determined to be validly proscribed under this law.

5. *Other Remedies.* The availability of relief under this law is not intended to be exclusive and shall not preclude, or be precluded by, the seeking of any other relief, whether civil or criminal.

6. *Limitation of Action.* Complaints under this law shall be brought within six years of the accrual of the cause of action or from when the complainant reaches the age of majority, whichever is later.

7. *Severability.* Should any part(s) of this law be found legally invalid, the remaining part(s) remain valid. A judicial declaration that any part(s) of this law cannot be applied validly in a particular manner or to a particular case or category of cases shall not affect the validity of that part or parts as otherwise applied, unless such other application would clearly frustrate the [legislative body's] intent in adopting this law.

23. *Effect of Pornography on Women and Children: Hearings Before the Sub-comm. on Juvenile Justice of the Comm. on the Judiciary,* 98th Cong., 2d Sess. 227–255 (1984) (testimony of Andrea Dworkin).

24. Such materials are readily available at any pornography store. Some materials in which women are treated in these ways are on file with Organizing Against Pornography/A Resource Center for Education and Action, Minneapolis, Minnesota. They include *Black Tit and Body Torture*, *Chair Bondage*, *Hard Boss*, *Hard Leather*, *Penthouse* 119–127 (Dec. 1984), *Slave Auction*, and *Tit Torture Photos*.

25. See *In Harm's Way* at 101–106.

26. See id. at 44–60.

27. See generally id. at 98–106, 108–109, 111–112.

28. See *Pornography and Sexual Aggression* (Neil M. Malamuth and Edward Donnerstein, eds., 1984).

29. *In Harm's Way* at 157–159 (testimony of Daryl Dahlheimer, psychotherapist).

30. Id. at 149–155 (testimony of Wanda Richardson, Harriet Tubman Women's Shelter, and Sharon Rice Vaughn, Minnesota Coalition for Battered Women).

31. Id. at 155–156 (testimony of Barbara Chester, director of the Rape and Sexual Assault Center).

32. Id. at 175–176 (testimony of Sue Santa, Minneapolis Youth Division).

33. Id. at 161–165 (testimony of Cheryl Champion, Washington County Human Services, Inc.).

34. See MacKinnon, 20 *Harvard Civil Rights-Civil Liberties Law Review* at 46–50 nn.107–108.

35. *In Harm's Way* at 143–145 (testimony of Bill Neiman, assistant county attorney, Hennepin County Attorney's Office); see generally Ann Jones, "A Little Knowledge," in *Take Back the Night: Women on Pornography* 179, 181 (Laura Lederer, ed., 1980).

36. See generally Donnerstein, "Pornography: Its Effect on Violence Against Women,"; MacKinnon, 20 *Harvard Civil Rights-Civil Liberties Law Review* at 52–53 nn.116–118 (collecting studies).

37. Neil M. Malamuth, "Aggression Against Women: Cultural and Individual Causes," in *Pornography and Sexual Aggression* 19, 34–39; Daniel Linz, et al. "The Effects of Multiple Exposures to Filmed Violence Against Women," 34 *Journal of Communications* 130, 142 (Summer, 1984).

38. Professor Donnerstein told me in conversation that it was proving impossible to make a film for laboratory purposes of *only* violence against women in which a significant number of subjects did not see sex.

39. See, i.e., Lovelace and McGrady, *Ordeal.*

40. See *Pornography and Sexual Aggression*; *In Harm's Way* at 46–60 (testimony of Dr. Donnerstein); see also above note 33.

41. Indianapolis, Indiana, City-County General Ordinance 35 (June 11, 1984) (amending ch. 16 of the Code of Indianapolis and Marion County). See above, note 22 for the definition of "pornography" in the Model Ordinance.

42. See, e.g., U.S. v. Smith, 794 F.2d 841, 848 n.7 (9th Cir. 1986) ("An assertion that certain pictures depict 'sexually explicit conduct' prohibited by [18 U.S.C.] sections 2251 and 2252 does not require of the affiant extensive knowledge of the prurient interest of the average person, of what portrayals of sexual conduct are patently offensive, or of literary, artistic, political, or scientific criteria for 'serious merit.' The affiant need only be able to identify the specific, clearly defined acts listed in section 2255. . . . This identification is certainly 'conclusory' to a certain extent, but it is a conclusion based on observation and not, as in the case of 'obscenity,' one based on evaluation. The statement that the photographs depict sexually explicit conduct is similar to many other factual conclusions routinely accepted by courts in applications for warrants"); Pennsylvania Liquor Control Bd. v. J.P.W.G., Inc., 489 A.2d 992, 994 (Pa. Cmwlth. 1985) ("[H]ere the fact-finder specifically found that the activity described by the Board's agent was *not* lewd, immoral or improper. There was no testimony of sexually explicit gyrations or badinage with patrons and no evidence of appeal to prurient interest other than bare breasts"); Pennsylvania Liquor Control Board v. Ronnie's Lounge, Inc., 383 A.2d 544 (Pa. Comwlth. 1978) (affirming a trial court finding that dancers had performed in a lewd and immoral manner when they engaged in sexually explicit gyrations simulating sexual intercourse while on the stage); In Interest of K.L.M., 496 N.E.2d 1262 (Ill. App. 1986) (father charged with neglect testified that he had not allowed his daughter to watch sexually explicit or X-rated movies); Swope v. Lubbers, 560 F. Supp. 1328 (D.C. Mich. 1983) (challenge to College policy directing that "no institutional funds of this College shall be used by student organizations for the acquisition of X-rated films, such films being the type which, by their nature show excessive violence and/or sexually explicit material"); Walnut Properties, Inc. v. City

of Whittier, 808 F.2d 1331, 1336 (9th Cir. 1986) ("There is no claim that distributors or exhibitors of adult films are denied access to the market or, conversely, that the viewing public is unable to satisfy its appetite for sexually explicit fare"); Moses v. Kenosha County, 649 F. Supp. 451, 453 (E.D. Wis. 1986) ("The Odyssey is in the business of selling and renting sexually explicit books, magazines and films, euphemistically called 'adult bookstores'"); Brown v. Pornography Com'n of Lower Southampton Tp., 620 F. Supp. 1199, 1209–1210 (D.C. Pa. 1985) ("It is clear under Pennsylvania law that the words 'adult products' refer to sexually explicit materials rather than to products commonly used by adults. . . . Furthermore, in the context of ordinances dealing with zoning and pornography the word 'adult' is commonly used to mean sexually explicit or erotic").

43. The foregoing discussion of subordination draws directly on Andrea Dworkin's lucid conceptualization in Andrea Dworkin, "Against the Male Flood: Censorship, Pornography, and Equality," 8 *Harvard Women's Law Journal* 1 (1985).

44. See i.e., "Two Accused of Murder in Snuff Film," *Oakland Tribune*, A6 (August 6, 1983) (two teenage girls reported murdered in the making of a pornographic movie).

45. See Ruth Colker, "Pornography and Privacy: Towards the Development of a Group Based Theory for Sex Based Intrusions of Privacy," 1 *Law and Inequality* 191 (1983).

46. Members of the City Council of Los Angeles v. Taxpayers for Vincent, 466 U.S. 789, 794 (1984). The legal argument made here is discussed and documented more fully in MacKinnon, 20 *Harvard Civil Rights-Civil Liberties Law Review* 1 (1985).

47. The finding of harm by the Minneapolis City Council:

> Special Findings on Pornography: The Council finds that pornography is central in creating and maintaining the civil inequality of the sexes. Pornography is a systematic practice of exploitation and subordination based on sex which differentially harms women. The bigotry and contempt it promotes, with the acts of aggression if fosters, harm women's opportunities for equality of rights in employment, education, property rights, public accommodations and public services; create public harassment and private denigration; promote injury and degradation such as rape, battery and prostitution and inhibit just enforcement of laws against these acts; contribute significantly to restricting women from full exercise of citizenship and participation in public life, including in neighborhoods; damage relations between the sexes; and undermine women's equal exercise of rights to speech and action guaranteed to all citizens under the constitutions and laws of the United States and the State of Minnesota.

These findings, as part of the Minneapolis Hearings, were entered into the legislative record in Indianapolis.

48. American Booksellers Ass'n v. Hudnut, 598 F. Supp. 1316 (S.D. Ind. 1984).

49. American Booksellers Ass'n v. Hudnut, 771 F.2d 323 (7th Cir. 1985).

50. Plessy v. Ferguson, 163 U.S. 537 (1896).

51. Dred Scott v. Sandford, 60 U.S. (19 How.) 393 (1856).

52. On February 24, 1986, true to this prediction, the United States Supreme Court summarily affirmed the Seventh Circuit's opinion, 475 U.S. 1001 (1986), on a 28 U.S.C. §1254(2) direct appeal, without argument, opinion, or citation—suggesting, inter alia, that power is not having to give reasons.

25. Pornography as Defamation and Discrimination

This lecture was given in the Boston University School of Law Distinguished Lecturer Series on February 16, 1990; it was delivered in a prior form, to the Hofstra University Conference on Group Defamation and Freedom of Speech, April, 1988. It was orginally published in 71 *Boston University Law Review* 793 (1991) and, in part, in *Only Words* (1993). The comments of Owen Fiss and Burke Marshall were especially helpful, as was the research assistance of Carmela Castellano. The contributions of Andrea Dworkin, as always, were formative.

1. Edward J. Bloustein, "Holmes: His First Amendment Theory and His Pragmatist Bent," 40 *Rutgers Law Review* 283, 299 (1988) (discussing Oliver Wendell Holmes's approach to freedom of speech).

2. The ordinance received 42 percent of the vote. The Nation, *L.A. Times*, 2 (November 12, 1985) (reporting that 9,419 people voted for the measure and 13,031 against it, while 1,931 voters abstained).

3. "Whoever publishes any false written or printed material with intent to maliciously promote hatred of any group of persons in the commonwealth because of race, color or religion shall be guilty of libel and shall be punished by a fine of not more than one thousand dollars or by imprisonment for not more than one year, or both. The defendant may prove in defense that the publication was privileged or was not malicious. Prosecutions under this section shall be instituted only by the attorney general or by the district attorney for the district in which the alleged libel was published." Mass. Gen. Laws Ann. ch. 272, §98C (West 1990).

4. See, e.g., International Convention on the Elimination of All Forms of Racial Discrimination, *opened for signature* Mar. 7, 1966, 660 U.N.T.S. 195, 218–220, reprinted in 5 I.L.M. 352 (1966) (entered into force Jan. 4, 1969) ("State parties . . . shall declare an offence punishable by law all dissemination of ideas based on racial superiority or hatred . . ."); see also *Positive Measures Designed To Eradicate All Incitement To, Or Acts Of, Racial Discrimination, Implementation Of The International Convention On The Elimination Of All Forms Of Racial Discrimination*, 1986, U.N. Doc. CERD/2, U.N. Sales No. E.85.XIV.2 (1986).

5. Examples of its official documentation include *Final Report Of The Attorney General's Commission On Pornography* (1986) (U.S.); *Pornography And Prostitution In Canada: Report Of The Special Committee On Pornography And Prostitution* (1985) (Can.); *Report Of The Joint Select Committee On Video Material* (1988) (Austl.); *Sexual Offenses Against Children: Report Of The Committee On Sexual Offences Against Chil-*

dren And Youths ch. 55 (1984) (Can.). For further analysis, see Diana E. H. Russell, "Pornography and Rape: A Causal Model," 9 *Political Psychology* 41 (1988) (analyzing how pornography causes rape by undermining inhibitions to raping and facilitating its social acceptance).

6. For citations from which this description is drawn, see Catharine A. MacKinnon, *Toward a Feminist Theory of the State* 276 n.2 (1989).

7. For sources, see Catharine A. MacKinnon, "Reflections on Sex Equality Under Law," 100 *Yale Law Journal* 1281, 1298 n.83, 1301 n.100 (1991). See supra at 116.

8. See MacKinnon, *Toward a Feminist Theory* at 17.

9. Andrea Dworkin and I discuss these issues, and those in the paragraphs following, in these terms in Andrea Dworkin and Catharine A. MacKinnon, *Pornography And Civil Rights: A New Day For Women's Equality* 25–26 (1988).

10. See Gloria Cowan, Carol Lee, Daniella Levy, and Debra Snyder, "Dominance and Inequality in X-Rated Videocassettes," 12 *Psychology of Women Quarterly* 299, 306–307 (1988) (finding that pornography contains abuse and violence that is directed primarily against women); Park E. Dietz and Alan E. Sears, "Pornography and Obscenity Sold in Adult Bookstores: A Survey of 5132 Books, Magazines, and Films in Four American Cities," 21 *University of Michigan Journal of Law Reform* 7, 38–43 (1987–1988) (documenting violence, bondage, sado-masochism, and gender differences in pornography); Neil M. Malamuth and Barry Spinner, "A Longitudinal Content Analysis of Sexual Violence in the Best Selling Erotic Magazines," 16 *Journal of Sex Research* 226, 226–227 (1980) (documenting increases in violent sex in pornography).

11. Andrea Dworkin and I discuss this in these terms in Dworkin and MacKinnon, *Pornography and Civil Rights* at 32–35.

12. See *In Harm's Way: The Pornography Civil Rights Hearings* 60–68 (Catharine A. MacKinnon and Andrea Dworkin, eds., 1997) (testimony of Linda Marchiano).

13. Id. at 264–265.

14. Id. at 125–128 (testimony of Shannon McCarthy Bicha); id. at 88–89 (testimony of Commissioner Wanda Laurence describing her neighborhood "innundated" with pornography); id. at 121–124 (testimony of J. B. describing pornography in her workplace).

15. Id. at 107–108 (testimony of G. C.).

16. Id. at 181–182 (testimony of Michael Laslett).

17. Id. at 146 (testimony of S. G.).

18. Id. at 108–114 (testimony of R.M.M.).

19. Id. at 101 (testimony of R. M.).

20. Id. at 114–120 (testimony of T. S.).

21. Id. at 106–107 (testimony of N. C. ("He put his genitals in my face and he said, 'Take it all.' Then he fucked me on the couch in the living room. All this took about five minutes. And when he was finished he dressed and went back to the party. I felt ashamed and numb, and I also felt very used.")).

22. Id. at 65 (testimony of Linda Marchiano).

23. Id. at 151 (testimony of Wanda Richardson).

24. Id. at 179 (testimony of Sue Schafer).

25. Id. at 70 (testimony of Pauline Bart, citing to a study by Larry Barron and Murray Strauss, later published as "Sexual Stratification, Pornography and Rape in the United States," in *Pornography and Sexual Aggression* 185 (Neil M. Malamuth and Edward Donnerstein, eds., 1984)).

26. Id. at 44–60 (testimony of Edward Donnerstein).

27. Id. at 44–60, 290–310 (testimony of Edward Donnerstein). See also Neil M. Malamuth, "Aggression Against Women: Cultural and Individual Causes," in *Pornography and Sexual Aggression* 19, 34–39; Michael J. McManus, Introduction, *Final Report of Attorney General's Commission on Pornography* xvi–xviii (1986) (reporting consensus among pornography researchers).

28. See James V. P. Check and Ted H. Guloien, "Reported Proclivity for Coercive Sex Following Repeated Exposure to Sexually Violent Pornography, Nonviolent Dehumanizing Pornography and Erotica," in *Pornography: Research Advances And Policy Considerations* 159, 171, 177 (Dolf Zillmann and Jennings Bryant, eds., 1989); Edward Donnerstein, "Pornography: Its Effect on Violence Against Women," in *Pornography and Sexual Aggression* 53, 78–79 (Neil M. Malamuth and Edward Donnerstein, eds., 1984); Edward Donnerstein and Leonard Berkowitz, "Victim Reactions in Aggressive Erotic Films as a Factor in Violence Against Women," 41 *Journal of Personality and Social Psychology* 710, 720–723 (1981); Neil M. Malamuth, "Predictors of Naturalistic Sexual Aggression," 50 *Journal of Personality and Social Psychology* 953, 960 (1986); Neil M. Malamuth, "Factors Associated with Rape as Predictors of Laboratory Aggression Against Women," 45 *Journal of Personality and Social Psychology* 432, 440–441 (1983); Neil M. Malamuth and James V. P. Check, "The Effects of Aggressive Pornography on Beliefs in Rape Myths: Individual Differences," 19 *Journal of Research in Personality* 299, 313–314 (1985); Neil M. Malamuth and James V. P. Check, "The Effects of Mass Media Exposure on Acceptance of Violence Against Women: A Field Experiment," 15 *Journal of Research in Personality* 436, 442–443 (1981).

29. Daniel Linz, Edward Donnerstein, and Steven Penrod, "The Effects of Multiple Exposures to Filmed Violence Against Women," 34 *Journal of Communications* 130, 142 (Summer 1984) (documenting that men exposed to filmed violence against women judged a rape victim to be less injured than did the control group); see also Neil M. Malamuth and James V. P. Check, "Penile Tumescence and Perceptual Responses to Rape as a Function of the Victim's Perceived Reactions," 10 *Journal of Applied Social Psychology* 528, 542–543 (1980) (documenting that exposure to rape depictions affected future reactions to rape).

30. Most of the researchers define sexual violence as requiring the appearance of the use of physical force. Pornography researchers commonly define the term to include rape when the materials expressly present sex they call rape, or when the women in the materials are shown to resist sexual intercourse that is then imposed on them. See James V. P. Check and Neil M. Malamuth, "Pornography and Sexual Aggression: A Social Learning Theory Analysis," 9 *Communications Year Book* 181, 189 (1986). The problem is that not all force is physical and many women are coerced offstage. Another problem is that not all forced sex involves conventional sex acts.

31. Check and Malamuth, 9 *Communications Year Book* 181; Russell, 9 *Political Psychology* 41; Dolf Zillmann and Jennings Bryant, "Effects of Prolonged Consumption of Pornography on Family Values," 9 *Journal of Family Issues* 518 (1988); Dolf Zillmann and Jennings Bryant, "Effects of Massive Exposure to Pornography," in *Pornography and Sexual Aggression* at 115, 130–131; Dolf Zillmann and James B. Weaver, "Pornography and Men's Sexual Callousness Toward Women," in *Pornography: Research Advances* at 95; James G. Buchman, "Effects of Nonviolent Adult Erotica on Sexual Child Abuse Attitudes," paper presented at a meeting of the American Psychological Association (Aug. 1990) (Boston, Mass.) (on file with author).

32. The effect on women of consumption of pornography is just beginning to be studied systematically. The best work to date is Charlene Y. Senn, *The Impact of Pornography in Women's Lives* (1991) (unpublished Ph.D. dissertation, York University) (on file with author). Prior useful studies include Charlene Y. Senn and H. Lorraine Radtke, "Women's Evaluations of and Affective Reactions to Mainstream Violent Pornography, Nonviolent Pornography, and Erotica," 5 *Violence and Victims* 143 (1990); Carol L. Krafka, *Sexually Explicit, Sexually Violent, and Violent Media: Effects of Multiple Naturalistic Exposures and Debriefing on Female Viewers* (1985) (unpublished Ph.D. dissertation, University of Wisconsin ([Madison])) (on file with author); Charlene Y. Senn, *Women's Reactions to Violent Pornography, Nonviolent Pornography and Erotica* (1985) (unpublished master's thesis, University of Calgary) (on file with author); Charlene Y. Senn and H. Lorraine Radtke, "A Comparison of Women's Reactions to Violent Pornography, Nonviolent Pornography, and Erotica," paper presented at the Annual Convention of the Canadian Psychological Association (1986) (Toronto, Can.) (on file with author).

33. The Model Ordinance defines "pornography" as:

> the graphic sexually explicit subordination of women through pictures and/or words that also includes one or more of the following: a. women are presented dehumanized as sexual objects, things or commodities; or b. women are presented as sexual objects who enjoy humiliation or pain; or c. women are presented as sexual objects experiencing sexual pleasure in rape, incest, or other sexual assault; or d. women are presented as sexual objects tied up or cut up or mutilated or bruised or physically hurt; or e. women are presented in postures or positions of sexual submission, servility, or display; or f. women's body parts—including but not limited to vaginas, breasts, or buttocks—are exhibited such that women are reduced to those parts; or g. women are presented being penetrated by objects or animals; or h. women are presented in scenarios of degradation, humiliation, injury, torture, shown as filthy or inferior, bleeding, bruised or hurt in a context that makes these conditions sexual.

The use of "men, children, or transsexuals in the place of women" in this definition is also pornography. Model Ordinance, reprinted in Dworkin and MacKinnon, *Pornography and Civil Rights* at 138–139. For the entire Model Ordinance, see supra at 493 n22. The Cambridge ordinance contained a similar definition. See Bill to Amend

§E, ch. 25, "Human Rights" of City of Cambridge, Mass., reprinted in MacKinnon and Dworkin, *In Harm's Way* at 457–461.

34. Model Ordinance, above note 33. In the Indianapolis ordinance, by contrast, the scenarios were limited by a specific defense so that only victims of coercion or assault could sue for materials that did not show violence. See Indianapolis and Marion County, Ind., Code ch. 16, §16–3(g)(8) (1984), reprinted in MacKinnon and Dworkin, *In Harm's Way* at 443–444. In the Bellingham version of the ordinance, defamation through pornography was also included as a cause of action.

35. It may be that much of the pleasure of dominance enjoyed in racial defamation is also sex, but further evidence and analysis would be required to sustain this argument.

36. 376 U.S. 254 (1964).

37. But compare, Doe v. University of Mich., 721 F. Supp. 852, 868 (E.D. Mich. 1989) (holding that the University of Michigan's policy against discriminatory harassment of students was invalid because it covered "verbal conduct" protected as speech under the First Amendment).

38. Davis v. Passman, 442 U.S. 228, 230 (1971).

39. Palmer v. Thompson, 403 U.S. 217 (1971) (holding that the closure by the city of Jackson, Mississippi, of public swimming pools formerly available to "whites only" did not violate Equal Protection Clause of the Fourteenth Amendment because both Blacks and whites were denied access); Jones v. Alfred H. Mayer Co., 392 U.S. 409 (1968) (prohibiting discriminatory sale or rental of property to "whites only"); Blow v. North Carolina, 379 U.S. 684 (1965) (holding that restaurant serving "whites only" violated Civil Rights Act of 1964); Watson v. Memphis, 373 U.S. 526 (1963) (holding that city's operation of large percentage of publicly owned recreational facilities for "whites only" due to delays in implementing desegregation violated the Fourteenth Amendment); see also Hazelwood Sch. Dist. v. United States, 433 U.S. 299, 302–305 (1977) (stating that, in employment discrimination claim against school district, plaintiffs alleged that district's newspaper advertisement for teacher applicants specified "white only"); Pierson v. Ray, 386 U.S. 547, 558 (1967) (holding that Black and white clergymen did not consent to their arrest by peacefully entering the "White Only" designated waiting area of bus terminal).

40. Pittsburgh Press Co. v. Pittsburgh Comm'n on Human Relations, 413 U.S. 376, 391 (1973) (holding that sex-segregated job advertisements violate human rights laws and are not protected under the First Amendment).

41. Morgan v. Hertz Corp., 542 F. Supp. 123, 128 (W.D. Tenn. 1981) (issuing injunction in sexual harassment case against making such statements), *aff'd*, 725 F.2d 1070 (6th Cir. 1984).

42. In Alexander v. Yale University, 459 F. Supp. 1, 3–4 (D. Conn. 1977), *aff'd.* 631 F.2d 178 (2d Cir. 1980), "Plaintiff Pamela Price asserts that she received a poor grade . . . not due to any 'fair evaluation of her academic work,' but as a consequence of her rejecting a professor's outright proposition 'to give her a grade of "A" . . . in exchange for her compliance with his sexual demands.'" Allegations that the university

lacked a grievance procedure for sexual harassment complaints were found to state a cause of action for sex discrimination under Title IX.

43. Price Waterhouse v. Hopkins, 490 U.S. 228, 235 (1989) (quoting statements as evidence of sex-discriminatory stereotyping in promotion evaluation).

44. Meritor Sav. Bank v. Vinson, 477 U.S. 57, 65 (1986) (holding that unwelcome verbal conduct of a sexual nature constitutes sexual harassment creating a hostile working environment).

45. Not until very recently was this possibility even raised. See *In re* R.A.V., 464 N.W.2d 507, 511 (Minn. 1991) (upholding conviction for burning cross under city ordinance that prohibits bias-motivated disorderly conduct on the ground that the ordinance could be interpreted to prohibit only expressive conduct that falls outside of First Amendment protection), *cert. granted sub nom.* R.A.V. v. St. Paul, 59 U.S.L.W. 3823 (U.S. June 10, 1991) (No. 90–7675); see also State v. Miller, 398 S.E.2d 547, 551–552 (Ga. 1990) (holding that wearing a Klan hood is not protected expression).

46. See United States v. Lee, 935 F.2d 952, 956 (8th Cir. 1991) (concluding that the act of crossburning is an overt act of intimidation that, because of its historical context, is often considered a precursor to violence, and thus invades the victim's privacy interests). In our amicus curiae brief for the National Black Women's Health Project in R.A.V. v. St. Paul, Burke Marshall and I make this argument, offering an equality defense for a Minnesota statute prohibiting crossburning. *Brief for the National Black Women's Health Project,* R.A.V. v. St. Paul, 505 U.S. 377 (1992).

47. Convergence is implicit in the design of international instruments for the regulation of racist speech, which casts group defamation as a practice of discrimination, International Convention on the Elimination of All Forms of Racial Discrimination, above note 4, and the extensive national legislation that parallels this convention. See, e.g., 1988 E.D.L.A. 114, leg. 23.592 (Arg.); Act of July 1, 1972, No. 72–546 (amending C. Pén. art. 24, ¶5) (Fr.); Laws of October 13, 1975, art. 654 (ratifying convention), Gazz. Uff. art. 337, Dec. 23, 1975, Parte I, 1976 Lex, p. 6, Law No. 654 art. 3(b) (Italy).

48. See Brown v. Board of Educ., 347 U.S. 483, 494 (1954) ("To separate them from others of similar age and qualifications solely because of their race generates a feeling of inferiority as to their status in the community that may affect their hearts and minds in a way unlikely to ever be undone"). *Brown* thus did not decide that these children were offended by segregation, and that the harm was therefore subjective, and hence irrelevant or nonexistent. Rather, it decided that the children were harmed by it in their feelings and self-concept, hence in their ability to learn. See also Charles R. Lawrence III, "If He Hollers Let Him Go: Regulating Racist Speech on Campus," 1990 *Duke Law Journal* 431, 438–440 (arguing that *Brown* may be read as regulating the content of racist speech).

49. See, e.g., R.S.C., ch. C-46, §319(3)(a) (1985) (Can.) (providing under the Canadian Criminal Code that no one who willfully promotes hatred against any identifiable group shall be convicted "if he establishes that the statements communicated were true").

50. The question whether the onus should be on the speaker to prove truth or on the victim to prove falsity, or whether truth is not relevant, is subject to varying legal treatments worldwide.

51. See, e.g., Ill. Rev. Stat. ch. 38, ¶471 (1949) (repealed 1961) (statute litigated in Beauharnais v. Illinois, 343 U.S. 250, 251 (1952), which outlawed publications that expose "the citizens of any race, color, creed or religion to contempt"); R.S.C., ch. C-46, §319(1) (1985) (Can.) (proscribing public communication that incites hatred against an identifiable group).

52. The most illuminating discussion of the subject I have seen is Patrick Lawlor, "Group Defamation: Submissions to the Attorney General of Ontario" (Mar. 1984) (on file with author).

53. Animal rights advocates and defenders of sadomasochism among humans would likely see this example differently from me and from each other.

54. See, e.g., R.S.C., ch. C–46, §319(2) (1985) (Can.) (creating under the Canadian Criminal Code an offense for the willful promotion or incitement of hatred against an identifiable group through statements other than in private conversation); §130–131 *StGB* (1987) (Ger.).

55. In the United States, violations of the Equal Protection Clause and disparate treatment violations of Title VII must be intentional to be discriminatory. Personnel Adm'r v. Feeney, 442 U.S. 256, 274 (1979); International Bhd. of Teamsters v. United States, 431 U.S. 324, 335–336 (1977); Washington v. Davis, 426 U.S. 229, 238–241 (1976). But disparate impact violations of Title VII need not be intentional to be actionable as discriminatory. Griggs v. Duke Power, 401 U.S. 424, 431 (1971). Under international law, dissemination of ideas based on racial superiority and racial hatred is prohibited "despite lack of intention to commit an offense and irrespective of the consequences of the dissemination, whether they be grave or insignificant." *Positive Measures*, above note 4, ¶83.

56. The Women's Legal Education and Action Fund (LEAF), with my participation, successfully made the argument outlined in the following paragraphs of the text in defense of the constitutionality of the hate propaganda provision of the Criminal Code of Canada under which the defendant had been convicted in R. v. Keegstra, [1991] 2 W.W.R. 1, 6 (S.C.C.). Keegstra was prosecuted for teaching Holocaust denial to schoolchildren under a law that criminalized willful propagation of racial and religious-based hatred. In response to the defendant's argument that criminalizing hatemongering violated his constitutionally protected freedom of expression, LEAF argued that the provisions were protected under the Charter's equality provisions. Found to limit freedom of expression, the provisions were nonetheless upheld by the Supreme Court of Canada as justified in a free and democratic society largely on an equality rationale.

57. The U.S. Supreme Court in Beauharnais v. Illinois saw this clearly, upholding Illinois's libel statute outlawing publications that denigrate a class of citizens by virtue of their race or religion: "[A] man's job and his educational opportunities and the dignity accorded him may depend as much on the reputation of the racial and religious

group to which he willy-nilly belongs, as on his own merits." Beauharnais v. Illinois, 343 U.S. 250, 263 (1952).

58. See *They Don't All Wear Sheets: A Chronology Of Racist And Far Right Violence—1980–86* (Chris Lutz comp. 1987) (compiling data on incidents of racial, religious, and homophobic violence); Richard Delgado, "Words That Wound: A Tort Action for Racial Insults, Epithets, and Name-Calling," 17 *Harvard Civil Rights-Civil Liberties Law Review* 133, 143–149 (1982) (discussing the emotional and psychological harms of racial insults); Mari Matsuda, "Public Response to Racist Speech: Considering the Victim's Story," 87 *Michigan Law Review* 2320, 2335–2341 (1989) (detailing negative effects of racist hate messages).

59. For example, as defined in the Canadian Criminal Code, R.S.C., ch. C–46, §318(2)(a)–(b) (1985) (Can.).

60. Of course, to succeed, this approach requires that constitutional equality mandates be interpreted properly. For an example of an approach conducive to protecting group libel laws, see the equality approach under the Canadian Charter of Rights and Freedoms in Andrews v. The Law Society, [1989] 1 S.C.R. 143, 171 (interpreting the purpose of §15(1) equality guarantees of the Charter as ensuring equality in the formulation and application of the law, including promoting a society in which all of its members are recognized by law as equally deserving of concern, respect, and consideration), as applied in Keegstra, 3 S.C.R. 697.

61. See Keegstra, 2 W.W.R. at 50 (quoting LEAF's factum to this effect).

62. This generally describes the respective tests in the United States and Canada. In the United States, the two steps are collapsed into one: does the provision violate freedom of expression? See, e.g., Beauharnais. 343 U.S. at 266–267. In Canada, whether freedom of expression is violated is one step; whether it can be justified as a limit on expression in a free and democratic society is determined separately. See, e.g., Keegstra, 2 W.W.R. 1; Irwin Toy Ltd. v. Quebec [1989] 1 S.C.R. 927, 991–1001; R. v. Oakes, [1986] 1 S.C.R. 103, 139. Germany provides an instructive comparison. See Eric Stein, "History Against Free Speech: German Law in European and American Perspective," in *Verfassungsrecht und Völkerrecht: Gedachtnisschrift für Wilhelm Karl Geck, Wilfried Fiedler und Georg Ress* 855–856 (Hrsg.) (Carl Heymanns Verlag K.G.) (1989).

63. Gertz v. Robert Welch, Inc., 418 U.S. 323, 339 (1974) ("Under the First Amendment there is no such thing as a false idea").

64. Compare, International Convention on the Elimination of All Forms of Racial Discrimination, above note 4 (requiring state parties to criminalize "all dissemination of ideas based on racial superiority or hatred").

65. This seems to be what is at stake in the discussion about campus hate speech codes, most of which, in essence, extend sexual harassment prohibitions to racial and ethnic slurs and insults, and some to sexual orientation as well. Literature in this area includes Kent Greenawalt, "Insults and Epithets: Are They Protected Speech?" 42 *Rutgers Law Review* 287 (1990) (considering legal claims against those who engage in harmful speech); Rodney Smolla, "Rethinking First Amendment Assumptions About Racist and Sexist Speech," 47 *Washington and Lee Law Review* 171 (1990) (advocating

narrowly drawn restrictions on racist and sexist speech); and especially the insightful Lawrence, 1990 *Duke Law Journal* 431. I do not think that the discrimination rationale on which sexual harassment law is based, and the sexual nature of the harassment which makes it so act-like, can be so simply transposed into the racial and ethnic defamation context. It is equally clear, however, that what is harassment in the gender context does not suddenly become pure idea in the racial context and that an equality theory can support such codes when properly drawn.

66. See Norwood v. Harrison, 413 U.S. 455, 470 (1973) ("Invidious private discrimination may be characterized as a form of exercising freedom of association protected by the First Amendment, but it has never been accorded affirmative constitutional protection").

67. American Booksellers Ass'n v. Hudnut, 771 F.2d 323 (7th Cir. 1985), *aff'd mem.*, 475 U.S. 1001 (1986).

68. Hudnut, 771 F.2d at 328–329.

69. Id. at 329.

70. Id.

71. Id. at 328.

72. In *Hudnut*, the court held that the ordinance prohibiting pornography, defined as "[s]peech that 'subordinates' women," "establishes an 'approved' view of women," and was thereby "thought control." Id. In so holding, the court missed that "subordinates" is a verb, an act, not a thought about an act.

73. For a discussion of "the inseparability of the idea and the practice of racism," see Lawrence, 1999 *Duke Law Journal* at 443–444.

74. Andrea Dworkin and I discuss this example in these terms in our book *Pornography and Civil Rights* at 60–61.

75. See, e.g., James R. McGovern, *Anatomy of a Lynching* 84 (1982) (stating that "disappointed late-comers were willing to pay fifty cents for a photograph" of Claude Neal's lynching).

76. Morris Dees, *A Season for Justice*, photograph reproduced at page facing 181 (1991).

77. 16 *Penthouse* 118 (Dec. 1984).

78. Hudnut, 771 F.2d at 329. On February 27, 1992, the Supreme Court of Canada explicitly held to the contrary in Butler v. The Queen, [1992] 1 S.C.R. 452 (S.C.C.), adopting LEAF's argument that pornography damages social equality. The Court ruled unanimously that pornography's harm to women justifies its criminal prohibition as obscenity. The Court recognized the substantial body of opinion holding that pornography "results in harm, particularly to women and therefore to society as a whole," in concluding that harm to women violated community standards. In addition to applying to violent materials, the Court's opinion found that "degrading and dehumanizing" materials can be prohibited because they "place women (and sometimes men) in positions of subordination, servile submission or humiliation. They run against the principles of equality and dignity of all human beings." Butler, 1 S.C.R. at 479 (Sopinka, J., majority opinion).

79. See New York v. Ferber, 458 U.S. 747, 758 (1982) (holding that child pornography's harm outweighs its value as expression, if any).

80. David Riesman, in "Democracy and Defamation: Control of Group Libel," 42 *Columbia Law Review* 727 (1942), explains how German courts espoused a general doctrine that only an individual could be defamed, thereby protecting favored groups. Id. at 765–766. Riesman recounts the use of defamation and manipulation of the law against defamation as a major weapon in the Nazi rise to power, making it possible systematically to defame Jews in a way calculated to lower their public esteem and to lure them into ruinous lawsuits. Id. at 728–729. Members of the government were exempt from legal responsibility for defamation. See also David Riesman, "Democracy and Defamation: Fair Game and Fair Comment II," 42 *Columbia Law Review* 1282, 1310–1311 (1942) (arguing that American courts of the period failed to use the law of defamation to "protect those weaker groups and weaker critics who cannot rely on wealth or power over public opinion as their safeguard"). By contrast, the *Hudnut* court equates the role of Nazi propaganda in the Nazi rise to power with the role of pornography in the status of women as an argument for protecting pornography. Hudnut, 771 F.2d at 329.

26. Pornography Left and Right

This book review of Richard Posner, *Sex and Reason*, and Edward de Grazia, *Girls Lean Back Everywhere*, was originally published in 30 *Harvard Civil Rights-Civil Liberties Law Review* 143 (1995). It was given as a talk at the conference "Laws and Nature: Shaping Sex, Preference, and Family" at Brown University (Feb. 6, 1993) and as the Sumner Canary Memorial Lectureship, Case Western Reserve University School of Law (Mar. 25, 1993).

1. The original attribution of this statement or view to me seems to be *Playboy*'s. James R. Petersen, "Politically Correct Sex," *Playboy*, 66, 67 (Oct. 1986) ("the antiporn feminists have their own brand of mercurial language: Sex is Rape . . ."). Subsequent versions include Asa Baber, "A Significant Shift," *Playboy*, 30 (Apr. 1992) (claiming my *New York Times* op-ed piece on rape implies that "all men are rapists"); James R. Petersen, "Mixed Company," *Playboy*, 47, 137 (Feb. 1992) ("The Catharine MacKinnons of the world view all sexuality as hostile"). It was subsequently published by Rush Limbaugh in its most pithy form. Rush Limbaugh, *The Way Things Ought To Be* 126 (1992) ("Ms. MacKinnon teaches, and I assume therefore believes, that all sex is rape, even the sex in marriage. . . . You laugh or you disbelieve, but I assure you this is true. I don't make things up"). Limbaugh often stated words to this effect on his radio program. See also James R. Petersen, "Catharine MacKinnon: Again," *Playboy*, 37, 38 (Aug. 1992) (cutting and using quotations of my work out of context to attempt, among other things, to substantiate this lie). This false characterization has undoubtedly been given momentum, elevation, and credibility by repetition in legitimate venues, such as Wendy Kaminer, "Feminists Against the First Amendment," *Atlantic*, 110, 114 (Nov. 1992) (claiming that Andrea Dworkin and I suggest that, due to sex inequality,

"there can be no consensual sex between men and women . . ."). For an attempt to raise *Playboy*'s concept as articulated in Rush Limbaugh's precise words to the facticity of a legal citation, see Susan Estrich, "Teaching Rape Law," 102 *Yale Law Journal* 509, 512 n.10 (1992) ("For the position that all sex is rape, see, e.g., Catharine A. MacKinnon . . ."). This attribution was corrected by an errata sheet to indicate that this was the author's opinion. Id. at errata ("Replace with 'For an analysis that seems to me to imply that all sex is rape, see Catharine A. MacKinnon . . .'").

It is, of course, difficult to provide citations to pages on which something is not said. Discussions of sexuality in the context of an analysis of gender inequality can be found in Catharine A. MacKinnon, *Toward A Feminist Theory of the State* 126–154, 171–183 (1989).

2. Pornographers and the mainstream media have told the same lie far longer about Andrea Dworkin, beginning in the late 1970s. Recent examples include Roundtable, "A New Sexual Ethics for Judaism?" *Tikkun*, 61, 62 (Sept.-Oct. 1993) (Kimmelman: "Andrea Dworkin suggested that all heterosexual intercourse is rape . . ."); John Casey, "The Case that Changes How We See Rape," *Evening Standard*, 9 (Oct. 20, 1993) ("The extreme radical wing of the feminist movement has long insisted that all men are rapists. One of its chief ideologues, Andrea Dworkin, argues in effect that all heterosexual intercourse is rape."); Richard Cohen, "The Wide Net of Sexual Harassment," *Washington Post*, A21 (June 15, 1993) ("In the lexicon of some radical feminists such as Andrea Dworkin, even willing sexual intercourse in marriage is a form of rape."); Richard Eder, "The Left and Right May Cheer Witty Debate of Culture," *Los Angeles Times*, E2 (Apr. 15, 1993) (book review) ("Andrea Dworkin's insistence on using rape for heterosexual intercourse in general . . ."); Suzanne Fields, "Tyson Jury Sends Strong Message," *Chicago Sun-Times*, 40 (Feb. 13, 1992) (editorial) ("Andrea Dworkin . . . stops just short of calling every episode of intercourse rape."); Wendy Kaminer, "Feminism's Identity Crisis," *Atlantic*, 51, 67 (Oct. 1993) ("Dworkin devoted an entire book to the contention that intercourse is essentially a euphemism for rape"); Charles Krauthammer, "Defining Deviancy Up: The New Assault on Bourgeois Life," *New Republic*, 20, 24 (Nov. 22, 1993) (including, in partial reference to Dworkin's work, "if there is no such thing as real consent, then the radical feminist ideal is realized: all intercourse is rape"); David Rubenstein, "Feminism that Degrades Women," *Chicago Tribune*, 15 (Jan. 31, 1992) (discussing Andrea Dworkin's views: "[i]f intercourse is virtual rape, women who seek it virtually seek to be raped"); David Sexton, "Focus the Sex War: It's So Bad Being a Man," *Sunday Telegraph Ltd.*, (London) 21 (Nov. 7, 1993) ("In America, Andrea Dworkin proclaims that all sexual intercourse whatsoever is exploitation and violation and must stop if women are to become equal"). Stripping these false statements of their qualifiers, this campaign of defamation was then expanded by *Time* magazine: "Andrea Dworkin has simplified the discussion by asserting that every act of sex between a man and a woman, no matter what, is rape." Lance Morrow, "Men: Are They Really that Bad?" *Time*, 58 (Feb. 14, 1994). Challenged on the veracity of this statement, head of *Time*'s research department Betty Satterwhite asserted the magazine's "confidence" in the statement and her assistant referred to

Andrea Dworkin's *Intercourse* at pages 122, 126, and 133. When confronted with the fact that *Intercourse*, apart from being a work of literary criticism, is about intercourse, not "all sex," and that those pages did not support this statement in any case, Ms. Satterwhite stated that *Time*'s characterization was true of "her work as a whole." She remained, however, unable to point to a single example that substantiated it. Ms. Satterwhite also stated that *Time*'s "policy" gave them no obligation to demonstrate that what they published is true. Conversation with Betty Satterwhite, chief of *Time*'s research department (approx. Mar. 3, 1994). No further willingness to correct, or citation to supportive passages, was obtained from *Time*'s legal department.

3. A certain crescendo was reached in Camille Paglia, "The Return of Carry Nation," *Playboy*, 36 (Oct. 1992).

4. The Moral Majority has long supported obscenity law. See *In Harm's Way: The Pornography Civil Rights Hearings* 96–97 (Catharine A. MacKinnon and Andrea Dworkin, eds., 1997) (statement of Eugene Conway, Morality in Media) (discussing obscenity law while saying he supports the ordinance, support he later withdrew in an unrecorded session, stating that obscenity law was enough).

5. See generally Andrea Dworkin and Catharine A. MacKinnon, *Pornography and Civil Rights: A New Day for Women's Equality* (1988).

6. At least, they warmed to obscenity law considerably. See, e.g., Appellee's Motion to Affirm or Dismiss at 16–17, Hudnut v. American Booksellers Ass'n, Inc., 475 U.S. 1132 (1986) (No. 85–1090). I have participated in scores of discussions in which liberals who criticized the ordinance asserted that any real problem pornography poses is adequately addressed by obscenity law.

7. Miller v. California, 413 U.S. 15, 24–26 (1973).

8. See Catharine A. MacKinnon, "Not a Moral Issue," in *Feminism Unmodified* 146 (1987).

9. This charge began as a political critique by pornography's defenders, transmuted into an assertion of fact—the right opposes pornography, so whoever opposes pornography must be allied with the right. It was applied to the ordinance—"feminists allied with right-wing moralists"—in an article in the *Village Voice*. Lisa Duggan, "Censorship in the Name of Feminism," *Village Voice*, 13 (Oct. 16, 1984) (purporting to report on the circumstances of passage of the Indianapolis ordinance). This account, full of fabrications (from stating that Andrea Dworkin played no part in the ordinance work there to reporting that I wore "gold jewelry") and distortions, credited the passage of the Indianapolis ordinance to the "political activism" of Reverend Greg Dixon, a fundamentalist preacher. He had nothing to do with it. After the hearings on the law, at which Duggan admits that no right-wing support surfaced (isn't inventing dark conspiracies *based on* absence of evidence a right-wing methodology?), Duggan says its main sponsor called Dixon and "asked for his help" because the ordinance was "in trouble." Id. The bill was not in trouble and its sponsor did not ask for his help. Based on Dixon's presence with a group of parishioners in the public audience at the final vote on the bill, Duggan invented his "decisive role in passing the anti-porn law in Indianapolis." Id. It seems that "during the final discussion before the vote many

council members were equivocating." Id. Supporters of the bill were expressive during the debate, legislators "felt the pressure," and the measure passed. Id. This post hoc ergo propter hoc fantasy is based on ignorance of the legislative process both in general and in particular. Political scientist Donald Alexander Downs credited this false account. Donald Alexander Downs, *The New Politics of Pornography* 124 (1986). Had either bothered to ask, they would have learned that enough votes for passage existed prior to the final vote. This right-feminist "alliance" did not exist, so pornography's defenders had to invent it. By force of endless repetition, it has become considered the deus ex machina of antipornography feminism. See, e.g., Pete Hamill, "Woman on the Verge of a Legal Breakdown," *Playboy*, 138 (Jan. 1993); Marcia Pally, "Misalliance Against Pornography," *Sacramento Bee*, F1 (Feb. 21, 1993); James R. Petersen, "Catharine MacKinnon: Again," *Playboy*, 37 (Aug. 1992). It is repeated by Judge Posner, in a passage excerpted by Edward de Grazia, in Edward de Grazia, *Girls Lean Back Everywhere: The Law of Obscenity and the Assault on Genius* 614 (1992). My favorite response to it is J. C. Smith's, who reportedly said, "[I]f right-wing women would spend more time in bed with [Ann] Scales, MacKinnon, and Dworkin, and less time in bed with their right-wing husbands, the world would be a better place." Ann Scales, "Avoiding Constitutional Depression: Bad Attitudes and the Fate of *Butler*," (1994) 7:2 *Canadian Journal of Women and the Law*, 349–492; see also Ann Scales, "Feminist Legal Method: Not So Scary," 2 *UCLA Women's Law Journal* 1, 5–10 (1992).

10. She is Beulah Coughenour, the Indianapolis legislator selected for her political skills, which were exceptional, by the moderate Republican (pro-affirmative action, pro-choice) Mayor William Hudnut, see William H. Hudnut III and Judy Keene, *Minister/Mayor* 146–147 (1987), to shepherd the ordinance through the City-County Council. Beulah Coughenour supported this human rights law out of an understanding that pornography harmed women and violated their equality. Even Downs learned this about her. See Downs, *The New Politics* at 110–112. In Indianapolis the ordinance was modified significantly, most importantly by exempting from the trafficking provision materials that did not show what is considered violence, a feature we termed the "*Playboy* exception." The fact that the Indianapolis ordinance covers *only materials that were made from, show, or are proven to cause violence*, Indianapolis and Marion County, Ind., Code ch. 16, §16–3(g)(8) (1984) (defense from the trafficking provision for so-called nonviolent materials) reprinted in MacKinnon and Dworkin, *In Harm's Way* at 443–444, has been routinely ignored in the press and case law, from *Hudnut* on, or misreported, even in scholarly literature. See, e.g., Deborah Rhode, *Justice and Gender* 266–271 (1989). The definition of pornography is also routinely garbled and simply misquoted. See, e.g., Downs, *The New Politics* at 114; Rhode, above, at 266. That a conservative legislator would preside over a compromise designed to save *Playboy*, certainly a left-right convergence, has produced no public comment whatsoever.

Using "conservative" as epithet, in effect requiring that only women who first present liberal credentials can work for women, shows no respect for the process of consciousness and organizing that has defined the women's movement, and no comprehension of the resulting politics of which the ordinance is a part. Downs is so dumbfounded at the "unusual alliance," Downs, *The New Politics* at 109, of women uniting against their common oppression that he simply cannot see the organizing of women *as women* that facing sexual violence as sex inequality makes possible. But then, he also misses the sexual violence and the sex inequality.

Entirely obscured in the desperation to tar this civil rights initiative with a right-wing brush have been the progressive politics of its first defenders and longest and strongest supporters. Completely ignored are the African American liberal Democratic man who was one of the bill's first two sponsors in Minneapolis and the lesbians and gay men and African American women who have sponsored it, fought for it, and voted for it in legislative settings. Their invisibility in these accounts *is* politics as usual.

11. Compare, e.g., American Booksellers v. Hudnut, 598 F. Supp. 1316 (S.D. Ind. 1984) (Barker, J.), with American Booksellers v. Hudnut, 771 F.2d 323 (7th Cir. 1985) (Easterbrook, J.) (holding that Indianapolis antipornography statute defining pornography and prohibiting coercion, force, assault, and trafficking in pornography as sex discrimination is a violation of First Amendment right to free speech), *aff'd mem.*, 475 U.S. 1001 (1986) (6–3 summary affirmance).

12. See Jean B. Elshtain, "The New Porn Wars," *New Republic*, 15 (June 25, 1984); Hamill, above note 19, at 138; Franklin E. Zimring, "Sex, Violence and the Law," *New York Times*, 18 (Jan. 28, 1990) (reviewing Downs, *The New Politics*) (uncritically repeating "strange bedfellows" as fact); see also Downs, *The New Politics*, generally and at 97, 109 ("strange bedfellows"; "unusual alliance").

13. Thomas Carlyle, *The French Revolution: A History* 174 (1934).

14. These politics are powerfully articulated in Andrea Dworkin, "Woman-Hating Right and Left," in *The Sexual Liberals and the Attack on Feminism* 28 (Dorchen Leidholdt and Janice G. Raymond, eds., 1990); see also Andrea Dworkin, *Pornography: Men Possessing Women* 98–99, 207–209 (1981) (articulating the left's attachment to pornography); Andrea Dworkin, "Why So-Called Radical Men Love and Need Pornography," in *Letters from a War Zone* 214 (1989).

15. De Grazia, *Girls Lean Back Everywhere*, above note 9.

16. Richard A. Posner, *Sex and Reason* (1992).

17. Id. at 441.

18. See Attorney General v. A Book Named "Naked Lunch," 218 N.E.2d 571 (Mass. 1966) (Edward de Grazia for intervenor Grove Press, Inc.).

19. See Grove Press, Inc. v. Gerstein, 378 U.S. 577 (1964) (Edward de Grazia for Grove Press, Inc.); see also Jacobellis v. Ohio, 378 U.S. 184 (1964) (applying reasons given for reversal of judgment of obscenity conviction by several justices in companion case to Grove Press v. Gerstein).

20. See de Grazia, *Girls Lean Back Everywhere* at 421–425.

21. See id. at 91, 109, 477.

22. Id. at 524.

23. "I see biology as explaining the drives and preferences that establish the perceived benefits of different sexual practices to different people." Posner, *Sex and Reason* at 7.

24. See, e.g., id. at 106–107.

25. See Frederick Engels, *The Origin of the Family, Private Property and the State* (International Publishers Co. 1942) (1892).

26. Posner, *Sex and Reason* at 438. Posner's theory of the relation between the biological and social in sex is well laid out on page 87. There, he opposes "a given" to "choice," as if biology is a given, a constraint, and society provides choices. Id. at 87. That society may be as, or even more, constraining than biology is not considered.

27. Id. at 29.

28. Id. at 7, 88.

29. Id. at 99 ("[T]he stronger male sex drive requires more spillways"); id. at 354–355.

30. Clitoridectomy was practiced in the past in Europe as psychotherapy, see "Sex, Lies, and Psychotherapy," see infra at 333 and continues to be practiced today as female genital mutilation (FGM) in many parts of the world. Posner does notice some literature on the clitoral orgasm but says it does not support a stronger (never equal?) sex drive in women because "capacity for orgasms and desire for them are two different things." Posner, *Sex and Reason* at 92. How he knows women have less desire for orgasms is unspecified. He separately notes the reality of clitoridectomy and its role in controlling women. Id. at 214.

31. See id. at 100–102, 106, 295–298.

32. Id. at 125.

33. He does mention in passing that sexual abuse of children can produce promiscuity, id. at 396, but without connecting it to his discussion of individuals' being "highly sexed" as a presumptively genetic trait.

34. Id. at 359.

35. For illustrative literature, see id. at 37 n.1, 359–360.

36. Id. at 179–180, 299–300.

37. Id. at 180, 299–300.

38. The common epithet that feminism is lesbianism in disguise contains an important truth. If a woman resists sexual subordination by men, her heterosexuality is often called into question. This is telling as to what heterosexuality is seen to be about, but it does not tell a biological story, unless (again) the subordination of women to men is supposed biological. It is a further problem for Posner's theory that the biological data on homosexuality he uses relies entirely on evidence collected on men.

39. Posner concedes that the genetic explanation for lesbianism is weak. Posner, *Sex and Reason* at 102. He attributes much "opportunistic" lesbianism to deprivation of male sexual companionship, id. at 137, meaning the old canard that lesbians would not be lesbians if they could have a man, which serves to keep men central to women's sexual definition. He also notes the possible contribution of sexual abuse by men to women's choice to be sexual with women, but again sees this as producing "opportunistic" rather than "real" lesbians. Id. at 299–300.

40. For a stunning example of this critique, see John Stoltenberg, *Refusing to Be a Man* (1989).

41. Posner says it makes "biological sense," Posner, *Sex and Reason* at 401, that stepfathers would be more likely to engage in incest than biological fathers, but he never addresses why an adult's sexually abusing *any* child makes evolutionary sense.

42. Nancy W. Thornhill and Randy Thornhill, "An Evolutionary Analysis of Psychological Pain Following Human (Homo sapiens) Rape: IV. The Effect of the Nature of the Sexual Assault," 05 *Journal of Comparative Psychology* 243, 247, 251 (1991).

43. I thought I made this up in its entirety until I read Nancy W. Thornhill and Randy Thornhill, "An Evolutionary Analysis of Psychological Pain Following Rape: I. The Effects of Victim's Age and Marital Status," 11 *Ethology and Sociobiology* 155 (1990) (asserting that reproductive-aged women are more severely traumatized by rape than older women or girls).

44. Posner, *Sex and Reason* at 92 n.14, 94, 106, 123, 354.

45. De Grazia, *Girls Lean Back Everywhere* at 577.

46. As it turns out, the child victims may not have told the researchers anything. Their caretakers may have "helped the child interpret the interview questions, or with very young victims the caretaker gave the responses to questions based on the caretaker's perception of the effect of the assault on the child." Thornhill and Thornhill, 11 *Ethology and Sociobiology* at 245. The children were previously interviewed by social workers. The researchers themselves did not even attempt to interview the children, but "received the data in the form of computer printouts." Id. at 243, 245.

47. Douglas T. Kenrick et al., "Evolution and Social Cognition: Contrast Effects as a Function of Sex, Dominance, and Physical Attractiveness," 20 *Personality and Social Psychology Bulletin* 210 (1994).

48. No changes in the rape law, or anything else, have addressed the drastic disparity between rape as a pervasive fact in women's lives and the legal system's inadequate response to it. See Catharine A. MacKinnon, "Reflections on Sex Equality Under Law," 100 *Yale Law Journal* 1281, 1298–1308 (1991), reprinted supra at 116. As to rape rates, Posner concludes that rape is decreasing based on one sample interview study that contradicts every other study on the subject, a study that has not been replicated. See Posner, *Sex and Reason* at 33 n.39. Age cohorts studies and annual FBI reports, supported by the experience of rape crisis centers, none of which Judge Posner mentions, document both that rape is far more prevalent than has been known and that numbers of rapes may be increasing. Diana E. H. Russell, *Sexual Exploitation: Rape, Child Sexual Abuse, and Workplace Harassment* 52–57 (1984); *Women and Violence: Hearing Before the Senate Comm. on the Judiciary on Legislation to Reduce the Growing Problem of Violent Crime Against Women*, 101st Cong., 2d Sess. 27–46, 67–68 (1990) (testimony of Mary Koss). Posner's choice of study is particularly bizarre in light of the repeated cautions in the source he cites for it that its odd results are unreliable. See Tamar Lewin, "25% of Assaults Against Women Are by the Men in their Lives," *New York Times*, A12 (Jan. 17, 1991) (stating that Bureau of Justice Statistics sample study showing rape rate dropped from 1973 to 1987 "should not be considered conclusive" as against FBI reports showing large annual increases, particularly as the sample

population (64 rapes in 1987, 136 in 1974) was too small a number from which to generalize).

49. Gillian K. Hadfield, "Flirting with Science: Richard Posner on the Bioeconomics of Sexual Man," 106 *Harvard Law Review* 479, 490 (1992) (book review).

50. See Simone de Beauvoir, *The Second Sex* (1961).

51. Although not extinct, sociobiology of race that offers genetic or evolutionary explanations for white supremacy or racial inequality in society is generally criticized as science for bigots and raises tremendous controversy. It is not a recognized specialization in social science. No federal judge has yet written a book arguing for it.

52. Posner, *Sex and Reason* at 114.

53. Id. at 43.

54. Sequoia Books, Inc. v. McDonald, 725 F.2d 1091, 1093 (7th Cir. 1983) (Posner, J.), *cert. denied*, 469 U.S. 817 (1984).

55. The definition of the word pornography used here and throughout is from the Model Antipornography Civil-Rights Ordinance, Section 2, reprinted supra at 493 n22.

56. De Grazia, *Girls Lean Back Everywhere*, frontispiece.

57. When women defend pornography, it seems as though pornography could not be hurting women. Fronting women thus has obvious strategic benefits for pornographers—and also makes women who are willing to perform this role comparatively valuable. The fact that some women are hurt less by pornography than others, and the fact that some women stand to gain by saying no women are, does not mean that many other women are not badly hurt by it—or, that all women, because they are women, are not limited and diminished by its existence in society.

58. Posner, *Sex and Reason* at 395–398.

59. De Grazia, *Girls Lean Back Everywhere* at 557, 582, 607, 609 (attacking laws against child pornography and defending sex photographs of children in artistic terms).

60. For a discussion of this aspect of Judge Posner's theory, see William N. Eskridge Jr., "A Social Constructionist Critique of Posner's Sex and Reason: Steps Toward a Gay Legal Agenda," 102 *Yale Law Journal* 333 (1992) (book review); Pamela S. Karlan, "Richard Posner's Just-So Stories: The Phallacies of Sex and Reason," 1 *Virginia Journal of Social Policy and Law* 229, 243 (1993) (book review) (asserting that male homosexuality is a "central preoccupation" of *Sex and Reason*).

61. De Grazia, *Girls Lean Back Everywhere* at 557, 582, 607, 609.

62. See Posner, *Sex and Reason* at 366, 369, 373, 374, 384, 385 ("since rape is a form of intercourse . . ."). This is also the import of his view that men who cannot get women to have sex with them become rapists. Id. at 106, 107, 107 n.54, 368.

63. Id. at 366; see also id. at 370, 385.

64. Id. at 385.

65. Id. at 367.

66. Id. at 371.

67. Id. at 366, 367, 371.

68. Id. at 371.

69. Id. at 85.

70. Douglass v. Hustler, 769 F.2d 1128 (7th Cir. 1985), *cert. denied*, 475 U.S. 1094 (1986).

71. Mishkin v. New York, 383 U.S. 502, 505 (1966) (finding that instructions to the author included that he "deal very graphically with . . . the darkening of the flesh under flagellation . . ."). For the titles, see id. at 513–515.

72. Brief Amicus Curiae of Marshall Cohen et al. in support of Appellant, Mishkin v. New York, 383 U.S. 502 (1966) (No. 49) (representing Marshall Cohen, Jason Epstein (Random House), Paul Goodman, Warren Hinckle (*Ramparts*), Eric Larrabee, Walter Minton (G. P. Putnam's Sons), Norman Podhoretz (*Commentary*), Richard Poirier (*Partisan Review*), Barney Rosset (Grove Press), Robert Silvers (*The New York Review of Books*), and William Styron).

73. Brief Amicus Curiae of the Law and Humanities Institute in Support of Respondent at 29, Massachusetts v. Oakes, 491 U.S. 576 (1989) (No. 87–1651).

74. Massachusetts v. Oakes, 491 U.S. 576, 580 (1989).

75. Commonwealth v. Oakes, 551 N.E.2d 910, 912 (Mass. 1990).

76. Id. at 912; John H. Kennedy, "High Court Set to Hear Mass. Child-Porn Appeal," *Boston Globe*, 13 (Jan. 16, 1989).

77. Posner, *Sex and Reason* at 381.

78. Id. at 378.

79. Anaïs Nin, *The Journals of Anaïs Nin (1939–1944)* 56–60, 66, 69–70, 72, 176–178 (1966). Posner notes that many legitimate artists have made pornography, Posner, *Sex and Reason* at 360, but seems to be of the view, basic to obscenity law, that aesthetically superior materials cannot be pornography.

80. Posner, *Sex and Reason* at 376.

81. De Grazia, *Girls Lean Back Everywhere* at 441.

82. 771 F.2d 323 (7th Cir. 1985), *aff'd*, 475 U.S. 1001 (1986).

83. Id. at 325.

84. Id. at 329.

85. Posner, *Sex and Reason* at 371. Posner makes a qualified exception for children. Id. at 395.

86. Id. at 381.

87. Id.

88. This happened to Linda "Lovelace," among others. See Linda Lovelace and Michael McGrady, *Ordeal* (1990).

89. Posner, *Sex and Reason* at 380.

90. See generally Catharine A. MacKinnon, "Prostitution and Civil Rights," supra at 151.

91. Miller v. Civil City of South Bend, 904 F.2d 1081, 1100 (7th Cir. 1990) (Posner, J., concurring), *rev'd sub nom.* Barnes v. Glen Theatre, 501 U.S. 560 (1991).

92. De Grazia, *Girls Lean Back Everywhere* at 584–585.

93. MacKinnon and Dworkin, *In Harm's Way;* see also Attorney General's Commission on Pornography, *Final Report* 31–46, 197–290 (1986) [hereinafter *Final Report*]; *Pornography: Women, Violence and Civil Liberties* (Catherine Itzin, ed., 1993)

[hereinafter Itzin]; Diana E. H. Russell, "Pornography and Rape: A Causal Model," 9 *Political Psychology* 41 (1988).

94. Posner, *Sex and Reason* at 366 ("[B]y facilitating masturbation, pornography may actually reduce the demand for rape . . .").

95. Id. at 366, 368–371. Part of the problem here seems to be that, inexplicably, Judge Posner does not discuss the best research on pornography's harm, including that on the effects of nonviolent materials. See MacKinnon and Dworkin, *In Harm's Way*; *Final Report*, above note 93; Itzin, above note 93.

96. *Final Report*, above note 93.

97. Posner, *Sex and Reason* at 370–371. He also discusses pornography as a "victimless crime," while apparently having considered the ordinance, which makes coercion, force, assault, and trafficking subordination civilly actionable. Id. at 371. Judge Posner, in a decision on nude dancing that predated his book, noted of the ruling on the ordinance in *Hudnut*, "We held that the ordinance violated the First Amendment because it was an effort to control the way people think about women and sex." Miller v. Civil City of South Bend, 904 F.2d 1081, 1092 (7th Cir. 1990) (Posner, J., concurring), *rev'd sub nom.* Barnes v. Glen Theatre, 501 U.S. 560 (1991). *Hudnut* did so rule. However, coercion, force, assault, and subordination are neither victimless nor thoughts.

98. This is discussed and documented in Itzin, above note 93, at 11–12.

99. De Grazia, *Girls Lean Back Everywhere* at 617. See American Booksellers Ass'n, Inc. v. Hudnut, 771 F.2d 323, 328–329 (7th Cir. 1985) ("[W]e accept the premises of this legislation. Depictions of subordination tend to perpetuate subordination. The subordinate status of women in turn leads to affront and lower pay at work, insult and injury at home, battery and rape on the streets. In the language of the legislature, '[p]ornography is central in creating and maintaining sex as a basis of discrimination. Pornography is a systematic practice of exploitation and subordination based on sex which differentially harms women. The bigotry and contempt it produces, with the acts of aggression it fosters, harm women's opportunities for equality and rights [of all kinds].'"); see also Village Books, et al. v. The City of Bellingham, No. C88–1470D, Memorandum and Order at 9 (D. Wash. Feb. 9, 1989) (in litigation on civil rights ordinance against pornography passed by referendum, ". . . it is undisputed that many societal harms are caused by pornography"); Schiro v. Clark, 963 F.2d 962, 971–973 (7th Cir. 1992) ("This Court previously addressed the issue of pornography in [*Hudnut*]. There we accepted the premise of anti-pornography legislation that pornographic depictions of the subordination of women perpetuate the subordination of women and violence against women . . . The recognition in *Hudnut* that pornography leads to violence against women does not require Indiana to establish a defense of insanity by pornography"), *aff'd sub nom.* Schiro v. Farley, 114 S. Ct. 1341 (1994).

100. De Grazia, *Girls Lean Back Everywhere* at 614–615 (quoting Richard A. Posner, *Law and Literature: A Misunderstood Relation* 334–335 (1988)).

101. Id. at 615 (radical feminist movement against pornography a "danger to literary values").

102. See de Grazia, *Girls Lean Back Everywhere*, frontispiece.

103. Miller v. California, 413 U.S. 15, 24 (1973) (defining obscene works as those "which, taken as a whole, appeal to the prurient interest in sex, which portray sexual conduct in a patently offensive way, and which, taken as a whole, do not have serious literary, artistic, political, or scientific value").

104. E.g., Judge Posner, in the excerpt de Grazia uses, describes the project of "[a] group of radical feminists [that] invites us to consider the obscene less as a matter of excessive frankness in the portrayal of sex than as a point of view harmful to women. . . ." Posner, *Law and Literature* at 334. Obscenity is already defined; the ordinance defines pornography. Obscenity is about a point of view; the ordinance makes *actual harm* civilly actionable. Judge Posner goes on to discuss the "sexually graphic," which is not the statutory language. Id. at 335–336.

105. "Sexually explicit" is a term in common use, see, e.g., Posner, above note 104, at 334, referring to an explicit presentation of sex. For example, in litigation by women whose photographs were used by *Penthouse* without their permission, *Penthouse* is referred to as "a sexually explicit men's magazine." Fudge v. Penthouse Int'l, 840 F.2d 1012, 1014 (1st Cir. 1988), *cert. denied*, 488 U.S. 821 (1988). In litigation concerning prisoners' access to pornography, one court found that "sexually explicit publications" posed a danger to rehabilitation. Dawson v. Scurr, 986 F.2d 257, 262 (8th Cir. 1993) (finding that the prison's rule provided "access to sexually explicit materials while advancing the legitimate penological interests in rehabilitation and security"), *cert. denied*, Shearon v. Lynch, 510 U.S. 884 (1993); see also Carpenter v. South Dakota, 536 F.2d 759 (8th Cir. 1976), *cert. denied*, 431 U.S. 931 (1977). In a sexual harassment case, one court said, "Although Romero's actions were not sexually explicit, they were attempts to pressure and intimidate plaintiff into renewing their sexual relationship and thus his actions constitute conduct of a sexual nature." Fuller v. City of Oakland, No. C-89–0116, 1992 U.S. Dist. LEXIS 2546, at *31 (N.D. Cal. Feb. 10, 1992). Courts thus have no trouble distinguishing the sexually explicit from mere conduct of a sexual nature. Obscenity law similarly clearly distinguishes "sexually explicit nudity" from mere nudity. See Erznoznik v. City of Jacksonville, 422 U.S. 205, 213 (1975).

Often, "sexually explicit" is deemed so clear that it is employed to define other unclear terms. See United States v. Western Electric, No. 82–0192, 1989 U.S. Dist. LEXIS 12513, at *1 (D.D.C. June 26, 1989) ("'[A]dult' audiotex programs [are] defined by Bell Atlantic as 'obscene, sexually explicit, lewd or indecent'); Young v. Abrams, 698 F.2d 131, 134 (2d Cir. 1983) ("Young defined X-rated films as those having 'more violence and more sexually explicit scenes than an R film [Restricted to adults] would have'"); see also Heise v. Gates, 197 Cal. Rptr. 404, 407 (1984) (using "sexually explicit" to clarify "obscene" and "pornographic"). Rarely is the term defined itself, and then most often in laws criminalizing abuse of children. See 18 U.S.C. §2256(2)(a)–(e) (1988) (sexually explicit conduct), W. Va. Code §61–8C-1(c) (1994); or to limit access by children to sexual materials using adults, for example, Ga. Code Ann. §16–12–100(a)(4) (1994); Mich. Comp. Laws §722.673, sec. 3(b) (1992); Wash. Rev. Code §9.68A.011(3) (1994).

The term is commonly used to describe that larger category of materials of which a smaller part may be obscene, in the same way that the Model Antipornography Civil Rights Ordinance uses "sexually explicit" to describe a larger category of materials, of which a smaller part may be sex-discriminatory. For example, one court noted, "before a person may be found guilty of promoting obscenity, the materials he promotes must be more than sexually explicit, they must be obscene under the statutory definition." People v. P.J. Video, 68 N.Y.2d 296, 300 (Ct. App. 1986), *cert. denied*, 479 U.S. 1091 (1987). Courts often note that "sexually explicit as defined by the Supreme Court in *Renton* [is] expression that the Court held could be constitutionally regulated." MD II Entertainment, Inc. v. City of Dallas, No. 3-92-CV-1090-H, 1993 U.S. Dist. LEXIS 8487 at *27 (N.D. Tex. Apr. 15, 1993) (citing Renton v. Playtime Theatres, 475 U.S. 41, 49 (1986)). The term "sexually explicit" is merely used, not defined, in Renton, 475 U.S. at 49, by reference to the decision in Young v. American Mini Theatres, in which, also undefined, "sexually explicit" designated a category of materials presumptively entitled to less First Amendment protection. 427 U.S. 50, 51 (1976).

106. The ordinance does not define pornography as graphic sexually explicit "depictions of" subordination, but as a practice of subordination. Women are often subordinated to make depictions of subordination, and as a result of the consumption of such depictions; but the subordination still must be proven to be *done*, not only shown. In addition, if materials criticize subordination, it will be difficult or impossible to prove that they subordinate.

107. Both also see us as obsessed with *Playboy*. See de Grazia, *Girls Lean Back Everywhere* at 583; Posner, *Sex and Reason* at 33, 365 n.33, 371–372. Discuss murder as the ultimate sex act in pornography, the sexualization of death and torture, the elements of objectification common to all pornography, and mention *Playboy* as part of it, and it will be said you are obsessed with *Playboy*. *Playboy* is such an icon, one of left and right's common nerves, that one need only touch it to be charged with obsession. For a discussion of "the Playboy standard," see Catharine A. MacKinnon, "More Than Simply a Magazine: Playboy's Money," in *Feminism Unmodified* 134, 138 (1987). Both writers seem unable even to perceive that it is *the harm Playboy does* that is documented, analyzed, and made civilly actionable.

108. Grove Press, Inc. v. Maryland State Board of Censors, 401 U.S. 480 (1971); Grove Press, Inc. v. Maryland State Board of Censors, 397 U.S. 984 (1970); Grove Press, Inc. v. Brockett, 396 U.S. 882 (1969); Grove Press, Inc. v. Gerstein, 378 U.S. 577 (1964).

109. For texts of the ordinance with its causes of action, see MacKinnon and Dworkin, *In Harm's Way* at 426–461.

110. Lovelace and McGrady, *Ordeal*.

111. MacKinnon and Dworkin, *In Harm's Way* at 265 (testimony of Ms. J.) ("I'm 15 and in the 9th grade. . . . Many of my friends and I have been attacked in and out of our homes with the use of pornography"). On questioning by the press, she described the events in the text.

112. Id. at 147–149 (testimony of Carole laFavor).

113. Mimi H. Silbert and Ayala M. Pines, "Pornography and Sexual Abuse of Women," 10 *Sex Roles* 861, 865 (1984).

114. *Final Report*, above note 93; MacKinnon and Dworkin, *In Harm's Way* at 39–160 (Minneapolis Hearings) (see also *Massachusetts State Hearings on Bill H. 5194*, Legislature's Joint Comm. on the Judiciary (Mar. 16, 1992), id. at 361–425).

27. From Silence to Silence

This speech was given to the National Press Club on November 22, 1993. It is published for the first time here.

1. Judy Klemesrud, "Women, Pornography, Free Speech: A Fierce Debate at N.Y.U.," *New York Times*, D10 (December 4, 1978).

2. Judy Klemesrud told John Stoltenberg of this conversation with Mr. Rosenthal. John Stoltenberg told me.

3. Alan M. Dershowitz, "Free–*Free*–Speech," *New York Times*, 31 (February 9, 1979); Opinion, "How Not to Fight Pornography," *New York Times*, 10E (December 24, 1978).

4. "Minneapolis Rights Attack on Pornography Weighed," *New York Times*, 44 (December 18, 1983). This headline is from the physical copy sold in Minneapolis that day. The online headline for the same article is "Minneapolis Asked to Attack Pornography as Rights Issue."

5. "Minneapolis Gets a Statute on Smut," *New York Times*, 24 (December 31, 1983). This headline is from the physical copy sold in Minneapolis that day. The online headline for the same article is "Minneapolis Gets Rights Law to Ban Pornography."

6. Fred Strebeigh, "Defining Law on the Feminist Frontier," *The New York Times Magazine*, 28 (October 6, 1991).

7. Judy Klemesrud, "Joining Hands in the Fight Against Pornography," *New York Times*, B7 (August 26, 1985).

8. See Catharine A. MacKinnon, "The Roar on the Other Side of Silence," see infra at 359.

9. Renate Adler, *Reckless Disregard: Westmoreland v. CBS, et al., Sharon v. Time* 17 (1986). ("[O]nce a journalist has been the first to publish certain 'facts' amounting to a 'story' all other journalists tend to go after the *same* story. . . . [I]t is exceptionally rare for a story in one publication to contradict, or even to take the mildest exception to, a story published in another. . . . [W]hatever rivalry exists . . . it is the rivalry of a pack going in one direction . . . and journalists are notoriously vindictive when the work of any of their number is criticized in print.")

10. Susan B. Trento, *The Power House* 192 (1992).

11. Steven G. Michaud and Hugh Aynesworth, *The Only Living Witness: A True Account of Homicidal Insanity* (1983).

12. Eugene L. Roberts, from a speech given at the National Press Club, November,

1993. See Eugene L. Roberts, "Nothing Succeeds Like Substance," *American Journalism Review* (December 1993); Eugene L. Roberts, "Newspapers' Thin Gruel," *The Baltimore Evening Sun*, Editorial Page (December 10, 1993).

13. Schiro v. Farley, 510 U.S. 222 (1994).

14. Robinson v. Jacksonville Shipyards, Inc., 760 F. Supp. 1486 (M.D. Fla. 1991).

15. Susan Faludi, *Backlash: The Undeclared War Against American Women* (1992).

16. See Rush Limbaugh, *The Way Things Ought To Be* 126 (1992) ("Ms. MacKinnon teaches, and I assume therefore believes, that all sex is rape, even the sex in marriage. . . . You laugh or you disbelieve, but I assure you this is true. I don't make things up."). This reference is a lie.

17. See James R. Petersen, "Politically Correct Sex," *Playboy*, 66, 67 (Oct. 1986) ("[T]he antiporn feminists have their own brand of mercurial language: Sex is Rape . . ."). Subsequent versions include Asa Baber, "A Significant Shift," *Playboy*, 30 (Apr. 1992) (claiming my *New York Times* op-ed piece on rape implies that "all men are rapists"); James R. Petersen, "Mixed Company," *Playboy*, 47, 137 (Feb. 1992) ("The Catharine MacKinnons of the world view all sexuality as hostile."); James R. Petersen, "Catharine MacKinnon: Again," *Playboy*, 37, 38 (Aug. 1992) (cutting and using quotations of my work out of context to attempt, among other things, to substantiate this lie).

18. See Susan Estrich, "Teaching Rape Law," 102 *Yale Law Journal* 509, 512 n.10 (1992) ("For the position that all sex is rape, see, e.g., Catharine A. MacKinnon . . ."). This attribution was corrected by an errata sheet to indicate that this was the author's opinion. Id. at errata ("Replace with 'For an analysis that seems to me to imply that all sex is rape, see Catharine A. MacKinnon . . .'"). People are entitled to inaccurate opinions.

19. See Katie Roiphe, "Date Rape's Other Victim," *The New York Times Magazine*, 26 (June 13, 1993).

20. See Carlin Romano, "Only Words" (book review), *The Nation*, 563 (November 14, 1993).

28. Vindication and Resistance

This analysis was first published in 83 *Georgetown Law Journal* 1959 (1995). It is dedicated to Marty Rimm.

1. For documentation of the harm of pornography, see generally U.S. Dep't of Justice, Att'y Gen. Comm'n on Pornography: *Final Report* (1986); Diana E. H. Russell, "Pornography and Rape: A Causal Model," 9 *Political Psychology* 41 (1988); Mimi H. Silbert and Ayala M. Pines, "Pornography and Sexual Abuse of Women," 10 *Sex Roles* 857 (1984); Evelyn K. Sommers and James V. P. Check, "An Empirical Investigation of the Role of Pornography in the Verbal and Physical Abuse of Women," 2 *Violence and Victims* 189 (1987); Catharine A. MacKinnon and Andrea Dworkin, *In Harm's Way: The Pornography Civil Rights Hearings* (1997).

2. See Andrea Dworkin, *Pornography: Men Possessing Women* 70–100 (1989).

Dworkin writes, "[Sade's] life and writing were of a piece, a whole cloth soaked in the blood of women imagined and real." Id. at 70. Sade's pornography also celebrates murder. One new development in computer technology will shed some light on the centrality of the use of real women to pornography's sexual effectiveness. "Interactive" pornography allows customers to customize on screen the desired stimuli, both visual and auditory, without the acts' first being performed on a live woman. If this form of pornography works sexually, pornography could end as a slave trade, while its harms to other women throughout society continue. The more active relation of the user to the material, combined with freeing production from the limitation of human flesh, could escalate the harms done through consumption. Taking this a step further, do we want "mirror world" pornography? See generally David H. Gelernter, *Mirror Worlds, Or, the Day Software Puts the Universe in a Shoebox* (1991).

3. See Robinson v. Jacksonville Shipyards, Inc., 760 F. Supp. 1486, 1526–1527 (M.D. Fla. 1991) (pornography at work actionable as sexual harassment). *Robinson* was settled after appeal was argued before the Eleventh Circuit. But compare Rabidue v. Osceola Refining Co., 805 F.2d 611, 622 (6th Cir. 1986), *cert. denied*, 481 U.S. 1041 (1987) (pornography at work not actionable as sexual harassment because "[t]he sexually oriented poster displays had a de minimis effect on the plaintiff's work environment when considered in the context of a society that condones and publicly features and commercially exploits open displays . . ." of such materials).

4. Indictment and Superseding Indictment, Criminal No. 95–80106, United States District Court, Eastern District of Michigan, Southern Division, Feb. 14, 1995, and March 15, 1995. See also Kaethe Hoffer, "Jake Baker's Pornography Is a Real Threat to Real Women," *Detroit Free Press*, A11 (Mar. 20, 1995). The indictment against Jake Baker was dismissed because the facts were not considered to pose a true threat by legal standards. United States v. Baker, 890 F. Supp. 1375 (1995) (opinion of Cohn, J.), judgment affirmed United States v. Alkhabaz, 104 F.3d 1492 (6th Cir. 1997).

5. It may be that it was more possible to see this woman as harmed because she was *not* physically sexually violated. Women lose human status when sexually assaulted, hence tend to be seen not as harmed but as treated appropriately to their less-than-human condition. On this analysis, this woman's name, having been made into pornography, lost its human status, but she herself did not.

6. One episode illustrates this. A digital rapist took over a woman's online identity, raped and otherwise tortured her, and made her behave as though she enjoyed it. This was widely termed "a rape in cyberspace," not a fantasy of a rape, or a story of a rape, or a discussion of a rape in cyberspace. Julian Dibbell, "A Rape in Cyberspace," *Village Voice*, 36 (Dec. 21, 1993). Netniks have suggested to me that verbal rape is taken seriously when it occurs in cyberspace because the community itself is constructed of words. I am not sure what they think other human communities are constructed of, or why whatever they are constructed of is not violated when a woman is raped. They have also suggested that in a virtual community, all are witnesses to rape. But consumers of visual pornography are also witnesses to rape, only they enjoy it. Why virtual rape can be more real than actual rape remains the question.

7. See generally Dworkin, *Pornography*; Catharine A. MacKinnon, *Only Words* (1993).

8. See Marty Rimm, "Marketing Pornography on the Information Superhighway," 83 *Georgetown Law Journal* 1849, 1904–1905 (1995) [hereinafter *CMU Study*].

9. Id. at 1857 n.17.

10. Id. at 1900; see also id. Figure 10.

11. Id. at 1901.

12. See id. at 1891 Table 5; see also id. at 1891 Figure 7.

13. Id. at 1892.

14. Id. at 1900 Figure 10.

15. Id. at 1899.

16. Hopefully, future studies of the same database will pursue the longitudinal dimension of user patterns, likely confirming what experiments have found and predicted: men enter the market at the "soft" end and quickly escalate sexually to using the "harder" or more intrusive and violating materials. See Dolf Zillman, "Effects of Prolonged Consumption of Pornography," in *Pornography* 127, 144–145 (Dolf Zillman and Jennings Bryant, eds., 1989) (two weeks into pornography study, participants who had been watching "common" pornography, largely defined as not showing sexual aggression, regularly chose to watch "less common" and more violent forms). See also William O'Donahue and James Geer, *Handbook of Sexual Dysfunctions* 67–68, 81 (1993). The Carnegie Mellon study also poses the potential, with all its dangers to privacy, that the prior pornography consumption of a campus rapist might be able to be studied after the fact of the rape. See *CMU Study* at 1911–1912.

17. Nan D. Hunter & Sylvia A. Law, "Brief Amici Curiae of Feminist Anti-Censorship Taskforce, et al. in *American Booksellers Association v. Hudnut*," 21 *University of Michigan Journal of Law Reform* 69, 100 n.2 (1987).

18. Id.

19. *CMU Study* at 1867, 1914.

20. Id. at 1874. It is unfortunately typical of legal discussions to manage to overlook such huge proportions of reality when that reality is pornography. See, e.g., Symposium, "Emerging Media Technology and the First Amendment," 104 *Yale Law Journal* 1613 (1995) (discussing computer networks extensively and pornography on them virtually not at all, the closest being a passing reference at 1695 n.43).

21. This is deducible from the data in Table 5, although the categories used make this less than conclusive.

22. *CMU Study* at 1854, 1895.

23. See generally Howard Rheingold, *The Virtual Community: Homesteading on the Electronic Frontier* (1993) (describing the social aggregate of relationships that forms out of webs of exchanges in cyberspace).

24. *CMU Study* at 1906; see also id. nn.130–131.

25. See id. at 1857, 1892, 1906.

26. United States v. X-Citement Video, 513 U.S. 64, 75–77 (1994).

27. See *CMU Study* at 1902–1903; see also id. Figures 7, 8, 9, 11.

28. See "Exploited and Missing Children: Hearing Before the Subcomm. on Ju-

venile Justice of the Senate Comm. on the Judiciary," 97th Cong., 2nd Sess. 39 (1982) (statement of Dana E. Caro, Criminal Investigative Div., FBI) ("It has been determined that the largest percentage of child pornography available in the United States today was originally produced for the self-gratification of the members of this culture and was not necessarily produced for any commercial purpose. Pedophiles maintain correspondence and exchange sexual [sic] explicit photographs with other members of this subculture"); Albert H. Belanger et al., "Typology of Sex Rings Exploiting Children," in *Child Pornography and Sex Rings* 79 (Ann W. Burgess and Marieanne L. Clark, eds., 1984) (thirty-two of thirty-eight child pornography rings studied were either strictly or partially producing materials for personal use); Gregory Loken, "The Federal Battle Against Child Sexual Exploitation: Proposals for Reform," 9 *Harvard Women's Law Journal* 105, 112 (1986).

29. See "South Pointe, The Adult Entertainment Company Adds Software Development Team with Acquisition," Pr Newswire (Nov. 3, 1994) (chronicling South Pointe's purchase of Innovative Data Concepts, a high-tech software developer); John R. Wilke, "Porn Broker: A Publicly Held Firm Turns X-Rated Videos into a Hot Business," *Wall Street Journal*, A1 (July 11, 1994) (describing Kenneth Guarino, South Pointe's largest shareholder (and until July 28, 1994, its chairman, CEO, and director) and longtime pornographer, with government-alleged links to the Gambino crime family).

30. See Andrea Dworkin and Catharine A. MacKinnon, *Pornography and Civil Rights: A New Day for Women's Equality* (1988), for a detailed discussion of this approach and examples of civil laws that could be used against injuries proven to be produced by pornography, however trafficked.

31. See McIntyre v. Ohio Election Comm'n, 115 S. Ct. 1511 (1995) (speech value of anonymity); Comment, "Who Are You? Identity and Anonymity in Cyberspace," 55 *University of Pittsburgh Law Review* 1177, 1185–1194 (1994) (discussing the historical protection of anonymity in law and the difficulties of continuing that protection in cyberspace); Lindsay Van Gelder, "The Strange Case of the Electronic Lover," *Ms. Magazine*, 94 (Oct. 1985) (deception through anonymity). Anonymous remailers raise special difficulties.

32. This seems implicit in Eugene Volokh's observation that while "the advent of electronic communications may change how child pornography is distributed . . . I don't see how it would change the rules relating to child pornography." Eugene Volokh, "Cheap Speech and What It Will Do," 104 *Yale Law Journal* 1805, 1844 (1995) (footnote omitted). This is because existing child pornography laws, like the sex equality approach, address the *harm* done by the materials, making how they are trafficked incidental. Volokh does not discuss pornography of adult women.

29. The Roar on the Other Side of Silence

This essay was first published as an introduction to *In Harm's Way: The Pornography Civil Rights Hearings* 3 (Catharine A. MacKinnon and Andrea Dworkin, eds., 1997).

1. Everywoman published only the Minneapolis hearings, and those only in Britain, in 1988. *Pornography and Sexual Violence: Evidence of the Links* (1988). Everywoman noted in its introduction,

> Publication of this material . . . is an historic event because strenuous efforts have been made . . . to persuade a publisher in the United States to make them publicly available. It has proved impossible to persuade any publisher, in the very country where pornography is itself protected as "freedom of speech", to risk any association with evidence about its harmful effects on society—and especially on women and children. This is one of many indications that in the United States, freedom of speech is available only to the assailants and not to the victims. The power and wealth of the pornography industry, and interconnections with "respectable" publishing, distribution, and sale outlets, mean the power to censor those who do not participate, do not agree with what is being said, and seek to expose the harm they are doing (p. 1).

2. As with all social movements, the process began substantially earlier—here with the women's movement as a whole, and more particularly with the feminist movement against pornography, "Take Back the Night" demonstrations and rallies, Women Against Pornography in New York City, and formatively with Andrea Dworkin's pathbreaking *Pornography: Men Possessing Women* (1981).

3. The ordinance has been actively considered in many other jurisdictions in the United States and was introduced before legislative bodies in Germany, Sweden, and the Philippines. No Canadian legislature or court has considered the civil rights ordinance. The Supreme Court of Canada upheld Canada's preexisting *criminal obscenity* law on the constitutional ground that pornography harms women and equality. R. v. Butler, [1992] 1 S.C.R. 452 (S.C.C.). Widely circulated false reports of the role of *Butler* in customs seizures of gay and lesbian pornography in Canada, and an analysis of the contribution of the civil rights approach to pornography to promoting gay liberation, are discussed in Christopher N. Kendall, "Gay Male Pornography After *Little Sisters Book and Art Emporium:* A Call for Gay Male Cooperation in the Struggle for Sex Equality," 12 *Wisconsin Women's Law Journal* 21 (1997).

4. We also worked with the cities and citizens of Bellingham, Washington, and Cambridge, Massachusetts, to pass these ordinances by referendum on direct vote of the people. The ordinance in Bellingham passed with 62 percent of the vote. The ordinance in Cambridge failed to pass but received 42 percent of the vote. A bastardized version was introduced in Suffolk County, New York, which we helped to defeat.

5. Testimony of Linda Marchiano, Minneapolis Hearings, pp. 60–65.

6. Letter of Women Against Pornography, Minneapolis Hearings, pp. 131–133.

7. Letter from Valerie Harper, Minneapolis Hearings, pp. 140–142.

8. Testimony of R. M. M., Minneapolis Hearings, pp. 108–112.

9. Testimony of S. G., Minneapolis Hearings, pp. 145–147.

10. The details of this account were provided at the press conference on July 25, 1984, by the young woman whose statement appears on p. 265.

11. Testimony of N. C., Minneapolis Hearings, pp. 106–107.
12. Testimony of G. C., Minneapolis Hearings, pp. 107–108.
13. Testimony of Carole laFavor, Minneapolis Hearings, pp. 147–149.
14. Testimony of J. B., Minneapolis Hearings, pp. 121–124.
15. Minneapolis Exhibit 11, letter of Marvin Lewis, p. 227.
16. Testimony of T. S., Minneapolis Hearings, pp. 114–120.
17. Id.
18. Id.
19. Minneapolis Exhibit 16, pp. 230–232.
20. The ordinances all appear in *In Harm's Way*, above note 1, at 426–461.
21. Increasingly, since then, they do. *Sex Exposed: Sexuality and the Pornography Debates* (Lynne Segal and Mary McIntosh, eds., 1992); Nadine Strossen, *Defending Pornography: Free Speech, Sex, and the Fight for Women's Rights* (1995); Wendy McElroy, *XXX: A Woman's Right to Pornography* (1995).
22. American Booksellers v. Hudnut, 771 F.2d 323 (7th Cir. 1985). "Therefore we accept the premises of this legislation. Depictions of subordination tend to perpetuate subordination. The subordinate status of women in turn leads to affront and lower pay at work, insult and injury at home, battery and rape on the streets." *Hudnut*, 771 F.2d at 328. Given that its author Judge Easterbrook strongly concludes that pornography as defined does the harms the ordinance makes actionable, some statements in its footnote 2 (see MacKinnon and Dworkin, *In Harm's Way*, Appendix, p. 481) ("MacKinnon's article collects empirical work that supports this proposition. The social science studies are very difficult to interpret, however, and they conflict. Because much of the effect of speech comes through a process of socialization, it is difficult to measure incremental benefits and injuries caused by particular speech. Several psychologists have found, for example, that those who see violent, sexually explicit films tend to have more violent thoughts. But how often does this lead to actual violence? National commissions on obscenity here, in the United Kingdom, and in Canada have found that it is not possible to demonstrate a direct link between obscenity and rape or exhibitionism. The several opinions in Miller v. California discuss the U.S. commission. See also *Report of the Committee on Obscenity and Film Censorship* 61–95 (Home Office, Her Majesty's Stationery Office, 1979); Special Committee on Pornography and Prostitution, 1 *Pornography and Prostitution in Canada* 71–73, 95–103 (Canadian Government Publishing Centre 1985). In saying that we accept the finding that pornography as the ordinance defines it leads to unhappy consequences, we mean only that there is evidence to this effect, that this evidence is consistent with much human experience, and that as judges we must accept the legislative resolution of such disputed empirical questions") have generated confusion. Contrary to footnote 2, the empirical studies on the effects of exposure to pornography do not "conflict"; the older studies have merely been superseded, as often happens when science progresses. The legislative record did not "conflict" either. The legislative record before the Seventh Circuit contained only empirical studies and victims' testimony documenting harm. There were no empirical studies that showed no harm. Legal briefs before the Seventh Circuit by ordinance

opponents *did* contain in their arguments references to prior governmental bodies elsewhere that, based on the superseded empirical studies and no testimony by victims, had concluded that the empirical record on harm was divided. This, however, presented no conflict in the legislative facts of record. Further, contrary to the suggestion implicit in footnote 2, no court is constrained to conclude that a legislature's factual record adequately supports its legislation if that record is not strong enough. That is, there was no empirical conflict of legislative fact before the Seventh Circuit on the question of harm, and the Seventh Circuit was not compelled to find that Indianapolis was permitted to legislate on the basis of the facts it had.

23. The hearings also show some differences among the ordinances in specific localities, distinctions that have been previously obscured. Unlike the Minneapolis ordinance, the Indianapolis ordinance requires that violence be shown or done for the materials to be actionable. MacKinnon and Dworkin, *In Harm's Way* at 444 (defense to trafficking claim that materials are only subsection [6] of definition). The Massachusetts ordinance effectively limits its trafficking provision to visual materials. Id. at 460. Both of these features were thought by politicians to make the bills more acceptable to the ordinance's opposition, but they did not help it in that respect at all. The judge who invalidated the Indianapolis ordinance did not even notice that it was limited to violence, and the Massachusetts ordinance was just as politically untouchable as if it had also made words-only materials actionable.

24. Notable examples can be found in accounts of the Indianapolis hearings in Donald Alexander Downs, *The New Politics of Pornography* (1989) ("Downs"), which was not based on a transcript, but on a document footnoted by him as "Administration Committee Notes." Errors resulted. For example, Edward Donnerstein's appearance before the Council was not, as Downs asserts, a "surprise move" (Downs, p. 123). It had been clearly announced before by Deborah Daniels. MacKinnon and Dworkin, *In Harm's Way*, Indianapolis Hearings, at 283. Downs states further: "As at Minneapolis, MacKinnon questioned Donnerstein, eliciting testimony on his research to support her legal points" (Downs, p. 123). I was not present when Donnerstein testified in Indianapolis. The ordinance's proponents did not manipulate these events, as Downs implies. Downs did. Presumably, the publication of the hearings makes distortions like these less possible. It should be noted that the official videotape on which the transcript of the Indianapolis hearings published in MacKinnon and Dworkin, *In Harm's Way* at 269–331, is based was incomplete when received. Attempts to locate sources for the hearings beyond the partial videotape proved fruitless. Asked for the source documents he referenced, Downs said he no longer had them (Letter of Donald A. Downs to author, July 19, 1996). John Wood and Sheila Seuss Kennedy, asked for written copies of their testimony, said they could not find them. The Records office at the City-County Council in Indianapolis said they keep official documents for seven years only (which is legally standard). Media sources who videotaped the hearings independently said they did not keep the tapes.

25. Altering the record to weaken the case on causality is illustrated by comparing two editions of the first national story the *New York Times* ran covering the Minne-

apolis hearings. One included in its report of the testimony of R. M. her direct how-to causal sentence: "When he convinced me to be bound, when he finally convinced me to do it, he read in a magazine how to tie the knots." "Minneapolis Rights Attack on Pornography Weighed," the *New York Times*, Sunday, December 18, 1983, p. 22. A different edition of *the same article*, headlined "Minneapolis Asked to Attack Pornography as Rights Issue," omitted *only this sentence*, leaving the witness with only her testimony stating by simile a weaker relation between using pornography and his actions: "My husband would read the pornography like it was a textbook." Sunday, December 18, 1983, p. 44.

26. For example, Wendy McElroy, *XXX: A Woman's Right to Pornography* (1995) stated: "Dworkin and MacKinnon orchestrated the public hearings at which the ordinance was aired. They called only the witnesses they wished to hear from" (p. 92). In Minneapolis, Andrea Dworkin and I were hired as expert consultants to present relevant witnesses. As the transcript amply shows, we did not control who was called or who was allowed to speak. MacKinnon and Dworkin, *In Harm's Way* at 39–268. Everywhere, the hearings were public. Notably, Wendy McElroy was listed third of those who were to speak against the ordinance at the Los Angeles hearing, but she did not present herself to speak.

27. E. R. Shipp, "A Feminist Offensive Against Exploitation," the *New York Times*, sec. 4 p. 2 (June 10, 1984).

28. Minus the claim about Charlee Hoyt and plus many additional false or misleading details, essentially the same "report" was recycled six months later in Lisa Duggan, "Censorship in the Name of Feminism," *Village Voice*, 13 (October 16, 1984), as if it were news.

29. The *New York Times*, note 27 above.

30. Beulah Coughenour was chosen by Mayor William Hudnut to shepherd the bill through the process largely on the basis of her political skills, which were exceptional. She also chaired the Administration Committee, through which the bill had to pass in order to be voted on by the City-County Council.

31. *Brief of the Neighborhood Pornography Task Force, Amicus Curiae, in Support of Appellant*, American Booksellers v. Hudnut (No. 84–3147), 771 F.2d 323 (7th Cir. 1985).

32. *Brief Amici Curiae of Women Against Pornography et al.*, American Booksellers Association, Inc. v. Hudnut (Docket No. 84–3147), 771 F.2d 323 (7th Cir. 1985) (brief for groups including The Minnesota Coalition for Battered Women, "a coalition of fifty-three local, regional, and state-wide organizations that provide services and advocacy to battered women and their families"); *Brief of Amici Curiae Trudee Able-Peterson, WHISPER et al. in support of Defendant and Intervenor-Defendants*, Village Books v. City of Bellingham, No. C88–1470D Memorandum and Order (D. Wash., Feb. 9, 1989) (unpublished) (brief of organizations of and for formerly prostituted women); *Memorandum of Amici Curiae Institute for Youth Advocacy, Voices in Action, et al.*, Village Books v. City of Bellingham, No. C88–1470D Memorandum and Order (D. Wash., Feb. 9, 1989) (unpublished) (brief on harms of pornography to children).

33. That this was a concerted strategic decision is clear from the fact that the FACT brief, adopting this same tactic, was filed on April 8, 1985. See Nan D. Hunter and Sylvia A. Law, "Brief *Amici Curiae* of Feminist Anti-Censorship Taskforce, et al.," 21 *University of Michigan Journal of Law Reform* 69 (1987/1988).

34. In contrast, many Hollywood actors, producers, and directors had actively lobbied for the passage of the Minneapolis ordinance, and some supported the Los Angeles one.

35. *Time* magazine, for one example, refused to publish the following letter signed by Gloria Steinem, Kate Millett, Alice Walker, Susan Brownmiller, Diana E. H. Russell, and Robin Morgan:

> The reasons feminists oppose pornography as a practice of sex discrimination [were] invisible in your story (*Sex-busters*, July 14, 1985). We oppose the harm pornography does to those who are coerced to make it, forced to consume it, defamed through involuntary appearances in it, assaulted because of it, and targeted for abuse and exploitation through its eight billion dollar a year traffic. When pornography's victims—mostly women and children—are believed, its harm is amply documented. Unlike the right wing's approaches, the civil rights approach to pornography was created to permit the injured access to court to try to prove that pornography *did* harm them in these ways. Inflicting such devastation on human beings is no one's civil liberty.

This unanimity was particularly remarkable in light of Kate Millett's signature on the FACT brief, although many who signed the FACT brief seem not to have read it.

36. *Task Force Hearing on Ordinances to Add Pornography as Discrimination Against Women, June 7, 1984*, p. 81 (Testimony of E. M.). This task force was set up by Mayor Fraser to look responsive after his second ordinance veto. Nothing came of it.

37. *Task Force Hearings on Ordinances to Add Pornography as Discrimination Against Women, June 7, 1984*, p. 45 (Testimony of Therese Stanton).

38. Id.

39. Id., p. 46.

40. See *NOW Hearings on Pornography, Materials on the Personal Testimony of NOW Activists on Pornography* (Lois Reckitt, Twiss Butler, and Melanie Gilbert, eds.), National Organization for Women, Inc., May 23, 1986. NOW also adopted a national resolution that pornography violates the civil rights of women and children and testified against pornography in Congress. NOW Resolution of June 1984 National Conference; Testimony of the National Organization for Women, presented by Judy Goldsmith, President, on the Impact of Pornography on Women before the Subcommittee on Juvenile Justice, Committee on the Judiciary (September 12, 1984). It has done little to nothing to implement this position since.

41. See, for example, Diana E. H. Russell, "Pornography and Rape: A Causal Model," 9 *Political Psychology* 1, 41–73 (1988); Gloria Cowan, Carole Lee, Daniella Levy, and Debra Snyder, "Dominance and Inequality in X-Rated Videocassettes," 12

Psychology of Women Quarterly 299–311 (1988); Wendy Stock, "The Effects of Pornography on Women," in *The Price We Pay* 80–88 (Laura Lederer and Richard Delgado, eds., 1995); James Check and Ted Guloien, "Reported Proclivity for Coercive Sex Following Repeated Exposure to Sexually Violent Pornography, Nonviolent Dehumanizing Pornography, and Erotica," in *Pornography: Research Advances and Policy Considerations* (Dolf Zillmann and Jennings Bryant, eds., 1989); E. Sommers and James Check, "An Empirical Investigation of the Role of Pornography in the Verbal and Physical Abuse of Women," 2 *Violence and Victims* 189–209 (1987); *Pornography: Women, Violence and Civil Liberties* (Catherine Itzin, ed., 1992); Andrea Dworkin, "Against the Male Flood: Censorship, Pornography, and Equality," 8 *Harvard Women's Law Journal* 1 (1985); Catharine A. MacKinnon, *Only Words* (1993).

42. Commission on Obscenity and Pornography, *The Report of the Commission on Obscenity and Pornography* (1970).

43. Attorney General's Commission on Pornography, *Final Report* (U.S. Department of Justice, July 1986) (hereafter cited as *Final Report*), p. 393.

44. *Final Report*, p. 396. The Commission also said that no remedy could reach coerced materials that were not also legally obscene (p. 396)—an unnecessary restriction on relief for proven injury.

45. *Final Report*, pp. 393–395.

46. *Final Report*, p. 749. New Zealand's *Pornography: Report of the Ministerial Committee of Inquiry* (January 1989) adopted the ordinance's definition of pornography for its own investigation, on p. 28, and called the ordinance "a brilliant strategy for expunging pornography from the face of any society that might adopt it" (p. 152). It recommended that the Human Rights Commission Act be reviewed and "that pornography be considered a practice of sex discrimination which can be expressly identified" by the Act (p. 155). The Human Rights Commission of New Zealand, before the Committee, recommended that the coercion, forcing, assault, and defamation provisions be added to the causes for complaint under the act (p. 153).

47. *Final Report*, p. 756.

48. Id. Accordingly, Carole Vance's claim, in reference to Andrea Dworkin's and my work, that the Commission "decisively rejected their remedies" and that "the Commission's Report summarily rejected Minneapolis style ordinances" is false. Carole S. Vance, "Negotiating Sex and Gender in the Attorney General's Commission on Pornography," in *Sex Exposed: Sexuality and the Pornography Debates* 37 (Lynne Segal and Mary McIntosh, eds., 1992). Her charge that we publicly misrepresented the Commission's results when we said it supported our approach—"Even more startling were MacKinnon's and Dworkin's statements to the press that the Commission 'has recommended to Congress the civil rights legislation women have sought,'" p. 38—is defamatory as well as false.

49. *Final Report*, p. 393.

50. 98th Cong. 2d Sess., S13191–13193, S. 3063 (October 3, 1984) and S13838–13839 (October 9, 1984); S. 1187 (1985), 99th Cong. 1st Sess., S6853–6855 Cong. Rec. (May 22, 1985). The bill proposed to "allow victims of child pornography and

adults who are coerced, intimidated, or fraudulently induced into posing or performing in pornography to institute Federal civil actions against producers and distributors." S6853 Cong. Rec. (May 22, 1985).

51. Originally S. 1226, the McConnell bill gave a civil right of action to victims of sexual crimes against pornographers if the victims could prove that "sexually explicit materials" influenced or incited the assault. 101st Cong. 1st Sess., S7281–7283 Cong. Rec. (June 22, 1989). In 1991, as S. 1521, the bill addressed "obscene materials and child pornography" instead. Its purpose was to require that those who trafficked such material "be jointly and severally liable for all damages resulting from any sexual offense that was foreseeably caused, in substantial part, by the sexual offender's exposure to the obscene material or child pornography." S. 1521, 102d Cong. 1st Sess. (July 22, 1991), Sec. 2(b).

52. 108 Stat. 1796 (1994). In one early case, the performer La Toya Jackson sued her former husband under the VAWA for systematically beating her until she performed for *Playboy* and other pornography. Complaint, Jackson v. Gordon, D. Nevada, Case No. CV S 00563 DWH (RJJ).

53. American Booksellers v. Hudnut, 771 F.2d 323 (7th Cir. 1985).

54. Hudnut v. American Booksellers, 106 S. Ct. 1172 (1986) (affirming without opinion). For the dissent see *In Harm's Way*, Appendix, at 482.

55. Robert L. Stern, Eugene Gressman, Stephen M. Shapiro, and Kenneth S. Geller, *Supreme Court Practice*, 7th ed. (BNA, 1993), 264–268.

56. In January 1984, constitutional scholar Laurence Tribe wrote Minneapolis City Council President Alice W. Rainville "to express dissent and dismay at Mayor Donald Fraser's veto of your ordinance to define pornography as a violation of civil rights. . . . While many hard questions of conflicting rights will face any court that confronts challenges to the ordinance, as drafted it rests on a rationale that closely parallels many previously accepted exceptions to justly stringent First Amendment guarantees. While remaining uncertain myself as to the ultimate outcome of a judicial test, I urge you not to allow an executive to prevent the courts from adjudicating what may eventually be found to be the first sensible approach to an area which has vexed some of the best legal minds for decades." (Letter of Laurence Tribe to The Honorable Alice W. Rainville, January 8, 1984.) See also Catharine A. MacKinnon, *Only Words* (1993); Cass R. Sunstein, "Pornography and the First Amendment," 1986 *Duke Law Journal* 589 (1986); Frank I. Michelman, "Conceptions of Democracy in American Constitutional Argument: The Case of Pornography Regulation," 56 *Tennessee Law Review* 291 (1989); Owen M. Fiss, "Freedom and Feminism," 80 *The Georgetown Law Journal* 2041 (1992).

57. Village Books et al. v. City of Bellingham, C88–1470D (W.D. Wash. 1989).

58. Senator Specter, under intense pressure from liberals, exempted traffickers in coerced adult materials. Senator McConnell, under pressure from across the political spectrum, adopted the obscenity definition for the materials his bill covered. Senator Specter's bill thus left the material incentive for coercion into pornography squarely in place, permitting pornographers to coerce women into sex for pornography and run

with the products and profits. He was told this. Senator McConnell's bill was rendered useless for victims because the legal definition of obscenity makes harm to victims irrelevant and is nearly impossible to prove. He was told this.

59. "If we had a keen vision and feeling of all ordinary human life, it would be like hearing the grass grow and the squirrel's heart beat, and we should die of that roar which lies on the other side of silence. As it is, the quickest of us walk about well wadded with stupidity." George Eliot, *Middlemarch* 177 (Bantam Books, 1985 ed. [from 1874 ed.]).

60. Id.

61. See Catharine A. MacKinnon, "Pornography Left and Right," 30 *Harvard Civil Rights-Civil Liberties Law Review* 143 (1995), reprinted infra at 327; Andrea Dworkin, "Woman-Hating Right and Left," in *The Sexual Liberals and the Attack on Feminism* 28 (Dorchen Leidholdt and Janice G. Raymond, eds., 1990).

62. To document specifically most instances of the treatment that forms the basis for this and the next paragraphs would further target those subjected to it. Here are a few examples that can be mentioned.

The Attorney General's Commission on Pornography was sued as a whole, and its members individually, on the basis of a letter sent by the executive director asking distributors of adult magazines whether they were selling pornography. Penthouse International, Ltd. v. Meese et al., 939 F.2d 1011 (1991). The fact that the case was thrown out on appeal as baseless did not prevent it from operating as an instrument of intimidation and silencing of the commissioners.

Al Goldstein, editor of *Screw*, a pornography magazine, sued Women Against Pornography and Frances Patai, an individual member of WAP, for libel for Patai's statement on WCBS-TV that *Screw* "champion[ed] abuse of children." Goldstein said he did not champion or defend abuse of children. Goldstein and Milky Way Productions, Inc. et al. v. Patai and Women Against Pornography, Summons and Complaint (Supreme Court of the State of New York, County of New York, October 10, 1984). The defendants produced extensive examples of eroticization of incest and other sexual use of children in *Screw* magazine over time. Having seriously damaged those sued, the case was settled.

Marty Rimm, undergraduate author of a sound and methodologically creative study, "Marketing Pornography on the Information Superhighway," 83 *Georgetown Law Journal* 1849 (1995), as analyzed in "Vindication and Resistance," infra at 352, described accurately the pornography that is available on computer networks and measured patterns of its actual use. He documented the simple truth, for example that the more violating the materials are to women, the more popular they are. Once some of his findings were given visibility and credibility in a *Time* magazine cover story, he was hounded, harassed, probed by journalists, and attacked in *Playboy*; excoriated as a censor and subjected to an intense rumor campaign of vilification on the Internet; likely deprived of a scholarship offer for graduate school at MIT; canceled before a congressional committee, where he was to testify; and threatened with the loss of his degree by his sponsoring institution, Carnegie Mellon University, which convened a formal inquiry into bogus charges that went on for years, although he was eventually cleared of all the serious charges. His initially sought book proposal, an analysis of the approximately 85 percent of his data that was not discussed in the article, suddenly could not find a publisher. No lawyer could be found to defend his academic freedom.

Shots were fired into the windows of the office of Organizing Against Pornography in Minneapolis when the ordinance was pending there.

Andrea Dworkin and I have each been attacked in most of the ways described in this and subsequent paragraphs, and in others as well. Andrea Dworkin discusses some of her experiences in *Letters from a War Zone* (1988).

Exploring the attacks on Martin Garbus, a well-known defender of rights of free speech, for the sin of suing the press for a plaintiff in a libel case, *The New Yorker* said this: "Robert Sack, who represents the *Wall Street Journal*, likens First Amendment law to a religion. 'Switching sides,' he concludes, 'is close to apostasy.'" Reflecting the pressure brought on him, Garbus was also quoted as saying: "I've told my colleagues within the First Amendment world that I would *never* take another plaintiff's case." *The New Yorker* author commented, "Undoubtedly, membership in the club does have its privileges. . . ." Susie Linfeld, "Exile on Centre Street," *The New Yorker*, 40, 42 (March 11, 1996).

63. Susan B. Trento, *The Power House* 192 (1992).

64. Letter from Steve Johnson to John M. Harrington, June 5, 1986, pp. 2, 1.

65. Id., p. 4.

66. Id.

67. *Hustler* magazine has often attacked critics of pornography in their "Asshole of the Month" feature. Peggy Ault, Dorchen Leidholdt, and Andrea Dworkin sued them for libel. Ault v. *Hustler* Magazine, Inc., 860 F.2d 877 (9th Cir. 1988); Leidholdt v. L.F.P. Inc., 860 F.2d 890 (9th Cir. 1988); Dworkin v. *Hustler* Magazine Inc., 867 F.2d 1188 (9th Cir. 1989). All three cases were held legally insufficient before reaching the facts, the courts holding in essence that pornography is unreal, hence not factual in nature, hence protected opinion. Both Gloria Steinem and Susan Brownmiller were used in pornography by *Hustler*. See Brief of *Amici Curiae* in Support of Plaintiff-Appellant, Dworkin v. *Hustler* Magazine Inc., 867 F.2d 1188 (9th Cir. 1989) (App. No. 87–6393) (pornography of both women in appendix). Andrea Dworkin and I have been used in visual pornography.

68. This is particularly apparent in reports of rapes and sexual murders (in which the presence of pornography is usually just left out, particularly of national coverage), on child pornography, and on the technological frontiers of the pornographers' coveted new markets, such as computer networks.

69. Linda Lovelace and Mike McGrady, *Ordeal* 177–179 (1980).

70. James V. P. Check and D. K. Maxwell, "Pornography and Pro-Rape Attitudes in Children," paper delivered at 25th International Congress of Psychology, Brussels; July 19–24, 1992. Check and Maxwell found, in a survey of 276 ninth-grade students in Canada, that nine out of ten boys and six out of ten girls had viewed video pornography. The mean age of first exposure was just under twelve. Boys who were fre-

quent consumers of pornography and/or reported learning useful information about sex from pornography were more accepting of rape myths and violence against women. Forty-three percent of the boys in one or both of these categories agreed that it was "at least maybe OK" to force a girl to have sexual intercourse "if she gets him sexually excited."

Examination of the Department of Justice's *Uniform Crime Reports* from 1991 to 1995 shows a steady increase in the double digits in the number of arrests for sex crimes reportedly committed by perpetrators under eighteen years of age up to 1993, then a small decrease thereafter. FBI, U.S. Department of Justice, *Uniform Crime Reports for the United States*, 1991, 1992, 1993, 1994, 1995. Closer scrutiny of the affected groups, beyond simply reported crime, suggests that sexual assaults are increasingly being committed by younger and younger perpetrators. Melinda Henneberger, "Now Sex and Violence Link at an Earlier Age," *The New York Times*, sec. 4, p. 6 (July 4, 1993); Claudia Morain, "When Children Molest Children," *San Francisco Chronicle*, F7 (May 4, 1994). "The 'portrait' of the American sex offender increasingly 'bears the face' of a juvenile." Sander Rothchild, "Beyond Incarceration: Juvenile Sex Offender Treatment Programs Offer Youths a Second Chance," 4 *Journal of Law and Policy* 719 (1996). In the same publication, see a report of a 1992 study at the University of New Hampshire's Family Research Laboratory concluding that "forty-one percent of sexual assaults on children ages 10 to 16 were done by other children," p. 720.

71. This passage was inspired by Louis Begley, "At Age 12, A Life Begins," *New York Times Magazine*, 101 (May 7, 1995): "Hitler was dead and the 10 days of miracles had begun . . . finally I could believe the Germans had been wrong. I had not, after all, been marked at birth as unfit to live. My disgrace was not inside me; it was their invention. I had the right to a place in the world."

Index